DEMOCRACY, SOCIALIZATION AND CONFLICTING LOYALTIES IN EAST AND WEST

Democracy, Socialization and Conflicting Loyalties in East and West

Cross-National and Comparative Perspectives

Edited by

Russell F. Farnen
Director and Professor of Political Science
University of Connecticut at Hartford

Henk Dekker
Associate Professor of Empirical Political Science
Leiden University, The Netherlands

Rüdiger Meyenberg
Professor and Head of Political Science
University of Oldenburg, Germany

and

Daniel B. German
Professor of Political Science
Appalachian State University

First published in Great Britain 1996 by
MACMILLAN PRESS LTD
Houndmills, Basingstoke, Hampshire RG21 6XS
and London
Companies and representatives
throughout the world

A catalogue record for this book is available
from the British Library.

ISBN 0–333–65958–9

First published in the United States of America 1996 by
ST. MARTIN'S PRESS, INC.,
Scholarly and Reference Division,
175 Fifth Avenue,
New York, N.Y. 10010

ISBN 0–312–16060–7

Library of Congress Cataloging-in-Publication Data
Democracy, socialization, and conflicting loyalties in East and West :
cross-national and comparative perspectives / edited by Russell F.
Farnen . . . [et al.].
p.   cm.
Includes indexes.
ISBN 0–312–16060–7 (cloth)
1. Political socialization. 2. Democracy.   3. Nationalism.
4. Comparative government. I. Farnen, Russell Francis, 1933–
JA76.D37   1996
321.8—dc20   96–19545
                                                            CIP

Selection and editorial matter © Russell F. Farnen, Henk Dekker, Rüdiger
Meyenberg and Daniel B. German 1996
Chapters 1–22 © Macmillan Press Ltd 1996

10   9   8   7   6   5   4   3   2   1
05   04   03   02   01   00   99   98   97   96

Printed in Great Britain by
The Ipswich Book Company Ltd
Ipswich, Suffolk

Contents

Part III
Socialization Processes: Case Studies

Part IV
Democratization Trends and European Integration

Part V
Politics and/of Education

Part VI
Conclusions, Synthesis, and Summary Comments

Notes on the Contributors

Margaret Conway, Professor, Department of Political Science, University of Florida, Gainesville, FL, USA.

György Csepeli, Professor of Social Psychology, Department Head, Institute of Sociology, Eötvös Loránd University, Budapest, Hungary.

Alfonso J. Damico, Professor, Department of Political Science, University of Florida, Gainesville, FL, USA.

Sandra Bowman Damico, Professor, Division of Educational Studies, Emory University, Atlanta, GA, USA.

Henk Dekker, Associate Professor of Empirical Political Science, Department of Political Science, Leiden University, Leiden, the Netherlands.

Russell F. Farnen, Professor, Department of Political Science, University of Connecticut, Storrs, CT, USA.

Barbara Fratczak-Rudnicka, Lecturer and Deputy Director, Institute of Sociology, Warsaw University, Warsaw, Poland.

Daniel B. German, Professor of Political Science, Department of Political Science/Criminal Justice, Appalachian State University, Boone, NC, USA.

E. I. Golovakha, Researcher and Department Head, Institute of Sociology, Ukrainian Academy of Sciences, Kiev, Ukraine.

Louk Hagendoorn, Professor of General Social Sciences, Utrecht University, Utrecht, the Netherlands.

László Kéri, Senior Researcher, Institute for Political Science, Hungarian Academy of Sciences, Budapest, Hungary.

Cees A. Klaassen, Associate Professor of Educational Sciences, Department of Educational Sciences, University of Nijmegen, Nijmegen, the Netherlands.

Hub Linssen, Assistant Professor, Faculty of Social Sciences, Department of General Social Sciences, Utrecht University, Utrecht, the Netherlands.

Darina Malová, Assistant Professor, Department of Political Science, Comenius University, Bratislava, Slovakia.

Ludo Mateusen, Secondary School Teacher, Strabrecht College, Geldorp, the Netherlands.

Jos Meloen, Social Scientific Researcher, LISWO, University of Leiden, Leiden, the Netherlands.

Rüdiger Meyenberg, Professor and Department Head, Department of Political Science, University of Oldenburg, Oldenburg, FRG.

Siebren Miedema, Professor, Section of Philosophy and History of Education, Leiden University, Leiden, the Netherlands.

N. V. Panina, Researcher and Department Head, Institute of Sociology, Ukrainian Academy of Sciences, Kiev, Ukraine.

István Stumpf, Senior Researcher, Institute for Political Science, Hungarian Academy of Sciences, and Director, Budapest School of Politics, Budapest, Hungary.

Remko Theulings, Graduate Student, Department of Political Science, Leiden University, Leiden, the Netherlands.

Wilma A. M. Vollebergh, Researcher, Department of Youth, Family and Lifecourse, Utrecht University, Utrecht, the Netherlands.

Meredith W. Watts, Professor of Political Science, Department of Political Science, University of Wisconsin, Milwaukee, WI, USA.

Rolf Willemse, Graduate Student, Department of Political Science, Leiden University, Leiden, the Netherlands.

Preface

This book is an outgrowth of certain individual, joint, or group research activities undertaken during 1994. All of these studies were conducted with the support and encouragement and under the aegis of the International Political Science Association's Research Committee on Political Socialization and Education (RCPSE #21).

This research committee sponsored two international meetings in January 1994 (Boca Raton, Florida) and August 1994 (Berlin and Potsdam, Germany). These conferences centered on three major organizing themes: democratization, pluralism, and nationalism/ethnic minority relations. In addition to committee sponsorship, we received support from the International Political Science Association in Oslo, Norway; Florida Atlantic University, Boca Raton, Florida; the University of Connecticut, Storrs, Connecticut; Social Issues Resources Series, Boca Raton, Florida; the German Political Science Association's (DVPW) Section on Political Science and Political Education, Hanover and Darmstadt, Germany; and the University of Oldenburg, Oldenburg, Germany.

We would also like to take this opportunity to thank the University of Connecticut Research Foundation (UCRF) for its continuing support of these publications. This is the fourth RCPSE volume produced with the financial support of UCRF. Also, this is the fourth volume for which Ms. Martha Bowman has managed the word processing/desktop publishing, general copy editing and organization, indexing, and diskette preparation. We continue to be in her debt and are thankful that she does what she does so well.

We, the editors of this volume, also want to acknowledge the help of our immediate family members and loved ones for their understanding and encouragement, without which all of our efforts would certainly have less personal meaning or significance in our lives. We also want to acknowledge the helpful support and spur to motivation which our respective universities (Connecticut, Leiden, Appalachian State, and Oldenburg) have provided over the years. It is far more rewarding to engage in research, writing, and publication when these activities are encouraged and assisted, rather than discounted, and when one's university removes impediments rather than erecting barriers which hinder such work.

All in all, we hope the 22 essays in this volume will be of interest to our international audience of readers. We trust that they will shed some light on contemporary trends in democratization, nationalism, political socialization, authoritarianism, and other topics treated on these pages. Since we have authors from seven different countries contributing to this volume, we believe the reader will benefit from our international, comparative, and cross-national perspectives on these important issues in contemporary politics, socialization, and public education.

Unless indicated otherwise, all tables and figures appearing in this volume are based on the outcomes of original research by the chapter author(s).

Russell F. Farnen
Farmington, Connecticut, USA

Henk Dekker
Zandvoort, the Netherlands

Daniel B. German
Boone, North Carolina, USA

Rüdiger Meyenberg
Wiefelstede, Metjendorf, FRG

Editors

Part I

Setting the Context

1   *Introduction*

Russell F. Farnen

ABSTRACT

This chapter introduces the reader to a collection of empirical research findings and scholarly syntheses of quantitative and qualitative research efforts on the themes of democracy, authority, pluralism, nationalism and internationalism, and minority rights. Another major emphasis in these studies is on assessing the impact of socialization forces and political education of youth in various countries. Some of the studies are quasi-longitudinal (for example, Farnen and German, Chapter 4) and focus on Eastern Europe, two contributions (Meloen in Chapter 2; Farnen in Chapter 3) emphasize the significant role of authoritarianism as the major alternative to democracy, internationalism, antimilitarism, pluralism, multiculturalism, and democratic educational processes. Different chapters also stress either different regions, for example Eastern Europe (Farnen and German in Chapter 4; Csepeli in Chapter 9), Western Europe (Linssen et al. in Chapter 11; Meyenberg in Chapter 15; Dekker and Willemse in Chapter 16), or particular countries, such as Slovakia (Dekker, Malová, and Theulings in Chapter 5), Germany (Watts in Chapter 6; Meyenberg in Chapter 15), Hungary (Csepeli et al. in Chapter 7; Stumpf in Chapter 8; Kéri in Chapter 12), the Netherlands (Vollebergh in Chapter 13; Meloen in Chapter 20, which also includes Flanders, Belgium); Poland (Fratczak-Rudnicka in Chapter 14); the United States of America (Conway et al. in Chapter 21), or the Ukraine (Golovakha and Panina in Chapter 10). Still other chapters emphasize the themes of racism, intolerance, xenophobia, and/or stereotyping (Watts in Chapter 6; Linssen et al. in Chapter 11; Vollebergh in Chapter 13), national loyalties (Farnen in Chapter 3; Dekker, Malová, and Theulings in Chapter 5; Csepeli et al. in Chapter 7), the European Union (Meyenberg in Chapter 15; Dekker and Willemse in Chapter 16), and democratic political philosophy (Miedema in Chapter 17), values (Klaassen in Chapter 18), citizenship (Dekker in Chapter 19), and socialization (Kéri in Chapter 12; Klaassen in Chapter 18; Conway et al. in Chapter 21).

All in all, this combination of 24 contributors from seven different countries provides a mix of American and Western, Central, and Eastern European analysts who, since they have each shared their work with the other contributors, are mutually informed about the topics, methods, and major conclusions their colleagues have reached in their research projects and published writings.

Of the six major parts of this book, the first provides an introduction to the subject of democratic transitions in East and West, including the force of nationalism, democracy, and authoritarian trends in the modern world, with special emphasis on political, economic, education, mass media, and environmental changes (including nationalism/minority relations and pluralism) in Central and Eastern Europe.

Part II deals with case studies of xenophobia in eastern Germany, nationalism and politics in Hungary, and postcommunist anomie in the Ukraine. Part III emphasizes intolerance and stereotyping and the dynamics of socialization processes. Part IV covers democratization, the EC and the EU, and (like Chapter 4) European elite political perspectives. Part V discusses politics of/and education, including democratic philosophy, values, morality, competence, citizenship, school socialization, and the role of education in a democratic society. Part VI sets forth the major general and specific conclusions which flow from the studies in this volume.

BACKGROUND

This book is the latest in a series of research projects which have been jointly sponsored by the IPSA/RCPSE and various US and European universities and institutes (such as the University of Connecticut, Oldenburg University, and the Hungarian Academy of Sciences Institute of Political Science and Center for Political Education in Budapest). The work of the IPSA research committee has been published in the International Studies in Political Socialization and Political Education Series which Verlag Peter Lang, Frankfurt am Main, FRG has sponsored (for example, representative volumes are Csepeli's *Structures and Contents of Hungarian National Identity*, 1988; and Farnen's *Integrating Political Science, Education, and Public Policy*, 1990).

The work of this committee has frequently appeared in Oldenburg University's European Studies Series. This includes Dekker and Meyenberg (eds.) *Politics and the European Younger Generation* (1991) and *Perceptions of Europe in East and West* (1992) and Farnen (ed.) *Reconceptualizing Politics, Socialization, and Education* (1993). The present volume is the first in a new BIS international series (edited by H. Dekker, R. Farnen, and R. Meyenberg) on international studies in political socialization and political education. The committee's work is often found in its official and co-supported international journal of political socialization and political psychology *Politics, Groups and the Individual* (Department of Political Science, Wassenaarseweg 52, 2333 AV Leiden, the Netherlands) as well as in the Hungarian Academy of Sciences publications, such as Csepeli et al. *State and Citizen* (1993) and *From Subject to Citizen* (1994).

With these introductory and context-framing remarks finished, now let us turn our attention to a summary of some of the major features of Chapters 2 through 21, grouped in a part-by-part analysis.

PART I: SETTING THE CONTEXT

This section introduces the reader to the major features of the book and ties the volume into past group activities of the IPSA/RCPSE *Gesellschaft* from the late 1980s to the present. Here, the work of Meloen on authoritarianism, Farnen on nationalism and authority, and Farnen and German on political perceptions of elites in Central and Eastern Europe is presented. My intention here is not to oversummarize these chapters, but rather to direct the interested reader's attention to those chapters containing material which may be of particular interest to someone who shares these same academic concerns.

Meloen (Chapter 2) lays out the relationships between dictatorships and authoritarian attitudes/regimes (in 70 countries) on the one hand and their antithesis found in democratic attitudes and state practices on the other. He cites a Freedom House 1993 report that 55 countries were judged to be 'not free' with a minority of only 19 per cent of the world's peoples living in 'free' societies. This is the worst such setback on these freedom measures since 1976.

Meloen's 70-nation analysis is unique in the literature. Meloen presents international data on authoritarianism measures as well as some national data on the Netherlands and its internal regions. Among his major findings based on his collection of demographic and politically descriptive data on other factors (such as women's rights violations, human rights obstructionism, censorship, intolerance of homosexuals, state terrorism, and capital punishment), the correlations between these measures of nondemocratic state practices (which yield state authoritarianism scores) and high authoritarianism attitudes are quite high (.85; p<.001) as is the case with two other similar measures (the Freedom Rating and the Human Freedom Index). State authoritarianism also predicts lower political participation; one-party, military, nondemocratic governments; undemocratic politics; economic irregularity/deprivation; educational deficits; nonurbanization; lower life expectancy and other population indices; low mass media exposure; linguistic incorporation; gender gap; and military dominance. His model of state authoritarianism relates authoritarian government type, attitudes (state authoritarianism also predicts authoritarian attitudes from scores on several national measures over time), and low educational attainment which, through state authoritarianism, predicts the levels of high ethnic diversity, larger military size, authoritarian government practices, and more severe gender differences (which is negatively correlated with educational attainment). Urbanization, gross national product, mass media, and climate (contrary to the 19th century political philosopher, Baron de Montesquieu) were excluded in this analysis of the relationships among cross-national indices of authoritarianism, state authoritarianism levels, and independent global indicators and demographic indices of education, gender, population, ethnicity, military conflict, and like variables.

The topics of nationalism, democracy, and authority are introduced in Chapter 3 (Farnen) along with cultural, civilization, and democratic/authoritarian differences. The basic elements of nationalism are also summarized, along with an overview of what we mean by minority, ethnicity, patriotism, and both strong and weak democracy. The results of several surveys of democracy, authoritarianism, and nationalism in North America and Central/Eastern/Western Europe are also presented in this chapter. Some of the Rose (University of Strathclyde Centre) findings on democracy, nationalism, and authoritarianism are presented as a backdrop to answer the question: 'Can civic education make a difference?' In answering this question, the first piece of information presented is that, of all the indices which predict nonauthoritarianism, the level of education is by far the most stable cross-national predictor appearing in study after study. A second set of data on the utility of civic education for school instruction showed that, in the US, it was effective, despite some shortcomings in serving the needs of minority students.

Five major generalizations about political socialization and education are also presented. These relate to persistence and change in the light of developmental patterns, the key importance of the middle school years for influencing student knowledge and values, the similar significance of current events and an open classroom climate for democratic growth, and some suggestions provided for improving the civic education of all students (including members of minority groups). Reference is also made to the need for a heuristic model in order for teachers to plan their civics lessons. A single example of playing out one basic question about national identity is used as an illustration of what has been proposed as the process of how we must make some hard choices about the particulars of democratic civic education.

The last chapter in this part presents the results of Farnen-German's (Chapter 4) follow-up study of elites from universities and health professions in Central and Eastern Europe regarding their impressions in 1993 of how national changes in politics, communications, education, economics, and the environment have been in democratic or undemocratic directions. This chapter discusses the role of intellectual elites, summarizes results from a 1989-91 survey on the same basic topics, provides some theoretical structures, and presents the 1991-3 findings. While there was some evidence of a smoother transition to democracy in some countries more than others, it is clear that politics, communications, and education have changed in the most positive way in some countries, but not in others. There is also hope for civil rights/pluralistic education. But, while the economic area may show some gradual improvement, the two environmental variables are dismal, indeed, showing no change/decline for 10 of the 14 countries included in the study.

The overall composite scores indicate little change for politics, communications, nationalism, and education; a significant overall decrease in minority toleration; some significant economic, but no significant environmental changes for the better. The alpha scores reported in the measures employed from 1991 to 1993 indicated some (for example, political education and ethnonationalism measures) were lower in reliability than others, whereas the others were at an acceptable level for international research. However, the most disturbing result may be that only the Slovakian respondents indicated that Slovakia was high on the minority toleration measure. Other researchers questioned this estimate because treatment of ethnic Hungarians (11 per cent of the Slovak population) is sometimes discriminatory. The Slovakian public's harsh treatment of (and unfavorable attitudes toward) Gypsies, Hungarians, and other minorities in the country and the high degree of anti-Semitism recently recorded in surveys (even in the absence of Jews actually living there) lead us, as well as other observers, to seriously question this result as evidence of wishful rather than reality-based thinking.

Other respondents scoring low were Croatians, the Czechs, Hungarians, and Poles. The rest were only at a medium level. These results bear further watching since they have the potential to be explosive in the near future.

PART II: AREA/NATIONAL CASE STUDIES

This part of the volume deals with case studies of Slovakia, Germany, Hungary, and the Ukraine.

Dekker, Malová, and Theulings (Chapter 5) examine what makes a Slovak a nationalist. They interviewed Slovak academicians and politicians and analyzed public opinion survey data. Based on their studies, between one-quarter and one-third of Slovaks demonstrated nationalism-related orientations between 1992 and 1994. Currently, Slovakia possesses many of the theoretical requirements for increased nationalism, including a political, economic, and identity crisis with politicians who serve as nationalistic 'entrepreneurs'.

Because nobody is born with nationalism intact, they use system, individual, and socialization variables to show how this attitude has developed in Slovakia. Charismatic nationalistic political leaders, a severe economic crisis, a political and cultural crisis, and ideological (moral) crisis, and 'nationalistic entrepreneurs' (including politicians, religious leaders, and mass media) promote the growth of nationalism in Slovakia. However, since empirical research is limited, there is a need for a longitudinal (preferably cross-national) panel study to determine the growth and pacification of nationalism in Slovakia and elsewhere.

Watts (Chapter 6) says that it has been generally argued that the terms 'left' and 'right' had no specific meaning in the formerly socialist societies in Central and Eastern Europe. While 'conservative' often meant 'Stalinist' and 'liberal' often meant 'reform socialist' or 'pluralism', it is not surprising that the conventional Western terminology could not easily be applied to developments in the former German Democratic Republic or such nations as Hungary, Poland, or Czechoslovakia. However, since the breakdown of the socialist regimes, there has been a rapid change in the political terminology and consciousness of those nations. Most of all, the young are particularly sensitive to such changes; they may serve as a sign of the emerging meaning of left and right. More specifically, they may provide an indication of the lines of conflict and resolution forming in the process of democratization.

Selection of the German case provides a unique opportunity to compare youth socialized in two different systems and affected differently by the unification process. Eastern youth cannot be taken to be 'typical' of the other formerly socialist nations, but they are subject to a number of similar stresses associated with the transition process (for example, loss of political orientation and occupational perspective and a combination of generalized apathy toward the conventional system as well as sensitivity to xenophobia and extremism). This set of problems seems to be common in the formerly socialist societies, though taking a somewhat different form in each nation.

The specific theoretical problem has at least three alternative hypotheses to be tested. Each predicts a different form of ideological conflict, each a different meaning of 'left' and 'right'. Which form is emerging will have significant consequences for the way in which the current youth generation will relate to the political process.

The first hypothesis holds that political parties represent 'frozen' conflicts of the past (whether religious, ethnic, regional, or industrial). Though these structural factors continue to influence the meaning of left and right, the traditional conflicts over the class-based distribution/redistribution of material values has declined. This has led to the formation of the second hypothesis, whose strongest form holds that the classic 'industrial' cleavages are being replaced with a conflict based on 'postmaterialist' values of participation, environmentalism, and personal development. A related theoretical orientation holds that the key factor is 'individualization' in the life course of youth which sets free personalized, but often politically unpredictable, processes of choice and development. This has led to a rethinking of the role of 'structural' factors in political and social behavior, though this critique of 'static' sociology has a long tradition.

A third hypothesis is more topical and concerned with specific developments in Germany (particularly the eastern part) since formal unification. Eastern German youth researchers have argued in their studies that youth in the new federal states (the former GDR) have become increasingly polarized ideologically during the transition process. This polarization, they believe, does not fall along traditional 'industrial' left-right conflict lines, but is increasingly defined by acceptance/rejection of foreigners and violence, and by a cluster of attitudes that relate primarily to racism and xenophobia. According to this thesis, then, the primary 'left' and 'right' split may be over racism and ethnic pluralism.

Watts maintains that the most likely explanation is a synthesis of the second two hypotheses. Other studies have found polarization along the lines suggested by the Leipzig researchers, but there are also clear signs of value change that affect ideology and party preference. The question is which structural and social-psychological factors are emerging in the postunification period as the primary conflict lines among youth. We know that this is a particularly sensitive period of politicization for German youth, that there are distinct age-gender interactions, and that the political effects may be a heightened sensitivity to demonstrations as well as apathy toward conventional political behavior. What is unclear is the course of these changes and the form in which they are likely to crystallize.

Watts examines this process using three types of data on German youth: 1) studies conducted by the former Zentralinstitut für Jugendforschung of the GDR, by its former members, or by current members in its new form as a branch of the German Youth Institute (Außenstelle Leipzig des Deutschen Jugendinstituts), 2) the 1991 all-German ALLBUS study (1991 Basisstudie in Gesamt-deutschland), and 3) the continuing series of Politbarometer studies of Forschungsgruppe Wahlen Mannheim. Data in 1) provide an intensive (but statistically nonrepresentative) view of eastern German youth; 2) provides a general framework for estimating the generalizability of information in 1) and allows comparison across age groups in both regions of Germany; 3) provides longitudinal information on left-right self-placement, party preference, and issue preferences in the primary areas of conflict examined in this study.

Watts finds signs of the 'ethnicization' of ideology among adult eastern and western Germans. High levels of anomie are also associated with xenophobia and rightist ideology as well. Foreigners are more closely linked (as targets of hatred) in the east more than in the west as economic competition/threats. There is also a clear indication that ideological conflict in both regions is 'ethnicized' on an overall basis of potential out-group conflicts/threats.

In Chapter 7, Csepeli, Kéri, and Stumpf present their findings from a 1992 survey of 4000 Hungarian youth aged 11 to 17 years. This study measured levels of national consciousness and identity formation. The five clusters of statistical/conceptual groupings which emerged after data analysis produced the following groups: conformists, loyalists, Christians, patriots, and naive citizens.

These five groups materialized on the basis of youth's answers about the extent of their personal commitment to Hungary and to Europe; how respondents would respect or memorialize different groups of dead in a cemetery (heroes of the 1848-9 war for independence or the remains of an old Roman villa or factory, or members of an old Jewish community); to which levels of government (local, national, international) the smallest or largest amount of tax income should be allocated; to the naming of un-named streets and to the erection of patriotic statues; to the support of Hungarian nationals in the then-ongoing Olympic Games in Barcelona, Spain or to the support of European and white athletes there in general; willingness to accept refugees from Asia or from ethnic

Hungarian families; willingness to demonstrate for the Hungarian minority in Romania (Transylvania) versus Bulgarian Turks, Hungarian Germans, Jews, 'Gypsies', or gays; and the pattern of beliefs regarding different religious categories, including God, UFOs, parapsychology, the devil, communism, and so forth.

This study found that decentering from less complex constructs to more ideologically based identities occurs over the ages from 11 to 17. Children from homes with better-educated parents perform these ideological transitions more smoothly and more completely just as was true of older versus younger students. By contrast with the naive group of younger respondents with more poorly-educated parents, those who developed a Christian or national patriotic identification were both older and had better-educated parents. The new generation of Hungarian youth is also different from other generations in that there is no longer a dual system of official and private education and socialization agencies as existed in the past under real socialism. Today's youth can also respond freely and unhindered by fear to a survey form that allows honest choices among ideological, religious, political, decisional, and policy alternatives within the context of a family generated values system. What they will do with their newfound freedom, pluralism, and diversity under a democratic civil society and free markct cconomy (should that soon become a reality in Hungary) remains to be seen.

Stumpf (Chapter 8) discusses the democratic transition process in Hungary in terms of political participation, voting behavior, and partisan political attitudes. He examines the role of age and religion in the formation of political party preferences as well as using the Michigan, rational choice, and socialization/postmodern models to analyze Hungarian's voting and political behavior. While Stumpf finds the politics of the transition to be uncertain, participation rates erratic, voting behavior unclear, and development of partisan attitudes in a state of flux, it is clear that there are certain political changes under way in Hungary. While social and structural changes in the West are having their influences on postindustrial/postmodern politics (for example, greater higher education, concern for environmental issues, and liberal economic values), such changes in Hungary are tied to generational/age, socioeconomic class, and religious differences among the polity. These factors are determinative for both adults and youth in that family religious values, for example, have their influence on youth especially when school-based religious education reinforces such views. Party membership/support is also clearly linked to religious preferences (for example, Christian Democratic supporters are 94 per cent religious, that is, by doctrine [55 per cent] or personal faith [39 per cent], whereas 53 per cent of the HSP [old communists, new socialists] are religious, many [49 per cent] in a personal, nondoctrinal way).

The data collected in this study revealed definite and specific differences among conservative, Christian, nationalistic, and liberal groups as well as the connections between ideological views on the one hand and age/generational, socialization, and religious background variables on the other. Owing to the unpredictability, inconsistency, and short-term data available on Hungarian voting behavior, it is no surprise that the newly enfranchised two-thirds of the electorate in Hungary are only slowly making their way toward democracy, pluralism, and civil society. However, it is true that many Hungarians both young and old learned useful survival strategies in the past in order to beat the official system through their 'second economy' efforts with its form of rational economic behavior. The Inglehart - socialization - cultural change - postmodern approach to Hungarian political analysis should, in the long run, be a useful method of analysis for charting Hungarian patterns of political behavior. One key element in this analysis will be the extent to which the new Hungarian government is both indebted to and concerned with the political demands of the 33 per cent of voters who are under 35 years of age. For the foreseeable future, economic factors will likely be more important than rational choice/activist motivations for political behavior in Hungary in the 1990s.

In Chapter 9, Csepeli deals with the topic of divided nations in Central and Eastern Europe, along with their resurgent nationalism, a lack of historical correspondence between nation-state and ethnic national groups, and their inexperience with democracy and universal human rights standards. The foregoing all combine with authoritarian trends to put rapid transition to democracy in jeopardy. Illiberal and dogmatic elites can exploit these internal and external ethnonational rivalries for their own advantage to forestall US, international, and Western European help, influence, and guidance.

Csepeli also discusses the meaning of nation and national identity in Central and Eastern Europe as well as the problems these states will likely encounter as they move toward democratization. Some of these factors include a history of regional conflict, a static period of nondevelopment toward modernity during the Communist period, and the difficulties of putting the red armies and nuclear genies back in their bottles through nuclear nonproliferation accords, denuclearization, and cooperative US/Russian/third country dismantling of the dispersed Soviet nuclear arsenals and their delivery mechanisms.

Other divisions in the area revolve around Occidental or Western social values versus Eastern or Byzantine cultural practices and the continuing effects of real socialism's grip on the populations for over 40 years. These factors keep countries in Central and Eastern Europe both backward and separate from the West in its economic, political, and social development. However, one feature citizens in Central and Eastern Europe did learn together was that of equality (even if this meant equal poverty or uniform subjugation). A second was that of the parallel or second economy, which was based on market rather than official redistributive principles. As a result, the citizenry have accepted reforms which are based on inequality, private property, market civil/human rights, and pluralism. These are the antithesis of the old, moribund system of real socialism, which had been applied in a region which lacked the Western tradition of citizen and national identity and equal rights for its members. While these traditions developed in France and the United Kingdom, they did not do so in Germany until later in the 19th century when the classic distinctions between *Gemeinschaft* and *Gesellschaft* were accepted there. And it happened even later in Central and Eastern Europe, particularly since these states were small in size, yet expansionistic, with their goals to reconstruct some ancient period with its imperial size and greatness. With the *Gemeinschaft* national orientation, these nations promoted exclusion and dichotomization, exaggerated national patriotism, compensatory self-aggrandizement, and blaming others/enemies for a history of national shortcomings.

Citizens and leaders in Central and Eastern Europe have yet to look realistically at the unfairness of their old redistribution schemes, the continuing grip which security and bureaucratic forces have on these societies, and the longstanding lack of a positive self-/national identity. The old myth of internationalist proletarian solidarity was verbally approved, but actually vetoed, in Moscow, which feared such international cooperation. The Soviets actually preferred to divide and conquer. Nationalistic roads to communism were promoted, resulting in ethnic purges in Rumania and Bulgaria, whereas only Tito and Stalin could keep the lids on their ethnic divisions to prevent them from boiling over. When this long-repressed nationalism did burst out, elites used this as an excuse to put democracy and the market on hold for the time being. Meanwhile, trivial debates over old national symbols were allowed to flourish in the parliaments and the press.

Such divisions which exist in Central and Eastern Europe today are less severe in those countries with no Byzantine tradition, that were closer to the West, and are more likely to adopt the *Gesellschaft* over the *Gemeinschaft* model of national development. Those countries lying further east in Europe still are being subjected to a more dangerous brand of militant nationalism; still have their old bureaucracies, security, and military apparatuses; and have made few moves to discard state socialism for one after the other declared official states of emergency or martial law. Should this state of affairs continue for long in Eastern Europe, then increased migration of refugees will likely pick up once again and further endanger any hope for a new long-lasting peace.

In Chapter 10, Golovakha and Panina discuss democratization (or the lack of it) in the Ukraine (which is beset with anomie) as well as the need for a new human rights strategy that would universalize the process for all citizens. These authors recognize that anomie cannot serve the cause of democracy well. The extent of social and economic malaise is so severe in Ukrainian society that it endangers the shared existence of social and political values. With social dissatisfaction come anomic demoralization, cynicism, anarchy, and paternalism.

The cure for this malady which is destabilizing Ukrainian society is decreased social anxiety through improved living conditions and increased life satisfaction. This requires a greater measure of personal responsibility and self-reliance, which would also improve the chances for increased democratization. Using survey data, these authors show the increasing ambivalence and contradictory nature of public opinion, which is split along radical-democratic and conservative-totalitarian lines. Members of the public, for instance, support both private property and limiting bourgeois ideology or unearned profit using strong mechanisms of public order. Consequently, there is no growth in a Ukrainian middle class, no growth in private institutions and organizations, little trust in politics, and decreasing faith in democracy. The people remain powerless and not politically efficacious so that a complete reform of the educational, socialization, communications, and political system is needed to correct these views.

Within the Ukraine, there has been some progress made in the field of human rights, but the threat of a return of authoritarian government remains real as long as the state has a monopoly on the economy and promotes a nationalistic ideology. Old farming systems, bureaucracy, military metaphors, continuing learned helplessness, conformism, and nihilism all exist side by side in Ukrainian political culture along with ethnic rivalries and mixed views toward Russia. These two authors propose a new human rights strategy which is principled, legal, tolerant, protective, international, verifiable, popularly based, organizationally supported, friendly toward privatization (both elite and popularly co-directed), and spread through new techniques of political socialization and education. Without such immediate changes in the society, the public may well initiate its search for a strong leader who will bring power, strength, order, direction, and authoritarian control to the society. This option is a distinct possibility for the Ukraine in the not too distant future.

PART III: SOCIALIZATION PROCESSES: CASE STUDIES

Linssen, Hagendoorn, and Mateusen (Chapter 11) begin this section with a discussion of the effect of international written contacts on nationality stereotypes of high school students. They hypothesized in their 12-nation survey that casual, frequent, voluntary, and cooperative contact of different nationals would reduce specific national stereotypes, but not those which applied to equivalent nations. The contact hypothesis proved to be true in three-fourths of the observed cases. Self-categorization theory is used to explain and contextualize the results.

Specifically, in 12.5 per cent of the cases, specific changes in stereotyping were observed after only six months of written contact. While a change in national stereotyping occurred in three out of four instances, this hypothesis was falsified in three other instances where, for example, a national categorization shifted to a religious one and then to a generalization. Such contacts and information exchanges reduce negative nationality stereotypes depending on given contextual situations, which activate resultant changes. The chapter also discusses situational, societal, and individual antecedents and effects of contacts, describes the research design and methods used, and covers north-south and country-size contact effects.

Kéri (Chapter 12) describes alternatives for socializing Hungary's new political elites. In the post-1989 world, governing and influential leadership groups are quite varied. They may be classed into six types on the basis of their political cultures, behaviors, and attitudes. These categories are the survivors, humanistic intellectuals, demagogic leaders, political professionals, newly born, and new capitalist entrepreneurs. They may also be called, respectively, the old guard, researchers, populist leaders, professional class, 'clean' young democrats without a past, and business-oriented political dilettantes. Since we now have a better opportunity to analyze these ideal types, we can see that the old clear-cut duality between the formal and informal (or overt and covert/hidden) socialization patterns served not only to combat the official party line, but they also had other side effects as well.

What is surprising is that the old Hungarian official political elite disappeared so quickly and was so rapidly replaced with new elites of a totally different stripe. This result provides convincing evidence of the failure of the old system as well as the force of those hidden family/socialization/education mechanisms which proved to be so powerful and effective. The resultant conclusion is that the same socialization agents, while supposedly operating in a uniform way, actually produced very different political products, depending on the school, family, age group, or workplace and their relative personal influence. In effect, each of these agents was able to transmit the political culture as a whole from its unique perspective and, while in competition with other (as well as official) agents of socialization. This pattern undoubtedly applies to other countries as well, just as the influence of over 40 years of formal socialist political education/socialization has had its present-day effects as well (for example, are the 'new' Hungarian communists successful today in part because they were successful in the past as 'old' communists?).

Vollebergh (Chapter 13) presents her empirical findings regarding social group identification and intolerance among adolescents in the Netherlands. She discusses authoritarianism, ethnocentrism, social groups, and self-identification; the outcome of a utopian experiment; and other research results. This study is based on the observation that while democratic theory is founded on political equality, social groups and one's social identity stem from inequality, selectivity, and choice. Therefore, this research looks at the relationships among affiliation, (non)authoritarianism, self-identification, and intolerance toward out-groups.

This study found that ethnocentrism was not the exclusive property of authoritarians since they and nonauthoritarian adolescents used similar classification categories in some respects to classify groups along a good-bad axis. However, authoritarians alone associated this axis with group power and strength and gave more positive values to groups which represented order, normality, God, and the supernatural. For the activists, the exact reverse was true. Both groups selected in-groups which were considered morally superior to the out-groups, but authoritarians chose masculine morality to a given feminine variant, which the nonauthoritarians preferred.

Characteristically, the authoritarians also identified with power, convention, toughness, and masculinity. But the nonauthoritarian activists also identified, excluded, and projected along feminist, nonpower, nonconventional, and less tough lines to construct their form of in-group favoritism and out-group exclusion. Consequently, there is a difference of degree or gradualism between authoritarians and nonauthoritarians. There is not a polar differentiation as opposites (which has often been maintained) regarding their differing opinions and psychological composition (that is, both groups practice in-group favoritism). It is just that the objects of this common in-group favoritism seem to vary from group to group.

To complete this part of the book, Fratczak-Rudnicka (Chapter 14) describes the current social consciousness of Polish youth based on a national survey of 15- to 25-year-olds conducted in April 1994. There is both 'good' and 'bad' news reported in this survey.

The 'good' news is that youth are more optimistic today than they were just a few years ago. Furthermore, many young people believe that education pays off in terms of later job successes and upward SES. Among today's youth, there is also increased support for market reform, increased economic realism, greater self-responsibility, and less fatalism about the future. However, they either remain uninformed or uninterested in politics, political views, or politicians.

As for the 'bad' news, the least independent, most fearful, most threatened, and least family supported are those youth whose parents are poorly educated, low income, unemployed, or live in a rural/small farm setting. This means that wealthy, well-educated, higher SES parents have children who are most interested in additional education, support private business ventures, approve of democracy and a market economy, and expect parental support. Therefore, there is a clear dichotomy based on SES/class divisions in which the better-educated, wealthier families have more social, economic, and political capital to spend on improving the lot of their offspring than do those who are not so equipped. Whether or not more of these potential 'winners' can be developed to offset the large number of 'losers' in the society remains to be seen, but recent developments have been positive in this respect.

PART IV: DEMOCRATIZATION TRENDS AND EUROPEAN INTEGRATION

Meyenberg (Chapter 15) discusses the democratization of the European Union (EU), while Dekker and Willemse (Chapter 16) approach the topic of linkages between masses and elites in the context of the European Community (EC) and EU. Meyenberg maintains that democracy requires popular sovereignty and either direct or indirect representation and participation in person or through democratic institutions. Such intermediaries are parties, interest groups, the press, and private organizations. He also discusses why the Germans fear (in public opinion surveys) the increasing power/role of the EU, its shortcomings, and confusion about the meaning of democracy in Europe. His concern is not with putting the EU on hold, but rather with democratizing it. That is, a basic power balance between its parliamentary and administrative branches can be maintained through direct representatives of the people from member countries. He also raises such questions as why not less standardization; greater subsidiarity; more national parliamentary directives to EU governmental representatives to protect national parliamentary rights; improved public knowledge of EU activities and a better-informed citizenry; and simultaneous movements to nationalize the EU while Europeanizing national parliaments?

Dekker and Willemse's chapter poses two questions about the existence of a gap or consensus in the Netherlands on the EU and how either result can be explained. To test elite/mass agreement, the responses which parliamentarians gave and those which the public had in a Eurobarometer poll were compared. The result showed consensus on all but two issues. Various standard models (that is, voters', party members', and pressure group members' sanctions, consensus, and role models) and two new models (that is, propaganda and socialization) were used in this analysis to explain the results obtained.

These results indicated that, regarding European integration, there is widespread elite/mass consensus with gaps only on the single market and pro-European feelings. The three traditional models were useless in explaining these results. The propaganda and (particularly) socialization models have far more promise for their explanatory power because the elected believe their job is to inform the electors and because, while information sources vary, there is a certain consistency on representatives' public positions and voting records. The overall results of this study illustrate that inter-age, cross-gender, multiple educational levels, income, and residence variations do not seem to matter when it comes to Dutch agreement on European integration, unlike results seen elsewhere in England, France, Denmark, and Germany.

PART V: POLITICS AND/OF EDUCATION

This section of the book is concerned with political philosophy, values, and civic competence, democracy, socialization, and schooling.

Miedema (Chapter 17) uses philosophical and analytical methods (including some extrapolation) to apply Hannah Arendt's political theory to political education and development using her analysis of totalitarianism to relate politics to pedagogy. His conclusion is that Arendt's concepts of democratic pluralism, individuality, identity, freedom, subjectivity, community, and solidarity are opposites of totalitarianism in its dark individual and oppressive communal forms. Education creates an intersubjective world, a public and communicative space, where individual and social identity, agency, and personality can develop an active citizenry which is engaged in the democratic project.

Klaassen (Chapter 18) tackles the difficult question of the correspondence among democracy, values, and morality as integral components of citizenship today, in both Eastern and Western Europe and North America. Two present lines of argument for the redefinition of citizenship include first, the civil society and historical approach, while the second emphasizes socialization, education, and political participation factors.

Redefinitions of citizenship are currently underway because of conflicting trends such as localism versus regionalism, national sovereignty versus international integration, legal and political individual rights and responsibilities versus social dependency and the welfare state, majority rule versus minority rights, capitalism versus democracy, individualism versus solidarity, self-interest versus human rights, and multiculturalism versus a new form of integrating and inclusive majoritarian nationalism.

Through self-reflexivity and self-actualization activities, citizenship education can help individuals develop a sense of identity, political participation skills, and a moral basis for evaluating individual and public policy alternatives, values, standards, and principles. Such political education needs to focus on providing situations where students can debate ethical choices, grapple with political and personal dilemmas, and develop those participatory and decision-making skills (as individuals and group members). Citizens so educated will help democracies to work their way through the moral anarchy so widespread in the contemporary world in which peace, equality, freedom, and justice are just as elusive as they were for the last half century.

Dekker (Chapter 19) makes a direct approach to defining democracy (strong and weak or direct/participatory versus indirect/republican forms), democratic citizenship, and citizenship competence. He also asks several questions, such as: What is the present level of democratic citizenship competence among youth? What are the main explanatory variables for these competencies? When do children first know/value democracy? Is this a stage/developmental process? Do such concepts/values change over time? If individuals are socialized to democracy, can we develop a model for this process?

The answers to these questions should help both Central and Eastern European countries and Western European and American polities increase their levels of political commitment, involvement, and action. To do so, it is necessary to conceptualize what democracy is, the individual rights and duties of citizenship *vis-à-vis* others and the state, the socioeconomic and politico-civic demands of citizenship, the legal and psychological conceptions of citizenship, and the peculiarities of democratic citizenship requirements and competencies. Such distinctions separate citizens into voters and decision makers, individuals and community members, the apathetic and the involved, and distrustful versus efficacious citizens.

Some of the key variables related to civic competence include level of education, SES, gender, personal health, and general socialization proclivities (that is, the major influence of socialization agents and individual/group political orientations, such as knowledge, affect, actions, and basic personality character-istics). From previous studies of such variables, it is possible to create a list of the key indices for a democratic citizenship competence study. Examples of these indices are democratic values, party/pressure group membership, political behaviors, and mass media interests. The framework for a longitudinal panel study is also detailed in this chapter. Such a project would be of widespread value to both old and new, developing and developed, and fragile and stable political systems.

'Authoritarianism, never again' is the theme of Meloen's (Chapter 20) contribution which surveys youth's attitudes toward anti-Semitism in the Netherlands and Belgium (Flanders). Meloen broke anti-Semitism into several component parts, but found them to be indistinguishable from one another. Of all the background variables, knowledge/interest in the Holocaust/World War II and degree of authoritarianism were linked to anti-Semitism (that is, such knowledge/interest may help reduce anti-Semitism levels). Anti-Semitism was also related to antiminority prejudices, nationalism, xenophobia, antifeminism, pro-apartheid, racial party preferences, and authoritarianism. Education also plays an intermediating role, it was found, in that type of school relates to ethnocentrism, anti-Semitism, and authoritarianism.

The Conway-Damico-Damico (Chapter 21) discussion of democratic theory, school socialization, and democratic results (for example, political participation) concludes that secondary schooling is an important factor (for example, extracurricular activities) in determining democratic beliefs, commu-nity, and later political behaviors. The 1972, 1974, and 1976 national surveys of secondary school students were used in this study. The findings served to prove that high school participation in extracurricular activities predicts one's holding democratic beliefs which, in turn, later leads to increased young adult participation in political and community activities.

PART VI: CONCLUSIONS, SYNTHESIS, AND SUMMARY COMMENTS

In this concluding section, Farnen (Chapter 22) summarizes the major specific and general conclusions drawn from the preceding contributions. These overall findings are interrelated, compared, and contrasted. Some of these specific conclusions apply to both the concrete and general levels (for example, authoritarianism). This syndrome or conceptual/theoretical artifact is handled at a basic level in several chapters (2, 3, 13, 19, and 20) so that we can see that it is related to anti-Semitism, intolerance, militarism, nationalism, educational conservatism, right-wing party support, ethnocentrism, and political regime type. At a higher level of generalization, these chapters indicate that whatever the socialization study, civic education research project, or political survey undertaken, authoritarianism should be one major dependent variable in the analysis. Other such factors discussed in this final chapter include citizenship, nationalism, democracy, racism, human rights, stereotyping, socialization, and European integration.

2   *Authoritarianism, Democracy, and Education*

A Preliminary Empirical 70-Nation Global Indicators Study

Jos Meloen

ABSTRACT

An empirical investigation of relevant data for 70 nations sought to find the meaning of authoritarianism and its possible relationships to dictatorial and antidemocratic political regimes. There were four levels of analysis. 1) Cross-national authoritarianism - the first problem investigated asked: Are there any measures of authoritarianism that are predictably different for different countries? If so, why do these differences exist? For this purpose, an estimate of authoritarianism scores was based on the results of 32 countries from which large numbers of authoritarianism data were available from a worldwide review. 2) State authoritarianism - next, a score for state authoritarianism was developed from these global indicators for some 70 selected countries. These included all the major countries on all continents. 3) Relationship between state authoritarianism and authoritarian attitudes - the state authoritarianism score was related to the previously developed estimate of authoritarianism levels in 32 countries. Surprisingly, both were highly correlated. 4) Preliminary analyses regarding causes of state authoritarianism - to understand the possible relationship between authoritarian attitudes and state authoritarianism, models were tested based on results of, and our experience with, 40 years of authoritarianism research. These models included independent global indicators of politics, economics, population (for example, density and urbanization), education, communications, ethnicity, the gender gap, military conflict, family-type, and religion. Conclusion and discussion - these models are presented and the most plausible explanations (in terms of the various guiding theories of authoritarianism) are discussed.

INTRODUCTION

This empirical investigation was conducted to discover the current operational meanings of authoritarianism and its possible relationships to dictatorial and antidemocratic regimes in the 1990s.

CROSS-NATIONAL LEVELS OF AUTHORITARIANISM

The first research question was: Are there any levels of authoritarianism that are predictably different for different countries? If so, why do these levels exist? Consequently, cross-national levels of authoritarianism were investigated. For this purpose an estimate of authoritarianism level was computed (based on results from 32 countries) from which large numbers of authoritarianism scores were available from a worldwide authoritarianism review (Meloen, 1983 and 1993). These data included some 20 000 students and 10 000 nonstudents, as well as many random samples and separate cross-national studies. Linear regression techniques were used to estimate student levels, as well as population levels.

Table 2.1 presents standardized authoritarianism scores and estimates from 32 countries using multiple studies from 1945 to 1993 as well as estimates of authoritarianism intercorrelations between these countries.

Initially, there was little social scientific basis for such estimates, except that they were based on many decades of research experience on authoritarianism. We also now have a formal statistical way to compute these estimates from known means in international samples. However, the meaning of such estimates was not entirely clear. Why would any variation in authoritarianism levels exist between countries? So many relevant differences exist that isolating those that would influence authoritarianism levels seemed to be an almost impossible task.

CROSS-NATIONAL LEVELS OF STATE AUTHORITARIANISM

To interpret these different observed levels, some logical authoritarianism measure (which could be computed from sources independent of the previous attitudinal estimates) applicable to these various countries was sought. Additionally, to be convincing, it should be related to the fundamental, theoretical ideas basic to the phenomenon of authoritarianism. Consequently, a score for state authoritarianism was developed using certain global indicators. A large number of sources for such indicators are available; for instance, those which Freedom House (a nonpartisan US human-rights monitoring group, which Eleanor Roosevelt founded in 1941 to combat antidemocratic forces abroad) used. Every year, they produce a worldwide distribution of 'free', 'partly free', and 'not free' countries. The preponderance of countries in the latter category are in Africa, the Middle East, and Southeast Asia. There were many other sources available. These included various United Nations bodies (for example, UNESCO's World Education Report [1991] and the UN Development Programme's Human Development Report [1991]), several international human rights groups (for example, Amnesty International), and the US State Department's and the CIA's World Fact Book data.

Table 2.1 Cross-national authoritarianism studies and estimates of standardized authoritarianism scores (SF) in 32 countries (column abbreviations described in notes on next page)

	Alb. nst.	Mea. st.	Sim. st.	Sim. nst.	Mel. st.	Mel. total	1945-80 st.	1945-80 nst.	Fst. st.	Fpop. nst.
Years (19)	59	67	72	72	93	45-80	45-80	45-80	93	93
(1)	(2)	(3)	(4)	(5)	(6)	(7)	(8)	(9)	(10)	(11)
Country										
1. USA	-	3.16	3.27	4.03	4.15	3.57	3.43	3.90	3.40	4.33
2. Canada	-	-	-	-	-	-	3.36	-	3.33	4.31
3. UK	4.15	-	-	-	-	3.87	3.75	3.99	3.70	4.40
4. Australia	-	-	-	-	-	-	-	3.98	3.45	4.34
5. New Zealand	-	-	-	-	-	-	3.52	4.37	3.48	4.35
6. S Africa-wh.	-	-	-	-	-	4.01	4.02	4.00	3.95	4.46
7. S Africa-bl.	-	-	-	-	4.68	-	-	-	4.57	4.61
8. Lebanon	-	5.06	-	-	-	-	4.93	-	4.80	4.66
9. Egypt	-	-	-	-	-	-	4.87*	-	4.75	4.65
10. Yugoslavia	-	-	-	-	-	-	4.53	-	4.43	4.58
11. Greece	-	-	-	-	-	-	4.11	-	4.03	4.48
12. India	-	5.06	-	-	5.17	5.08	5.06	5.11	5.03	4.72
13. Hong Kong	-	-	-	-	-	-	4.61	-	4.50	4.59
14. Germany-W	5.08	-	-	-	3.14	4.51	3.72	4.80	3.12	4.26
15. Austria	-	-	-	-	-	-	4.17		4.09	4.49
16. Italy	-	-	-	-	-	3.83	3.01	4.84	3.00	4.23
17. Brazil	-	4.02	-	-	-	-	4.04	-	3.97	4.47
18. Zimbabwe	-	4.91	-	-	-	-	4.91	-	4.79	4.66
19. Netherlands	4.53	-	-	-	2.72	4.10	2.53	4.43	2.73	4.17
20. Belgium	5.05	-	-	-	3.59	-	-	5.05	3.55	4.36
21. France	4.66	-	-	-	-	-	-	4.66	3.56	4.37
22. Sweden	4.41	-	-	-	-	-	-	4.41	3.43	4.34
23. Norway	3.81	-	-	-	-	-	-	3.81	3.16	4.27
24. Israel	-	-	-	-	-	-	4.59	-	4.49	4.59
25. Finland	-	-	3.51	3.98	2.98	-	-	-	2.97	4.23
26. Spain	-	-	-	-	3.57	-	-	-	3.53	4.36
27. Estonia	-	-	-	-	4.34	-	-	-	4.25	4.53
28. Poland	-	-	-	-	4.55	-	-	-	4.45	4.58
29. Hungary	-	-	-	-	3.10	-	-	-	3.09	4.25
30. Russia	-	-	-	-	4.74	-	-	-	4.63	4.62
31. Mexico	-	-	4.49	4.67	-	-	-	-	4.39	4.57
32. Costa Rica	-	-	3.76	4.32	-	-	-	-	3.71	4.40
N (Countries) =	7	5	4	4	12	7	18	13	32	32

Table 2.1 (continued)

Notes: nst.=nonstudents; st.=student sample(s); pop.=population; wh.=white; bl.=black; W=West. All F scores recomputed to Standard F (SF) scale: 1.00-7.00 scale range. Columns: 2=Albinski (1959); 3=Meade and Whittaker (1967); 4=Simpson (1972); 5=Simpson (1972); 6=Meloen, Farnen, and German (1993); 7,8,9=Meloen (1983); 10=SF-estimate 1993 students; 11=SF-estimate population (1993); columns 10, 11 estimated from 2 to 8 using linear regression analysis; *: estimated from 'Dogmatism' scores.

A number of indicators relevant to authoritarianism were available for some 70 (initially) selected countries. These included all the major countries on all continents. The quantified indicators were all based on the work of the previously mentioned well-recognized international bodies. See Tables 2.2 and 2.3 for 12 (plus one composite) indicators of state authoritarianism and the internal reliability of state authoritarianism measures (Cronbach's alpha correlations). The variables included acts of state terrorism, suppression of deviant attitudes, denial of gay rights, imposition of state beliefs on individuals/groups, excessive use of capital punishment, suppression of labor unions, censorship, designation of abortion as illegal, incarceration of political prisoners, obstruction of the work of human rights bodies, and existence of a large gender gap.

The statistical reliability of this short measure appeared to be rather high (Cronbach's alpha: .85 and .86 for the 10- and 12-item versions, respectively).

The rank order of these state authoritarianism scores showed that on these measures, all known dictatorships scored high while the free, democratic countries scored low. Table 2.4 presents these results of the highest (for example, Iran, Libya) and the lowest (for example, the Netherlands, Canada) scoring countries (that is, the external validity of these measures).

State authoritarianism was also highly (negatively) correlated (***=$p<.001$; **=$p<.01$; *=$p<.05$ throughout below) with the international UN Human Freedom Index (1985) (.81*** for 48 countries) and Freedom House's freedom rating (1992) (.83*** for 52 countries).

RELATIONSHIPS BETWEEN STATE AUTHORITARIANISM AND AUTHORITARIAN ATTITUDES

The state authoritarianism score was related to the previously developed estimate of authoritarianism levels in 32 countries. (See Table 2.5 for the intercorrelations between F-scale results by country with external state authoritarianism indicators.) Surprisingly, both were highly correlated (.85*** for 27 countries).

Table 2.2 State authoritarianism indicators

1.	Unions (91)	Trade Unions Illegal (1991) Range: legal; legal but controlled; legal but harassed; legal but repressed; illegal or nonexistent
2.	Cappun (91)	Capital Punishment Legal (1991) Range: abolished for all crimes; abolished for ordinary crimes only; abolished in practice, but not in law; retained and used for ordinary crimes
3.	Terror (91)	State Terroristic Practices (1991) Range: no infringements on human rights; repression and moderate infringement of human rights; terror and torture used; disappearance or assassinations rife
4.	Supres (91)	State Suppression of Deviation (1991) Range: affirmative action practiced; neglect; discouragement; criminalization or legal discrimination; suppression
5.	Gays (91)	Gays Not Tolerated/Unlawful (1991) Range: lawful and tolerated; lawful and repressed; unlawful and tolerated; unlawful and repressed
6.	Beliefs (91)	State Beliefs Imposed (1991) Range: no stated beliefs, all tolerated; no stated beliefs, but favoritism in practice; stated beliefs, others tolerated; stated beliefs imposed, others repressed
7.	Censor (91)	State Censorship (1991) Range: rules implicit; bureaucratic, but flexible; bureaucratic, but rigid; arbitrary
8.	Abort (91)	Illegal Status of Abortion (1991) Range: legal, on request; legal for sociomedical reason; legal, to protect mother; legal, to save mother
9.	Mildoc (86)	Military per 100 Physicians (1986) Range: 0-400 soldiers; 400-2000 soldiers; 2000-10 000 soldiers; >10 000 soldiers per 100 physicians
10.0	Oppos (90)	PCONSC (91)+OBSTR (90) Anti-Opposition 1990: includes both indicators
10.1	Pconsc (91)	Prisoners of Conscience (1991) Range: no prisoners; prisoners
11.	Obstr (90)	Obstructive to Human Rights Bodies (1990) Range: not obstructive; obstructive
12.	Gender (89)	Unequal Opportunities for Women (1989) Range: most equal; less equal; little equality; least equal

Sources: Adapted from Population Crisis Committee; Amnesty International; US State Department; Minority Rights Group; World Directory of Minorities; International Lesbian and Gay Association; International PEN Adopted Prisoners of Conscience; Index on Censorship; and others. See A Note on Sources at the end of this chapter.

Table 2.3 Internal consistency of state authoritarianism measures

Reliability Analysis			Item-Rest Correlations	
Nr.	Code	Variable	Staut12	Staut10
1.	Unions (91)	Trade Unions Illegal (1991)	.44	.51
2.	Cappun (91)	Capital Punishment Legal (1991)	.64	.64
3.	Terror (91)	State Terror Practices (1991)	.69	.67
4.	Supres (91)	State Suppression of Deviation (1991)	.63	.65
5.	Gays (91)	Gays Not Tolerated/Unlawful (1991)	.61	.61
6.	Belief (91)	State Beliefs Imposed (1991)	.26	.30
7.	Censor (91)	State Censorship (1991)	.60	.59
8.	Abort (91)	Illegal Status of Abortion (1991)	.44	.44
9.	Mildoc (86)	Military per 100 Physicians (1986)	.62	.63
10.0	Oppos (90)	PCONSC91+OBSTR90 Anti-Opposition (1990)	-	.48
10.1	Pconsc (91)	Prisoners of Conscience (1991)	.28	-
11.	Obstr (90)	Obstructive to Human Rights Bodies	.50	-
12.	Gender (89)	Unequal Opportunities Women 1989	.85	-
Number of countries in parentheses ( )			50	52
Cronbach's alpha			.86	.85
Standardized item alpha			.86	.85

Note that both lists of variables in Table 2.5 were computed from completely independent sources, using separate types of research. The national authoritarianism estimate was an indication of average levels of attitudes among the country's population. Such attitudinal authoritarianism was also strongly (negatively) related to several other independent indicators (that is, the Freedom Rating [-.79***, 30 countries] and the UN Human Freedom Index [-.68***, 27 countries]).

It also predicted (see Table 2.6) levels of democratic participation (suffrage) in government (-.59**, 29 countries).

These authoritarianism estimates also predicted (see Table 2.7) the group of dictatorial types of government as being quite different from the group of democratic ones (.51**, 32 countries).

Once again, all such indicators were taken from independent sources. The inference from this relationship between state authoritarianism and attitudinal authoritarianism is that in dictatorships, high levels of authoritarian attitudes are predictable, while in free countries, much lower levels exist. This widespread, but causal inference now has support using empirical data. This result is rather unique because it has never before been measured in this way since dictatorships have usually denied us access to do critical empirical research. Nor has it ever before been possible to relate corresponding attitudinal levels to these causative and/or interactive dictatorial state practices in an empirical way.

Table 2.4 External validity: state authoritarianism ranking by country in the early 1990s

Highest = 100			Lowest = 0		
1.	Iran	93	1.	Netherlands	0
2.	Libya	80	2.	Canada	3
2.	Pakistan	80	3.	Sweden	7
3.	Iraq	70	4.	Finland	10
4.	Syria	67	4.	France	10
4.	Bangladesh	67	4.	Denmark	10
6.	China	60	5.	Germany	12
6.	South Africa	60	7.	USA	20
7.	USSR	57	8.	Japan	23
			10.	UK	30

Notes: Data base: 70 countries worldwide (including all major nation-states).
High = authoritarian; Low = free countries.

THE CAUSES OF STATE AUTHORITARIANISM: PRELIMINARY ANALYSIS

To understand possible relationships between attitudinal authoritarianism and state authoritarianism (which is not at all obvious), several theoretical models were tested. These were based on results of, and experiences with, 40 years of authoritarianism research. Independent global indicators of politics, economics, population (for example, density and urbanization), education, communications, ethnicity, the gender gap, military conflict, family types, and religion were used in these analyses. Table 2.8 displays the political, economic, educational, demographic, mass media, ethnic, gender, and military indices and their intercorrelations with state authoritarianism and authoritarian attitudes.

A preliminary test model (see Figure 2.1) showed that, instead of economics, state authoritarianism was almost completely ($R2=.86$) explained by the political (authoritarian) system, the (low) level of educational attainment, and the (high) level of authoritarian attitudes.

This, in turn, explained authoritarian state practices (for example, lack of popular participation in government [$R2=.48$] with no other variables included). State authoritarianism also predicted widening the gender gap and, to some extent, military conflict potential. All other indicators used in the analysis showed no (direct) influence (family type and religion were not yet included). Furthermore, the sole predictor of attitudinal authoritarianism was state authoritarianism ($R2=.72$) to the exclusion of all other variables.

Table 2.5 Authoritarianism national samples intercorrelated with state authoritarianism indicators

F Scale Estimates for Authoritarianism National Samples	Code Variable Name	State Authoritarianism		Freedom Rating	Human Freedom Index
		Staut10 1991	Staut12 1991	Free92 1992	HFI85 1985
1. F Population 1993	Fpop93	.85*** (27)	.85*** (27)	.79*** (30)	.68*** (27)
2. F Students 1993	Fst93	.85*** (27)	.85*** (27)	.79*** (30)	.68*** (27)
3. F Students 1991-92	F10	.89** (9)	.88** (9)	.78** (12)	.48 (8)
4. F Students 1983	Fst83	.86*** (19)	.86*** (19)	.79*** (20)	.79*** (19)
5. F Population 1983	Fpop83	.34 (13)	.35 (13)	.50 (13)	.40 (13)
6. Albinski Nonstudent	FAlbin	-.06 (7)	-.10 (7)	.21 (7)	-.15 (7)
7. Meade F Students	FMeade	.97** (5)	.96** (5)	.95** (6)	.79 (5)
8. Simpson F Population	FSimPop	.98* (4)	.99* (4)	.88 (4)	.95* (4)
9. Simpson F Students	FSimSt	.91 (4)	.91 (4)	.93 (4)	.94 (4)

Notes: number of countries in parentheses ( ); *** = p<.001; ** = p<.01; * = p<.05; for all indicators: high = authoritarian, low = free. See Table 2.1 for information on sample populations and studies used in this analysis.

Table 2.6 Participation in government (suffrage) and authoritarianism

Participation in Government	(Autgov91):	Range: Universal suffrage (1. full participation) to nonelected or military governments (5. no participation)			
(1) State authoritarianism scores, authoritarianism levels and freedom ratings	(2) State Auth.	(3) Population Auth. Est.	(4) Student Auth. Est.	(5) Freedom Rating	(6) Human Freedom Index
Year(s)	1990-91	1993	1993	1992	1985
Variable	Staut10	Fpop93	Fst93	Free92	HFI85
Range	0-100	1-7	1-7	1-7	0-38
	Means/N	Means/N	Means/N	Means/N	Means/N
Participation levels for all states	39 (51)	4.43 (32)	3.84 (32)	2.92 (59)	18.4 (51)
1. Full	15 (4)	4.33 (2)	3.41 (2)	2.00 (4)	18.0 (4)
2. Some	32 (33)	4.40 (23)	3.70 (23)	1.98 (33)	13.0 (33)
3. Slight	45 (2)	4.54 (3)	4.30 (3)	3.33 (3)	25.0 (3)
4. Virtually none	65 (10)	4.59 (3)	4.48 (3)	4.54 (14)	33.1 (9)
5. None	71 (2)	4.66 (3)	4.80 (1)	5.10 (5)	31.0 (2)
F-between groups	11.0***	2.6(*)	2.6(*)	11.4***	7.5***
Pearson-r	.69***	.51**	.52**	.66***	.55***
F-linearity	43.4***	9.9**	10.1**	43.1***	23.2***

Notes: Presented are the means and the number of states in parentheses (); all high scores indicate high authoritarianism, while all low scores indicate more freedom; column (2) Staut10: state authoritarianism, 10 indicators; column (3) Fpop93: estimate for total population of authoritarianism; column (4) Fst93: estimate for student level of authoritarianism; column (5) Free92: most recent Freedom House 'freedom rating'; column (6) HFI85: UN Human Freedom Index 1985; *** = $p < .001$; ** = $p < .01$, two-tailed; * = $p < .05$; (*) = $.05 < p < .10$.

Table 2.7 Government type and authoritarianism

(1) State authoritarianism scores, authoritarian- ism levels and freedom ratings	(2) State Auth.	(3) Population Auth. Est.	(4) Student Auth. Est.	(5) Freedom Rating	(6) Human Freedom Index
Year(s)	1990-91	1993	1993	1992	1985
Variable	Staut10	Fpop93	Fst93	Free92	HFI85
Range	0-100	1-7	1-7	1-7	0-38
	Means/N	Means/N	Means/N	Means/N	Means/N
For All States	39 (50)	4.43 (29)	3.84 (29)	2.90 (60)	18.4 (48)
1. Parl. Dem.	28 (18)	4.38 (12)	3.60 (12)	1.58 (19)	12.6 (18)
2. Fed. Pres. Dem.	14 (5)	4.35 (5)	3.48 (5)	1.10 (5)	4.0 (4)
3. Pres. Parl. Dem.	36 (10)	4.46 (5)	3.97 (5)	2.56 (17)	23.1 (10)
4. Pres. Leg. Dem.	27 (1)	4.40 (1)	3.71 (1)	1.00 (1)	7.0 (1)
5. Fed.Pres.Leg.Dem.	42 (2)	4.47 (1)	3.97 (1)	2.50 (2)	16.5 (2)
6. Parl. Dem. under mil. influence	69 (2)	-	-	5.00 (2)	33.0 (2)
7. Mil. Dominated Gov't.	60 (4)	4.62 (2)	4.59 (2)	5.88 (4)	30.8 (4)
8. Pres. Parl. Mil. Dominated Dem.	63 (1)	4.66 (1)	4.80 (1)	4.50 (1)	-
9. One-Party Gov't.	64 (6)	4.61 (2)	4.59 (2)	5.41 (6)	31.4 (5)
10. Mil. Gov't.	80 (1)	-	-	6.17 (3)	31.0 (2)
F-Between Groups	6.3***	1.96	1.92	26.0***	6.4***
Pearson-r	.70***	.59**	.58**	.86***	.64***
F-Linearity	47.1***	11.9**	11.7**	207.3***	37.0***

Notes: Presented are the means and the number of states in parentheses ();all high scores indicate authoritarianism, all low scores freedom; column (1) Parl.=Parliamentary, Dem.=Democracy, Fed.=Federal, Pres.=Presidential, Leg.=Legislative, Mil.=Military, Gov't.=Government (2) Staut10: state authoritarianism, 10 indicators; column (3) Fpop93: estimate for total population's authoritarianism; column (4) Fst93: estimate for student authoritarianism; column (5) Free92: most recent Freedom House 'freedom rating'; column (6) HFI85: UN Human Freedom Index (1985); *** = p<.001; ** =p<.01, two-tailed.

Table 2.8 Intercorrelations of indices with authoritarian attitudes and state practices

(1)	(2)	(3)	(4) Authoritarian Attitudes	(5)	(6) Authoritarian State Practices	(7)
Number of States Included (Nmin-Nmax)			6-13	11-33	8-52	10-63
	Year 19__	Nmin-Nmax	F10	Fpop93	Staut10	Free92
Political Indices						
1. Democratic Attitudes	92	9-12	.05	.07	.27	-.02
2. Pro-Dictator	92	8-11	.81**	.80**	.91**	.61(*)
3. Human Freedom Index	85	8-51	-.48	-.68***	-.81***	-.81***
4. Political Rights	93	12-62	-.76**	-.77***	-.78***	included
5. Civil Rights	93	12-62	-.77**	-.77***	-.85***	included
6. Authoritarian Gov't.	91	12-59	.67*	.51**	.69***	.66***
7. Gov't. Type (Auth.)	92	12-60	.36	.59**	.70***	.85***
8. Fukuyama's Democratic	92	13-59	-.43	-.61***	-.77***	-.71***
Economic Indices						
1. Human Development	90	9-58	-.75*	-.72***	-.74***	-.47***
2. Human Development	70	8-52	-.71*	-.72***	-.78***	-.58***
3. Personal Buying Power	92	9-54	-.49	-.75***	-.77***	-.60***
4. Gross National Product	92	11-55	-.52(*)	-.69***	-.75***	-.58***
5. Govt. Expenditures	91	12-62	-.83**	-.68***	-.70***	-.52***
6. % Industrial GNP	91	9-48	-.18	.06	-.34*	-.27
Educational Indices						
1. Literacy	90	12-63	-.49	-.61***	-.71***	-.40**
2. Literacy	91	12-58	-.49	-.53**	-.67***	-.36**
3. Adult Literacy	85	9-58	-.71*	-.72***	-.80***	-.49***
4. % Literacy	90	12-62	-.49	-.64***	-.76***	-.43***
5. Enrollment 4-23 Years	88	8-55	-.55	-.50**	-.70***	-.44**
6. Years of Schooling	80	9-58	-.49	-.67***	-.79***	-.60***
7. Educational Attainment	(3+6)	9-58	-.70*	-.73***	-.81***	-.50***
8. % University Students	88	8-54	-.26	-.57**	-.66***	-.57***
9. % Govt. $ on Ed.	88	6-39	-.20	-.01	.18	.05
10. % GNP Govt. $ on Ed.	88	8-48	-.62	-.29	-.29(*)	-.20
11. % Students in Ed.	88	7-49	-.31	.16	.30*	.26(*)
12. % Students in Human.	88	7-49	.68(*)	.27	-.13	-.21
13. % Student in Soc.Sci. /Law/Sci.	88	7-49	-.22	-.01	-.14	-.27(*)
14. % Students in Eng.	88	7-49	-.13	-.07	-.01	.20
15. % Students in Med./Prof.	88	7-49	-.30	-.56**	-.14	-.06

Table 2.8 (continued)

(1)	(2)	(3)	(4)	(5)	(6)	(7)
			Authoritarian Attitudes		Authoritarian State Practices	
Number of States Included (Nmin-Nmax)			6-13	11-33	8-52	10-63
	Year 19__	Nmin-Nmax	F10	Fpop93	Staut10	Free92
Population/Demographic Data						
1. Population (millions)	93	12-62	.55(*)	.32(*)	.18	.26*
2. Population Density/Km2	93	9-57	-.06	.21	.03	.02
3. Life Expectancy	92	12-62	-.71**	-.74***	-.75***	-.44***
4. Urbanization	91	13-62	-.75**	-.47**	-.57***	-.39**
5. 'Human Suffering' Index	91	13-61	.64*	.70***	.84***	.59***
6. Climate: Mod.-Tropical	94	13-64	.43	.47**	.57***	.35**
7. Rain in cm/year	94	13-64	.02	-.34(*)	-.30*	-.19
Communications/Mass Media (per capita)						
1. Newspapers	88	8-57	-.69(*)	-.46*	-.68***	-.50***
2. Paper Consumption	88	8-52	-.49	-.69***	-.70***	-.59***
3. Radios	88	8-57	-.24	-.58**	-.63***	-.53***
4. TVs	88	8-56	-.48	-.73***	-.79***	-.64***
Ethnicity/Minorities						
1. % Speak Dominant Lang.	93	9-59	-.70*	-.49**	-.51***	-.40**
2. Number Ethnic Groups	93	12-62	.33	.19	.10	.19
3. % Ethnic Persons	93	6-34	.81(*)	.42	.34(*)	.07
Gender Gap/Male vs. Female						
1. Children Born/Woman	93	10-59	.79**	.70***	.78***	.55***
2. % Women in Labor Force	91	13-61	-.17	-.40*	-.59***	-.38**
3. Missing Women	90	6-46	.74(*)	.51*	.53***	.40**
4. Life Expectancy/% Male	90	9-59	-.54	-.58**	-.60***	-.39**
5. Women in school/% Male	80	9-58	-.69*	-.76***	-.71***	-.55***
6. % Women in Labor Force	88	9-58	-.19	-.41*	-.57***	-.35**
7. % Women in Parliament	88	8-52	-.52	-.45*	-.38**	-.11
Military						
1. % Military 18-22 Years	93	9-56	-.65(*)	-.03	-.03	.11
2. % Military Spend/Capita	89	9-56	-.13	-.34(*)	-.25(*)	-.19

Notes: *** = p<.001; ** = p<.01; * = p<.05; (*) = .05<p<.10; column (4) most correlations were not significant because of the small number of countries (6-13) for which data were available; F10: F -scale used in 13 countries, Meloen, Farnen, and German, 1993; Fpop93: population authoritarianism estimate in 32 countries based on F-scale means; Staut10: State authoritarianism based on 10 indicators in over 60 countries; Free92: Freedom House 'freedom rating' for 1992.

Figure 2.1 State authoritarianism: a preliminary model

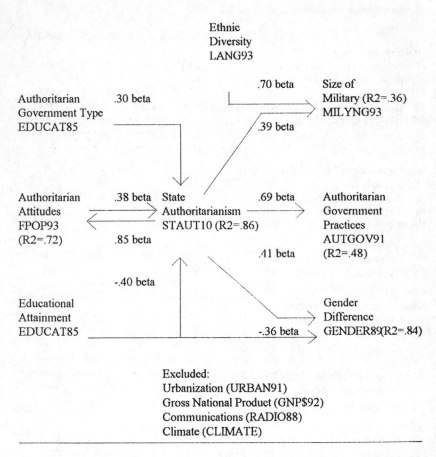

Excluded:
Urbanization (URBAN91)
Gross National Product (GNP$92)
Communications (RADIO88)
Climate (CLIMATE)

Abolishing dictatorships and installing democratic systems may not immediately result in a quick change of personal authoritarian attitudes due to factors that maintain such personality characteristics. According to our results, for instance, one such factor is the lack of adequate education (that is, there are still countries in this world with a national average of no more than two years of schooling). Indeed, there is some evidence from free countries that (the already low levels of) authoritarian attitudes may change somewhat over decades, but not over short periods. Relative regional stability (see Table 2.9 for this analysis), apart from some modest changes, was shown for the Netherlands (between 1970 and 1980 as well as since then) in national random samples.

Table 2.9 Regional stability in Dutch authoritarianism levels: 1970-1980

Region (1)	1970 (2)	1975 (3)	1980 (4)	1970-80 (5)
National	4.41	4.33	4.10	4.28
Provinces/Cities				
Groningen	4.42	4.27	4.02	4.24
Friesland	4.29-	4.59+	4.16+	4.35+
Drenthe	4.25-	4.28	4.01	4.18-
Overijssel	4.49+	4.28	4.12	4.30+
Gelderland	4.47	4.32	3.95--	4.25--
Utrecht	4.42	4.13-	4.18+	4.24
North-Holland	4.24--	4.04--	3.96-	4.08-----
South-Holland	4.42	4.31	4.15	4.29
Zeeland	4.54+	4.64+	4.05	4.41++
North-Brabant	4.57++	4.39+	4.23+	4.40++++
Limburg	4.56+	4.80++	4.26++	4.54+++++
Amsterdam	4.01---	x	x	x
Rotterdam	4.36	x	x	x
The Hague	4.42	x	x	x
N of Respondents	1925	1803	1859	5587
Standard Dev	1.16	1.12	1.13	1.14

Notes: Middendorp's National Random Samples of 1970, 1975, and 1980 were used. See Meloen and Middendorp (1985, 1991) where only 1975 and 1980 surveys were used. The F Scale mean scores wer 1.00 (low) to 7.00 (high) with a scale mean of 4.00.

The same seems to be true of the US (between 1953 and 1993) in various surveys, including random samples or large, nationwide samples. (See Table 2.10 for these longitudinal data.)

CONCLUSIONS

The relationship between authoritarian attitudes and state authoritarianism (with its minor images of democratic attitudes and democratic state practices) has never before been assessed so clearly in empirical research, nor has it been empirically investigated on such a broad group of nations. The strength of the relationship between such attitudes and state practices may even be rather surprising to skeptical researchers. Although such a relation has often been suggested, sufficient empirical support to date had been meager and fragmented due to the inaccessibility of dictatorships and communist regimes. This lead to a great deal of speculation about sources of authoritarianism.

Table 2.10 Regional stability in US authoritarianism levels: 1945-90

	Altem	Meloen	Meloen	Meloen	Middlt	Will
	Politi-cians	All samples	Student	Non-student	Random National	Random National
	1986-90	1945-80	1945-80	1945-80	1964	1953
	SRWA	SF	SF	SF	MF	SF
USA Region	(1)	(2)	(3)	(4)	(5)	(6)
1. North East	3.98	3.41	3.32	3.66	49.71	3.67
2. Mid West	4.25+	3.68+	3.60+	3.87+	x	x
3. North Central	4.07	3.38	3.03	3.56	49.48	3.86
4. West	4.10	3.50	3.45	3.56	48.23	3.07
Non-South	4.09	3.47	3.49	3.77	49.71	
5. Border South	4.58+	3.65+	3.51+	4.08+	49.90+	-
6. South	4.71++	3.90++	3.77++	4.19++	52.17++	4.50++
South+Border	4.69**	3.88**	3.75**	4.18**	50.63**	

Notes: *Columns*: (1) Altemeyer study (1993) of 549 Republicans, 682 Democrats, 2 Independents in House and Senate in 40 US states using RWA scale as recategorized by Meloen; (2) Meloen (1983) reanalysis of 201 (unweighted) samples of SF scales in 28 US states, including 18 161 students and 8035 nonstudents; (3) as in (2): only nonstudents; (4) as in (2): only students; (5) Reanalysis by Middleton (1976) of 1964 US national survey, with 1975 adult respondents; (6) Reanalysis of Williams (1966) of a 1953 US national survey of 1174 adult white respondents. *Scores*: SRWA: standard 1-7 range RWA-scores; SF: standard 1-7 range F-scores; MF: Middleton F-scores, range unknown, most likely standardized mean = 50. *Rows*: Categorization by Middleton (1976): South: Virginia, North and South Carolina, Georgia, Florida, Tennessee, Alabama, Mississippi, Arkansas, Louisiana, Texas; Border South: Oklahoma, Kentucky, West Virginia, Maryland, Delaware, District of Columbia); West: Washington, Oregon, California, Idaho, Nevada, Utah, Arizona, Wyoming, Colorado, New Mexico; North East: Maine, Vermont, New Hampshire, Massachusetts, Rhode Island, Connecticut, New York, New Jersey, Pennsylvania, Delaware, Ohio, Michigan; Mid West: Indiana, Illinois, Nebraska, Kansas, Missouri; North Central: North and South Dakota, Montana, Wisconsin, Minnesota; Middleton and Williams: Mid West probably included in North Central and Border in South. *Differences*: +: higher score; ++ highest score; South versus non-South: ** = difference in means is significant at the <.05 level.

Researchers had to rely on extrapolations from research on democratic citizens in free countries (as shown by Meloen in 1983 and 1993). Such extrapolations have so far been unsuccessful in eliminating the least likely sources of authoritarianism. Therefore, an ever-growing number of causative factors have been suggested. During the Cold War, hardly any progress was made on the theoretical basis for authoritarianism research. Consequently, many researchers were forced to reinvent the wheel time and again. Little new knowledge about authoritarianism was accumulated. Studying the subject was often discouraged, as Sanford and Levinson reported (Meloen, 1991).

Investigators themselves were being intimidated by those who used the same undemocratic methods and means which authoritarianism research was revealing (Billig, 1985).

The present results also show why the discussion of left- and right-wing authoritarianism has become almost completely obsolete. That is, there is no basic difference between the two. Instead, there is only dictatorship, largely hidden behind various extremist ideologies or political belief systems, both for left and for right.

This current approach may be the beginning of a breakthrough for this so often and so unjustly criticized research paradigm on authoritarianism. After more than 40 years of research, it now may be possible to start looking for the real roots of this incompletely understood phenomenon.

AUTHORITARIANISM: SOME POSSIBLE EXPLANATIONS

From these results, one may speculate about the following general explanation for these findings. A complex world is hard to understand without any education. This lack of understanding may also be counter-productive for escaping from extreme hierarchical leadership and those attendant social relationships that may undergird dictatorships, such as defensive group reactions favoring a strong leader. Such relationships have existed for a very long time. They were successful as long as people had to fight the evolutionary battle over natural threats and human hostility. Modern society all too easily views such behavior as irrational or emotional. This may, however, explain the continuous relationship between authoritarianism and ethnocentrism and, consequently, with other basic views about the inequality of human beings and groups.

The success of dictators may be their emotional appeal to the uneducated and the irrational, who unfortunately have no better explanations for how to integrate their reality. This social paranoia may be especially successful when dictators can convincingly portray real or presumed external threats. Poorly educated supporters of dictatorship may dream of better times in the past and may believe in authoritarian social solutions. Typically, these include super male 'military' behavior and no mercy for its victims or for the social minorities and outcasts who cannot defend themselves politically or who are so easily portrayed as enemies of the people/state. Also, mythical 'tribal' fantasies (based on superstition to explain reality) maintain the belief that if everyone would act in the same conformist manner, everything would turn out better for us, the glorified in-group. This suggests the utility of a cognitive (or better, a lack of cognitive understanding) approach to authoritarianism (like those of Goldstein and Blackman, 1978, pp. 15-61, or Rokeach, 1960) or of the learning (or better, 'unlearning') approach (like Altemeyer, 1988).

However, all of these important and various elements cannot be synthesized without using Adorno et al.'s (1950) study. They tried to make sense of the various and particular recurring and irrational elements of authoritarianism (such as mythical and superstitious tendencies, 'anti-intraception' or harshness toward out-groups, or often-present projective sexual preoccupations, mental rigidity, cynicism, and destructiveness). Such elements are denied or ignored in these cognitive and rational approaches. Additionally, much of the functioning of cognitive and rational individuals seems so much more a feature of democratic and free persons than of that among those believing in dictatorship. Such rational cognitive functioning may not always be possible for the illiterate or ill-educated who have nothing to rely on other than the behaviors of those around them and those who raised them. This encompasses social groups and parents, including their behaviors and mythical stories. Such practices may widely differ from those experienced in highly developed, well-educated nations as compared to the experiences of those in the developing world.

However, we shall never understand such general human processes if we must find a way to encourage more clarity than was produced in the last 50 years. It may be time to try out new ways in carefully directed international research. The hope that democracy would prevail, as Fukuyama (1992, pp. 49-50) expressed it only a few years ago, may be valuable, but this may also not be enough.

According to Freedom House (1993, 1995, 1996) reports, there was an increase of formal democracies in the early 1990s, but the number of countries judged 'not free' has hardly decreased (in 1986, there were 55 countries; in 1996, there were 53 countries). Also, a minority of only 20 per cent of the world's population lives in 'free' societies in 1996, compared with 36 percent in a 1986 Freedom House report. This may suggest that the period of post-Cold War democratic expansion paradoxically resulted in an increase of formal democracies, even though less of the world's people enjoyed full democratic rights in that same period.

A NOTE ON SOURCES

The country statistics and ratings are based on and adapted from the UNDP (1991), UNESCO (1991), Kidron and Segal (1991), MacKay (1993), and CIA (1993). Cited sources are the Population Crisis Committee, Amnesty International, US State Department, Minority Rights Group, World Directory of Minorities, International Lesbian and Gay Association, International PEN Adopted Prisoners of Conscience, Index on Censorship. Other national data are taken from Fukuyama (1992), Meloen (1983, 1993), Meloen, Farnen, and German (1994), Simpson (1972), Meade and Whittaker (1967), Albinski

(1959), Altemeyer (1993), Williams (1966), Middleton (1976), the Human Freedom Index, and the Human Development Index in UNDP (1991).

REFERENCES

Adorno, T., E. Frenkel-Brunswik, D. Levinson, R. Sanford (1950). *The Authoritarian Personality.* New York, NY: Harper & Row.

Albinski, M. (1959). De Onderwijzer en de Cultuuroverdracht (The Teacher and the Transfer of Culture). Assen, the Netherlands: Van Gorcum.

Altemeyer, B. (1988). *Enemies of Freedom.* London, UK: Jossey Bass.

Altemeyer, B. (1993). Personal communication with the author.

Billig, M. (1985). 'The Unobservant Participator: Nazism, Anti-Semitism and Ray's Reply', pp. 444-9 in *Ethnic and Racial Studies*, Vol. 8, No. 3.

CIA, Central Intelligence Agency (1993). *The World Fact Book 1993-94.* New York, NY: Maxwell Macmillan Company.

Freedom House News (1996). 'Global Gains for Democracy as Threats Loom', pp. 1-16 in *Freedom Review*, Vol. 27, No. 1.

Freedom House Survey Team (1993). *Freedom in the World: The Annual Survey of Political Rights and Civil Liberties 1992-1993.* New York, NY: Freedom House.

Freedom House Survey Team (1995). *Freedom in the World: The Annual Survey of Political Rights and Civil Liberties 1994-1995.* New York, NY: Freedom House.

Fukuyama, F. (1992). *The End of History and the Last Man.* London, UK: Penguin Books.

Goldstein, K. and S. Blackman (1978). *Cognitive Style.* New York, NY: Wiley & Sons.

Kidron, M. and R. Segal (1991). *The New State of the World Atlas.* New York, NY: Simon and Schuster.

MacKay, J. (1993). *State of Health Atlas.* New York, NY: Simon and Schuster.

Meade, R. and J. Whittaker (1967). 'A Cross-Cultural Study of Authoritarianism', pp. 3-7 in *Journal of Social Psychology*, Vol. 72.

Meloen, J. (1983). *De Autoritaire Reactie in Tijden van Welvaart en Crisis* (The Authoritarian Response in Times of Prosperity and Crisis). Amsterdam, the Netherlands: University of Amsterdam, unpublished Ph.D. dissertation.

Meloen, J. (1991). 'The Fortieth Anniversary of "The Authoritarian Personality,"' pp. 119-27 in *Politics and the Individual*, Vol. 1, No. 1.

Meloen, J. (1993). 'The F Scale as a Predictor of Fascism: An Overview of 40 Years of Authoritarianism Research', pp. 47-69 in W. Stone, G. Lederer, and R. Christie (eds.) *Strength and Weakness: The Authoritarian Personality Today.* New York, NY: Springer Verlag.

Meloen, J., R. Farnen, and D. German (1994). 'Authoritarianism and Democracy', pp. 123-52 in G. Csepeli, D. German, L. Kéri, and I. Stumpf (eds.) *From Subject to Citizen.* Budapest, Hungary: Hungarian Center for Political Education.

Meloen, J. and C. Middendorp (1985). 'Potentieel Fascisme in Nederland' (Potential Fascism in the Netherlands), pp. 93-108 in *Jaarboek van de Nederlandse Vereniging van Marktonderzoekers.* Haarlem, the Netherlands: De Vriegeborgh.

Meloen, J. and C. Middendorp (1991). 'Authoritarianism in the Netherlands: Ideology, Personality or Sub Culture', pp. 49-72 in *Politics and the Individual*, Vol. 1, No. 2.

Middleton, R. (1976). 'Regional Differences in Prejudice', pp. 94-117 in *American Sociological Review,* Vol. 41.

Rokeach, M. (1960). *The Open and Closed Mind.* New York, NY: Basic Books.

Simpson, M. (1972). 'Authoritarianism and Education: A Comparative Approach', pp. 223-34 in *Sociometry,* Vol. 35, No. 2.

UNDP, United Nations Development Programme (1991). *Human Development Report 1991.* Oxford, UK: Oxford University Press.

UNESCO, United Nations Education Scientific and Cultural Organization (1991). *World Education Report 1991.* Paris, France: UNESCO.

Williams, J. (1966). 'Regional Differences in Authoritarianism', pp. 273-7 in *Social Forces,* Vol. 45.

3   Nationalism, Democracy, and Authority in North America and Europe since 1989

Lessons for Political Socialization and Civic Education

Russell F. Farnen

ABSTRACT

This chapter focuses on the post-Cold War world and the tensions among nationalism, democracy, and authoritarianism on the one hand and the implications these developments have for political socialization and civic education on the other. It describes the cultural divide between Western and non-Western civilizations and nations, the new roles of religion and ethnicity in political affairs (especially in Central and Eastern Europe), as well as defining the major outlines of national, democratic, and authoritarian trends through reference to public opinion analysis and other research findings. It also provides suggestions about the role of civic education and political socialization research in teaching and studying these three political phenomena.

A major conclusion reached in this study is that the manifestation, reinforcement, and growth of authoritarianism at the individual level and fascism at the state level are the root causes of rabid and excessive nationalism, prejudice, and xenophobia. The curriculum of Western schools during the Cold War years was obsessed with teaching anti-Communism as a left-wing aberration from (and enemy of) democracy, while right-wing fascism was allowed to rest silently on the sidelines, undisturbed by critical analysis or pedagogical treatment.

Since 1989 with the near death of communism as a world ideology, we have discovered that the likely heir of communism is not democracy, but rather the rebirth or continuation of those same fascist/authoritarian elements which gave rise to World War II and the ensuing Cold War or 'long peace'. Merely teaching the pro-democracy catechism in any form is insufficient to counter the fascist menace at either the individual or state level. Why? Because fascism's appeals are so basic, seductive, simple, and ethnocentric. Everyone, in the East or West, may espouse the virtues of democracy, but all too many simultaneously embrace authoritarian values, ideologies, and states, however contradictory they seem to be. Political socialization research and civic education must be reinvented in North America and Europe in order to address this newly reborn ideological and psychological enemy of freedom, humanity, and the democratic personality, process, and political system.

INTRODUCTION
Scope of This Study

This analysis discusses the questions of the cultural divides that lead to a clash of civilizations and/or nations in the absence of any new world order which will replace the long peace which prevailed from 1945 to 1989. It also describes the roles of ethnicity, religion, and identity as factors which are politically salient today and are likely to become even more so tomorrow. Definitions and descriptions of democracy, nationalism, and authoritarianism are presented through a summary of some of the major findings about each of these concepts as well as survey research and empirical analyses. To answer the question 'How can political socialization research and civic education make a difference?', several suggestions based on the outcomes of this study are presented. The conclusion is that civic education can be very useful in combating authoritarianism and promoting democratic processes and practices and that political socialization research can also assist this process if redirected in an appropriate manner to include an analysis of authoritarian tendencies in its ongoing projects both nationally and cross-nationally.

Cultural Divisions, Civilization Fault Lines, and Global Indicators of Democracy/Authoritarianism

No sooner had we in the West stopped discussing Fukuyama's (Summer 1989) thesis regarding 'the end of history' with the victory of Western liberal enlightened values of freedom, democracy, the market, and social justice over the dark forces of collectivism, communism, the command economy, and state-directed equality, than we took up the challenge to seek new models for explaining the post-Cold War new world order. Some of these were old theories, such as the division of intellectuals into the micro and macro camps of internationalists. Still others look at the emerging world in terms of growing East-West cosmopolitanism, nationalism, and liberal transnationalism scenarios for differing degrees of war, peace, or cooperation. A third such *Weltanschauung* looks at the new world as the continual battle between authoritarianism and democracy, both at the regime and individual/personality levels.

The passage of time and events in Eastern Europe, Africa, Latin America, the Caribbean, and Asia have proved that Fukuyama's prediction was not only overly optimistic, but even somewhat naive. On the other hand, the macro-micro theorists take their lead from a more lengthy tradition of realism versus idealism in foreign affairs in which either the nation state or the *Zeitgeist* of the major civilizations determine the fate and direction of much of the world. For example, Huntington's *The Clash of Civilizations* in 1993 divided present Europe into the Western Christians (using a map from circa 1500 AD) as versus Orthodox

Christians and Islamics who live east of a line drawn from Finland through the Baltics and south to Croatia, splitting other states along the way. Huntington sees the cultural clash of civilizations as the old, new, and future forces of hegemonic battle between 'the West and the rest' over the forces of modernity, liberalism, technology, democracy, the market, secularism, and settling the global consumers' quest for more Sony products rather than more soil. However, Huntington recognizes that nation states will remain 'the most powerful actors in world affairs', but he emphasizes intercivilization conflict, rather than the more familiar intracivilization civil wars. This emphasis reminds one of Kennedy, Toynbee, Spengler, or Wright and their sweeping generalizations about 'imperial overstretch' challenge and response, the decline of the West, and the predicted follies of naturally warlike and bellicose peoples. With over 30 hot wars now raging throughout the post-Cold War world within and between so many ethnic, cultural, and nation-state contexts, it is difficult to see how these grandiose pronouncements help us clear up our shared fuzzy thinking on these matters. (On these points, see Fukuyama, Summer 1989, pp. 3-18; Pietras, May/June 1994, pp. 31-2; Weeks, September/October 1993, pp.24-5; and Huntington, Summer 1993, pp. 22-49.)

Still a third way to understand the world is to examine the growth of democracy and the rise of authoritarianism in the post-1989 world. In this regard, we have two relevant studies, the first by Freedom House (a nonpartisan, US-based, nonprofit, public service agency) and the second a global indicators survey of 176 nations worldwide. The Freedom House (January-February 1994) report, 'The Comparative Survey of Freedom: 1994', focused on free elections, party competition, minority rights, citizen participation, power sharing, protest rights, ethnic pluralism, citizen equality, worker organization, religious freedom, and equal opportunity. This survey found increased repression in 1993, an end to post-1989 liberalization, and increased ethnic tensions and human rights/democratic restrictions. Nevertheless, the number of democracies grew from 99 in 1992 to 107 in 1993. However, the world seemed rapidly to be splitting into free democratic and unfree dictatorial or authoritarian regimes.

After looking at the 1993 Freedom House annual survey, one observer (Bartley, September/October 1993, p. 16) commented on the 'amazing speed' of democracy's spread to Latin America, the former Communist bloc, and both Africa and Asia. That is, only 31 per cent (most in China) lived under repressive regimes (a minor 11 per cent decrease in a decade) and the number of free states increased to 75 (or 20 more than in the previous decade). By contrast, the Meloen report decried the 'massive increase in worldwide repression'. Despite an increase in the number of free countries, the actual number of people living in such countries declined from 36 to only 19 per cent of the world's population (Meloen, August 1994, p. 4). Consequently, whether the glass with the free democratic cocktail is half full or half empty depends a lot on who is pouring the drinks, the size of the glass, and whether it is looked at from above, below, or the side.

Meloen conducted two studies (a 70-nation and a 170-nation global indicators survey) of state authoritarianism, democracy, and education (see Chapter 2 in this volume and Meloen, January 1994 and August 1994). The indicators used in the first study included the absence of state terrorism as well as no suppression of moral deviation, denial of gay rights, imposition of state beliefs, use of capital punishment, suppression of labor unions, prohibition of abortion, imprisonment of dissidents, gender inequality, and state antihuman rights activity. He found that all of the dictatorships listed scored high and free democratic countries low on the overall state authoritarianism measure. State authoritarianism correlated .81 (48 countries) with the UN Human Freedom Index and .83 (52 countries) with the Freedom House measures (Meloen, January 1994, pp. 1-6; see Chapter 5 in this volume and Farnen and German, August 1994, pp. 7-8).

In his 170-nation expanded study, Meloen (August 1994) demonstrates that it is the cultural climate of state authoritarianism which creates dictatorships, violates human rights, and is statistically related to authoritarian attitudes, authoritarian governmental type, and traditional family structures. These hierarchical cultural frameworks provide a favorable climate for the growth of authoritarianism at the state and personal levels. Low educational attainment levels and economic developmental levels also influence the growth of authoritarianism. Dictatorships use state authoritarianism to control the populace by monopolizing political power, repressing opposition movements, and using violence. Its instruments are the military, police, and legal system. These strong men need fanatic supporters to uphold their antidemocratic hegemony. Dictators often assume the guises of democratic processes through voting rituals and claims of majority rule by the nation's 'folk' or native people. In most countries of the world, using rabid nationalism, racism, ethnic and religious xenophobia, and chauvinism as vital parts of the ideological belief system prevents the growth of democratic norms, processes, and behaviors (Meloen, August 1994, p. 31).

In sum, the major causes of authoritarianism and the lack of freedom are: traditional family/hierarchical structures and socialization processes; lack of educational development; existence of an authoritarian government; higher degree of authoritarian personality attributes; cultural features such as hierarchical, nonegalitarian interpersonal and social relations; low level of material economic development, which promotes crisis solutions to desperate problems; and, finally, interactions among and the interrelatedness of the previous six factors allow the creation of a multicausal model which explains state authoritarianism, its primary inputs/causes (that is, GNP, education, family, culture, attitudes, and government type), and its most obvious outputs/products (that is, gender discrimination; rigged elections; ethnic, religious, and nationalistic military conflict within and between states; state violence and terrorism; and minority suppression or discrimination) (Meloen, August 1994, pp. 31-2 and his Figure 5).

Religion and Ethnicity in Central and Eastern Europe

In discussing cultural divisions, I mentioned nationalism, national identity, and ethnicity. In contrast to Western Europe (which is relatively homogeneous), much of the peoples in Central and Eastern Europe are a mixture of either very similar or very different religious and ethnonationalist groups (see Tables 3.1a and b). For example, England is overwhelmingly English in ethnicity and Anglican in religion, with some Irish and Commonwealth immigrants and some Roman Catholic, Jewish, and Eastern religious groups in the distinct minority. The western part of Germany prior to reunification was 41 per cent Roman Catholic, 40 per cent Protestant (Lutheran/Evangelical), 2.5 per cent Muslim (mostly Turkish immigrants and guest workers), and 11 per cent others. By and large, even with the increased pace of asylum seekers' (from Central and Eastern Europe, the Balkans, and elsewhere) in-migration, these immigrants constitute 10 per cent of Germany's population. Where cultural/ethnic divisions exist, they occur among 'native' Germans (many of whom immigrated there after 1945 from Silesia, East Prussia, Pomerania, the Danzig Corridor, and from folk German communities in Central and Eastern Europe) and guest workers (Turks and Yugoslavs), Gypsies (Roma or Sinti), and new asylum seekers and political/economic refugees. Despite a small Sorbish minority in the state of Brandenburg and a sizable Danish minority in the Schleswig-Holstein region, these groups are nonconflictual, essentially bilingual (or multilingual), and pluralistically integrated in a Dutch type pilloried fashion into the Cottbus and Flensburg communities.

Elsewhere in Western Europe, different countries contain small minority or ethnic groups (such as Algerians, Yugoslavs, Mollucans, Surinamese, Basques, Catalans, and Laplanders) and one or more predominant religious group(s) (such as Protestants and Roman Catholics, along with the inconspicuous presence of small Jewish, Islamic, and other religious minorities). Just as there are some predominantly single-ethnic-group or one-religion countries in the West (for example, Spain, Italy, Ireland, Portugal, and the Scandinavian nations) and Protestant (Lutheran/Evangelical) and Roman Catholic partitions (for example, western Germany, and the Netherlands), similar situations exist in Central and Eastern Europe. For example (see Table 3.1b), Poland is majoritarian Roman Catholic (95 per cent), as is Croatia (77 per cent), Slovakia (62 per cent), and Slovenia (85 per cent); Romania (87 per cent), and Bulgaria (89 per cent) are predominantly Eastern Orthodox; Albania (70 per cent) is mostly Islamic-Muslim; Estonia (60 per cent) is predominantly Lutheran; whereas other states in the region are religiously fractionated, with either one large or several small religious groups which pluralize those cultures/societies. For example, Latvia is divided among Roman Catholic, Protestant, and Eastern Orthodox groups; eastern Germany is primarily Evangelical/Lutheran, with some fewer Roman Catholics. In the countries of Central and Eastern Europe, the predominant religion, shared hegemony religions, or co-religions, and any large minority religions of 10-15 per cent or more are not likely to be victims of persecution as would be the case with small religious groups (such as Jews everywhere or Muslims in Bulgaria, Serbia, and Poland or Roman Catholics in Romania) in other countries.

When religion is tied to an ethnic group's identity (such as Islamic Turks in Germany, Eastern Orthodox Yugoslavs in Sweden, or Jews in Western and Eastern Europe), then the forceful elements of national divisiveness, ethno-nationalism, xenophobia, chauvinism, irredentism, and illiberal or nonliber-ationist nationalism come into play. For example, Greeks and other minorities are endangered in Albania, just as the Sinti/Roma ('Gypsies') are fair game for stereotyping, violence, and discrimination (in Bulgaria, Croatia, eastern Germany, Hungary, Romania, and Slovakia) because of their small minority status. Rarely is there discrimination against members of a large minority group who can move freely in a given society. However, the situation is different if members of that group differ from majority group members in terms of race, lifestyle, skin color, or dress;they then take on minority, class, and caste distinctiveness, thereby attracting or becoming targets for majority discrimina-tion (as is the case with Gypsies in Central and Eastern Europe and African Americans in the US, but less so for either new Caucasian immigrants to the US who are fluent in English or Jewish citizens today). In Central and Eastern Europe, the connections between the dominant ethnic group and the dominant religion (for example, Poles and Slovenes - Roman Catholic; Romanians and Bulgarians - Eastern Orthodox; and Albanians - Islamic) not only spell danger for smaller ethnic/religious groups, but also threaten neighboring states which have minorities belonging to the majority in another country (for example, Hungary, it is said, is a country surrounded by Hungarians in Romania, Slovakia, Serbia, Slovenia, Croatia, and the Czech Republic). This same situation applies to Albanians in Serbia, Russians in Estonia and Latvia, Slovaks in the Czech Republic, Hungarians in Slovakia, Turks in Bulgaria, and Greeks in Albania.

Table 3.1a Ethnic groups in Central and Eastern Europe in the 1990s

Country	Population in millions (date)	Majority Ethnic Groups (in %)	Minority Ethnic Groups (in %)
Albania	3.3 (1991)	Albanian-90.	Greek-9; Others (Macedonian, (Montenegrin, Serbian, Croatian)-1.
Bulgaria	9.0 (1992)	Bulgarian-76.	Moslem Turks-13; Moslem 'Pomaks'-3; Roma/Gypsy-7; Others (Macedonian, Armenian, Russian)-1.
Croatia	4.8 (1991)	Croatian-78.	Serbian-12; Slovene-.5; Hungarian-.5; Italian-.4; Czech.-.3; Albanian-.2; Montenegrin-.2; Roma/Gypsy-.1; Macedonian-.1; Slovakian-.1; Others:-7.6.
Czech Republic	10.4 (1990)	Czech-94.	Slovakian-4.1; Hungarian-.2; German-.5; Polish-.7; Ukrainian/ Russian-.1; Others-.4.
Eastern Germany	16. (1993)	German-96.5	Sorb-.5; Vietnamese-.5; Mozambican-.5; Others (Sinti/ Roma/Gypsy, Asylum Seekers/ Immigrants from Yugoslavia, Romania, Poland, Russia)-2.
Estonia	1.6 (1992)	Estonian-61.5	Russian-30.3; Ukrainian-3.1; Byelorussian-1.8; Finn-1.1; Others-2.2.
Hungary	10.3 (1992)	Hungarian-90.6	German-1.6; Slovakian-.1; Romanian-.2; Roma/Gypsy-.7; Others (Croatian, Serbian, Slovene, Jewish)-.5.
Latvia	2.7 (1992)	Latvian-53.5	Russian-34; Byelorussian-4.4; Ukrainian-3.4; Polish-2.2; Lithuanian-1.3; Others-1.2.
Lithuania	3.8 (1992)	Lithuanian-80.4	Russian-8.9; Polish-7; Byelorussian-1.6; Ukrainian-1.1.
Poland	3.8 (1990)	Polish-95	German-3; Others (Ukrainian, Byelorussian, Lithuanian)-2.
Romania	23. (1990)	Romanian-78	Hungarian-11; Roma/Gypsy-10; Others (Germans, Jews)-1.
Serbia (incl. Vojvodina, Kosovo, Montenegro)	11. (1991)	Serbian-62.	Albanian-17; Montenegrin-5; Hungarian-3; Yugoslavian-3; Others (Bulgarian, Hungarian)-10.

Table 3.1a (continued)

Country	Population in millions (date)	Majority Ethnic Groups (in %)	Minority Ethnic Groups (in %)
Slovak Republic	5.3 (1991)	Slovakian-85.7	Hungarian-11; Roma/Gypsy-1.5; Czech, Moravian, Silesian-1.0; Ruthenian (Russyn) and Ukrainian-.6; German-.1; Others (Polish, Russian)-.1.
Slovenia	2.0 (1991)	Slovene-87.	Others (Hungarian, Croatian, and Italian)-13.

Sources: Adapted from Hunter (ed.), 1994 (pp. 74, 78, 243, 463, 465, 484, 533, 536, 690, 696, 870, 872, 895-8, 1097, 1103, 1120, 1125, 1170, 1172, 1174, and 1619); *The Europa World Year Book*, 1993 (pp. 284, 288, 294, 600, 612, 613, 857, 861, 867, 905, 910, 918, 1203, 1232-4, 1310, 1371-2, 1735, 1738, 1742-3, 1803-13, 2315, 2330-1, 2537, 2544, 2545, 2375, 3225, 3232, and 3242.

Table 3.1b Religious groups in Central and Eastern Europe in the 1990s

Country	Population in millions (date)	Majority Religious Groups (in %)	Minority Religious Groups (in %)
Albania	3.3 (1991)	Islamic/Muslim-70.	Eastern Orthodox-20; Roman Catholic-10.
Bulgaria	9.0 (1992)	Eastern Orthodox-89.	Islamic/Muslim-9; Others (Roman Catholic, Jewish, Protestant)-2.
Croatia	4.8 (1991)	Roman Catholic-77.	Eastern Orthodox-11; Islamic/Muslim-1; Others (Protestant, Jewish)-11.
Czech Republic	10.4 (1990)	Roman Catholic-39; Others-30.5; None-30.	Protestant-.5
Eastern Germany	16. (1993)	Lutheran-41; None-32.	Roman Catholic-7; Others-20.
Estonia	1.6 (1992)	Lutheran-60.	Eastern Orthodox-30; Others (Adventist, Methodist, Baptist)-10.
Hungary	10.3 (1992)	Roman Catholic-60.	Protestant-25; Others (Jewish, Eastern Orthodox or None)-15.
Latvia	2.7 (1992)	Roman Catholic-26; Protestant-26; Eastern Orthodox-34.	Jewish-1; Others or None-13.
Lithuania	3.8 (1992)	Roman Catholic-80.	Eastern Orthodox-12; Others (Protestant, Jewish, or None)-8.

Table 3.1b (continued)

Country	Population in millions (date)	Majority Religious Groups (in %)	Minority Religious Groups (in %)
Poland	3.8 (1990)	Roman Catholic-95.	Others (Eastern Orthodox, Protestant, Jewish, Islamic/ Muslim)-5.
Romania	23. (1990)	Eastern Orthodox-87.	Roman Catholic-6.5; Protestant-4.0; Others (Jewish, Islamic/Muslim)-2.5
Serbia (incl. Vojvodina, Kosovo, Montenegro)	11. (1991)	Eastern Orthodox-60.	Islamic/Muslim-3; Roman Catholic-4; Others or None-33.
Slovak Republic	5.3 (1991)	Roman Catholic-62.	Others (Eastern Orthodox, Protestant, Jewish)-8; None-30.
Slovenia	2.0 (1991)	Roman Catholic-85.	Others (Eastern Orthodox, Islamic/Muslim, Jewish)-10; None-5.

Sources: Adapted from Hunter (ed.), 1994 (pp. 74, 78, 243, 463, 465, 484, 533, 536, 690, 696, 870, 872, 895-8, 1097, 1103, 1120, 1125, 1170, 1172, 1174, and 1619); *The Europa World Year Book*, 1993 (pp. 284, 288, 294, 600, 612, 613, 857, 861, 867, 905, 910, 918, 1203, 1232-4, 1310, 1371-2, 1735, 1738, 1742-1743, 1803-13, 2315, 2330-1, 2537, 2544, 2545, 2375, 3225, 3232, and 3242.

WHAT IS NATIONALISM?

This section discusses nationalism and some of its related concepts, such as minority status, ethnicity, patriotism, and racism. (For a more complete discussion of these themes and concepts, see Farnen, 1994, pp. 23-102; Farnen and German, August 1994; and Chapter 5 in this volume.)

Although the words *nationalism, minority, patriotism, racism*, and *ethnicity* are often used in a self-evident fashion above, it may be helpful to define these terms before proceeding. The definitions will focus on their relevance to political socialization research findings and to concepts of that field of study, all of which have public and educational policy implications.

Nationalism

Nationalism is, above all, 'a state of mind, in which the supreme loyalty of the individual is felt to be due the nation-state' (Kohn, 1955, p. 9). It assumes a common descent or lineage, a territory, a political system, and certain characteristic customs, traditions, language, or religion. These preconditions are neither necessary nor sufficient to constitute a nation, however. Israel was a nation before it became a state in 1948, US citizens have no common heritage, and the Swiss speak several different languages - yet each of these nation-states has a national identity and 'a living and active corporate will'. That is, this 'state of mind' inspires (or claims to inspire) all of its members while maintaining that 'the nation-state is the ideal and the only legitimate form of political organization and that the nationality is the source of all cultural creative energy and of economic well-being' (Kohn, 1955, p. 10).

Brinton (1953, pp. 220-1) called nationalism 'the strongest single factor in the existing networks of interests, sentiments, and ideas binding men into territorially based political groups.' It was also 'a complex blending of almost everything that goes into Western life' and provided a 'backlog for all the more abstract political forms' (such as communism, Nazism, and US democracy) he discussed. He saw no hope for necessary environmental or constitutional changes (such as the UN or world federalism) that would wipe out this strong, worldwide, nationalistic faith. This civil religion served many purposes. Namely, 'it bulwarks the weak and the inadequate with their membership in the great whole, their share of the pooled self-esteem of patriots. . . . But it does not take the place of a consoling God' (Brinton, 1953, pp. 52-3). For Brinton, the only antidote for nationalism was neither an idealistic nor a cynical democracy but rather a realistic (even pessimistic) democracy. This type of system requires ordinary citizens to meet moral and political questions while remaining cognizant of their own and others' imperfections (as successful farmers, physicians, and other workers do). But this realistic democracy would be a most demanding (if potentially very successful) political culture for its citizens.

Nationalism stems from a combination of one or more basic value orientations: (a) blood, 'race', soil, language, and ethnic affinity; (b) ideology, 'sacred' tenets and beliefs, and moral objectives; (c) personal, symbolic heroes and leaders; and (d) attachment to civic values, roles, institutions, and political processes, laws, and principles that promote the common polis, civil society, and unity amidst diversity (Andrain, 1971, pp. 27-8).

Minority

By contrast to a national group, a political, social, or economic minority is more than the smaller of two or more groups. A minority group is part of a national population that differs in some major characteristics (for example, race, language, political power, ethnicity, national origin) from the predominant members of a population. As such, minority groups are subject to differential treatment by the majority or predominant coalition group(s) in a given society. Minority group members also have a sense of self-identification and group membership plus a feeling of depreciation, discrimination, or denial because of their lack of economic wealth, political power, or general social or cultural influence on the society as a whole.

Ethnicity

An ethnic group is formed along racial or cultural lines; its members allegedly possess common traits and customs. In the US, for example, African Americans may be categorized as a minority group (being 12 per cent of the total population) whereas Jewish Americans, also a minority group (3 per cent of the population), may be further classified as an ethnic group because of their nonmajoritarian religion, language, customs, traditions, and history. Although African Americans and Jews may be nationalistic in their patriotic feelings toward the US, some of the former may be adherents of African-American nationalism and some of the latter may also have basic affinities toward the historic Jewish nation, the State of Israel, or Zionism. These multiple loyalties are tolerated in the US, provided that open conflict or confrontation with the majority culture does not seriously endanger public education, health, safety, well-being, morals, or national security interests.

Patriotism

Political communities and nations expect allegiance from their citizens as the reciprocal of the protection the state affords its members. Patriotism thus serves a functional purpose. Political loyalty to the nation-state is an expression of support for, and consent to be governed by, the regime that represents the sovereign public as a whole. Obedience to legitimately constituted laws can be expected in democratic societies. Moreover, reasoned patriotism is compatible with privacy, choice, criticism, and individual judgment (Cleary, 1971, pp. 25-6). The tensions that arise when citizens abjure allegiance, duty, order, and law observance because of calls from individual conscience or higher-law principles test the allowable limits of responsible citizenship and accepted forms of civil disobedience. Reasoned patriotism and the exercise of citizens' rights to nonparticipation or oppositional participation against state action are both compatible with a democratic political system. One such case, for example, is conscientious objection to the military draft for religious reasons. Indeed, part of the definition of national identity in countries such as the Netherlands, Canada, the US, and Germany is allowance for just this sort of exception to the general rule that the citizen of a nation state must risk life and limb if called upon to protect the survival of the body politic.

The degree to which people are expected to respond with mindless obedience (as opposed to individual choice) to orders from state officials may even be construed as a measure of the strength, maturity, or health of a given political community or nation. When a community tolerates such dissent against its most vital security interests while surviving these challenges to its legitimacy and very existence, the system can truly be said to evidence characteristics of a strong, functional, and effective democratic polity.

Patriotism and loyalty to one's country frequently display nationalistic overtones. A recent study comparing two different types of patriotism in New Zealand (apolitical) and the US (political, ideological, and power projection) helps us to distinguish between two forms of patriotism as well as their objects. The 20-year-old university students in their study associated New Zealand with their islands, landscape, a secure home, and pride in its natural beauty, environment, and sports. By comparison, while over 40 per cent of Americans and New Zealanders were proud of their country, two-thirds of the American subjects used the word 'freedom', 38 per cent the word 'democracy', over 50 per cent mentioned the American flag, one third the incumbent president, and 35 per cent the word 'powerful' to describe their country. New Zealanders have no revolutionary war or military tradition to speak of; their commonwealth status and connections to England prevent the growth of national symbols. New Zealand's founding myth is based on an 1840 treaty with the native Maoris. Since New Zealand has only contributed to other people's wars and its closest neighbor (Australia) is 1000 miles distant, citizens are more proud of their sports victories, independence, environmentalist and antinuclear stances, and other unique accomplishments than they are of more typical national symbols (Hirshberg, 1994).

The Authoritarian Personality (Adorno et al., 1950, pp. 107-8) addressed this bifurcated concept of 'positive' and 'negative' patriotism. It defined negative patriotism as 'blind attachment to certain national cultural values, uncritical conformity with the prevailing group ways, and rejection of other nations as out-groups.' Positive or genuine patriotism, by contrast, meant love of country and connectedness to national values; yet, the positive patriot 'can appreciate the values and ways of other nations . . . ', is 'permissive toward much that he cannot personally accept for himself . . .', and 'is free of rigid conformism, out-group rejection, and imperialistic striving for power.' Still other definitions refer to the patriot's personal links to the power and culture of his society and its preservation or expansion. It also means community devotion, pride in - and love of - country, and popular loyalty through feelings of identity and attachment. More recently, Bar-Tal (1993) claimed that positive patriotism can fundamentally be applied to every group. For him, it means 'attachment of group members toward their group and the country in which they reside' (Bar-Tal, 1993, p. 48). Bar-Tal says that in lay persons' minds, patriotism encompasses attachments to their own group and their land of residence, is motivational, contains positive evaluations and affections, and expresses national/group love, loyalty, pride and care. As such, Bar-Tal believes it is an inevitable occurrence and is necessary for developing a necessary sense of community. He also tries to differentiate patriotism from nationalism by saying that while nationalism may be ethnocentric, claim national superiority, and propose dominance, patriotism is a 'more general and basic sentiment' which is only dangerous in its 'negative', 'blind', or 'fervent' forms. However, he does admit that patriots 'draw the line between in-groups and out-groups . . ., [and] unite group members by emphasizing their similarity in contrast to the different out-groups' (Bar-Tal, 1993, p. 56). Nationalism seeks a separate, distinct, and independent state, whereas patriots do not conceive of themselves as a national group in pursuit of their own state (Bar-Tal, 1993, p. 51). In sum, although a healthy individual may require positive self-esteem which, in turn, may produce good interpersonal relations, can it be that nations need a positive patriotic spirit for their survival and that this positive feeling will reduce tendencies toward war?

New Zealanders demonstrate a form of positive and peaceful patriotism while American patriotism is more negative, bellicose, and hegemonic. In part, Israeli patriotism is surely defined through the exclusion of its Arab and Muslim residents and neighbors with whom they waged many wars. Therefore, the degree of positive and negative patriotism in a country may largely depend on its military tradition, historical experience, sense of world leadership or threats to its hegemony, or the geopolitical reality of a given age. American patriotism was very different during the Revolutionary, Civil, First and Second World, Korean, Vietnam, and Persian Gulf Wars in part because the duration, nature, and size of the threat, the objects fought, and the enemies demonized were all different. Nationalism, then, readily uses patriotism in its positive or negative sense whenever the need arises. Patriotism is not nationalism to be sure, but both positive and negative patriotism certainly are necessary preconditions or co-conditions for attaining nationalistic goals and nation-state internal unity, especially when combined with nationally defined internal/external exclusivity (Dekker, January 1994, pp. 3-4; Dekker, Malová, and Theulings, Chapter 5 in this volume).

Some Additional Observations about Nationalism

Nationalism, then, may exist in various forms. The former USSR and Yugoslavia were once multinational states just as was the Austro-Hungarian Empire (which had Czechs, Slavs, Italians, Poles and other nationalities as constituent elements). There are nationalities without a state and there are states that do not base their identity on one nationality. Consequently, nationalism helps to create a political consciousness, mobilizes the citizenry behind the leadership, and unifies and integrates the populace behind a common ideology. It is emotional, thrives on sacrifice, and resembles a religion in terms of its followers' fanatical fervor. Moreover, it creates a sense of organic community, requires allegiance and patriotism, and gives citizens some higher meaning for their political life. In its total concern for complete loyalty and obedience from its citizenry, it may also serve the cause of fascist or neocommunist totalitarianism. Newly emerging nations with less-developed economies also seem more prone to nationalist wars as compared with more highly developed democratic nation-states (with notable exceptions). In sum, since nationalism promotes a consciousness of national superiority and it touts the interests of the nation-state above all others, the potential for violence and war thereby produced makes nationalism, as Kenneth Boulding once said, 'the only religion that still demands human sacrifice' (Kegley and Wittkopf, 1981, p. 365; Macridis, 1980, pp. 269). So, although we all may understand what nationalism means in theory and practice, the most important question that remains is how to temper it and turn its force in more peaceful and productive directions. Nationalism is now appearing in different guises in many of the former Soviet republics and client states in that the authoritarian neocommunists have unified their party groups under newly legitimized nationalistic banners (for example, in Russia, Serbia, Croatia, Slovakia, and Romania), thus seeking to preserve their monopoly of state power.

More Recent Trends

In November 1991, Vaclev Havel (then President of a united Czechoslovakia) opened a symposium in Bratislava on minorities in politics (Havel, November 1991, pp. 14-17 in Plichtová [ed.], 1992) by speaking about 'the freedom of a prisoner'. He likened the new states in the area which were emerging from the confines of the Soviet-dominated past to a freed prisoner who walks out of his solitary, dark cell into the light of day, is startled, and then longs for the simple security of his familiar, past life behind bars. Havel said societies in Central and Eastern Europe are in an analogous situation in their search for quick fixes and simple solutions to complex problems which are the products of recent history. This situation is a breeding ground for intolerance, xenophobia, and the search for a culpable criminal or enemy who can be brought to justice so that they can recreate the order and peace of the prison society in their new world. If they cannot readily find such an enemy, then they ask, 'Who else is at hand to blame?' Is it a member of some other nation, race, or ethnic group? In such moments, anti-Semitism (one of the traditional flash points to which people try to direct their metaphysical grievances and find a scapegoat) gets revived. However, there are some other types of intolerance, including persecution of the Gypsies, the Vietnamese, and so on. Havel added that societies in Central and Eastern Europe were so isolated for 50 years that they could not properly interact with different peoples today, so that the 'enemy' or flashpoint,

. . . is the one who is easily at first sight identified as an outsider. Who else could it be than a person speaking a different language, or who has a different color of skin? This is a great danger and, moreover, such a danger is growing out in a situation when the authority and trustworthiness of democratic institutions is being built . . . when such institutions do not function as they should. And this is a very dangerous subject that should be given attention by all of us (Havel, November 1991, p. 17 in Plichtová [ed.], 1992).

At this same conference, a Dutch political scientist questioned whether nationalism was going 'back to Sarajevo or beyond Trianon?' (Koch, November 1991, pp. 34-44 in Plichtová [ed.], 1992). He saw this renaissance of nationalism as either escalating to the interstate level, thereby endangering European security (the 'Sarajevo Syndrome'), or emphasizing the domestic nature of the phenomenon. This interpretation points to the rightist, authoritarian connotations of the problem as threats to democratization, economic liberalization, and the viability of post-totalitarian societies in which democratic dissident movements have ironically paved the way for authoritarian regimes. Instead, Koch first assumes that not all that is described as nationalism in Central and Eastern Europe is actually so and that its appeal is really weaker than it seems on the surface. Second, he finds that Central and Eastern European nationalism is 'neither inevitable nor natural' and depends especially on national conditions and ideologies. Third, he maintains that the rebirth of nationalism there does not mean that Sarajevo II will reappear because we now have a new European state system. Instead, the real targets of such a nationalist revival will be democratization and liberalization as well as the security of the region's internal ethnic minorities. His fourth thesis is that nationalism is the 'unhappy history' of this region; it prevented the gradual growth of 'natural' territorial entities so that current unsatisfied claims for states, national homogeneity, and a homeland for each national group are based on a long history of regional violence.

Koch describes nationalism as joining the political and national units to make a congruent whole. All subjects of the state must belong to the same nation and every nation should fulfill its common destiny through the actions of its own state agency. Nationalists exclude 'us' from 'them' on the arbitrary basis of ethnicity, a common history, language, or blood. The elite-led political program of nationalism espouses internal homogenization, forced assimilation, deportation, or genocide, although this may mean irredentism and the use of violence to change borders.

Nationalism is also not to be confused with postcommunist ethnic emancipation or cultural autonomy in religion and language use (that is, cultural pluralism for the Hungarian minority in Slovakia is quite different from the claims for Hungarian irredenta heard in the parliamentary halls in Budapest). Not all outbursts of violence, racism, or ethnic claims are evidence of nationalistic trends. The post-1989 breakdown of law and order, violence containment, and crime control were co-products of the 1989 revolutions which produced a kind of Lebanonization in Central and Eastern Europe (such as the civil wars in the trans-Caucasus region). Such violence is internally, but not internationally, dangerous and explosive. Instead, the rebirth of national consciousness, regional and cultural autonomy, democracy, and pluralism can develop hand in hand in the region. In light of these observations, Koch proposes that NATO/WEO-led antinationalist military plans will be less effective than engineering an expeditious 'return to Europe' for these countries. This can happen by promoting democracy, modernity, and economic prosperity in the region in cooperation with the enlarged European Community (Koch, November 1991).

Dekker, Malová, and Theulings (January 1994 and Chapter 5 in this volume) provide a different perspective on nationalism. This group of Slovak/Dutch political scientists distinguished among elite, organizational, ideological, and individual levels of nationalistic political orientations. Since the picture they assembled was a puzzle with so many missing pieces, they abstracted six national orientations which were the opposites of internationalism, cosmopolitanism, or higher law doctrines on the one hand and national alienation on the other. These constructs included cognitions such as national awareness, consciousness and distinctiveness, and the attitudes of national feeling, liking, pride, preference, superiority, and nationalism in an hierarchical, pyramidal fashion. Nationalism was conceived as the combination of considering one's own people as a 'nation' with a common origin (kinship); wishing congruence of 'nation' and state; realigned borders; forced assimilation or deportation of ethnic national groups; and rejection of international cooperation. They also hypothesized that one must move through these stages of national orientations from bottom to top as one would through Piagetian cognitive growth or Kohlbergian moral developmental stages (but other alternatives of alienation and internationalism are not excluded). The explanatory variables identified in this survey include system (international, political, economic), individual social-demographic variables, personal characteristics, individual political and nonpolitical orientations, and political socialization variables.

Their case study of Slovakian nationalists demonstrated the existence of nationalistic orientations among one-third to one-fourth of the populace in light of the current economic, ideological, and political crisis in the country when entrepreneurial politicians regularly play the nationalist appeal card in this great game. They predicted that the growth of nationalism in Slovakia will be accelerated if a charismatic leader appears.

WHAT IS DEMOCRACY?

This section discusses two major Western views of democracy, namely the 'strong' or participatory view versus the 'weak' or elitist representative view. It also briefly describes the implications of these two theories for a definition of democratic citizenship, democratic citizen education, and nationalism.

'Strong' Versus 'Weak' Democracy

Tables 3.2 and 3.3 present a combination of theories of democracy and citizenship in the form of participatory *versus* representative democracy theories regarding essential citizen rights, duties, and roles. These two theories are labelled 'strong' versus 'weak', direct versus indirect, mass versus elite, classical versus modern, normative versus empirical, and communitarian versus liberal (European) or republican (US). In this schematic presentation, particular attention is paid to the place and relative importance of policy- and decision-making and problem-solving roles for the democratic citizen or the leadership (Dekker, 1992, pp. 2-6).

Strong Democracy

Participatory or 'strong' democracy theory stresses that politics relates to all of human existence, not merely to government. Politics happens wherever conflict occurs, where decisions are made, and where power and authority are expressed. Citizen participants are believed to be concerned with making decisions regarding problem-solving and public policy questions. Citizens are considered equal in their power and right to influence and make decisions. Through practice, education, and experience, the mass of citizens can improve their civic involvement and participation. Such participation improves the development of one's political personality and democratic character, citizen proficiency, and improved decisions and their implementation. Shared responsibility and popular acceptance will result, along with an increasing sense of belonging to one's political community. Citizens can also decide to replace elected officials with others (including themselves). Shared decision making obviates the need for violent protest or revolution since any pent-up antagonisms can be regularly released. Since mass political decisions are founded on values, morals, and opinions (as well as on information and experience), the citizenry is as qualified as experts and leaders to make sound judgments and to choose correct problem solutions and policy options.

Table 3.2 Representative/'weak'/indirect versus 'strong'/direct/participatory democracy: policy/decision-making and problem-solving

Political Processes and Relationships	Representative Democracy Elements	Participatory Democracy Elements
Politics concerned with:	Public sector and formal officials who *decide* politically	All social, economic, and human life where *decisions* regarding power, values, authority are made
Democracy is:	An electoral process and methods for replacing elites	A process of personal, group, and public *decision making* and *problem solving*
Democratic process evidenced through *citizen* roles:	Voting to select elite *decision makers* (indirect)	Participating in *making political decisions* and *solving public problems* (direct)
Citizen participation observed in:	Voting and elections to choose representatives and *decision makers*	Whenever politics happens: elections, home, work, school, community *decision making*
Concept of equality means:	*Citizens* are eligible to run for office, to join the elite meritocracy of talents and wealth	*Citizens* share power/influence without discrimination for popular *decision making*
System stability/ instability happens when:	Elites insure stability; mass rule creates anarchy	An educated, participatory citizenry insures shared responsibility for *decisions*; disintegration happens when elitism, authoritarianism, discrimination, apathy, alienation, and bureaucratization are rife
Knowledge basis for theory is:	Survey research and 'realistic' analysis of voter misinformation, disinterest, intolerance, and low voter turnout	*Democratic* norms and values (such as informed *citizen decision making*) are idealistic, yet realistic; *democracy* is the worst form of government, except for all the others which have been tried
Democracy and *citizen efficacy/ effectiveness* are:	Incompatible since *citizens* are relieved of all *decisions*, except voting influence and power	Compatible in that individuals and groups share responsibilities and duties with their leaders in *decision making*

Table 3.2 (continued)

Political Processes and Relationships	Representative Democracy Elements	Participatory Democracy Elements
Degrees of theoretical convergence/ agreement:	Basic agreement on minimum individual levels of education, information, participation, system support for elementary *democracy/decision making*; choice of leaders is important as is availability for recruitment in an open elite	Stress on the importance of political information, education, and skillful personal/group *decision making*; choice of leaders is informed through party, reference group, and mass media; participation extends beyond voting to petitions, protests, campaigning, office holding, and group/ class/interest representation

Sources: Adapted from Dekker, 1992, p. 3; Dekker, January 1994, pp. 2-7; and Farnen, 1993c. Also see Chapter 19 in this volume.

Table 3.3 Key concepts of 'strong'/participatory versus 'weak'/representative democracy

Political Concept	Representative Democratic View	Participatory Democratic View
Primary political object or goal:	Individual self-fulfillment and freedom	Group and social betterment and the common good through individual and collective action
Human beings, by nature, are:	Autonomous, irrational, selfish, emotional, untrustworthy, and capable of great evil and much banality	Autonomous, social, rational, emotional, educable, and capable of both good and evil
The social cement or bonds come from:	Social contract, constitutions, laws, courts, law enforcement	Community norms, values, customs, and *democratic* habits of the heart, such as consultation, compromise, fairness, persuasion and common sense
Source of political interest/motivation:	Self-interest and freedom from personal or state hindrance	Public welfare and fulfilling common group and individual needs
Individual rights, duties, and identities:	Based on the duty to lead, serve, or follow and laws, courts, rights, and government exist to protect elite rights from the tyranny of the majority	Balanced with a view that for every right, there is a corresponding duty and the public good is not served by championing individual rights over community well-being

Table 3.3 (continued)

Political Concept	Representative Democratic View	Participatory Democratic View
Political participation occurs through:	Exercising the right to vote, to choose leaders who will protect individual and elite interests and ensure individual freedom	Voting and more extensive political activity to perform the rights and duties of the office of citizen to better oneself and the community while improving *citizenship* competence and quality *decisions*
Qualifications of political leaders assessed by:	Independent judgement, choice of party/power elite, and qualifications of elite candidates for public office	Stand on issues, party responsibility, class and representational interests, pre-election popular candidate selection by polls, party convention, and citizen involvement
Key activities of the ideal *citizen*:	Voting regularly, maintaining individual autonomy, independence, and obedience	*Decision making/problem solving* on a daily basis as an individual or group member to recreate or reinvent government to serve human needs

Sources: Adapted from Dekker, 1992, p 3; Dekker, January 1994, pp. 2-7; and Farnen, 1993c. Also see Chapter 19 in this volume.

Wherever politics is found, citizen participation is needed, particularly at the local level and in the workplace, schools, families, religious groups, and community fora (such as US National Issues Forums) modeled on the Athenian city state/forum and the New England town meeting. Since citizens gain competence through participatory practices, systemic stability is further assured through practical experience in education for democracy. Citizens feel efficacious because they are actively involved and can see the results of their political labors. They develop shared conceptions of the common good and change their individual opinions into informed public opinion through public discourse. Citizens learn to trust and respect one another as they participate in joint public decision making, thus supporting the ideological foundation of normative democratic theory. Civic education's role in participant-oriented democracy stresses citizen empowerment ('knowledge is power'), participatory skills, intelligent problem solving and decision making, and social reconstruction on a regular basis. Citizens can learn daily to recreate themselves and to reinvent their society while handling conflict through experience with practical politics and policy analysis. Schools provide experiences in democratic life and encourage democracy in other social institutions, such as the family.

Weak Democracy

Representative or 'weak' democratic theory more narrowly construes politics as the concern of political authorities, governments, and legislatures, exclusively those in the public domain. Emphasis is placed on political realism and the results of empirical political theory, which show that most voters are uninformed, uninterested, unpredictable, politically irresponsible, uninvolved, and unwilling to take the time needed to govern their societies. These theorists trust the elites of power, intelligence, education, and wealth, who (with their staunch bureaucratic allies) can maintain a stable society. A guiding theme is conservative governance based on constitutional grounds implementing a long-range and responsible public philosophy. Since democracy is conceived of as a political method or competitive process whereby incompetent voters reluctantly participate in elections to choose a governing elite, it does not matter which set of party elites rules. It is believed that they have more in common with one another than they do with the masses. The public role in governing is limited to acquiring information about candidates (rather than evaluating complicated public policies and discussing alternative choices) and voting in open, free elections. This provides enough popular control over elected leaders. Citizens are granted this right because the leaders they choose may hurt or benefit their private interests. Political participation, then, is limited to choosing the legitimate decision makers and to replacing one elite with another more preferable set of political aristocrats. Equality in this system means 'one man, one vote' as well as equal opportunity to participate in elections to choose the elite.

Leaders direct the major operations of government (which, itself, is considered just another organization, best run like a business). When citizens become too actively involved in politics and governance, the elite worries that smooth governmental operations are threatened and political stability or system maintenance is at risk. They cite supporting evidence to show that the elite is more civil-libertarian and civil-rights oriented and less authoritarian than the mass of citizens. Therefore, mass participation is considered a threat to a stable and free government functioning under democratic laws, not under the whims of men. The leaders fear that when the masses become too politically involved, the result will be violence, protests, social divisions, or even revolution, none of which is believed to be good for security, order, or business-as-usual. This elite believes that it is best to leave the mass to consumerism, entertainment television, and sports since normal people cannot really understand complex political issues.

Representational theory is excessively legalistic, individualistic, and autonomy oriented. It stresses realism, empirical theory, and elite training (especially through private education). It also emphasizes duties and responsibilities; hierarchy, order, and authority in schooling; the social reproduction function of public schooling; and passive, obedient, and respectful citizen roles. Elitists' favorite school courses are historical study, constitutional and legal studies, and geographic knowledge. Political education and practical politics or policy making are considered an expensive and dangerous waste of time since schools need to train workers for the national service and production industries. The hidden curriculum, which helps the elite to reproduce itself, is endorsed as is training the upcoming elite in its leadership roles through emphasis on higher-order cognitive skill training. Historical, literary, artistic, and music studies teach the elite to accept proper leadership roles while the masses must learn to respect their betters (that is, those who appear on every page of history texts).

The Two Theories Compared

These two sets of theories have been discussed in Western political theory since the days when Plato and Aristotle categorized political regimes as philosophical, aristocratic, oligarchic, democratic, and tyrannous. Jean Jacques Rousseau in the 18th and John Stuart Mill in the 19th centuries espoused democratic participatory theories, just as modern theorists (such as Barber and Newmann) have done in recent years. Socrates, Plato, and Aristotle advocated elite rule by the intellectual aristocracy, just as Schumpeter, Dahl, Converse, and Luskin have maintained at different times in the last 50 years. For example, Barber (October 1989, p. 355) writes:

> Yet if democracy is to sustain itself, a richer conception of citizenship is required that meets the test of what may be called strong democracy. Strong democracy is not simply a system whereby people elect those who govern them, but a system in which every member of the community participates in self-governance. It entails not merely voting and overseeing representatives but ongoing engagement in the affairs of the civic community at the local and national levels. Citizenship defined in this strong manner is far more burdensome and far more meaningful than the other version with which we tend to be content.

By contrast, Luskin (December 1990) reanalyzed the 1976 American national election study data to create a model explaining the political sophistication (or lack thereof) levels of mass publics. He concluded that interest (motivation) and intelligence (ability) have an effect on one's developed level of political sophistication but that informational variables (namely, education and print media exposure) do not. As he summarized it, '. . . the combination of limited cognitive resources and competing attentional demands may keep politics a minority pursuit, as it seems to have been even in ancient Athens.' He continued, 'This is not the place to dilate on democratic theory, but these results suggest that a highly sophisticated, participatory public is not even [a] feasible prescription. How distressing this is is unclear. But theory, if these results are right, must accommodate itself to fact' (Luskin, December 1990, pp. 331 and 353).

Tables 3.2 and 3.3 show some points of convergence between strong and weak democratic theories. On several points (namely, individual education, basic political information, political participation, decision making, and upward mobility into leadership roles), both theories agree on the basic worth of the concept if not on the degree of information, participation, or decision making required. Strong democrats agree with these basic political needs in a democracy, but they stress the need for more information, more education, additional forms of participation, and more sophisticated political decision making, public policy formulation, and problem solving on the part of the citizenry.

Table 3.4 summarizes other aspects of the divergence between strong and weak democrats regarding the nature of civic education. Table 3.5 lays out the views of the strong democrats (and their opposites) regarding citizenship competence and incompetence. In Table 3.4, we find once again the difference between elite versus mass knowledge; systemic stability versus change; the hidden versus the democratic curriculum; the stress on history versus practical politics and problem solving; and schooling conceived of as a corporate enterprise or assembly line to be privatized versus the school as a political setting where emancipation and critical thought are encouraged, and where social reform and liberation take place via democratic processes.

Table 3.5 could also be divided into strong and weak democratic columns since elitists/weak democrats are more likely to produce incompetent democratic citizens than are strong/participant-oriented democrats. For example, the elitists espouse limited political knowledge, discourage involvement, and, thereby, promote apathy and cynicism. Although the weak democrats do not foster nationalism, terrorism, stereotyping, racism, xenophobia, or enemy images since they fail to consider these elements in their description of what an effective or competent citizen must be aware of, they let these tendencies develop or wither away if only by accident. Since the elitists endorse nonvoting, politics avoidance, and shallow political knowledge, citizens are left to themselves to accept or reject war and violence as the simple means to resolve conflict.

By contrast, the strong democrat espouses developing and sharing relevant political information, fostering the growth of a coherent democratic ideology, and encouraging political sophistication. The participatory democrat proposes that politics become a part of everyday life, that no political view be left unchallenged, that mass media be used and interrogated, and that holding public office is both a public trust and an honorable profession. The strong democrats also endorse using conflict resolution, compromise, mediation, and negotiation at all levels of individual, interpersonal, group, and public life so that resorting to violence is the last (rather than the first) public policy option.

Table 3.4 'Strong' participatory versus 'weak' representative views of public and civic education

Educational view or philosophy	Representative Democratic View	Participatory Democratic View
Nature of knowledge to be learned, transmitted:	Competence and knowledge of leaders are more important than ignorant, confused, and inactive *citizenry*; media provides consumer information, entertainment, and pro-government propaganda within a narrow focus on nonabstract individual, home, and family matters	Through direct political participation, *citizens* can learn from media and experts all they need to know about complex political questions, problems, and issues so that informed public opinion is critical for public *policy making*
Purpose of schooling to encourage:	Depoliticized electorate, nonpartisanship, interest in law and order, system maintenance, and reproduction of modes of production and learning	Partisan *citizens* and choices, liberation, empowerment, social reconstruction, and deconstruction of hidden curriculum
Purposes of *civic education* to promote:	Order, obedience, law observance, authority, inequality, the hidden class-based curriculum, cognitive knowledge, and passive *citizenship* role	Heightened political interest and involvement, improved participant knowledge and skills, social reconstruction; *democratic* schools, proficiency in *decision and policy making, problem solving*, and critical thought, and active *citizen* roles as leaders and followers
Typical modes/ subjects favored for civic education include:	Pre-1945 history, geography, constitutional analysis, economics, and consumer skills	Practical politics, international affairs, political problems, democracy, citizenship, civic education, social studies, political behavior, public opinion analysis, comparative government, and post-1945 history

Table 3.4 (continued)

Educational view or philosophy	Representative Democratic View	Participatory Democratic View
Politics and/of education positions/questions include:	Accepting hidden curriculum as elitist and class-based, like the society; no professional training for politics teachers; no testing of politics in state or national examinations; restricting political education to basic minimums, stressing work-related skills of reading, writing, mathematics, and university preparation; nonunion and independent voters are lauded; schools are organized like corporations, hospitals, and prisons in a bureaucratic hierarchical fashion	Hidden curriculum is rejected; teachers are given training in politics; state examinations and assessments include politics and *citizenship* education; school, classroom, peer, and work group *democracy* encouraged; partisanship is accepted as an alternative personal choice; critical attitudes are endorsed as part of a theory of informed participation in groups and as individuals to improve public *problem solving and decision making*

Sources: Adapted from Farnen, 1990 and 1993c. Also see Chapter 19 in this volume.

Six Definitions of Democratic Citizenship at the National (US), International (IEA), and European (Council of Europe) Levels

Here, I want to summarize six different definitions of (and perspectives on) democratic citizenship. These come from the US (two), IEA (international) and Western European levels (Meyenberg, FRG, and Dekker, NL), and two other Western/Eastern European summary views from two separate 1992/1994 collections of Council of Europe documents.

The USA I - 1980s

The first definition from the US in the 1970s and 1980s describes 17 components (from a conceptual/content perspective for the end of schooling), ranging from patriotism and national loyalties to history, constitutions, structures and functions, politics (international and comparative), critical thinking, problem solving, decision making, and contemporary events. It is also divided into knowledge, understandings, affects, and behaviors. The least stress in this curriculum is on politics and comparative government and the most on critical thinking, decision making, problem solving, basic concepts, and national loyalties (see Farnen, 1990, pp. 118-22).

Table 3.5 Positive and negative components of democratic citizenship

Competent Democratic Citizenship Component	Incompetent Democratic Citizenship Component
Developing political knowledge about public *policy making*	Demonstrating political ignorance of *democratic* processes and procedures
Possessing well-developed opinions, attitudes, and cognitive schema about politics, *democracy*, freedom, equality, social welfare, and tolerance	Demonstrating the lack of any political interest or coherent political attitudes, opinions, or schema in regard to parties, ideologies, or the dangers of intolerance
Manifesting political interest, party identification, ideological coherence, a cosmopolitan view, balanced *nationalism*, human solidarity, and civic courage	Showing evidence of political alienation, anomie, overzealous *nationalism*, obsessive political fanaticism, approval of state fascism/ terrorism, stereotyping, xenophobia, racism, and 'enemy' images
Practicing political behaviors, such as acquiring political information, talking politics, questioning others, defending one's views, revising schemata, matching personal and policy preferences, interest group, and party activity; standing for party, group, or political office; using conflict resolution effectively; consuming quality information sources and reliable comparative political mass media; and informed voting	Shunning things political, ignoring politics, and isolating one's views; confusion about personal views and policies; no group activity; being apolitical, independent, neutral, and nonpartisan or middle-of-the-road; stances to hide political cynicism, distrust, or apathy; nonvoting; avoiding political media and information; and headline news and sound bites accepted
Practicing conflict resolution, mediation, persuasion, and peaceful resolution of disputes through diplomacy, negotiation, and compromise	Espousing war, police, violent, and nondiplomatic violence as the solution for national and international problems of group conflict, treaty violation, and violations of international law or UN sanctions

Source: Adapted from Dekker, January 1994, pp. 5-7. Also see Chapter 19 in this volume.

The USA II - 1993

The second definition (also for the end of schooling in the US) deals with government and its tasks, the US political system and its foundations, democracy and the US Constitution, US politics and world affairs, and citizen roles. This October 1993 document from the CIVITAS Project (Quigley and Bahmueller [eds.], 1991) stresses topics such as the rule of law; limited government constitutions; comparative political systems; political culture, democratic values, individualism, humanism, and participation; power, federalism, structures and functions, public policy, foreign policy and international organizations, citizenship, rights, responsibilities, and public goals; leadership; and service (*National Standards for Civics and Government*, October 1993, pp. ix-xiii).

The IEA Report - 1975

A third perspective (from a mid-1970s international report by Torney, Oppenheim, and Farnen, 1975, pp. 94-5) is from the IEA civic education project. In formulating its models of civics as an international subject, the IEA civic education committee (from 1966 to 1971) developed a series of models of the affective domain of civics, which dealt with key concepts (such as equality, toleration of dissent/opposition, women's rights, legitimacy, efficacy, and democratic values), a perceptual domain of 'how society works' from the student perspective (that is, police, courts, laws, legislatures, welfare organizations, political parties, unions, and the UNO), and content areas of politics. The six content areas agreed upon for the ten-nation study were deemed applicable to countries as geographically distant as Israel, New Zealand, the Netherlands, and the US (Britain also accepted the measures, but failed to participate for economic reasons). These six content areas of citizenship, political processes and institutions (national and international), economic processes and institutions, and social processes and institutions presented a broad-based international model of common concerns in political education, which could be measured cross-nationally. As administered, because of curriculum-imposed content restraints, certain areas were stressed (for example, citizenship concepts and political and economic processes), whereas other areas (for example, communications and mass media, interdisciplinary approaches, and socialization processes) were minimized in the testing (this report is summarized in Farnen, 1990, pp. 229-34).

EC/EU - 1993

A fourth definition comes from two 1993 studies on all-European citizenship (Meyenberg, 1993, pp. 358-74; and Dekker, 1993, pp. 519-45). Meyenberg's contribution (also see Chapter 12) pointed out the following goals for civic education in Europe and the FRG:

◆ Increasing political knowledge and interest of youth
◆ Developing a European attitude and common values
◆ Developing a sense of European community; understanding European integration and interdependence
◆ Understanding European treaties, decision-making processes of EC/EU institutions, and their competencies
◆ Developing democratic citizenship participation, critical analysis, and opinion formulation skills
◆ Defining democracy as a principle, type of state, way of life, and school process (that is, democratic behaviors)

Dekker's study (also see Chapters 16 and 19 in this volume) is more comprehensive because it asks how European are youth expected to be (answer: quite a bit) and how European they actually are (answer: not very much). Nevertheless, Dekker's especially valuable contribution is his summary (taken from research findings and policy documents from 1988 to 1991) of the goals of European citizenship. It also uses a knowledge, opinions, and attitudes breakdown about the EC/EU/EP along with basic facts, trust, national member-ship roles, problems and policies, identity, democracy, social justice, human rights, pluralism, unification, patriotism, nationalism, and Europeanism.

Council of Europe - 1992

A fifth perspective on what is democratic citizenship competence for the 1990s comes from the research reports flowing from two Council for Cultural Cooperation (October 1992a and 1992b), and Council of Europe research workshops in Valletta, Malta from 6-9 October 1992, and in Nitra, (former) Czechoslovakia from 27-30 October 1992.

The first workshop on the secondary school curriculum (according to the *Rapporteur's* summary) decided that for East and West, teaching humanitarian values was better left to the home and community or the indirect effects of or 'ethos' of the school. School autonomy, local reforms, and teacher independence were endorsed (especially in the East). A focus on the economic transition process in the East, educational self-development, and less reliance on foreign experts were all outcomes of this meeting as well.

Summarizing the Western European concerns and interests from the second workshop on political education, the Germans (two reports) were interested in authoritarianism, stress prevention, handling xenophobia and prejudice, exploring fascism, and preventing an escape from freedom. Other topics of interest were studying Europe, multiculturalism, foreign workers, environmental-ism, third world studies, ethical and moral studies, the European Union, Turkish studies, right-wing extremism, basic laws, nationalism, German federal state history and studies, peace studies, international studies, bureaucracy, the handicapped, conflict resolution, political economy, political history, and national socialism in Germany. A French report stressed the study of school democracy and antiracism as alternatives to the prevailing 'market logic' of civics. An Austrian report discussed conflict resolution strategies in schools, while a Spanish project mentioned democratic values, civil rights, and participation as well as moral development, democratic school reform, authoritarianism, conflict resolution, pro-social behavior, and justice, freedom, toleration, happiness, moral autonomy, human rights, and peace through moralization. An Italian contribution stressed the need for solidarity, toleration, equality, interculturalism, the handicapped, co-responsibility, and school reorganization, whereas a British report described civics as moral education, peace studies, self-responsibility, interculturalism, community, pluralism, rights and duties, democracy, values education, justice, and active citizenship.

An Irish report mentioned European studies in detail through a study of self, school, community, the UK and Ireland's history, colonization in the 17th century, World War I, and contemporary migration patterns. A Swiss monograph stressed the study of childhood, citizenship, democratic values, and human rights, whereas a Norwegian professor described his country's civics curriculum as dealing with responsibility, social knowledge and history, geography, environmentalism, interculturalism, and conflict resolution. Pluralism, multiculturalism, and student participation in the real community were other goals described in this same report. So we see here a typical Anglo-Irish focus on history, the German interest in authoritarianism and multiculturalism, and the Norwegian emphasis on communitarianism.

One Romanian report from the Malta conference laid out the changes under way in Central and Eastern Europe with respect to a new philosophy of education, school decentralization, de-indoctrination and sanitizing the old Marxist ideological projects, reforming humanities and social sciences, de-bureaucratization, and teaching about democracy and free markets. His national report mentioned the current study of humanism, history, religion, and the social sciences as well as geography and civics (to a modest degree). A Bulgarian report stressed certain civic themes, such as respect for others, human rights, civil conduct, rules, problem solving, democracy, conflict resolution, inter-culturalism, environmentalism, and school reform.

Two reports on Slovenia and the Czech Republic described their concerns. In Slovenia, they stressed the legal system, human rights, and democratic society as well as ethics, tolerance, peace, ecology, and world religions. In the Czech Republic, they emphasized the study of self, home, family, community, native land, and state as well as ecology, law, economics, and anthropology. The Hungarian report mentioned democracy, participation, values, deviance, law, morality, citizenship, problem solving, conflict resolution, empathy, and social knowledge. Poland (where a new, officially approved civics curriculum is now in place) emphasized school democratization and humanization along with self-government, autonomy, and civil liberties in a democratic and open society with a free mass media. In Lithuania, they were concerned about de-Stalinization, democratic school reform, humanism, morality, ethnicity, ecology, mutuality, tolerance, and self-government. The Russian model focused on Comenius' (ca. 1750) democratic humanism and liberalism to teach democracy through everyday life (that is, complete depoliticization). The Ukrainian report discussed the general need for a 'scientific world outlook' through the study of the scientific method of problem solving, including the historical approach. The topics of interest were strengthening 'the spiritual life of the modern society', encouraging flexible thought among youth, and democratizing human relations.

These results indicate that when it come to democratization and civic education, Eastern Europeans are 'flying blind', to paraphrase the title of a 1992 Hungarian political science report on developing civil societies in Eastern Europe. Studying philosophy, science, or history, and practicing school/teacher autonomy may still produce good Marxists, fascists, or democrats, depending on the philosophers, scientists, or historians studied, or the spirit of the school and style of the teacher doing the civic education. My conclusion is that we find a very confused picture of the goals of civic education and citizenship competence in the East. There is much more agreement in the West and the US on citizenship, politics, participation, democracy, peace, conflict resolution, internationalization and Europeanization, and other common trends. (Copies of the October 1992 and 1994 reports can be obtained from the Council of Europe, Strasbourg.)

Council of Europe and Institute of International Education, Stockholm University - 1994

The sixth perspective on citizenship comes from a Council for Cultural Cooperation (Council of Europe) conference in October 1994 on minority education. It included an expanded view on civic education and identity conflict, which Mitter (October 1994) from Frankfurt am Main presented that same month in Stockholm. The Council conference (held in Bautzen, Germany) discussed minority education issues, languages, the Basques of Spain, and research themes (for example, on the subjects of racism, ethnic groups and nondiscrimination principles in school textbooks, ethnic prejudice, bilingualism, multiculturalism, national minorities, identity, primary and secondary language instruction, and Gypsy children in the Netherlands, the UK, Italy, Hungary, the Czech Republic, Finland, Austria, and Germany).

This conference discussed theoretical constructs for including minority education and multiculturalism in civic education and national history instruction. Participants discussed various projects, such as the Mercator minority linguistic documentation network, the Sorbish people in Germany, the connections between Basque sociopolitical power and the educational situation of the Spanish Basque community, and the best or most useful theoretical constructs for minority education (including sociopolitical and cultural contexts, identity and loyalty questions, legal and administrative provisions for schooling, curricular, pedagogic, linguistic, civic, and history teaching, and human rights/democracy as core values for minority education for human dignity and toleration). Mitter (October 1994) also discussed national loyalty and cultural identity conflicts. He emphasized education's role in harmonizing such conflicts which occur regarding individual and group rights and decision making (using majority rule while maintaining coherence) in modern democratic states which are beset with so many conflicting loyalties. Sociopolitical tensions also arise when defining just what are the majority (or mass) and the minority, economic or linguistic superordinate or subordinate positions, educational practices which accept or reject minority language(s) and administrative autonomy, and devices to encourage or negate minority connections to their 'mother nation'.

Civic education is considered a school subject representing broad educational and curricular principles. It is a field which uses political language, pedagogy, objectives, and processes to identify basic intrasocietal loyalty conflicts and to harmonize ethnic and social relations. In this respect, the subject of national history is most in need of a general overhaul since it pits national loyalty against cultural identities (dual or multiple). Teachers can play a key role in this process as productive agents for democracy and toleration or as raucous cheerleaders for intolerance and hatred for nondominant groups (Council for Cultural Cooperation, October 1994).

WHAT IS AUTHORITARIANISM?

Political scientists are usually more interested in studying authoritarian or totalitarian regimes or political theory than they are in the authoritarian personality or syndrome. Nevertheless, there is some congruence between such actual regimes and individual personality traits or characteristics. These include the use of aggression or force, political indoctrination, unquestioning support or submission, nationalistic and militaristic traditionalism, lack of respect for civil rights and liberties, anticommunism, ethnic intolerance, chauvinism, and right-wing party support (see Figure 3.1, box F).

At the individual level, authoritarians support middle-class conventions, accept the authority of power wielders, disparage minority groups, and have a moralistic obsession about sex. They need to express power over others from whom they expect obedience; are concerned with hierarchy, authority, and status; deem women as inferiors to be exploited; have elitist views of education; demand homage and withhold praise; play the father, God, boss, or tyrant roles on the job; are humorless and overly serious; cannot brook challenges to their authority; use Machiavellian power plays and intrigue; employ stereotyping; lack ethical norms; express anti-Semitism and prejudice; and drive to dominate. Authoritarians are also less postmaterialistic, less interested in politics and political information, distrust democracy, employ nationalistic symbolism, sanction capital punishment, prefer the 'old days' and 'a strong leader', deplore their 'degenerated' society, reject third-world aid and environmental preservation, and admire both aristocrats and private property.

Figure 3.1 Theoretical, multivariable, and interactive (multiple causality) model of three political culture types and authoritarian personality characteristics

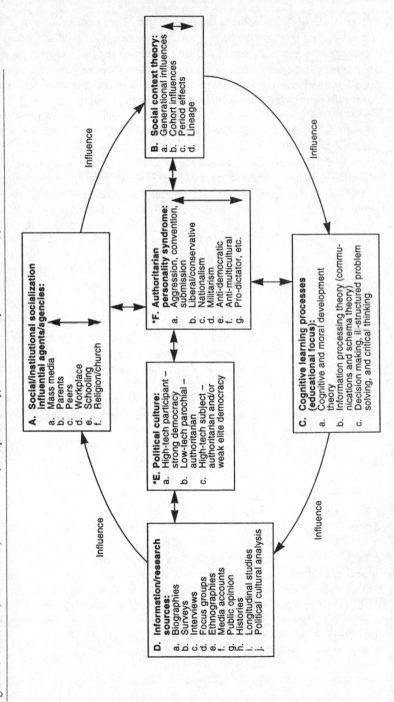

Figure 3.1 (continued)

Notes: Determinants of authoritarianism and political culture/environment of a given 'age', time (1, 2, 3, or past, present, future). The dynamic influences and interactive processes produce political patterns, waves, figures, and chaotic outlines of political cultures in regards to authority/democracy - conservatism/liberalism. Double-headed arrows indicate interacting forces/influences for political stability and change.
* Since the authoritarian personality reinforces an authoritarian political culture and vice versa, these two factors may be considered as either independent or dependent variables in different research designs. (On this point, see Meloen, Chapter 2, in this volume.)

Authoritarians also oppose economic nationalization measures, equal opportunity and affirmative action policies, and call themselves 'traditionalists', 'antisocialists', 'right-wingers', and 'conservatives'. They advocate harsh police action, enjoy the traditional family and 'normal' sex roles, dislike homosexuals, and endorse strict child-rearing practices. They are also pro-native-white and pro-racist in their views. Many of these views are shared with their parents, suggesting intergenerational transfer of these values. Authoritarians tend to be older, less educated, rural or industrial workers, small shopkeepers, farmers, or fishermen. Authoritarians also are anti-Semites, dogmatists, ethnocentric, and endorse inequality. They have a high level of distrust, paranoia, ambivalence, using fear, threats, and punishment to the extreme. They also advocate 'realism' and *Realpolitik* in foreign affairs. Particulars describing 'ideal types' of authoritarianism differ from society to society. The prevailing political culture, family child-rearing practices, gender roles, socioeconomic levels, and other factors (such as degree of education or urbanization) are responsible for intercultural variations. In Soviet Russia, for example, authoritarians were antidemocratic and anticapitalist, yet shared preferences for ethnocentrism, ethnic prejudice, nationalism, and sexism with their Western counterparts (see Altemeyer, 1981 and 1988; Meloen, Farnen, and German, July 1993; and Meloen, van der Linden, and de Witte, November/December 1992).

One reason for this description of the authoritarian as an 'ideal type' is that the degree or salience of authoritarianism has profound meaning and importance for any discussion of democratic decision and policy making. On the basis of this personality trait, right-wing authoritarians have been labelled 'enemies of freedom' (Altemeyer, 1988). Authoritarians will have very different modes of decision making than would democratic 'ideal' personalities. For example, the degree of societal, group, and personal authoritarianism will have its effect on types of decisions allowed, the decisional process itself, outcomes, and evaluations of policy effectiveness. Someone who is undemocratic and looks to a strong leader; is personally aggressive; displays sexism, racism, or ethnocentrism; does not treat others with toleration and respect; and abhors politics and lacks political information will be very different in a decision-making group than will someone with directly opposite or mixed characteristics. Therefore, in addition to generational factors, the type of democratic theory one advocates, and previous socialization experiences, the authoritarian personality syndrome is another important situational or environmental characteristic. The person interested in schooling and democratic decision making must consider all of these factors when discussing and implementing democratic decision-making processes in classrooms, community groups, workplaces, or other settings. The overall cycle of authoritarianism levels based on scale scores in Western countries indicates that general authoritarianism levels were high in the 1950s, lower from 1960 to 1971, rose until the mid 1970s, and stayed there through the end of the 1980s. Since we are only now gathering data on the early 1990s, we can only venture a guess that these average levels (with intracountry group variations) will be higher in some countries (for example, the former USSR, US, Canada, and the UK) and lower in others (for example, the Netherlands, the FRG, Finland, and Sweden) because of personality/societal interactions as mediated through these various political cultures.

At any rate, authoritarianism can be a major impediment to democratic learning since it is so dependent on stereotyping, submission, dependency, and subject roles in decision-making practices. By contrast, field independence and reflective thinking are more effective solution strategies than authoritarians' related impulsive thinking and conformist or field-dependent learning strategies. Authoritarians' greater dependence on attitudinal anchors (such as high social prejudice levels, religious conventionalism, and a view of the modern world as a mean and scary place) also interferes with their development of useful adaptive and creative learning/reasoning strategies. Consequently, their democratic and informal decision-making skills often become attenuated, restricted, and maladaptive.

The major purpose of Figure 3.1 is to show some of the major features of authoritarianism and its positive relationship to nationalism, militarism, conservatism, and antidemocratic orientations. However, it also illustrates the connections among the degree of authoritarianism, the level of political culture within the context of generational/cohort/period effects on its development, combined with the influence of socialization agents (such as parents and schools), and the connection between it and stage developmental, information processing, and problem solving educational formats. The people of different political cultures also learn their politics from media and other sources as well as through their respective socialization process. In sum, this schematic shows on a broad scale the dynamic and interactive processes which produce patterns, waves, and aberrations in the outlines or map charting the ebb and flow of political authority/democracy, conservatism/liberalism, or nationalism/internationalism.

INDICES OF NATIONALISM, DEMOCRACY, AND AUTHORITARIANISM IN EUROPE AND THE ATLANTIC COMMUNITY

This section describes some general public opinion research findings for Western and Eastern Europe and North America from 1989 to 1994, focusing on recent Central and Eastern European results which are only recently coming into print. Also described are the results of the Slovakian Centre for Social Analysis and the survey research findings on Central and Eastern Europe from the University of Strathclyde reports.

Organized political parties and movements based on authoritarian principles are typically neither powerful nor popular today either in Western Europe or North America. However, there is some evidence of the increasing appeal of fascist political ideology and authoritarian populism in both the West and East. By contrast to totalitarian regimes still extant in Cuba, Vietnam, North Korea, and China and fascist governments in South Korea, Serbo-Yugoslavia, Taiwan, Indonesia, Thailand and elsewhere, North America and Europe as a whole (excepting certain 'holdover' countries, such as Albania, Romania, and Russia - in its Parliament) do not have authoritarian governments, major parties, or popular movements based on radically antidemocratic principles. Where organized authoritarianism exists, it still plays a discordant major (as in Russia) or minor (as in eastern Germany) role in the democratic pageant. However, the existence of authoritarian ideologies, sentiments, value structures, personality traits and behaviors is quite another matter. Despite their receiving some 10 per cent of the vote in national and European Parliament elections and up to 30 per cent of the vote in Antwerp and Marseilles local elections, we may be able to dismiss the political importance of right-wing politicians (such as David Duke in the US or Enoch Powell in the UK) or parties (such as the Flemish Block, the Center Party in the Netherlands, the National Front in France and in Belgium, the National Republican Party in Germany, or nationalistic movements such as Pamyat in Russia). Yet, these ideological fascists and their willingness to slavishly abide by social conventions, to submit to authoritarian dominance, and to act aggressively toward their 'inferiors' or the 'underclass' is quite another matter which we cannot so easily put aside.

AUTHORITARIANISM AT BAY AND DEMOCRACY AT RISK: SOME 1991/92 SURVEY RESEARCH FINDINGS

To extract a few from the many instances of such pro-authoritarian tendencies in our everyday lives (balanced with some contrary evidence of pro-democratic sentiments), let us consider the following facts taken from 1991 surveys:

♦ Out of 12 Western and Eastern European nations, only the Germans (eastern and western) and Czechs said they were not losing interest in politics. Large majorities in Italy and France and a nearly even split in the other surveyed countries (the UK, Spain, Hungary, Poland, Bulgaria, Russia, the Ukraine, and Lithuania) said they were losing interest in politics.

♦ When asked to choose between freedom and economic security or equality, Americans, Ukrainians, Russians, western Germans, and Czechs preferred personal freedom over security/equality, whereas the other ten countries (including eastern Germany) chose the opposite.

♦ Overwhelming majorities (87-96 per cent) in 12 Eastern and Western European countries endorsed the state's role in caring for the poor in contrast to 67 per cent of American respondents.

♦ A group of seven Eastern European countries opposed having homosexual teachers in schools, whereas a majority of the Americans, Germans, English, Italians, Spanish, and French would accept them.

♦ No majority in any of the surveyed countries wanted socially 'dangerous' books to be allowed to remain in public school libraries.

♦ When asked how 'recent changes' affected 'relations between ethnic groups', only small percentages (5-31 per cent) in Eastern Europe said this was a 'good influence', with either a plurality or a vast majority in the other Eastern European nations responding that such recent events had a 'bad influence'.

♦ Citizens (27-70 per cent) of certain Eastern European countries (for example, former Czechoslovakia, Hungary, Lithuanian, and, above all, Poland) agreed that the churches' political role was 'too great', but only token numbers (except in Poland with 30 per cent) said that the church was a 'bad influence'. However, majorities throughout all of Europe oppose the Roman Catholic church's stand against abortion.

♦ Eastern Europeans also believed that newspaper and television were a 'good influence', wanted the state to operate radio and television stations, and preferred state and private newspaper ownership.

♦ Unlike the US, France, Spain, Bulgaria, and Lithuania (which endorsed the personal efficacy of voting in 1991), only a bare majority in the UK, western Germany, and former Czechoslovakia agreed that 'voting gives people like me a say.' A larger number in eastern Germany and Poland disagreed with the statement then agreed. Nearly even splits between the two options were registered in Italy, Hungary, Russia, and the Ukraine.

♦ The large majority of Eastern Europeans favored democracy, but women were less inclined to do so. This was particularly true in Bulgaria and Russia, where only a narrow majority of women were pro-democratic.

♦ Eastern Europeans were more favorably disposed toward a multiparty system, but many countries (unlike opposing majorities or pluralities in the US, the UK, France, Spain, former Czechoslovakia, Poland, Bulgaria, and

Lithuania) would outlaw those parties that did not believe in a democratic system.

♦ Except for Russia and the Ukraine which disapproved, the large majority (in Hungary, a plurality of 47 per cent) in other Eastern European countries approved of the basic societal changes since Autumn 1985. However, majorities in nearly every eastern European state (except Poland and eastern Germany) said their countries and lives had gotten worse. This is to be compared with western Europeans' sense of personal betterment, if not national improvement (except for Spain), in the last five years. Fortunately, expectations for improvements in both personal and national satisfaction levels for the next five years were nearly universal, with the exception of France, where it was believed that personal fortunes will improve and the nation's situation will remain stable. (Source for above statistics: *Times Mirror*, 1991, pp. 27-43.)

♦ Anti-Semitism was guarded. There were large numbers of 'do not know'/'no opinion' answers; however, higher levels (about 20 per cent on average) of anti-Jewish sentiment were found in the East than in the West, with the highest levels (33 per cent) registered in Catholic Poland and Slovakia.

♦ Large numbers of Eastern Europeans disliked the ethnic minorities with whom they lived and expressed discontent with their neighbors. Germans regarded Poles, Romanians, and Turks unfavorably. Poles disliked or distrusted Germans and Ukrainians. Czechs disliked Hungarians. French views about North Africans were negative.

♦ Countries which were ethnically homogeneous (such as Poland and Hungary) and pluralist countries (such as former Czechoslovakia) perceived internal groups as more threatening than external dangers.

♦ Citizens in many countries believed that essential parts of their countries still lie in bordering nations. This intensified their dislike of these neighbors, with the most extreme example being Hungarian antipathy toward Romanians.

♦ The Sinti/Roma ('Gypsies') were among the most universally despised groups, being most disliked in Hungary, Bulgaria, former Czechoslovakia, and eastern Germany.

♦ Eastern and Western Europeans as a whole were equally high (about 70 per cent) on patriotism measures though not as high (88 per cent) as the US. (Sources for the preceding data are *Times Mirror*, 1991, pp. 27-43; *Times Mirror*, 27 January 1993, pp. 1 and 1 to H7 and HA-HD; and *Times Mirror*, 16 September 1991, pp. 1-6.)

Possible conclusions to be drawn from these 1991 survey results indicate that while Western Europeans are enjoying economic prosperity and generally support democratic values (with notable exceptions), the more authoritarian-prone Eastern Europeans have a long way to go in their quest to build democratic political systems. Evidence of these trends can be seen in lessened political interest, preference for security/equality over freedom, fear of homosexual teachers in the East, popular reliance on - or fear of - the political role of the Church, pronounced pro-censorship feelings (in both East and West) threatened diminution of women's economic roles in Eastern countries in favor of traditional male economic dominance, intolerance of ethnic strife, widespread support for the inefficacy of voting and outlawing certain political parties, and increasing distrust of politicians and lack of personal political efficacy. These trends do not portend well for the future of democracy as we know it, particularly in the East. This generalization is further reinforced by significant anti-Semitic feelings, dislike of domestic minorities, 'gypsies', and neighboring countries, and very high patriotism levels (hopefully, liberation-oriented or reasoned) which the positive end of the cold war, increasing economic integration and security, and other more positive democratic trends could reinforce. The latter include caring for the poor, accepting homosexual teachers in the US and the West, declaring equality for spousal work options in the West, viewing mass media favorably in the East, supporting a multiparty system and voting as a process among majorities in eight Eastern and (mostly) Western countries, and expressing pro-democratic sentiment in the East (if less so among women) Consequently, there are signs of hope for a democratic resurgence to accompany the growth in personal and social optimism seen in both East and West, providing fascist trends do not stage a triumphant return as they have in Serbia, Croatia, and elsewhere.

This broadly painted picture is not as rosy as it seems. Follow-up surveys in Russia, the Ukraine, and the Baltic Republics in 1992 indicated that, in the main, while the Lithuanians were pleased with their steady progress toward democracy (if not with their slow economic recovery), the political situation in the Ukraine was less sanguine (though fairly stable), and that in Russia was absolutely bleak. There, disillusionment with Russia's present leadership, with democracy, and with the Russian version of free market economics was nearly complete. For example, in November 1992, 51 per cent of Russians favored a strong leader, rather than a democratic form of government, to solve their problems. This fact is in contrast to just the opposite result found only 17 months earlier in the 1991 survey. (Other Russian survey data indicate that Russians, when asked specifically about it, do not want a dictator to return.)

This 1992 survey also found a rising popular disappointment with the Russian parliament, a decreasing sense of political empowerment, and a declining interest in politics. Russians were clearly disappointed with present conditions and free market reforms, had low expectations for the future, and increasingly supported a return to authoritarianism. These results are not surprising in light of the fracture of the Soviet Union into its separate rival parts, a dim future forecast for cooperation among the Commonwealth of Independent

States (for example, between Russia and Georgia, and the Ukraine), political and economic chaos, and the intense rivalry for hegemony between President Boris Yeltsin and a Russian Parliament in which former communists and conservative nationalistic forces continue to be dominant. The new Russian 'right wing' was unfavorable toward Yeltsin, economic reform, and increasing democratization. Clearly, democratic sentiments in Russia are declining just as a preference for authoritarianism is rising.

Other relevant and politically significant trends in Russia included a steep rise in a belief in God across all demographic groups as well as an increase (to 30 per cent) in the number of Russians who said they had little in common with other ethnic groups or races. Unfavorable ratings of other former Soviet states also remained high, but anti-Semitism in Russia was stable at 22 per cent (as compared with, for example, 6 per cent of Americans). Increasing nationalism was also evident in Russia with respect to recovering lost territories and support for Serbian 'ethnic cleansing' as a model proposed for use in Russia for dealing with its national/ethnic minorities. Russian women also tended to be more conservative, antidemocratic, anticapitalistic, more in favor of press censorship, and more positive toward church and God. Most Russian youth preferred capitalism to socialism in contrast to older Russians who favored returning to some form of socialism or communism. Rural Russians were also more conservative, feared change, distrusted democracy, and preferred a strong leader; however, their support for the church decreased, while their evaluations of entrepreneurs were increasingly positive. Press support also increased, while half the population opposed greater media censorship. Yeltsin supporters opposed - while nationalistic, anti-Semitic, Pamyat adherents favored - more press censorship.

Results from the Lithuanian and Ukrainian surveys also validated the explosive, changeable, and mercurial nature of the electorates there with a decrease in middle-of-the-road, centrist, middle-class, and pluralist views. Support for democracy (still a majority) in these two nations decreased since 1991. In contrast to Lithuanians who wanted more free markets, 52 per cent of Ukrainians disapproved of recent economic reforms, as did the same number of Russians. Lithuanians remained staunch supporters of democracy and free market reforms, but the number who favored a strong leader was up to 25 per cent. Significantly, the number of 'no opinion' responses in all three former Soviet states increased appreciably regarding the 'democracy' versus 'strong leader' choice as well as with respect to the 'socialism' versus 'capitalism' dichotomy (for example, more than doubling to one-third or more in Russia and the Ukraine). Ukrainians still favored democracy as did Lithuanians, who also preferred the capitalism option. Ukrainians and Lithuanians were still over-whelmingly in favor of private land ownership and property sales; their belief in God also rose inversely with the decrease in their economic and political optimism. Ukrainians and Lithuanians increased their ethnic exclusivity sentiments, whereas anti-Semitism dropped in the Ukraine and increased in Lithuania. Nationalist sentiment in the Ukraine (symbolized by RUKH support for 'national consciousness') has increased at the expense of favorable views toward the Russians, but the Russianized eastern Ukraine was much more pro-Russian, pro-authoritarian, antidemocratic, antiparliament, less patriotic, and more pessimistic than the ethnic Ukrainian western region.

By contrast, Lithuanians have rejected the Sajudis independence movement in favor of reinstalling its formerly despised and now democratically elected communist rulers in the form of its Democratic Labor party. They also tended to believe that voting empowered them, supported democracy and human/civil rights, and positively evaluated the political and economic changes of recent years. Lithuanian (like Ukrainian) women were also more conservative, less democratic, more pro-censorship, and more likely to have 'no opinion' on all questions, except for support for the church and belief in God. Russian youth were also more pessimistic, less democratic, less capitalistic, and more conservative than either Ukrainian or Lithuanian youth. However, youth groups in all three countries were generally more in favor of democracy, free markets, and rapid change than were their seniors or other identifiable groups, such as rural people. Attitudes toward press censorship were polarized in all three societies, with large numbers who favored or approved it. One might legitimately expect (given that anti-Yeltsin and pro-Pamyat groups in Russia were pro-censorship) the Ukrainian RUKH supporters and the Lithuanian Democratic Labor supporters to be antipress and pro-censorship. Unexpectedly, both of these groups opposed press censorship (despite recent heated electoral campaigns) and had generally favorable attitudes toward their mass media. (Source: *Times Mirror*, 27 January 1993, pp. 1-45.)

These more recent poll results clearly indicate that pro-democratic sentiments in Russia and the Ukraine are on the wane and are stronger in Lithuania. The balance between more democracy or a strong authoritarian leader could go either way in Russia, whereas the Ukrainians and Lithuanians could both turn to more dictatorial party rule as the pace of their economic reform increases. With significant groups of seniors, women, rural citizens, anti-Semites, communists, and nationalists losing faith (if they ever had any) in democratic government, authoritarianism in one form or another has a very good chance of staging a strong comeback in Russia and the Ukraine (if probably not in Lithuania), especially if the military decides to lend a helping hand to one side or the other.

The Slovakian Case

A 1993 Centre for Social Analysis survey (Bútorová et al., March 1993, pp. 23-7) indicated most Slovaks objected to independence, blaming the split on Czech injustices. Slovaks prefer trading most (85 per cent) with Austria and the Czechs, but least (25 per cent) with Moslem countries and Israel. Slovaks least prefer Gypsies as prospective neighbors (98 per cent), followed by Hungarians and Jews (ca. 30 per cent). (Also see Chapter 5 in this volume.)

Despite the fact that there are few Jews living there, 22 per cent of Slovaks are anti-Semitic. Social distance toward Jews is relatively high. For example, Slovak reluctance to having Jewish neighbors increased from 32 per cent in January 1991 to 33 per cent in January 1992, dipped to 27 per cent in March 1993, and most recently rose to 42 per cent. In Slovakia, anti-Semitism is:

a. Demonstrated by those who do not want Jews as neighbors. They believe Jews are disloyal; are engaged in a world conspiracy; are selfish over money, profits, and personal gain; and excessively influence Slovak economic and political life.
b. Only neutral or unbiased to the extent that Slovaks disagree with the Jewish disloyalty thesis (38 per cent), do not fear excessive Jewish political and economic influence (44 per cent), and do not mind having a Jew for a neighbor (67 per cent) or relative (51 per cent).
c. Reflected in the positive stereotype toward Jews regarding business skills (88 per cent), scientific and cultural achievements (66 per cent), and economic prowess (38 per cent).

If our general hypothesis relating authoritarianism and social prejudice/anti-Semitism rings true, there should be certain characteristics which anti-Semitic, prejudiced, more authoritarian Slovaks share regarding nationalism, militarism, ethnicity, party politics, and public policy options. Therefore, predictably, Slovakian anti-Semites often:

a. Belong to the Slovak majority.
b. Are prejudiced against Hungarians, Czechs, and Gypsies, too.
c. Are nationalists, support the Czech-Slovak split, the nationalistic government in power, and nationalistic political parties and movements.
d. Are militarists, support continuing weapons production and arms exports.
e. Espouse Slovak autarchy or neutrality in foreign policy, are anti-internationalists, anti-Western, and against regional cooperation activity.
f. Oppose widespread civil rights guarantees.
g. Oppose private ownership of communist state property.
h. Espouse state ownership of major production companies, egalitarianism, and state paternalism.
i. Are anticapitalistic.

From this summary, we can see that Slovak, Russian, and other Eastern authoritarians mirror the prevailing social/economic and cultural conformity images.

The Strathclyde Centre for the Study of Public Policy New Democracies CEE Barometer: 1991-3

Between 1991 and 1993, Rose (Rose and Haerpfer, 1993) at the University of Strathclyde, Glasgow, directed a series of surveys on Central and Eastern European countries while occasionally using Austria for a comparative Western versus Eastern European perspective. These studies help us to further discern some of the trends underway with respect to key variables, such as support for democracy, authoritarianism, ethnic diversity, old/new regime approval, and political values. Rose found many similarities in the economics and politics in the ten countries in the region which are all undergoing the double (market and democratic) revolution and share the common historical experience of Soviet rule. Some of the national specific findings he reported are:

◆ Bulgaria is the most economically strapped country, is still the most collectivist, and the citizenry largely prefers a strong man to take charge rather than depending on parliamentary debate and action.
◆ The Czech Republic clearly favors the market and democracy more so than other countries in the survey. Its citizens are most likely to be democrats and to have greater confidence in the future, perhaps because they are relatively better off economically at present.
◆ The Slovak Republic is often characterized as 'backward' when compared with the Czechs, but their overall political patterns are very much like both the Czechs and the other participating Central and Eastern European countries. Despite the continual competition in Slovakia for a strong political leader, the Slovaks (like the Czechs) are less in favor of a strong-man government than are other nationals.
◆ Hungary had a somewhat more favorable past under Communism and have a troubled present. Therefore, they are more approving of their old economic and political system, are average in most of their survey responses, and are above average in their economic survival skills and in being democrats, confident in the future.
◆ Romania is also more economically underprivileged, yet the people are optimistic about their economic and political future and clearly reject the old regime.
◆ Slovenia is very confident about its current and future economic and political prospects partly because it escaped the Yugoslavian wars.

♦　Croatia, by contrast, has suffered more than Slovenia from the regional war which has somewhat diminished its former prosperity. Croatians are very much against the old Belgrade regime and reject (at an above-average level) the idea of suspending parliament.

♦　Byelorussia and the Ukraine, both part of the former Soviet empire, are very pessimistic about their present and future economic prospects and still prefer the old Soviet type economic system. Their citizens are also much more likely to support the old political regime and are negative about their present and future governmental possibilities. These two countries are the least democratic in orientation; the Byelorussians favor government by a strong man.

In sum, among these ten countries, the Hungarians are most and the Croats least in favor of the old regime; the Czechs, Romanians, and Slovenes are most in favor of the current regime; and the Hungarians, Croats, Byelorussians, and Ukrainians are most against their current rulers; whereas the Czechs, Slovaks, Romanians, and Slovenes are most politically optimistic about the future; and the Byelorussians and Ukrainians are most pessimistic in this respect. On average for all ten countries, approval of the old regime stood at 43 per cent, the current regime at 53 per cent, and their future political system at 72 per cent.

The average numbers of democrats across the ten countries stood at 32 per cent and reactionaries at 23 per cent. Most democratic were the Czechs, Romanians, and Slovenes; least democratic were the Hungarians, Byelorussians, and Ukrainians. (The picture of reactionaries was the mirror image of the pro-democratic one.) Across the ten countries, 35 per cent of all respondents believed that parliament was likely to be suspended; 24 per cent would approve the suspension. Overall, 42 per cent favored government by a strong man, despite the number of 'hopeful authoritarians' being only 15 per cent on average and the number of 'confident democrats' 57 per cent across these countries. The perceived threats from internal ethnic groups averaged 52 per cent across these countries, with the greatest threats seen in Croatia, Romania, Hungary, Slovakia, and the Czech Republic. The fewest threats were seen in Bulgaria, Byelorussia, and the Ukraine. Threats from past enemies (Germany and Russia) averaged 34 per cent internationally, with the Czechs, Poles, and Romanians as the most threatened. In comparing a preference for individualistic values (46 per cent international mean) with collectivistic values (26 per cent international mean), the most individualistic were the Czechs, Slovaks, and Croats; the most collectivistic were the Bulgarians and Romanians (Rose and Haerpfer, 1993, pp. 72-82).

CAN CIVIC EDUCATION MAKE A DIFFERENCE POLITICALLY?

This section reviews some of the findings on the general relationships between increasing levels of education, college major or field of study, exposure to civic education, and political orientations, attitudes, and belief structures (such as liberalism/conservatism or authoritarianism levels).

Education and Personal Political Development in the US

In 1993, Jennings (1993) reported the outcomes of a longitudinal three-wave political socialization study of the Vietnam generation under way in the US from 1965 to 1982. He found that the college-educated population was initially most highly volatile just after high school, when their political attitudes were most in flux, after which they maintained higher rates of continuity. Furthermore, educational level remained politically salient in terms of differentiating respondents both within and between age cohorts and between parents and their offspring. Higher education also tended to both reinforce and stabilize pre-existent political dispositions and behaviors (which are a result of family, personal, previous educational, and other socialization influences) with the addition of a more liberal attitude toward civil liberties and toleration being a more generalized result. In turn, the influence of choosing a specific college major and course of study are not only affected by pre-existent predispositions which influence the choice of a major, but also result in further influences which are a result of the college experience and postcollege adult life experiences and environments (Jennings, 1993, pp. 1 and 18-19).

Among the most significant outcomes of this research projects are specific examples of these developmental patterns. College graduates often (40 per cent) reported that their political and religious views were frequently challenged in their educational experience. The more highly educated also reported important political disagreements with their parents at a higher rate than less-educated groups. Jennings found that the higher the level of education, the higher the level of political interest, efficacy, factual knowledge, sophistication, and political activity level at each time point in the study. However, this was not solely a result of more education since home, previous schooling, and prior political influences were also instrumental in this process. College-educated respondents became increasingly liberal over the years on matters such as political tolerance, opposition to school prayers, and pro-school integration (to a lesser degree). For example, the college-educated tolerated the fascist party and the Ku Klux Klan, but had little good to say for the religiously oriented Moral Majority.

The data on college majors are also interesting. On measures of ideological sophistication, political knowledge, and personal political efficacy, humanities and social science majors either started out and/or finished high on these measures over the years, whereas the opposite was true of education, business, or science majors. On the topics of civic tolerance, antischool prayer, and school integration, the social science and humanities majors were also more liberal in 1982, regardless of where they started out in 1965 or stood in 1973. They were also more pro-labor union and antibig business than were the other three groups. Also, they were more pro-Democratic Party in their politics. Finally, the humanities and social science majors outdistanced the other three groups in their support of the proposition that government should ensure everyone a job and a good level of living. They were also far more liberal than conservative on self-ratings and were decidedly pro-choice on the abortion question (Jennings, 1993, pp. 2-18).

Education and Authoritarianism in the Netherlands: Two Dutch Studies

Dekker and Ester (1993) reported the results of national random probability sample analysis of Dutch citizens from 1975 to 1991. Some of the major content areas concerned ideology, age groups, authoritarianism, social discrimination, and income inequality. Among their findings on authoritarianism, education, nationalism, racism, and social discrimination, the following general results stand out. Youth attitudes generally mirror those of the wider Dutch society so that there is no distinctive youth political culture in the Netherlands. This same generalization applies to the elderly group. Negative stereotyping of older and younger people is a result of one's authoritarian ideas and the general tendency to discriminate using rigid categories to form opinions. The category of youthful 'Yuppies' proved to be a 'media mirage' because these young, urban profession-als are not at all conservative and, if anything, belong to the new left-of-center professional class and hold quite liberal views. The survey questioned and rejected the existence of a so-called 'working class authoritarianism'. Instead, education is more relevant than social class in determining high or low levels of authoritarianism in Holland. Authoritarianism is positively related to having stereotyped views of the unemployed. Age, education, and authoritarian attitudes are key explanatory variables for knowledge of AIDS, acceptance of AIDS patients, and a negative attitude toward homosexuals. These studies also found that racial attitudes are predicted by authoritarianism, even controlling for socioeconomic factors. Another hypothesis about connections between race and education (while controlling for authoritarianism) was rejected; authoritarianism still remained as the strongest predictor of racial prejudice. Finally, these findings indicated that the typical respondents believed that others (that is, the general public) held more conservative views on racial minorities than was actually the case. Influential institutions (such as mass media and education) can have some social impact on the supposed public 'conservative bias' by correcting these erroneous personal views on prevailing public opinions (Dekker and Ester, 1993, pp. 14-17).

As for nationalism scores, they found that increases in age (life cycle), not generational effects, were more important, just as was the case for support for democratic freedoms and women's rights (but not for left-right self-ratings, which were neither life-cycle nor generational effects). Both nationalism and right-wing self-identification increase with age and decline by recency of survey year/cohorts, while support for democratic freedoms and women's rights decrease with age and increase over time and all cohorts. The elderly are more authoritarian, anomic, skeptical, less democratic, nonparticipatory, and less in favor of women's rights. They are also more conservative, traditional, anti-socialist, more worried about war/peace, and more pro-defense/military in their views. The group of nonauthoritarians in Dutch society include females, younger, educated, employed, and semi-autonomous workers who rate themselves more liberal politically (Dekker and Ester, 1993, pp. 13-17, 23-34, 62-83, 85-7, 122-9, 139-50, 152-62, and 188-206).

Vollebergh (1994) also contributes to our understanding of the relationship between education and authoritarianism among Dutch adolescents over a two-year period. Her research confirmed that increases in educational level was a predictor of lowered authoritarian levels, which had been corroborated in previous research on the subject. Increasing education by itself was not the causal factor here so much as the improved educational standards and acquisition of cultural status that accompanied higher education. Gender differences favoring girls' lower authoritarianism in earlier years disappeared as males were better educated. For example, nonauthoritarian, lower-educated subjects increased most in an authoritarianism direction, while authoritarian, better-educated ones became less authoritarian over this time period. Authoritarians with less education and nonauthoritarians who were better educated remained as authoritarian as they were originally. As long as education is taking place, changes in authoritarianism can be expected to occur, especially during the important developmental period of adolescence (Vollebergh, 1994, pp. 70-1).

What about European Political Socialization/Education in the EC/EU?

Dekker (1993, pp. 519-45) has described some of the significant system, social, and individual political variables/orientations which are related to the EC, EU, and EP voting. These include knowledge, opinions, attitudes, and interests regarding the EC/EU as well as key socialization variables.

- System variables: the EP's changing powers; and the economic situation and outlook
- Social variables: nationality, the socioeconomic position of the respondent (and/or his/her parents); and level of urbanization
- Individual characteristics and variables: age, gender, health, intelligence, or level of education
- Individual political orientations variables:
  - Politically relevant orientations, including religion, opinion on emancipation of women (or girls), self-confidence, and social ambition
  - National political orientations, including political knowledge, political opinions, political interest, political efficacy, party preference, and party identification
  - EC/EU political orientations, including:
    - Knowledge of goals, policies, member states, and EU institutions in general and the EP in particular, and perception of consequences of (not) voting for the EP
    - Opinions on EU goals (un)importance of EU policies, effectiveness of EU policies, EU membership of one's own country, benefits of EU membership, scrapping of the EU, one's own country's leaving the EU, (un)importance of the EP and having a party preference in next EP election, and (evaluation of) the perceived consequences of (not) voting for the EP
    - Attitudes such as interest in EU politics and policies; attitude about the EU, political efficacy with respect to EU problems, and attitude about voting for the EP; and Europeanism
- European political socialization variables:
  - Socialization agencies such as family, church, school (including European politics courses), mass media, peer group, contacts abroad, workplace politics, and politicians and their political messages
  - Socialization processes including, among others, the likelihood that relevant others (parents, friends) want the respondent to (not) vote, and personal willingness to conform (or not) to these expectations.

Dekker has operationalized these variables into an East/West European political competence survey regarding the European Community and integration. The survey tested opinions and knowledge about the EC and contains questions about a particular country and its European connections. Some preliminary results were included in a Polish report by Fratczak-Rudnicka et al. (May 1993, pp. 1-5). This report said some of the questions were not relevant to Eastern European students (in this case, a group of 160 Warsaw University students) and had to be revised after a pretest on 30 students. On a test of seven items about EC facts (for example, date established, charter organizations and countries, and main institutions/locations), 73 per cent of students got 0, 1, or 2 correct answers; only 27 per cent had from 3 to 6 answers correct. Students said they knew little about (but were interested in) the EC and that they got most of their relevant information from television and newspapers. Despite their ignorance (also shared by Western European students), 71 per cent supported European integration and were opposed to its isolation, restriction, or limitation, instead of its expansion and development. Almost all (96 per cent) of the students felt 'European' always or sometimes, yet the large majority (73 per cent) were skeptical about being able to democratically influence the course of European events. They also did not talk about the EC in private conversations and had no fixed opinions on the topic. Most (70 per cent) Polish students believed that the EC is important for Poland's future. More than half believed Poland would benefit from EC membership. The students were also able to determine 'most' from 'least' to 'not' European nations (for example, French, Russian, and American, respectively). They also wanted to join European nature, ecology, antiwar/nuclear weapons movements/organizations.

NATIONALISM AND SOME POLITICAL SOCIALIZATION RESEARCH FINDINGS

Let us now turn to a summary of three recent research reports on nationalism and political socialization in three countries (Hungary, Poland, and the US) (also see Farnen, 1994a, pp. 23-102). The following major points were made:

a.   A Polish study of students (average age of 21 years) indicated different degrees of social distance toward Germans, Hungarians, and Canadians (who were rationalized, affectively treated, or sentimentally imagined), respectively (Holly, August 1988).

b.   Authoritarian personality characteristics in Hungary are associated with an exclusive sense of nationalism, ethnocentrism, anti-Semitism, and the lack in humanistic, enlightened, cosmopolitan, and internationalist personality characteristics. A Hungarian national identity study between 1976 and 1985 also indicated that children positively evaluate citizens and reject photos of foreigners, exaggerate their country's size, and gradually move from the fantasy realm to more social depictions of country between grades 4 and 8. Temporal sequencing of cognitive elements went from parents and birthplace to language and group; then to country awareness, jobs, and geography; and, finally, to politics, social system, and group cohesion. Nationalistic elements among youth are more pronounced than among adults and are associated with citizenship and language among youth. Youth agree with adults' positive statements about country, yet lack conceptual integrity. Ethnocentrism and positive stereotyping of country are widespread among youth, but socialist internationalism in the media and education have increased their ambivalence regarding youth's positive nationalistic sentiments and their learned rejection of ethnocentrism in general. Youth were more pessimistic about their national history than were adults. They ascribed Hungary's past failures to 'enemy' strength, rather than to in-group weakness. They, thereby, avoided cognitive dissonance. Youth's national identity feelings may be divided into those associated with birthplace, well-being, and national affirmations. These naturalized, operational, and existential elements produce an identity which is part of everyday life. Personal history and common experiences provide youth with a sense of personal meaning and identity plus group cohesion. History and geography curricula in the schools ignore ethnic minority questions, nationality issues and feelings, and reasoned patriotism since it tends to be dull, faceless, ideological, and both uninformed and uninformative (Csepeli, 1989).

c. A longitudinal panel study (repeated from 1965 to 1973 and in 1982) of college-educated Vietnam protestors tested the theory of persistence. While nonprotestors were solidly Republican, protestors identified strongly with the Democrats, with whom they solidly allied by 1972. This loyalty lasted at least into the 1980s, when they were in their 30s. Protestors had higher support for civic tolerance/liberties, opposed school prayer, supported integrated schools, and failed to support the military, big business, and the police at higher levels than did nonprotestors. These differences mellowed over the years; however, ratings of those groups seen as having too little influence (African-Americans, youth, women, and welfare recipients) were still much higher among protestors. Both groups gave high ratings in favor of women's rights, but the protestors were still more liberal on most public policies and on civil liberties. Although the college protest generation did not differ much from nonprotestors in high school on civic tolerance, by 1973, they were very tolerant and rejected provincial and nationalistic statements as: 'The American system of government is one all nations should have.' They were also more tolerant of Communists and anticlerics and had positive views on women's equality, minority aid, legal rights, and minority equality. Consequently, there are clear associations here between these views and American social welfare liberalism, pro-democratic, antiauthoritarian, antifascist, and nondogmatic political orientations (Jennings, June 1987).

SCHOOLING AND SOCIALIZATION INTERACTIONS AND EFFECTS: A BRIEF SUMMARY

Political socialization research findings are useful input, process, and output measures for assessing the effectiveness of civic education when combined with personality, structural, developmental, and other historical or social institutional (family, religion, peer and work groups, individual experiences, and socioeconomic political events) factors. These studies also provide some guidelines, however crude at the moment, for how curriculum changes may be directed for schools of the future. Based on literature and research findings, we can say (with a reasonable degree of probability) at least four things:

1. Certain forms and types of schooling have positive influences on democratic development and citizenship education, skills, and training. Since billions of dollars are spent worldwide on public education which has citizenship improvement as a major goal, it is important that we be able to assess sources, processes, outcomes, and interrelationships among socialization agents, teachers, students, and curriculum variations.

2. Cross-nationally in ten Western democracies patriotic rituals, flag salutes, rote memorization, and student passivity in the classroom did not promote civic knowledge or democratic beliefs (such as political equality, support for dissent opposition, tolerance, antiauthoritarianism, and increased participant orientations). In other words, a democratic classroom climate (which fosters student interest in predicting future trends, encourages student-teacher discussion of political choices, recognizes the value of voting and creative political conflicts, allows free access to information and political media needed to make political decisions, and promotes willingness to take political action) was more likely to increase support for pro-democratic values and greater political knowledge (if not for more active political participation and support for national governmental policies) in all of the countries surveyed. Indeed, it may be that encouraging support for patriotism may be contrary to acquiring democratic values (such as a critical view of government, equal rights, tolerance, and press freedom) cross-nationally (Torney, Oppenheim, and Farnen, 1975, pp. 15-21).

3. We also know that the relative influence of schools and parents in fostering political information cross-nationally shows some school effects, but is a shared result of school influence, SES and educational levels, and the home environment. But merely acquiring political knowledge does not mean that students will also favor democracy, current national policy, and participant views of citizenship. Knowledge may be convertible to power, but it does not necessarily produce active, loyal democrats, regardless of the prevailing current educational philosophy.

4. The relative influence of schools, media, and parents in fostering democratic orientations and skills is just as important as how long these beliefs last or which ones are regularly reinforced. How children develop a sense of national identity, how they perceive minorities, how minorities perceive the majority, how these constructs fit into a definition of one's political self (that is, a person's cognitive maps, schemata, or scripts), and how these factors influence students' conflict resolution, decision and policy making skills,

information processing, and political reasoning are all important questions which socialization, cognitive studies, moral development, and informal reasoning research can help us to answer within the context of schooling.

DOES POLITICAL EDUCATION/SCHOOLING MAKE A DIFFERENCE?

As for the effects of schooling, itself, we know (also with a certain degree of accuracy) that teaching about democracy can make a difference; that different forms of civic education can affect knowledge levels, political attitudes, and participant orientations; that majority group students may be significantly affected by political education; and that the nature and type of classroom climate (for example, democratic, elitist, or authoritarian) can influence students' political orientations. For example, Patrick's (December 1988) survey of US curriculum effects concluded that course content exposure is directly related to increases in the students' political knowledge. He said that youth's values and attitudes are greatly influenced by 'a supportive classroom environment' as well as the 'analysis, appraisal, and discussion of civic issues.' 'Critical thinking about civic issues' and classroom discussions with a 'free exchange of information and ideas' increase the 'potential for developing democratic values and attitudes' among students. Youth community service programs may also have an impact on students' political behaviors if 'collective reflection on the experience' is collaterally practiced (Patrick, December 1988, pp. 1-13).

Litt's (February 1965, pp. 69-75) early study of Boston, Massachusetts, high schools found a concurrence between students' middle class social status and their acceptance of those democratic norms which textbooks, school teachers, administrators, and the community endorsed. Anyon's (1980, pp. 317-41) later study of New Jersey elementary schools with students from different socioeconomic levels discovered vast differences in decision making skills taught in the various types of schools. In workers' schools, schoolwork was mechanical and rote, providing little opportunity to demonstrate choice or decision making. Middle-class schools focussed on grades and correct answers, allowing some choices about decisions. The affluent schools had far less structure and stressed creativity, independent work, concepts, ideas, thought, choice, and decision-making skills. Finally, the executive-class/elite school had schoolwork which was analytical, intellectual, reasonable, conceptual, and emphasized quality in decision-making and problem-solving abilities. These different forms of schooling inculcated different cognitive and behavior skills which were closely related to social class expectations and the development of useful 'symbolic capital' for upper-class students. The affluent schools produced students prepared to lead, make decisions, plan and control others, and take ownership of the economic system. Based on this analysis, Anyon proposed an alternative agenda for schooling. She advocated schools where most students could exercise critical thinking, be creative, use power and planning, and effectively help to manage their own schooling and later work life (with less conflict) in socially useful directions.

Other evidence that schooling makes a difference for youth's political socialization can be found in several other studies. For example, Hess and Torney (1967, pp. 200, 365, and 377) claimed the school was an important instrument for childhood political socialization, particularly regarding partisan political commitments. Almond and Verba (1963, pp. 315-18) also pointed to education as the principal determinant of political attitudes in their five nation comparative study. Follow-up studies to the 1975 IEA study reported above (Torney, Oppenheim, and Farnen, 1975) have also documented the degree to which classroom climate can have an impact on students' political learning. Encouraging pupils to study controversial issues, to express their opinions, and to practice critical thinking often results in increased empathy, respect for the truth and others' reasoning, more sources of information, higher motivation to learn, more accurate perceptions of alternative perspectives, more positive attitudes toward political conflict and public controversy, greater curiosity to learn, and improved problem-solving abilities (Torney-Purta, 1985, pp. 91-9). In 1976, the US National Assessment of Educational Progress found nearly a 20 point spread in mean scores when comparing those who studied politics either 'very little' or a 'good deal'. Student reports also indicated that US classroom practices may be more democratic than we realize in that students characterized them as open and comfortable, encouraging independent thought, creating a supportive climate for teacher-student disagreements and opinions, and allowing students to make real decisions about school affairs. Political education courses also were credited with being useful, nonredundant, realistic, relevant, and innovative. They also promoted, according to student reports, independent learning about political decision making, controversies, and issues as well as how to analyze values and alternative approaches to political questions (National Assessment of Educational Progress, November 1976, p. 31). Other National Assessment reports (National Assessment of Educational Progress, October 1983, pp. 19-29) on US student performance through 1983 showed that 9-, 13-, and 17-year-old students met testing objectives at the 50 per cent average level, except for African American and disadvantaged urban youth who significantly scored below average on all but one major objective (that is, respect for others' rights).

Moreover, political curriculum, teaching, and learning projects in more than one country have repeatedly shown the degree to which students in the experimental groups consistently outscored those in control groups. These experimental curricula have also served to increase student political interest as well as learning; to stimulate discussion, debate, and written work; and to take students into the community to contact political officials. Such results are often achieved with a 70 per cent passing grade expectation, which is no mean feat (Strecher, May 1988, pp. 1-52).

Similar results have been reported in polities as different as the US, the UK, Sweden, and Papua, New Guinea (PNG). For example, Wormald (August 1988, p. 7) reported that the PNG social science curriculum for grades 7 to 10 provided a conceptual focus on conflict, political change and development, decision making and analysis, contemporary society, and ideology. Wormald's survey of these students found evidence that the schools helped to increase political knowledge, interests, political aspirations and skills, a critical view of political leaders, critical political opinions, and faith in democratic processes. (PNG students also took pride in teaching their parents much of what they, themselves, learned about democratic politics.) Over two decades ago, Abrahamson (1967 and 1970) found the (recent UK preschool reforms) English educational system to be segmented, tracked, and elitist. It taught the low and middle classes the virtues of law observance, deference, and subject orientations. The elite students learned to be motivated, efficacious, powerful, and competent leaders. More recently, Denver and Hands (August 1988, pp. 1-19) reported on the effects of an experimental English secondary school politics course. This course aimed to develop 'transferable skills, a framework of knowledge and concepts, and procedures for assessing the validity of political information, beliefs, and values.' Studying politics for one or two years had discernible effects as compared with central groups in terms of increased political knowledge and sophistication, improved ideological and issue awareness, more political discussion and media usage, increased toleration and openness to political participation, and less cynicism. Students also became more political-issue-oriented voters rather than dependent on others' views. Regarding issue awareness, for example, the politics course students were better able to identify political issue positions, to link them to partisan political party positions, and to assign appropriate political policy positions to these parties. A second year of such study showed an even greater impact (Dekker, 1992, p. 15).

A Swedish study (Westholm, Lindquist, and Niemi, 1987, pp. 1-29) of school types, exposure to civics and history instruction, and a crude test of political knowledge (that is, just 12 items on international organizations and warfare) also found some school program and political education effects. The highest scores or the greatest gains were registered for students who were in the natural or social science tracks and who were university bound. By contrast, vocational students started out and ended up lower on the measures. They concluded that 'the social studies curriculum does have a considerable impact on cognitive development in mid to late adolescence' (Westholm, Lindquist, and Niemi, 1987, pp. 27-9). Exposing all students to equal amounts of political education would have the potential for greater education achievement across different programmatic and school types, something which vocational students were then being denied.

Niemi and Junn (September 1993) conducted a study using 1988 US National Assessment of Educational Progress civics tests. These forms consisted of 150 items of which individual students answered from 50 to 75 different test items. Data on these students (who were aged 17 and above and were high school seniors) were analyzed regarding ethnicity, parents' education, television viewing habits, course exposure, home environment, and achievement characteristics. After reviewing the 30-year literature on exposure to civics instruction and effects on students' knowledge, behaviors, and attitudes, these authors report mixed research findings in the US and other countries. Part of the problem with previous research is the lack of sufficient scope for testing civics knowledge (that is, sampling the content domain) as well as failure to estimate the extent of exposure (that is, opportunities to learn) to civics course material as well as interest, motivation, or self-selection of the political information to be learned. That is, there are structural (home and curriculum) as well as individual (motivational) factors, with students having more control over the latter than the former. Specifically with respect to exposure (structural) features, coursework, current events, topics, home factors (books, language, number of parents) were examined. These were contrasted with selection (individual) factors such as parental education, television viewing habits, student government activity, liking for civics, college plans, and grades, as well as race, which was treated in both categories.

The findings indicated that 92 per cent of US high school seniors had taken some civics courses. Those who were so exposed scored much better than those who were not, particularly if they had a recent course. However, having had just one (as contrasted with several) courses does not appear to be of great significance. Recent course exposure also seems to have a positive effect on understanding presidential responsibilities, on the value of popular elections, and on positive governmental orientations, whereas some school practices showed no effects on civics knowledge (for example, group projects or textbook reading in class). However, the more students discussed current events in class, the better their average test scores were. Minority status and female gender also repeatedly predicted less civics knowledge as did absence of reading materials at home, non-English-speaking home environment, single-parent homes, less-educated parents, and high television usage.

While the Langton and Jennings (September 1968) study of civics course impact attributed only a 4 per cent positive difference to having taken civics and a number of related political dependent variables, Niemi and Junn's study of recent course exposure (as compared with no civics course exposure) also yielded a 4 per cent positive difference, but the latter find these results both meaningful and no reason to do away with such coursework, especially since this result (as they say) '. . . is net of all the other influences' (Niemi and Junn, September 1993, p. 11). Furthermore, courses which had a broader variety of content coverage helped students to score better, as did current events discussions, plans for a college education (a surrogate for educational achievement), and participation in student government. (Minority respondents also showed more cynical responses to an attitudinal question regarding the degree to which the Reagan government in 1988 paid attention to the people.) These authors concluded that a broad-based civics curriculum has its effects on the students' 'psyches', provide context or cognitive maps which allow students to deduce answers to unfamiliar material, and '. . . when it comes to high school seniors' knowledge of American government and politics, the school and the civics curriculum do matter' (Niemi and Junn, September 1993, p. 13).

As a follow-up to their earlier study, Niemi and Junn (August 1994) examined the relationships between ethnicity in the US and high school seniors' performance on a 1988 civics/citizenship achievement test. This was a nationally representative sample of terminal year secondary school students. Niemi and Junn's study was based on the National Assessment of Educational Progress nationwide citizenship examinations. They reported many interesting findings about the differential performance on the same test for students belonging to different racial and ethnic backgrounds, including the following:

♦ Regardless of ethnic group/race, students liked studying government, found it interesting, and were both regularly and recently exposed to civics coursework (which displayed a variety of topics and political coverage). They also were equally exposed to current events in class and often reported their participation in student government. However, they were different in some other important respects. That is, whites came from homes where their parents were better (college) educated, where more reading and reference materials were available, and where two parents lived at home.

♦ Contradictory to the conventional wisdom of the Langton and Jennings (September 1968) study (which indicated that civics courses did not make any difference, except for minority youth), this study (like their 1993 report) indicated that civics coursework does matter. However, exposure to civic education did not make any unique or particular difference for African-American students' overall test performance.

♦ Upon closer examination of the data, when civic education is divided into its various subcategories (such as governmental structures and functions, civil rights and civil liberties, and practical politics), this is where the racial/ethnic gap either widens or narrows. For example, white students clearly outperform Latinos and African Americans on structures and functions items (for example, Congress has the power to tax), but there is less of a score difference for Latinos - and especially for African Americans - compared with whites on civil rights and liberties questions (for example, the US Bill of Rights, poll taxes, and social contract theory).

♦ Among these three groups, there are differential rates of daily television viewing (whites view less) and intentions to attend college (whites and

African Americans more often plan to attend than do Latinos). Yet, these background or independent factors and others mentioned previously (for example, books and reference materials, a parental education) explain 40 per cent of the difference between whites' and Latinos' lower scores and only 25 per cent of the difference between whites' and African Americans' scores. Whites from reading-oriented homes (where they speak only English, have two college-educated parents living in the house, and view less television) tend to score highest on these measures, especially when combined with the influence of school factors (such as more civics course-work, participation in student government, liking governmental studies, more current events discussions, and a greater variety of topics studied). For whites, male gender also predicted higher scores. For African Americans, these school factors are less important and may even be considered insignificant, despite the fact that they report greater interest in civics than whites. Instead, home factors (that is, language, reading, and education) are more important, but not gender, television viewing, or two parents in the home. For Latinos, home factors are less important (except for two parents at home), including the home language spoken or gender. For Latinos, current events discussions and civics variety are also important for learning.

♦   When it comes to knowledge of civil and individual rights as contrasted with structures and functions, schooling is less relevant for the former than for the latter, except for discussing current events (which helps to increase knowledge about civil rights). Structures and functions are aided by broad coverage, student government roles, and current events discussions. Television viewing does not impact rights knowledge as it does structures/functions and it may actually increase students' knowledge of criminal rights. Home reading interests also influence rights knowledge, but not structures/functions. Media effects, then, are quite complicated matters and less simple than gender (which does not show a rights - but does reveal a structures/functions - effect) (Niemi and Junn, August 1994, pp. 1-8 and tables 1-5).

Five Major Generalizations

Political education research and political socialization findings can be used to construct five major generalizations regarding a citizen's developmental patterns and competing sources for important influences on one's political knowledge and attitudes.

1.   Based on the US experience, we can trace a pattern whereby basic political loyalties (such as national patriotism, ethnicity, trust, racism, and religiosity) are formed early in life during the primary grades (ages 6-10 years). By the

upper elementary or middle school (ages 12-14 years), attitudes and knowledge become more differentiated, factually based, and more unstable, but not yet sophisticated. By grade seven or eight (ages 13-14 years), students become interested in sociopolitical ideas, develop firmer attitudes and consistent conceptualizations, and are concerned about 'the real' versus 'the ideal'. By late high school (ages 17-18 years) and into the university period (ages 18-22 years), one's fund of political knowledge increases, contradictions are negotiated, and political efficacy emerges, unless cynicism and alienation interfere with its development. From the time of their mid-20s, citizens are politically involved or distant, focus on personal goals, and may develop a reasoned commitment for those ideas and attitudes they took wholesale from their childhood or youth. Most older adults (except for middle-aged establishment citizens) are neither very interested nor involved in politics, vote when able to do so, and have deficient political issue positions. They dislike controversy, seek consensus, like democracy in the abstract (but dislike deviants and practicing civil libertarians, who upset the social order), and demonstrate fairly stable party and social group evaluations, however devoid they are of critical or in-depth knowledge about political issues and important public interests.

2. The second generalization is that while children and adults seem to be fairly stable in this respect, middle-school students (ages 12-14 years) may be most open to new knowledge and ideas about commitment and participation as well as reconsideration of their cognitive and attitudinal stances, such as one's political partisanship. These students are most receptive to discussing the relative virtues of conflict, partisanship, participation, and commitment while embracing the free expression of all opinions. The standard curriculum fare in the US exposes students to 'the American way' in the early grades; to state and national history in 4th and 5th grades (ages 9-10 years); to an often-chauvinistic discussion of other peoples, cultures, and societies in 6th to 8th grades (ages 11-13 years); to civics in 9th grade (14 years old); to US history (for the third time) in 11th grade (17 years old); and to government in 12th grade (18 years old). Consequently, when middle-school students are most ready to discuss partisanship, conflict, and policy issues, the schools downplay conflict, stress factual coverage, curtail debate, and cautiously delay such discussions until 9th grade civics or even 12th grade government. By that time, the cognitive developmental boat has left the then more clearly delineated educational shore. However, merely by raising such questions in the middle-school years, without realistic discussions of normative and ideological questions, might be a cure worse than the disease. That is, students are perfectly capable of holding ambivalent, contradictory, or factually incorrect views even when they contradict or challenge their own overall political schemas and cognitive frames of reference. Consequently, before warranting any civic education invasion of

the middle school, we should further research the parameters of political resocialization during this neglected period of political development for students aged 12-14 years. If these are truly the most impressionable years with students most open to critical self-examination, then it may be during this time period that civic educators should focus their attention (Jenness, 1990, pp. 192-5).

3. A third major generalization drawn from these studies is that school and classroom climate, the hidden curriculum, and the democratic ethos of free-wheeling discussion, debate, critical inquiry, and informed decision making can make a significant difference in students' civic knowledge, attitudes, and behaviors. The 1975 IEA study is one cross-national example of this research finding. There are several others (for example, Ehman, November 1970 and Spring 1980) which also corroborate this finding. When asked about the meaning of 'citizenship', American students' responses did not mention facts or participation, but rather focussed on interpersonal morality, cooperativeness, tolerance, good judgment, and wise decision making. Teacher educators also stressed a preference for thinking and analytical skills over factual knowledge or participation. This goal was best achieved through emphasis on effective and ethical decision making and reasoning with democratic values, rather than indoctrination, values clarification exercises, or exaggerated exhortations about practicing full-fledged, adult, participatory decision making. This type of curriculum would be most compatible with the democratic classroom in the democratic school. Reasoning in a critical fashion about democracy and politics is surely an accomplishment which could counter claims for more 'essential' and factual learning, something which takes much time and hard work, but which leaves our memories so quickly and easily thereafter that we scarcely notice its absence (Jenness, 1990, pp. 198-9).

4. A fourth relevant generalization is that for majority youth and civics, the Niemi and Junn (September 1993) findings for course influence and current events' discussion are encouraging as is the more positive evaluation of government associated therewith. The study of politics in schools may make a difference if it is recent, current, varied, and reinforced. Once again, the future task is to alter what and how such pupils are taught and, then, to see what effects a new curriculum (for example, one based on authoritarianism versus democracy, critical inquiry, conflict resolution, informal decision making, and public policy analysis) might have on both the majority and minority as well as the university and noncollege-bound youth.

5. Despite the contradictory outcomes of the Langton and Jennings (September 1968) and Niemi and Junn (August 1994) studies regarding minority youth and civic education, it is clear that African American and Latino students are somewhat closer to white students on civil and individual rights items than on governmental structures and functions questions. Yet, these

results still show an information gap between the majority and minority student populations that is exacerbated in the scores for the more traditional civics topics which are learned in school. The gap may narrow between majority and minority performance on some test questions, but it remains wide for the tests as a whole. However, if we look at the significant inter-correlations between test score and structural/individual characteristics across the entire white, African American, and Latino groups, the critical element for improved civics scores are current events discussions, liking for the subject, and planning to go to college. For whites and African Americans, the shared items of significance are reading/reference material at home, English speaking, and parental educational level; and for whites and Latinos, variety of topics studied and two-parent household. Therefore, eight of the 11 school and civics curriculum, home environment, and individual achievements are shared between whites and the two minority populations, with only student government participation, less television viewing, and amount/recency of civics coursework applying to higher-scoring whites alone. The schools, then, seem to be contributing to an increase in students' knowledge about civics and government. However, the way to motivate minority youth to learn more in school is not to encourage them to watch more police, courtroom, and criminal television programs, but rather to use the reading/reference materials they have at home, to become informed about current events, to take more civics courses which have a variety of subject matter, to watch less entertainment television, and to maintain an active interest in school governance. There is not any deficit reduction formula or magic curriculum which will offset the differences of minority youth, but there are proven methods to raise the political compe-tence of all students simultaneously so that minority students can benefit from civic education reform.

WHAT SHOULD WE TEACH ABOUT DEMOCRACY, NATIONALISM, AND AUTHORITY? AND WHEN, WHERE, AND BY WHOM SHOULD IT BE TAUGHT?

One proposal mentioned in the previous section focuses on the basic dimensions of knowledge, attitudes, and behaviors (with respect to authority-democracy, critical habits of thought, effective decision making processes, and public problem solving with conflict resolution and policy analysis skills). This proposal is based on a recent analysis of how to reconceptualize politics, education, and socialization for the 21st century (Farnen, 1993a, pp. 376-459, and 1994b, pp. 129-52). This study, combined with other work focusing on authoritarianism and the authoritarian personality (for example, see Farnen, 1993b, pp. 212-91), convinced me that the answers to at least six fundamental political questions (such as: How do we develop our political cognitions? How do we promote critical self-examination? How do we solve political problems? How is public policy made in authoritarian and democratic regimes? Is authoritarianism the root cause of undemocratic behavior? How do people participate in democratic settings to resolve conflict?) should be at the core of any new civics curriculum proposals. (For a more complete discussion of national perspective on political decision making and education, see Farnen [1993c].)

CONCLUSIONS AND INTERPRETATIONS

The foregoing analysis of authoritarianism, nationalism, ethnicity, minority status, and political socialization serves as a backdrop for a brief discussion of national educational policies in general and political education in particular. These comments relate to national ideologies and the treatment of national, ethnic, and racial minorities in various school systems. Elsewhere (Farnen, 1990, pp. 287-93), I have described a synthetic, analytic, and policy process model useful for an examination and reconstruction of the political education curriculum. This model incorporates the key features of teaching and learning (for example, texts, teachers, and school organizations), individual orientations (for example, values, skills, and knowledge) across different levels (for example, from group to international) with respect to political environments, systems, and problems (that is, public policy and decision making).

With respect to national identity/minorities, using this model would raise hundreds of basic questions about these topics. These questions relate to nationalism, racism, human rights, majority rule, pluralism, immigration, and other topical or problem areas which cut across the school curriculum. Nationalism, political identity, and minority-majority interactions are essential parts of the political culture/environment, the political decision-making processes, and the political problems dimensions of policy analysis (that is, political situations, rules, agendas, issues, decisions, implementation, evaluation, modification, and feedback).

An example of one such basic question would be: 'What has the student been taught and what does the student know about national identity and its influence on one's positive self-image (that is, conceptions of self and one's citizenship) at the individual or everyday level of life?' This basic question opens the door to multiple levels of analysis across different age groups and different classes of students in different classroom settings. That is, students and teachers can examine the sources of knowledge (flags, songs, and symbols), the extent to which conceptions are shared by others, the likely differences and similarities that occur across societies, and the close connections between one's self-ascriptions ('Who am I?') and societal definitions of citizen, patriot, hero, traitor, minority, majority, race, and nation.

These basic operations have not been systematically questioned or examined in many national school systems. Usually, if questioned about their national identity or political self, respondents give stock answers. The expectation of such communication is the acceptance of stock answers as part of our shared, everyday, and conventional wisdom. This process requires no critical self-examination because it is in the realm of 'common sense' by age ten and hardens thereafter into socially acceptable and expected ethnocentrism and prejudice. Teachers, parents, administrators, and politicians neither expect (nor probably want) these fundamental questions to be asked or answered since the outcomes are unanticipated and unexpected and may be deemed confused, dangerous, subversive, unsettling, unpredictable, or unpatriotic.

The answers to these fundamental questions of self-examination (if handled in a stepwise, systematic, and increasingly sophisticated manner across age groups) could result in self-doubt, self-criticism, alternative conceptions, and/or more reasoned patriotism and loyalties. The societal elite (the carriers or role models for these accepted truths) will also not readily accept such formulations since they challenge the very essence of the purposes of schooling and its basic functions. The primary purpose of both democratic and undemocratic schooling is control rather than enlightenment or liberation (that is, system and regime maintenance). Consequently, the teacher's usual role is to ensure conformity to national traditions rather than to examine or challenge them in a critical fashion. The rhetoric of democratic citizenship education may well apply to a critical treatment of political participation, voting, or minority rights (usually at the abstract or conceptual, but not concrete or case study, levels), but it will seldom extend to basic controversies over political loyalties or patriotism.

Adopting the proposition that the 'unexamined life is not worth living' or the belief that challenges to social certainties will produce thoughtful, informed, and involved citizens is not a likely prospect for timid teachers. They serve as keepers of the holy writ of national supremacy, military might, and thinking in accord with the familiar dictum my country, may it always be right, but right or wrong, my country nevertheless. There is little faith in the rule of reason when the patriotic stakes are so high and imagined risks to national security or personal survival may lurk in the background.

When examining such fundamental questions, the apparent dangers (costs) to the folkways, mores, customs, and traditions will probably always outweigh the presumed benefits of reasoned patriotism and loyalty. Early on, immigrant groups learn about the need to conform to basic social and political values. Some even become superpatriotic, conservative, and authoritarian in their political outlook (for example, Cuban Americans in Florida), which indicates a desire not only to adopt but also to die for their new (or to regain their old) country. This allows them to prove their loyalty, which may be challenged daily (though probably more by the media or themselves than by other citizens, as a rule).

Other groups with a lengthier national history are able to safely challenge these obligations of patriotism. For example, dedicated and ideologically strong religious groups can safely pit religious scruples against the state. In the US, the Seventh Day Adventists and Jehovah's Witnesses do this by refusing to participate in patriotic rituals. They reason that their loyalty to a higher power ('God') permits no 'idolatry' or worship of 'graven images', such as the US flag. African American citizens have also adopted the higher-law doctrine in their challenges to legalized segregation by claiming that the democratic principles of equality and civil disobedience precede the social contract and the Constitution. They protest in the name of natural rights, popular sovereignty, individual conscience, and religious/Biblical values - a 'higher law'.

Normally, schoolroom discussions of these matters deal with the peculiarities of such behavior or the errant groups' voting rights, equal treatment, or equal opportunity goals in elections, laws, jobs, schooling, affirmative action, housing, transportation, and so forth. The underlying conflicts and tensions between individual conscience, higher-law principles, civil disobedience, passive resistance, minority rights, and the social compact are not discussed in schools, government, homes, or the mass media. Instead, the focus of discussion and debate (that is, the pragmatic compromise) is on the particular goal or concrete economic, political, or legal redress, stripped of its underlying principles or concepts.

These actions (legitimate parts of the democratic policymaking process in a pluralistic society) are not subjects of focus or sources of strength for the polity. The goals of tolerance, compromise, respect, appreciation, understanding, empathy, and enlightenment are not key elements in public discourse when civil disobedience occurs. Instead, this is conceived of as a source of weakness (that is, a public 'problem' needing resolution) rather than a source of strength (that is, examples of citizen involvement, participation, the right to petition the government, religious freedom, and minority rights). Adherents to the accepted political environment and culture (no matter how democratic the individual or that culture is) find it difficult to accept the legitimacy of these basic challenges to continuing social and ideological survival. The threat to the basic valuative underpinnings of the society is too great to permit short-term (especially during times of military crisis) or bothersome long-term challenges to the ideational foundations of even the most pluralistic societies.

ACKNOWLEDGEMENT

An earlier draft of this chapter was presented at the Deutsche Vereinigung für Politische Wissenschaft section meeting on Political Science and Political Education in Potsdam, FRG in August 1994. I want to thank Dr Stephanie Schulze (formerly of Humboldt

University, Berlin, and presently at Brandenburg University, Potsdam, FRG) and Professors Adolf H. Noll and Axel Shulte of the University of Hannover, FRG for extending this invitation to discuss these findings. The University of Connecticut Research Foundation's financial support for this project is also gratefully recognized.

REFERENCES

Abrahamson, P. (Summer 1967). 'The Differential Political Socialization of English Secondary School Students', p. 246-69 in *Sociology of Education*, Vol. 40.

Abrahamson, P. (1970). 'Political Socialization in English and American Secondary Schools', pp. 68-75 in *The High School Journal*, Vol. 54, No. 2.

Adorno, T. et al. (1950). *The Authoritarian Personality.* New York, NY: Harper and Row.

Almond, G. and S. Verba (1963). *The Civic Culture.* Princeton, NJ: Princeton University Press.

Altemeyer, B. (1981). *Right Wing Authoritarianism.* Manitoba: University of Manitoba Press.

Altemeyer, B. (1988). *Enemies of Freedom.* San Francisco, CA: Jossey-Bass.

Andrain, C. (1971). *Children and Civic Awareness: A Study in Political Education.* Columbus, OH: Merrill.

Anyon, J. (1980). 'Social Class and the Hidden Curriculum of Work', pp. 317-41 in H. Giroux, A. Penna, and W. Pinar (eds.) *Curriculum and Instruction.* Berkeley, CA: McCutchon Publishing Corp.

Bar-Tal, D. (1993). 'Patriotism as a Fundamental Belief of Group Members', pp. 45-62 in *Politics and the Individual,* Vol. 3., No. 2.

Barber, B. (October 1989). 'Public Talk and Civic Action: Education for Participation in a Strong Democracy', pp. 355-6 and 370 in *Social Education,* Vol. 53, No. 6.

Bartley, R. (September/October 1993). 'The Case for Optimism', pp. 15-18 in *Foreign Affairs,* Vol. 72, No. 4.

Brinton, C. (1953). *The Shaping of the Modern Mind: The Concluding Half of Ideas and Men.* New York, NY: New American Library.

Bútorová, Z. et al. (March 1993). *Current Problems of Slovakia After the Split of the CSFR.* Bratislava, Slovakia: Centre for Social Analysis.

Cleary, R. (1971). *Political Education in the American Democracy.* Scranton, PA: Intext Educational Publishers.

Council for Cultural Cooperation (October 1992a). *The Secondary School Curriculum.* Strasbourg, France: Council of Europe.

Council for Cultural Cooperation (October 1992b). *Workshop on Political Education.* Strasbourg, France: Council of Europe.

Council for Cultural Cooperation (October 1994). *Minority Education.* Strasbourg, France: Council of Europe.

Csepeli G. (1989). *Structures and Contents of Hungarian National Identity.* Frankfurt/Main: Verlag Peter Lang.

Dekker, H. (1992). 'Socialization and Education of Young People for Democratic Citizenship. Theory and Research.' Paper presented to the Institute of Political Studies and IPSA/RCPSE Conference on 'Political Consciousness and Civic Education During the Transformation of the System', 30 November to 3 December 1992, Warsaw, Poland.

Dekker, H. (1993). 'European Citizenship', pp. 519-45 in R. Farnen (ed.) *Reconceptualizing Politics, Socialization, and Education: International Perspectives for the 21st Century*. Oldenburg, FRG: Bibliotheks- und Informationssystem der Universität Oldenburg (BIS).

Dekker, H. (January 1994). 'What is a Democratic Citizen? Democratic Citizenship Competence of the Young: Conceptualization, Variables, and Indices.' Paper presented to the IPSA/RCPSE Conference on 'Reinventing and Fostering Democracy and Human Rights', 11-15 January 1994, Florida Atlantic University, Boca Raton, Florida.

Dekker, P. and P. Ester (1993). *Social and Political Attitudes in Dutch Society*. Rijswijk, Netherlands: Social and Cultural Planning Office.

Dekker, H., D. Malová, and R. Theulings (January 1994). 'Nationalism: Concepts, Conceptualizations, and Indices. Description and Explanation. Case: Slovakia.' Paper presented to the IPSA/RCPSE Conference on 'Reinventing and Fostering Democracy and Human Rights', 11-15 January 1994, Florida Atlantic University, Boca Raton, Florida.

Denver, D. and G. Hands (August 1988). 'Does Studying Politics Make a Difference? The Political Knowledge and Perception of School Students.' Paper presented to IPSA XIV World Congress, Washington, DC.

Ehman, L. (November 1970). 'Narrative Discourse and Attitude Change in the Social Studies Classroom', pp 76-83 in *The High School Journal*, Vol. 54.

Ehman, L. (Spring 1980). 'The American School in the Political Socialization Process', pp. 110-14 in *Review of Educational Research*.

Farnen, R. (1990) Integrating Political Science, Education, and Public Policy: International Perspectives on Decision-Making, Systems Theory and Socialization Research. Frankfurt/Main, FRG; Bern, Switzerland; New York, NY; and Paris, France: Verlag Peter Lang.

Farnen, R. (1993a). 'Reconceptualizing Politics, Education, and Socialization: Cross-National Perspectives on Cognitive Studies, Problem Solving, and Decision Making', pp. 375-459 in R. Farnen (ed.) (1993), *Reconceptualizing Politics, Socialization, and Education: International Perspectives for the 21st Century*. Oldenburg, FRG: Bibliotheks- und Informationssystem der Universität Oldenburg (BIS).

Farnen, R. (1993b). 'Cognitive Maps: The Implications of Internal Schemata (Structures) Versus External Factors (Content and Context) for Cross-National Political Research', pp. 212-91 in G. Csepeli, L. Kéri, and I. Stumpf (eds.) (1993), *State and Citizen*. Budapest: Institute of Political Science, Hungarian Center for Political Education.

Farnen, R. (1993c). 'Cross-National Perspectives on Political Decision Making and Education.' Paper presented to the XIIth International Human Sciences Research Conference, 10-14 August 1993, University of Groningen, Groningen, Netherlands.

Farnen, R. (1994a) 'Nationality, Ethnicity, Political Socialization, and Public Policy: Some Cross-National Perspectives', pp. 23-102 in R. Farnen (ed.) *Nationalism, Ethnicity, and Identity: Cross-National and Comparative Perspectives*. New Brunswick, NJ and London, UK: Transaction Publications.

Farnen, R. (1994b). 'Political Decision Making, Problem Solving, and Education: American and Cross-National Perspectives', pp. 129-52 in S. Miedema et al. *The Politics of Human Science*. Brussels, Belgium: VUB Press.

Farnen, R. and D. German (August 1994). 'Central and Eastern European Elite Perspectives on Political Communications, Educational, Economic, and Environmental Changes (1989-93).' Paper presented to the XVI World Congress of the International Political Science Association, 21-25 August 1994, Berlin, Germany.

Fratczak-Rudnicka, B. et al. (May 1993). 'Opinions of Polish Students on European Community and Integration.' Paper presented to the IPSA/RCPSE Round Table Conference on 'From Subject to Citizen', Balatonföldvár, Hungary, 23-28 May 1993.

Freedom House News (January-February 1994). 'Freedom House Reports Massive Increase in Worldwide Repression', pp. 1-21 in *Freedom Review*, Vol. 25, No. 1.

Fukuyama, F. (Summer 1989). 'The End of History?', pp. 3-18 in *The National Interest*, Vol. 16.

Havel, V. (November 1991). 'A Freedom of a Prisoner', pp. 14-17 in J. Plichtová (ed.) (1992) *Minorities in Politics*. Bratislava, Slovakia: Czechoslovak Committee of the European Cultural Foundation.

Hess, R. and J. Torney (1967). *The Development of Political Attitudes in Children*. Chicago, IL: Aldine Publishing.

Hirshberg, M. (1994). *Apolitical Patriotism: The New Zealand National Self-Image*. Christchurch, New Zealand: Department of Political Science, University of Canterbury.

Holly, R. (August 1988). *Young Poles About Germans, Hungarians, and Canadians: Stereotyped Imaginations of Nationalities* (unpublished manuscript). Warsaw: Institute of Political Science in the Polish Academy of Sciences.

Hunter, B. (ed.) (1994). *Statesman's Year Book (1993-94)*. New York, NY: St. Martin's Press.

Huntington, S. (Summer 1993). 'The Clash of Civilizations?', pp. 22-49 in *Foreign Affairs*, Vol. 72, No. 3.

Jenness, D. (1990). *Making Sense of Social Studies*. New York, NY: Macmillan Publishing Co.

Jennings, M. (June 1987). 'Residues of a Movement: The Aging of the American Protest Generation', pp. 367-82 in *American Political Science Review*, Vol. 81, No. 2.

Jennings, M. (1993). 'Education and Political Development Among Young Adults', pp. 1-24 in *Politics and the Individual*, Vol. 3, No. 2.

Kegley, C. and E. Wittkopf (1981). *World Politics: Trend and Transformation*. New York, NY: St. Martin's Press.

Koch, K. (November 1991). 'Back to Sarajevo or Beyond Trianon?', pp. 34-44 in J. Plichtová (ed.) (1992) *Minorities in Politics*. Bratislava, Slovakia: Czechoslovak Committee of the European Cultural Foundation.

Kohn, H. (1955). *Nationalism: Its Meaning and History*. Princeton, NJ: D. Van Nostrand.

Langton, K. and M. Jennings (September 1968). 'Political Socialization and the High School Civics Curriculum in the United States', pp. 862-7 in *American Political Science Review*.

Litt, E. (February 1965). 'Civic Education, Community Norms, and Political Indoctrination', pp. 69-75 in *American Sociological Review*, Vol. 28, No. 1.

Luskin, R. (December 1990). 'Explaining Political Sophistication', pp. 331-61 in *Political Behavior*, Vol. 12, No. 4.

Macridis, R. (1980). *Contemporary Political Ideologies: Movements and Regimes.* Cambridge, MA: Winthrop.

Meloen, J. (January 1994). 'Authoritarianism, Democracy, and Education: An Empirical 70-Nation Global Indicators Study.' Paper presented to the IPSA/RCPSE Conference on 'Reinventing and Fostering Democracy and Human Rights', 11-15 January 1994, Florida Atlantic University, Boca Raton, Florida.

Meloen, J. (August 1994). 'State Authoritarianism Worldwide: A 170-Nation Global Indicators Study.' Paper presented to the XVI World Congress of the International Political Science Association, 21-25 August 1994, Berlin, Germany.

Meloen, J., R. Farnen, and D. German (July 1993). 'Authoritarianism, Democracy, and Symbolic Political Leadership in the New World Order: Evidence from Twelve Countries Worldwide.' Paper presented at the XVI Annual Scientific Meeting of the International Society of Political Psychology, 6-10 July 1993, Cambridge, MA.

Meloen, J., G. van der Linden, and H. de Witte (November/December 1992). 'Authoritarianism and Political Racism in Belgian Flanders.' Paper presented to conference on 'Political Consciousness and Civic Education During the Transformation of the System', Institute of Political Science, Polish Academy of Science, 30 November to 3 December 1992, Warsaw, Poland.

Meyenberg, R. (1993). 'Political Education, Germany, and Europe', pp. 358-74 in R. Farnen (ed.) *Reconceptualizing Politics, Socialization, and Education: International Perspectives for the 21st Century.* Oldenburg, FRG: Bibliotheks- und Informationssystem der Universität Oldenburg (BIS)

Mitter, W. (October 1994). *Civic Education in the Mirror of Identity Conflict.* Stockholm, Sweden: Institute of International Education, Stockholm University.

National Assessment of Educational Progress (November 1976). *Education for Citizenship.* Denver, CO: Education Commission of the States.

National Assessment of Educational Progress (October 1983). *Citizenship and Social Studies Achievement of Young Americans: 1981-1982, Performance and Changes Between 1976-1982.* Denver, CO: Education Commission of the States.

National Standards for Civics and Government (October 1993). Calabasas, CA: Center for Civic Education.

Niemi, R. and J. Junn (September 1993). 'Civics Courses and the Political Knowledge of High School Seniors.' Paper presented to the annual meeting of the American Political Science Association, 2 September 1993, Washington, DC.

Niemi, R. and J. Junn (August 1994). 'The Political Knowledge of White, African-American, and Latino High School Seniors.' Paper presented to the XVI World Congress of the International Political Science Association, 21-25 August 1994, Berlin, Germany.

Patrick, J. (December 1988). *Schools and Civic Values.* Bloomington, IN: Social Studies Development Center of Indiana University.

Pietras, Z. (May/June 1994). 'Scenarios for East-Central Europe', pp. 31-2 in 'The Future of East Central Europe' Conference Program Abstracts, 29 May to 1 June 1994, Maria Curie-Sklodowska University, Lublin, Poland.

Quigley, C. and C. Bahmueller (eds.), 1991. *CIVITAS: A Framework for Civic Education.* Calabasas, CA: Center for Civic Education.

Rose, R. and C. Haerpfer (1993). *Adapting to Transformation in Eastern Europe: New Democracies Barometer II.* Glasgow, Scotland: Centre for the Study of Public Policy, University of Strathclyde.

Strecher, B. (May 1988). *Instructional Effects of the National Bicentennial Competition on the Constitution and the Bill of Rights.* Pasadena, CA: Educational Testing Service.

The Europa World Year Book (1993). London: Europa Publications, Inc.

Times Mirror (1991). 'The Outlook for Business in the New Europe', pp. 1-51. Washington, DC: Center for People and the Press.

Times Mirror (16 September 1991). 'Old Europe Persists Despite Revolutions; Russia Largely Unchanged Despite Coup Attempt, Survey Finds', pp. 1-6. Washington, DC: Center for People and the Press.

Times Mirror (27 January 1993). 'The Russians Rethink Democracy: The Pulse of Europe II', pp. 1-45. Washington, DC: Center for People and the Press.

Torney, J., A. Oppenheim, and R. Farnen (1975). *Civic Education in Ten Countries: An Empirical Study.* New York, NY: John Wiley and Stockholm: Almquist and Wiksell.

Torney-Purta, J. (1985). 'Evidence for Balancing Content with Process and Balancing Answers with Questions', pp. 91-9 in A. Jones (ed.) *Civic Learning for Teachers: Capstone for Educational Reform.* Ann Arbor, MI: Prakken.

Vollebergh, W. (1994). 'The Consolidation of Educational Differences in Authoritarianism in Adolescence', pp. 57-71 in *Politics and the Individual,* Vol. 4, No. 1.

Weeks, A. (September/October 1993). 'Do Civilizations Hold?', pp. 24-5 in *Foreign Affairs,* Vol. 72, No. 4.

Westholm, A., A. Lindquist, and R. Niemi (1987). 'Education and the Making of the Informed Citizen: Political Literacy and the Outside World.' Paper presented to the Workshop on Political Socialization and Citizenship Education in Democracy, Tel Aviv University, Israel.

Wormald, E. (August 1988). 'Political Literacy in a Newly Independent Country: Papua, New Guinea.' Paper presented to IPSA XIV World Congress, Washington, DC.

4 Central and Eastern European Elite Perspectives on Political, Communications, Educational, Economic, and Environmental Changes (1989 to 1993)

Russell F. Farnen
Daniel B. German

ABSTRACT

In 14 Central and Eastern European nations, a nonrandom sample of 210 elite respondents (social science and health professionals) have rated their country's transition from 1991 to 1993 from communism to a new transitional system. Measures of change toward democratic political processes and institutions on a composite score show perceptions of a slight decline. On an overall rating, communications democratization also shows slight overall improvement. Political education composite change is nonexistent. Nationalistic orientations overall are moderate (except for Serbia and Croatia) and have mostly remained about the same cross-nationally. Compared to the 1989-91 period, respondents' perceptions about minority toleration overall are that this is actually worse in 1993. These economies are perceived to be better off, but performance here is rated even worse than for the political, communications, and educational dimensions. Environmental quality is rated very low and shows no overall change in conditions. Country-by-country transitions are presented on each measure employed. (The time periods involved are January 1989 to early January 1991 [time period a] and late January 1991 [time period b] to January 1993.)

INTRODUCTION

In 1989, the Central and Eastern European nations broke away from Soviet hegemony and began moving from communist governments toward more democratic political processes and institutions. We conducted a 'Survey of Eastern European Politics, Communications, and Education Before and After the Central and Eastern European Revolutions of 1989' in January 1991a. One hundred forty-one people from Bulgaria, Czechoslovakia, Eastern Germany, Hungary, Poland, Romania, and Yugoslavia responded to the mailed 1991 survey. (The 1989-91a results can be found in Farnen and German, 1994.)

In 1993, we began Phase II of monitoring changes in the countries of Central and Eastern Europe. This report represents the results of responses from 210 higher-education academicians and upper-level officials to our 'Follow-up Survey of Trends in Central and Eastern European Politics, Communications, Education, and Economics Since January 1991' (see each table for the number of elite respondents for the 1991b/1993 period in each nation). We added questions about economic and environmental change in these nations to the original questionnaire because it was important to obtain benchmark data on such changes. The 1993 survey includes the 1989-91a nations as well as responses from representatives of the Baltic states (Estonia, Latvia, Lithuania), Albania, the new nations of Serbia/Montenegro, Croatia, and Slovenia, as well as the newly created Czech and Slovak Republics.

In the 1989-91a survey, respondents perceived Romania to be the least democratic nation in the pre-1989 period, followed by the Czech and Slovak Federative Republic (CSR), Bulgaria, and eastern Germany; Hungary, Poland, and Yugoslavia were seen to be the most democratic. The Czech and Slovak Federative Republic was rated as being the most democratic by 1991a; Romania, Bulgaria, Hungary, Poland, and eastern Germany were ranked next; while Yugoslavia was last. By then, all nations had changed from their former single-party communist-dominated form of government. The bulk of the following data represent the changing response patterns between 1991b and 1993.

POLITICS AND THE ROLES OF INTELLECTUAL ELITES

We have deliberately chosen a group of well-educated elites because they were adept at English, willing to participate in this survey, and are likely to be part of the emerging power structures either sooner or later in many (if not all) Central and Eastern European countries. There is every reason to believe that one's higher educational level more so than age will significantly influence the development of a common view of political attitudes and beliefs both within and across countries in Central and Eastern Europe. This result, for example, was found to be the case in a 1988-90 study of 80 ethnic Russians from Moscow and Voronezh in the Russian Republic. There, younger and older highly educated respondents had much more similar responses to rapid social change than did another group of younger and older, but uneducated, respondents (Sloutsky and Searle-White, September 1993, pp. 511-26).

Moreover, as Schöpflin (1993) says in his discussion of the road from postcommunism: 'A key role is being played and will be played in the construction of democracy by intellectuals. In many ways, this was predictable given the traditionally important position that intellectuals and intellectual ideas have held in Central and Eastern Europe' (Schöpflin, 1993, p. 193). Nevertheless, whereas the intellectual elite may have played a significant role in delegitimizing and replacing the old Communist Party *nomenklatura* and other 'real socialist' elites in certain countries (such as the Czech Republic, Slovenia, Poland, and Hungary), they played either a less-significant role (for example, in Albania and Bulgaria), were coopted by nationalists (as in Serbia), or were prevented from any real political action or expression (the Romanian case) because they were scapegoated as parasites or lacked any moral capital gained from the absence of pre-revolutionary political resistance activity/roles. In Poland, for example, there has also been a growing populism driving political parties, movements, and Solidarity. This has led to a certain climate of anti-intellectualism. Nevertheless, the old Communist elites everywhere (except in eastern Germany, of course) have often taken advantage of popular discontent with privatization to benefit themselves since they were frequently well-educated, best connected, well off, and available to return to power after the dust settled and popular apathy and discontent solidified. The Hungarian political elites were also increasingly abstract, irrelevant, and at odds with popular political sentiments and simple goals, despite the fact that some politicians (such as President Arpad Goncz) were former literary figures (Schöpflin, 1993, pp. 193-4).

Although it would require a comparative study of less-educated non elites or novices versus well-educated intellectual elites, professionals, or experts, there is a steady stream of evidence indicating that the belief and cognitive structures of elites (that is, their schemas or political maps) are quite different from those of the mass public. Experts, for example, have more coherent, consistent, and constrained information processing and belief systems. Their schemas are more complex and interrelated. Their whole reasoning process in a problem-solving routine also differed remarkably from novices' solutions. For example, novices tend to be more particularistic, less-forceful in argument or reasoning, and less-capable of abstracting or generalizing in problem solving. Consequently, the research results described here are useful for depicting the overall national and international patterns of elite beliefs, attitudes, and perceptions about democracy, education, mass media, nationalism, economics, and environmentalism. Consequently, the broad outlines of these cognitive structures can be mapped. In this respect, these findings may be useful for these purposes. (On these points, see Voss et al., 1983, pp. 165-213; Larson, March 1994, pp. 17-33; and Farnen, 1993, pp. 212-91.)

We must also acknowledge the important role which elite conflicts have played in the national unification and fragmentation processes in Central and Eastern Europe since 1989. Such old and new political elites struggle for power, domination, and national unification versus regional confederational, local, or ethnic definitional unity. They also seek popular support for their 'imagined' or historical images of a culturally uniform ethnic, religious, or national group. These elite-defined fundamental categorizations determined the political and cultural social context in which public policy alternatives are debated (that is, the terms of debate are defined by different political, economic, social, media, religious, and other elites). For example, old and new political elites often speak of either recreating a lost cultural identity or using nationalism to create a new cohesive national state. Along the way, anti-Semitism and negative attitudes toward Sinti-Roma (Gypsies) enlist scapegoating prejudice and negative reference grouping so that a new sense of cultural distinctiveness or unity can be created. Such struggles within and between elites is especially pronounced during times of ethnic, social, and military crisis or when strong national rule or a loose confederation have been dissolved, including the destruction of Soviet hegemony. Therefore, the perceptions of intellectual elites are useful in ascertaining the paths different emerging nations will follow.

THE 1989-91a SURVEY

Elsewhere, we (see Farnen and German, 1993 and 1994) reported findings from our nonrandom survey of 130 elite or professional Eastern Europeans regarding their perceptions of changes in political processes and institutions, communications mass media, and political education from pre-1989 to early 1991a. The countries involved, followed by the number of social and political science professors and occupational safety and health professionals responding in each country, were as follows: Bulgaria, six; CSR, fourteen; eastern Germany (former GDR), ten; Hungary, forty-eight; Poland, thirty-five; Yugoslavia, three; and Romania, fourteen. From the outset, it should be stressed that our focus was on charting the perceptions of this group of elite scholars and professionals. Two compelling reasons among others were that they were both well-informed and willing to cooperate with an English language research project.

Four of the countries surveyed had (a) sizable indigenous minority(ies) (such as Roma, Ukrainians, Hungarians, or Slovaks). Eastern Germany had only a small Sorbish group in the southeast, along with recent immigrants and foreign students and workers. Respondents indicated only a moderate level of ethnic tolerance in Eastern Europe toward minorities prior to 1989. All the nations surveyed (except eastern Germany) reportedly experienced a higher level of minority toleration. However, no nation fell into the highest group of possible scores, indicating a possible source of difficulty for establishing and consolidating basic democratic practices and pluralism in the region in the near future. Compared with the pre-1989 period, the nationalism index declined significantly in only one country, Romania; by contrast, it rose significantly in Hungary and Serbia.

Using factor analysis of the five indices employed in the survey for all seven nations (including former Yugoslavia and Bulgaria), we found communality (h^2) scores ranging from .63 to .83. The factor loadings indicated that the politics, communications, and education indices tracked together, whereas the nationalism index tracked negatively with the toleration index (which, itself, tracked positively with the politics, communications, and education indices). Our other composite index of overall democratization for all seven countries (including former Yugoslavia and Bulgaria) indicated that Bulgaria, the former CSR, and Romania emerged with the three highest rankings and the greatest positive scale score changes. Hungary and Poland fell in the middle range of rankings with fewer prodemocratic changes. Eastern Germany ranked in the middle range of prodemocratic relative increase, behind the former CSR, Bulgaria, and Romania, but ahead of Hungary, Poland, and Yugoslavia in the latter respect.

In 1993, this survey was expanded to fourteen countries, including all seven of these aforementioned nations (or former nations in the cases of Yugoslavia, Czechoslovakia, and eastern Germany) as well as their successor states and others (for example, Serbia, Slovenia, Croatia, the Baltics, and Albania). Also, two environmental and economic dimensions were added. Consequently, we shall be able to compare some of these earlier results with more recent ones as we move further away from that watershed year of 1989. Thus far, our analysis on a country-by-country basis of these 1993 results indicates increased open communications, no progress on education, and lessened democratization trends, stable or increased nationalism, decreased ethnic toleration, and increasing economic and environmental pessimism. (See our 14-nation composite score in Table 4.9 for comparative purposes.) We asked respondents to reply to each item using a format of 1 to 7, with 4 as a mid-point (that is, a semantic differential dichotomy relating to a specific variable).

SOME THEORETICAL CONSIDERATIONS
Related Work

Our approach (examining relevant political, communications, and educational trends) is in the tradition of cross-national studies previously conducted mostly in Western democratic nations. This theoretical work includes *The Civic Culture* (Almond and Verba, 1965), *Political Action* (Barnes and Kasse et al., 1979), *Citizen Politics in Western Democracies* (Dalton, 1988), and *Continuities in Political Action* (Jennings and van Deth et al., 1989). We have also employed analytic categories used previously in *Politics in Eastern Europe* (Volgyes, 1986). Based on these works, our own research, and our theoretical interests, we have created a survey questionnaire with indices for political, communications, and educational conditions and developments immediately prior to and since the Eastern European revolutions that took place in the Autumn of 1989. The survey instrument (see Appendix) a follow-up 'Survey of Trends in Eastern European Politics, Communications, Education, and Economics Since 1991' employs questions relating to a diversity of political parties, citizen involvement, communications outlets, censorship, educational content and practices, environmental impacts, and market economics. The survey was administered early in 1993 to political/social scientists, allied health professionals, and other highly educated 'elites' within 14 Central and Eastern European nations.

This approach has several obvious faults. Among these are the lack of a representative national sample of either respondents or of elites, the fact that these are elite perceptions, and the fact that the passage of time and recent political changes make these observations outmoded very quickly (that is, the political shelf life of these results will last only a couple of years at most). This research project represents a focus on aspects of change which could and will be affected by both internal variables and external (that is, relations with other nations) developments. It is not our intention to address all aspects of change in the nations under consideration, but only to measure these explicitly defined aspects of overall changes.

Our survey research may also be appropriately faulted for many of the same reasons that Central and Eastern Europeans have criticized other approaches (such as *The Civic Culture*). That is, we use what could be considered 'Anglo-American' and Western European concepts of political democracy as measures of progress toward generalized democracy. We have also not carefully detailed the history of each nation's political cultures. By using identical indicators in various nations, we run the risk of oversimplification, despite the fact that we readily admit that such developments are vastly more complex than our simple set of indices (see Wiatr, 1980, pp. 103-23).

Indeed, some of our respondents to both surveys referred to the survey instrument using classic terms such as 'American bourgeois', 'tendentious', and not being based on sufficient personal or practical experience in the region. While we recognize limitations in our approach, the instrument was returned largely without criticism by the large majority of respondents to whom the survey was mailed. Since each recipient also received four additional copies of the survey form and was asked to distribute it to colleagues, we received additional questionnaires from other respondents. We believe our measures are genuine indicators of an overall movement from centralized, totalitarian rule to more-democratic political frameworks/processes. At the system level, evidence pertaining to the shift from Communist Party dominance to popular, multiparty mechanisms is presented (for example, measures of popular input, voting/participation patterns, interest articulation, and dissent/opposition behaviors). Regarding communications media, the measures locate the transition from tight state media control toward greater print and nonprint press freedom. In education, the inquiry examines developments such as decentralization and democratization of the formal political education curriculum, textbooks, policy, and the 'hidden' curriculum/classroom environment. As for the few questions on environmental and market economic trends, these only touch the surface of these two dynamic areas.

Our primary hypothesis is that movement until 1993 away from pre-1989 more-centralized control will vary from one nation to another dependent on a) pre-1989 and 1989-93 trends, b) the relative success of new political participation practices, c) the emergence of multiple communications sources, d) the degree to which new democratic educational processes emerge, e) the extent to which the market is opened up, and f) the environment cared for. It is obvious that each nation evolves from a different starting point. For example, in 1991, one respondent from Thuringia in eastern Germany commented that the former GDR differs from all other Eastern European nations in the extent to which Germans were previously exposed to Western media as well as in their economic, cultural, and family connections to the West. The role of media in support for revolutionary developments in eastern Germany has been examined in detail elsewhere (Buhl, 1990). In order to be more meaningful, this research project has been an on-going one since each nation has only just begun a journey which may end not necessarily in democracy, but rather in several other possible scenarios. These include right-wing fascist authoritarianism or military dictatorship or a variant of 'third way' reformed socialism, 'big party socialism', or benign Communist totalitarianism. Another major aim of this effort is to create a baseline body of evidence which might help predict later outcomes in the 14 nations/political subcultures whose small groups of elites we surveyed.

Questions 1 and 3-21 of our questionnaire form a Political Index (see Appendix). Questions 22-30 and 32-38 form a Communications Index and questions 39-48 and 50 form a Political Education Index. Questions 2, 47, and 49 form a separate Nationalism Index; numbers 13-14 and 48 form a Toleration for Minorities Index; and questions 51-55 tap economic and environmental responses. Question 31 sought information on the role of television in each nation. Respondents were asked to reply to each item using a format of 1-7, with 4 as a mid-point (that is, a semantic differential dichotomy relating to a specific variable). Response patterns on each set of questions for each nation are given in a set of eight tables. Here, we also examine the results from each index for each nation. These indices may be considered more complex, complete, or generalized measures of elite perceptions since they go beyond election results, institutional behavior (such as a parliament), media ownership, and other similar measures.

Nationality, Ethnonationalism, and Minority Groups

Throughout this study, we refer to nationalism, ethnonationalism, and minority toleration measures. It is clear in the Western tradition that we speak of nationalism as representing factors such as patriotism or supreme loyalty to the nation state (regardless of race, creed, or ethnicity) and that the concept of an ethnic, racial, or national minority refers to given subgroups in a pluralistic political culture (such as American Jews, African Americans, or various Latino or recent Asian emigres). However, in the Eastern European tradition, a more frequently used term is that of ethnonationalist groups (such as the Croatians, Serbs, Germans, Slovenes, or Russians). This means that different national, cultural, or linguistic groups may exist within a national state, speak a different national language, and live in a wholly separate and ethnically intact community. Germans in the Zips (Tatra Mountains) region of Slovakia, for example, maintained their separate German language and cultural identity for hundreds of years, were not assimilated in Slovakian/Slavic culture, and were treated as *Volksdeutsche* (folk Germans) after 1945, when they were expelled from Slovakia as were the Germans from Silesia, Pomerania, and East Prussia.

In sum, the idea of ethnonationalism means that it does not apply to the Sorb minority in eastern Germany or to Gypsies anywhere or to Bosnians (there are Serbs, Croats, and Muslims in the region, but no Bosnians, per se). Yet it does apply to the Volga Germans in Russia, the Jews in Russia who want to be reunited with the Israeli state, and to Hungarians living in Romania, Slovakia, or Kosovo, for instance. Citizenship by blood line (ius sanguinis) is compatible with this concept rather than by place of birth (ius solis). Therefore, second- or third-generation Turks born and living in Germany are not automatically granted citizenship unless they apply for it, which is a very different case from citizenship by birthright in England, Canada, or the United States, for example.

Democratic Political Cultures

There are a variety of ways we may estimate the relative democratic levels of political cultural development for different political systems. Among these are the use of global indicators, surveys of authoritarianism and democracy in different countries, or a common list of criteria for political rights (for example, free elections) and civil liberties (for example, free press, assembly) which are universally applied worldwide.

The latter approach is that used in Freedom House's report on 'The Comparative Survey of Freedom: 1994.' The criteria which this study used for democratic rights/liberties include free elections, political party competition, minority rights, citizen participatory power, regional decentralized/shared power, right to petition, ethnic pluralism, citizen equality, worker organization, religious freedom, and equality of opportunity. This survey found an increase in worldwide repression in 1993, an end to earlier post-Cold War liberalization, and a rise in ethnic tensions and restrictions on human rights and democracy. However, the number of democracies grew from 99 in 1992 to 107 in 1993, with Estonia, Hungary, and the Czech Republic particularly noted for their democratic gains. The world increasingly seemed to be splitting into democratic/free and dictatorial/unfree groups at a rapid pace.

As for the countries in our survey, Albania, Croatia, Romania, Latvia, and Slovakia were listed as partly free; the Czech Republic, Estonia, Germany, Hungary, Lithuania, Poland, Bulgaria, and Slovenia as free; and Serbia/Montenegro as not free (*Freedom House News*, January-February 1994, pp. 1-15).

A second approach is that used in Meloen, Farnen, and German (July 1993) which assessed authoritarianism, democratic attitudes, multiculturalism, support for dictatorship, and nationalism among high school and university students in 12 North American, Western and Eastern European, and Third World countries in 1992-3. In this study, it was found that Western Europe had the lowest relative authoritarianism scores and very strong democratic attitudes, whereas Third World countries had both high authoritarianism and supportive democratic attitudes, with the US in the middle of both these extremes. Nearly all Eastern European countries (Russia, Estonia, and Poland) had both moderately high authoritarianism and low democratic support scores (except for Hungary, which had very low authoritarianism and high democratic attitude scores).

Across all these countries, it was found that high authoritarianism predicted: lower support for multiculturalism; high support for militarism; pro-nationalistic educational practices; and high self-ratings as right-wing in one's personal political views. By contrast, high democratic attitudes predicted: support for multiculturalism; antimilitarism; antinationalistic education; pro-liberal (or process-oriented) education; and non-self-ascription as right-wing.

Our third example is also drawn from the recent corollary work of Meloen (January 1994). Meloen (see Chapter 2 in this volume) first estimated the cross-national relative levels of authoritarianism in 32 countries. The data used included 20 000 students and 10 000 nonstudents in these samples. He then asked what could account for the variations seen. Thereafter, a state authoritarianism measure was developed using global indicators, such as those found in the Freedom House survey, UNESCO, Amnesty International, the US CIA and State Department, and others for 70 countries. These indicators included the relative absence of state terrorism, suppression of moral deviation, denial of gay rights, imposition of state beliefs, use of capital punishment, suppression of labor unions, prohibition of abortion, imprisonment of political dissidents, gender inequality, and state antihuman-rights activity.

As a result of this analysis, Meloen found that all dictatorships listed scored high and free, democratic countries scored low on the state authoritarianism measure. State authoritarianism correlated .81 (for 48 countries) with the UN Human Freedom Index and .83 (52 countries) with the Freedom House measures. When state authoritarianism was correlated with the derived cross-national authoritarianism scale scores, they also were highly intercorrelated at the .85 level (27 countries). This national personality or attitudinal authoritarianism was also negatively related to the UN (-.68; 27 countries) and Freedom House (-.79; 30 countries) ratings/indices and negatively predicted

(-.59; 29 countries) popular participation in government as well as the probable existence of a dictatorial form of government (.51; 32 countries).

In searching for the underlying causes of nondemocracy and authoritarianism, Meloen found it was not economics, but rather a combination of the authoritarian political system, low levels of popular education, and high levels of authoritarian attitudes that produced or were correlates of state authoritarianism ($R^2 = .86$). This, in turn, explained authoritarian state practices such as lack of popular political participation ($R^2 = .48$). It also predicted gender inequality and discrimination and, possibly, military conflict propensity. Using state authoritarianism as the sole predictor of attitudinal authoritarianism, the R^2 was .72. Consequently, we may safely assume that dictators can manipulate the poorly educated using real or presumed external threats for which military solutions are offered. These factors can be combined with mythical and superstitious appeals to the in-group's rigidity and restricted action, as well as their capacity for aggression, punitiveness, and submissiveness.

This background helps to elucidate the theoretical structures we have used and which underlie our survey of democratic politics, education, and communications as well as public policy options regarding a free market and environmentalism. To illustrate, our political processes and institutions scale used 20 questions on party control over the political system, multiparty mechanisms, popular political activity, and governmental use of force or intrusions into personal life. Our communications index (or scale) covered governmental censorship, diversity of media ownership and programs, and use of media as propaganda outlets. The 11-question political education index asked about school democracy, the ideology of school subjects, textbooks, and practices. The three-item nationalism index tested international cooperation and patriotism levels. Three items formed a minority toleration index on ethnic toleration and civil rights. The three-item economic index tapped government privatization efforts, a hard currency policy, and market competition. Two environmental policy questions asked about postmaterialist ideas (à la Ronald Inglehart) regarding protective environmental actions and improvements. (Factor analysis loadings on five indices for the 1989-91 data for all seven nations combined demonstrated that political, communications, and educational democratization indices were positively associated with the minority toleration index and negatively related to the nationalism index. These findings are in accord with acceptable Western political theory.)

As a whole, it was hypothesized that these measures would adequately assess democratization trends in these 14 countries from 1989 to 1993. Our survey questions cover the major areas of political, communications, educational, free market, and environmental change. We also address matters of regional significance (such as communist ideology, nationalism, and ethnic toleration for minorities). That this is not a random or representative national survey of public opinion in the countries surveyed goes without saying; we merely accept their reports for what they are worth on face value. However, many of their responses can be biased, of course, depending on a variety of factors such as respondents' privileged positions in their countries prior to 1989, their own support for democratic change, and their own nationalistic or internationalistic bias. On the whole, these elite survey responses seem to be true to other scholarly or informed opinions in those countries which gave a large response (for example, Hungary, Poland, Romania, Bulgaria, and Lithuania) and less accurate in some cases (such as Albania and Slovakia). On the whole, however, we are satisfied that these elite survey results accurately portray present perceptive reality in the large majority of these countries, better even than some Western newspaper or journalistic reports, which have their own set of biases and distortions.

1991b to 1993 TRANSITION TOWARD DEMOCRACY

The course of change (although always in the direction of democracy) in the Central and Eastern European countries has been neither uniform nor easy. Western and eastern Germans have experienced strained relationships for a variety of reasons; two of these include eastern Germans' complaints about Bonn's domination and the re-emergence of neofascist movements which have exhibited violence toward minorities. Unemployment is very high in eastern Germany and many western Germans complain about the high cost of rebuilding the eastern *Länder*. Yugoslavia is torn apart and warfare is currently raging in Bosnia-Herzegovena. Czechoslovakia has separated into the Czech Republic and the Slovak Republic. The Baltic states are grappling with ethnic hatred toward Russian minorities. Albania is experiencing renewed nationalism and rampant economic deterioration. Hungary faces problems over ethnic Hungarian discrimination in Romania, possible problems with Hungarian ethnic minorities in Slovakia, and the immigration of poverty-stricken Hungarian refugees from Romania. In Poland and Slovakia, as well as in other nations, anti-Semitism is also on the increase, even with the absence of big groups of Jews there.

The political future is not clear in any nation. As one of our Lithuanian respondents wrote: 'Changes in Eastern Europe are extremely important and, as in [the] case of Lithuania, unpredictable.' Diversity is obvious throughout the region. A second Lithuanian respondent added:

I also think that when examining the forms [surveys], you need to remember that we have only started the transition from the totalitarian society to the democratic one. Somebody has already changed his way of thinking and somebody has not. As a consequence, our today's society is greatly nonhomogeneous and so are our answers.

POLITICAL PROCESSES/INSTITUTIONS VARIABLES

In this analysis of the survey results, we present mean index scores for each nation. Nations are ranked on their reported response patterns for time periods 1991b and 1993. Our report details those changes occurring between 1991a and 1993. In some cases, there is no change; in others, it is not significant; but all changes are not always in a democratic direction. In some cases, the nations do not differ appreciably on the indices; in other instances, they differ considerably. The mean scores are based on a scale of 1-7. Cronbach's alpha (internal reliability coefficients) on each of the indices which we treated as scales are also reported in each table for the 1989, 1991a and b, and 1993 periods.

Table 4.1 shows the results from responses to questions 1-21. All nations are grouped closely in the mid-range on political democratization. Other indices show much more variation. Serbia/Montenegro, Poland, and Hungary are perceived to be the least democratic. (It should be noted that the perceptions about Poland apply to the previous, pre-1994 political regime, not to the present coalition in power.) The previous regime was more committed to economic shock therapy than is the new neoleft alliance. In Poland, a new leftist alliance of former/neo-Communists, peasants, and ethnonationalists reemerged in 1994 since this survey was completed; and in Hungary, a right-wing, authoritarian-nationalist, anti-Communist alliance is currently in power, but has run behind the Socialists in first round May 1994 elections. Responses to question 1 indicate that the old Communist Party, while split apart and weakened, is more alive in Serbia/Montenegro than in any other nation surveyed. As one respondent from Beograd, Yugoslavia, wrote:

> Extremely opposite answers are [a] result of different respondents' views on [the] Socialist Party of Serbia (ruling party) - as a party successor of [the] Communist party, or as a new party. SPS is in a sense [a] leftist party, but also could be placed on the right, due to its nationalistic program and praxis. [The] formal successor of [the] former Communist party - Communist Alliance - Movement for Yugoslavia is politically minor, meanwhile [the] Socialist Party of Serbia with some help [from the] Serbian Radical Party (left and right program, too) control[s] [the] political system.

Compared with the 1991a results, all eight countries are considered less democratic at the start of 1991b. In 1993, Slovenia just makes it into the high column. All of the other 1989-91a surveyed countries report less democratization than in 1991a results. Surprisingly, Slovenia is alone at the high level. Serbia, Poland, and Hungary are grouped together at the lower end of the spectrum, which is a result totally unanticipated for these countries, except for Serbia. The Cronbach's alpha reliability statistic based on the entire cross-national elite group of 210 respondents for democratic processes and institutions averaged .61 over the four different points in time from 1989 to 1993. This is quite an acceptable level (.70 or higher is optimal for intranational scaling). Therefore, there is some conceptual clarity and consistency among our respondents in their views on democratic principles/practices. (The use of the alpha statistic in political psychology surveys with only 100 or more respondents is also a well-known practice, quite acceptable as long as statements are limited to the sample members' perceptions, since this is not a national random sample of adults or elites.)

Table 4.1 Extent of change from 1991b to 1993 in the Central/Eastern European development of democratic political processes and institutions (1989-91a in parentheses)*

Nation (1993 n = 210)	(1989 and 1991a)	1991b Rank[1]	Mean[2]	1993 Rank[1]	Mean[2]
Albania (15)	(NA)	M	4.59	M	4.85
Bulgaria (28)	(2.7 - 5.3)	M	4.67	M	4.63
Croatia (3)	(NA)	M	4.80	M	4.40
Czech Republic (9)	(2.5 - 5.4)	M	4.76	M	4.50
Eastern Germany (9)	(2.5 - 4.8)	M	4.53	M	4.43
Estonia (7)	(NA)	M	4.70	M	4.93
Hungary (36)	(3.2 - 5.0)	M	4.56	M	4.29
Latvia (6)	(NA)	M	4.79	M	4.78
Lithuania (15)	(NA)	M	4.72	M	4.53
Poland (42)	(3.5 - 5.0)	M	4.33	M	4.28
Romania (18)	(2.3 - 4.9)	M	4.45	M	4.56
Slovakia (8)	(2.5 - 5.4)	H	5.09	M	4.81
Slovenia (6)	(NA)	M	4.70	H	5.11
Serbia (8)	(3.1 - 4.7)	M	4.37	M	4.33

Key:
NA = Not applicable
[1] Rank (low [L] = 1.0-3.0; medium [M] = 3.1-5.0; high [H] = 5.1-7.0)
[2] Mean score
* Democratic political process and institutions scale (20 items) alpha scores and (n)
$$1989 = .71 \ (101)$$
$$1991a = .66 \ (101)$$
$$1991b = .44 \ (158)$$
$$1993 = .62 \ (147)$$

The old Communist party is dead in Slovenia, eastern Germany, and Estonia, and is nearly so in Latvia, the Czech Republic, Slovakia, Hungary, and Poland. It is relatively intact in Serbia and still exists to some degree in Albania, Croatia, Romania, Lithuania, and Bulgaria. New variations of 'neo-' or 'reformed communists' have arisen in some countries. For example, eastern Germany still has the Party for Democratic Socialism (which is its 'old left' alliance) along with a resurgence of rightist groups and parties there (such as the

Republikaner). As of 1994-95, former communists have been freely elected to run the governments of Poland and Hungary. Members of these groups refer to themselves as 'social democrats' and are not oriented to Moscow or one-party rule.

But why did 13 of 14 countries' means indicate either practically the same (excepting Slovenia) or even less democratic transformation in 1993 than in the 1991a or b time periods? This may be a result of previous high expectations for sweeping changes in those nations, whereas actual progress toward the realization of democracy has been much slower. For example, a drop in 'popular/public tolerance level toward ethnic and linguistic minorities' was reported in six of these countries in 1993. However, the greatest declines on this question from 1991a and/or b to 1993 were reported in Hungary, Poland, Serbia, the Czech Republic, and Croatia (eastern Germany remained essentially unchanged, though slightly declining). In one case, Hungarians reported that the ruling party, the Hungarian Democratic Forum, has become more nationalistic in 1993. The level of nationalism is moderate, although increasing to a rank of second (behind Serbia) in 1993 (see Table 4.6). On the single survey question of 'government support of nationalistic orientations', national responses placed Hungary in the high category. They also report a drop in 'spontaneous demonstrations' and mass attendance at party meetings and public gatherings. Popular contacts with officials/politicians to promote political reform have declined as have political discussions with friends and peaceful circulation of petitions to change governmental practices. According to reports from survey respondents, Hungarians appear to have moved away from a consistent pro-democratic momentum to a kind of political quiescence, staying afloat in a political backwater. Corroboration of these results comes from Rose and Haerpfer's survey findings. As is true of this elite survey, Rose and Haerpfer's national random sample survey places Slovenia ahead in popular confidence about their democratic future (Rose and Haerpfer, 1994, p. 20).

EXTENT OF CHANGE IN DEMOCRATIC COMMUNICATIONS

Table 4.2 shows the results from questions 22 through 30 and 32 through 38. The alpha scores for these 16 items averaged .82, which is quite high for this kind of a cross-national comparative group. This statistic indicates a great deal of conceptual clarity and consistency (reliability) among respondents on the democratic political communications variable. The democratic communications index again shows a mixed series of comparative and multi-year results. From 1989 to 1991a, there was clear overall improvement. The two 1991 response patterns show an overall negative or no change situation (except for the Czech Republic and Serbia!). By contrast, the 1991b to 1993 pattern shows that a majority reported improvement. However, six countries had minus or no change and several had scores lower than those we charted for them in 1991a (for example, Hungary, Poland, and Romania).

Respondents in Slovenia in 1993 claim to have the most democratic communications system, perhaps because they continue to have a strong economy and remain intact without war; Croatians report having the worst media. Czech respondents indicated a high level of governmental support for freedom of the press from 1989 to 1993, so their consistency in responses makes sense in terms of increasing privatization of mass media.

Table 4.2   Extent of change from 1991b to 1993 in Central/Eastern European development of democratic communications (1989-91a in parentheses)*

Nation (1993 n = 210)	(1989 and 1991a)	1991b Rank[1]	Mean[2]	1993 Rank[1]	Mean[2]
Albania (15)	(NA)	M	3.91	M	4.54
Bulgaria (28)	(2.2 - 4.8)	M	3.99	M	4.60
Croatia (3)	(NA)	M	3.31	L	2.94
Czech Republic (9)	(1.8 - 4.9)	H	5.10	M	4.89
Eastern Germany (9)	(2.6 - 5.0)	M	4.66	M	4.40
Estonia (7)	(NA)	M	4.35	M	4.89
Hungary (36)	(2.9 - 4.7)	M	4.44	M	3.86
Latvia (6)	(NA)	M	3.70	M	4.06
Lithuania (15)	(NA)	M	4.40	M	4.84
Poland (42)	(2.5 - 4.8)	M	4.17	M	4.37
Romania (18)	(1.2 - 5.0)	M	4.31	M	4.62
Slovakia (8)	(1.8 - 4.9)	Ḣ	5.04	M	4.87
Slovenia (6)	(NA)	M	4.43	H	5.11
Serbia (8)	(3.0 - 4.2)	H	5.09	M	4.83

Key:
NA = Not applicable
[1] Rank (low [L] = 1.0-3.0; medium [M] = 3.1-5.0; high [H] = 5.1-7.0)
[2] Mean score
* Democratic communications scale (16 items) alpha scores and (n)
$$1989 = .89 (110)$$
$$1991a = .73 (105)$$
$$1991b = .84 (166)$$
$$1993 = .81 (168)$$

Many nations showed progress toward a more democratic mass media environment. However, Hungarian (like Polish and Romanian) responses represent a serious decline in the level of democratic communications. They perceived less governmental support for the freedoms of speech and press; more censorship; regulation of word-of-mouth interpersonal communications; and less trust in television, radio, newspapers, and news magazines. Perhaps the government's continuing control over Magyar Television (MTV) in Budapest precipitated this trend. (On survey questions 21 and 32 which dealt with police, party, or agency interference into private, family, or group affairs, the Hungarian respondents were uniquely and uniformly high in their responses to these questions, indicating a widespread belief that such intrusions are regularly occurring.) Serbia also showed an increase in democratic communications scores, with press freedom levels lower in 1993 than in 1991, but higher than the average in eight other countries (including Latvia, Hungary, Poland, Croatia, and four others).

EDUCATIONAL DEMOCRATIZATION

Alpha scores on the democratic political education variable averaged .50 over the four time periods in the survey. This indicates less conceptual clarity cross-nationally in respondents' consistent answers regarding pro- and antidemocratic educational practices. Trends in the development of democratic political education indicate that in 1991b, five nations had a lower average score than that previously reported in the 1989-91a period, two indicated no change at the start of the period (Czech Republic and eastern Germany), and only one (Serbia!) had an increase. In the 1991b to 1993 period, there were three no-change indications, six positive changes, and five negatives.

The results of questions 39-50 are presented in Table 4.3. Slovenia and the Czech Republic stand out as reportedly having the most democratic educational systems. Estonia and Serbia (perhaps indicating respondent bias, confusion about or unfamiliarity with the concept, or continuing support for the traditional system) are also relatively high on this 1993 measure. There is more variation on this measure than on other (for example, political and communications) indices. Croatia lags behind the others because of its continuing lack of a new, revised, and more democratic educational system.

Czech respondents indicate that their government has relinquished nearly all control over political education in the schools. In Croatia, the exact opposite is the case. The Croatian survey answers indicate that the government controls the production of political education textbooks used in the schools, whereas this is much less the case in the Czech Republic, Lithuania, Slovenia, Slovakia, and (especially) Estonia.

While some nations reported progress in the transition toward a more democratic educational system, Hungary and Poland show a decline on this measure. The Hungarians and Poles mention increased governmental attempts to control political education in the schools as well as through textbook production. (A new, centralized Polish social studies, history, and civics curriculum plan from the Ministry of Education was introduced and accepted in

1993-4. This liberalized curriculum is more democratic and pluralistic on paper. A final verdict on its effects must await actual experience with its implementation.)

Table 4.3   Extent of change from 1991a to 1993 in Central/Eastern European development of democratic political education (1989-91a in parentheses)*

Nation (1993 n = 210)	(1989 and 1991a)	Rank[1] 1991b	Mean[2]	Rank[1] 1993	Mean[2]
Albania (15)	(NA)	M	3.26	M	4.30
Bulgaria (25)	(2.3 - 4.5)	M	3.74	M	4.08
Croatia (3)	(NA)	L	2.73	L	2.39
Czech Republic (9)	(2.3 - 5.0)	M	4.91	M	4.78
Eastern Germany (9)	(2.7 - 3.9)	M	3.93	M	3.85
Estonia (7)	(NA)	M	4.13	M	4.69
Hungary (36)	(3.0 - 4.5)	M	4.28	M	3.73
Latvia (6)	(NA)	M	4.09	M	4.42
Lithuania (13)	(NA)	M	4.09	M	4.17
Poland (42)	(2.9 - 4.4)	M	3.74	M	3.50
Romania (18)	(2.2 - 4.9)	M	3.77	M	4.00
Slovakia (8)	(2.3 - 5.0)	M	4.27	M	4.34
Slovenia (6)	(NA)	M	4.13	M	4.88
Serbia (8)	(3.0 - 3.7)	M	3.97	M	4.69

Key:
NA = Not applicable
[1] Rank (low [L] = 1.0-3.0; medium [M] = 3.1-5.0; high [H] = 5.1-7.0)
[2] Mean score
* Democratic political education scale (11 items) alpha scores and (n)
          1989 = .48 (107)
          1991a = .51 (96)
          1991b = .44 (177)
          1993 = .58 (175)

CIVIL RIGHTS EDUCATION

Table 4.4 shows responses to the question on the extent of minority civil rights education in political education. Predictably, except for Serbia, the brightest picture of all measures employed in this paper is demonstrated in Table 4.4. More nations report political education about support for the civil rights of minorities in the high category, with Slovenia, Albania, eastern Germany, and Latvia perceptions being outstanding in this regard. Certainly, this is good news; but reality discloses that education toward an objective lacking in the actual political sociocultural milieu could mean very little. For many years, political education in Eastern Europe was geared toward creating the 'new socialist man'. *Gesellschaftswissenschaft* (the science of society) was infused into the entire curriculum from mathematics to geography. The collapse of communism in

Eastern Europe demonstrated that the real socialist model of political education has failed at least (if not entirely) to a considerable degree.

Table 4.4 Civil rights education in Central/Eastern European nations in response to the question: 'Extent to which respect for civil rights of minorities is taught in political education'

Nation (1993 n = 210)	1991b		1993	
	Rank[1]	Mean[2]	Rank[1]	Mean[2]
Albania (15)	M	3.73	M	4.93
Bulgaria (25)	M	3.24	M	3.32
Croatia (3)	M	3.33	M	3.67
Czech Republic (7)	M	4.14	M	3.42
Eastern Germany (9)	M	4.33	M	4.56
Estonia (7)	M	3.14	M	3.86
Hungary (34)	M	3.21	M	3.21
Latvia (5)	M	2.40	M	4.20
Lithuania (13)	L	2.85	M	3.15
Poland (42)	M	3.19	M	3.14
Romania (18)	M	3.67	M	4.11
Slovakia (8)	M	3.88	M	4.12
Slovenia (6)	M	3.83	H	5.17
Serbia (8)	M	4.00	L	2.75

Key:
[1] Rank (low [L] = 1.0-3.0; medium [M] = 3.1-5.0; high [H] = 5.1-7.0)
[2] Mean score

Now, a new experiment with democratic political education is evolving. But as Gazsó states, '. . . democratic education has little tradition in the Hungarian educational system' (Gazsó, 1993, p. 65). Since successful education depends on 'know-how', it will be necessary in the broader political environment for the development of experience with toleration and moderation of nationalistic sentiments, which have not to date characterized the countries in Central and Eastern Europe.

EXTENT OF MINORITY TOLERATION AND NATIONALISM

To measure the extent of minority toleration and nationalism in each country, we employed an index of three questions. The three questions on minority toleration used between 1991b and 1993 (as well as from 1989-91a) concerned:

♦ Popular/public tolerance level toward political minorities
♦ Popular/public tolerance level toward ethnic and linguistic minorities

♦ Extent to which respect for civil rights of minorities is taught in political education

The questions on nationalism between 1991b and 1993 (as well as 1989 and 1991a) asked about:

♦ Extent of dominant political party or government support for patriotism
♦ Extent to which the need for international cooperation is taught in political education (for example, United Nations, European Community/Union, Helsinki Accords, and Conference on Security and Cooperation in Europe)
♦ Extent to which nationalism is taught in political education.

Tables 4.5 and 4.6 contain the results of these measures along with benchmark data for Phase I (1989-91a). The bad news is that minority toleration only increased in one nation (Slovakia) and is only moderate to low for all nations, except Slovakia. Perhaps the economic downturn has produced this negative phenomenon. Nationalism is not very low (but it is also not extremely high) in any nation (except Serbia). It also increased in Croatia, which engaged in open warfare with Serbia (Yugoslavia was a country already high on our earlier 1989 to 1991a nationalism index).

Changes in ethnonationalism from 1989-91a indicated four decreases and four increases. From 1991b to 1993, the pluses and minuses were about equal; one country was unchanged. Higher nationalism scores in Croatia and especially in Serbia (which is off the charts) are understandable. Alpha scores only averaged .33 for this short scale, indicating a quite scattered response pattern. Perhaps this is partly because of the varying understandings regarding national identity, nationality, ethnicity, and ethnonationalism.

The Slovakian response on minority toleration merits special discussion because the finding appears to (and actually may) contradict reality. As Roskin observed, 'Slovaks have memories of being exploited, oppressed, and ignored not only by Czechs but, earlier and much longer, by Hungarians' (Roskin, 1994, p. 183). It remains to be seen whether or not democracy is fragile in Slovakia; our analysis indicates the need for a tentative wait-and-see attitude. Respect for 'Gypsies' is not legendary. In fact, they are considered inferiors. Slovak treatment of the Hungarian minority has led to an 'overall hardening of the political climate', which includes an atmosphere of something closer to 'raw majoritarianism' as opposed to political pluralism in the regional/national political spheres. An immediate confrontation and environment of suspicion has evolved out of events 'including the removal of Hungarian inscriptions from traffic signs in the municipalities of Southern Slovakia' (Bútorová and Bútora, 1994, pp. 319-39).

Table 4.5 Extent of change in minority tolerance from 1991b to 1993 in Central/Eastern European nations (1989-91a in parentheses)*

Nation (1993 n = 210)	(1989 and 1991a)	1991b Rank[1]	1991b Mean[2]	1993 Rank[1]	1993 Mean[2]
Albania (15)	(NA)	M	4.93	M	4.93
Bulgaria (28)	(2.3 - 3.6)	M	3.24	M	3.45
Croatia (3)	(NA)	M	4.67	L	3.00
Czech Republic (9)	(2.6 - 4.1)	M	4.26	L	2.76
Eastern Germany (9)	(3.5 - 3.4)	M	3.37	M	3.26
Estonia (7)	(NA)	M	3.86	M	4.24
Hungary (36)	(3.7 - 4.3)	M	3.66	L	2.96
Latvia (6)	(NA)	M	3.03	M	3.83
Lithuania (15)	(NA)	M	3.61	M	4.37
Poland (42)	(3.3 - 4.1)	M	3.37	L	3.07
Romania (18)	(3.1 - 4.6)	M	3.80	M	4.48
Slovakia (8)	(2.6 - 4.1)	M	4.92	H	5.17
Slovenia (6)	(NA)	M	4.78	M	4.89
Serbia (8)	(3.4 - 3.9)	M	4.71	M	3.25

Key:
NA = Not applicable
[1] Rank (low [L] = 1.0-3.0; medium [M] = 3.1-5.0; high [H] = 5.1-7.0)
[2] Mean score
* Minority tolerance scale (3 items) alpha scores and (n)
    1989 = .50 (121)
    1991a = .61 (120)
    1991b = .58 (197)
    1993 = .64 (199)

Despite a diminution of civil liberties, Slovakia has inherited the same associate membership in the European Union (EU), which the Czech Republic, Poland, and Hungary had already received. However, Slovakia and the other nations will have to demonstrate a higher degree of economic development and growth in their democratic civil societies before they gain full EU membership. Hence, pressure exists from outside to treat their national/ethnic minorities there in a democratic fashion. In sum, the EU imperative provides pressure for economic reforms, while Council of Europe membership for these countries increases the trend toward more minority toleration and democratization.

Furthermore, Slovak independence may have moderated a previously distinct nationalism, resulting from feelings of inferiority toward their Czech counterparts who were wealthier, better educated, and were often perceived as being somewhat arrogant. There is a new blush of national satisfaction and good will; now that they feel equal to the Czechs, the Slovak elites' increased security may result in a decline in selfish/divisive nationalistic orientations and a willingness to treat their own minorities with the respect they had not themselves previously received from Prague. A similar move toward moderation appeared after October 1968 (resulting from the Prague Spring) when the Slovaks were granted federal status. Slovak elites were then satisfied with their newly created jobs in Bratislava (Brown, 1988, pp. 300-1).

Table 4.6 Extent of change in ethnonationalistic sentiment from 1991b to 1993 in Central/Eastern Europe (1989-91a in parentheses)*

Nation (1993 n = 210)	(1989 and 1991a)	1991b Rank[1]	1991b Mean[2]	1993 Rank[1]	1993 Mean[2]
Albania (15)	(NA)	M	4.27	M	3.84
Bulgaria (28)	(5.6 - 4.5)	M	4.58	M	3.31
Croatia (3)	(NA)	M	3.89	H	5.11
Czech Republic (9)	(3.5 - 3.4)	M	3.30	M	3.59
Eastern Germany (9)	(3.7 - 4.0)	M	4.00	M	4.07
Estonia (7)	(NA)	M	4.67	M	4.57
Hungary (36)	(3.1 - 4.6)	M	4.31	M	4.76
Latvia (6)	(NA)	M	4.17	M	3.50
Lithuania (15)	(NA)	M	5.00	M	3.71
Poland (42)	(3.9 - 4.0)	M	3.72	M	3.88
Romania (18)	(5.4 - 3.3)	M	3.89	M	3.65
Slovakia (8)	(3.5 - 3.4)	M	3.12	M	3.29
Slovenia (6)	(NA)	M	3.89	M	3.17
Serbia (8)	(3.0 - 4.6)	H	5.13	H	6.19

Key:
NA = Not applicable
[1] Rank (low [L] = 1.0-3.0; medium [M] = 3.1-5.0; high [H] = 5.1-7.0)
[2] Mean score
* Ethnonationalism scale (3 items) alpha scores and (n)
        1989 = .33 (123)
        1991a = .29 (118)
        1991b = .34 (200)
        1993 = .37 (197)

ECONOMIC DEVELOPMENTS

In Table 4.7, the results of questions 51-53 are presented. While a Cronbach's alpha of .77 is very good for such a short scale, these market economics scores are among the lowest seen in this survey. Except for the initial ratings of Slovakia, Poland, the Czech Republic and eastern Germany, all of the other ten countries are in the low category in 1991b. For 1993, these same four countries (plus Slovenia) show improvement, but six countries still rank very low. Respondents in most nations report economic progress between 1991 and 1993; however, this development follows a dramatic decline in most economies after 1989. Initially, the slow switchover from state socialist economies was difficult, resulting in an economic downturn in most nations. Many rate themselves in the low category, indicating that some economies nearly collapsed. Most experienced high inflation rates, lowered production, higher unemployment, and lower incomes. Indeed, economic projections for this entire area for the 1990s forecast further economic decline in nearly all countries in the region (except eastern Germany) with some (for example, Albania, Slovakia, and Romania) more serious than others (for example, Hungary and the Czech Republic show some gains).

The results showing an economic upturn are very positive; no nation reports a significant slippage. Estonia and Slovenia report considerable improvement in their economic conditions. If true, this news bodes well for the development of democratic processes and institutions. If economic deterioration similar to that which occurred immediately after the 1989 revolutions should continue, the transition from state-controlled economies to democratic civil society and politics will be even more difficult.

Table 4.7 Extent of development toward a market economy in Central/Eastern Europe (1991-3)*

Nation (1993 n = 210)	1991b		1993	
	Rank[1]	Mean[2]	Rank[1]	Mean[2]
Albania (15)	L	1.62	M	3.80
Bulgaria (28)	L	1.71	L	2.45
Croatia (3)	L	1.22	L	1.94
Czech Republic (9)	M	3.96	M	4.78
Eastern Germany (9)	M	4.70	M	4.56
Estonia (7)	L	1.22	M	4.19
Hungary (36)	L	2.55	M	3.32
Latvia (6)	L	1.22	L	3.06
Lithuania (15)	L	1.97	L	2.36
Poland (42)	M	3.39	M	3.72
Romania (18)	L	1.93	L	2.35
Slovakia (8)	M	4.33	M	4.63
Slovenia (6)	L	1.89	M	4.72
Serbia (8)	L	2.46	L	2.36

Key:
[1] Rank (low [L] = 1.0-3.0; medium [M] = 3.1-5.0; high [H] = 5.1-7.0)
[2] Mean score
*Market economics scale (3 items) alpha scores and (n)
　　　　　　　1991b = .78 (194)
　　　　　　　1993 = .75 (206)
** Economic questions were not part of the 1989 or 1991a survey.

ENVIRONMENTAL CONDITIONS

Table 4.8 shows the results of rating each country's environmental condition. One of the worst legacies the Central and Eastern European countries inherited from the communist years was appalling environmental conditions. Environmental controls were lax. The heavy use of brown coal (which emits sulfur) and the sole use of leaded automobile fuel (which emits lead and carbon monoxide) are just two of the unregulated assaults on environmental quality. Of all the variables used in this survey (see Table 4.9), the quality of the environment has the lowest scale score means.

Table 4.8 Response to 'Rate the general condition of your country's environment (1 = worse and 7 = better) as getting better or worse since January 1991' (1991-3)*

Nation	1991b		1993	
(1993 n = 210)	Rank[1]	Mean[2]	Rank[1]	Mean[2]
Albania (15)	L	2.03	L	2.70
Bulgaria (28)	L	1.63	L	2.09
Croatia (3)	L	1.50	L	1.33
Czech Republic (9)	L	3.00	L	2.39
Eastern Germany (9)	M	4.17	M	3.89
Estonia (7)	L	1.75	L	2.00
Hungary (36)	L	2.54	L	2.03
Latvia (6)	L	1.42	L	2.08
Lithuania (14)	L	2.25	L	2.00
Poland (42)	L	2.43	L	2.75
Romania (18)	L	1.97	L	2.03
Slovakia (8)	M	3.81	M	4.25
Slovenia (6)	L	2.00	M	4.00
Serbia (8)	L	2.00	L	1.69

Key:
[1] Rank (low [L] = 1.0-3.0; medium [M] = 3.1-5.0; high [H] = 5.1-7.0)
[2] Mean score
* Environmental rating scale (2 items) alpha scores and (n)
         1991b = .65 (195)
         1993 = .63 (207)
**Environmental questions were not part of the 1989-1991a survey

Even though the Albanians, Bulgarians, Estonians, Latvians, Poles, Romanians, Slovakians, and Slovenes report some progress, the other nations indicate worsening conditions (for example, the eastern German, Czech, Croatian, Lithuanian, Hungarian, and Serbian responses). In most nations, the economy will have to improve radically before substantial amounts of money are devoted to environmental improvement. However, this task is one which needs to be addressed immediately. Although the equivalent of millions of US dollars are now being put into environmental improvement, ameliorating or solving the problem will require billions of new international, private, and social invest-ments.

COMPOSITE SCORES AND CONCLUSIONS
Composite Score Results

Finally, let us examine the composite score on each of the survey measurements. Table 4.9 presents the 1991 and 1993 overall Central and Eastern European mean scores.

Table 4.9 Composite scores from 1991b to 1993 on each measure employed for all Central/Eastern European nations combined (1989-91a in parentheses)

Measure (1989 - 1991a scores in parentheses)	1991b Mean Score	1993 Mean Score	t Value	Probability Level 2 tailed test	1991b-1993 n
Politics (2.8 - 5.1)	4.59	4.51	2.23	.03*	210
Communications (2.3 - 3.0)	4.32	4.45	-.24	.01*	210
Education (2.6 - 4.5)	3.94	3.98	-.75	.45 (NS)	205
Minority Toleration (3.0 - 4.0)	3.78	3.64	2.07	.04*	210
Nationalism (4.0 - 4.0)	4.03	3.99	.55	.59 (NS)	210
Economics (NA)	2.47	3.00	-7.35	.00*	202
Environment (NA)	2.33	2.46	-1.61	.11 (NS)	202

Key:
* Statistically significant at the >.05 level
NA = not applicable to 1989 - 1991a
NS = not significant at >.05 level

These composite ratings illustrate that maintenance or stability in the level of democratic processes and institutions and the slight increase of the democratic communications mean score are the most healthy conditions among all of the variables examined. Although education is not ranked the highest, it is not worsening. Minority toleration is rated lower; nationalism stays at a moderate level; economic conditions mean scores are lower than other measures, but improving; and environmental quality is the lowest. (Four of the seven mean scores showed significant T test mean differences, adjusted for sample size, from 1991b to 1993.)

Measures of change toward democratic political processes and institutions show a slight relative overall decline. Communications democratization shows only a small positive change. Educational democratization has not improved. Nationalistic orientations are moderate and show little change. Minority toleration actually is worse in 1993 compared to 1991b. Economic performance has improved, but is still very poor (as the 3.0 on a 7-point scale clearly indicates). No change is reported in improving the dismal level (2.46) in 1993 of overall environmental quality.

Comparing these overall results with the figures obtained in 1991a for a composite index on seven countries (Bulgaria, CSR, East Germany, Hungary, Poland, Romania, and former Yugoslavia) on the same politics, communications, and education scores, we saw very different results (see Farnen and German, 1993, pp. 35-66).

At that time, the 1991a scores ranged from 4.2 to 5.1 with an international mean of 4.7 (that is, a mean score scale increase of 2.1 points) (Farnen and German, 1993, p. 62). Here, these results are below the previous international means for democratization and education. All three show either a small decline (politics), no significant change (education), or a significant positive increase (communications). In that the toleration levels are significantly lower and nationalism remains relatively moderate, with the economy/environment scores being very low, the picture of Central and Eastern European countries which emerges is bleak and definitely not rosy, with only marginal improvement appearing in some areas (for example, communication and economics).

Conclusions

As to whether the democratic glass is half full or half empty in these countries, only the passage of time will prove if continual Western private and public efforts to include Central and Eastern European countries in the emerging community of nations which comprise a sort of new world order will succeed or fail. Thus far, the situation in former Yugoslavia forecasts failure, but new efforts for joint ventures, foreign aid, the Council of Europe and EC/EU associate members, the North Atlantic Cooperation Council (NACC), joint military operations, revised CSCE operations, and a 'Partnership for Peace' or full NATO membership between East and West may help to turn this bleak situation around in the next few years. As private, bilateral, and multinational efforts more directly address special social, economic, political, and security concerns and realities in the East, it may yet be that a combination of related factors (for example, foreign aid, joint ventures, IMF, GATT, Council of Europe, OECD, the EC/EU, and MFN status) will serve to further democratize, pluralize, and Westernize these emerging democracies. Only then can economic, political, environmental, educational, and communications reforms produce something closer to what these nations are actually seeking. This may be summed up in the terms free markets, civil societies, and pluralistic/democratic political cultures and institutions.

ACKNOWLEDGEMENT

An earlier draft of this chapter was presented at the Deutsche Vereinigung für Politische Wissenschaft section meeting on Political Science and Political Education in Potsdam, FRG in August 1994. We want to thank Dr. Stephanie Schulze (formerly of Humboldt University, Berlin, FRG) and Professors Adolf H. Noll and Axel Shulte of the University of Hannover, FRG for extending this invitation to present our findings. Support provided by the University of Connecticut and Appalacian State University Research Foundations is also gratefully acknowledged. Preliminary versions of this ongoing research were published elsewhere (see Farnen and German, 1995a and 1995b).

REFERENCES

Almond, G. and S. Verba (1965). *The Civic Culture: Political Attitudes and Democracy in Five Nations.* Boston, MA: Little, Brown and Company.

Barnes, S. and M. Kasse et al. (1979). *Political Action: Mass Participation in Five Western Democracies.* Beverly Hills, CA: Sage Publications.

Brown, J. (1988). *Eastern Europe and Communist Rule.* Durham, NC: Duke University Press.

Buhl, D. (1990). 'Window to the West: How Television from the Federal Republic Influenced Events in East Germany', pp. 668-73 in *P.S. Political Science and Politics,* Vol. XXIII.

Bútorová, Z. and M. Bútora (1994). 'Political Parties and Slovakia's Road to Independence',pp. 319-39 in G. Csepeli, D. German, L. Kéri, and I. Stumpf (eds.) *From Subject to Citizen.* Budapest, Hungary: Institute of Political Science, Hungarian Academy of Sciences.

Dalton, R. (1988). *Citizen Politics in Western Democracies: Public Opinion and Political Parties in the United States, Great Britain, West Germany and France.* Chatham, NJ: Chatham House Publishers.

Farnen, R. (1993). 'Cognitive Maps', pp. 212-91 in G. Csepeli, L. Kéri, and I. Stumpf (eds.) *State and Citizen.* Budapest, Hungary: Institute of Political Science.

Farnen, R. and D. German (1993). 'Prospects for Democracy in Eastern Europe: An Elite Survey', pp. 35-66 in R. Farnen (ed.) *Reconceptualizing Politics, Socialization, and Education: International Perspectives for the 21st Century.* Oldenburg, Germany: Bibliotheks- und Informationssystem der Universität Oldenburg (BIS).

Farnen, R. and D. German (1994). 'Elite Perspectives on Political, Communications, and Educational Changes in Eastern Europe', pp. 77-104 in S. Nagel and V. Rukavishnikov, *East Europe Development and Public Policy.* London: Macmillan Publishers, Ltd.

Farnen, R. and D. German (1994). 'Political, Communications and Education Change in Eastern Europe: Implications for Political Socialization Research', pp. 218-35 in R. Holly (ed.) *Political Consciousness and Civic Education During the Transformation of the System.* Warsaw, Poland: Institute of Political Studies, Polish Academy of Sciences.

Farnen, R. and D. German (1995a). 'Minority Toleration and Political Education in Central and Eastern Europe: 1991-1993', pp. 3-25, and 'Central and Eastern European Elite's Perspectives on Political, Communication, Educational, Economic, and Environmental Changes (1989 to 1993)', pp. 75-118 in *A Political Portrait of Ukraine*. Kiev, Ukraine: Democratic Initiatives.

Farnen, R. and D. German (1995b). 'Minority toleration and Political Education in Central and Eastern Europe: 1991-1993', pp. 145-60 in *Collegium Antropologicum*, Vol. 19, No. 1.

Freedom House News (January-February 1994). 'Freedom House Reports Massive Increase in Worldwide Repression', pp. 1-21 in *Freedom Review*, Vol. 25, No. 1.

Gazsó, F. (1993). 'The Process of Political Socialization in the School', pp. 62-6 in G. Csepeli, L. Kéri, and I. Stumpf (eds.) *State and Citizen: Studies on Political Socialization in Post-Communist Eastern Europe*. Budapest, Hungary: Institute of Political Science, Hungarian Academy of Sciences.

Jennings, M. and J. van Deth et al. (1989). *Continuities in Political Action: A Longitudinal Study of Political Orientations in Three Western Democracies*. Berlin, FRG: Walter de Gruyter.

Larson, D. (March 1994). 'The Role of Belief Systems in Foreign Policy Decision Making', pp. 17-34 in *Political Psychology*, Vol. 15, No. 1.

Meloen, J. (January 1994). 'Authoritarianism, Democracy, and Education: An Empirical 70 Nation Global Indicators Study.' Paper presented to the IPSA/RCPSE Conference on 'Reinventing and Fostering Democracy and Human Rights' at Florida Atlantic University, 11-15 January 1994, Boca Raton, FL.

Meloen, J., R. Farnen, and D. German (July 1993). 'Authoritarianism, Democracy, and Symbolic Political Leadership in the New World order. Evidence from Twelve Countries Worldwide.' Paper presented to the Sixteenth Annual Scientific meeting of the International Society of Political Psychology, the Charles Hotel, Cambridge, MA, 6-10 July 1993.

Rose, R. and C. Haerpfer (1994). 'Mass Response to Transformation in Post-Communist Societies', pp. 3-28 in *Europe-Asia Studies*, Vol. 46, No. 1.

Roskin, M. (1994). *The Rebirth of East Europe, Second Edition*. Englewood Cliffs, NJ: Prentice Hall.

Schöpflin, G. (1993). 'The Road from Post-Communism', pp. 183-200 in S. Whitefield (ed.) *The New Institutional Architecture of Eastern Europe*. New York, NY: St. Martins Press.

Sloutsky, V. and J. Searle-White (September 1993). 'Psychological Responses of Russians to Rapid Social Change in the Former USSR', pp. 511-26 in *Political Psychology*, Vol. 14, No. 3.

Volgyes, I. (1986). *Politics in Eastern Europe*. Chicago, IL: Dorsey Press.

Voss, J. et al. (1983). 'Problem Solving Skill in the Social Sciences', pp. 165-213 in G. Barnes (ed.) *The Psychology of Learning and Motivation*. New York, NY: Academic Press.

Wiatr, J. (1980). 'The Civic Culture from a Marxist-Sociological Perspective', pp. 103-23 in G. Almond and S. Verba, *The Civic Culture Revisited*. Boston, MA: Little, Brown and Company.

APPENDIX: QUESTIONS FROM THE 'FOLLOW-UP SURVEY OF TRENDS IN CENTRAL AND EASTERN EUROPEAN POLITICS, COMMUNICATIONS, EDUCATION, AND ECONOMICS SINCE JANUARY 1991'

Note: A plus or minus has been placed next to each item to indicate whether or not agreement with it would signify a positive or negative value for each respective scale.

I. DEMOCRATIC POLITICAL VARIABLES

1. Degree of Communist Party control over the political system. (-)
2. Extent of dominant political party or government support for patriotism to nation. (-)
3. Extent of dominant political party or government support for anti-individualist values. (-)
4. Extent of dominant political party or government support for antibourgeois values. (-)
5. Presence of viable multiparty (more than one dominant political party) mechanisms. (+)
6. Degree of spontaneous (noncoerced) popular participation in elections. (Specify approximate per cent voting.) (+)
7. Popular mass attendance (noncoerced) at political party meetings and public gatherings. (+)
8. Popular contacts with official/politicians to promote political reforms. (+)
9. Popular discussions of politics with friends. (+)
10. Popular participation in spontaneous demonstrations. (+)
11. Political efficacy/civic competence of voting population. (+)
12. Popular participation in violent political demonstrations or protest activities. (-)
13. Popular/public tolerance level toward political minorities. (+)
14. Popular/public tolerance level toward ethnic and linguistic minorities. (+)
15. Popular and peaceful circulation of petitions to change governmental policies. (+)
16. Popular participation in peaceful demonstrations (such as strikes) to change government policies. (+)
17. Use of police forces against demonstrators/strikers. (-)
18. Use of military troops/armed forces against demonstrators/strikers. (-)
19. Level of attachment of voting population to political parties of the political left. (-)
20. Level of attachment of voting population to political parties of the political right. (-)
21. Degree of police, party, and other investigative agency's intrusion into private, family, or group affairs. (-)

II. DEMOCRATIC COMMUNICATIONS VARIABLES

22. Extent of government support for popular expression and freedom of speech. (+)

23. Extent of dominant political party or government support for freedom of press. (+)

24. Extent of government banning/censoring of movies, magazines, newspapers, television programs, or books considered politically dangerous. (-)

25. Diversity of programs and ownership/outlets of television stations. Specify type of ownership/control (for example, entirely governmentally owned/controlled to establishment of one or more privately owned media outlets). (+)

26. Diversity of programs and ownership/outlets of radio stations. Specify type of ownership/control (for example, entirely governmentally owned/controlled to establishment of one or more privately owned media outlets). (+)

27. Diversity of political viewpoints and ownership/outlets of newspapers. Specify type of ownership/control (for example, entirely governmentally owned/controlled to establishment of one or more privately owned media outlets). (+)

28. Diversity of political viewpoints and ownership/outlets of news magazines. Specify type of ownership/control (for example, from entirely governmentally owned/controlled to many privately owned media outlets). (+)

29. Diversity of political viewpoints and authorship of demonstrative arts (paintings, theater). Specify type of ownership/control (for example, from entirely governmentally owned/controlled to many privately owned media outlets). (+)

30. Extent of dominant political party or government use of communications media as an agent of political socialization and pro-government propaganda. (-)

31. Extent to which television was/is the most important single medium of mass communications. (+)

32. Extent to which government or dominant political party attempts to regulate/prevent/stifle word-of-mouth interpersonal political communications. (-)

33. Extent to which many listeners rely on foreign (for example, Radio Free Europe, BBC, Voice of America, Radio Paris, and Die Deutsche Welle) for news of the day. Specify foreign broadcasts listened to most frequently. (-)

34. Extent to which mass media news writers/editors feel free to present the news according to their own determination of what should be broadcast or printed. (+)

35. Extent to which the people trust the existing television communications media. (+)

36. Extent to which the people trust the existing radio communications media. (+)

37. Extent to which people trust the existing newspaper communications media. (+)
38. Extent to which people trust the existing news magazine communications media. (+)

III. DEMOCRATIC POLITICAL EDUCATION VARIABLES

39. Extent to which government or dominant political party attempts to control political education in schools. (-)
40. Extent to which there is a diverse and separate political education curriculum in the schools (that is, other than scientific socialism). Specify school level. Specify content of course (for example, Marxist-Leninism, civil rights, pluralism, free enterprise, and democracy). (+)
41. Extent to which government or dominant political party controls the production of political education textbooks used in schools. (-)
42. Extent to which government(s) exert(s) ideological control over all school curricula (for example, infuses and economic/political/social philosophy into economics, and biology courses). (-)
43. Extent to which a free and open democratic classroom environment exists in political education courses. (+)
44. Extent to which organized peer pressure is employed in schools to achieve approved educational/behavioral political objectives. (-)
45. Extent to which government-approved voting/participation behaviors are taught in political education. (-)
46. Extent to which interest articulation, popular participation, and dissent/opposition behaviors are taught in political education. (+)
47. Extent to which need for international cooperation is taught in political education (for example, United Nations, European Community, Helsinki Accords, and Conference on Security and Cooperation in Europe). (+)
48. Extent to which respect for civil rights of minorities is taught in political education. (+)
49. Extent to which nationalism is taught in political education. (-)
50. Extent to which actual political participation occurs in the schools (for example, experiential citizenship training such as actual participation in self-government, making decisions about classroom and school governance, and visiting government offices and meeting with legislators). Specify extent of participation. (+)

IV. FREE MARKET ECONOMIC VARIABLES

51. Rate your country's/government's success in privatizing state-owned companies since January 1991. (+)
52. Rate your country's success in establishing a hard and transferable currency since January 1991. (+)

53. Rate your country's success in moving the market toward open competition for goods, labor, services, and capital. (+)

V.   ENVIRONMENTAL VARIABLES

54. Rate your country's success in industrial restructuring that has been environmentally friendly. (+)

55. Rate the general condition of your country's environment as getting better or worse since January 1991. (+)

Part II

Area/National Case Studies

5   *What Makes a Slovak a Nationalist?*
A Case Study

Henk Dekker
Darina Malová
Remko Theulings

ABSTRACT

Many politicians and journalists who perceive a growth of nationalism in Central and Eastern Europe (in general) and in Slovakia (in particular) are very concerned about it. Is there, indeed, a growth in nationalism in Slovakia? And if so, what explains its continuation, rebirth, or growth? To answer these questions, we interviewed Slovak academicians and politicians. We also analyzed Slovak reports on public opinion survey data. Empirical data specifically on Slovakian nationalistic attitudes were not found. Consequently, statements on nationalism in (and the growth of nationalism among) the Slovak population are not based on empirical findings. However, there are certain indications about nationalism-related orientations. Between one-quarter and one-third of Slovaks had such orientations in 1992-4. Three categories of explanatory variables are distinguished: systemic, individual, and socialization. Many of the theoretical requirements leading to an increase in nationalism are present in Slovakia nowadays. These include a political, economic, and an identity crisis, with politicians acting as nationalistic 'entrepreneurs'.

INTRODUCTION: NATIONALISM, MYTH OR REALITY?

There is a serious concern about both the existence and growth of nationalism which paints 'the pointillist ethnic canvas of twentieth-century Eastern Europe' (Pearson, 1993, p. 61). Journalists and politicians see a growth in nationalism and are concerned about its uncertain effects. For example, 'Nationalism is the only real threat to democracy in Eastern Europe' and 'Europe hears beat of nationalism anew from Hungarians' are the titles of an article starting on the front page of an American newspaper. It is also said that 'Romania, with a 2 million-member Hungarian minority, and Slovakia, with 600 000 ethnic Hungarians, have also become increasingly nationalistic, accusing Hungary of stirring up ethnic discontent' (*Boston Globe*, 7 July 1993, p. 1). A Dutch newspaper reported 'The fall of socialism has created in the East a vacuum that is filled in by spokesmen of a rabid and xenophobic nationalism' (*NRC Handelsblad*, 8 July 1993, p. 9). The renaissance of nationalism is feared for internal reasons (threat of political democratization, economic liberalization, and personal safety for ethnic minorities) as well as for international reasons (Sarajevo syndrome; inevitable escalation from regional to the European level, and dangers to the peace and security of the continent) (Koch, 1992).

The Western press describes Slovakia (after Serbia and Croatia) as the black sheep of Central and Eastern European civilization. The negative image is echoed in meetings of international organizations such as the Council of Europe's Parliamentary Assembly and the European Parliament. A reporter for a Dutch daily newspaper wrote: 'It is becoming even worse in Slovakia than we already feared. Xenophobia is stirred up openly. Minorities like the Romanies and the Hungarians are teased. Anti-Semitism rises, and there is a wish to canonize the deceased leader of the nazist "puppet state of Slovakia" during World War II, the Roman Catholic priest Joseph Tiso.' It was reported that the Prime Minister of Slovakia has pled for 'stopping the unlimited propagation of the gypsies.' There was, according to this newspaper, 'a continuous bartering with lawmaking limiting the free movement of individuals and the using of non-Slovak first names is allowed one day and forbidden the other day with the result that no one knows what to do.' A columnist of the same paper requested the Dutch Foreign Minister and the Dutch ambassador at the Council of Europe to accuse Slovakia at the Council meeting and to consider evicting Slovakia from the Council. The CSCE High Commissioner for Minorities, the Dutchman Max van der Stoel, was asked to undertake action as well (*Algemeen Dagblad*, 11 September 1993). On the front page of another Dutch newspaper, Slovakia's Prime Minister Vladimir Mečiar was characterized as 'a nationalistic demagogue' (*NRC Handelsblad*, 29 December 1993, p. 1).

Many Slovaks are aware of these poor press reports abroad. Almost half of them (45 per cent) are concerned about this negative image (Bútorová, 1993). An overwhelming majority (91 per cent) see the importance of a good Slovak image to guarantee continuing foreign assistance (Bútorová, 1993). One of the pre-election promises for the 1992 winning party (HZDS) was to make Slovakia more visible in the world and to create a more positive image. However, in March 1993, one-third thought that the image was worse than before the 1992 elections (another third thought the image was better, while the remainder thought there was no change or had no opinion about it). Those optimistic about a positive change in Slovakia's foreign image numbered 43 per cent (Bútorová, 1993). A Bratislava daily newspaper reported: 'We are not the favorites of Europe, but other countries have no reason to hurt us. If the opinion against Slovakia arose due to an information shortage, we should remedy that' (*Pravda*, 22 June 1993, p. 3). There really are some serious doubts about the quality of the accurate information on Slovakia in other countries. For example, one map of Central Europe published in a Dutch newspaper showed Slovenia in the location of Slovakia (*De Volkskrant*, 2 October 1993, p. 28).

Having read these articles, we asked ourselves: Is there, indeed, a growth in nationalism in Slovakia? And if so, what are the plausible explanations for its rise? To answer these questions, we interviewed 18 Slovak scientists (from the disciplines of political science, sociology, ethnology, history, psychology, philosophy, and law), and eight Slovak politicians (including Members of Parliament and Chairpersons of several different political parties) in June 1993. We also conducted a study of the available literature and analyzed public opinion survey data. The theoretical basis for our research is presented in the next section (see also Dekker and Malová, 1994).

NATIONALISM

Nationalism includes four different phenomena: nationalism as an ideology, a movement, a process of nation-building, and an individual attitude. The latter is the most important category because the other three are ultimately based on individuals' attitudes and/or decisions. The first three phenomena are classified as elite nationalism, while the fourth is individual (both elite and mass) level. The attitude of nationalism is just one out of nine relevant national orientations that we have distinguished. There are three national cognitive orientations: national awareness, consciousness, and distinctiveness. The six national attitudes are: national feeling, liking, pride, preference, superiority, and nationalism, *per se*.

To develop an attitude toward an object, an individual needs to be aware of the object's existence. In the case of national attitudes, the individual is first expected to become aware of the country he/she is living in and of the nationality he/she possesses. We call this national awareness. (As for national orientations in Slovakia, it is signified in the statements: 'I live in Slovakia' and 'I am a Slovak'.) The next cognition is national consciousness; this means the consciousness of constituting (together with other nationals) a group with something in common besides the nationality that gives the country and people a particular identity (for example, signifiers are: 'Slovakia has its own identity' and 'Slovaks have other things in common besides their Slovak nationality'). The third cognition is national distinctiveness. This is the perception that one's own country differs from other countries and that nationals differ from non-nationals (for example, 'Slovakia differs from other countries' and 'Slovaks differ from other peoples').

The first national attitude is the feeling of being [one's own nationality]. We call this national feeling (for example, 'I feel I am a Slovak'). The second attitude (including an increasing intensity of positive affection) is national liking. That is, liking one's own country and people (for example, 'I like Slovakia', 'I like to be a Slovak', and 'I like the Slovaks in general'). National pride is the attitude of being proud of one's own country and people (for example, 'Slovakia can be proud of what it performs' and 'I am proud to be a Slovak'). Strong positive affections toward an object imply (and lead to) comparing one's own country and people with others, which may result in national preference. This means preferring one's own country and people above others (for example, 'I prefer to live in Slovakia', 'I prefer to have Slovak nationality', 'I prefer Slovaks in my contacts with other people in general'). The more positive the affection to one's own country and people becomes, the more negative the affection may become toward others. National superiority is the combination of attributing the 'best' characteristics (in the individual's own perceptions) to one's own country and people; having the willingness to force other nationalities living in the country to assimilate; and wishing to preserve national independence (for example, 'Slovakia is the best country to live in', 'The Slovak nationality is the best nationality to have', 'Slovak people are the best people with whom to be in contact', 'I like Slovaks more than people from other countries in general', 'Non-Slovaks living in Slovakia must accept Slovak customs and become Slovak', and 'Slovakia should preserve its independence in contacts with other countries'). Finally, the individual may develop the attitude of nationalism. Nationalism is the combination of a belief in a 'nation' with a common origin (kinship); the desire for congruence between 'nation' and state, including (if necessary) changing natural/state borders; the willingness to force other nationalities/'ethnic' groups/'nations' inside the country to leave; and the rejection of international cooperation (for example, 'The Slovaks have a common origin', 'All Slovaks should live in Slovakia', 'Slovaks living in Hungary should have Slovakia's protection', 'That part of Hungary where a majority of the population is Slovak should become part of Slovakia', 'Non-Slovaks living in Slovakia must leave Slovakia', and 'Cooperation with other countries does not benefit Slovakia and, therefore, should be rejected').

Each individual is expected to reach one of the following stages of national cognitive development: national awareness -> national consciousness -> national distinctiveness, and one of the following stages of national attitudinal development: national feeling -> national liking -> national pride -> national preference -> national superiority -> nationalism. The stages must be fulfilled in sequence since each stage incorporates the previous one and prepares for the next.

Our basic assumption is that no one is born with nationalism intact. We can distinguish three categories of explanatory variables: system, individual, and socialization variables. System variables (macro-level) cannot explain (differences in the level of) nationalism (micro-level) completely. Therefore, something must function as a bridge between society and individual. Most individual variables are also background variables. The main influence must come from political socialization. In spite of international insecurities, foreign domination, and economic deprivation, political crisis, and feelings of insecurity and disorientation, national orientations (in general) and nationalism (in particular) develop among individuals only when they are promoted. This promotion takes place in the national political socialization processes which each individual undergoes. To explain differences in national orientations (in general) and nationalism (in particular), one must examine political socialization agencies, the content and design of their messages, and the ways in which these messages are individually received and processed (socialization structures and processes). Individuals differ in their willingness to receive nationalistic messages from socialization agencies because of (among others) different perceptions of the political and economic situation and outlook and different levels of need for psychological security and identity acquisition or change.

Ultimately, nationalism develops when national socialization includes elements of a common ancestry and consanguinity and congruence of 'nation' and state. Political leaders acting as national(istic) 'entrepreneurs' (Kasinitz, 1992, uses the term 'ethnicity entrepreneurs') are expected to be the most important national(istic) socializers. Leaders of both majority and minority parties/groups may support and strengthen the perspective of 'one nation, one state' and may use the 'nation'/nationality issue to acquire political power (and to secure their prominent place in the national history). 'Nation'/nationality is a powerful rallying point for those eager to bolster their popularity in political (and economic) hard times. It is 'the widest possible mobilization that is available within a state' (Bloom, 1993, p. 81). The more charismatic these political leaders are, the stronger their expected influence. They are in a position to influence the individual directly (through their public statements or speeches) or indirectly (through other socialization agencies, such as parents, school, mass media, armed services, and so forth). Their tools include creating and prescribing/promoting one common language and excluding foreign languages; promoting and encouraging the display of the national flag or emblem and singing or playing the national anthem; initiating and supporting the commemoration of national historical personalities and events; restoring and/or building impressive national buildings, such as palaces and national history museums; employing national or nationalistic rhetoric to emphasize a common ancestry and consanguinity; initiating and strengthening conspiracy rumors; and blaming troubles on domestic 'ethnic' or minority and foreign 'enemies'. Under the influence of charismatic national(istic) political leaders, a considerable part of the population may be encouraged to strengthen their national orientations and to move upwards in the depicted stage hierarchy. This results in a larger group of people with national preference or feelings of superiority and a larger group of nationalists.

NATIONALISM AT THE ELITE LEVEL

If it is true that there is (a growing) nationalism in Slovakia, then there must be (an increase in) expressions of nationalistic ideology, activities of nationalist movements, activities of politicians who aim to build (and maintain) the 'nation'-state, and (a growing number of) individuals who show or express nationalistic attitudes. To confirm or reject these assumptions, we interviewed Slovak academic observers and politicians and analyzed public opinion survey data.

We first asked our Slovak respondents whether there is something that nationalists could call a Slovak 'nation'. Almost all gave a positive answer. Its roots could be found in the Great Moravian Empire of the middle ages. Second, a Slovak emancipation movement in the 19th century could be cited. Ludovít Stúr (1815-56) was named as one of the founding fathers of the Slovak 'nation'. He promoted Slovak culture and language, initiated publication of the first Slovak newspaper (the *Slovenské Národne Noviny*), and opposed the 'magyarization' of Slovakia (then part of the Hungarian Empire) and participation in the Hungarian war of independence against the Austrian Empire in mid 19th century. Third, respondents referred to the struggle to be free to use the Slovak language and speech, which was one reason Slovaks supported the establishment of Czechoslovakia after World War 1. Fourth, elements of a 'nation' could be seen in the independent state of Slovakia from 1939 to 1945. Within the Nazi *Neuordnung*, Slovaks were permitted to form their own state. 'Slovaks experienced their first tantalizing and unforgettable taste of (perhaps pseudo)nation-statehood in the Second World War. . . . It constituted an ambition-raising experience which became indelibly imprinted on the collective memory' (Pearson, 1993, pp. 63 and 67). Some of our respondents called this a 'clerical-fascist state'. Slovaks were not the only ones who competed for the favors of Nazi Germany. 'The newly created nation-states in Central and Eastern Europe were uncertain of themselves and territorially dissatisfied. This is why many of them seized the first opportunity to compromise their independence' (Csepeli and Örkény, 1993, p. 126).

The second question is whether there were/are any prominent nationalist ideologues, movements, and political leaders in recent history. Based on our respondents' answers, we composed the following description of the history of Slovakia, paying extra attention to national and nationalistic elements.

In 1946, the last free pre-communist elections took place in Czechoslovakia. In Slovakia, the Democratic Party won the elections (60 per cent; to the Communist Party's 30 per cent), while in Czechia, the Communist Party won. The President of the Slovak state, Jozef Tiso, was executed as a war criminal in 1947. No attempt whatever was made to deal with the 1940s Slovak state 'other than regarding nationalism and its concomitants as epiphenomena, as side effects or consequences of the class struggle' (Pick, 1993, p. 38). The communists took over the Czechoslovakian state in 1948. This regime was controlled mainly by the Czech Communists (the Slovak Communists were not as influential because of their relatively low electoral support in the 1946 elections). In the 1950s, leading communist personalities in Slovakia were accused of being 'bourgeois nationalistic' (for example, in favor of more autonomy for Slovakia).

The eight months of the 'Prague Spring' in 1968, offered 'socialism with a human face' under the leadership of native communists such as Alexander Dubcek, Ota Sik, and Josef Smrkovsky. It ended on the night of 20/21 August 1968. Tanks from the Soviet Union and its allies then introduced a 20 year period of intensified oppression (under the leadership of, among others, Gustáv Husak). According to our respondents, the Czecho-Slovak Federation (established in 1969) was more communist and Czech than a federation of Czechs and Slovaks.

The official communist policy aimed to destroy national identity in favor of an international, socialist one. In practice, political elites made opportunistic use of both communist internationalism and national orientations. In their private lives, Slovaks were able to enjoy Slovak culture. Slovak folklore and other beliefs received regime support in the early 1980s. 'Nationalism was . . . nurtured, rather than diluted, in the communist experience' (Brzezinski, 1989, pp. 2 and 4). This seems to be a more accurate observation than that nationalism was put in a deep freeze under communism, thereby 'remaining dormant in the people in the way [it] existed in the early 40s' (Pick, 1993, p. 38). Some of our respondents, themselves, thought it an act of resistance to commemorate national heroes (for example, visiting General Stefanik's grave on the day of his death to commemorate a Slovak World War I hero). People lived 'the lie' (the official ideology of formal socialization agencies, such as school, newspapers, and official meetings) and 'the truth' (for example, family, church, 'samizdat', dissident groups, and informal groups) (Havel, 1990, pp. 10 and 26). Since the official communist ideology contradicted everyday life, its influence was undermined. The 'freezer' metaphor seems to be only partly true; national orientations were never really put on ice since the communist regime frequently used them to manipulate the public. However, both communism and nationalism had some elements in common. These included perpetuating the idea of the organized society, insisting on the crucial importance of the collectivity (class or nation) at the expense of the individual, considering social engineering a political good, and basing 'their policies on absolute norms and values, on symbols to which concepts as compromise, negotiation and self-limitation are basically strange' (Gerrits, 1992, p. 9).

Independence from the Soviet Union and its communist allies was the result of the 'velvet (bloodless) revolution' of 1989; politically dominant were the Civic Forum in the Czech part and the Public Against Violence (PAV) in the Slovak area. In 1990, the Czechoslovak Federal Assembly decided to change the official name of the Czechoslovak Socialist Republic (CSSR) to the Czecho-Slovak Federative Republic (CSFR). Thus began the 'war over a hyphen'. Slovak politicians preferred the hyphen in the name Czecho-Slovakia, while Czech politicians preferred Czech and Slovak Federative Republic. From then on, there were two official names of the Federation, one in Slovak and one in Czech. Especially among political elites in the Slovak part, this 'war' strengthened distrust, resulting in the establishment of a National Council for the Liberation of Slovakia. This Council organized demonstrations and promoted the idea of Slovak independence. The Slovak Christian Democratic Movement began to advocate a looser form of coexistence with the Czechs in 1991. Large pro-Slovak independence demonstrations were held in Bratislava throughout the summer months. Vladimir Mečiar was fired as prime-minister of the Slovak government after disagreeing with the PAV. He established the center-oriented Movement for a Democratic Slovakia (HZDS). The right-wing Civic Democratic Union (ODU) was also established.

In 1992, 42 political parties, movements, and groups took part in the second parliamentary elections (the turnout was 85 per cent). Because of the threshold requirements (minimums: 5 per cent for parties, 8 per cent for movements, 10 per cent for coalitions of parties), 12 out of the 42 political parties got seats in the Federal Parliament. In the Slovak parliament, six parties got seats. The Movement for a Democratic Slovakia (HZDS), led by Mečiar, was the winner. HZDS received 34 per cent of the vote for the Federal Assembly and 37 per cent for the Slovak National Council (74 out of 150 seats). HZDS campaigned for a more equal partnership with the Czech Republic. Slovak independence was only one of the options, although its minimum requirements gave the impression a new Slovakia would have all the attributes of an independent state (that is, international recognition, its own constitution, and its own president). It also called for slowing the pace of reform and related negative economic development in Slovakia to a lack of Slovak influence in Prague's political decision-making. The Slovak National Party (SNS) gained 8 per cent of the vote (15 seats); its main program aimed to achieve Slovak independence. The Party of the Democratic Left (SDL) (the successor of the Communist Party) got 15 per cent, the Christian Democratic Movement (KDH) received 9 per cent, and two Hungarian parties, the Hungarian Christian Democratic Movement and Coexistence garnered 8 per cent (5 and 9 seats, respectively, totalling 14 seats) (FSU, 1992). HZDS (74 out of 150 seats) formed a (minority) government with Mečiar as Prime Minister.

Negotiations between the leaders of the two winning parties in the Czech and Slovak regions (Vaclav Klaus and Mečiar) resulted not in a new federation but in the 'velvet separation' in 1992. This separation signalled the success of nationalist elites. However, some of our respondents said that a key factor in the negotiations occurred when the negotiators, themselves, set a time limit (a new political entity had to be established by 1 January 1993). Consequently, the separation can be seen (or presented) partly as a 'working accident'. A referendum on the split was not held, although the federal constitution called for a one prior to a constitutionally valid separation. As a result, 'nationalism reigns over constitutionalism' (according to *The Prague Post*, 24 February 1993, p. 5).

During the first year of their independent existence, the Slovaks established a new national political system. The new Constitution of the Slovak Republic was ratified in September 1992. It established a parliamentary democracy with proportional representation and a unicameral parliament. A strong executive branch was included to protect the system from extreme political fragmentation. The Prime Minister, among others, has the right to recall a member of the cabinet, to return laws to the parliament, and to combine voting on a bill with a vote of confidence in the cabinet. Human and minority rights were protected in the Constitution and, particularly, in the Bill of Rights. A Constitutional Court was established to rule on the constitutionality of draft legislation and to review complaints on the violation of fundamental human and minority rights. A parliamentary vote of no confidence in March 1994 removed Mečiar from the premier's seat. Thus, the newspaper *Republika* wrote that the architect of Slovak independence (Mečiar) had become the victim of a Czechoslovak, communist, and Hungarian conspiracy. The SNS also pleaded for the national rehabilitation of Tiso. The new SNS chairman, Ján Slota (a member of Mečiar's governing coalition) also voiced public slurs against Jews, Hungarians, and Czechs.

Therefore, we may conclude that nationalists can use historical events as symbols of an existing 'nation' and that many of the political elites express/expressed national preference and national superiority, while only some of them demonstrate/demonstrated nationalism in their sentiments.

NATIONALISM AT THE INDIVIDUAL LEVEL

We have not found any specific empirical study on national orientations (including nationalism) among contemporary Slovaks. However, there are some survey- and content-analysis research data on nationalism-related political orientations. The Institute for Public Opinion Research of the Slovak Statistics Office, the Research Center of Social Problems at the Coordinating Center of Public Against Violence, and the Center (until 1992, Institute) for Social Analysis of Comenius University assembled these data. Bútorová (1993) compiled the research findings at the latter two institutions. These findings report standardized face-to-face interviews with a sample of 1132 respondents living in Slovakia between 12 and 21 March 1993. The analysis presented in this chapter is mainly based on Bútorová's report; if not the case, another source is named explicitly. The analyzed studies included data on the following nationalism-related political orientations: attitudes toward the 1940s Slovak state; attitudes toward the 1993 independent Slovak state; support for the nationalist party; support for a nationalist political leader; opinions on the desirable level of influence for nationalists on Slovak life; social distance; anti-Semitism; and belief in a foreign conspiracy.

Regarding attitudes toward the 1940s Slovak state, one-third (33 per cent) of the 1993 population was positive about this. These respondents thought its virtues outweighed its shortcomings. (However, 39 per cent had a negative attitude and 28 per cent were undecided). Jozef Tiso, the head of state, was described positively by 29 per cent (and negatively by 42 per cent, with 29 per cent taking no position). Tiso was seen as the most important Slovak historical personality by 5 per cent in 1992 (Misovic, 1993). Only 38 per cent approved of stopping the commemoration of Jewish deportations and exterminations during the 1940s in the Slovak state.

With respect to attitudes toward the 1993 independent state, Slovak public opinion polls between 1989 and 1994 repeatedly showed that a very small minority of the population wanted to split the common Czech-Slovak state. In June 1990, only 8 per cent of the Slovaks (and 5 per cent of the Czechs) supported the idea of two separate states. A majority of both Slovaks (57 per cent) and Czechs (72 per cent) expressed support for the common state, while 39 per cent of the Slovaks (and 16 per cent of the Czechs) supported confederation (Benes, 1990). In July 1992, only 16 per cent of the population in both parts of the federation favored two independent states (Malová, 1993b). The Federation was dismantled despite a clear absence of support in public opinion polls. After the 1993 split, 68 per cent of the respondents said they would have preferred a referendum before the division. Only 29 per cent indicated they would have supported Slovakia's independence (50 per cent would have been against, 13 per cent would not have voted, and 8 per cent did not know). Women, ethnic Hungarians, and the population of Eastern Slovakia less readily accepted the split (age, level of education, size of municipality, and other sociodemographic variables were statistically not significant). Slovak independence supporters were more in favor of an authoritarian regime's principles; were more reluctant to accept armaments conversion; had a lower tolerance with respect to Czechs, Hungarians and Jews; and judged the 1939-1944 Slovak state more leniently. SNS and HZDS adherents were more often pleased with the creation of the independent state, where they feel confident of their new opportunities. They interpreted the division more often as a result of the will of the Slovak people and of the reluctance of Czechs to accept Slovaks as equal partners. The strongest critics of the Federation's split were the supporters of Hungarian political parties. Even in May 1994, support for the division was limited: 27 per cent would have voted for and 57 per cent would have voted against the division of the Federation had there been a referendum. The predominant response (60 per cent) to Slovakia's independence was fear of the future. Other responses which received less support included embarrassment (42 per cent), new opportunities (40 per cent), joy (32 per cent), and sadness (29 per cent).

SNS (the only party which openly campaigned for independence) received 8 per cent of the vote in the June 1992 elections. HZDS won the elections with

37 per cent of the vote. HZDS related the negative economic development in Slovakia to the lack of Slovak influence in CSFR political decision-making, and campaigned for a more equal partnership with the Czech Republic, where Slovak independence was only one of several options. However, a majority of the HZDS voters supported the split afterwards. After the June 1992 elections, SNS kept its support and HZDS lost its backing, primarily from those who favored preserving the federative republic (8.3 and 18.6 per cent, respectively, in March 1993). Other nationalist parties (the Independent Party of the Slovaks, the Slovak People's Party, and the Slovak National Democratic Party) received only marginal popular support and were soon dissolved.

The leaders of SNS and HZDS, Ludovít Cernák and Vladimír Mečiar, received a mean sympathy rating score of 1.80 and 2.09 (1 = most sympathy, 3 = least sympathy) and received trust from 5.7 and 22.1 per cent. Trust in Cernák did not change in 1992 and at the beginning of 1993. Trust in Mečiar decreased. At the beginning of 1993, trust in Mečiar was 16.5 per cent less than in January 1992 and 22.1 per cent less than in April 1992. After he was removed as Prime Minister in 1994, popular trust in him increased again.

Respondents were also asked to indicate the influence of several different groups on Slovak life. 'Nationalists' had 'too little' influence according to 26.2 per cent (an 'adequate' influence according to 19.2 per cent, 'too much' according to 19.8 per cent, while 34.8 per cent did not know).

A relatively high percentage of Slovak respondents reportedly would not like to have a Hungarian as a close relative (43 per cent) or neighbor (39 per cent). In September 1990, 74 per cent of Slovaks and 85 per cent of Hungarians living in Slovakia stated that relations between Slovaks and Hungarians were good; however, 21 per cent of Slovaks and 9 per cent of Hungarians said that they were bad. Slovaks who had Hungarian friends were more positive in their evaluation of relationships and vice versa. Slovaks living in the Southern part of Slovakia thought that their language was the main problem in ethnic relations; therefore, 78 per cent favored a law to require Slovakian as the official language. One-fourth of those Slovaks and Hungarians were not satisfied with the Hungarian minority's representation in the Slovak parliament. Slovaks thought it was overrepresented, while Hungarians believed it was underrepresented (Statistics Office of the Slovak Republic, 1990; 376 Slovaks and 384 Hungarians were interviewed 20-26 September 1990). Most Hungarians agreed that they had the opportunity to send their children to mother-tongue nursery and primary schools (70 and 77 per cent, respectively, but 24 and 20 per cent of each group perceived no such opportunity). These same perceptions among Slovaks were 89 and 90 per cent 'yes' and 7 and 8 per cent 'no'. Regarding the opportunity to attend mother-tongue secondary schools, 53 per cent of Hungarians said 'yes' and 35 per cent 'no'; however, 10 per cent of the Slovaks said it was not possible for them to attend such secondary schools in their districts (Institute for Public Opinion Polls, reported in *Národná obroda*, 3 February 1994).

The social distance toward Romanies is much more negative (over 80 per cent). In 1990, only 18 per cent of Slovaks characterized their relations with Romanies as 'friendly'. According to the Opinion Window Agency, 43 per cent of the Romanies in May 1990 said their relations with other citizens were 'good', while 25 per cent said they were 'more good than bad' (this was a quota sample of 680 respondents collected in cooperation with the US-based Gallup organization). Social distance toward Czechs is much smaller (less than 20 per cent). Mutual trust and friendship between Slovaks and Czechs has declined considerably in the last ten years (Malová, 1993a). In 1993, 26 per cent thought such relations had deteriorated; only 3 per cent said they improved after the split (among this group, supporters of SNS, 7 per cent, and HZDS, 6 per cent, predominate). The reasons given for deteriorating relations are the governments of both republics (22 per cent), politicians' actions (17 per cent), the government and the National Council of Slovakia (15 per cent), and Czech politicians (13 per cent) (Statistics Office of Slovak Republic, 1993; 1268 respondents were interviewed during 19-28 February 1993).

High percentages of Slovak respondents reported they would not like to have a Jew as a close relative (42 per cent) or neighbor (27 per cent). Some 29 per cent feared excessive Jewish influence on economic and political life. Approximately the same percentage thought 'important events take place as a result of the worldwide Jewish conspiracy' (47 per cent had no opinion). One-fifth (21 per cent) of the respondents agreed with the statement 'Jews have never had a genuinely positive attitude to the Slovak people.' Two-thirds (63 per cent) believed the statement 'Jews are mainly concerned about themselves - their money and their profit.' The overall anti-Semitic population was estimated to be around 28 per cent (that is, those agreeing with at least three of these four statements and the neighborhood social distance question) (Bútorová, 1993).

'Selling out' Slovakia to foreign capitalists was also a common fear/concern (57 per cent). The anti-Slovak conspiracy was seen as the main reason for government's low performances by 10 per cent; however, 45 per cent believed Slovakia's negative image in the world resulted from the activities of 'those who do not wish Slovakia well'. This belief was doubly strong among Slovaks as compared with Hungarian minority members. It was highest among HZDS, SNS, and SDL supporters, and even higher among respondents who would have voted for the CSFR split in a referendum.

We may conclude that there are credible indications that about one-quarter to one-third of the Slovak population supported nationalism-related orientations in the 1992/1993 period. Assuming that these subgroups mainly consist of the same individuals, 33 per cent thought the 1940s Slovak state's virtues outweighed its shortcomings; 29 per cent would have supported Slovakia's independence if there had been a referendum; 32 per cent responded with joy to

Slovakia's independence; 8 per cent voted for SNS and 37 per cent for HZDS; 29 per cent fully agreed with the value of 'unity and togetherness'; 26 per cent thought nationalists had too little influence; and at least 28 per cent may be considered anti-Semitic. However, the question whether or not there is a growth in nationalism (or nationalism-related orientations) cannot be fully answered because of missing longitudinal panel study data. Any comparisons of pre- and post-1989 data are risky at best because, for obvious reasons, respondents are more likely to speak their minds after the revolution than before.

AN EXPLANATION OF NATIONALISM

No person is born a nationalist. Then, how are nationalists 'made' in Slovakia? When, how, why, and under what influences does a Slovak become a nationalist? We can distinguish among three categories of relevant variables: system (international and national political and economic), individual (social-demographic; nonpolitical, but politically relevant orientations; and political orientations other than the orientation under study), and socialization variables.

International Political System Variables

The international political system variables include the position of Slovakia in the former Czecho-Slovak Federation, the relationship between Slovakia and the Czech Republic after the division of the federation, the strained relationship with Hungary, and a strong desire for international recognition and improvement of Slovakia's image abroad.

The Slovak and Czech Republics' 'velvet divorce' soon changed into what has been called an 'emery-paper separation'. The monetary union ceased to function within two months (February 1993) when Czecho-Slovak banknotes were refused and new Slovak and Czech currencies were introduced. Since then, Slovakia has run a consistent deficit with the Czech Republic. (In February 1994, all such debts were repaid, however). The customs union suffered from serious tensions. At issue were the Czech government's request to the Slovaks for recompensation for the 1992 budget deficit, its decision to stop issuing privatization vouchers to Slovak citizens, and the establishment of new frontiers and border crossings.

The strained relationship with Hungary mainly hinges on the position of Hungarians in Slovakia and of Slovaks in Hungary (Ocovský, 1992; Bútorová, 1992; Bacová, 1992; Masarykova Universita, 1993). Hungarians (about 500 000 people or 10-11 per cent of the population) are still the largest minority group in Slovakia. The south Slovak region, where most of them live, was included in Czechoslovakia after the Austro-Hungarian monarchy collapsed.

Hungarian leaders' political statements in the 1990s have not only raised popular fears, but also some of the political elites in (Czecho)Slovakia have made self-serving political capital from them. In 1990, the Hungarian Prime Minister proclaimed himself the prime minister 'of all Hungarians' and later (in 1992) promised 'the motherland's support for kinfolk living abroad as minorities.' In 1992, the Hungarian Defense Secretary stated that 'the Hungarian nation lives in Hungary and seven adjacent countries . . . This dispersed entity of the Magyars does influence Hungarian foreign policy and Hungarian defense policy' (quoted by Griffiths, 1993, p. 22).

In 1990, language also became a major issue. The Public Against Violence proposed to limit the right to use the Hungarian mother tongue in local political processes in areas that were more than 10 per cent Hungarian. SNS objected and asked for a ban on all languages, save Slovak. The Public Against Violence agreed to a compromise (20 per cent) in the new language law, which Mečiar's first cabinet adopted in autumn 1990. However, Hungarians still felt threatened. The new Slovak constitution referred to Slovak as the official language. Hungarian parliamentary parties demanded the right to go to Hungarian-language schools, to broadcast Hungarian-language television and radio programs, to use Hungarian in daily business with local officials, and to elect their own (Hungarian) local governments. In return, the Slovak government said the Constitution and the Bill of Rights made every discrimination on the basis of ethnicity illegal. They also maintained the following positions: the actual language law guarantees the right to use a minority language in official matters in regions with a minority population of more than 20 per cent; there are hundreds of Hungarian-language schools at every level; there are 26 Hungarian newspapers; 14 ethnic Hungarians serve as representatives in the 150-seat Parliament; and more than 100 million Sk in governmental support was spent on minority institutions in 1992. Slovak Hungarians' demands became sharper in 1993 after the Slovak government went back on their earlier promise to give Hungarians more rights. For example, in September 1993, the government backed out of agreements to allow towns with large Hungarian or other minority populations to post road signs in Hungarian and to allow the use of first names and women's surnames in the original language. The government's proposal to provide parallel optional education in both languages in mixed regions displeased the Hungarian political elite. Tensions rose after the government proposed a new territorial and administrative reform. This would have divided southern Slovakia along a north-south axis, thus lessening the concentration of majority Hungarian settlements in these new territorial units. The Hungarian parties organized several demonstrations and rallies, while sending petitions to the Council of Europe. Subsequently, the Regional Council of the Association of Cities and Municipalities (in southern Slovakia) proposed to establish a separate province with its own self-administration (December 1993). The High Commissioner for the Minorities of the CSCE (the Dutchman, Max van der

Stoel) mediated between the government and the Hungarian minority. However, escalation of the Hungarian minority issue into a more severe conflict (or war) between Slovakia and Hungary is not expected. This is due to a mutually perceived interdependence, with national/'ethnic' minorities in both countries, and shared international political interests (for example, continued Council of Europe membership and the wish for full NATO and EU membership) (Bombík and Samson, 1993).

With respect to international recognition, the Slovak government had some success, but there was little or no improvement in Slovakia's image abroad. On 30 June 1993, Slovakia was voted into the Council of Europe (with the Hungarian representation abstaining). This required many diplomatic initiatives. By early spring 1993, Slovakian resolve was being tested when a Council Resolution detailed minority rights. By May, there were still two issues: surnames and road signs. Slovakia accepted these two 'recommendations' (conditions for admission): liberalizing name rights and tolerating bilingual signs. On 13 July (two weeks after Slovakia's membership on the Council was approved), the Prime Minister rejected a law that would have allowed 'ethnic' minorities to register their names in their own language. The following day, the Transport Ministry ordered the removal of Hungarian-language road signs. Despite their strong wish for international acceptance, nationalist aspirations may hamper this goal. Since individual foreign states and international organizations continue to blame and reject Slovakia, this may increase attitudes favoring national preference, superiority, and nationalism. As one observer noted: 'The best policy [for Western Europe] to counter the nationalist danger is to facilitate a "return to Europe" of the Eastern European countries as much as possible' (Koch, 1992, p. 39). Meanwhile, the government gathers the evidence that a brand new state exists and that it is internationally respected. It gives much attention in the media to every bank agreement (for example, an IMF loan June 1993) and presents its every admission into an international organization as proof that HZDS's policies have world 'approval'. Slovakia's admission to the Council of Europe led Prime Minister Mečiar to speak of a 'certificate of maturity'. He said, 'We were subjected to severe scrutiny, and the result is that Slovakia unambiguously belongs to this democratic world' (*Prognosis*, 20 August 1993, p. 7). In January 1994, the Slovak government put in a bid for the 2002 Winter Olympic Games for the High Tatra mountains. Thereby, officials declared, 'Slovakia will become world-famous in a positive sense' and 'Slovakia as such would lose its inferiority complex' (*Prognosis*, 17 February 1994, p. 5).

National Political System Variables

Some unclear provisions in the Constitution (among others, regarding the President's rights and powers) have led to tensions between the different government branches from the beginning. Fragmentation of the ruling political parties (HZDS and SNS) negatively influenced governmental stability. Since early 1993, the Slovak government suffered from serious crises. The Economics Minister (the SNS chairman), Ludovít Černák, resigned while complaining about the power of former communists in government. Next, the Foreign Minister, Milan Kňažko, was sacked (April 1993). He left the HZDS and formed (with seven others) the Independent Club of Deputies. The government (originally officially having only 74 HZDS MPs out of 150 Parliament seats) lost more and more support. This resulted in its inability to govern. The SDL demanded accelerated elections, but HZDS refused. However, there were fewer than the 90 opposition seats needed for approval of pre-term elections. Six weeks' negotiations (aiming at reconstructing a coalition government between the HZDS and the SNS) failed by the end of July 1993. Parliament rejected several other proposals, including the parliamentary political parties' request to sign 'a pact of acceptance of the state's interests', to declare a chancellor's system of government, and to implement a presidential system. Parliament also rejected a State Defense Council bill, which would have allowed Prime Minister Mečiar to declare a state of emergency and to act without parliamentary approval or control. Furthermore, HZDS tried (without success) to change laws regarding the Slovak Parliament. These would have allowed dissenting MPs to be replaced in order to regain a parliamentary majority. At the same time, the opposition could not come up with any acceptable alternatives due to their own deep divisions. Later that year, other negotiations were successful. In October, a coalition government (HZDS and SNS) started to work. In the meantime, no elections were held. That autumn, a serious conflict broke out between the Prime Minister and the President. The President sought cooperation with all political parties, while the Prime Minister continued to mobilize his supporters at rallies, regularly insulting other politicians, especially the President. In December 1993, six SNS MPs refused to agree on the next year's budget. They then left the SNS fraction and established a new parliamentary group under the leadership of Černak (who was included in the government as an 'independent'). See Table 5.1 for a picture of party strength in the Parliament and Cabinet as of December 1993.

Illustrative of the charged political atmosphere was a mysterious incident which occurred in February 1994. A letter from Milan Panic (the Prime Minister of former Yugoslavia) to Mečiar trickled out. He thanked Mečiar for offering to sell Slovak arms illegally to the rump Yugoslavian regime to be used for the Serbian war effort. (This, by the way, would have violated the UN embargo on arms sales to Yugoslavia and would have decreased any chance for loans from the World Bank and the IMF.) The letter said that an 'offer for weapons and explosives from Russia . . . is much more favorable both in terms of quality and price.' Another remarkable part of the letter said, 'Despite my recent failure in politics, I really cannot accept the commission you have offered me for this transaction. By the way, speaking of commissions, I would like to remind you of a common business procedure: it is not customary to demand a percentage of the commission.' Finally, Panic wrote that he had tried to phone the Slovak Prime Minister but 'your phone was not working.' The next day, Mečiar interrupted his Cabinet meeting and called in the editors of all the major Slovak newspapers for a briefing. They were asked not to leak any information. However, the Czech News Agency obtained a copy of the letter and distributed it. In the Parliament, Mečiar said that this letter was a provocation against him (and the Slovak Republic). The letter was written in English, sent from Prague in November (three months earlier) to the Slovak President's Office, and (after translation into Slovak) mailed to the government. He criticized the President for mailing the letter instead of personally delivering it, which he said was 'probably to make it sound feasible that the information leaked from the government's office.' After his speech, the Alliance of Democrats of Slovakia chair, Milan Kňažko (co-founder of Mečiar's HZDS), said that he was convinced that Mečiar had written the letter himself. 'He's insane! He creates an enemy, then fear, and then he comes on as the great savior,' Kňažko said (Prognosis, 4 February 1994, p.5).

Table 5.1 Party composition of the National Council and the Cabinet of the Slovak Republic (31 December 1993)

Party	Parliament seats		Cabinet seats	
	N	%	N	%
HZDS	65	43	13	81
SDL	28	19		
KDH	18	12		
SNS	8	5	1	6
Coexistence/HCDM	14	9		
Alliance of Democrats	8	5		
National Democratic Club	6	4		
Independent*	3	2	2	13

* A parliamentary fraction can be formed if there are at the least five members.

In February 1994, Foreign Minister Jozef Moravcik and Deputy Prime Minister Roman Kováč left the government. They supported and joined a new parliamentary group, the Alternative for any Political Realism. Consequently, the government once again lost its parliamentary majority. In March 1994, the President addressed Parliament; he criticized the Prime Minister and pleaded for a coalition's majority government. Mečiar lost his Premier's seat when Parliament voted no confidence. A new government was established as a coalition of the opposition (two clubs of 'independent MPs', formerly HZDS representatives, SDL, KDH, part of the SNS, and the two Hungarian parties). Parliament decided to hold a pre-term election in September. Surely, this political system may be characterized as having undergone several serious crises.

Economic Variables

In the early 1990s, Slovakia's factories had been laying off thousands of workers. Once, these factories supplied the Warsaw Pact bloc with rocket launchers and tank parts. Civilian production has not filled this gap. (Recently, military production was restarted. ZTS Dubnica now produces a new howitzer and Konstructa Trencín has developed a cannon with a 40-kilometer range. They hope to sell the cannons to foreign customers, but the first recipients will be the Slovak army.) Over the last couple of years, Slovakia's economy has generally deteriorated. It is in severe crisis with (each year) rising inflation (30 per cent), rising unemployment (14 per cent), falling industrial output, declining exports (resulting in a negative trade balance), increasing budget deficit (5 per cent), and diminishing foreign reserves (*The Economist*, 7 August 1993, p. 30). In July 1993, the Slovak crown was devalued 10 per cent (although 30 per cent would have been more appropriate according to some economists; *The Economist*, 7 August 1993, p. 30). Privatization has rapidly slowed down. The governmental privatization program favored alternatives to voucher privatization. The opposition disagreed with direct sales of public property to foreign companies or to state managers. Many Slovak citizens suffered from the lower standard of living (in the middle of 1993, almost one-fifth of the families lived below the poverty line). See Table 5.2 for unemployment data on Slovakia, the Czech Republic, Poland, and Hungary.

Table 5.2 Unemployment and currency data in the Visegrad countries (Spring 1994)

	Inhabitants (in millions)	Unemployment February 1994 (in %)	Hard currency reserves in state central bank (in US $)
Slovakia	5.3	14.4	0.8
Czech Republic	10.3	3.5	6.2
Hungary	10.3	11.0	6.8
Poland	38.5	15.7	4.3

Source: Adapted from *SME, v strednej Europe* (We are in Central Europe, monthly SME enclosure), 28 May 1994.

Meanwhile, a small economic elite (including former Communist Party officials) is successful in reaping profits. There is a radical decrease in satisfaction with the standard of living (Bútorová, 1993). Many Slovaks are disappointed (in part, due to their unrealistic expectations) and are pessimistic about the future. As Pick (1993, p. 38) observed, 'This produced a high level of frustration, anger and helplessness . . . , increasing the need for an outlet for the frustration.' Aggression cannot be directed toward political elites (because they were popularly elected), nor toward the old scapegoats (the exploiting capitalists and capitalist nations). 'As a result, the formerly functioning enemy images [Hungarians and Gypsies] were reinstalled in their original form, after having been dormant for nearly 50 years' (Pick, 1993, p. 38). At the same time, the Czech economy grew under the leadership of Prime Minister Vaclav Klaus and President Vaclav Havel (who are responsible for what has been called Klaus' 'capitalism with a [Havel's] human face').

Politically Relevant Orientations

Many Slovaks are expected to have 'lost' their ideology (communism), which had helped them make sense of the complex political environment for many years. Other Slovaks may believe the loss of that ideology is a welcome relief. Some of our interviewees said that in place of three partly conflicting identities (Communist, Czecho-Slovak, and Slovak), there is now just one (Slovak). Alternatively, the Slovak identity is a source of tension for those who disagreed with having a separate Slovak state and were dissatisfied with its actual performance. Loss of ideology may result in an identity threat and feelings of anxiety. If this is true of many Slovaks, it may be expected that they will either reinforce already held identifications or will actively seek new identifications (Bloom, 1990). Options to replace communism are religion and Christian democracy, capitalism and liberalism, social democracy, democracy, or nationalism (including 'nation' instead of working class, national instead of class enemy, and national instead of socialist leaders). However, embracing religion and Christian democracy require a radical break with one's former life (including possibly irrational, new, or contradictory orientations). Moreover, religious socialization structures are relatively less well-developed. On the other hand, the Roman Catholic Church (mainly) may still have some credibility because it was the only institutionalized alternative to the communist ideology. Capitalism and liberalism may be attractive to only the very smallest or richest part of the population. Social democracy may be too closely associated with the former regime. Democracy may be related to the period of political disorder created after 1989. What may remain is a 'new left' (a combination of a revised communism, social democracy, and liberalism) or nationalism. The dominant SDL political elites in opposition until March 1994 are former communists, yet they only now identify themselves as social democrats. The dominant HZDS political elites in power through March 1994 ('neither socialist nor capitalist') mainly supported nationalist themes.

Sentiments about other Slovakian political tendencies show a generally negative trend. Almost half the population (Commission, 1993) said Slovakia is going in the wrong direction. The feeling of contentment disappeared after the revolution. The general economic situation in Slovakia and the overall household finances got worse in the last year (according to 69 and 63 per cent of the public, respectively; Commission, 1993). Only 32 per cent of respondents had hopes for a better life for themselves and their families. People expected that the general Slovak economic situation and their personal financial circumstances will worsen (55 and 54 per cent respectively; Commission, 1993). Slovaks' main fears and concerns are increasing crime and chaos (88 per cent); further restricting cooperation and contacts with the Czech Republic (78 per cent); foreign mafia 'laundering dirty money' in the country (74 per cent); political representatives' inability to represent ordinary people's interests (69 per cent); more economic decline and increasing poverty (68 per cent); heightened tensions with Hungary (66 per cent); a new wave of strikes and social unrest (60 per cent); lack of industrialized countries' interest in Slovakia (58 per cent); and 'selling out' Slovakia to foreign capitalists (57 per cent). Political distrust is increasing overall. A very small minority (8 per cent) were satisfied with the government's problem solving. Most people were (both before and after the revolution) alienated from political life (Malová, 1993a). A majority (59.4 per cent) said they cannot understand what is going on in 'our' politics (Bútorová, 1993).

National(istic) Socialization

Political leaders, churches, and mass media contributed to national(istic) socialization. HZDS' leader and (former) Prime Minister Mečiar's national entrepreneurship can be illustrated. He changed his statements on cooperation with the Czechs within one year (after the Slovak National Council dismissed him). At the end of 1990 (for the first time as the Prime Minister with the Public Against Violence nomination), he stated that, concerning the Czechs, 'Slovakia has always confirmed its interest in a common state' (Pehe, 1990, pp. 6-9). He also stated that 'the proximity in culture, language, geopolitical interests, and economic ties guarantee that our nations will want to live together' (interview with R. Havranova in *Práce Praha*, 25 August 1990). Just six months later, Mečiar emphasized 'national principles' and the importance of 'Slovakia's individuality' (interviewed with V. Popelka and I. Pokojny in *Pravda Bratislava*, 7 March 1991). Besides the leaders of HZDS and SNS, other party chiefs promoted Slovak national orientations. For example, the Christian Democratic Movement chief, Ján Čarnogurský, asserted that 'in Slovakia the idea of nationality plays an important part, it is alive and strong . . .' and that 'the idea of nationality as such is positive' (interview for *Československý rozhlas* in Bratislava, 7 June 1991, translated by the Foreign Broadcast Information Service in *FBIS Daily Report - Eastern Europe*, 10 June 1991, pp. 13-15).

The director of a human rights organization in Bratislava, Zuzana Szatmary, declared that 'the only problem is that politicians play the nationalistic card. The greatest fear for Hungarians among Slovaks is in the northern parts of the country where almost no Hungarians live. It is an artificial problem which is used to cover other problems' (interviewed for the Dutch newspaper *NRC Handelsblad,* 7 June 1993, p. 6). A Hungarian psychiatrist living in Slovakia's Bratislava added: 'The government in Bratislava manipulates the people, and the governments in Budapest and Bucharest do the same. Bratislava tells me continuously that I should demonstrate to be a loyal Slovak citizen. Budapest asks me to honor my Hungarian roots and culture' (interview for the Dutch newspaper *de Volkskrant,* 16 October 1993, supplement, p. 3).

Immediately after the establishment of the Slovak Republic, national symbols were chosen and, thereafter, promoted. They include (besides the language) a national coat of arms, flag, and anthem; a presidential residence (in the first months, a castle on top of a Bratislava hill; later, in response to a public debate, in downtown Bratislava, nearer the Parliament) with a detachment of guards; Devin Castle (in remembrance of the Great Moravian Empire); and the Jánošík story.

The national coat of arms shows three mountains and the Byzantium double cross. The same coat of arms was used during the Hungarian Empire as a symbol for North Hungary. It was also used in the 1940s Slovak state. The mountains (Tatra, Mantra, and Fatra) are symbols of the geography of Slovakia and represent those three rather separate communities. The cross symbolizes the bishops Cyrilius and Methodius who arrived in Nitra in 863 to preach Christianity. They also wrote a liturgy (in an earlier Slovak language) called *staro-sloviencina.* They are considered the founders of the first Slovak alphabet. The flag shows the pan-Slavic blue-white-red. The Jánošík story describes a medieval Slovak Robin Hood, who stole from the rich and distributed the proceeds among the poor. His coat of arms is pictured in Slovak folkloric dress. In 1994, new bank notes and a series of new state holidays were introduced (including 1 January for the Slovak Republic's creation in 1993; 5 July for Saint Cyril and Methodius day; 29 August for the Slovak national uprising; 1 September for approval of Slovak Constitution in 1992). The 28 October national holiday, commemorating the Czecho-Slovak Republic creation, was stricken from the list.

Not only do political leaders promote national(istic) orientations, but in September 1993, some religious leaders heralded President Tiso (whom the Czechs had killed) of the 1940s Slovak state as a martyr. They asked for his canonization. Both Slovak and Hungarian Christian Democratic Parties still argue over which language should be used during church services.

No analysis of mass media has been carried out regarding national(ist) messages. However, there are analyses of topics related to Jews, anti-Semitism, and the Holocaust in some Slovak periodicals (Bútorová, 1992; Dostál et al., 1993; and Bútorová, 1993).

The new political parties established their own newspapers immediately after November 1992 (Bútorová, 1993). Public Against Violence started to publish *Verejnost'*; the Christian Democratic Movement, the *Slovenský denník*; and the Slovak National Party, the *Slovenský národ* (a weekly, with 20 000 circulation in 1993). The government started the daily *Národná obroda* (published since 1990; its 80 000 copies were regularly read by 14 per cent in 1993). *Pravda*, the former Communist Party paper, is close to the SDL (regularly read by 34 per cent of the population in 1993). *Práca* is the daily trade unionist newspaper (in 1993, it claimed a regular readership of 26 per cent of the population). *Smena* was initially the Central Committee of Slovak Union of Youth daily (in 1993, its readership was 15 per cent of the population). The new *SME* (9 per cent of the readership in 1993) resulted from a split within the original *Smena*. It is the daily with the youngest readership. *Nový Slovák* is a daily with a nationalistic character (in 1993, it had a circulation of 20 000). The popular daily *Nový čas* (first published in 1991; in 1993, circulation was 270 000 copies; it has a readership of 39 per cent, with an above-average following among the 8- to 34-year-old age group) has no political party ties. Two other weeklies are the *Slovenské národné noviny* (7000 circulation) and the anti-Semitic *Smena* (80 000 circulation and 15 per cent readership in 1993).

In the daily *Nový Slovák*, the 1940s Slovak state was uncritically evaluated in an attempt to create a historical legend; the concept of 'Jew' often overlaps with that of 'enemy' and anti-Semitism is presented as an 'enemy's invention'. In *Smena*, the present Slovak state is presented as the restoration of the 1940s Slovak state. There, President Tiso is glorified as a martyr; Jews are characterized as aggressors and religious fanatics, who exert excessive influence in the world due to mysterious and impenetrable structures; and the anti-Slovak orientation is related to a Jewish 'world lobby'. In the *Slovenský Národ*, the 1940s Slovak state is evaluated positively, President Tiso is praised, the enemy image (who allegedly damages Slovak interests abroad) is constructed through raising the 'Jewish question', and a Jewish 'world conspiracy' is described. In the weekly *Slovenské Národné Noviny*, the 1940s Slovak state receives no criticism. The idea of the 'people' and their own statehood is considered to have supreme social value; however, a need for tolerance and understanding is emphasized. As Bútorová (1993, p. 76) concluded, 'the only openly anti-Semitic periodical among the analyzed periodicals published in Slovakia . . . is *Smena*. Others . . . also contain elements of anti-Semitism, but in most cases they have a covert form.' For example, in the *Národná obroda*, the 1940s Slovak state and its head are negatively evaluated, the 'Jewish question' is brought up as the most significant negative aspect of that state, and it criticizes the efforts to renew the tradition of a fascist Slovak state (pointing to the negative publicity it receives abroad), but it writes also that anti-Semitism in Slovakia is exaggerated abroad since minority rights are strictly respected.

CONCLUSIONS AND INTERPRETIVE PERSPECTIVES

We asked ourselves: Is there a growth in nationalism in Slovakia? And if so, what are the plausible explanations for its increase?

The attitude of nationalism is just one out of six relevant national attitudes (that is, national feeling, liking, pride, preference, superiority, and nationalism, *per se*), which must be acquired and developed sequentially since each incorporates the previous one and prepares for the next. Nationalism is the combination of a belief in a 'nation' with a common origin (kinship); the desire for congruence between 'nation' and state (including, if necessary, changing natural/state borders); the willingness to force other nationalities/'ethnic' groups/'nations' inside the country to leave; and the rejection of international cooperation.

We have not found any specific empirical study on national orientations (including nationalism) among the contemporary Slovak population. However, there are some survey- and content-analysis research data on nationalism-related political orientations (such as attitudes toward the 1940s Slovak state; attitudes toward the 1993 independent Slovak state; support for the nationalist party; support for a nationalist political leader; opinions on the desirable level of influence for nationalists on Slovak life; social distance; anti-Semitism; and belief in a foreign conspiracy). There are credible indications that about one-quarter to one-third of the Slovak population supported nationalism-related orientations between 1992 and 1994. However, the question whether or not there is a growth in nationalism (or nationalism-related orientations) cannot be fully answered because of missing longitudinal data.

Our basic assumption is that no one is born with nationalism intact. We distinguished three categories of variables: system, individual, and socialization. National orientations (in general) and nationalism (in particular) develop among individuals only when they are promoted. This promotion takes place in the national political socialization processes which each individual undergoes. Under the influence of charismatic national(istic) political leaders, a considerable part of the population may be encouraged to strengthen their national orientations and to move upwards in the depicted stage hierarchy. Many conditions for the growth of nationalism exist today in Slovakia. These include a severe economic crisis; a political and cultural crisis; an ideological (moral) crisis; and politicians, religious leaders, and mass media acting as 'nationalistic entrepreneurs'. There are good reasons to expect a growing nationalism in Slovakia in the coming years (that is, more individuals changing attitudes of national feeling, liking, and pride into national preference, superiority, or nationalism).

For Slovakia, much depends on whether or not the new broad coalition government (since March 1994) will survive and succeed in overcoming the economic crisis before another election. Political leaders/elites in the postcommunist transformation processes can have a relatively large influence on the future development of the political system and culture in their country. Mečiar, who is now opposition leader, still enjoys a lot of support among the population. He is well acquainted with effective strategies and techniques of campaigning and has a good chance to win another election. If he wins, resumption of his national superiority and nationalism promotion may be expected. We may also expect a revival of the old leftist ideology and growth of a 'new left'. Many Slovaks may end their present ideology and identity crisis by returning to their roots, thereby reinforcing their identification acquired after a long intensive communist socialization. They may prefer communist economic certainty to any free market uncertainty. Probably more Slovaks will opt for this ideology, but minus its undesirable parts, perhaps in combination with elements of social democracy and liberalism. The SDL, although presenting itself as social democratic, may become the representative of this 'new left'. This party may be more attractive thanks to the personality of its leader, Peter Weiss. He is also well-acquainted with effective strategies and techniques of campaigning (as confirmed in our personal interview with him).

The studies cited in this chapter as well as our own empirical work do not offer answers to all the empirical questions we asked at the start of this study. To understand the development of national orientations (including nationalism) in Slovakia, it is necessary to initiate a longitudinal panel study (preferably cross-national) into nationalism as well as the variables related thereto (in general) and the political socialization variables (in particular). Such a research project would make it possible to refine our nationalism theories. Moreover, it will make it possible to improve the public debate on the renewed growth of nationalism and its pacification in Slovakia and elsewhere. It may be inevitable, but we may regrettably fear it since nationalism 'tears the man out of all the identification groups that are characteristic for pluralist democracy and recognizes just one and only one: a nation and nationality. Each exclusiveness is aggressive, and so also the nationalistic one' (Kusý, 1992, p. 124).

REFERENCES

Bacová, V. (1992). 'Supporting and Retarding Factors of the Romanies' Integration in the Post-Communist Society of Slovakia', pp. 257-310 in J. Plichtová (ed.) *Minorities in Politics: Cultural and Language Rights.* Bratislava, Slovakia: Czechoslovak Committee of the European Cultural Foundation.

Benes, L. (1990). 'Danova reforma: Ale kdy?' (Tax reform: But when?) in *Hospodarske Noviny*, 29 August 1990.

Bloom, W. (1990, 1993). *Personal Identity, National Identity and International Relations.* Cambridge, UK: Cambridge University Press.

Bombík, S. and I. Samson (1993). 'Security Perspectives for Central Europe: A Slovak View', pp. 37-43 in *Perspectives*, Vol. 1.

Brzezinski, Z. (1989). 'Post-Communist Nationalism', pp. 1-25 in *Foreign Affairs*, Vol. 68, No. 5.

Bútorová, Z. (1992). 'Attitudes Towards the Jews in Slovakia', pp. 250-6 in J. Plichtová (ed.) *Minorities in Politics: Cultural and Language Rights.* Bratislava, Slovakia: Czechoslovak Committee of the European Cultural Foundation.

Bútorová, Z. (1993). *Current Problems of Slovakia after the Split of the CSFR.* Bratislava, Slovakia: Center for Social Analysis.

Commission of the European Communities (1993). *Central and Eastern Eurobarometer.* 'Public Opinion about the European Community.' Brussels, Belgium: Commission of the European Communities.

Csepeli, G. and A. Örkény (1993). 'Conflicting Loyalties, Citizenship, and National Identity in Hungary and Eastern Europe', pp. 118-32 in R. Farnen (ed.) *Reconceptualizing Politics, Socialization, and Education: International Perspectives for the 21st Century.* Oldenburg, FRG: Bibliotheks- und Informationssystem der Universität Oldenburg (BIS). And pp. 11-12 in *Studies in Cultural Interaction in Europe*, Vol. 3.

Dekker, H. and D. Malová (1994). *Nationalism: the Final Stage in the National Attitudes Hierarchy.* 'What Makes an Individual a Nationalist?' Leiden, the Netherlands: Department of Political Science, Leiden University.

Dostál, O., Z. Fialová, and M. Vasecka (1993). *Nacionalizmus a vybrané slovenské masmediá.* (Nationalism in the Slovakian News Media) Bratislava, Slovakia: Civic Institute.

FSU (Federal Statistical Office) (1992). *Volby 1992 HSFR.* Prague, Czech Republic: FSU.

Gerrits, A. (1992). *Nationalism and Political Change in Post-Communist Europe.* The Hague the Netherlands: Netherlands Institute of International Relations 'Clingendael'.

Griffiths, S. (1993). *Nationalism and Ethnic Conflict: Threats to European Security.* SIPRI Research Report No.5. Oxford, UK: Oxford University Press.

Havel, V. (1990). *Moc Bezmocných.* (The Power of the Powerless) Prague, Czech Republic: Lidové Noviny.

Kasinitz, P. (1992). *Caribbean New York.* Ithaca, NY: Cornell University Press.

Koch, K. (1992). 'Back to Sarajevo or Beyond Trianon?', pp. 34-43 in J. Plichtová (ed.) *Minorities in Politics: Cultural and Language Rights.* Bratislava, Slovakia: Czechoslovak Committee of the European Cultural Foundation.

Kusý, M. (1992). 'Collective Rights of Minorities', pp. 121-4 in J. Plichtová (ed.) *Minorities in Europe: Cultural and Language Rights.* Bratislava, Slovakia: Czecho-Slovak Committee of the European Cultural Foundation.

Malová, D. (1993a). 'Effect of Cultural Factors on the Promotion of the Relations of the Czechs and Slovaks', pp. 129-34 in D. Kováč (ed.) *History and Politics.* Bratislava, Slovakia: Czechoslovak Committee of the European Cultural Foundation.

Malová, D. (1993b). 'The Relationship Between the State, Political Parties and Civil Society in Post-Communist Czecho-Slovakia.' Paper presented to the East European Workshop at the Center for European Studies of Harvard University, Cambridge, MA, USA.

Masarykova Universita (1993). *Budováni státu.* (In 1992: Building of the State; from 1993: Building of the States) Reviews on Czechoslovak politics. Brno, Czech Republic: International Institute of Political Science, Masaryk University. Vol. IV, No. 1-12.

Misovic, J. (1993). 'Opinions on the Personalities of the Czech and Slovak History in the past and Today', pp. 24-7 in D. Kováč (ed.) *History and Politics.* Bratislava, Slovakia: Czechoslovak Committee of the European Cultural Foundation.

Ocovský, S. (1992). 'Interpretation of Statistical Data on Nationalities', pp. 94-9 in J. Plichtová (ed.) *Minorities in Politics: Cultural and Language Rights.* Bratislava, Slovakia: Czechoslovak Committee of the European Cultural Foundation.

Pearson, R. (1993). 'War and the Promotion of Nation-Statehood in Eastern Europe 1914-1945', pp. 61-71 in D. Kováč (ed.). *History and Politics.* Bratislava, Slovakia: Czechoslovak Committee of the European Cultural Foundation.

Pehe, J. (1990). 'Power-sharing Law Approved by Federal Assembly', pp. 6-9 in *Report on Eastern Europe*, Vol. 1, No. 51, 21.

Pick, T. (1993). 'Enemy Images', pp. 35-41 in D. Kováč (ed.). *History and Politics.* Bratislava, Slovakia: Czechoslovak Committee of the European Cultural Foundation.

Statistics Office of the Slovak Republic (1990). *Názory, Informačný bulletin Ústavu pre výskum verejnej mienky pri Slovenskom štatistickom úrade.* (Views. Information Bulletin of the Institute of Public Opinion Polls of the Slovak Statistics Office), Vol. 1, No. 3.

Statistics Office of the Slovak Republic (1993). *Názory, Informačný bulletin výskumu verejnej mienky, Štatistický úrad Slovenskej Republiky.* (Views, Information Bulletin of the Institute of Public Opinion Polls of the Slovak Statistics Office), Vol. 4, No. 1.

6   *Polarization and the Development of Political Ideology in Germany*

Race, Values, and Threat

Meredith W. Watts

ABSTRACT

In the formerly-socialist Central and Eastern European societies, the terms 'left' and 'right' had an indeterminate meaning, but those nations have rapidly changed their political terminology and consciousness. The young are particularly sensitive to emerging lines of conflict forming in the process of democratization. Using data on eastern German (GDR) youth from just before and after the *Wende* (the evaporation of the old GDR state), we examine the meaning of 'left' and 'right' with respect to attitudes toward 'values', and racism/xenophobia. There is evidence that the left-right continuum absorbed the lines of conflict over foreigners and refugees. This is particularly pronounced for the population of young eastern Germans, but signs of the 'ethnicization' of ideology are also present among adult eastern and western Germans. High anomie (an indicator of threat and social insecurity) is associated with antiforeigner and 'right' ideology as well. Differences between eastern and western Germany confirm that the 'targets' of xenophobia in the east are more closely related to economic threat than in the west, but the background of xenophobia is clear in both regions. In general, the results point to an 'ethnicization' of ideological conflict in which perceived threat and competition from out-groups play a significant role.

INTRODUCTION

Though the terms 'left' and 'right' have a history of some two centuries or more, they have shown a remarkable capacity for absorbing different shades of meaning as the substantive political content has changed (Fuchs and Klingemann, 1990). The same terms can represent a diversity of political meaning that will not only vary from one political culture to another, but within a given system as it undergoes historical change. 'Left' and 'right' of the early industrial era contained different content than the same terms in the late- or postindustrial era, reflecting shifts in the underlying lines of cleavage and conflict in developed societies (Inglehart, 1990).

Just as longer-term shifts from industrial economies based on classic 'work' and industrial production to societies based on 'service', 'information', and consumption produced changes in ideology, so too have the transitions of the formerly-socialist societies altered the understanding of left and right in those systems. Previously, whole societies could be officially characterized as 'left' (and others as capitalist and 'right'). More recently, the collapse of centralized state socialism has reorganized those terms. The newly emerging spectrum seems to be absorbing a mixture of industrial and postindustrial configurations. However, there are other phenomena that reflect the unusual transitional character of those societies; these phenomena may produce a left-right continuum whose content differs from that of their western counterparts. Eastern Germany plays a unique role in this process since it has elements of the older socialist system, a superimposed Western market system, and a few other unique elements which the transitional stress of unification and modernization has intensified. Of particular concern here is the emergence of political xenophobia, that is the manner in which animosity toward foreigners (*Fremdenfeindlichkeit*) in Germany may form a new basis for cleavages along ideological lines.

Hostility toward foreigners is not necessarily an essential part of the left-right continuum. Nevertheless, in various societies in may be absorbed into the spectrum and become an intrinsic part of its meaning. This was the case for apartheid in South Africa. It has appeared in various forms throughout the American past and has had many mutations throughout Western Europe as those nations react to increasing numbers of foreign immigrants, job-seekers, and refugees. Not only have conservative parties announced their concerns about these sometimes permanent visitors, but right-extremist groups have attempted to make 'foreigners' a central issue on the political agenda.

Let us now examine this potential 'ethnicization' of ideology in light of the following questions:

1. Have 'race' and the 'foreigner issue' become intrinsic cleavages in the German political culture?
2. Does xenophobia have different roots in the East than in the West? That is, does a formerly-socialist political culture react differently to the ethnicity issue than a Western democracy of longer duration?
3. Does age (or 'youth') of the citizen make a difference in the degree of sensitivity to the potential threat that foreigners may be perceived to represent?
4. To what extent are political values, anomie, and orientations toward economic competition related to one's ideology?

Germany is, of course, a unique situation for such an analysis. It now contains (within its post-October 1990 boundaries) a developed Western market-style society (the 'old' Federal Republic or FRG) and a transitional, formerly-socialist society (the five new federal states that comprised the former territory of the German Democratic Republic or GDR). This analysis will focus on the relationship of ideology and 'foreignness' in the period just before and immediately after formal unification. Using studies conducted in the former GDR, we will be able to test whether youth reacted with a particular sensitivity to the *Ausländer* (foreigner) theme and whether ethnicity played a special role in defining 'left' and 'right' in the postsocialist GDR. An all-German survey from the year after unification will allow a comparison of the 'ideologization' of foreignness in both regions of Germany.

However, before turning to the actual data, we must briefly look at the role and meaning of the left-right spectrum in the pre-unification FRG. We will have to touch on at least two other themes, though only tangentially: the role of values and value change in addition to the role of resentments and threat perceptions in political ideology.

THE POLITICAL LEFT-RIGHT SPECTRUM

What do political 'left' and 'right' mean? It is commonly understood that the answer to this question is relative to a given historical time and place. There is no single criterion of left and right which is valid for all societies and all historical periods (or even for all subsegments of a single political culture). In short, these meanings vary with a specific political context. Therefore, the real question is to find out what it means to people when they think of themselves and others as having a particular place on the left-right ideological spectrum.

Particularly relevant to this analysis is Barnes' discussion of rightist parties. It is a paradox, he suggests, at least in recent history in industrial societies. Youth has tended to be more leftist than older citizens (Barnes, 1991); yet, right-wing parties do not die out. Instead, they tend to change their content. Barnes suggests that the actual 'meaning' of the right (its agenda and content) takes on new forms with the passage of time. Thus, a 'right' always exists, but its actual substantive meaning may look different from one period to another. Thus, there may be no real paradox. That is, when 'youth' become older, the classic spatial continuum still has its metaphorical and communicative value. When people describe themselves as left or right, it conveys something meaningful to them. But in the case of 'leftist' youth, they grow up to (and help to create) a different right than existed when they were young.

According to Dalton, this change process involves a 'demobilization' of older political cleavages and the 'mobilization' of new political agendas (Dalton, 1991). If the changing lines of cleavage become firm, political parties will eventually modify their political programs. New parties may emerge to accommodate shifts in underlying lines of conflict in the society. These alternative lines of conflict do not completely replace one other, however. They may exist side by side. Some argue that this is happening in industrial societies where the older generations may hold on to the class conflicts of the industrial era, whereas postwar generations are more likely to reflect differences in current political values (Dalton, 1991; Inglehart, 1990). These arguments highlight two themes that are important to the current study. These are the likelihood of shifting meaning in the understanding of left and right and the possibility of generational differences in the emergence of new cleavages.

In the case of postwar Germany, there is evidence that the term 'left' has shifted its symbolic content from identification with the classic ideologies of the left (for example, socialism or communism) to concrete social issues (Wilamowitz-Moellendorff, 1993) in recent decades. The 'right' underwent less change during the 1970s and 1980s, retaining its identification with conservative-traditional values and with radical or extreme (right) political positions. Thus, though the left and right changed their meanings to a greater (left) or lesser (right) extent, the spatial metaphor remained useful as a generalized medium for expressing one's own political position and for understanding (at least in a general way) the general political positions of others. Fuchs and Klingemann (1990, p. 208) have estimated that 90 per cent of all (western) Germans understand the meanings of left and right. They can also employ them as a 'general code' for political discourse.

This political spectrum does not have to be a highly developed, intellectualized, system of thought. More important is the communication function of the left-right spectrum. This refers to its ability to serve as a 'generalizing mechanism' (Fuchs and Klingemann, 1990, p. 205) which facilitates understanding of the political world and which provides a framework for a mutually intelligible political discourse. In this view, the German 'right' is identified with (among other things) conservative social values, nationalism, and (in its extreme form) fascism. Minkenberg goes further to describe a 'value-based' redefinition of the right. He argues that 'postmaterialist' values typical of the German younger generations (particularly students and adherents of the so-called 'New Social Movements', such as feminists, peace and antiwar activists, and antinuclear group members) have produced a counter-reaction on the right. This new right brings together segments of the 'old right' (which was generally conservative, educated, and higher status) with lower-status groups (which are less educated and generally more 'materialist') (Minkenberg, 1992).

An important part of this argument is that this new cleavage does not follow the class-based political fronts of the industrial era. Instead, it often unites conservative elites and right-wing populists. They do not share common class interests, but they sense a common danger. A focal point of this danger in modern Germany is the presence of foreigners in increasing numbers; these increasing numbers imply not only an impact on the culture, but may be perceived (rightly or wrongly) to create economic burdens and job competition.

Elite segments of the population whose status, economic position, or cultural commitments are endangered may also share these perceived threats. But in Germany, as in many other late-industrial societies, there are also lower-status, less-well-educated members of this conservative reaction that perceive a large variety of such threats. These range from structural reorganization in the economy that threatens their positions, to a loss of trust in mediating institutions (for example, unions) to speak for their interests, to anxiety about a 'multi-cultural' society in which 'foreigners' compete for jobs, housing, and control over the symbolic 'culture' itself. These 'antimodernists' are likely to express their fears through a 'right'-oriented reaction to foreigners and to their domestic enemy, the 'multicultural' leftists, who favor a modern (or postmodern), pluralist, and culturally-differentiated society.

The result is a combination of 1) classic and elitist opposition to cultural change, 2) ethnic chauvinism and xenophobia expressed against 'outsiders', and 3) fearful confrontation with 'threatening' economic and cultural competition. These elements together have the potential for producing a realignment of the structure of political cleavages in the society. In such a realignment, elitist and populist elements of the society would coalesce to oppose outsiders who are defined on an ethnic basis. The result of these trends has, arguably, been a redefinition of the political spectrum. It produced an association of 'left' and 'right' with 'materialist' values and (to the extent that 'foreigners' are perceived to be a threat) an 'ethnicization' of the political spectrum.

The remainder of this analysis examines the extent to which ethnicity has, in fact, become important in defining the content of political ideology. We may hypothesize further that this tendency is likely to be more pronounced in the five new *Länder* of eastern Germany (where such perceived threats were greater) and among youth (who are more sensitive and responsive to political trends and are probably more readily motivated to orient themselves to new threats and challenges).

DATA AND MEASURES

Three separate surveys serve as the basis for examining the previously mentioned general working hypotheses in this analysis. The first two surveys from 1990 come from the former GDR Central Institute for Youth Research. The first survey dealt with 'Youth and Right-Extremism', the second with 'Youth and Hostility toward Foreigners.' Both reflected the traditional methodology of the Leipziger Central Institute in which nonrandom (but extensive) surveys were conducted. Subjects were pupils, students, and apprentices in the province of Saxony (usually in the cities of Leipzig, Dresden, and Chemnitz). These two studies (involving 1624 and 1228 young people, respectively) were the first systematic data available on right-wing and xenophobic attitudes of young eastern Germans.

The third study is the German General Social Survey (ALLBUS) conducted in both western and eastern Germany in 1991. It is referred to as the 'Baseline

Study' since it was the first of the ALLBUS series to be conducted in both regions of the united Federal Republic. The survey contains a large representative sample (n = 3058) of all Germans 18 years of age and older. The three studies are described in greater detail in Appendix A. Appendix B contains the original German text of the various items and scales in the analysis, along with an English translation.

THE LEFT-RIGHT DIMENSION AND RIGHT-WING EXTREMISM: EAST GERMAN YOUTH

If the terms 'left' and 'right' represent a generally understood, symbolic means for communicating one's social and political attitudes, the way people place themselves and others on such an imaginary scale should be correlated with other, more specific, political attitudes and values. If we know what those orientations are, we have a good indication of what the terms 'left' and 'right' mean in that particular political culture. In this first part of the analysis, we want simply to see how closely associated these factors were among young eastern Germans around the time of unification. Although these are admittedly not random samples of all eastern German youth, the samples are probably large enough to allow us some insight into the interrelationships among our various research factors. The nonrandomness gives us pause in trying to estimate exactly how many 'right' or 'left' youth there were in eastern Germany. Nevertheless, the data are reliable and valid enough to help us understand the theoretical and empirical relationship among the key variables that are of interest here.

Table 6.1 provides information on the extent to which left and right are associated with more specific measures of acceptance (or rejection) of right-extremist groups, ideas, and slogans. (See Appendix B for details of the various scales.)   The correlation coefficients are ranked from highest to lowest, indicating in descending order the amount of association that exists between each scale and the general left-right dimension.

The most powerful indicator of left and right seems to be 'nationalism', which consists of such statements as 'I am proud to be a German' and 'the Germans were always the greatest in history.' In contemporary German political discourse, both statements are associated with right-wing and nationalist sentiments far more so than similar statements might imply in other political cultures. Virtually as strong is acceptance/rejection of the right-extremist Republikaner party (REPS) and the degree of agreement with right-extremist slogans (for example, 'Germany for the Germans', 'Foreigners Out', and 'Jews are Germany's Misfortune'). Less closely associated, but still in a positive direction, are attitudes toward National Socialism (for example, 'Fascism also had its good points' and disagreement with 'I feel only contempt for Adolf Hitler'), positive evaluation of right-extremist and neo-Nazi groups (for example, the 'National Alternative' group, which was later banned, the Viking Youth, and the German People's Union), and identification with the Skinheads (who were popularly, though not always fairly, identified as a major source of antiforeigner aggression). Left-right self-identification is also associated with one's willingness to see a ban placed on right-extremist groups.

Table 6.1 Correlations of left-right self-placement with alternative measures of ideology, eastern German youth aged 14-20 (1990)

	Left-Right Self-Placement
Nationalism	.60
Republikaner	.58
Rightist Slogans*	.54
National Socialism	.46
Right Extremist Groups	.38
Skinheads	.36
Ban Right Extremist Groups	-.30

Sources: * Coefficient from Study B71, n = ca. 1100; all other coefficients are from Study B70, n = approximately 1624.

The fact that there is a correlation between the left-right continuum and, say, attitudes toward National Socialism, does not mean that all on the left are negative and all on the right are favorable toward the Nazi past. The former is almost universally true (that the left rejects the Nazi past), but the reverse does not necessarily hold. Those who rate themselves as 'right' may also reject the figures and emblems of the Third Reich, even though they find 'modernized' versions of its racism and nationalism attractive. At the symbolic level, the left rejects the Nazi era, contemporary neo-Nazis, and right-extremists; the right may distance itself from old and new Nazis, but accept elements of xenophobic nationalism or popular far-right slogans. This represents a redefinition of the left-right spectrum in which 'modern' xenophobia plays a stronger role than any explicit philosophical continuity with historical National Socialism and the Third Reich. Therefore, it may be argued that 'left' and 'right' play a role in generalizing and summarizing the primary elements of nationalism and xenophobia, but that explicit fascist ideology, while related, is less central to the practical ideological continuum that emerged among East German youth in the early days after the *Wende* (turning point).

LEFT-RIGHT AND XENOPHOBIA (*FREMDENFEINDLICHKEIT*)

As early as 1990, self-rating along a continuum from left to right obviously had assumed a meaning that included orientations toward right-extremist groups. The center of gravity of the xenophobic position did not seem to focus on an explicit ideology of National Socialism, but it might better be described as a kind of 'quasi-' or 'proto-ideology'. That is, this consisted of a loose collection of prejudices, beliefs, and vocabulary adopted in part from nationalistic, xenophobic, or right-extremist groups. This 'modernized' form of right-extremism does not require the Nazi past as a central metaphor but depends more on the concepts of ethnicity, fear of foreigners, and defense against real or imagined threats to culture and economy. Of course, this is implied in the correlations in Table 6.1, but Table 6.2 provides a more explicit view of the relationship between ideology and xenophobia.

The correlations are grouped according to three general concepts: affect (racism, prejudice) toward foreigners; perception of competition associated with foreigners; and approval of discrimination against foreigners. Each scale can be considered as measuring an aspect of the more general concept of political xenophobia.

Table 6.2 Correlations with left-right self-placement of eastern German youth aged 14-20 (1990)

	Left-Right Self-Placement
Prejudice	
Foreigners (-)	.68
Number of Foreigners (*)	.45
Competition	
Economic Competition	.67
Culture	.65
Discrimination	
Social Distance (high)	.64
Grant Asylum? (no)	.59
Discrimination/Expulsion (high)	.73

Sources: Study 1 (B70), n = 1624; Study 2 (B71), n = 1170 (actual n's differ somewhat due to missing data). Note: As a general rule, coefficients +/- .10 are generally significant at p < .001. The '*' indicates the coefficient is from study B70; all other coefficients are from Study B71.

As we might expect, 'left' and 'right' are closely associated with affect (emotional response) directed toward foreigners. The most general measure (positive or negative attitude toward 'threatening' foreigners, such as Turks, Poles, Vietnamese, Gypsies, and Africans) shows moderately strong correlations (.46 in one study and, in a somewhat modified form, .68 in another). A further test is the crudely stated item concerning the number of foreigners. In one study (see B71 in Appendix A), 39 per cent thought there were 'too many [foreigners] in East Germany', while an additional 15 per cent agreed with the more extreme statement that 'every one [foreigner] is too many'. In a second study (see B70 in Appendix A), the corresponding figures were roughly comparable at 35 and

10 per cent. However, left and right were not just related with an emotional reaction against foreigners, but also with a more intense perception that foreigners represented economic and cultural competition for Germans. This is consistent with the 'programs' and ideological fragments which right-extremist groups provided and which target foreigners as a concrete threat to jobs, housing, and other material resources in Germany. Antiquated racist biologism of the Nazi sort is scarcely a factor. Its replacements are to some extent 'normalized' through more legitimate-sounding attacks on the 'threat' which foreigners supposedly pose. This is both less 'racist' and more 'populist' than any archaic theory of racial purity. It is also more dangerous because it skirts the taboo of the Third Reich and 'sanitizes' the xenophobic semantics while translating it into a vocabulary of defense against troublesome 'outsiders'.

The next step in our analysis is to see whether xenophobic prejudice has a political form (that is, a desire to institutionalize discrimination). Logically, of course, it seems likely, though not necessary, that the negatively valued and feared group(s) should also be faced with a willingness to discriminate against them socially and politically. This relationship is tested in the last set of coefficients in Table 6.2. As might be expected, 'left' and 'right' are associated with a desire for social distance (in the workplace, in social surroundings, or in intimate relations), with a desire to limit their access to Germany's generally liberal asylum policy, and with a desire to actively discriminate against foreigners (releasing them first from jobs or expelling them from the country). In sum, the terms 'left' and 'right' among eastern German youth at the beginning of unification were strongly associated with xenophobic content, including the three dimensions of affect, perception of competition from the out-groups, and active approval of discrimination against foreigners who might either wish to enter as refugees or who were already there as part of the labor force.

Of course, the argument here is not that the topic of 'foreigners' fully defined the emerging left-right continuum in the former GDR region. 'Left' and 'right' no doubt have a variety of meanings and correlates that are not examined here. But the evidence is strong that attitudes toward foreigners did (at least in 1990 as formal unification began) play a significant role in the ideological self-perception of youth. This suggests that the traditional meanings of the left-right spectrum (for example, class conflict or anticlericalism) were likely to be less central in the changing eastern German political culture than the more-immediate and powerful issues of 'foreigners', nationalism, and ethnic chauvinism.

THE LEFT-RIGHT DIMENSION AND RIGHT-WING EXTREMISM IN THE GENERAL POPULATION

However central xenophobia seemed to be for the left-right self-identification of young eastern Germans, the youth studies cannot tell us anything about the prevalence of this ethnicization phenomenon among the general populations in eastern and western Germany. For a broader view, we must look to other data. Fortunately, an all-German survey was conducted in the following year (1991) to establish a basis for comparing developments in the two regions of the newly-unified Germany. This ALLBUS 'Baseline Study' does not allow a comprehensive test of all the components of left-right ideology that might be of interest here. However, the data do provide information on a variety of factors that allow a comparison of some of the correlates of left-right ideology in all of Germany. Here, we are interested in whether the eastern German youth were notably different from other groups and whether eastern and western Germans in general showed a different pattern of ideology with respect to foreigners.

These questions may be examined in two stages. First, we may analyze the general correlates of left-right placement to see whether the ideological spectrum is embedded in more or less the same social-psychological structure. Second, we can examine the relationship of these factors to xenophobia to see whether animosity toward foreigners has similar roots in the eastern and western regions. In both cases, it will be useful to look at youth separately for signs that the political discourse about foreigners affected them differently or more intensely than it did other Germans. Table 6.3 provides part of the answer.

In Table 6.3, we see significant differences between youth and adults, and between east and west, in acceptance of foreign migrants. Taking the western Germans first, it is perhaps surprising that the most 'acceptable' are not the Aussiedler of German origin, but potential workers from other parts of the European Union. In general, western Germans were more favorable toward, say, French, English, or Italian workers than to 'Germans' from Eastern Europe. The least popular potential in-migrants were the 'most foreign' - those seeking asylum and those job-seekers who came from outside the European Union. The rank order of acceptance is the same for youth and young adults in western Germany (see the first three columns, lower half of Table 6.3), but the younger generation somewhat more accepts foreigners than does the older. This is clear not only from the first two columns which display the levels of acceptance and rejection, but also the third column which measures the net difference between the acceptance and rejection expressed by each age group.

Table 6.3 Support for in-migration by type of migrant job seekers and region (western versus eastern Germany) and age (ALLBUS 1991)

	Total Sample					
	Western Region			Eastern Region		
Migrant Group	For	Against	Net	For	Against	Net
Ethnic Germans (*Aussiedler*)	22	10	12	16	12	4
Asylum Seekers	14	22	-8	15	15	0
EU Workers/Job Seekers	35	10	25	13	6	-13
Non-EU Workers/Job Seekers	11	28	-17	6	39	-23
	Youth/Young Adults					
Ethnic Germans (*Aussiedler*)	21	11	10	18	11	10
Asylum Seekers	25	14	9	17	16	1
EU Workers/Job Seekers	40	8	32	16	19	-3
Non-EU Workers/Job Seekers	16	22	-6	7	31	-24

Note: The 'for' category refers to unlimited in-migration, the 'against' category to 'complete prohibition'. The middle category is not neutral, but refers to certain 'limitations'. Thus, the net figures are only a rough measure of the 'center of gravity' of this public's opinion. The actual level of public affect is probably more negative than these data convey (depending on how such 'limitations' are publicly interpreted).

Eastern Germans showed a somewhat different pattern. For them, the essential dimension of conflict is the threat of foreign job seekers. Only the acceptance of asylum seekers is around the same level as western Germany; for all others, the levels of acceptance are lower. If there is any doubt that 'jobs' was the main factor for eastern Germans, the low ratings given western European workers (EU job seekers) makes it clear that the threat of more 'job seekers' in an unstable employment market was a more powerful reason for rejection than 'foreignness' *per se*. For non-EU job seekers, the combination of 'foreignness' and job threat was the most powerful combination of all, producing the highest level of rejection for any potential group of in-migrants. In short, the most critical mixture is that of the two dimensions: xenophobia on the one hand, fear on the other.

Eastern German youth, like their western German counterparts, resemble their broader regional political environment. To be sure, they seem to accept the various categories of potential foreign migrants more than do their elders; but the 'net' figures for both types of job seekers show that for youth and young adults (as with their parents' generation), the economic threat is powerful. The negative net figure for non-EU workers is a further sign of the explosiveness of the combination 'foreigner' plus 'competitor'. This convergence is powerful in the western region, but the 'multiplier effect' seems to be much more intense in the east.

Up to this point, we have been looking at evidence of differences in the way eastern and western Germans perceive foreignness and threat, but we have not yet begun to answer the question of how 'ideological' these threats are. We need now to look specifically at the relationship between rejection of in-migrants and our specific measures of political ideology. The relevant coefficients are presented in the first section of Table 6.4, under the heading 'foreigners'.

Table 6.4 Key intercorrelations with left/right ideology: eastern and western Germans, 1991

	Left/Right Self-Placement (High score = 'Right')			
	Western Region		Eastern Region	
	All	Youth	All	Youth
N (approximate) =	(1350)	(200)	(1350)	(150)
Foreigners				
Aussiedler	.03	-.08	.06	.12
Asylum-Seekers (refugees)	.19	.17	.12	.32
EU-Job Seekers	.10	.00	.03	.01
Non-EU Job Seekers	.15	.09	.14	.21
In-Migration	.16	.07	.12	.22
(*Zuzug* Index, sum of above 4 items)				
Values: General				
Traditional Social Values				
(Religion/Family/Neighbors)	.21	.23	.15	.21
Materialist Values (Inglehart Index)	.27	.23	.09	.02
Values: Work/Success				
Success (Machiavellianism)	.15	.11	.09	-.01
Success (Achievement)	.05	.10	.04	.12
Job Values (Useful)	-.01	.05	.03	.01
Job Values (Fulfilling)	-.02	.11	-.02	.05
Job Values (Income/Success)	.05	.18	.09	.12
Relative Deprivation/Resentment				
Anomie (high)	.19	.24	.21	.09
Educational Level (high)	-.16	-.13	-.10	-.18

Source: Adapted from ALLBUS Baseline Study (1991). Note: The ideology measure was self-placement on a scale from 1 (left) to 10 (right). 'Youth' = respondents 18-25 years of age. In general, coefficients +/- .10 are significant at the $p < .001$ level.

FOREIGNNESS AND IMPLIED 'THREAT'

As I have discussed elsewhere (Watts, 1994), not all 'foreigners' are perceived in the same way. They have distinctly different places in the German political culture, depending on their degree of cultural 'foreignness' and the threat of economic competition they represent. The ALLBUS data allow a comparison of the different types of 'foreignness' which eastern and western Germans perceive. The first section of Table 6.4 looks at four different categories of migrants: 1) the

Aussiedler (who are usually foreign nationals of German heritage) who have an automatic right to German citizenship; 2) asylum-seekers claiming refuge in Germany under Article 16 of the Basic Law (which offers refugee status to those who are politically persecuted); 3) workers and job-seekers from elsewhere in the European Union (that is, other Western Europeans); and 4) workers or job-seekers from outside the European Union. (A positive correlation coefficient indicates that respondents seeing themselves on the 'right' also tend to reject the arrival of non-German migrants.)

As would be expected from our previous analysis, the association between the 'right' and xenophobia is not limited to an allegedly hypersensitive eastern German youth. These data show that such sensitivity is also perceptible in the broader German population. Germans on the 'right' tend to reject outsiders, but there are differences according to the origin of the in-migrants. In both the western and the eastern regions, acceptance of *Aussiedler* is not specifically related to political ideology for the larger population (the correlations are near zero). There has been a tendency for the more politically conservative to favor in-migration of ethnic Germans. However, whatever leaning there was in that direction has become much less clear since unification. On the one hand, ethnic Germans are often perceived to be disadvantaged in the eastern European nations in which they live. This promotes a sympathy for them that goes beyond simple ethnicity and involves a degree of support for them as a politically-discriminated minority. On the other hand, various 'conservative' or even rightist Germans may not accept the *Aussiedler* as being 'really German' (consider the Volga German who may now wear a turban, come from Kazakstan, and speak no German). Status-threatened Germans may simply view the *Aussiedler* as another source of threat for social services, jobs, and housing. These complex reactions can be seen in youth's different reactions. In eastern Germany, youth on the right tend to reject the *Aussiedler*, while western German youth with rightist political leanings tend somewhat more to favor the return of ethnic Germans.

The reaction to asylum seekers (who are generally from non-Western, or less-developed nations) is more similar in both regions. The right's most universally rejected groups are asylum seekers. Eastern German youth are even more ideological in their rejection of refugees than are western German youth (with a correlation between ideology and rejection of .32). In fact, as we might expect from the earlier analysis, ideology for eastern German youth is more closely associated with rejecting foreigners than for any other subset of Germans we examined. This applies to the non-European-Union job-seekers as well.

Here, we see once again the difference in German acceptance of eastern and western European peoples. The West European job seekers are less enthusiasti-cally greeted by eastern German youth, but this acceptance is not significantly 'ideologized' (that is, correlated to the left-right political spectrum). This is also the case for western German youth. Ethnic sensitivities seem most to fit into an ideological framework for youth when the target group is non-European. The politicization of ethnic migration seems to be the highest in the former GDR, among youth, and directed against refugees and potential workers. This can be seen clearly in the summary coefficients for the overall index of in-migration.

To summarize, 'foreigners' are the most ideologized in the following order: eastern German youth, followed by eastern and western Germans generally, trailed by western German youth. The foreigners most ideologized in the western region are the asylum seekers and non-European workers, then European job seekers. For the eastern region, the most politicized groups are the asylum-seekers, then the non-EU workers. We cannot argue that the measures available are the best indices of attitudes toward foreigners that we might find, but what evidence we have indicates that those in the western and eastern regions reacted differently and that youth reacted with a distinctive sensitivity that was different in each region (more tolerant in the west, more xenophobic in the east).

Thus far, we have examined the extent to which foreignness is ideologized among eastern German youth and compared the eastern and western Germans with respect to the way they react to (and ideologize) various types of potential in-migrants. In the following section, we move to the next step, which is to focus on additional background elements that are related to acceptance or rejection of these foreigners. In doing so, we will look for common elements as well as differences between the two regions of Germany. As before, the emphasis is on the early unification period (in this case, 1991) when hopes and fears were both high, but also when residual differences between the social and political cultures of the two regions were perhaps greater than they would ever be in the future. For this analysis, we call again upon the German Social Survey (ALLBUS).

IDEOLOGY, VALUES, AND STATUS

One might have thought that the functional definition of 'conservatism' would have changed drastically in the eastern region of Germany. No doubt, it did in many respects. But in the re-emergence of a left-right political schema, we see signs of a familiar theme. In the second section of Table 6.4 (labelled 'Values...'), it is interesting to note that the 'traditional social values' of religion, family, and neighbors are about equally related to the conservative end of the spectrum in both eastern and western Germany. Such values were prized in the east and were, at least some argue, associated with communitarian or collectivist values. But 'community' is not just a socialist value. In fact, it appears in both regions to have been about equally associated with 'conservative' political self-placement. Thus, in spite of nearly a half-century of separation in different economic and political systems, such traditional social values as religion, family, and community ('neighbors') remain significant ideological anchors in both regions of Germany. Among younger and older, east and west, this traditional cleavage between 'left' and 'right' remains and is carried into the contemporary understanding of the left-right continuum.

One might, therefore, expect that the distinction between 'material' and 'postmaterial' values (using the Inglehart Value Index measure) might show a similar pattern. But 'material' values such as the preference for security and economic stability (as opposed to the 'postmaterial' values of political participation and personal fulfillment) are associated with political conservatism in western Germany only. The association in the east is small and insignificant for adults and youth. This may mean either that the understanding of 'left' and 'right' was still strongly anchored in traditional, materialistic concerns for economic stability for eastern Germans; or that various political elements (from 'old' to 'new' left, including newly 'conservative' groups) were not different among themselves in the way they valued participation and individual fulfillment (though they may have had different things in mind); or, more simply, that the modernization and affluence associated with the development of postmaterial values (Inglehart, 1990) were simply not available to most eastern Germans at the time of the survey.

The question of work-related values presents an interesting problem. There is clearly evidence that eastern German youth underwent a change in personal values and goals beginning roughly in the mid-1980s. This included a decline in enthusiasm for 'public' commitment in favor of significant increases in personal and hedonistic goals (advancement, income, recognition, and friends). This 'modernization', or 'anticipatory Westernization' produced a shift in goals and values that brought eastern German youth closer to their western counterparts.

Heitmeyer has focused on the darker side of this process, arguing that an exaggerated version of competitive, Western market values has produced an increase of right-wing extremism in western and eastern Germany (Heitmeyer, 1987 and Heitmeyer et al., 1992). He, thereby, refers to the development of a personal ideology that internalized the beliefs that economic struggle, manipulation of others, and 'success at any price' are necessary for success. In an extreme (even pathological) form, this 'ideology' provides the basis for extrapunitive aggression against competitors (for example, foreigners or the 'socially weak'). Although he is not clear about how the process occurs, he suggests that the market ideology is 'transformed' or 'deformed' into a right-wing version that is both Social Darwinistic (in its contempt for the weak and its emphasis on struggle and competition) and hierarchical (in its emphasis on 'natural' differences, dominance, and a general tendency toward racism).

It is not possible to test for the full 'syndrome' that Heitmeyer describes, but the ALLBUS data do allow us to test whether such a stylized version of the Western market system (often referred to in Germany as the 'elbow' society) is, in fact, associated with the right end of the political spectrum. Though it seems plausible enough that this would be the case, we wonder about the particularities of the eastern German case. It seems equally plausible that the intensity of economic threat would affect eastern Germans of all political colors in a similar fashion, producing a widespread (but not necessarily ideological) belief in the need for using sharp elbows to cope with the outcomes of the *Wende*.

As it turns out, however, the results are partly consistent with the prediction and partly contrary. The 'Machiavellian' version of the success scale (in Table 6.4) is generally associated with the right side of the political spectrum. This implies that those rating themselves as 'right' are also more likely to believe that one must be ruthless and manipulative. These individuals also place a high value on the goals of income and success. What is contrary to the Heitmeyer prediction is that the association holds for western Germans more so than for eastern Germans and for the general public more so than for youth. In other words, it is the eastern German youth for whom this type of economic and social 'Machiavellianism' is the least related to ideology, even though the Heitmeyer theory seems to imply that it should be particularly high for them.

Contrary to expectations, then, 'Machiavellian' success is more ideologized in the west than in the east and more among adults than youth. What is more ideologized for German youth in both regions is the perception that success is achieved through talent and achievement (for example, education, intelligence, and hard work). This is perhaps not surprising, but it is contrary to the general prediction that a perverse market-economy aggression should be associated with the right. Instead, what we find is the beginnings of a conventional, achievement-oriented, conservatism; and we find it among the youth. The association between the 'right' and a 'brutal' success-orientation remains more western and 'older' rather than younger. Exaggerating somewhat, we might say that what is typical of youth is not the ideologization of competitive ruthlessness, but rather of adaptation to 'traditional' achievement values.

There is additional, but nonconclusive, information concerning job values. We might expect that 'fulfilling' work would be more important to the so-called 'postmaterialist' left and that 'income and success' would be less important. However, this is not the case. The measures we have here show a more traditional pattern. Ideology is scantly related to the value placed on doing 'useful' work. Instead, it is related to the need for 'fulfilling' work among western German youth. 'Income' and 'success' were associated with the political right in both east and west.

Obviously, this does not constitute a tidy test of the presence of material and postmaterial values. However, it does point to differences between youth and adults as well as between east and west. The emerging pattern for eastern youth is for a self-perception as being on the political right to be associated with material values of income and success. Among the western youth, we do see a slight connection between 'fulfilling work' and the right (not the left). Here, we might actually have expected to find the association to be the reverse (with fulfilling work being associated with the 'postmaterialist left'), but it appears that a more subtle analysis is needed to clarify this relationship. It may be that the notion of 'fulfillment' is associated with a general achievement orientation. The scale items (Appendix B) refer to having interesting work, being able to work independently, and being able to develop a sense of responsibility. This may appeal to a 'postmaterialist' orientation toward personal growth, but it can also be read as the development of executive or management skills. These different contextual readings of the scale items may muddle any supposed relationship with materialist/postmaterialist values.

Our last analysis in this area concerns a broad category that might be loosely described using the terms 'relative deprivation' and 'resentment'. These terms are used in a general sense and do not imply that we can evaluate relative deprivation theory from these data. Instead, we want to point out an explicit connection to the relationship we found earlier in this analysis between left-right ideology on the one hand and perceived threat and vulnerability on the other. Once again, we can frame the question in the terms of Heitmeyer's argument. This time, we examine his thesis (Heitmeyer, 1987, 1991) that personal and social disorientation, collapse of values, and uncertainty play an important part in the growth of right-extremism and violence among youth.

Heitmeyer draws a clear developmental connection between social disintegration at the macro level and emergence of the right-extremist ideology on the micro level. It is possible to test this proposition (at least at the individual level) if we examine the relationship between rightist ideology and the perception of disintegration (which we operationalized here through the classic concept of anomie). Assuming that youth and adults in Germany can place themselves fairly accurately on such a left-right scale (Fuchs and Klingemann, 1990; and our analysis above suggest that they can) and assuming that the feeling of social normlessness and unpredictability is an important aspect of disintegration, then there should be a positive association between ideology and the anomie scale.

In short, the question is whether Germans seeing themselves as 'right' should feel a higher degree of anomie. According to our data, they do. Adults in both regions and western German youth who place themselves on the political 'right' feel a threatening loss in values, social organization, and future predictability. What is inconsistent with this theory is the lack of association for the younger eastern Germans who, overall, were probably more deeply threatened and disconcerted than those in the west. Obviously, there is not a simple relationship between social dislocation and ideology. We can only speculate as to why the proposition fits eastern German youth less well than the other groups. It might be that eastern German youth saw the perceived normative breakdown and threat as a positive opportunity and, therefore, did not produce the complex of threat and xenophobia. Or it may be that anomie was so widespread that it affected left and right, xenophobic and nonxenophobic, alike (thus reducing the predicted correlation). Or there may be a problem either in the measurement of 'education' for the eastern German youth or in the meaning of educational level itself during the German transition. All we can say at this point is that the correlations between anomie and education are generally in the predicted direction (western Germans = .19, and youth = .25; eastern Germans = .13), except for eastern German youth for whom the association was nonsignificant at the .07 level.

Aside from this puzzling finding for eastern German youth, there is a broader matter to be considered in the relationship between anomie, education, and ideology. Here, we may consider an explanation that begins with the negative impact of 'disintegration' phenomena (anomie), but attempts to focus more on the personal resources that individuals have at their disposal to cope with social and economic threat. To see how this might work, we can first look a bit more at the anomie scale and then at education as a coping resource.

Anomie (at least as measured by the ALLBUS scale) is at least, in part, an indicator of perceived social stress. This involves a belief that the situation of common people is getting worse, that the future is so bleak that it is irresponsible to have children, that politicians do not care about the common people, and that most people do not care about their fellow human beings. This attitude also implies that the individual does have the skills or resources to cope with external stressors. Success is unpredictable and even basic survival is problematic.

In this view, anomie reflects a general feeling that one is not equipped with the resources required to be successful or that one does not know or cannot employ the tactics and talents that are likely to be needed. Therefore, the environment is threatening and difficult to master. In such a situation, 'success' and 'income' will be highly valued, but the path to them is likely to be unclear. In the absence of the necessary cultural resources (such as education) and social resources (such as social networks or 'contacts'), one is likely to see success as a result of what one lacks (such as connections, luck, and material resources). An important aspect of this type of anomie is the inability to conceptualize the cultural and social resources that are needed. It is simultaneously a projection of a simple (and tendentiously brutal) 'understanding' that manipulation and disregard for others is the key to success. As a projection, it also is a refracted view of the values that one believes are dominant.

While we cannot test this alternative formulation in any detail, it is possible to examine one relationship that would be predicted from it. That is, if anomie reflects a perceived lack of resources, then a higher level of education should reflect a greater acquisition of resources and, therefore, be negatively associated with anomie. Furthermore, education should be moderately associated with leftist ideological self-placement.

In Table 6.4, educational level is indeed associated with ideology and, of course, negatively associated with anomie; that is, the better educated (who have more resources for achieving success) are less anomic. They are also more likely than the less advantaged to favor 'postmaterial' over 'material' values, and to favor 'usefulness' and 'fulfillment' as intrinsic elements of a job. The better educated are also less likely to favor 'Machiavellian' strategies and more likely to favor 'performance' criteria for success. Of course, this is consistent with the fact that they possess more of these resources and, therefore, see the environment as less threatening, unstable, and unpredictable. Unlike the correlations with anomie, however, the hypothesized association of education with ideology is consistent for all groups, including eastern German youth. This tends to confirm our argument that the 'right' among the broad German public is, at least under current conditions, associated with a poorer resource base for coping with economic and social threat.

This brings the discussion back to the central question of xenophobia and its relationship to ideology and other personal orientations. I have argued elsewhere (Watts, 1994) that ideology is a central factor in xenophobia because it can, in its rightist variations, politicize ethnicity and cultural differences. But this politicization is, in itself, not enough to energize a desire for political discrimination or exclusion. Required also is a belief that foreigners are harmful, threatening, and 'to blame' for perceived economic and cultural competition. This threat provides a motivation to discriminate, exclude, or expel. In the following section, we turn to the factors associated with one aspect of *Fremdenfeindlichkeit*, namely the degree of acceptance or rejection of 'foreign' groups' in-migration.

FACTORS ASSOCIATED WITH DISCRIMINATION/EXCLUSION

Elsewhere, I have presented evidence supporting the proposed correlation between threat and political xenophobia (Watts, 1994). It would be appealing if this specific relationship could be directly replicated here. Unfortunately, however, the ALLBUS survey does not contain all the needed measures. (For example, there is no good measure of threat.) By making a few allowances for the indirectness of some of the ALLBUS measures, however, we can construct at least a general test of this association between ideology, threat, and discrimination. For that, we have examined in Table 6.5 most of the same factors presented in Table 6.4, except that what we want to 'explain' is not ideology (as in Table 6.4), but 'acceptance/exclusion' of foreigners.

Noticeable once more is the fact that the association between this aspect of *Fremdenfeindlichkeit* and 'rightist' self-identification is the highest among eastern and the lowest among western German youth. Once again, this points to the fact that 'foreignness' is (or, at least, was in 1990/91) more politicized among young Germans in both east and west. Anomie and material/postmaterial values were associated with ideology, but the association with ethnic rejection is even stronger and more consistent. Simply stated, the more anomic the individual, the greater the tendency to reject in-migrants. The same is true of values: the more 'materialist', the higher the rejection of in-migrants.

I cannot test with these data whether there are long-term socialization differences that have produced variations by region. Various analysis 'after the Wende' point to residual differences between youth in east and west. That is no doubt also the case with values and a variety of sociopolitical attitudes. But in the case of hostility toward foreigners, there is a particularly strong reason for us to emphasize differences in the concrete challenges that Germans face. The intensity of the unification process (including the high level of threat and motivation that it produces) creates a different situational environment for youth and adults as well as in eastern and western regions.

Table 6.5 Correlations with *Zuzug* index: eastern and western Germans, 1991

	In-migration (*Zuzug*)*			
	Western Region		Eastern Region	
	All	Youth	All	Youth
N (approximate) =	(1350)	(200)	(1350)	(150)
General				
Ideology (right)	.16	.07	.12	.21
Anomie (high)	-.14	-.13	-.16	-.16
Values: General 'Traditional'				
(Religion/Family/Neighbors)	.05	.01	.02	-.06
'Material' (Inglehart Index)	.32	.10	.22	.19
Values: Work/Success				
Success (Machiavellianism)	.02	.02	-.03	.01
Success (Achievement)	-.05	-.08	.00	-.00
Job 1 (Useful)	.00	-.14	-.01	-.12
Job 2 (Fulfilling)	-.08	-.09	-.05	-.14
Job 3 (Income/Success)	.16	.07	.13	.10
Relative Deprivation/Resentment				
Subjective Class (high)	-.17	-.12	-.19	-.18
Fair Share (yes)	-.18	-.17	-.14	-.18
Educational Level (high)	-.32	-.31	-.22	-.18

Source: Adapted from ALLBUS Baseline Study (1991). Note: 'Youth' = respondents 18 to 25 years of age. This study did not include respondents younger than 18; the grouping here is older than the 'youth' in the earlier (there, 14 to 20 years of age) tables.

*'In-migration' is the summed index (as in Table 6.4) of attitudes, such as those toward asylum seekers and non-EU job seekers.

On the one hand, high anomie measures fears of instability, unpredictability, and social alienation/normlessness. On the other, the values scale indicates, among other things, the preference for material stability over other personal goals. Both of these factors are probably more intensely threatened in the east than in the west and among those with fewer social resources for coping with the challenge. 'Foreigners' have been defined as out-groups that directly affect such sensitivities and 'threaten' these needs for stability and predictability.

This is not the result of 'conservatism' *per se*. This interpretation is supported by the fact that 'traditional values' are not associated with rejection of foreigners. Placing high value on one's intimate 'in-group' (family, relatives, and neighbors) does not necessarily imply rejecting foreigners, but a threat from specific outsiders does. Anomie and 'material' values, therefore, appear to measure this connection to threat, while traditional values represent the conventional and less xenophobic face of conservatism. The danger which the ideologization of ethnicity represents is not in its possible connection with traditional values. What is more important is the degree to which the political 'right' may come to represent as xenophobia and hostility toward foreigners, which are less benign factors.

There are other tests we can make of the association between the 'benign' and 'malignant' aspects of the right. For one of them, we can call on Heitmeyer who has argued that certain central themes from the capitalist market economy are a major source of right-extremism. However, the relationship described here is more consistent with a 'normal' market- and achievement-oriented conservatism than with the Social Darwinist version he portrays. Contrary to Heitmeyer's view (1987, and Heitmeyer et al., 1992), 'Machiavellian' success orientations are not directly related to xenophobia. What is related, at least for youth in both regions, is the wish for 'useful', socially-productive work. A tendency to reject foreigners is associated with a de-emphasis on social usefulness and (for all German groups, adult and youth/young adults) with an emphasis on 'income' and 'success' as the most important aspects of work. This is not consistent with a theory of generalized Machiavellian dominance and manipulation, but rather with a personal need for success and achievement. To be sure, foreigners may threaten one's personal success and this may be enough to produce a 'political xenophobic' reaction, but there is no available evidence that the mechanism for xenophobia is a ruthless Machiavellianism.

DISCUSSION

Though it is often argued that the classic terms 'left' and 'right' lost their meaning in Eastern Europe during the early stages of transition from socialism, these data show signs that the classic left-right distinction 'absorbed' (in the ideological space of young East Germans) the intrasocietal cleavage which conflict over the presence of non-Germans in the nation has created. In the process of unification, there was a tendency for ideology among eastern youth to be 'ethnicized'. Shortly after the *Wende*, there emerged a strong association between ideology and beliefs about foreigners. The relationship was most certainly associated with prejudice and stereotypical thinking ('xenophobia'), but this was not the classic racism of the Nazi era. Its motor force in the mass public seems far more to be a perception of economic and cultural threat.

Xenophobia becomes politicized through this combination of 'ideologization' and the perception of threat. Both elements provide a cognitive and emotional connection between those defined as 'foreign' as well as approval for possible discriminatory actions that might be taken against them. It is this development of a 'political xenophobia' that represents an important aspect of what, in German, is referred to as *Fremdenfeindlichkeit* (hostility against foreigners).

To be sure, the objects of political xenophobia are not random. They are defined in conjunction with an ethnic chauvinism and racial prejudice. (The targets tend to be nonwhite, non-Christian, or non-Western.) But that is only one part of the story. The real intensifier is the sense that these foreigners constitute an economic threat, provide competition in the job and housing markets, and absorb more German resources than they produce. This explosive combination represented in the phrase 'foreign competitor' seems to be the prime motivation in the development of political xenophobia.

'Foreignness' is also not an absolute, easily definable factor. It is subject to a process of cultural definition. It seems to vary with the degree of presumed ethnic similarity and the nature of the perceived threat. Yet, these factors are, themselves, subject to a process of political and cultural definition. For the western Germans, ethnic Germans from Eastern Europe are more acceptable, as are Western European job-seekers. For eastern Germans, job seekers of all sorts are negatively viewed. All Germans are united in their ideologization of the most negatively viewed groups of all: the non-Western job seekers and asylum-seekers.

At the individual level, there is a set of attitudes and perceptions that are associated with ideology and xenophobia. Rightist ideology is associated with rejection of foreigners, but also shows an association with traditional social values (positive) and with postmaterialist values (negative). A hypothesized positive association between ideology and Machiavellian achievement values was only loosely supported (for the west), while traditional achievement values seemed to be associated with the conservative end of the scale for youth in both German regions. As hypothesized, anomie was associated with the political right, though not (as might be expected) for young eastern Germans.

The particular interpretation of 'education' used here may deserve a further explanation. The association of higher educational attainment and the center-left end of the political spectrum has been a consistent research finding for at least the last two decades. In fact, it has been so constant (at least for the younger generations) that it is often forgotten that in an earlier, more elitist era, advanced education was more closely associated with higher status and greater conservatism. A vast array of literature attests to this association, which is strongest for the young and well educated. (In Watts et al., 1989, Chapter 7, this phenomenon is clearly demonstrated among older and younger female generations. The better educated older women are more conservative, while in their 'daughters'' generation, education was associated with more leftist politics.) Thus, the 'prediction' that education is associated with tolerance and center-left ideology is not only common, but it is multiply predicted from a variety of positions and scarcely of much interest when taken alone. However, without denying any of the various other effects of education, it is useful in the context of the current discussion to emphasize the utility of education as a resource for coping with any dynamic and threatening social situation.

If this resource-based proposition has any value, it is in its emphasis on the combined effects of education (which is a cultural resource), anomie (which is related to a perceived ability to cope), and xenophobia (which is associated with lower resources and greater feelings of helplessness and resentment). In contemporary Germany as in other industrial societies, higher education has (at least since the expansion of educational opportunities of the 1960s) been associated with 'postmaterial' values and with less, rather than more, anomic threat and uncertainly. In contemporary Germany, 'anomie' is not associated with leftist criticism of the dominant culture, but more with a sense of threat and apprehension that comes from social insecurity. Therefore, this anomic form of alienation tends to be associated with xenophobia (which is, itself, a reaction to threat) and with the 'right'. In this view, contemporary anomie is part of a complex of insecurity, xenophobia, and the ethnicization of ideology.

It may be that anomie may be poorly measured for young eastern Germans or that the phenomenon is too widely diffused to have a specific ideological connotation for them. This, however, remains a puzzle, as does the absence of a significant relationship between postmaterialism and ideology among eastern Germans in general. If the problem is not at the level of measurement, then there is a truly interesting phenomenon at work here. Ideology in the east may not, as yet, be associated with such phenomena as fear of normative and social disintegration (anomie) or with the development of postmaterial values. Further development in this direction is likely to occur and probably will have significant consequences for political party structures. We may see, as Dalton (1991) argues, a process of demobilization of old cleavages and mobilization of new ones. These data suggest that the mobilization of the east is not (or, at least, was not in 1990/91) associated with fears of macro-level social disintegration or with postmaterial value change (as they were in the west).

However, there were clear signs of mobilization over the issues of foreigners, ethnic chauvinism, and nationalism. This points toward a lag in 'modernization' of the political cleavage structure, combined with a threat-based political xenophobia. We should not describe this *Fremdenfeindlichkeit* as a residual of the German Nazi past (though this is certainly the case for some groups), but as a 'modernized' version of xenophobia based on a sensed threat and competition. In the east, the question is whether the cleavage structure will develop into a modernized western form or whether it will (at least for a time) become more 'fixed' in the cleavage which political xenophobia represents.

For the west, the question is whether the incipient cleavage which xenophobia represents will increasingly define the political spectrum. Here too, it is of importance whether ethnic chauvinism and nationalism become central figures in the ideological structure and, in a more general sense, how they come to be related to the other cleavages in the overall German political culture. This analysis did not conduct a comprehensive examination of all the conceptual dimensions that are related to the left-right spectrum, but the results here suggest that the 'foreigner' issue may be on the way to becoming an important feature in the German ideological cleavage structure (cf. Fuchs and Klingemann, 1990; Wilamowitz-Moellendorff, 1993). It is unclear whether this cleavage will be further 'mobilized' (Dalton, 1991), thereby creating additional changes in party programs and party system structures.

REFERENCES

Barnes, S. (1991). 'On the Electoral Persistence of Parties of the Right', pp. 233-44 in K. Reif and R. Inglehart (eds.) *Eurobarometer: The Dynamics of Public Opinion*. New York, NY: St. Martins Press.

Dalton, R. (1991). 'The Dynamics of Party System Change', pp. 215-55 in K. Reif and R. Inglehart (eds.) *Eurobarometer: The Dynamics of Public Opinion*. New York, NY: St. Martins Press.

Friedrich, W. and W. Schubarth (1991). 'Ausländerfeindliche und rechtsextremistische Orientierungen bei ostdeutschen Jugendlichen' (Hostility Toward Foreigners and Right-Extremist Orientations Among Eastern German Adolescents), pp. 1052-65 in *Deutschland Archiv*. Vol. 24.

Fuchs, D. and H. Klingemann (1990). 'The Left-Right Schema', pp. 203-34 in M. Jennings and J. van Deth (eds.) *Continuities in Political Action: A Longitudinal Study of Political Orientations in Three Western Democracies*. Berlin, FRG/New York, NY: Walter de Gruyter.

Heitmeyer, W. (1987). (3rd expanded edition 1989). *Rechtsextremistische Orientierungen bei Jugendlichen*. (Right-Extremist Orientations Among Youth.) Weinheim/Munich, FRG: Juventa.

Heitmeyer, W. (1991). 'Die Widerspiegelung von Modernisierungsrückständen im Rechtsextremismus', pp. 100-15 in K. Heinemann and W. Schubarth (eds.) *Der antifaschistische Staat entläßt seine Kinder: Jugend und Rechtsextremismus in Ostdeutschland*. (The Reflection of Anti-Modernization in Right-Extremism. The Anti-Fascist States Sets Its Children Free: Youth and Right-Extremism in Eastern Germany.) Cologne, FRG: PapyRossa.

Heitmeyer, W., H. Buhse, J. Liebe-Freund, K. Möller, J. Müller, H. Ritz, G. Siller, and J. Vossen (1992). *Die Bielefelder Rechtsextremismus-Studie. Erste Langzeituntersuchung zur politischen Sozialisation männlicher Jugendlicher*. (The

Bielefeld Right-Extremism Study: The First Long-term Survey on Political Socialization of Male Youth.) Weinheim/München, FRG: Juventa Verlag.

Inglehart, R. (1990). *Culture Shifts in Advanced Industrial Society.* Princeton, NJ: Princeton University Press.

Minkenberg, M. (1992). 'The New Right in Germany: The Transformation of Conservatism and the Extreme Right.' pp. 55-81 in *European Journal of Political Research*, Vol. 22.

Watts, M. (1994). 'Youth and Xenophobia: Traditions and Transitions. Threat, Racism and Ideology Among East German Youth.' Paper prepared for presentation at the XIII World Congress of Sociology, International Sociological Association, 18-23 July 1994, in Bielefeld, FRG.

Watts, M., W. Fuchs, A. Fischer, and J. Zinnecker (1989). *Contemporary German Youth and Their Elders: A Generational Analysis.* Westport, CT: Greenwood Press.

Wilamowitz-Moellendorff, U. (1993). 'Der Wandel ideologischer Orientierungsmuster zwischen 1971 und 1991 am Beispiel des Links-Rechts-Schemas' (Changing Ideological Orientation Patterns Between 1971 and 1991 in the Case of Left-Right Schemas), pp. 42-72 in *ZA Informationen*, Vol. 32.

APPENDIX A: DATA BASES

All the studies described in this appendix were made available by Central Archive for Social Research (*Zentralarchiv für Sozialforschung*), University of Cologne. Of course, neither the original authors of the studies nor the *Zentralarchiv* are responsible for any analysis or conclusions presented here.

Study B70: 'Jugend und Rechtsextremismus '90' (Youth and Right-Extremism '90)

Data were collected in the fall of 1990 by means of a questionnaire distributed to 1624 pupils, students, apprentices, workers and employees in Leipzig, Dresden, and Chemnitz in schools and training sites. The study was conducted under the auspices of the former Central Institute for Youth Research (*Zentralinstitut für Jugendforschung*) of the German Democratic Republic, Leipzig. The original data were prepared for distribution through the Central Archive for Social Research (*Zentralarchiv für Sozialforschung*), University of Cologne, Federal Republic of Germany. Effective sample size after selection of 14- to 20-year-olds (and allowing for missing data) is roughly 1400.

Study B71: 'Jugend und Ausländerfeindlichkeit, 1990' (Youth and Hostility Toward Foreigners, 1990)

The study was conducted in the last half of 1990 (roughly six months after the fall of the Berlin Wall) and is available under the title *Jugend und Ausländer-feindlichkeit*, Codebuch B71, from the *Zentralarchiv für empirische Sozial-forschung*, University of Cologne, FRG. The study was conducted by the *Zentralinstitut für Jugendforschung Leipzig* and was prepared by that institute's staff in its new form as the *Außenstelle Leipzig, Deutsches Jugendinstitut*. The 1228 total respondents were a nonrandom sample, based on questionnaires distributed in selected classrooms in Dresden, Leipzig, and Chemnitz. Our analysis is based on a potential maximum of 926 respondents who fall between the ages of 14 and 23, though the effective number is sometimes smaller due to missing data (particularly where a large number of scales are employed).

For reports on the above data sets as prepared by former members of the Central Institute, see Friedrich and Schubarth (1991).

ALLBUS Baseline Survey, 1991

Representative random sample of 3058 adult Germans (18 years of age and older, living in private households) in the first German Social Survey that included the five new federal states. The sample included 1514 respondents from the west, 1544 from the east. Data were provided by the Inter-university Consortium for Political and Social Research, Ann Arbor, MI. They are available under ICPSR Number 9832 and from the *Zentralarchiv für empirische Sozialforschung*, Cologne, FRG.

APPENDIX B: MEASURES EMPLOYED IN THE ANALYSIS (BY STUDY)
East German Youth Studies, 1990: Study B70

Ideology Scales: For all, a high score indicates the right-wing position.

Ideology: Five-point scale, ranging from 1 ('left') to 5 ('right').

Nationalism: Ich bin stolz, Deutscher zu sein/Wem es in Deutschland nicht paßt, der soll auswandern/Die Deutschen waren schon immer die Größten in der Geschichte [I am proud to be a German/If someone does not like it in Germany, they should leave/The Germans were always the greatest in history].

Republikaner: Die Partei der Republikaner ist eine demokratiegefährdende Partei/Die Partei der Republikaner ist eine neue Nazi-Partei/Die Partei der Republikaner ist demokratisch/Die Partei der Republikaner ist ehrlich [The Republikaner party is a danger to democracy/ . . . is democratic/ . . . is honest].

NS (National Socialism): Wir Deutschen sollten wieder einen mit starker Hand regierenden Führer haben/Der Faschismus hatte auch seine guten Seiten/Für Adolf Hitler kann ich nur Verachtung empfinden [We Germans should have a leader again who rules with a strong hand/Fascism also had its good sides/I have nothing but contempt for Adolf Hitler].

Right-Extremist Groups: 'Ich fühle mich hingezogen zu ...' (1 = ja, 2 = nein): den Skinheads/den Republikanern/der Nationaldemokratischen Partei Deutschlands/der Freiheitlichen Deutschen Arbeiterpartei/Nationalen Alternative/der Nationalistischen Front/der Deutschen Volksunion/Aasgard-Bund-Wotans Volk/Wiking-Jugend [I feel myself attracted to the Skinheads/ . . . the Republikaner/ . . . the Free German Workers Party/ . . . the National Alternative/...the Nationalist Front/ . . . the German Peoples' Union/ . . . the Aasgard-League/ . . . Wotan's People/ . . . the Viking-Youth].

Skinheads: Haltung zu Skinheads [Attitude toward Skinheads] (from 1 'rejection' to 4 'am one').

'Ban Right-Extremist Groups': Rechtextremistische Parteien oder Gruppen sollten überhaupt verboten werden (1 = 'agree completely' to 5 = 'not at all')[Right-extremist parties or groups should be banned].

Contact: Sum of responses (1 = yes, 2 = no) to 'direct contact' with foreigners in each of the following areas: family, workplace, neighborhood, and circle of friends.

Discrimination: (Ausländer sollten) 'gleiche Rechte' haben/Wenn Arbeitsplätze knapp werden, dann sollte man zuerst die Ausländer entlassen/Ausländer sollten grundsätzlich ihre Ehepartner unter den eigenen Landsleuten wählen [Foreigners should have the same rights/If jobs become scarce, foreigners should be fired first/Foreigners should choose their marriage partners among their own people].

Distance: Sum of three items: Ich wäre bereit . . . mit Ausländer etwas zu trinken/Ausländer nach Hause einzuladen/eine(n) Ausländer(in) zu heiraten [I would be ready to go drinking with a foreigner/ . . . invite a foreigner to my house/...marry a foreigner].

(Attitude Toward) Number of Foreigners: Was würden Sie generell zu der Anzahl der Ausländer in den ostdeutschen Ländern sagen (for responses from 'jeder ist einer zu viel' to 'nicht viele')? [What would you say generally about the number of foreigners in the East German states - responses ranging from 'each one is one too many' to 'not many?']

(Understanding for) Anti-Semitism: In wieweit haben Sie selbst Verständnis für antisemitische Aktionen in jüngster Zeit auf deutschem Boden? (from 1 = 'completely' to 5 = 'not at all') [To what extent do you have understanding for recent anti-Semitic actions in Germany?]

(Affect Toward) 'Bad' Foreigners: Sum of affect ratings for each of the following: Poles, Russians, Turks, Arabs, Vietnamese, Africans, Gypsies (each

on a five point scale from 1 = 'große Sympathie' - 'great sympathy' to 5 = 'große Antipathie' - 'great antipathy').

East German Youth Studies, 1990: Study B71

Ideology: Five-point scale, ranging from 1 ('left') to 5 ('right').

Economic Competition: Ausländer kosten uns mehr Geld als sie selbst einbringen/Bei entsprechender Qualifikation sollten Ausländer prinzipiell dieselben Chancen auf dem Arbeitsmarkt haben wie Deutsche/Ausländer belasten den ohnehin schon angespannten Arbeitsmarkt in Deutschland [Foreigners cost us more money than they bring in themselves/Where qualifications are equal, foreigners should have the same chances in the job market as Germans/Foreigners burden the already-stressed job market in Germany].

Cultural Competition/Threat: Ausländer sollten ihre Lebensweise weitestgehend der deutschen Lebensart anpassen/Eine Einbürgerung von Ausländern bereichert die kulturelle Vielfalt unseres Alltags/Ein hoher Ausländeranteil führt zu einem Verfall der deutschen Kultur und Lebensweise [Foreigners should adapt their way of life as much as possible to that of the Germans/Making citizens of foreigners enriches the cultural diversity of our everyday life/A high proportion of foreigners leads to a decline of German culture and way of life].

(Affect Toward) 'Bad' Foreigners: Sum of Poles, Russians, Turks, Arabs, Vietnamese, Africans, gypsies (each on a five point scale from 1 = 'große Sympathie' - 'great sympathy' to 5 = 'große Antipathie' - 'great antipathy'). [Same as study B70.]

(Attitude Toward) Number of Foreigners: Was würden Sie generell zu der Anzahl der Ausländer in den ostdeutschen Ländern sagen (for responses from 'jeder ist einer zu viel' to 'nicht viele')? [What would you say generally about the number of foreigners in the East German states, responses ranging from 'each one is one too many' to 'not many?'] [Same as study B70.]

Distance: Sum of three items: Ich wäre bereit . . . mit Ausländer etwas zu trinken/Ausländer nach Hause einzuladen/eine(n) Ausländer(in) zu heiraten. [Same as Study B70 above.]

Asylum: Asyl sollte gewährt werden . . . wenn für den/die Antragsteller in ihren Heimatländern aus unterschiedlichen Gründen direkte Lebensgefahr besteht/...wenn Asylanten in ihren Heimatländern wegen ihrer politischen Gesinnung massiv verfolgt werden/ . . . wenn die Armut die Leute aus ihren Heimatländern vertreibt/...wenn Familien ihrem in Deutschland verdienenden Hauptverdiener nachziehen [Asylum should be granted . . . if the applicants lives are threatened in their home country/ . . . if they are persecuted in their home countries because of political beliefs/ . . . if poverty drives them out of their countries/ . . . if families follow their breadwinner who is already in Germany].

Discrimination: Sollen in Deutschland lebende Ausländer das kommunale Wahlrecht erhalten?/Ausländern sollte jegliche politische Tätigkeit in Deutschland verboten werden/Wenn Arbeitsplätze knapp werden, dann sollte man zuerst die Ausländer entlassen [Should foreigners in Germany be able to vote in local elections?/Foreigners should be barred from all political activities/When jobs are scarce, foreigners should have the same rights/If jobs become scarce, foreigners should be fired first/Foreigners should choose their marriage partners among their own people].

Right-Extremist Slogans: Deutschland den Deutschen!/Ausländer raus!/Rote raus!/Die Juden sind Deutschlands Unglück! (each scored from 1 = 'agree completely' to 5 = 'not at all') [Germany for the Germans/Foreigners Out/Reds Out/The Jews are Germany's misfortune].

Contact: Sum of responses (1 = yes, 2 = no) to 'direct contact' with foreigners in each of the following areas: family, workplace, neighborhood, and circle of friends [same as Study B70].

(Identification with) 'Rightist' or Aggressive: Republikaner, Skinheads, Faschos, Hooligans (on a five-point scale from 'belong to' to 'those are my enemies').

ALLBUS Baseline Study, 1991

Anomie: Index/Scale of four dichotomous items, high score = high anomie (recoded from original): . . . die Situation der einfachen Leute wird nicht besser, sondern schlechter/ . . . so wie die zukunft aussieht, kann man es kaum noch verantworten, Kinder auf die Welt zu bringen/ . . . die meisten Politiker interessieren sich in Wirklichkeit gar nicht für die Probleme der einfachen Leute/...die meisten Leute kümmern sich in Wirklichkeit far nicht darum, was mit ihren Mitmenschen geschieht [The situation of the common people is not becoming better, but worse/ . . . The way the future looks, one can hardly justify bringing children into the world/ . . . Most politicians are not interested in the problems of the common people/ . . . Most people are not actually concerned with what happens to their fellow human beings].

Values: Inglehart index with values from 1 = 'Postmaterialist' to 4 = 'Materialist'.

Subjective Class: High score = higher subjective social rating (from 1 = 'Unterschicht' - 'lower class' - to 5 = 'Oberschicht' - 'upper class').

'Fair Share?': Im Vergleich dazu, wie andere hier in Deutschland leben: Glauben Sie , daß Sie Ihren gerechten Anteil erhalten, mehr als Ihren gerechten, etwas weniger oder sehr viel weniger? (from 1 to 4)[In comparison to the way others live here in Germany, do you believe that you receive your fair share, more than your fare share, somewhat less, or much less?]

Success (1) ('Machiavellianism'): High score = high rating of traits/tactics (reverse scoring from original, where 1 = 'sehr wichtig' - 'very important' to 4 = 'unwichtig' - 'unimportant'): . . . Opportunismus, Rücksichtslosigkeit/Beziehungen, Protektion/Geld, Vermögen/Soziale Herkunft, aus der 'richtigen' Familie stammen/Bestechung, Korruption [opportunism, ruthlessness/connections/money, wealth/social background, coming from the 'right' family/bribery, corruption].

Success (2) ('Achievement'): High score = high rating of traits/tactics (reverse scoring from original, where 1 = 'sehr wichtig' to 4 = 'unwichtig'): ...Bildung, Ausbildung/Intelligenz, Begabung/Leistung, Fleiß/Initiative, Durchsetzungsvermögen [education, training/intelligence, talent/accomplishment, diligence/initiative, persistence].

Life Importance (religion/family/neighbors): High score = positive. Summed rating of importance of Verwandschaft/Religion und Kirche/Nachbarschaft (each on a scale from 1 = 'unwichtig' - 'unimportant' - to 7 = 'sehr wichtig' - 'very important').

In-Migration (*Zuzug*): Summed index of approval/rejection of in-migration of four groups; high score = rejection: Zuzug von ...Aussiedlern aus Osteuropa/ ...Asylsuchenden/...EG-Arbeitnehmern/...nicht-EG-Arbeitnehmern (items scored from 1 = 'soll uneingeschränkt möglich sein' - 'should be possible without limitation' - to 3 = 'soll völlig unterbunden werden' - 'should be completely stopped') [in-migration of . . . migrants - of German origin - from East Europe/refugees - asylum-seekers/workers from the European Union/workers from outside the European Union].

Ideology: Ten-point scale, ranging from 1 ('left') to 10 ('right').

Job 1 ('Useful'): Viel Kontakt zu anderen Menschen/ein Beruf, bei dem man anderen helfen kann/ein Beruf, der für die Gesellschaft nützlich ist/gibt einem das Gefühl, etwas Sinvolles zu tun [contact with other people/an occupation in which you can help others/an occupation that is socially useful/an occupation that gives the feeling of doing something useful].

Job 2 ('Fulfilling'): Interessante Tätigkeit/eine Tätigkeit, bei der man selbständig arbeiten kann/Aufgaben, die viel Verantwortungsbewußtsein erfordern [interesting work/a job in which one can work independently/tasks that promote responsibility].

Job 3 ('Income/Success'): Hohes Einkommen/gute Aufstiegsmöglichkeiten/ein Beruf, der anerkannt und geachtet wird [high income/good chances of advancement/a job that is recognized and respected].

7 Hungarians' Conflicting Identifications with the Homeland and Europe

György Csepeli
László Kéri
István Stumpf

ABSTRACT

This chapter discusses the results of a 1992 survey of 4000 Hungarian youth aged 11-17 years. The study addressed their sense of national consciousness and identity formation. At least five different patterns of belief or clusters emerged among the students: conformists, loyalists, Christians, patriots, and naive citizens. It was found that there are different levels of commitment to both nation and Europe and that respondents had different ideas about memorializing the dead, allocating taxes, reacting to the Olympic games (and support different athletes in competitions), as well as choosing religious orientations. All in all, age and parental education proved to be the two strongest explanatory variables. The old system of official and unofficial or dual socialization is now dead in Hungary so that youth can finally and fairly respond to a survey form, choose among meaningful alternatives, and have no reason to fear somebody is watching over their shoulders.

THE REVIVAL OF NATIONAL IDEOLOGIES IN CENTRAL AND EASTERN EUROPE AS A MEANS OF LEGITIMATION

The implosion of the great power which ruled Central and Eastern Europe resulted in the sudden collapse of state socialist systems throughout the region. Nation states in this part of Europe formerly had their own capitals, armies, administrations, and other prerequisites of independence; yet they were, in fact, ruled from Moscow, the Soviet empire's capital. State borders consequently lacked any real importance. Only the former Yugoslavia did not seem to fit this paradigm. But the simultaneous collapse of Yugoslavia suggests that this country was, in fact, only a part of the post-Yalta system. Its internal unity was probably maintained through the threat of force from both Belgrade and Moscow.

As a result of the USSR's fracturing, both the importance of state borders and the national independence of individual countries have increased from the Elbe to the Baltics. Eastern Germany, the sole exception, became part of a united Germany. As a consequence, the transition from state socialism to democracy in eastern Germany lacks any similarity to the democratic transitions which inhabitants in the rest of Central and Eastern European countries are experiencing. Other exceptions may be found in the Ukraine and Byelorussia; they have preserved important characteristics of their Soviet-dominated past through their continuing close affiliation with Russia. Most countries located between Russia and Germany have become independent, freeing themselves from unwanted foreign influences. This is a new and unparalleled experience for these countries. They had been unimportant parts of large empires and were long deprived of a right to self-determination.

Because of these new circumstances, the countries in Central and Eastern Europe were forced to look for new principles of legitimation and a justification for their right to exist. Due to the collapse of the internationalist and socialist 'brotherhood' under Soviet hegemony, the old ideologies of internationalism and socialism proved to be unusable. The European Union (EU) of Western European countries was quite reluctant to integrate (individually or collectively) the poor and backward Central and Eastern European countries as member states. Consequently, federalism was not a viable option in this region. National ideologies were the only means which enabled these countries to fulfill their legitimation needs. The transition from state socialism and social integration to a market economy, political pluralism, and a reward structure based on achievement also increased social conflicts in these countries.

The first postsocialist government of Hungary, formed in 1990, needed legitimation through national ideological development as well. Our survey, carried out two years after this government was elected, explores a basic political socialization question: How successful was the attempt to educate the new postcommunist generation in a renewed national identity? (On these points, see Csepeli et al., 1993 and 1994; Szabó and Csepeli, 1984.)

THE SAMPLE

Our sample consisted of 4000 young Hungarian respondents aged 11 to 17 years in 1992. The sample was nationally representative for place of residence, education levels, and parental social status. We found that the large majority of respondents (80 per cent) had studied at least one foreign language. German proved to be the most common foreign language studied (31 per cent), then English (29 per cent), Russian (12 per cent), and French (6 per cent).

Hungary's 20th century has been filled with painful political experiences which have caused much hardship for many Hungarian families. More than a quarter (27 per cent) of our respondents were able to recall some type of political persecution which had affected the lives of one or more of their family members in the past. Catholicism was the most common faith among respondents (56 per cent). Affiliation with the Calvinist reformed church was next with

15 per cent, while 3 per cent claimed to be Lutheran. One-fifth of the respondents failed to mention any religious affiliation at all.

WIDENING CIRCLES OF IDENTIFICATION

With respect to group feelings, there is no more important motive to assume a given identity than the answer one would give to the question, 'Why am I a member of the X or Y group?' In order to explore the motives leading to an adoption of a Hungarian identity, five alternative statements were given to the respondents. They rated them according to their perceived/relative weight. Our results can be seen in Table 7.1.

As Table 7.1 demonstrates, citizenship and mother tongue take the lead in Hungarian identification among Hungarian teenagers, while self-identification (personal choice), descent, and place of birth play less important roles. A twofold structure was later revealed using factor analysis. Four classification categories had high positive scores on the first factor. Only 'personal choice' was found in the second factor. This structure demonstrates that national identification based on self-categorization differs from the type of identification based on citizenship, mother tongue, descent, and place of birth. No matter what was behind being Hungarian, respondents were divided in their estimates of the total number of Hungarians to be expected at the beginning of the next century. Nearly half (43 per cent) of respondents anticipated increases in the number of Hungarians, while 33 per cent expected a numerical decrease. The rest (24 per cent) felt that the same number of Hungarians would be alive in the next century as there are today.

Table 7.1 Perceived weight given to aspects underlying Hungarian students' self-categorizations (in %)

	(Dis)Agreement Levels					
	strongly agree	agree	do not know	disagree	strongly disagree	
Source	1	2	3	4	5	total
Personal choice	27	21	24	10	18	100
Citizenship	35	24	22	9	10	100
Mother tongue	37	27	21	7	8	100
Descent	31	27	23	10	9	100
Place of birth	28	19	22	13	18	100

Symbols have generally played important roles in democratic transitions in Central and Eastern Europe. Symbols are very important because of their cognitive accessibility and their inexpensive costs. For example, instead of coping with tremendous economic and social problems, the national assembly of Hungary became involved in a hopeless discussion about a new national emblem immediately following the 1990 elections. Following a general tendency to revive the past, the nation's new coat of arms was to be an old one, of course. Members of Parliament, however, were embarrassed since there were so many alternatives. Two major versions came out on top in the debate. They were practically identical except for the fact that one used the Holy Crown (traditionally the symbol of the Hungarian feudal state), while the other had none. Liberals and socialists preferred the coat of arms without the crown, while nationalists pushed for the crowned symbol. Finally, after a long debate, the crowned version (although unsuitable for a democratic republic) was selected. Croats, Poles, and Bulgarians all had similar debates.

According to our data, the Hungarian transition from state socialism to democracy at the symbolic level was successful from a nationalist point of view. Our respondents were asked to choose among three versions of the Hungarian coat of arms. In preferring the royal version, 80 per cent of our respondents showed they approved of the government's choice. The republican version had 12 per cent approval, while 8 per cent still preferred the socialist coat of arms with its red star.

Being a member of a group means that one will probably occasionally think about one's membership. A third (30 per cent) of our respondents said that they frequently thought about their membership in a Hungarian national community. Less than half (46 per cent) said that they sometimes thought of being Hungarian; but only 10 per cent could not recall those times when they recognized themselves as being Hungarians. The feeling of being European was quite rare in our sample. Half of the sample never thought of their European identity. Even though 39 per cent of the respondents stated that they occasionally thought of themselves as Europeans, only 2 per cent reported that being European was a major concern.

Despite the ideological crusade which was fought intensively on the battlefields of mass communications and in classrooms, 29 per cent of the respondents felt no national pride in 1992. Another 45 per cent felt some national pride and 29 per cent were very proud to be Hungarians. The trend toward pride in their Europeanism was similar. Yet, on the average, when compared with national pride, respondents felt less pride in their European identity. Although 37 per cent of the sample said they were not proud of being European, 42 per cent felt some pride in their Europeanism, and 21 per cent felt good about being European. A majority of respondents (54 per cent) rejected national shame. Even more (61 per cent) rejected shame as an element of their European identity.

To explore the structure of positive and negative emotional components of national and European identities, we conducted a multivariate analysis; it resulted in two main components. National and European identification scored equally high on both main components, which showed marked differences in their emotional/attitudinal composition. In the first instance, positive and negative feelings scored equally high, while in the second, pride and shame scores both showed negative correlations.

The timing of our survey coincided with the Olympic games in Barcelona, Spain. It turned out that 90 per cent of the respondents watched the events on television. One overwhelming tendency in this respect was support for Hungarian athletes whenever and wherever they were involved. The tendency to support European athletes more than non-Europeans was much rarer; even fewer respondents manifested any racial preferences. The multivariate analysis resulted in two main components. The first component represented a preference for European and white athletes and the second showed high positive scores regarding preference for Hungarian athletes.

Although racial or national identification might have played a minor role in watching the Olympic games, attitudes about immigrants certainly were affected by the nature of one's identification. Most (71 per cent) of the respondents indicated a willingness to accept refugees, provided they were ethnic Hungarians. A willingness to accept refugees from Asia was much less the case. Only 12 per cent of the respondents agreed that an unlimited number of Asian immigrants should be allowed to enter Hungary.

Xenophobia, ethnocentrism, and conventionalism might be the underlying factors which resulted in a general tendency to avoid taking part in demonstrations for minority rights (see Table 7.2). The exception to this rule (in more ways than one) was respondents' willingness to protest for the Hungarian minority in Transylvania (Romania) (see Table 7.2). Since the Yalta Agreement in 1945, generations have grown up in Central and Eastern Europe who have had the experience of being both separated and banned from Western Europe. Some of our respondents seemed to continue to believe in this permanent separation, while others took another view.

Table 7.2 Hungarian students' willingness to participate in demonstrations for the rights of given minority groups (in %)

Minority Group	Willingness				
	strongly unwilling	unwilling	strongly willing	willing	do not know
Hungarians in Transylvania	14	17	37	25	7
Turks in Bulgaria	64	20	7	3	6
Germans in Hungary	29	32	22	8	9
Jews	33	29	20	9	9
Gypsies	47	26	12	8	7
Gays	74	14	4	2	6

One question in our survey aimed at detecting opinions concerning future borders in Europe. The majority of respondents (58 per cent) agreed with the statement that borders in Europe would eventually disappear and that the continent would be united. Some 18 per cent of the respondents disagreed with this statement; 10 per cent believed any unity in Western Europe would not include the countries of the former Soviet bloc; but another 10 per cent thought that Central (not Eastern) European countries (such as Poland, Hungary, the Czech and Slovak Republics) would be included in a united Europe, while Eastern European countries (such as Romania, Bulgaria, Serbia, Albania, Latvia, Estonia, and Lithuania) would not soon be a part of a united Europe.

The degree of broadening circles of identification was measured using a question group in which respondents had to distribute a tax amounting to 100 million forints between various institutions carefully chosen to represent different/competing circles of group identity. Local communities were most favored, while somewhat less money was delegated to the county and the national governments. The European Parliament and the United Nations each was granted an average of 15 million forints. In sum, 70 per cent of the tax money was kept within the country and 30 per cent was granted to international agencies. Three strategies for allocating tax resources were revealed through main component analysis:

1. To international agencies
2. To the national government
3. To the local government

INTERPRETING PATTERNS OF NATIONAL HISTORY IN THE CONTEXT OF POLITICAL SOCIALIZATION

History lessons are often a major element in the formal process of political socialization. Issues, personalities, and national events contribute to upholding national identity, viewed as an eternal continuity rooted in the distant past and leading into a remote future. The present is a function of how the continuity in national existence has been presented. Different national ideologies (which are not necessarily without conflicting elements) are responsible for these views. Events, persons, explanations, and narratives which are represented as history to the child have powerful political implications. Consequently, history becomes a battlefield for competing political ideologies.

Political socialization under state socialism traditionally had a duality of ideologies. The official ideology was not compatible with alternative ideological constructions, but conflicts between them never emerged openly. As a result of the transition from state socialism to democracy, conflicts between ideological alternatives have come to the fore. Schools and the mass media became the battlegrounds for the *Kulturkampf* (cultural struggles), where liberalism, socialism, and nationalism battled it out for the souls of the new generation.

To explore the impact of this *Kulturkampf*, we formulated some questions with historical content. In one set of questions, the respondents were confronted with the need to build a hypothetical highway which would inevitably destroy certain historical monuments which were in the way of the planned development. The respondents were told that a certain number of monuments would have to be destroyed, but that they could choose which ones they preferred to save. The tendency to preserve was most pronounced for monuments testifying to the Hungarian presence in the Carpathian basin, while the tendency to demolish was strongest in the case of the remains of a Roman villa, an old Jewish cemetery, and an abandoned factory building.

Another question measured the adolescents' political and ideological preferences through proposals to name unnamed streets. From a set of 12 proposals, the majority of respondents preferred prominent Hungarians whose names did not play a central part in the ongoing ideological campaign, but were familiar enough to be chosen. Some of these were Ferenc Deák, who created the compromise between Hungary and Austria in 1867, King Mathias who was the greatest Hungarian renaissance ruler, and Ferenc Kölcsey, author of the Hungarian national anthem. Also chosen were names which carried nationalist, Christian, or communist overtures, such as the Holy Spirit, while the People's Army had far less appeal. The same tendency was found when students were asked for whom they would erect commemorative statues. István Széchenyi (builder of the Chain Bridge in Budapest) and Zoltán Kodály (a composer) proved to be the most popular figures, while persons with strong ideological backgrounds (such as János Kádár, Miklós Horthy, and Imre Nagy) were not often chosen as subjects for memorial statues.

The largest group of respondents (46 per cent) said that Hungarian history as a whole was tragic, while 31 per cent evaluated it for its glory. As for attributing causes of national failures, external ones (such as bad luck and unfortunate geographical location) were not accepted as determining forces, while internal causes (such as lack of national solidarity and backwardness) were blamed. The only exception was enemy superiority, which was widely accepted as well. National success was viewed as a function of internal factors. Any important role for external factors was rejected. This pattern of attribution in times of failure represents a shift from traditional nationalist explanations, which overemphasize the role of bad luck (that is, *balsors*, in the Romantic terms of the Hungarian national anthem).

PERCEPTIONS ABOUT HUNGARY'S PLACE IN THE WORLD

International comparisons are major sources for national self-evaluation for any national group. A negative self-evaluation among young Hungarians can be inferred from the fact that 77 per cent of the respondents believed that Hungary had to catch up with certain other countries in contemporary Europe. Countries such as Germany (34 per cent), Austria (13 per cent), Switzerland (11 per cent), France (11 per cent), and Great Britain (11 per cent) topped the list of those believed to be more developed than Hungary. Another element of national negative self-representation was tapped using a question which asked respondents to name the happy and unhappy countries in Europe. Not a single respondent mentioned Hungary as a happy country, while 17 per cent referred to it as an unhappy one. In a similar poll ten years ago, not a single respondent viewed Hungary in negative terms, while the majority of them identified it as a happy country (Szabó and Csepeli, 1984). These results support the position that the old 'iron curtain' has been replaced by a new 'cognition curtain'. The happy countries listed were invariably Western European, while unhappy ones were, without exception, those in Central and Eastern Europe.

Another controversial perception pattern was revealed in this study. A set of questions explored how young Hungarians perceived the international scene around them in terms of relative levels of harmony and conflict. All countries mentioned as being Hungary's major partners had played a direct role in Hungarian history or shared borders with the country (with the exception of the US, which is currently a major positive protagonist). Interestingly enough, Turkey (a major negative protagonist in the past) was also mentioned, though the Ottoman occupation of Hungary ended centuries ago. Hungary was generally viewed as being a victim of hostile intervention in the past. Some of the negative protagonists of the past were simultaneously viewed as positive protagonists today (for example, Russia, Germany, and Austria). According to their general perceptions, young Hungarians say that some countries which currently provide aid to Hungary did much harm in the past. Only one country (Poland) was consistently seen in terms of a relationship of mutual harmony. The tendency prevailed to perceive all neighboring countries in terms of suspicion and mistrust (with the exception of Austria).

Hungary's international position was ambiguously perceived. The immediate international environment elicited feelings of fear and mistrust, while countries some distance away were perceived in positive (though unreciprocated) emotional terms. The great Western European powers (like one's parents) were seen simultaneously as sources of both rewards and punishments. The only country to which nearly divine powers were attributed was the one farthest away: the United States.

Table 7.3 Hungarian student response to 'In what do you believe?' (in %)

Religious Category	Not at all		Range <---------->		Very much	Do not
	1	2	3	4	5	know
God	18	11	18	17	36	0
UFOs	17	12	26	21	23	2
Acupuncture	13	13	24	27	19	4
Life after death	26	14	23	15	21	1
Resurrection	40	17	17	11	15	0
The Last Judgment	31	19	20	8	10	2
Destiny	37	16	19	13	13	2
Parapsychology	21	16	27	18	14	4
Reincarnation	29	17	22	15	14	3
Astrology	22	19	28	18	13	0
The devil	60	13	11	7	8	1
Communism	55	21	13	3	2	6

FAITH AND RELIGION

One of the most immediate consequences from a transition from ideological repression under state socialism to pluralism and democracy is freedom to publicly confess one's faith of choice. Table 7.3 shows the proportion of respondents (in percentages) according to religious beliefs. Most respondents tended to believe in God and UFOs, while they were least prone to believe in the devil and communism. After main component analysis was carried out, a more regular pattern emerged. In the first category, beliefs based on traditional religious teaching were found. Fad beliefs (for example, UFOs, parapsychology, and reincarnation) were located in the second grouping. In the third type, strangely enough, beliefs about astrology and communism were closely associated.

CLUSTERS

Cluster analysis revealed five political and ideological profiles. The different cluster groups of respondents apparently share some common beliefs which we describe in the following paragraphs.

1. Conformist Citizens. The largest group of respondents (33 per cent) simultaneously felt both shame and pride in their national and European identities. They opted to preserve the 1848/1849 war heroes cemetery rather than an old Jewish one. Regarding national identification, citizenship requirements were chosen over one's self-categorization. Regarding distribution of taxes, this group favored giving money to international

institutions. Attribution of national success was seen as a function of external causes. Hungarian, European, and white athletes (as opposed to non-Hungarian, non-European, and nonwhite ones) were most likely to be supported in the (Barcelona, Spain) Olympics. Christian beliefs were weak for this group, but beliefs in irrational and religious fads were quite strong.

2.   Citizen Loyalists. The second largest group represented 30 per cent of the sample. They were more reluctant to demolish the old Jewish cemetery and discounted the role of international institutions for tax distributions. In national identification, citizenship also seemed relatively more important than any self-categorization. They were more concerned with explaining national failures than successes, preferring external causes to internal ones. Hungarian athletes enjoyed their support in the Olympics. Christianity failed to attract them, but they also rejected modern fads/beliefs.

3.   Christian Citizens. One-fifth of the respondents expressed pride in their national and European identification and chose to preserve the old Jewish cemetery. Self-identification was more important than citizenship for national identification. National self-criticism was reflected in the attribution patterns for national successes and failures. In both cases, a strong preference for internal causes emerged. Impartiality was their dominant mood when watching the Olympic games. Spiritual bonds to Christianity proved to be very strong with this group, but they equally and strongly rejected superstitions, religious fads, and communism.

4.   Citizen Patriots. Some (9 per cent) of the respondents belonged to this cluster. Group members shared feelings of pride in being Hungarian and European and favored preserving the cemetery to commemorate heroes of the 1848/49 War of Independence. The tendency to allocate taxes to local governments was dominant. In the national self-justification category, members of this cluster resorted to external causes to explain national failures, while internal ones were mentioned as reasons for successes. Hungarian, European, and white athletes were clearly preferred in the Olympic games. Religious faith was less important than other modern types of irrational belief.

5.   Politically Naive Citizens. Pride in being Hungarian and European was characteristic of this small cluster. A preference to preserve the national heroes' cemetery was predominant. Citizenship proved to be stronger for national identification than self-categorization. A kind of national helplessness could be inferred with a tendency to cite external factors as causes for both national failures and successes. European and white athletes were more likely to be supported in the Olympic games. A strong superstition level was found, including continuing faith in the old communist society.

DISCUSSION AND CONCLUSIONS

Developmental studies treating national identification demonstrate the tendency for increasing decentralization to occur. This is likely to result in cognitive maps containing a stock of basic categories with elements of various group identities. According to our results, this decentralization process accelerates between the ages of 11 and 17. A tendency to identify with more and more categories then develops. Simultaneously, the affective components of identification become more complex. Conventional identifications are gradually replaced when ideological constructs (religious, national, and supra-national identities) supersede them.

The growth of sensitivity to identification alternatives and the readiness to resort to cognitive means of interpreting the social environment in terms of collective identities is related to one's social background. The immediate impact of family communication is transmitted through the construction of family history and education levels (which determine access to ideological and political contents and structures in identity formation). The higher the education level of the parents, the more likely that the child will acquire ideological content and structure which will enable him/her to think and feel in a conscious way about his/her place in a socially constructed world, which was originally founded on the basis of certain spontaneous identifications.

Our regression analysis supports the former descriptive/developmental pattern. Members of the 'naive' group clearly tended to be younger, but older members of this group tended to be children whose parents had a poor education. A similar pattern emerged for members of the 'loyal citizens' and 'citizen patriot' clusters. 'Conformists' were clearly a product of age (that is, the lower the respondent's age, the higher the degree of conformity). Development of a conscious identity (in terms of Christianity and national affiliation) was clearly seen to be a result of age increases and increasing level of parental education.

The transition from state socialism to democracy has resulted in the disappearance of the old duality in political socialization for postcommunist Hungary. According to our results, any attempts to restore the duality of official and private spheres for political socialization have failed. These transition-period youth coped well with pluralism and could orient themselves within various given interpretations of ideological, religious, and political categories. The disappearance of ideological constraints, however, has not changed the decisive role of the family and social structures in the political socialization of postcommunist youth. The latter have lost their parents' paradise of equally poor subjects and are now faced with meeting the challenge of civic freedoms, diversity, pluralism, and self-responsibility in an increasingly civil/free market society.

ACKNOWLEDGEMENT

This research project received generous support from the Hungarian Scientific Research Fund (OTKA) and the Ezredforduló Alapitvány.

REFERENCES

Csepeli, G., L. Kéri, and I. Stumpf (eds.) (1993). *State and Citizen: Studies on Political Socialization in Post-Communist Eastern Europe.* Budapest, Hungary: Institute of Political Science and Hungarian Center for Political Education.

Csepeli, G., D. German, L. Kéri, and I. Stumpf (eds.) (1994). *From Subject to Citizen.* Budapest, Hungary: Hungarian Center for Political Education.

Szabó, I. and G. Csepeli (1984). *Nemzet és Politika a 10-14 Éves Gyerekek Gondol-kodásában* (The Nation and Politics in the Cognition of 10-14-Year-Old Children). Budapest, Hungary: Tömegkommunikációs Kutatóközpont.

8   *Problems of Transition to Democracy in Hungary*

Political Participation, Voting Behavior, and Partisan Attitudes

István Stumpf

ABSTRACT

In spring 1994, general elections were held in Hungary. Since one-third of the voters were under 35 years old, the future of Hungary's democratic system and the policies of the new government will reflect their influence, attitudes toward political parties, and motivation to participate in the electoral process. Recent empirical research on Hungarian youth's political attitudes and experiences includes types of conventional and nonconventional political participation and their consumption of various sources of political information. Our analysis of Hungarian public opinion revealed definite differences between conservative Christian, nationalistic, and liberal trends. The chapter reveals the varying roles which differing generational, religious, and socialization experiences play in the development of specific ideological viewpoints. Since voter behavior is extremely unpredictable, the classic models for analyzing Western political attitudes can be used in Hungary only to a strictly limited degree.

INTRODUCTION: THE UNCERTAINTIES OF TRANSITION

In the light of what we now know since systemic changes occurred in Eastern Europe at the end of the 1980s, it is evident that there are fundamentally differing cultural and political features (many of which have been influenced by each country's historical development) behind these seemingly homogeneous institutions. After the fall of the communist regimes, these differences greatly contributed to the fact that various pluralist (multiparty) systems came into being. Basically, three factors decisively influenced political events, with competing multiparty systems at one end of the scale and centrist noncompetitive parliamentary systems at the other (Körösényi, 1991). These factors are the existence, the level of development, and the activities of opposition movements during the period of communist rule; parliamentary traditions, including free elections; and basic characteristics of the political cultural heritage.

Despite the many specialized works on 'the transition', no agreement has yet been reached concerning a consensus view about its different paths in Eastern Europe. Research on Latin-American and, later on, the South-European transition may have resulted in a 'revolution' in comparative political science (Agh, 1993), but the peculiarities of Eastern European transitions displayed many more differences than similarities (Hankiss, 1990; Szoboszlai, 1991, 1992; Bozóki et al., 1992).

If we apply Powell's (1982) five factors for the comparative study of stability in present-day democratic regimes, then Hungary (thanks to its achievement of governmental stability) seems to be a politically successful and consolidated country in comparison with other new Eastern European democracies. Powell's factors are 1) voter participation and citizen involvement, 2) government stability and performance, 3) strength of the party system, 4) constitutional setting and rule of law, and 5) management of violence and crisis and maintenance of democracy. However, behind the facade of a relative institutional stability (especially with regard to political attitudes and voters' permanent party orientation), one finds less steadiness and a blurred picture.

In view of the large-scale sociopolitical changes taking place in Hungary, it is very difficult to formulate any general statement concerning the voters' attitudes. Political-sociological researchers suggest that the most characteristic feature of the Hungarian voters' attitude is that it is situation-bound and flexible. At the same time, one can see that (easily recognizable) structural and (less easily recognizable) socialization or symbolic processes influence the formation and changes in voters' attitudes toward political parties. In the light of the researches carried out up to now, we can conclude that approximately one-third of the 1994 Hungarian voters possessed stable party preferences. The number of nonparticipants can be estimated around 30 per cent; these are the people who simply cannot be persuaded to vote. In fact, parties try to win over these potential voters (35 to 40 per cent of the electorate) who are ambivalent, possess no definite party preferences, and may not even take part in the elections. After a brief survey of theoretical models of voters' attitudes, the present study analyzes the roles of age and religion in the formation of Hungarians' party preferences.

MODELS AND THEORIES FOR THE ANALYSIS OF THE VOTERS' ATTITUDES

The subject of voters' attitudes has been a favorite topic in the Western political and sociological literature since the 1960s. Politicians are also concerned with those factors which influence electoral participation and party preferences. Scholarly work in this area seeks improved insights into those social processes which determine stability and crisis in political regimes. American research on citizen participation and voting behavior (Niemi and Weisberg, 1993a and b; Dalton, 1988; Barnes et al., 1979) distinguishes those factors which have short- and long-term influence. These classic studies emphasize the following effects on voting: socioeconomic status (SES), age, gender, strength of party identification, political efficacy, and political dissatisfaction.

Of course, some of these variables (such as SES and political efficacy) overlap; others (such as age and religious affiliation, which we will discuss later) influence one's participatory levels. Among those which most strongly and directly influence participation, Campbell et al. (1960 and 1966) mentioned strength of partisanship, issue opinions, and candidate images. Some comparative research conducted in the mid-1970s (for example, Barnes et al., 1979) registered significant differences from country to country regarding those which had the most decisive influence on voter turnout. For example, in the US, the most significant factors were educational attainment, age, and (to a lesser degree) party preference. In England, party identification proved to be the most important factor, while educational level had less relevance than the voter's age. In Germany, the one factor of party identification played the most significant role. Current scientific interest in citizen political behaviors recognizes a devaluation of traditional forms of participation (such as voting, campaign work, and political membership) and citizens' disappointment with political life, the deepening legitimization crisis of regimes, and the political elites which govern (Dalton, 1988; Inglehart, 1990). Recently, various political participation models were applied to electoral analyses in Western democracies. Some experts self-confidently alleged that they were often able to predict in advance an individual's voting preference better than the individual himself/ herself could foretell.

Several dominant and competing models vie to provide the best explanation for differences in voters' participatory and voting behavior. One theory known as the University of Michigan Survey Research Center model emphasizes voters' party identification, partisan commitment, and party loyalty. This model's theory of political socialization considers the family as crucial with respect to formation of party identification. It assumes that by age ten, children already possess a party preference. This party identification is connected with their parental loyalty so that this family influence can persist for a lifetime. A basic assumption of this theory is that nearly every voter forms a party preference and that this is usually inherited. Party identification, then, directly influences one's voting behavior and, indirectly, candidate choice and associated policy choices. In developed democracies, a steep decrease in party loyalty in the last two decades questioned the explanatory value of the 'Michigan model', though efforts were made to rescue it to provide an adequate explanation for the general decrease in party identification.

In Western democracies, three factors explain the growth of political independents. These include a radical decrease in class loyalties/identification, which transformed the SES basis for the major parties; the increased levels of education, which enabled voters to analyze political events and reach their own decisions without political party help; and the increased political role played by television, which diminished the importance of the parties as communications channels to the public.

A significant challenge to the 'Michigan model' was the 'rational choice model' (Downs, 1957), which maintained that a citizen would choose the party which best suits the voter's own political interests, values, and priorities. Using rational criteria, the voter will choose a certain party to get the most from it. A starting point for this theory is that the voter is well aware of his/her real interests. The voter does not vote for a party because he/she is merely following advice from family or friends, but rather because he/she wants to obtain some social, political, or economic capital out of this decision. Before deciding, the voter obtains as much political information (both pro and con) as possible. Another consideration is whether it is worth more to squander one's time gathering information or not to vote at all. Citizens' decisions are determined using strictly rational criteria. The voter's decision also depends on his/her retrospective evaluation of past governmental performance, not merely on current political issues in the contest. Rational choice theory has become a popular explanatory device in recent decades, but its limitations are also evident. This is especially true in those countries where the political role of religion is very strong, such as in the Islamic world, Latin America, and Poland.

International comparative research has produced the 'theory of generational value changes' that also competes with the Michigan and rational choice models (Inglehart, 1977 and 1990). One of its representatives, Ronald Inglehart, states that a 'silent revolution' is taking place in the Western highly industrialized countries. Those generations which were born after World War II and which were raised during good economic times tend to give priority to the so-called 'postmaterialist' values (connected with the quality of life) more than to material needs and values. This reconsideration of societal values is related to important social changes, such as the technological and information revolutions (which contributed to increased efficiency, transformed the mass media, modified the demands of the various trades and professions, and extended the so-called intellectual, bureaucratic, communications, service, or 'third sector'). The international balance of power made it possible for these new generations to live a life without a total war. Additionally, the opportunities to learn were significantly extended, especially after higher education was available to the masses.

These socioeconomic changes transformed not only the value system, but also allowed a majority of the population to participate actively in political life. Instead of a society which elites managed and mobilized, another type of society began to crystallize. This is one where various civic groups are active and can limit the influence and power of elites (Inglehart, 1990). It was the younger and better-educated generation that best used opportunities which the 'information society' afforded for broader participation in the decision-making processes both at the national and international levels. New lines of political division came into being so that traditional party structures and systems also began to crumble. So-called 'alternative movements' and 'green' parties appeared on the political scene and, in many countries, they successfully fought for parliamentary seats.

In his discussion of 'culture shift', Inglehart (1990) discusses these changes in values. On the basis of a cross-national survey carried out in more than 24 countries, he arrives at the conclusion that changes in the younger generations' value system constitute only a part of a more extensive cultural transformation. At its core, one finds not only the weakening of traditional religious, social, and sexual norms, but also the appearance of new types of economic, cultural, and political behavior. Although economics continue to play a major role in industrialized countries, it may no longer be considered as the crucial explanatory factor. What can now be seen is the slow advance of those values which are related to prestige motives, self-realization, and values which are defined primarily in cultural terms and which have become the strongest motivators for human behavior.

Cultural change theory maintains that citizen political behaviors are based on more than external life circumstances and environmental effects. Cultural learning, socialization experiences, interconnections among various majority cultures and minority subcultures also fulfill a very important role in shaping our thoughts and actions in public life. In this sense, culture is a system of attitudes, values, and knowledge for a given society, which is transmitted from generation to generation. Consequently, unlike laws and legal decisions, it cannot be transformed overnight. Historically developed values and the accumulated knowledge of a nation's political culture persist in hidden forms, even if there is a complete change in political leaders, regimes, or governments. For example, over many decades, communist regimes could not abolish those traditional cultural and religious attitudes and values which lurked beneath the surface of society. In those first democratic elections held in postcommunist countries, the successes of those parties which offered Christian-national slogans and programs demonstrated the validity of a theory of cultural resistance. Simultaneously, other Eastern European political developments indicated that former communist governments' political propaganda and indoctrination had some influence on citizens' political attitudes.

STRUCTURAL CHANGES IN THE WEST AND EAST

If we analyze the pattern of relationships between voters' socioeconomic background, their political participation, and their attitudes, we find significant differences between Central and Eastern Europe and the West. After 1945, economic development took off in Western Europe and the US. Despite continuing debates about the state's economic role, governmental involvement in solving social problems was significantly expanded. Structural economic changes basically transformed labor-market structures as well. The number of agricultural workers also drastically decreased, while many other workers left the industrial sector for service-sector jobs. In industrialized countries, over half the work force have jobs in the service sector and in public administration. Thanks to expanded opportunities for tertiary learning, in many Western countries, more than one-third of each younger generation experience some form of higher education.

Parallel to this expansion, the quantity and quality of the information sources also grew incredibly. The electronic and print media have created a communications revolution and a global information superhighway. The use of devices such as narrow-casting and computers increases data processing efficiency. These were just a few of the factors which make it possible for an enlarged public to obtain more political information, which promised to improve effective political participation. Along with these structural changes, there were new developments in the political sphere as well. Stable party preferences, so characteristic of Western party systems, became weaker along with erosion in the importance of class status and religion. Personal and party stands on concrete issues proved to have much more influence on voting behavior than did traditional party preferences. However, manifest differences between election promises and actual policies, along with frequent cases of corruption and public scandals, also inspired popular distrust in political institutions and elites.

Following radical changes in the political systems in Central and Eastern Europe, local economies everywhere were in deep crisis. All new governments immediately had to cope with these new (as well as inherited) economic difficulties, while simultaneously putting their respective countries on the road toward the market economy. These governments found themselves in a very complicated and contradictory situation. On the one hand, they had to curtail drastically the extent of the state-owned sector and, on the other, they had to preserve the role of the state in the social sphere. After dismantling large, state-run enterprises, many people lost their jobs. With a shrinkage in the market for agricultural products and the removal of state price supports, fewer people found work in this sector (which previously had a state monopoly on the agricultural cooperatives). Economic development in the service sector was not rapid enough to absorb the superfluous labor force. The old middle class began to disappear, while growing unemployment became one of the worst problems in the infant democracies. Furthermore, the state-run higher education system had provided opportunities only for some 10 per cent of each young generation and private educational institutions did not grow to meet increased demands for more professional and technical training.

Citizen expectations regarding the complete changeover from the previous system were not fulfilled and popular trust in new democratic institutions and new political elites began to diminish. Whereas in the West, the outlines of a new type of 'postmodern politics' appeared on the horizon, in parts of Central and Eastern Europe, bloody ethnic conflicts have occurred along with the rise of nationalistic populist parties (which made political capital out of increasing social and political tensions); the increases in unemployed workers, new immigrants, and asylum seekers; and the growth of a new authoritarian spirit.

Despite many internal divisions and tensions, Hungarian parliamentary democracy and its political institutions have preserved their stability and their ability to function. As the time for the Spring 1994 general elections approached, basic political divisions seemed to deepen. In contrast with parallel processes underway in the West, in Hungary, more traditional factors of division which influence party support and voters' attitudes (for example, social status and religion) are increasingly significant today. Since the Hungarian multiparty system has not yet fully crystallized because it is a relatively new phenomenon, citizens tend to give priority to generational differences, traditional class strata identifications, and religious commitments instead of to party performance and ideologies.

GENERATIONAL CLEAVAGES AND PARTY ATTITUDES

The large-scale involvement of young people in the overthrow of one-party systems in Central and Eastern Europe had already determined that a marked generation change would take place within the political elite as well. In fact, this generational change took place, but not in its anticipated direction. The group of politicians (predominantly middle-aged people who, by 1989, had some political experience) (Gazsó, September 1992, p. 85) was soon replaced; another group of politicians came to the fore. They were older, invoked Hungarian historical traditions and the pre-communist political culture and ways of thinking, but had no real experience in practical politics (Róna-Tas, 1991, p. 379). Thus, the first wave of systemic changes here did not result in the political ascendancy of the younger people. However, this lack of generational change in the political leadership does not mean that this opportunity has been lost forever for the younger people. In many cases, a separate analysis of political generations only becomes important after a given system of political socialization proves to be a complete failure (Delli Carpini, 1989, p. 14). In view of these antecedents for the Hungarian revolution (in terms of the political socialization), it is not surprising that a historically unique party consisting of young people under 35, the Federation of Young Democrats (FYD), became a part of the first freely elected parliament as the fifth largest party in the country.

After the 1990 elections, the 386-strong Hungarian parliament was comprised of six parties. The Hungarian Democratic Forum (HDF) had 164 seats (42 per cent) and was a moderate to conservative, Christian, nationalist party. Other Hungarian political parties were the Alliance of Free Democrats (AFD) with 92 seats (24 per cent), a social-liberal party; the Independent Small-holders Party (ISHP), which had 44 seats (11 per cent), a populist-conservative party; the Hungarian Socialist Party (HSP), with 33 seats (9 per cent), a reformed communist, social-democrat party; the Federation of Young Democrats (FYD) with 22 seats (6 per cent), a radical-liberal, nationally-oriented party; and the Christian Democratic People's Party (CDF), with 21 seats (5 per cent), a Christian-democratic party.

Under the leadership of the HDF, along with participation of the ISHP and CDP, a conservative, Christian, national coalition government was formed. Within the Hungarian parliament, a significant number of deputies changed sides from 1990 to 1994 so that the governing coalition's majority dwindled. Even after Prime Minister József Antall's death in December 1993, the HDF coalition government did not lose its majority so that the Hungarian government was the only regime in Central and Eastern Europe that was continuously in power between 1990 and 1994.

Since the FYD was a very popular political party for many years (especially among voters aged 18 to 50), it provides a basis for the generation-specific analysis of voters' party preferences. In Hungary, we find that the voter's age is an important indicator of various types of political activity as well as of one's willingness to vote.

In autumn 1992, we conducted a nationwide political socialization survey by sampling 4000 people (representative of the teenage Hungarian population). The Szonda Ipsos Public Opinion Research Institute conducted the survey and processed the resulting data for us. The sample consisted of four subgroups, each with 1000 respondents (10-11, 12-13, 14-15, and 16-17 years old).

Our primary aim was to discover the effects and characteristic features of the processes of political socialization which had started since 1989, after the change in the political system. We wanted to find out what was the relative standing of politics among young people. We learned they not only did not appreciate politics, but from a list of nine topics, politics got the worst ranking (Figure 8.1). When combined with other data from youth research, apathy toward politics signifies the dangerous condition of traditional forms of political participation in a situation where only 2.8 per cent of the young generation belong to any youth organization.

Willingness of younger citizens to participate in democratic politics has a different history in Western Europe and the US since, in the former countries, the proportion of young voters has declined. The US 1992 presidential election reflected Bill Clinton's successful mobilization of young voters, minorities, women, and other key groups.

Other researchers besides Inglehart also mention that there is a close relationship between the age effects (generations) and voters' attitudes. For example, Harrop and Miller (1987) emphasize four trends regarding youth and elections. Namely, young voters are more favorable toward social welfare, environmental, or 'leftist' policies than older voters; young people are more supportive of political extremism (either 'right' or 'left'); the young are much more open to new parties or independent candidates; and those voting for the first time are more likely influenced by current (rather than historical) events. Furthermore, in his analysis of 'protest politics', Dalton (1988, pp. 69-70) says that this type of political behavior is characteristic of the younger generation (which has more leisure time) and those still enrolled in higher education.

Figure 8.1 Answers to the question: To what extent are you interested in the following? (averages within the age group of 10-17 years; range: 1 = not interested at all, 5 = very much interested) (November 1992)

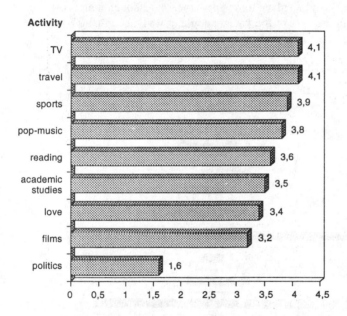

Note: Sample size = 4000 persons.

Since the political behavior of young voters is extremely unpredictable, special attention must be paid to the dual effects of socialization and generational influences. Younger voters also constitute a significant proportion of the Hungarian electorate. Among those who voted in Hungary for the first time in 1994, we find three age cohorts or so-called 'large' generations. The 770 000 young people (aged 18-21) who voted for the first time played a crucial political role, if only because of their numerical strength. Neither the educational institutions nor the labor market could absorb this group. Some 30 per cent of this group consisted of uneducated or poorly educated young people with higher rates of unemployment than other groups. The 13-33-year-old cohorts together made up almost one-third of those who were eligible to vote (that is, 2.3 million people). If using the age classifications from the political public opinion polls, we can say that the largest age group consists of the 34-39-year-olds (that is, 2.6 million people). The Hungarian data reveal that voters under 50 years of age make up two-thirds of the electorate.

In analyzing data from the political public opinion polls, we relied on Szonda Ipsos Public Opinion Research Institute. For years, this institute has conducted a monthly survey of citizens' shifting party preferences using a nationally representative sample of 1000 people. By November 1993, the Federation of Young Democrats had lost its first place in total public popularity. It had previously held this place for over two years. Although it also lost some of its prestige in the eyes of the young people, it was, nevertheless, the most popular party for them (Figure 8.2).

Figure 8.2 Party preferences for two Hungarian age groups (in %, March and November 1993)

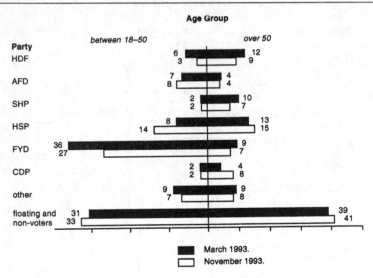

If we analyze the average age of the voters for each party, we can see even more clearly the generation structure of the Hungarian electorate (Figure 8.3). The average age of FYD voters is 35 years. While this fact bodes well for the FYD future, at the same time, it is potentially dangerous because the number of the independent, between-party, or 'floating' voters is relatively high (as are nonvoters) in these younger generations. It may also pose a threat to the new Hungarian democracy because if the popularity of FYD falls significantly, then younger voters may decide not to vote at all if they are unable to find an appropriate party to support.

Figure 8.3 Average age (in %) of the nonvoters and voters for specific political parties (March 1993)

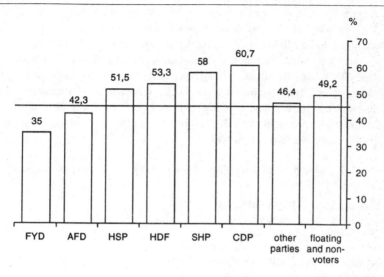

Note: Average age of citizens with voting rights is 46.3.

THE RENAISSANCE OF RELIGIOSITY

Besides the generation-related characteristics of the Hungarian voters' attitudes, another feature of many of the postcommunist countries is the spectacular renaissance of religion. New governments have helped the established 'historical' churches so that they can now exert political influence and ensure that religious interests are represented. Religious parties in the governing coalition are probably guided by power interests as well as principles. They can easily make political capital out of the present religious renaissance and augment the number of their supporters. This political advance of religion has not occurred without widespread social debate and conflict. Two such examples are the debates about laws regulating television in Poland and the problems connected with the return of church property in Hungary.

Even after decades of compulsory Marxist indoctrination, a majority in most of the populations in Central and Eastern European countries can be considered religious. However, a natural resistance develops against the return of any officially-promoted 'religiousness', just as was the case with respect to the previously endorsed 'irreligiousness'. Quite often, these spectacular demonstrations of a party's/candidate's religious fervor and identity are meant to compensate for the lack of any clear political commitments. Thus, it may even serve as a test of faith if one joins the newly emerging political elites.

Our previously mentioned survey of Hungarian youth included a group of questions about their religious beliefs. The responses revealed some surprising facts, such as that 51 per cent of youth (aged 11-12 and 13-14) declared themselves to be religious. This proportion was not much lower in the case of the older youth either since for the 15-16-year-old cohort, it was 45 per cent and for the 17-18-year-old cohort, it was 41 per cent (Table 8.1). In each age cohort, approximately 20 per cent also replied, 'I believe in God, but I am not religious.' These data indicate that among youth, religious beliefs have a stable basis. These responses also reveal that more than 80 per cent of the two youngest cohorts get regular religious education in school.

Table 8.1 Self-reports of 16-17-year-olds about their relationship to religion (in %) (November 1992)

Religious, follows church teachings	8
Religious in a personal way	33
Believes in God, but not religious	21
Not religious, not interested in such issues	19
Not religious, but has other convictions	10
Does not know	10
Another answer	2

Note: Sample size - 1000 persons.

If we analyze the party preferences of would-be voters in the 17-18-year-old cohort, we find overwhelming support for the FYD (52.2 per cent) and minimal support for the other parties (AFD, 4.7 per cent; HDF, 4.0 per cent; ISHP, 1.3 per cent; CDP, 0.7 per cent; and HSP, 0.2 per cent). Among these would-be (first-time) voters who are religious or who believe in God, a majority support the FYD, although average support will not differ from the average of other not-religious/nondeist FYD supporters. Almost every CDP supporter (though their number is very small) is either definitely religious or at least believes in God. This same pattern occurs for the other parties: ISHP (77 per cent), HFF (72.5 per cent), AFD (66 per cent), and FYD (62.9 per cent). (The HSP is not mentioned because the degree of support is so low that the data cannot be evaluated without danger of distortion.)

In summer 1993, we also conducted a survey called 'Political Structure, Party Structure, and Voters' Attitudes', involving a national probability sample of 2000 people representing the Hungarian general electorate. We asked the survey respondents to characterize themselves from a religious attitudes standpoint. They had to choose from among five alternatives (Tables 8.1 and 8.2):

1. I am religious and follow church teachings.
2. I am religious 'in a personal way'.
3. I cannot tell whether I am religious or not (do not know).
4. I am not religious.
5. I have some other conviction. I have nothing to do with any religion.

Taking everything into consideration, we see no essential difference between the self-evaluation of the older and younger Hungarians. Nearly two-thirds (64.6 per cent) of those eligible to vote declare themselves to be religious in some form. This proportion is similar to the aggregate data concerning the 15-18-year-old cohort, but it is lower than the share of religious persons among the youngest cohorts. What we have been able to establish is that some two-thirds of all citizens have some religious orientation and Hungarian youth also share these beliefs at an even higher level of support.

Table 8.2 Self-reports of party voters' religious views (in %) (May 1993)

Party	Religious follows church teachings	Religious in personal way	Does not know	Not religious	Not religious but has other convictions
HDF	23	51	4	17	5
AFD	10	42	9	27	12
SHP	28	61	1	8	2
HSP	4	49	5	30	12
FYD	10	50	6	26	8
CDP	55	39	1	5	
Other	7	48	7	27	11
Floating/ nonvoters	18	50	7	20	5

Note: Sample size = 2000 persons.

Juxtaposing party support at the overall national level and religious self-evaluation, we can establish even more subtle connections between voters' preferences and these attitudes. Those religious persons who follow church teachings primarily tend to support the Christian Democratic Peoples' Party (17.3 per cent) and, then, the FYD (17.0 per cent). The proportion of religious persons who support the CDP is four times the average level of general popular support for this party. However, for the FYD, the opposite is true in that religious persons support this party at a level 10 per cent below that for the whole population's level of overall support.

Among those who declared themselves religious 'in a personal way', the FYD has the largest proportion of their support (28.4 per cent), which is somewhat higher than the national average of its overall support. It is surprising that in the last-mentioned category, the second place nationally is held by the Hungarian Socialist Party, which is the least popular nationwide among those who follow the teachings of the church (10 per cent).

Other connections between religion and party can be seen if we analyze the distribution of the voter base for each party *vis-à-vis* attitudes toward religion (Table 8.2). Among those who declared themselves religious 'in a personal way', the proportion of those not voting or not choosing a specific party (floating voters) is significantly higher (49.8 per cent) than the overall national average for this group, whereas in all other religious categories, the proportion of floaters/nonvoters is far below this figure.

The stable Christian Democrat supporters (93.7 per cent) are recruited almost exclusively from the ranks of the religious citizens, the majority (55.2 per cent) of whom follow church teachings. Among Independent Smallholders Party members (farmers), the number of religious persons is also high, but the proportions differ radically from those of the CDP. Among ISHP supporters, the absolute majority is those who are religious 'in a personal way' (61.3 per cent), whereas those who follow church teachings constitute only 28 per cent. Among Hungarian Democratic Forum supporters, the proportion of the religious persons is also high (74 per cent), with more than half (51.2 per cent) declaring themselves to be religious 'in a personal way' or following church teachings (22.8 per cent). Among FYD supporters, religious persons also form a majority (59.8 per cent), but within this category, the majority are religious 'in a personal way'. Religious persons also are in the majority among the supporters of the Alliance of Free Democrats (52 per cent) and the Hungarian Socialist Party (52.2 per cent). However, internally, those in the AFD who follow church teachings are twice as numerous as those among the HSP.

Looking at voters at the other end of the scale (those who say they have no religious beliefs), we find that their proportion is the highest among the HSP (29.7 per cent), the AFD (27 per cent), and the FYD (25.5 per cent). The ISHP (with only 7.5 per cent support) is contrasted with the HDF's (17.1 per cent) relatively strong support from nonreligious people.

CONCLUSIONS

What conclusions can we draw from the three classic models (Michigan, rational choice, and socialization/postmodern) of voter behaviors as well as from these data on generational and religious factors and their influence on political behavior in Hungary?

We can apply these classic models for the time being only to a limited degree as a framework for analyzing Hungarian voting/party/political behavior. Hungarians' party preferences and the party system, itself, both display a high degree of flux and uncertainty. In view of the fact that more than two-thirds of the Hungarian voters have had no personal experience with the workings of a pluralist political system, the formation of party identification through the influence of religious and family ties can be considered as something relevant and useful.

For decades, most Hungarians were compelled to survive and to evade the communist power structure's rules (including their working in the so-called 'second economy'). They relied on rational calculations and personal connections and stayed independent of the official redistributive system as much as possible. These skills were very efficiently transmitted to young family members. Even in the new postcommunist political situation, they provide a viable strategy of life for many. Hungarian society does not lack the tradition of a rational political behavior. However, in the long run, a modified version of socialization and culture change theory (adapted to Hungarian circumstances and religious/generational aspects thereof) can provide a suitable and more comprehensive explanation for recent and current changes in the realms of Hungarian political culture and political behavior, including party loyalty and voter preferences.

One of the great dilemmas both before and after the 1994 elections is whether or not there will be a generational breakthrough within the Hungarian political elite. Despite the decrease in the FYD's popularity, such a development can be envisaged in the light of the present data. In all probability, the extent of its realization will depend on the policies of the new coalition government.

The dynamic economic processes shaping the structure of Hungarian society have led to a situation in which the majority feel uncertain and insecure about the future. Behind the renaissance in religion, there is also (among other factors) the driving force of poverty. Previous religious orientations and recent political socialization are likely to play an increasingly important role in influencing voters' attitudes and behaviors. Any party would meet serious resistance if it tried to pursue an openly antireligious policy. Considering everything (and owing to the popular uncertainty about the political, social, and economic environment), it seems to us that the 1994 parliamentary elections were primarily based on traditional (for example, religious and former Communist Party loyalties) affiliations, preferences, and feelings. Consequently, rational, independent, free-thinking, and well-informed voters will form only a small minority at best.

ACKNOWLEDGEMENT

We acknowledge financial help from the National Scientific Research Fund (OTKA) and the Turn of the Millennium (Ezredforduló) Youth Foundation in Hungary for supporting this research project.

REFERENCES

Agh, A. (1993). 'The Comparative Revolution and the Transition in Central and Southern Europe', pp. 231-52 in *Journal of Theoretical Politics*, Vol. 5, No. 2.

Barnes, S., M. Kaase, M. et al.(1979). *Political Action. Mass Participation in Five Western Democracies*. Beverly Hills, CA and London, UK: Sage Publications.

Bozóki, A., A. Körösényi, and G. Schöpflin (1992). *Post-Communist Transition. Emerging Pluralism in Hungary*. London, UK: Pinter Publisher. New York, NY: St. Martin's Press.

Campbell, A., P. Converse, W. Miller, and D. Stokes (1960). *The American Voter*. New York, NY: John Wiley & Sons, Inc.

Campbell, A. et al. (1966). *Elections and the Political Order*. New York, NY: John Wiley & Sons, Inc.

Dalton, R. (1988). *Citizen Politics in Western Democracies*. Chatham, NJ: Chatham House Publishers, Inc.

Delli Carpini, M. (1989). 'Age and History: Generations and Sociopolitical Change', pp. 11-56 in R. Sigel (ed.) *Political Learning in Adulthood: A Sourcebook of Theory and Research*. Chicago, IL and London, UK: The University of Chicago Press.

Downs, A. (1957). *An Economic Theory of Democracy*. New York, NY: Harper and Row.

Gazsó, F. (September 1992). 'Cadre Bureaucracy and the Intelligentsia', pp. 76-90 in *The Journal of Communist Studies*, Vol. 8. No. 3.

Hankiss, E. (1990). *East European Alternatives*. Oxford, UK: Calderon Press.

Harrop, M. and W. Miller (eds.) (1987). *Elections and Voters: A Comparative Introduction*. New York NY: New Amsterdam Books.

Inglehart, R. (1977). *The Silent Revolution: Changing Values and Political Styles Among Western Publics*. Princeton, NJ: Princeton University Press.

Inglehart, R. (1990). *Culture Shift in Advanced Society*. Princeton, NJ: Princeton University Press.

Körösényi, A. (1991). 'Revival of the Past or New Beginning? The Nature of Post-Communist Politics', pp. 52-74 in *Political Quarterly*, Vol. 62. No. 1.

Niemi, R. and H. Weisberg (eds.) (1993a). *Classics in Voting Behavior*. Washington, DC: Congressional Quarterly Press.

Niemi, R. and H. Weisberg (eds.) (1993b). *Controversies in Voting Behavior*. Washington, DC: Congressional Quarterly Press.

Powell, G. (1982). *Contemporary Democracies*. Cambridge, MA and London, UK: Harvard University Press.

Róna-Tas, Á. (1991). 'The Selected and the Elected: The Making of the New Parliamentary Elite in Hungary', pp. 357-93 in *East European Politics and Societies*, Vol. 4, No. 3.

Szoboszlai, G. (ed.) (1991). *Democracy and Political Transformation: Theories and East-Central European Realities*. Budapest, Hungary: Hungarian Political Science Association.

Szoboszlai, G. (ed.) (1992). *Flying Blind: Emerging Democracies in East-Central Europe*. Budapest, Hungary: Hungarian Political Science Association.

9   *Deluded Nations*
Dynamics of Nationalism in Central and Eastern Europe

György Csepeli

ABSTRACT

This chapter deals with the symptoms of nationalism which have resurfaced in Central and Eastern Europe. New, emerging challenges have to be properly understood during the transition from state socialism to democracy and a market economy. This contribution argues that a legacy lacking correspondence between the state and nation, with concomitant trends of authoritarianism, can hinder development. This applies especially to democratic institutions and citizenship based on universal standards of human rights. Present antiliberal and dogmatic national ideologies serve the interests of the previous ruling elite, who can exploit historical and symbolic conflicts among ethnic nationals. The conclusion of this chapter is that malignant international processes should be foreseen if they are to be sidetracked. The international community and democratic countries of Western Europe and North America must share leadership roles, otherwise global disorder, barbarism, primitiveness, xenophobia, nativism, and other uncivilized behaviors will become all too characteristic of civic life in Central and Eastern Europe during the 21st century.

INTRODUCTION

This chapter is about what 'nation' and 'national identity' mean in Central and Eastern Europe and what new challenges we can be sure to encounter during the transition there from state socialism to postsocialism. This study then discusses future prospects as well as recent research findings.

The first matter which we have to face when examining ethnonational problems is that the future often looks back at us from the past. It is a cliché of postmodern historical writings that certain great narratives which served as stories of the past have been lost and that the major units of time (that is, the past, present, and future), which are seemingly so easily distinguishable, have actually been fused together. However, countries in Central and Eastern Europe are only now waging their battles for modernity. During the period of state socialism, time stopped here. The Czechs, Germans, Poles, Slovaks, Hungarians, Romanians, Serbians, Croatians, and Slovenes were sentenced to forget their past.

Many reasons support this forced forgetfulness. History was not merciful to these peoples. They lived beside each other for centuries, though they never truly knew each other. The relations between them were not built on harmony, but rather on eternal conflict. The passage of time saw an entire array of prejudices, hatreds, negative experiences, and ill-intentioned international processes. Moreover, in the course of the 20th century, both world wars originated out of this explosive region. We do not see (and have not been offered) a guarantee that this unfortunate historical scenario will not repeat itself. The ethnic nations of Yugoslavia today stand in bloody conflict. In place of the beleaguered Soviet Union, hungry and frustrated ethnic nations are emerging. Their basis for secure national identities is, at best, unsure. The extent of the nuclear arsenal accumulated by the old Red Army is also frightening. Therefore, this chapter is conceived in the hope that an attempt to provide a proper understanding of the present situation may help us decrease threatening dangers from this part of the world. One can properly act only with correct information.

'Where is Central and Eastern Europe?' I believe that this question was not frequently posed in America between 1945 and 1989. Perhaps it did not even need to be asked. In 1945, President F. D. Roosevelt answered this question when he gave in and agreed that the Americans would allow the Red Army to press as far as the Elbe. Thus, all the space to the East of the Elbe lies in Eastern Europe, including the Central area of this region. There are at least 15 ethnonational groups which have lived in Eastern Europe for the last millennium.

In the reign of Charles the Great (747-814) the first European territories to the West of the Elbe River were separated from the lands beyond it. Thus, the 'Occident' came into being. It was a symbiosis of the Greco-Roman legal and political traditions, Christian values, and the 'barbaric'-German cultural elements of previous times. Since the Latin usage, 'Occident' refers to 'the West' in modern European languages. This word 'West' is not just a point on the compass; it means much more than this. As Anderson (1974) maintains, the West is where freedom, the interests of property, and equality reign supreme. Over the centuries together with these interests, those institutions which today are spread throughout the Western world came into being. These include guarantees of societal peace, dynamic economic development, and human security.

The separation of these areas lying to the East of the Elbe from the rest of Europe was a *fait accompli* even during the era of Charles the Great. Szücs (1988), whose article on the regions of Europe appeared in 1981 in Hungarian, was rightfully surprised that when the authors of the Yalta agreement (Roosevelt, Winston Churchill, and Joseph Stalin) agreed on the postwar division of Europe, it was as though they had carefully studied the previous borders of the Western Roman Empire. However, what Stalin inherited was not homogeneous. Upon the ruins of the Roman Empire, a successor empire centered in Byzantium emerged in both the West and East. Dynamic developments leading to modern 'citizen-identity' began in the Western area of the divided Roman Empire; however, in the Eastern part of the empire, servitude, the principles of authoritarianism, and the consciousness of being a subject was strengthened. Byzantium did not recognize the Roman pope as the head of Christianity; therefore, in opposition to the Catholic faith of Rome, Christians in the East clung to orthodoxy.

While the Western Roman Empire's border stretched to the Elbe, the Eastern Roman Empire did not quite reach it. It became a question of which influence over the lands stretching from the Black Sea to the Elbe would assert itself. The force of Byzantine Orthodox Christianity spread on to Bulgarians, Romanians, Russians, Greeks, Serbs, and Albanians. This influence, however, was broken at the Carpathians, where wooded areas separated Russian and Polish lands. It could not extend its influence to the Estonians, Lithuanians, and Latvians situated on the shores of the Baltic Sea. Thus, a middle region appeared and took over the Western Roman influences, recognized the authority of the Roman pope, and created the basis of Western institutional structures. But all this happened later. The Poles, Czechs, Slovaks, Hungarians, Croatians, Slovenians, Estonians, Latvians, and Lithuanians lived in this central region, where they remain today. The paradox is that, although originally not considered a part of the 'West' (a metaphor for a particular political ideology and culture), this is exactly what the Baltics became. Meanwhile, since they lay very close to the East, the West at any time could culturally renounce them. Since they often were incapable of defending themselves, they often turned to the West for help in fighting to preserve their identity (which occurred several times in the 20th century).

Marx wrote in 1848 that the specter of communism was Europe. Though this specter was able to trample with his foot only Eastern Europe, after 150 years, his sojourn in Europe has come to an end. Following the collapse of the Eastern European state socialist systems, history was renewed in every country. Stalin once said to Churchill that history belongs to God. By this, he meant that the past has no power over the present and the future. In light of past former Soviet successes, it appears that Stalin was right. Socialism in Eastern Europe endeavored to erase the pre-Marxist/Leninist past once and for all, to obliterate the old national traditions rooted in the past, to eliminate social inequalities and the remnants of feudalism, and to create the 'New Socialist Man'. This 'New Man', made out of individual and national self-interest coupled with an open heart and soul, would take part selflessly and joyously in the building of a rationally planned and organized 'new society', which ceaselessly would satisfy all human needs.

Stalin's proposed program was popularly attractive. The people of the areas spreading from the Elbe to the East lived in poverty and backwardness. Who would not have happily made the sacrifice to achieve these noble goals? They put an end to an economy based on private property; every source of economic power became the socialist state's. The 'new life' had begun. However, a shadow was cast on these beginnings: the Red Army preserved order; the secret police guarded the public conscience; and every competing political and public organization was either forbidden or severely restricted in its activities, except for the ruling Communist Party.

Mass poverty and underdevelopment came to an end. The average life span increased, school and health access became free, unemployment became a foreign notion, industry took off, and cities (which attracted the peasant masses from the nearby villages) popped up almost daily. The modern goals of socialism had begun to be realized. But the people were not happier. Coercion, intimidation, narrowed possibilities, and lack of freedom stifled them. Paradoxically, the more the promises of socialism were realized, the more industry and urbanization advanced, the more cultural standards rose, then the more dissatisfied the people became. The Red Army (or at least the local power behind the Soviets) suppressed this dissatisfaction. It became increasingly more difficult to convince the Eastern Germans, Poles, Hungarians, Czechs, Slovaks, and Romanians that the building of this 'new society' was in their personal interests. The practical means contradicted the idealistic goals. In the course of employing the means of terror, intimidation, coercion, and subjugation, the Eastern European socialist societies split apart. The possessors (party functionaries, bureaucrats, technocrats, police, and soldiers) of these means came face to face in a catastrophic confrontation with those who lacked such power or means. In fact, it turned out that there was to be no 'new society'.

With the passing of decades, however, it also developed that state socialism had effected some irreversible changes. Although the promises of modernization were not fulfilled, members of East European nations learned what it meant to be equal - even if this meant the equality of subjugation. Previous social barriers fell. In times of turbulence (even if they had been beaten into order by the authorities), they learned that they had strength in numbers. They also discovered that the promised 'new society' was a lie since next door in the West freedom, security, and prosperity ruled. They began to long for the West, which they first encountered in the form of consumer goods. Western popular culture brought them these ideas. Later, on the basis of personal experience, they also became convinced of the joy of consumerism because, even if only in small numbers, they were able to travel to the West and Western tourists were able to visit them.

The state socialist systems centralized society-produced goods and later redistributed them. However, in the course of redistribution, those directing it took a portion of these goods. Society had to satisfy itself with the remains. These remains were too few and too small to motivate the workers who, in every possible way, withdrew themselves from the power of the center. The workers, themselves, began to engage in economic activities with one another. And thus, in the shadow of redistributed wealth, there arose a second economy which followed market principles. The two parallel economic modes hindered rather than helped each other. When conflicts arose, state-imposed redistribution always won.

Time and again, consumers encountered shortages. There were just not enough supplies or consumer articles for a respectable daily subsistence. Meanwhile, workers noticed waste in their workplaces time and time again. Kornai's (1980) writings perfectly captured the socialist economy as a symbiosis of shortage and waste. This economy made rational development impossible. To the contrary, it resulted in a waste of resources, pollution of nature, and the decline in the quality of human life. When, under pressure from the Soviet Union at the end of 1981, suppression of Solidarity occurred and dissatisfaction in Poland ensued, it became obvious in the entire Central and Eastern European region that the socialist economy and the oppressive political and ideological order were irreformable. Therefore, a classic revolutionary situation arose. It is the joke of history that it was Lenin who, before the Bolshevik revolution of 1917, defined a revolutionary situation as one in which the ruling group no longer could rule in the old way and the subjugated groups no longer wanted to live in the old ways. Thus, a revolutionary situation prevailed in a society when the given method of societal coexistence suited no one, when everyone believed he/she was the injured party.

The realization of socialism was built on the negation of history. In time, however, socialism acquired its own history, which indicated that the socialist goals were unobtainable. In the wake of realizing the goals of socialism by means of terror and oppression, there surfaced popular suffering, disillusionment, and dissatisfaction. In the course of the history of socialism, negative experiences multiplied. In those Central and Eastern European societies which observed developments in the West, the impression easily arose that the only choice for Central and Eastern Europeans disenchanted with socialism was to accept the positive interests of the West along with the institutions based on them. It appeared that they longed for fundamental civil and human rights; they wanted to create a market economy; they desired ideological pluralism. Moreover, they were capable of such societal inequalities which are formed a) when the means of production are in private hands, and b) when privilege arises as a consequence of individual success. In Central and Eastern Europe, many people believed that opposition to socialism contained both affirmation of civil society and recognition of private property.

This is where that history (which Stalin said belongs to God) enters the picture. The Central and Eastern European societies, under the influence of the Soviet Union as dictated in the Yalta Agreement, were never really freed from their cursed legacy. This legacy was rooted in the hierarchical social organization of the Eastern Roman Empire along with the long overdue adoption of Western models. While in Central and Eastern Europe various empires (such as the Ottoman, the Habsburg, or the Russian empires) were ruling over various peoples, in Western Europe, national states with distinct borders were emerging.

The West European national states had their own rulers, capitals, national banks, currencies, languages, symbols, armies, administrations, and autonomous scientific and cultural institutions. By contrast, Central and Eastern Europe lacked independent states; if there were such, they were merged within the various empires. Consequently, since social development possibilities were so limited, this hindered the growth of stable identity structures for Central and Eastern Europeans.

In the course of the social revolutions of West European states, democratic rights were extended to the population, resulting in clarifying not only the national identity of every individual state, but also the conscious identity of individual citizens. After the 1789 French Revolution, along with citizen and national identity came the presumption of equality. Whoever was a part of the nation also had equal rights to freedom, property, and participation in state life. On the basis of mutually possessed rights, religious, cultural, or ethnic differences could emerge. But these differences could never be allowed to become so strong that they would neutralize the other cohesive forces of identity as conceptualized in democratic political, ideological, and economic rights. Certain conflicts have remained (for example, between church and state), but they were not interpreted as being over one's national identity.

An Hungarian political scientist, Bibó (1991) points to those profound differences which (in contrast to the formation of Western European national states) characterized the formation of Central and Eastern European national states. The criteria for establishing German national identity best exemplify these differences. (For this analysis, I am also indebted to Kornai, 1980; Sugar and Lederer, 1971; and Szücs, 1988.)

GERMAN NATIONAL IDENTITY FORMATION

At the beginning of the 19th century, when Napoleon attacked Germany and the Germans were forced to defend themselves, they discovered their identity. Having to defend oneself is a particularly negative position which produces both anxiety and aggression. It aggravated the German situation in that during Napoleon's military attack, the Germans had an extraordinary political configuration. There was no common state; no uniform economic order; no coherent social classes. The Germans lived divided among many states. In such a way, when they awakened to their own identity (and it was Napoleon who provoked them to do so for, in contrast to the French, it was necessary that they first recognize their 'German-ness'), it was necessary that they found their identity in spiritual and cultural ways in the absence of relevant state, administration, law, and commerce practices. In the first place, their language offered them direct consciousness of their identity. More indirectly, the basis of a shared language provided a sense of identity through literature and everything else one can express with words, including philosophy, ethnography, and psychology. Thus, in this unique situation, they initially became German. This meant that, in the first place, nation as an idea had to come into being. As a consequence of this, German-ness was realized. In the course of this realization, the unity of the German state belatedly emerged (again, in contrast to the French) in 1871 - and on French territory to boot. William the First, victorious over the French, was crowned as the German Emperor in Versailles.

Despite the emergence of the German Empire, anxieties about their overdue arrival among the ranks of European national states did not subside. The fear that they would not be able to surpass the English and the French further lingered in the German consciousness. These feelings of national tardiness did not permit a period of needed calm so that the German Empire did not become a democratic state. Instead, the state became centralized and authoritarian. It turned its efforts to stockpiling armaments, obtaining overseas possessions, and achieving security. From this basic picture, we can understand the impatient German national attitudes and their readiness for constant geographical expansion. Realistic perspectives changed completely. The unreal (expansion) appeared to be a realistic task, while a more realistic program (the spread of democratic rights, a search for peaceful development, and preservation of international harmony) became unreal. A new standard glorified perceived German national interests. According to this measure, the entire German population was classified into either 'good' or 'bad' groups by the authoritarian rulers. Germany's enemy turned out to live on the inside. It soon appeared that 'bad' Germans were not even Germans, despite the fact that they spoke German, lived in Germany, and paid taxes to the German state.

The German defeat in World War I only exacerbated the complexities of German national identity. The list of 'bad' Germans grew longer. Not only did members of national minorities and Jews end up on this list, but so did communists, social democrats, Catholics, and homosexuals. One of the consequences of this list appeared when a representative of the most hysterical variant of the German national idea, Adolf Hitler, came to power in 1933. He established concentration camps to filter out 'bad' and 'phony' Germans. Dachau, where one of the first concentration camps was established, lies next to Munich, a center of German culture. In the camp's museum, there is an exhibit which shows the symbols the guards used to distinguish among the camp population. Though every prisoner was defined as harmful from a German point of view, the German Jew, the German communist, the German Catholic, and the German homosexual each had his/her own symbol. World War II brought about the complete defeat of this hysterical German national idea. The Federal Republic of Germany (under American, English, and French occupation) developed a democratic constitution. Following this, the Germans set off on that road which the English (in 1649) and the French (in 1789) had already taken.

In sociology, there are two German words which are generally not translated; rather they are left in the German. The one word is *Gemeinschaft* and the other is *Gesellschaft*. By the former, we mean a collective whose members share the knowledge of a common lineage. They believe that their kinship is naturally given; they endow the existence of the collective with transcendental understanding. Members consider the whole of the group to be more important than the life of the individual. The primary value, then, is the group itself. *Gesellschaft* signifies a group whose members are united under contractual relationships where the body of common interests are defined clearly and rationally. While one enters the first group primarily through birth, anyone who willingly undertakes responsibilities of membership may enter the second. While this group also has common goals, there is open debate and constant renegotiation; if someone maintains a minority opinion, he/she does not end up on a black list; the group does not consider him a traitor. The dignity and the sanctity of individual life is of special importance in this group's value system. Whereas the obligations of the members of the group rest primarily on political and economic views, the collective's cultural, moral, and spiritual characteristics do not force one to play a role as in the former collective group type. The members of the *Gesellschaft* collective do not consider each other brothers. They do not project paternal features onto their leader and do not want to 'develop' at any cost, or to grow organically, like a tree. It is not individuals, but rather the laws which they, themselves, have created which rule over all their members.

Classic Western European national development unambiguously points toward a preference for the *Gesellschaft* type of social organization. A consciousness of some common lineage must exist in Western European nations, but from the point of view of classifying citizens living today, it is not at all clear just who has been born into which group. The nation is the collective based on political will, sustained by a collective of economic interests. On the basis of this political and economic joint collective, a pluralist ideology and a variegated religious, cultural, and moral life emerges. It is only in times of war that such nations close ranks; as soon as the war ends and troop movements cease, peaceful life returns and continues undisturbed.

Certain characteristics of German national development clearly correspond to the *Gemeinschaft* social type. Here, the components of what constitutes national existence are diametrically opposed to the social situation previously discussed. First, the idea of a cultural, moral, and spiritual collective emerges. Upon these foundations, one begins to look for political, legal, and economic grounds. Consequently, it is necessary that such a state be in a condition of constant mobilization; the ideal view and reality can never be resolved or come completely together. Reality stands in need of constant improvement. Collective/elite will becomes paramount, perspectives of action narrow, and success is overestimated. Failures are buried/hidden and made to appear to be the work of foreign or domestic enemies. A closed national consciousness emerges; this serves as the essential characteristic of a closed national mind.

CENTRAL AND EASTERN EUROPEAN *GEMEINSCHAFTEN*

The recent awakening of Central and Eastern Europe followed the pattern of the previous German national awakening. It could not have occurred otherwise. As we saw earlier, social development was different from the West. Countries in Central and Eastern Europe adopted Western models only much more recently. However, there is a unique, but significant, difference between the development of the German nation and Central and Eastern European nations. Except for the Russians, these countries are small in size. They occupy relatively small territories and have small populations. Their small size, however, is not just a simple mathematical problem in the self-perceptions about these ethnic nations; indeed, it is a painful/embarrassing point for all of them. Their small size is one source of the fear that that which is small may become smaller or even disappear altogether. This fear results in their frequent and spasmodic attempts at expansion. These nations constantly want to grow in territory, population, and international influence. In principle, they have chosen the intensive path to national growth. However, to follow it they must reform their domestic relations, give up their hysterical reflexes, and free themselves from their ideology-manufacturing rulers whose interests actually run counter to a strategy of intensive growth. When a nation wants to grow extensively, its expansion can only be accomplished at the expense of another. It follows from this that a classic zero-sum game is the hotbed for the growth of insecurity, inability to communicate, suspicions, and hatreds.

The past is kept alive in these countries because their zero-sum games continue mostly (as long as there is no war) because of this past. It is the joke of history that in the more than 1000 years since the collapse of the Roman Empire, every nation in Central and Eastern Europe can claim a mythical period of time when it was large. In Hungary, people look back with nostalgia to the time of King Louis the Great, when what is now the territory of such a small country was so large that three seas washed its shores. Even little Slovakia was previously independent, but only for five years and then only by the grace of a fascist Germany. Other Slovak nationalists dream of coming from the Great Moravian Empire which existed for a couple of decades before the Hungarians entered the Carpathian basin in 896 AD. Romania also considers itself a direct descendant of the Roman Empire and traces its history back more than 2000 years. Croatians consider themselves descendants of 'Illyria' (which never existed) (Sugar and Lederer, 1971). Although the Serbs initiated the 1991 war against the Croatians seeking 75 per cent of Croatia's territory, they do not want to hear about their million-plus Albanian minority's right to join Albania nor about the rights of its Hungarian minority (half a million people). History has severely tormented the Poles since neighboring empires have divided its territory among themselves on several occasions. This country was like a shuttlecock batted between Germany and Russia; its borders were always fluid and unstable. One could continue with such examples. Each such proves that this megalomania of historical origins is one of the most dangerous legacies with which people in Central and Eastern Europe must finally come to terms if they want to eventually live with free and democratic social structures.

The essential components of the *Gemeinschaft* type of national consciousness, therefore, are the following:

1. Dichotomization (for example, unyielding discrimination, prejudices, stereotypes, arbitrary immigration policies).
2. Artificial evaluation based on closed-mindedness (for example, emphasis on the nation as symbolizing the greatest value and the artificial or contrived endorsement of its every accomplishment, be it in art, morality, behavior, or even *vis-à-vis* types of flora and fauna).
3. Overcompensation (for example, compensating for one's small size by national accomplishments, believed to be big. These accomplishments could be historical or from any other area so that Hungarians, for example, are extremely proud of the fact that in their forests live deer whose antlers are the largest in the world!).
4. Attribution (including the record of manufactured causes when past failures and successes are explicated). The favored explanations for successes are moral and psychological factors through which the ethnic excellence of the nation can be emphasized. However, when explaining failures, foreign causes (of a lasting or temporary nature) always come to the forefront. The numerical superiority of the enemy and the threat of the outside world play an important role in the self-perceptions of all small nations. The Yugoslavian Serbs, when they seem to be losing from the current Serbo-Croatian War, blame their failures on Germany, accusing it of manipulating the European Community. It is also a history-based wound to the Hungarian national identity regarding the indifference of fellow Hungarians to the repeated deportations in 1944. Then, the Hungarian police crammed hundreds of thousands of Hungarian citizens into ghettos, packed them into trains, and sent them to certain destruction in extermination camps. Several opinion polls questioned present Hungarians about this unforgivable sin. Most people consistently refused to accept any personal responsibility, saying that the occupying Nazi German army carried out these deportations. They dismiss any opinion that the Hungarian churches and public opinion could have done anything to prevent this national disgrace. The Regent, Miklós Horthy, who retained his position during the German occupation, placed direct blame on 'fate' in his memoirs - as though he had not been the

one who agreed with Hitler at Klessheim Castle to allow the Germans (on 15 March 1944) to occupy Hungary without resistance. Since ill fate can produce failures at any time, attributing failure to its inevitability and unpredictability is an ideal means for both creating and maintaining false national self-perceptions. Another very popular cause of failure is betrayal. Where there is betrayal, there are traitors, about whom it is soon discovered that there is something foreign in their origins or mentality. Consequently, one should only expect these people to have become traitors. No matter how we look at it, the communist past lasted for more than four decades in all the Central and Eastern European nations. As previously mentioned, there were disturbances, protests, and other manifestations of public opposition (for example, in 1948, 1952, 1956, 1958, 1980, and 1989), but these decades essentially passed without open revolt or civil warfare. The failure of the state socialist systems made it obvious that the active or passive consent of millions made it possible to keep such systems in power in every country. The euphoria from the collapse of the autocratic communist parties has already passed by the early 1990s. It became more and more unpleasant to face the fact that these communist parties were mass parties (as were the parties which ruled during the fascist era). The proportion of party members in every former socialist country reached 10-15 per cent of the active adult population. Together with their family members, this is indeed an unpleasant fact which involves many people and which cannot be denied. Because the postcommunist transition in the short run has not brought the advantages which the masses were promised or expected during the 'silent revolutions' of 1989, new legal witch hunts have begun. First, ex-party functionaries were put on public trial. Next will be hundreds of thousands of former Communist Party members. Meanwhile, a hunt continues for the former network of secret police informers.

5. Comparison (includes employing artificially developed patterns to secure a positive national self-image. To an observer coming from Western to Central and Eastern Europe, it is most notable that, when there is discussion of a given country's position *vis-à-vis* the West, the same response of 'we are the bridge between West and East' is heard in each country. Meanwhile, in each country, the opinion whispered about its East Central European neighbors is 'they have an Eastern mentality', 'their development has come to a standstill', or 'they are backward.' Thus, the small country-big accomplishment peoples come by their new Western identities without having to create a Western infrastructure, democracy, bank system, and work-ethic culture. Comparison is just another way that the countries in Central and Eastern Europe equate themselves with the West, so that the result will be positive. For instance, in contrast to taking the risks inherent in democratic political relations, they prefer paternalism and authoritarianism which emphasizes/produces security; instead of accepting

emphasis on an alienating consumption, they stress spiritual and cultural advantages; in contrast to negative individualism, they elevate their collectivist feelings as though they are national virtues.

COMMUNIST INTERNATIONALISM

State socialism in Central and Eastern Europe reached an end after the 'silent revolutions' of 1989/90. Both in the West and the East, to those people who had counted on the quick arrival of a civil society and a market economy, this must have been a disappointment. It is as difficult for the former state socialist countries to free themselves of the state just as it was easy to free themselves of socialism or Russian domination. The postsocialist countries inherited a strong bureaucratic apparatus devoted to economic redistribution; this elite will not easily give up either its privileged position or power. This apparatus, furthermore, centralized the lion's share of the economy to the greatest extent possible and only afterwards divided what was left among their clients. The question yet remains as to why these old aspirations do not meet with more significant contemporary societal resistance.

One of the reasons for this lack of resistance is that the generations which grew up under state socialism do not welcome competition based upon the principle of achievement. They do not like any social inequalities separating winners from losers. Thanks to central redistributive mechanisms, during state socialism, the people became used to making a minimal effort to keep their jobs, live in low-rent apartments, have generous/free health provisions, enjoy low-cost mass transportation, take vacations, and receive free state-funded education, leisure, and public education. It is a paradox that previous sociological investigations have shown that in every state socialist country, the old method of redistribution results in at least as much economic inequality as does a market economy. In the first place, it was exactly those who governed redistribution (bureaucrats, well-educated technocrats, and members of the party apparatus) who obtained most scarce resources. These studies, however, were not made public; the authors (for example, Iván Szelényi) were silenced or chased out of the country. It became an *idée fixe* in many circles that, under socialism, societal inequalities diminished and security was adequate for all. Society ended up supporting 'learned inertia inaction/dependence', consequently expecting the all-powerful state to satisfy its needs. The collapse of the state socialist order's ideological and political structures was not able to banish these expectations. As a result, the bureaucracy was able to re-establish itself as indispensable in the new era.

In addition to the state redistributive bureaucracy, there is another powerful group, namely the state administration, police, and military machinery. Typically, people had a negative self-identity under state socialism. Severe, political, and ideological oppression regularly eliminated potential/rival sources of positive identity (that is, having competing religious and worldly identities was prohibited). Collectivization of agriculture and industry consequently led to mass emigration, which also weakened preexistent local and regional ties. The search for alternative political identities was impossible under a one-party system. The one category of social identity permitted was the psychologically empty notion of the international 'proletariat'. As a demonstration of how empty this word was, we can cite the results from one relevant survey. In the 1980s, a survey of functionaries in the communist youth union in Hungary sought to define the following sentence: 'Proletarians of the World Unite!' Despite the fact that during 40 years, one could read this slogan on the heading of almost every daily newspaper, hardly anyone among the survey participants could correctly explain its meaning.

Under state socialism, nobody really knew who he/she was. At best, people only knew where they did not belong; therefore, the one and only measure of their self-definition was negative. On the basis of negative identity, the most diverse pathological symptoms developed: alcoholism, drug use, crime, moral nihilism, cynicism, everyday aggression, lack of solidarity and helpfulness, and a whole network of effects based on primitive collective experiences (for example nepotism, protectionism). These asocial responses were not able to counterbalance the general deep-seated reign of public distrust and suspicion.

The state socialist social order thus began a general attack on identity categories. This attack was quite successful. Ironically, just one category escaped total devastation: national identity consciousness. The endurance of the national category under state socialism is ironic because the founding fathers of socialism (Marx, Engels, and Lenin) intended theirs to be an internationalist doctrine. The socialists viewed previous national identity and consciousness as a means whereby the exploiting classes obscured the exploited's vision so that they share a rational solidarity with the very people with whom they should not (that is, their native interests are diametrically opposed). According to classic/textbook socialists, national identity may be dangerous because a feeling of national separateness could hinder the proletariat in individual nations from expressing solidarity with each other. (Indeed, if they related to one another as foreigners, they could even be capable of war.) According to the doctrine, if socialism wins in a society, it is followed by the decline of national identity and the end of national feeling. There would no longer be a national bourgeoisie which is interested in keeping these reactionary sentiments alive.

Contrary to this naive expectation, the historical reality presents an opposite view. During the initial period of state socialism, it became obvious that living under Soviet rule in Central and Eastern Europe, national traditions lived on; even if under the ashes, the fiery embers of nationalism continued to glow. Following the communist takeover in every Soviet satellite, they organized show trials against high-ranking communist functionaries (the Rajk, Slansky, Kostev,

Gomulka, and Pauker trials). They modelled these trials after the Roman Catholic Inquisition proceedings against heretics in the Middle Ages. In order to carry out the death sentences (which had already been decided upon), the authorities had to obtain forced 'confessions'. These confessions systematically contained acknowledgements of 'nationalist deviation'. Nationalism apparently qualified as a communist heresy. Stalin and his followers perpetuated this in the interest of hindering collaboration among Central and Eastern European states. Stalin greatly disapproved of the ideas of the Bulgarian communist leader Georgi Dimitrov, who suggested that there be a federation of the newly-born socialist states. Dimitrov was a true internationalist who recognized that the only possible countermeasure to the misery of East European nationalism could be the promotion of cultural, political, legal, and economic integration within the region.

From the beginning, the Soviet Union treated the nationalism question using a 'double bind' method. On the one hand, they pursued the question ideologically. On the other hand, it was in this superpower's interest that the individual small states live hermetically sealed from one another. Thus, simultaneously, Moscow could thereby place each small satellite state in a separate transmission belt. This model is exactly what obtained before World War II, when Berlin was the center and Hitler bound the Central and Eastern European states to himself, just as Stalin did later. Thus when the opportunity arose, both tyrants were able to employ without resistance the basic principle which the Roman Emperors used to maintain a unified Roman Empire. This basic principle was conceptualized as *divide et impera* (divide and conquer/rule)!

The isolation and the creation of its own party and state bureaucracy in every former socialist state once again served to produce the foundations of nationalism. Thus emerged a national political and economic elite which was interested in its own survival. Participation in any international division of labor would threaten their existence because it would have meant introducing a market economy or aligning with a world economy. The socialist elites were naturally incapable of doing or accepting this because their skills were limited to central planning and operating the oppressive machinery that went with it.

When it turned out that socialist promises could not be fulfilled (or, more precisely, that it was impossible to supply in mass quantities the modern necessities promised by socialism), frustration and disillusionment increased in socialist societies. These elites had two options. The first was that, by degrees, they could loosen the shackles on the planned economy and make room for market mechanisms to mitigate the effects of their most critical shortcomings. (We may refer to this as the reformed socialist's alternative.) The other possibility is for the elite to fiercely protect mechanisms for 'building socialism'. While it resisted every change, it strove to win the ideological acceptance from the restless population. It was obvious that another ideology (such as nationalism) could not present itself. As we have already noted, socialism pulverized every other possible basis for one's social identity. (This we may call the alternative of the national communist.)

The reformed socialist alternative reached its apex in Hungary following the failure of the 1956 revolution. A new political elite came to power. It recognized that the revolution would not be repeated if they allowed some autonomy in private life and made room for private initiatives (naturally within tightly circumscribed boundaries, relegating major decisions only to questions of their legality or illegality). Therefore, any concession/decision was retractable. Consequently, 'goulash communism' appeared in Hungary and the Hungarian standard of living sharply increased compared with that of the other socialist countries. In Czechoslovakia, the 1968 Soviet intervention put an end to experiments with reform socialism, although the Czechs/Slovaks supported it. The Czechoslovak Communist Party leader, Alexander Dubcek, then acquired unparalleled popularity. In Poland, the collectivization of agriculture never got off the ground; therefore, the germs of a private economy remained. The national ideology in these countries was alive, but the political elite (in the interests of legitimizing its power) saw it as increasingly unnecessary to strongly emphasize its own national identity because it was able to demonstrate its relative economic success.

The party and state leadership in charge of reform under the alternative of national communism realized that it could support its power if it could make the population believe that 'building socialism' was compatible with the culture-nationalist program for national survival from the last century. This idea, itself, originated with Stalin who, in the blood-soaked days of World War II, discovered that he could mobilize the Russian masses behind him if he could present the war of national defense against the Germans as a struggle for the survival of the Russian imperial identity.

Romania is the ideal example of such national communism. The communist dictator ruling in Romania only surpassed his fascist predecessors in nationalist fervor. His system maintained the mindless planned economy, which resulted in only suffering and misery for the Romanians. Meanwhile, a grand-scale national assimilation program began to be realized. The dictator chased out the Jews, ransomed the Romanian Germans to Germany, and began annihilating the cultural identity of the two-million-strong Hungarian minority. The assimilation program enjoyed the support of Romanian national public opinion, behind which, naturally, stood the bureaucratic elite. Bulgaria began a similar enterprise with the Turkish minority living on its territory. In the Balkans, President Josep Broz Tito was able to keep a balance among the individual member states of the Yugoslavian union.

But while in every individual member state there was a centrally planned economy that went with a powerful party and state bureaucracy, it was only a question of time before the lid would pop off the boiling pot. That is, individual member republics could easily fall upon each other with their national slogans and armies waving national flags. In the case of the member republics comprising the disintegrating Soviet Union, the situation is completely analogous. One can expect that the bureaucratic elite of the former member republics, sounding their slogans of national independence, are fighting the same battle for the protection of their own privileges and their rigid redistribution mechanisms (this was the same type of battle which we witnessed between the states comprising the former Yugoslavia). It aggravates the situation that some former Soviet member states possess a significant arsenal of nuclear weapons, the control of which is not entirely secure/satisfactory.

REBIRTH OF THE NATIONAL PAST

The collapse of state socialism brought with it the legitimate rebirth of a national past. On the one hand, the only identity factor which remained was concerned with just where the nation belonged. In a time of insecurity, such needs for identity increase anyway. On the other hand, the traditional type of national ideology became an obvious helpful means to postpone any real societal changes, to delay the introduction of market structures, and to prevent laying a foundation for a civil society.

The most striking manifestation of this national revival is the increased role for (and resurrection of) national symbols. After the 'silent' revolution, every former socialist country has feverishly brought back the ancient national symbols while eliminating Soviet-based ones. They tore down Lenin's many statues, ripped down red stars, and cut out the socialist symbols from formerly red national flags. One such example already existed when the Hungarians in 1956 struck down the behemoth statue of Stalin, an eyesore on one of Budapest's most beautiful squares. They marched against Soviet tanks under flags with holes cut in the center. (The flags had holes because they had excised the Soviet red star, exactly as the people of Bucharest later did when they erupted against communism in 1989.) They also changed street names and, once again, gave cities and mountains their old names. National martyrs were rehabilitated and old exiles were brought home and reburied. They re-tailored the uniforms of the army and the police, changed the dates of national holidays, and reopened old sites for national remembrances and pilgrimages.

Symbolic attacks on national systems caused heated debates in many countries because the multiplicity of national traditions leaves room for a variety of options. In Hungary, for example, the new government spent long months discussing which version of the coat of arms should become the official symbol of the state, recalling the previous case during the communist takeover. There was an almost identical debate in Poland. In both countries, the question was whether or not there was a place in the republic's coat of arms for a king's crown. In Croatia, knives were pulled in the debate over whether the country's coat of arms, which resembles a chessboard, should begin with a red or a white square. (As for the presence of a hammer and sickle, the conservatives have obviously had enough of these socialist symbols, but the final debate has not yet been decided.) In the beginning, the ease and quickness with which these symbolic changes have happened helped us to forget that the transition from state socialism to postcommunism is a rough road paved with many obstacles. Basic questions of state naturally go far beyond mere questions of political symbols.

The countries located beyond the historic Occident of yesteryear must sober up from their intoxication with national fervor. The signs indicate that countries in Central Europe may actually have a greater chance to do this than do those states which were never able to get out of the grip of their Byzantine traditions. The collapse of the Soviet empire guarantees a chance that the people of Eastern Germany, Poland, the Czech Republic, Slovakia, Hungary, Slovenia, and Croatia can find their way back to the path leading to the West. State socialism in these countries wreaked great destruction as well. Socialist reform efforts and a rebirth of national identity-consciousness (thanks to geographic proximity to the West) both contain their democratic elements. However, new postcommunist elites in these countries are profoundly divided about the question of which changes they should approve for building a new national identity. Those people who believe in the *Gemeinschaft* pattern of nation building and wish to move further along its trajectory (of force) can say they have significant societal support. Nevertheless, simultaneously, societal forces which are drawn to the *Gesellschaft* pattern carry just as much public legitimacy. The latter group also works on building up citizen consciousness, which corresponds to modern Western democratic political norms. They are also convinced that, using this model, the values of freedom, property, and equality can develop unhindered. The development of such appropriate supportive institutions, naturally, cannot alone erase the tensions, prejudices, hatreds, and conflicts which the Central European nations acquired in the past. However, one can count on the fact that in the course of opening up class structures which in the future will be based on opportunity-equality, a market economy, and the introduction of democratic politics, we shall likely find an opportunity for national, ethnic, religious, and minority conflicts to be expressed constructively in the future. Hence, it will be more possible for such conflicts to be discussed and resolved through open societal communication.

Choosing among various alternatives which nationalists, liberals, and others have proposed is one factor which divides the nations. These disputes still stand unresolved. Perhaps toward the end of the 1990s, we shall be able to say which path they will follow. East Germany will probably model itself on democratic West Germany, so it is not very probable that a unified Germany will be tempted to revive the dangerous tradition of expansionistic and militant German nationalism. Supporters of the *Gemeinschaft* type of national consciousness in

Poland, the Czech Republic, Slovakia, Hungary, Slovenia, and Croatia may sooner than later realize that if they continue to advance their national identity at one another's expense, then not only will their mutual alienation increase, but the West may well continue to reject them. This result will produce continuing technological backwardness, a hopeless struggle among neighbors, and increased Balkanization. The more increased privatization, currency convertibility, and international economic and cultural exchange develop, the better the chances are that civil society will win in these countries. By contrast, those principles underlying personal authority and supporting bureaucratic elite powers will thereby likely lose support.

The countries lying to the East of Central Europe are also more open to the forces of malevolent nationalism. The collapse of state socialism in these countries still left central redistributive apparatuses there relatively untouched. Already during the old socialist times, these bureaucrats had successfully experimented with the use of national ideology based on the *Gemeinschaft* model, basically to legitimize their own unchallenged powers. The transition from state socialism to postcommunism in Romania, Serbia, Bulgaria, Albania, the Ukraine, and Russia has only been cosmetic. Strong liberal opposition forces there did not step forward so that the central redistributive power foundations and mechanisms remain functionally intact. These elites in these countries, consequently, want to convince the people that they are living in a real or quasi-real state of emergency. At the moment, it still appears hopeless to break the old magic circle established long ago among the major bureaucratic, military, and ideological personnel/institutions/structures in the society. The continued role of this elite helps to maintain both compulsive and paranoid national consciousness and a permanent sense of war/emergency that is closely linked to it.

The big question for the next century in Europe will be whether the West will have enough power to prevent any major conflicts which malevolent East European nationalism may cause. If the West views with indifference the struggles of the Central and Eastern European nations, then they must accept a new wave of refugees and 'illegal' immigrants or asylum seekers as well as continued force, warfare, conflict, and barbarity in regional and international relations. All of these trends amount to an enormous threat to world security. If we add this to the other dangers threatening world security and prosperity (for example, environmental pollution, the population explosion, and the rise of fundamentalist ideologies in the Third World), then we can say that fear and anxiety are just two of the legitimate and well-founded emotions that will characterize life for much of the next century.

REFERENCES

Anderson, P. (1974). *Passages from Antiquity to Feudalism*. London, UK: NLB.
Bibó, T. (1991). 'The Distress of the East European Small States', pp. 13-86 in K. Nagy (ed.) *Democracy, Revolution, Self-Determination: Selected Writings*. New York, NY: Boulder.
Kornai, J. (1980). *Economics of Shortage*. Amsterdam, the Netherlands: North Holland.
Sugar, P. and J. Lederer (1971). *Nationalism in Eastern Europe*. Seattle, WA and London, UK: University of Washington Press.
Szücs, J. (1988). 'Three Historical Regions of Europe', pp. 291-331 in J. Keane (ed.) *Civic Society and the State*. London, UK: Verso.

10 Democratization in the Ukraine under Conditions of Post-Totalitarian Anomie

The Need for a New Human Rights Developmental Strategy

E. Golovakha
N. Panina

ABSTRACT

Post-totalitarian anomie in the Ukraine threatens the realization of basic democratic goals, such as social transformation. There is a serious danger if the Ukraine again goes down the totalitarian path toward the sole obsessive goals of 'equality' and economic 'fairness'. The population is tired of further social experiments, angry with their worsening life situations, and perceive themselves as unprotected in an insecure atmosphere of normlessness. If the people's living standards further decrease, this will produce nostalgia for the 'good old times' of barrack socialism.

Our studies indicate that the dominant mass consciousness prefers the 'equality of poverty'. This is a specific feature of mass psychology and consciousness (which politicians help to promote); it produces 'social helplessness' rooted in totalitarian state paternalism and a post-totalitarian ambivalence about one's personal consciousness. These results of post-totalitarian anomie are considered in this chapter in the context of a problem for democratic social development which, itself, must be solved/resolved.

Postcommunist society still requires a number of preconditions to preserve elements of a rudimentary democracy within the confines of the present authoritative political regime, a state economic monopoly, and propagation of an archaic national ideology. From the viewpoint of progress in the field of human rights protection, the task at hand is not merely to protest some particular cases of state restrictions on individual rights and liberties with the purpose being to focus public attention on restoring the violated rights, but rather to actively develop a strategy advocating broader human rights for all as well as human personality rights. Post-totalitarian social development requires a) general principles of democratic state policy and civic society to increasingly protect the public; b) a program for legal consciousness development (for both citizens and public authorities), including elements of legal education and political socialization to spur democratic civic consciousness; and c) principles and means for harmonious ethnic relations, national tolerance, and maintenance of international peace.

DEMOCRACY AND ANOMIE

The new conditions of postcommunist society shocked the Ukrainian people with a new reality, after a long-term period of stability and an existence 'without problems' in the former totalitarian society. There are critical changes in life modes and people's psychology in postcommunist times.

The continuing economic crisis, destruction of the old ideology, and disintegration of the old state machine typify the modern social situation. This is only the visible part of the social iceberg which provokes psychological tension since each person is both an eye-witness and participant in the old society's destruction. Anomie is characteristic at each major transitional state in a society, but it is only under exceptional historical circumstances that it reaches a total social scale. Under these conditions, one's life undergoes serious changes and major deformations which spread through all strata of the population.

For the majority of the population, the stable society (traditional, hierarchical, and based on fixed customs and traditions or totalitarian, based on total state control over all spheres of social life) gives everyone an opportunity to believe one's own life is sensible within these narrow, exclusive limits. A freer normative structure to a much lesser extent predetermines the people's normal living activities. The loss of regulative functions which social institutions and groups perform produces anomie (an absence of norms). This also leads to total disorganization of those social structures and norms which have already lost their regulative power.

Sociologists' attention often turns to anomie when concrete historical changes create social crises and a break in social stability. 'Anomie' is a key sociological concept associated with political instability. The problems of anomie and social disorganization concerned sociologists after World Wars I and II as well as during days of considerable economic and social crises.

The main subjective precondition for the appearance and growth of anomie in modern postcommunist societies is mass renunciation of the old system and its basic values. The mass character of this previous support was documented in 1989-90 surveys. The old system of values has been destroyed to a considerable extent at the level of individual consciousness, while the ruling ideology was reflected to a greater extent in the prevailing system of social values. Individuals embraced this system only superficially under threat of official sanctions for any infringement of normative behavior.

The Ukrainian elites (political, religious, economic, and social) believe that the modern state of Ukrainian mass consciousness borders on insanity or even goes beyond this limit. This testifies to the fact that they are poorly informed about certain common tendencies in the normal processes of social integration and disintegration with the appearance of corresponding sociopsychological syndromes. We also observe a psychological paradox in the making: a person may feel he/she previously had more security and freedom in a strict or closed system (with a narrow choice among occupations and limited opportunities for social advancement) than under conditions of uncertainty in a mobile open system with more universal norms. The recent study of these phenomena was based on the previous research of Fromm (1966 and 1974), Merton (1964), Bekker (1961), Lemert (1972), and others.

POPULAR WELL-BEING AND TENDENCIES TO FORM A VALUE-BASED NORMATIVE SOCIAL SYSTEM
Social Dissatisfaction

Social belonging (contentment, support) is perhaps the most generalized indicator of social well-being. Its major satisfaction component or indicator is the degree of personal contentment with one's own social position, the degree of contentment with what each person gives to society, and with what each person receives from it.

The Kiev Institute of Sociology, Ukrainian Academy of Sciences, conducted nationally representative research on social well-being in the Ukraine in April 1992 with a random sample of 1752 people. This survey provided an opportunity to ascertain that the level of social satisfaction was so low that it documented the prevalence of mass feelings of social discontent that could lead to total estrangement of people from their own society. Nearly half the adult population (50.7 per cent) were not content with their position in Ukrainian society to some extent; one-third (33.2 per cent) found it difficult to determine their own relative position; while only 16.6 per cent were content. Three-fifths (60.2 per cent) of the population were not content with what they got from the society (social rewards) and 8.7 per cent were content. Nearly one-fourth (25.7 per cent) of the population was content with their social contributions (that is, those social conditions which would provide opportunities for self-realization and for making a positive contribution to social development), while 23.9 per cent were not so content. The majority also found it difficult to determine their degree of satisfaction with what they actually gave to the society.

The comparative analysis of social satisfaction among different socio-demographic groups showed that practically all groups evidenced social estrangement. One may suppose *a priori* that social estrangement is more characteristic of older generations than of youth and middle-aged people, of the unemployed than of working (as is usual in stable societies), but our data completely contradicted these assumptions.

There are certain differences in these data regarding varying satisfaction with the different components of social satisfaction. Some population subgroups (for example, the middle-aged generation, the intelligentsia, and skilled workers) have little satisfaction with what they give to the society, while others (for example, youth, pensioners, and technical and service personnel) have little satisfaction with what they receive from the society. But in the present situation, it is not so important which population groups have little satisfaction with certain aspects of their social life; it is more important to note that in the total population one practically cannot find any sufficiently large social group(s) in which the majority of their members closely identify with their society as it is undergoing major social transformation. No group(s) uniformly feel(s) that they are both necessary to and useful transformers of their society.

Anomic Demoralization

Earlier (1990-91) survey research data showed that Ukrainians were increasingly pessimistic, which was reflected in their mainly negative estimates of their own current life situation and future positions (Golovakha and Panina, 1993). For our empirical research on the Ukrainian population's social well-being, we used special methodologies to measure the degree of demoralization resulting from the general reaction to anomie. We based our scale of anomic demoralization on MacClosky-Srole's methodology (adapted by Popov), which we used in 1990 on a representative sample of Kiev's population (Golovakha et al., 1992).

In April 1992, our new data allowed us to conclude that anomie had caused a high degree of demoralization among practically all levels of the Ukrainian population. One or more degrees of demoralization was characteristic of 85 per cent of the population. Comparative analysis of different subpopulation categories showed that, despite certain differences (for example, the lower the age and higher the educational level, the less anomic demoralization), overall means on the demoralization index testified to a high level of anomic demoralization among all social groups.

If we look at mass consciousness, one such nonempirical/qualitative indicator is the growth in apocalyptic moods and bleak public expressions of imminent 'ruin' or forthcoming 'catastrophe'. Such reactions may be indicative of public demoralization or a normative reaction to anomie. Looking at the state of public consciousness in the Ukraine from 1989 to 1992, we can see that by the end of 1992, such apocalyptic moods had become widespread, if not dominant. Press materials, political speeches, and survey data show that such reactions appeared immediately after the early splash of social optimism characteristic of the 1987-8 period; yet, more and more pessimistic reactions emerged, encouraging more catastrophic prognoses and gloomy expectations.

Analyzing connections between public demoralization and sociopolitical characteristics showed us that people who favored capitalistic economic development and the introduction of market principles were less demoralized than those who approved of the old ideological system (socialistic state principles) or those who were confused about their own sociopolitical positions. So the acceptance of new values helped some groups overcome their demoralization (which the destruction of previous value-normative rules probably caused) to some extent. Our analysis further showed that people who did not experience anomic demoralization were more often ready to use (or to participate in) illegitimate means (for example, illegal strikes, seizure of buildings, and formation of illegal armed unites) of struggle to achieve their interests.

So it may be that the absence of demoralization, itself, does not mean the absence of destructive anomic influences. It is also not an effective precondition for forming a proper value-normative personal system. Merton (1964) defined situations where people received aid, yet simultaneously lacked supportive institutional means as being typically anomic for American society in the 1930s. Another possible type of response to anomie seems to be the so-called unnormative reaction that produces indifference about the means for goal achievement. Internalized indifference to the means of goal achievement (or norms) leads to cynicism.

Is Cynicism a Typical Reaction to Anomie?

One way that cynicism results from the absence of norms is when this situation, itself, becomes part of the individual's sense of consciousness and behavior. A main component of cynicism is its high levels of skepticism, not only in terms of norms for individual behavior, but for people in general.

We measured the level of public cynicism in our research project. Using a cynicism scale from the MMPI test (which Guiliasheva [1983] had adapted and restandardized for use in the USSR), our results testified to the fact that a high level of cynicism is characteristic of people who are directed toward constructing a state on some new, more highly valued basis (for example, capitalist, according to the Western model, or national-state development, according to 'its own way'). Those who supported the old value system and those who could not determine their own value directions were less cynical. However, these latter groups exhibited more anomic demoralization, as mentioned previously.

Some believe that cynicism is an abnormal reaction to anomie. In sociological analyses regarding individuals' integration into a new social system, it may also be considered a new type of value-normative subsystem. But the way each such subsystem develops is rather unpredictable, even if the main goal is to construct a democratic society. Democratic institutions are constructed not only on the basis of declared goals, but also on the formation of democratic means to achieve their determined aims. Nevertheless, the absence of any clear directions toward legitimate aims during the short term both complicates, and considerably extends, the process of democratic reformation. As a matter of fact, an abnormal reaction to anomie leads to a more intense anomie, which promotes formation of archaic, but not democratic, societies.

Normative Reactions to Anomie: Archaism and Paternalism

Anomic demoralization (despondence and confusion over values and norms) results from normative reactions to anomie. According to Bekker (1961, pp. 203-5), when long-term normative behavioral regulators are absent or when many people think that anything can happen, demand for a 'return to the good old times' often arises. Bekker points out that one way out of this anomic impasse for mass consciousness is to search for an 'authoritative interpreter'. This means for a leader (chief) who knows the correct path to the future and who can force others to follow his commands.

The formation of two types of value-normative subsystems as a result of anomic demoralization is either traditional-archaic (based on demands to return to the older value system) or authoritative (based on the necessity to give power to a dynamic person who can establish a 'new strong order'). The question remains: to what extent is one or another of these value-normative subsystems characteristic of the Ukraine during the present period of new state system formation?

Those who prefer returning to the old system of values wax nostalgic about the 'good old times'. In a representative sample of the Ukrainian population (Institute of Sociology, Ukrainian Academy of Sciences, November 1991), more than two-thirds of the people affirmatively answered the question: 'Do you agree with the fact that people lived better in the past?' (even though 'the past' was deliberately not defined). Such results may document a total feeling of social nostalgia, but this is not a concrete or well-considered conclusion. For example, answers about people's personal lives revealed another character. That is, only 33 per cent were satisfied with their past lives, while 57 per cent thought they missed much in their previous lives. These differences between personal estimates of one's past and the 'past on the whole' illustrate typical reactions to anomie. For example, 'in the past, people felt better about themselves because each of them knew how to act correctly' (67 per cent agreement). This is a primary expression of the nostalgia about the past which exists in the present unstable Ukrainian society. By themselves, nostalgic moods do not constitute a value-normative subsystem. However, nostalgia about a past 'when a certain order was in the society' is a sufficiently dangerous emotional basis to support concrete political programs. If authoritative political forces were to lead this reactionary mood, the previous political system would regain control.

Paternalistic motivations among the public support a return to the traditional system of values. These current opinions are very close to the old system of socialist values. Although socialist and communist values are rejected if their specific names are used in a majority of cases (that is, the socialist platform is supported by 5.5 per cent of Ukrainians, the communist by 2.9 per cent), paternalistic convictions (reflecting these unconscious socialist tendencies) are more widespread. The socialist system (which the majority of the population now rejects) has a different connotation in the social sciences (for example, it means 'paternalism' in sociology, 'learned helplessness' in psychology, or 'political ineffectiveness' in politology). The main result of these definitions indicates an absence of personal responsibility not only for society's fate on the whole, but also for one's own.

Current sociological and sociopsychological research efforts in the Ukraine show the spread of these paternalistic tendencies. For example, although a growing number of people acknowledged a declining living level, only 28 per cent responded to the question 'What are you going to do in order to avoid poverty?' by saying they were going to earn more, while 49 per cent thought that they 'could do nothing or that it would be necessary to conserve money on everything' (12 per cent chose to spend their savings, 5 per cent to ask for help from family and friends, 3 per cent to leave the country, and 2 per cent to move). When asked 'Who has to assume responsibility for the peoples' material state?', only 17 per cent indicated that a person has to rely on himself/herself in the first place. Most others relied on state structures at different levels for this responsibility.

No modern industrialized country's government refuses to support a certain minimum living wage for its citizens. But just what do citizens of a country with socialist values understand as a living wage? The question was 'What costs should a living wage pay for?' The most widespread answer was that 'it had to pay for all expenses, giving one the possibility to live as well as the majority of people' (47 per cent). Only 19 per cent thought the minimum wage had to pay for basic food, clothing, and dwelling needs. When asked about the people's readiness to work more to achieve a higher material state, only 15 per cent said 'they felt the necessity to work to such an extent which would give them prosperity.' Three-fifths (60 per cent) thought that 'such prosperity would be reasonable if it may be achieved without any loss of health or contacts with children and family', while 12 per cent said 'there was no sense in aspiring to make a lot of money while one can be satisfied by a collection of modest and necessary things.'

Paternalism shows up in the absence of personal responsibility for one's own material-economic state as well as in the evaluation of one's significance in the political sphere. Only 13 per cent of the Ukrainian population believe they can do something when local authorities infringe on people's interests; even fewer (9 per cent) think they can do something if the Ukrainian government is involved in the case. So the people transfer personal responsibility to the government and political authorities, even though the public thinks it cannot influence public political decisions and actions. The culmination of paternalistic attitudes was integral to the communist system of socialization and, normally, could provide a concrete basis for a return to socialist society. However, communist values are declaratively rejected as viable value-goals in the Ukrainian mass consciousness.

Under conditions of social anomie, we can also see a rise in widespread authoritarian orientations, with an increasing belief in the need for a strong national leader. More than half of the Ukrainian population agreed with the statement that a 'few strong leaders could do more for our country than all the current laws and discussions.' The index of authoritarianism (using a seven-item F-scale [Adorno et al., 1950]) for the adult Ukrainian population was 4.28 in April 1992. In any case, popular reactions to anomie lead to increasing totalitarian orientations in the society. Of course, this could mean an archaic-traditionalist, socialist, or (neo)fascist society.

If such a viewpoint spreads to mass consciousness, it can become the basis for a rebirth of a socialist value-normative social system. Traditional tendencies (as one way to overcome anomie) can lead to the return to socialist principles if the society has insufficient psychological resources to cushion the blow of the democratization process and construction of a legal democratic society with a market economy and political pluralism. The question here is about the psychological stability of the population under stressful conditions. Economic crisis and political instability create high stress levels in post-totalitarian development.

PSYCHOLOGICAL RESOURCES FOR OVERCOMING ANOMIE AND STABILIZING A SOCIETY

Our experience in using different psychological indicators for characteristic modes of living under stable and unstable social conditions indicated that the most reliable indicators for constructing an effective system of psychological stability were to reduce anxiety, ensure total living satisfaction, and internalize norms about personal responsibility. An individual's level of anxiety is an integral psycho-physiological indicator of his/her mental health. This is the most dynamic indicator of a psychological state connected with organic psycho-physiological features which allows the individual to spontaneously react to stress in his/her surroundings.

Satisfaction with life is the most stable indicator of a psychological state reflecting one's attitude to life as a whole, one's moral spirit, and psychological stability in stressful conditions. Internalizing personal responsibility for one's own fate is an integral characteristic of a person's confidence in himself/herself. This helps someone survive psycho-traumatic conditions and actively influence the transformation of these very conditions.

Social Anxiety

Conditions which produce widespread anxiety include social instability, a decline in economic development, a falling standard of living, a growth in criminality, an increasing number of international conflicts, and other problems. The worsening social well-being under anomic conditions has led to the tendency toward self-diagnostics of mental health of the population. The most extreme of these tendencies may be called 'hyperdiagnostics' (meaning the inclination to dramatize when describing the population's mental health). The majority of Ukrainians estimate that other people increasingly manifest negative psychological characteristics (irritability, animosity, and tiredness). At the same time, estimates about their own feelings and states (not dealing with social problems) were more satisfactory. For example, 88 per cent thought the majority of people were characteristically irritable, while only 17 per cent reported their own irritability.

Such contradictions are explained by the fact that popular estimates of social well-being were the bases for evaluations of general mental health. Here, one must distinguish between a rational, deliberate attitude about social problems or a natural, normal reaction to abnormal conditions and anxiety or the total psycho-emotional state of a person. An individual may not always realize why his/her anxiety level is rising. Some increase in the anxiety level is a normal reaction to a situation threatening one's survival. However, a general rise in the social anxiety level which exceeds these limits disrupts normal living activities and leads to poor mental health.

The best methodology for measuring anxiety levels in sociological research is Spielberger's scale, which Khanin (1976) adapted and which we used in our investigations. Our research showed that in April 1992, the anxiety level approached (but did not exceed) the upper limit of the norm on sense of social well-being and the psychological state of the Ukrainian population. Different factors (for example, demoralization, cynicism, and social estrangement) affect the level of social well-being and influence rising anxiety levels. But personal living conditions and circumstances have the greatest influence. Persons going through crisis events (for example, death of spouse/family members, natural calamities, criminal incidents, crushing insults, and severe humiliation) preceding the survey showed anxiety levels exceeding the norm's upper limits. This may be seen as one symptom of psycho-neurotic deviation. The strongest stress factor leading to an increase in anxiety is a general threat to physical health. Approaching the upper limit of the anxiety indicator norm is rather typical for a people under conditions of anomie, producing an unstable Ukrainian social life. The population's somatic health is the most significant risk factor, causing a lowered level of psychological stability in the Ukraine.

Life Satisfaction

We used the ILS scale (Index of Life Satisfaction, Neugarten et al., 1961) to measure the general level of life satisfaction (that is, 'moral spirit', 'strength of mind', psychological comfort, and so forth). If anxiety indicators allow us to measure the citizens' functional psychological state, the life satisfaction index is a more stable indicator with intensified changes in surrounding environmental factors.

When comparing the peculiarities and influence of one's mode of living on his/her psychological state in both socialist and transitional societies, one can make the following observations:

1. In both transitional and stable societies, the main factor determining life satisfaction is one's personal perspectives on life (that is, people who have clear personal goals and plans exhibit high levels of psychological comfort, whereas those who lack them have a negative view of their well-being).
2. On the whole, subjective more than objective factors determine one's psychological stability (that is, a generally optimistic person can more readily maintain his/her total psychological stability).
3. In a stable socialist society, certain objective sociodemographic factors (for example, sex, age, nationality, and material living standard) do not influence one's degree of life satisfaction as much as in transitional societies, although they have an influence on psychological differentiation among people. Therefore, in transitional Ukrainian society, we examined those sociodemographic factors which directly influence a population's differentiated responses and psychological resources to overcome anomie. As stated previously, age is a leading sociodemographic factor for determining one's psychological stability. With increases in age, the level of anxiety in an unstable society is significantly higher and life satisfaction is considerably lower. Representatives of older age groups, particularly pensioners, have catastrophically low levels of life satisfaction because of poor health, poor material conditions, and social dissatisfaction, all of which exhaust their psychological resources.
4. On the whole, the average index of life satisfaction for adult Ukrainians did not significantly change during the last ten years. Thus, we conclude that there are probably sufficient psychological resources banked in the society which can keep anomie and its effects at bay, despite pessimistic estimates of Ukrainians' overall mental health.

Internalization of Personal Responsibility/Self-Reliance

One of the most important personal social characteristics is that psychological quality called 'locus of control' (Rotter, 1966). This quality is connected with more things and persons which are responsible for something happening. If a person takes on the main responsibility (that is, explaining them in terms of one's own behavior, character, and abilities), this demonstrates his/her 'inner control'. Such a person is called 'internally controlled'. One who makes outside factors (other people, surroundings, fate, or chance) responsible demonstrates external control. Social paternalism favors externality by shifting responsibility for major decisions to governmental structures. Successful transition to a democratic society cannot happen if the psychological basis for a new society (that is, development of personal responsibility of people for one's own fate, for social decisions, and for public acts) does not change.

Our investigations have shown varieties in such positions among different population segments. Research data from April 1992 showed internality was characteristic of less than one-fifth (19 per cent) of the population. A majority (55 per cent) of the population has an external position. The incidence of internality-externality was approximately the same for people living in Russia's South Ural border region, the NPP zone (also called the Cheliabinsk region). This fact demonstrates extreme externality among persons living in a totalitarian society.

One principal tendency we noted was that the younger generation more often overcomes this external (dependent) position *vis á vis* society and differs from older generations in their readiness to accept responsibility for their own fate. Externality was 68 per cent among persons over 55 and 56 per cent among those between 18 and 31. Internality grows in inverse proportion to lower age levels (15 and 25 per cent respectively for each of these age groups). Additional surveys of senior high school pupils in Kiev and the Chernobyl region in April 1992 (a 1424 person sample) showed that the new generation's internality predominated (Nesvetailov, 1992). Among all the surveyed pupils, internalization was 37 per cent, while externalization was 24 per cent.

SOCIOPOLITICAL ORIENTATIONS OF UKRAINIANS: PERSPECTIVES ON DEMOCRATIC SOCIAL DEVELOPMENT

According to the results of a series of representative surveys from 1991 to 1993, the majority of Ukrainians from different social groups and regions support the development of a democratic society based on the principles of political and economic pluralism, equality of all citizens before the law, personal freedom, and social justice. For example, 54 per cent of adults (in June 1993) expressed the opinion that the Ukraine required the same type of development as in

Western countries, with only 19 per cent against that developmental model (survey by independent Center for Democratic Initiatives, 1799 respondents). These people represented the entire Ukrainian population based on major sociodemographic characteristics.

Nevertheless, in transitional societies, declared political and economic values/goals have no firm support in real choices about actual activities. This conflict usually appears between innovational goals and conservative means. Merton (1964) described this conflict as one of the manifestations of anomie under a destabilized society. In this time of transition from totalitarianism to democracy, we see parallel orientations regarding democratic goals for societal development and using/supporting quasi-totalitarian means for their realization.

The Ambivalence of Mass Political Consciousness

In an active search for concrete ways out of the current crisis state using the democratization process to build a legal state, the proposed means for achieving these democratic goals are often both conflicting and contradictory. Two main types of means (differing according to their political orientation) exist: radical-democratic and conservative-totalitarian. In our 1990-91 research, we asked lawyers, philosophers, sociologists, economists, and politologists about this typology of means. Thus, we composed our list of democratic goals (for example, construction of a free economy, and freedom of movement) for social development and conservative-totalitarian means (for example, struggle, unearned income, and establishing strong order). In two representative adult surveys in Kiev (542 people in July 1990 and 431 in July 1991), this parallel orientation toward contradictory goals and means was also evident.

People raised in a totalitarian system learn that the term 'rights' does not mean broadening the privileges of all, but rather subjecting one's own interests to those of the state machine. They cannot imagine other ways to achieve certain social goals except through a struggle to 'strengthen public demands or to establish a strong social order'.

An example of this expressed contradiction in the sociopolitical orientations of the majority of the population is that 27 per cent of those who agreed with the right to private property also believed that it was still necessary to fight 'bourgeois ideology'. However, 38 per cent of the supporters of this struggle with 'bourgeois ideology' limited themselves to the idea of introducing private property. More diffuse responses supported repressive formulations (for example, 'unearned profit', and 'strong order'). In general, we find more widespread democratic orientations among youth, particularly regarding the economy and politics; but this does not hold true in the sphere of international relations, perhaps confirming the fact that international dissention most perniciously overburdens the new generation.

Features of Post-Totalitarian Political Culture

Under these conditions, with widespread ambivalence in sociopolitical orientations (regarding the democratic transformation of social structures with support for totalitarian means to solve worsening public problems), the dangers to the democratic content of public transformation become more real. The public orientation for sharing 'equality in poverty' remains the most publicly dominant.

According to objective criteria, even people with an above-average income consider themselves middle class and very rarely as representatives of an upper income group. This means that the process of forming a Ukrainian middle class similar to those in stable democratic countries is only at the first stage. The majority of the population belongs to the lowest social strata and, correspondingly, is not extremely interested in stability or active political participation. So there is little political participation among the population in this sociotransformational process. According to our data, less than one-third of citizens take part in organized public activity. Here, we see the as yet unmet potential for the formation of a civil society with people capable of defending their civil and human rights.

In 1991, when the Ukraine became a sovereign state, the main power structures (parliament and government) did not have majority support since the population had not connected their hopes to political struggles in parliament. Later on, the level of confidence in political institutions continued to fall, first affecting political parties. Taking into account the fact that parties are one of the main political institutions of democratic society, any fall in the level of confidence in such an institution may be interpreted as the backward step on the road to democratization. With increasing satisfaction about the process of democratization, combined with more skepticism about political parties, this contradiction testifies to the rather low level of democratic political culture because parties struggling for votes (confidence) from voters (by legitimate means) is a major attribute of a democratic society. And when no political party enjoys the peoples' confidence, then the natural result is increasing skepticism about the whole process of democratization.

Our data indicate that most Ukrainian voters support peaceful forms of protest; however, another type of political personality (far fewer in number) is oriented toward radical, illegitimate protest. This type is also important for the future development of the national political situation. Summarizing our data, we see that radicals tend to support the political opposition and its leaders, whereas most common persons support the President of the Ukraine. Radicals also have a considerably higher level of political efficacy and demonstrate less authoritarianism. On the whole, radicals are ready for illegitimate political actions and protests more often than 'moderates', except during a time of economic difficulties. Though radicals have a lot of charm and view themselves as disinterested fighters for progress, one can see their resemblance to the earlier romantic Bolshevists, who gave birth to waves of violence and political terror.

One of the most serious democratic deficiencies is the insufficient political competence of the Ukrainian population. A majority of the republic's inhabitants cannot determine their own political position *vis-à-vis* general sociopolitical development in the Ukraine. The first year of Ukrainian independence saw an increase among people who displayed their fundamental ignorance about interpreting the basic elements of political life. Ukrainians, as a rule, believe they are helpless to do something even if the authorities infringe on their rights. When asked: 'Can you do something against governmental decisions which infringe on people's rights?', only 8 per cent (in June 1993) gave a positive answer. Such a low estimate of one's political efficacy leads to continuing reproduction of the 'learned helplessness' directly inherited from the old totalitarian system.

To increase the population's political competence level, we must look to several factors, such as capability of political leaders and legitimization of overall power structures. It also will require a reliable system of democratic political socialization and political education, an independent and competent mass media, and a basic level of civil society guaranteeing citizens the possibility to participate directly in political life. The theoretical basis for the continuous reconstruction of a civil society and legal state apparatus must be reflected in effective programs of democratic political education. Without the experience of such a system in the Ukraine as in other developed democratic states, it is impossible to regularize normal processes for political socialization and the formation of a democratic civil consciousness.

Human Rights and Strategic Development

The dramatic attempt of the former USSR states, including the Ukraine, to join with other societies through real acknowledgement of democratic human rights is one of the major factors (as well as the existence of social, class, and ethnonational intolerance) for strengthening democratic development to counterbalance totalitarian theory and practice. Searching for the way out of previous historical predicaments in which the Ukrainians joined other victims of communism has a simple solution: join the Universal Declaration of Human Rights and international pacts on economic, social, cultural, civic, and political rights. As for those hundreds of international legal standards that regulate human rights procedures, former Communists must learn to follow both the letter and the spirit of these documents.

However, the path to achieving human rights and liberties since 1945 has been tortuous and thorny. Human rights adherents from developed Western countries see in their own countries wide variations in the protection of rights and interests of various social groups. Of course, we no longer agree with that which Soviet ideologists condemned in the past (such as the unjust treatment of Angela Davis or Hider, which were purely politically based Cold War propaganda). Some current issues still trouble human rights champions. These include the position of national minorities, women, elderly and sick people, AIDS victims, immigrants, *Gastarbeiter*, destitute people, and other social groups that are subjects of discrimination, even in the Western democracies. It is not merely a coincidence that the 1993 International Human Rights Conference held in Strasbourg recognized the further evolution of the human rights concept itself. Conferees confirmed the universal character of this issue in which political, economic, social, and cultural rights are inseparable and combine to provide a dignified and civilized existence for human beings in all societies.

Post-Totalitarian Society and Progress in the Field of Human Rights

Within a very short time, the Ukraine actually managed to free its population from a permanent threat of political reprisal. Some dissidents were pursued via illegal laws or directives from the ruling party. Political restrictions in the Civic Code, censorship, limitations on visas, and secret elections of political executives have been abolished. Seemingly, there is no longer a basis for concern as far as prospects for human rights are concerned. Nevertheless, with deepening socioeconomic crisis threatening the democratic social transformation, the most serious danger is that, once more, Ukrainian society may go down the totalitarian path since the citizens are tired of recent social experiments and angry with worsening living standards. They prefer equality, fairness, and security to the present atmosphere of continual crisis.

This recurrent threat is just one potential route for the Ukraine's development since the legally elected administration has declared its adherence to democratic principles and human rights. Nevertheless, the society still demonstrates a number of rather significant tendencies if not to restore totalitarianism and lawlessness, then at least to restrict the growth of their rudimentary democracy. Democratic disincentives include helping an authoritative political regime to grow, supporting the state's economic monopoly, and continuing to propagate an archaic state/national ideology.

Among these tendencies is the existence of a half-decayed socialist economic system, which is ineffective and under control of the state collective farm sector. This sector actively uses trading firms and other groups to convert noncash goods into cash at a pace that exceeds production capacity and encourages a high inflation rate. The second tendency is maintaining the old nomenclatura in major legislative and executive positions. Although they have changed the color of their banners, they did not waste any time restoring their habitual use of ideological, rather than pragmatic, principles of governing. In turn, certain forces (such as national democratic parties and movements) which initially opposed the Communists have decided that out of all issues (human rights included), strengthening the national state system is the highest priority, even if this means revived anti-Semitism, xenophobia, and ethnic stereotyping. The third tendency is the residual totalitarian political and legal culture of the society and corresponding levels of mass consciousness. No doubt, in the past, a confrontational strategy for 'survival' required that any creative process had to be considered as a struggle. This meant a struggle against omnipresent 'outer and inner foes', a struggle for 'execution and overexecution of plans', for 'peace and friendship' between people, and for economic 'yield'. This fight on all 'battlefields' created a peculiar 'trench psychology', that says to everyone that it is dangerous to 'show oneself' before the general 'signal to attack' the 'enemy' in the name of national greatness. Consequently, values supporting a 'fight' are of greater significance to many people than are those of 'creation'.

A specific feature of Ukrainian mass psychology and politicians' consciousness is 'learned helplessness', whose roots are found in totalitarian state paternalism. This basic personality type cannot take responsibility for oneself or for the society in which he/she lives. Communist theory and practice and the system of communal relations reproduced this social helplessness. 'Omnipotence of the party in our movement toward a bright future' has been replaced by the idea of banning the 'communist devil' and, thus, to raise democratic prospects without any unusual personal effort at democratization expected in our society.

This post-totalitarian dual consciousness, with conformist and nihilistic tendencies, is widespread today. A person with this consciousness may support the market economy and fixed prices, freedom to move and to maintain the system of living permits, or the complete independence of the Ukraine and, yet, be against its departure from the Soviet Union. In the March 1991 Referendum, the Ukrainians simultaneously voted for both federation and confederation (see Golovakha and Panina, 1993). This is a typical example of conformity and contradictory reactions. People are ready to support mutually exclusive positions just because they believe that those who ask the questions best know the hidden answers. Remember, there is just a short step from conformism to negativism when all public choices are rejected. We considered this as a precondition for rebellion, anarchy, and chaos. Even though the population almost unanimously supported the Independence Act in the December 1991 Referendum, this does not mean they will unanimously support future nation state building plans. Polls held long before this referendum showed that half the population supported the Ukraine's participation in the USSR's revival. Ukrainian independence is now associated in the mass consciousness with aggravated crisis, increased enmity, and economic loss. Consequently, we can expect stronger separatist tendencies in several regions. Ethnic conflict (which, in post-totalitarian society, is a major source of human rights violations) threatens everyone's right to a life with civic and human dignity.

The issue of ethnic relations is especially significant today for the Ukraine, an independent state with dozens of ethnic groups. Though the Ukraine has experienced some open ethnic conflicts, there are multiple sources for these tensions in different regions. These include reestablishment and absorption of the Crimean Tatars, anxiety in regions with Russian-speaking citizens about the possible 'Ukrainization of Ukraine', the problem of the Transcarpathian Russians, the spreading idea of a 'Novorussia revival', and so forth.

The public account for the appearance of such problems as 'intrigues of the party and bureaucratic mafia'. This was the case in polls held during the first two to three years of *perestroika*. But the experience of those republics where so-called 'democrats' hold power shows that neither democratic slogans nor goals are sufficient protection against extreme nationalism. They will not guarantee a civilized character for the process of national revival.

Principles of a New Strategy

From the point of view of continuing progress in the field of human rights protection, the task of the movement is not limited to protesting particular restrictions on personal liberties to attract public attention to help restore these violated rights. Rather, the task involves actively developing a strategy advocating the rights of the entire population under the specific conditions of post-totalitarian social development, with deep economic crisis, and permanent tensions in its ethnic relations. This strategy should include the following essential elements:

1. Developing general principles of democratic state policy and civic society aimed at increasing security for the general population.
2. Developing programs to increase legal consciousness (among citizens and authorities), including legal and political education.
3. Discussing principles and means to harmonize ethnic relations and to promote national toleration as an important precondition for maintaining domestic and international peace.

The detailed development of an authentic strategy for human rights protection needs rather significant preparatory work, such as:

1. Analyzing the theory and the practice developed democratic countries use to provide social protection and security for people.
2. Sharing the reports and experiences of the international and national human rights organizations.
3. Reporting on the general results of human rights protection in the Ukraine (for example, the historical experience and real situation).

4. Analyzing citizens' mass, political, economic, and legal consciousness, their attitudes about a legal state, and civilized ethnic relations.

Major trends in the human rights theory and practice are closely related to democratic political cultural development in post-totalitarian society through:

1. Promotion of numerous civic unions, groups, and organizations to replace the postcommunist state with a democratic civil society.
2. Privatization of public land, lodgings, small-scale and middle-scale enterprises. This will undermine the absolute bureaucratic domination over socialist-type society and will draw many citizens into the process of ethical reformation. This will also increase their democratic political activity, competence, and efficiency.
3. Attraction of the most competent and democratically oriented intelligentsia to develop human rights protection strategies using mass consciousness development and education, combined with sociological monitoring.
4. Organization of mass human rights protection movements which unite citizens to protest human rights and political liberties abuses.
5. Establishment of permanent control over the law enforcement system to overcome the old image of 'corrupted law and its guardians', which is still imbedded in the mass consciousness.
6. Development of political education principles which can help to overcome antidemocratic and aggressive feelings. These principles include:
    a. Propagation of national and social class tolerance as the way to avoid social conflict and civil war during this crisis.
    b. Consolidation of basic shared liberties (speech, press, movement, and consciousness) as absolute values for which the society is willing to endure all of the difficulties of post-totalitarian development.
    c. Destruction of the psychological stereotype of 'learned helplessness', which is connected with a conviction that an adequate life is possible elsewhere, 'but not here' and that 'we' are doomed to a pitiful existence. Depending on charity from prosperous Western countries must also end.
    d. Construction of a new image of the Ukraine as a united house for all who live there. The country must be open to contacts with other civilized states, but first with its nearest neighbors since peace in nearby houses helps guarantee peace in one's own.
    e. Development of citizens' democratic political education system at all educational levels as now exists in all highly developed democratic states. It is impossible to ensure the normal process of political socialization and promote civic consciousness without meeting this basic requirement.

CONCLUSIONS

As the result of this investigation into the problems of democratization and human rights under prevailing conditions of post-totalitarian anomie, we found a number of explanatory phenomena applying to citizens living in a transitional society.

1. The Ukrainian sense of social well-being has been broadly demoralized among all strata of the population. This is based on a mass feeling of social goal-lessness, resulting from increased social status uncertainty from living under conditions of total anomie.

2. Post-totalitarian society has rather widespread contradictory value systems, such as democratic equality and the inequalities of a market (capitalist) economy, traditionalism (directing us to the past 'in general'), social isolationism (characteristic of archaic societies), paternalism (valuable for maintaining totalitarian elements), and social cynicism (a basis for an archaic society).

3. The lack of any clear and dependable democratic political orientations has left the majority of the population ambivalent. This means there are two parallel citizen orientations which increase human rights and democratic goals for social development, use totalitarian means to realize these, and continue the problems involved with political ineffectiveness, lack of efficacy, ignorance, and incompetence which further hinder the furtherance of human rights and democratic development of the Ukrainian Republic.

In the final analysis, the psychological state of the Ukrainian population (which is enduring extreme social anomie while experiencing the concurrent formation of value orientations under these conditions) produces the following trends: widespread paternalistic attitudes, declarative rejection of communist value-goals, increased cynicism, and support for aggressive extremism. This explosive mix of attitudinal and value orientations may lead inevitably to a retreat from declared democratic goals and a renewed search for a leader who proclaims ideas stressing strength, power, and social order. Such a cynical, authoritarian leader would reject common human values and espouse fascist (authoritarian) orientations. So, we can see only three ways to escape from anomic deadlock. These include using old norms to reach a new goal; moving without norms toward a new goal; or knowing nothing about norms and, instead, believing in a strong leader who knows everything. In light of all the previously mentioned trends, if we are allowed the luxury to predict the probable future direction that a considerable part of the Ukrainian population would follow, we believe they will choose the last alternative. If the continuing state of severe anomie continues, the most probable popular choice would be for such an alternative way and for such a leader.

REFERENCES

Adomo, T., E. Frenkel-Brunswik, D. Levinson, and R. Sanford (1950). *The Authoritarian Personality.* New York, NY: Norton & Company, Inc.

Bekker, H. (1961). 'The Modern Theory of Sacred and Secular and its Development', pp. 158-218 in H. Becker and A. Boskoff (eds.) *Modern Sociological Theory and its Succession and Changes* (in Russian). Moscow, USSR: Publishing House for Foreign Literature.

Fromm, E. (1966). *Escape from Freedom.* New York, NY: Rinehart & Winston, Inc.

Fromm, E. (1974). *The Anatomy of Human Destructiveness.* London, UK: J. Cape.

Golovakha, E. et al. (1992). 'Kiev - 1990-1991: Sociological Reports' (in Russian). Kiev, Ukraine: Naukova Dumka.

Golovakha, E. and N. Panina (1993). 'Political Consciousness, Legitimacy, and Personality: Transition from Totalitarianism to Democracy in the Ukraine', pp. 139-52 in R. Farnen (ed.) *Reconceptualizing Politics, Socialization, and Education: International Perspectives for the 21st Century.* Oldenburg, FRG: Bibliotheks- und Informationssystem der Universität Oldenburg (BIS).

Guiliasheva, I. (1983). 'Questionnaires as the Method for Investigations with Persons', pp. 62-81 in *Methods of Psychologic Diagnostics and Correction in Clinics* (in Russian). Leningrad, USSR: Medicine.

Khanin, U. (1976). *A Brief Guide for Using the Scale of Reactive Personal Anxiety by Spielberger* (in Russian). Leningrad, USSR: LNIIFK.

Lemert, E. (1972). *Human Deviance, Social Problems, and Social Control.* Englewood Cliffs, NJ: Prentice-Hall.

Merton, R. (1964). *Social Theory and Social Structure.* London, UK: Collier-Macmillan, Ltd.

Nesvetailov, G. (1992). 'Chernobyl from the Point of View of the Sociology of Catastrophes', pp. 54-64 in *Vestnik of Russian Academy of Sciences, No. 4.*

Neugarten, B. et al. (1961). 'The Measurement of Life Satisfaction', pp. 135-43, *Journal of Gerontology, No. 3.*

Rotter, J. (1966). 'Generalized Expectancies for Internal versus External Control of Reinforcement', pp. 1-28 in *Psychological Monographs, Vol. 80, No. 1.*

Part III

Socialization Processes: Case Studies

11   *Changing Nationality Stereotypes through Contact*

An Experimental Test of the Contact Hypothesis among European Youngsters

Hub Linssen
Louk Hagendoorn
Ludo Mateusen

ABSTRACT

In a European 12-nation study, the contact hypothesis was tested according to an experimental within-subject repeated measurement/between-subjects research treatment design. It was hypothesized that informal, frequent, and cooperative contact between members of different nationalities would reduce their reciprocally held nation-to-nation stereotypes and that this reduction would not be generalized to equivalent nations. The results revealed that 75 per cent of all contact effects were positive and that no generalization to equivalent nations occurred in 75 per cent of the instances where contact had a positive or negative effect. The results are discussed within the framework of self-categorization theory.

INTRODUCTION

Since the onset of intergroup research, it has been assumed that direct contact between members of different groups reduces stereotypes and prejudices. The observed (presumably atypical) behavior in these direct contact situations supposedly refutes and enfeebles any prior stereotypes (Allport, 1954). It was initially believed that mere contact, alone, would be enough to have a beneficial effect. Over time, numerous other factors have been identified as favorable or unfavorable to stereotype and attitude change. Equal-status between contacting groups, counterstereotypical behaviors of out-group members, cooperation in pursuit of a common goal with a positive outcome, high acquaintance potential, or positive support of authorities were identified as having a positive effect (see Hewstone and Brown, 1986, and Stephan, 1987, for a more complete literature review). We have been constantly accumulating still other factors, such as a balanced ratio of in- and out-group members (Amir, 1976; Hallinan and Smith, 1985), demographic variables (Williams, 1964), task competence in relevant skills (Blanchard and Cook, 1976; Rosenfield, Stephan, and Lucker, 1981), or favorable prior relations between participating groups (Tajfel, 1978). Therefore, the contact hypothesis developed into, as Stephan (1987, p. 17) puts it, 'a bag lady who is so encumbered with excess baggage that she can hardly move.' Therefore, Stephan (1987) proposed an overall conceptual model in which he distinguished three major contact-affecting antecedents: societal, situational, and individual antecedents.

SITUATIONAL, SOCIETAL, AND INDIVIDUAL ANTECEDENTS AND THE EFFECTS OF CONTACT

Traditionally, situationally determined antecedents relating to the effect of contact (for example, setting, nature of interaction, group composition, and task content) were main objects for research, probably because they were more accessible for manipulation. Societal and personal factors (for example, historical and current relations between groups or individual cognition and affect) were controlled through selection, while possible mediating factors (for example, cognitive attention, encoding, and retrieval) have been studied outside the setting of intergroup contact, leaving their influence yet unclear (Stephan, 1987). Which repercussion the change in attitude has for the person or society has (probably due to methodological obstacles) seldom been addressed.

In recent years, the manipulation of situational antecedents has been directed at the characteristics of the situation and their impact on attitudes regarding the out-group. The influence of group characteristics (such as numerical size, minority or majority position, and group culture) on contact was manipulated. Researchers either conducted laboratory experiments with artificial groups (Brewer and Miller, 1984; Brown and Abrams, 1986; Deschamps and Brown, 1983; Diab, 1970; Norvell and Worchel, 1981) or studied contacts between natural groups (Amir, 1976; Biernat, 1990; Caspi, 1984; Clement, Gardner and Smythe, 1977; Commins and Lockwood, 1978; Cook, 1978; Marín, 1984; Revenson, 1989; Riordan, 1987; Wilder and Thompson, 1980). The nature of the interaction was often manipulated in that cooperative or competitive tasks were created (Brown, 1984; Brewer and Miller, 1984; Cook, 1978; Deschamps and Brown, 1983; Desforges et al., 1991; Geartner et al., 1990; Miller and Davidson-Podgorny, 1987; Wilder and Shapiro, 1989), contact frequency was controlled (Wagner, Hewstone, and Machleit, 1989; Wilder and Thompson, 1980), or formal or informal contacts were studied (Bornman and Mynhardt, 1991; Clement et al., 1977; Commins and Lockwood, 1978; Schofield, 1979; Spangenberg and Nel, 1985; Wagner et al., 1989). Positive as well as neutral effects were found when the contact had a cooperative and formal character. The best results for a positive contact effect however occurred when the frequency of contact was high and when it occurred in an informal setting

(Bornman and Mynhardt, 1991; Wagner et al., 1989; Wilder and Thompson, 1980).

A common feature of the cited investigations concerns the fact that the assessment of contact uses *ex post facto* research. Although (in general) a division between a control and an experimental group were made, only one single assessment was pursued (that is, after the contact experience already had occurred). Assessments of attitudes or stereotypes preceding the contact experience were virtually absent in all of these investigations. Such shortcomings in these researches severely impair the validity of attributing attitudinal differences to the contact experience itself (Hewstone and Brown, 1986). A more valid approach to test the contact hypothesis is possible when a repeated within-subject (prior to treatment and follow-up assessment) between-groups (control versus experimental group) research design is applied and contact is considered to be a treatment. Given the previously mentioned interaction determinants, we hypothesize that informal, frequent, and cooperative contact between members of different nations will reveal a positive effect on their reciprocally held stereotypes when assessed according to an experimental within-subject repeated-measurement/between-subjects treatment design.

Thus far, we have mentioned antecedents which influence the contact situation. We can raise an additional question about the influence of contact, *per se*: Is the change in stereotyped perception generalized to all the out-group members to which the contacted person belongs? Or alternatively, will it be limited to the subgroup to which he/she belongs or to the contact person alone? In recent years, the possible generalization of a changed stereotype to the larger population to which the contact person belongs has been discussed in the framework of the intergroup versus interpersonal contact controversy. One hypothesis is that generalization of attitude change toward an out-group is less likely to occur when the contact is based on personal rather than group interaction (Brewer and Miller, 1984; Hewstone and Brown, 1986). It is argued that personal or private interaction is prone to 're-fencing' (Allport, 1954), which refers to the phenomenon that a contacted out-group member gets labelled as an exception to the rule. Intergroup contact which accentuates the similarity of the contacted member with the out-group as a whole results in a more likely transfer of the changed attitude to all out-group members.

This as yet rather hypothetical reasoning concerning the generalization of a contact experience leaves untouched the issue of how the definition of in-group/out-group membership itself gets established. Self-categorization theory (Turner, 1987) suggests that a person (conceived as a self-categorizing identity) 'exists as a part of a hierarchical system of classification.' This means that an individual can identify with several groups simultaneously. Which social self-concept becomes salient or which in-group/out-group distinction becomes relevant is situation- or context-dependent (Turner, 1987). Following Rosch's (1978) categorization principle, self-categorization theory posits that the situation determines whether superordinate or ordinate levels of in-group/out-group distinctions become salient. For instance, in a global geographical context, one can, identify with Europe as opposed to America, using a continental super-ordinate level of categorization. Within Europe, one can identify oneself at an intermediate level of categorization with southern as opposed to northern nationalities or small as opposed to big countries. Finally, on a subordinate level of categorization, one can identify oneself with one's own nationality as opposed to others. Evidence for the existence of an intermediate level of categorization has been found. For example, Linssen and Hagendoorn (1994) demonstrated that, within a larger European context, north-south latitude and country-size-related stereotypes existed, which transcended the individual-subordinate-national level.

Now, the question arises: Will the effects of intergroup contact occurring on a subordinate level of categorization be generalized to the intermediate level of categorization or not? In other words, at which level will the effects of contact occur? Will it be the level of categorization activated by the intermediate intergroup setting or by the subordinate contact situation? More specifically, in a European context, are changes in stereotypes activated in a European nation-to-nation contact experience, generalized to a European north-south (or big-small) level of categorization when the stereotypes are assessed within a larger European context?

With respect to the last question, Turner (1987) suggests that in-group/out-group evaluations are based on comparisons in terms of a higher-order category prototype. Applied to a European context and in line with Linssen and Hagendoorn's (1994) findings, this implies that an in-group/out-group nation-to-nation evaluation would be based on an intermediate north-south, or big-small, higher-order category prototype. Furthermore, Turner (1987) claims that a change in the in-group/out-group evaluation will not affect the higher-order category prototype. After all, generalization of the effect of contact in a setting in which a lower (or subordinate) categorization (for example, nationality) is activated would imply that the higher-level category prototype has been redefined. Therefore, we hypothesize that, within a European context, changes in in-group/out-group evaluations (due to nation-to-nation intergroup contact) will not be generalized toward other nations belonging to the same intermediate higher-order level of categorization as the contacted nation. Thus, the intergroup setting will determine the content and structure of the activated stereotype, while the contact setting will determine the level of generalization of the contact effect.

METHOD
Subjects

The subjects participating in this experiment were students of the second highest grades of secondary schools in 11 European countries. (In the original research, 12 European countries participated. Due to a nonresponse of the French participants in the second assessment, their contribution was excluded.) In total, 416 subjects were involved on a voluntary basis. Divided according to nationality, the numbers were: Luxembourg (44), Danish (33), Belgian (55), Dutch (50), German (28), English (23), Irish (31), Italian (42), Spanish (53), Portuguese (39), and Greek (18) subjects. All subjects were between 16 and 18 years of age and took part in an international exchange program, called 'Europroject'. Some 42 per cent of them were male, 56 per cent were female, and 2 per cent no data. All the Belgians were male; while, for the other countries, the male/female percentages were between 68 and 32 per cent in the Netherlands and 12 and 88 per cent in Italy.

Survey Materials

The national stereotypes were assessed using a questionnaire. Respondents were asked to indicate on a scale of 0 per cent ('hardly any') to 100 per cent ('[almost] all') how many representatives of a national group would have a certain characteristic? This is a comparatively sensitive and reliable method to assess pre-existent national stereotypes.

Twelve nationalities (including the nationality of the respondent) had to be judged on the basis of 12 trait adjectives, yielding 144 responses per subject. The other nationalities to be judged were: Luxembourg, Denmark, Belgium, the Netherlands, Germany, England, Ireland, Italy, Spain, Portugal, and Greece. The surveyed trait adjectives were: efficient, friendly, religious, rich, emotional, assertive, enjoying life (from this point on, labelled 'hedonistic'), intelligent, competitive, honest, aggressive, and scientifically minded.

The questionnaire and all the trait adjectives were administered in the subjects' native language. The trait adjectives were translated from an English master-questionnaire into eight European languages. In the Greek questionnaire, the contemporary Greek character set was used. Due to time-limits, no reverse translation procedures were employed.

Procedure

The questionnaires were administered twice in class to the same subjects (in both May and October 1991). We employed devices in the research to control for possible sequential response effects, incomplete counterbalancing of the trait adjectives over countries to be judged (hereafter referred to as 'targets'), incomplete counterbalancing of targets over respondent-countries, and incomplete counterbalancing of targets over time (May versus October 1991).

After the first assessment, pupils in the participating schools were (on a voluntary and informal basis) urged to begin written contact with pupils from other countries who also participated in the exchange program (a Dutch school launched this initiative; see Discussion and Conclusions section). To guarantee that the contact reflected an intergroup interaction, each pupil was instructed to act as a representative of his/her own country during the first contact. Once contact was made, any interference with the nature of the communication was prohibited..

In order to trace those subjects who had contact with a foreign nationality, an auxiliary questionnaire was administered after the second assessment was completed. This auxiliary questionnaire included queries about the nationality of the foreign contact, frequency of contact, content of exchange themes, and meeting the correspondent in person.

Research Design

In order to test the hypothesis that contact affects stereotyped perceptions, the research was conducted according to a 2 (treatment: contact/no-contact) x 2 (time: repeated within-subject measurement) experimental design. Between factor levels were subjects who had foreign contact (experimental or contact groups) versus subjects who had no foreign contact (control or no-contact groups).

To test the hypothesis that generalization of changed stereotyping to other targets within the same or intermediate level will not occur, a third between-factor level was added to the experimental and control levels. This third (or 'generalization') level represents the judgement of a subject about a group of targets within the same intermediate level with which no contact was made, although the subject did have contact with one single target at this intermediate level. Due to this third between-factor level, the final analysis was conducted in accordance with a 3 (treatment: contact/generalization/no-contact) x 2 (time: repeated within-subject measurement) design.

RESULTS
Data

The data set consisted of 12 (targets) x 2 (time) repeated measurements, including auto-stereotypes, within each subject. To test the two hypotheses on a between-factor basis (contact/generalization/no-contact), each target judgement of a subject was treated as a separate response. Therefore, the 12 (x 2) responses of one subject were considered as 12 responses of 12 subjects. To accomplish this, the data-matrix was partially transposed (using the SPSS routine 'FLIP'). This resulted in a data-matrix which consisted of 4992 (=416 x 12) repeated within-subject responses. Such a transposition is a legitimate procedure for transforming a within-subject factor into a between-subjects factor when the homogeneity of variance is not violated (Stevens, 1992). Hence, any analysis in which the homogeneity of variance was violated was excluded from the testing of the hypotheses. All analyses were confined to hetero-stereotypes.

Analysis

Because the testing of the hypotheses is based on the assumption that two intermediate levels of categorization are present in 12 European countries (north-south and big-small), prior analyses on seven European nations and 22 traits (Linssen and Hagendoorn, 1994) were replicated. An oblique rotated factor analysis of the 12 administered traits revealed a three-factor solution, with a factor intercorrelation less than .10 and explaining 62.2 per cent of the total variance. One factor was associated with the trait-adjectives 'scientifically minded', 'intelligent', 'efficient', and 'rich', all having factor-loadings ranging form 0.80 to 0.75. A second factor was associated with the trait-adjectives 'emotional', 'hedonistic', 'religious', and 'friendly', with factor-loadings ranging from 0.83 to 0.58. The third factor clustered the trait-adjectives 'aggressive', 'competitive', 'honest', and 'assertive', with factor-loadings ranging from 0.80 to 0.47. The trait-adjectives 'friendly' and 'honest' exhibited a dispersed factor-loading, positive on the second factor (0.60 and 0.35) and negative on the third factor (-0.47 and -0.52).

Linssen and Hagendoorn (1994) found a similar pattern with respect to the factor solution of 22 trait-adjectives and identified the dispersed loading trait-adjectives as being a statistical subcluster. Following their procedure, averaged and rounded sum scores were computed to ascertain those trait-adjectives loading on each factor. An exception to this rule was made concerning the subcluster containing 'friendly' and 'honest'. These scores where summed, averaged, and rounded separately. Subsequently, these four scores were entered as dependent variables in a one-way analysis of variance, with the target-nation as the independent variable. The goal was to check whether the means of the four dependent variables would align according to the intermediate levels of categorization (Tables 11.1 and 11.2).

Table 11.1 North-south factor (in %)

Efficient			Emotional		
Target	Portugal (1)	43	Germany (1)	51
Nation	Spain (2)	46	England (1)	51
	Greece (2)	47	Denmark (2)	55
	Italy (3)	50	Ireland (2)	55
	Ireland (3)	50	Luxembourg (2)	57
	France (4)	54	Belgium (3)	59
	Belgium (5)	57	France (4)	62
	Denmark (5)	58	Netherlands (4)	62
	England (5)	50	Portugal (4)	64
	Netherlands (5)	60	Greece (5)	66
	Luxembourg (5)	60	Spain (6)	67
	Germany (6)	66	Italy (7)	72

$F[11,4311] = 109.10; p<.0001$ $F[11,4391] = 86.34; p<.0001$

Note: The numbers 1 through 7 (in parentheses) denote homogeneous subgroups (multiple comparison test: BTukey HSD p<.05) in that target nation.

As can be seen in Table 11.1, the distribution of attributed emotionality and efficiency is aligned according to a north-south intermediate level of categorization. Southern European nations are perceived as emotional and inefficient while northern European nations are believed unemotional and efficient. In Table 11.2, the distribution of attributed aggressiveness and friendliness is aligned according to a country-size determined, intermediate level of categorization. Small European nations are perceived as peace-loving and friendly, big European nations as aggressive and unfriendly.

Given the previous experience with two intermediate determined levels of (nationality) categorization, we used a clustering of target and response countries to test the three hypotheses. Countries located below 48° north were clustered as 'Southern' and those above 48° north as 'Northern'. The alternative clustering (according to an intermediate categorization) was based on the numerical proportion of a country's population. Countries with less than 15 million inhabitants were characterized as 'small' and those with more than 15 million inhabitants as 'big'. As a result, France, Italy, Spain, Portugal, and Greece were categorized as southern targets; Denmark, Ireland, the Netherlands, Belgium, Luxembourg, Germany, and England as northern targets. Denmark, the Netherlands, Belgium, Luxembourg, Ireland, Portugal, and Greece were categorized as small targets; England, France, Germany, Spain, and Italy as big targets. In the analysis, these two categorizations will be used separately. Contact effects in the north-south categorization will be analyzed independently from those in the country-size categorization.

The subdivision into northern versus southern and small versus big nations was subsequently used to define the direction of an attribution to a target. To illustrate: one can consider the attribution of a northern respondent concerning a southern target or the attribution of a northern respondent concerning a northern target. Both attributions imply differentially directed judgements from one and the same source. As a result, four distinct target-directed attributions can be distinguished within a north-south context. These are attributions from 1) northern response nations concerning northern targets; 2) northern response nations concerning southern targets; 3) southern response nations concerning northern targets; and 4) southern response nations concerning southern targets. A similar division in target-directed attributions applies for the country-size, namely, attributions from 1) small response nations concerning small targets; 2) small response nations concerning big targets; 3) big response nations concerning small targets; and 4) big response nations concerning big targets.

Table 11.2 Nation-size factor (in %)

	Aggressive		Friendly	
Target	Luxembourg (1)	49	Germany (1)	51
Nation	Portugal (1)	46	France (2)	54
	Denmark (2)	52	England (2)	55
	Greece (3)	53	Spain (3)	57
	Belgium (3)	53	Italy (4)	60
	Ireland (3)	55	Ireland (4)	60
	Netherlands (4)	58	Portugal (5)	61
	Spain (4)	58	Luxembourg (5)	62
	France (4)	60	Denmark (5)	63
	Italy (5)	62	Greece (5)	63
	England (6)	64	Belgium (6)	64
	Germany (7)	71	Netherlands (7)	66
	$F[11,4375] = 99.73; p<.0001$		$F[11,4426] = 32.50; p<.0001$	

Note: The numbers 1 through 7 (in parentheses) denote homogeneous subgroups (multiple comparison test: BTukey HSD p<.05) in that target nation.

The two divisions resulted in 2 x 48 MANOVA's (2 types of intermediate categorization levels x 4 judgement directions x 12 trait adjectives), structured according to a 3 (between-subjects: contact and generalization, versus no-contact) x 2 (repeated within subjects: May versus October 1991) research design. Analyses resulting in a significant 2-way -time-by-treatment-interaction were considered to reveal a contact effect. After deleting those 2-way interactions which revealed a violation of the homogeneity of variance, simple effects analyses of variance over time (May/October 1991) were performed on any remaining significant analyses. These last analyses were performed to discover in what direction the contact effect was pointing.

Only significant simple effects over time in the two treatment groups (contact or generalization) coinciding with nonsignificant, or significant but opposing simple effects over time in the control group (no-contact) refer to changes in stereotyping due to contact. They are to be considered as a general verification of the contact hypothesis. Whether these changes are positive or not depends on the direction of the change in mean attribution over time. The hypothesis concerning the generalization of stereotype changes would be confirmed if treatment groups (contact and generalization) have a significant simple effect over time within the same direction.

North-South Contact Effects

With regard to testing the two hypotheses concerning the intermediate north-south categorization, significant 2-way time-by-treatment interaction effects were found for: 1) attributed religiousness from southern respondents concerning northern targets ($F[2,1018]= 4.69$; $p<.01$; see Figure 11.1; for the simple effects analysis results associated with this interaction, look in the upper left-hand corner of Figure 11.1); 2) attributed 'emotionality' from southern respondents concerning northern targets ($F[2,1013]= 5.08$; $p<.01$; see Figure 11.2; same as Figure 11.1); 3) attributed 'emotionality' from southern respondents concerning southern targets ($F[2,451]= 4.54$; $p<.01$; see Figure 11.3); 4) attributed 'hedonism' from southern respondents concerning southern targets ($F[2,453]= 3.69$; $p<.05$; see Figure 11.4); 5) attributed 'friendliness' from northern respondents concerning northern targets ($F[2,1432]= 8.56$; $p<.001$; see Figure 11.5); 6) attributed 'aggressiveness' from northern respondents concerning southern targets ($F[2,1058]=12.63$; $p<.001$; see Figure 11.6).

No significant 2-way interaction effects of other attributions from northern or southern respondents were found. Thus, the contact hypothesis was corroborated since the southern respondents' demonstrated a positive re-appraisal of perceived northern 'emotionality' after having contact (Contact: Mmay=54 per cent versus Moct=60 per cent; increase=+6 per cent; see Figure 11.1) and a reduction of perceived southern 'emotionality' (Contact: Mmay=66 per cent versus Moct=52 per cent; decline=-14 per cent; see Figure 11.2) and 'hedonism' (Contact: Mmay=72 per cent versus Moct=59 per cent; decline=-13 per cent; see Figure 11.3). Whether the reduction in perceived northern 'religiousness' (Contact: Mmay=51 per cent versus Moct=44 per cent; decline=-7 per cent; Generalization: Mmay=46 per cent versus Moct=42 per cent; decline=-4 per cent; see Figure 11.4) is to be interpreted as positive or negative is not clear. The fact of the matter is that this effect represents a reinforcement of a previously held northern stereotype.

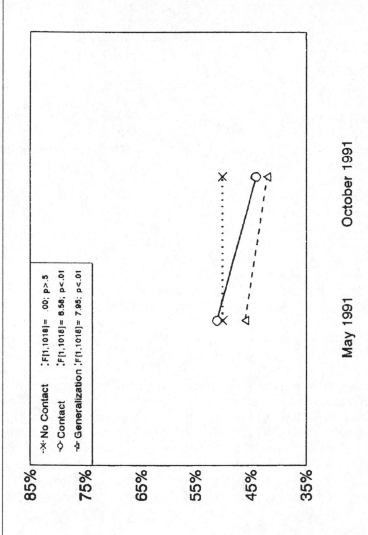

Figure 11.1 Attributed religiosity by contacting, generalizing, and noncontacting Southern respondents to Northern countries

Figure 11.2 Attributed emotionality by contacting, generalizing, and noncontacting Southern respondents to Northern countries

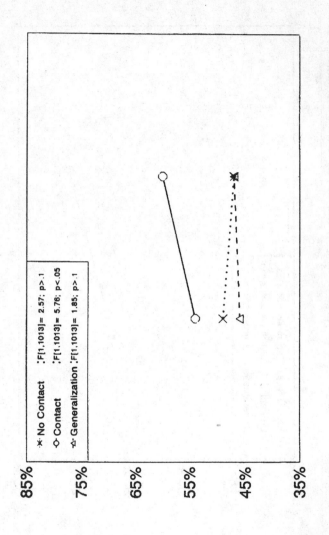

Figure 11.3 Attributed emotionality by contacting, generalizing, and noncontacting Southern respondents to Southern countries

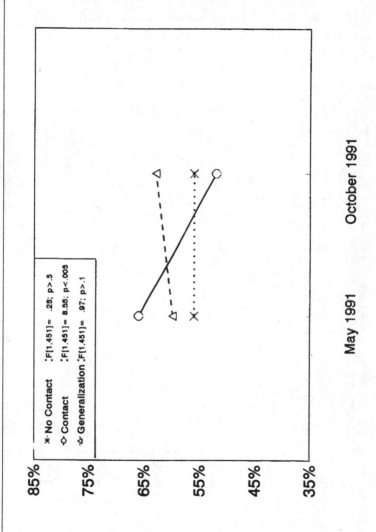

85%

75%

65%

55%

45%

35%

* No Contact   ;F[1,451]= .28; p>.5
◇ Contact   ;F[1,451]= 8.55; p<.005
△ Generalization ;F[1,451]= .97; p>.1

May 1991   October 1991

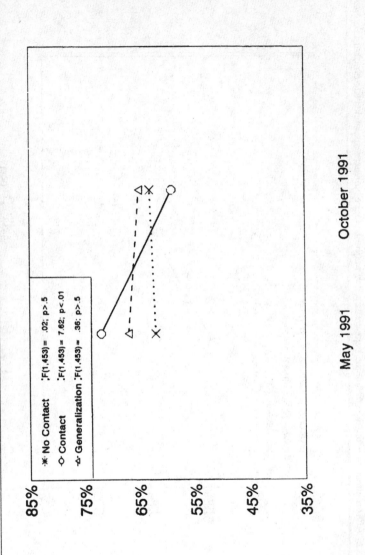

Figure 11.4 Attributed hedonism by contacting, generalizing, and noncontacting Southern respondents to Southern countries

Figure 11.5 Attributed friendliness by contacting, generalizing, and noncontacting Northern respondents to Northern countries

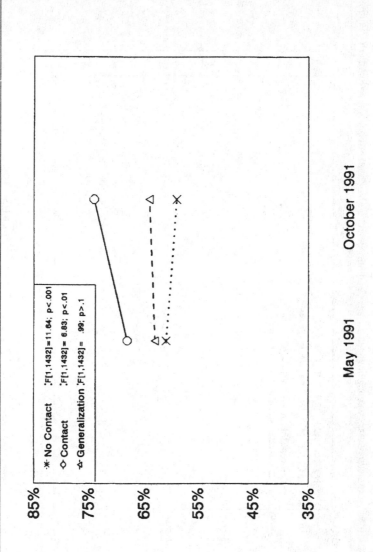

* No Contact   'F[1,1432]=11.84; p<.001
◇ Contact   'F[1,1432]= 6.83; p<.01
△ Generalization 'F[1,1432]= .99; p>.1

85%

75%

65%

55%

45%

35%

May 1991   October 1991

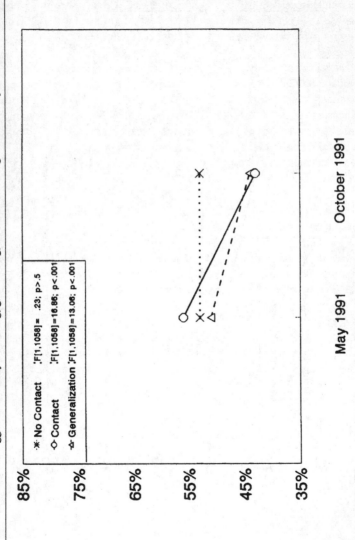

Figure 11.6 Attributed aggressiveness by contacting, generalizing, and noncontacting Northern respondents to Southern countries

Northern respondents re-appraised their attributions about northern targets with respect to attributed 'friendliness' (Contact: Mmay=68 per cent versus Moct=74 per cent; increase=+6 per cent; see Figure 11.5) and about southern targets with respect to attributed 'aggressiveness' (Contact: Mmay=56 per cent versus Moct=43 per cent; decline=-13 per cent; see Figure 11.6). Both changes represent a positive effect of contact and, therefore, confirm the contact hypothesis.

The second hypothesis (concerning the absence of intermediate generalization) had to be rejected for the re-appraisal of the northern trait 'religiousness' (by southern respondents) due to contact and the re-appraisal of the southern trait 'aggressiveness' by northern respondents. In all other cases where contact had an effect, the second hypothesis was confirmed in that the (positive) contact effects were limited to the re-appraisal of traits attributed to the population of only one nationality. In these latter cases, subtyping did occur concerning the re-appraisal of the traits on an intermediate level of categorization.

Country-Size Contact Effects

With regard to the testing of the two hypotheses concerning the intermediate level of country-size categorization, significant 2-way interaction effects were found for: 1) attributed efficiency from respondents from big countries concerning big targets (F[2,496]= 3.27; p<.05; see Figure 11.7; for the simple effects analysis results associated with this interaction, look in the upper left-hand corner of Figure 11.7); 2) attributed 'friendliness' from respondents from big countries concerning big targets (F[2,499]= 3.70; p<.05; see Figure 11.8; same as Figure 11.7); 3) attributed 'assertiveness' from respondents from big countries concerning big targets (F[2,499]= 3.57; p<.05; see Figure 11.9); 4) attributed 'assertiveness' from respondents from small countries concerning small targets (F[2,1412]= 6.29; p<.005; see Figure 11.10); 5) attributed 'honesty' from respondents from small countries concerning big targets (F[2,1132]= 4.59; p<.01; see Figure 11.11); 6) attributed 'aggressiveness' from respondents from small countries concerning big targets (F[2,1131]= 3.60; p<.05; see Figure 11.12).

Figure 11.7 Attributed efficiency by contacting, generalizing, and noncontacting respondents from big countries to big countries

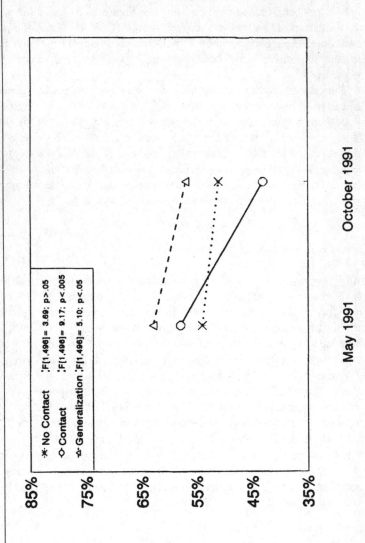

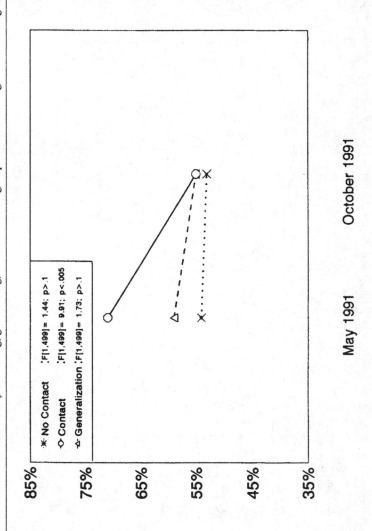

Figure 11.8 Attributed friendliness by contacting, generalizing, and noncontacting respondents from big countries to big countries

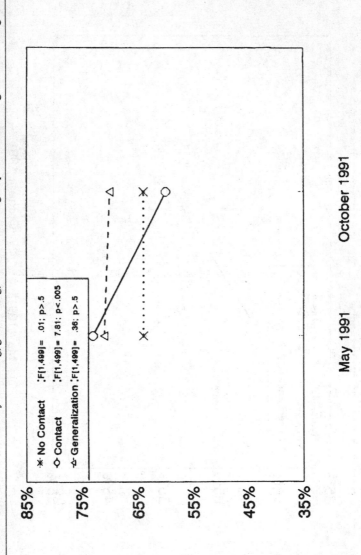

Figure 11.9 Attributed assertiveness by contacting, generalizing, and noncontacting respondents from big countries to big countries

* No Contact   ¹F[1,499]= .01; p>.5
◇ Contact   ²F[1,499] = 7.81; p<.005
△ Generalization ³F[1,499]= .36; p>.5

May 1991   October 1991

85%
75%
65%
55%
45%
35%

Figure 11.10 Attributed assertiveness by contacting, generalizing, and noncontacting respondents from small countries to small countries

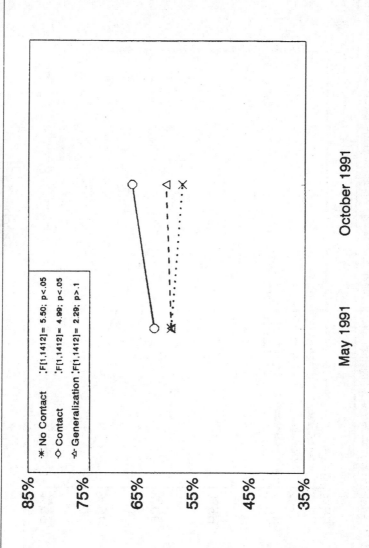

Figure 11.11 Attributed honesty by contacting, generalizing, and noncontacting respondents from small countries to big countries

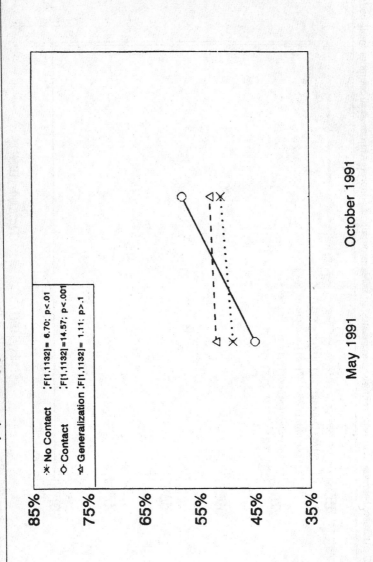

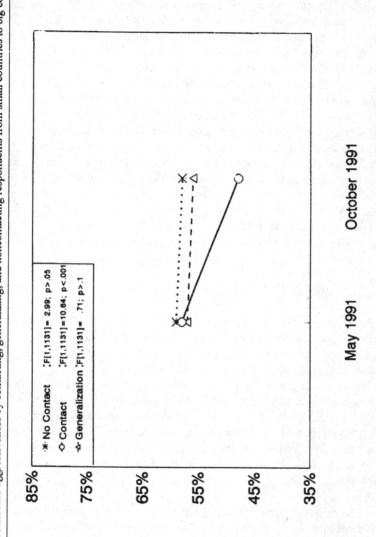

Figure 11.12 Attributed aggressiveness by contacting, generalizing, and noncontacting respondents from small countries to big countries

The contact hypothesis was corroborated. We found positive re-appraisals with respect to the attribution of 'honesty' (Contact: Mmay=48 per cent versus Moct=58 per cent; increase=+10 per cent; see Figure 11.11) and 'aggressive-ness' (Contact: Mmay=58 per cent versus Moct=48 per cent; decrease=-10 per cent; see Figure 11.12) by respondents from small countries concerning big targets after contact and in the attribution of 'assertiveness' (Contact: Mmay=62 per cent versus Moct=66 per cent ; increase=+4 per cent; see Figure 11.10) by respondents from small countries concerning small targets. A negative effect of contact was found in the changed attributions of respondents from big countries concerning big targets. The attribution of 'efficiency' (Contact: Mmay=58 per cent versus Moct=43 per cent; decrease=-15 per cent; Generalization: Mmay=63 per cent versus Moct=56 per cent; decrease=-7 per cent; see Figure 11.7), 'friendliness' (Contact: Mmay=71 per cent versus Moct=55 per cent; decrease=-16 per cent; see Figure 11.8), and 'assertiveness' (Contact: Mmay=73 per cent versus Moct=60 per cent; decrease=-13 per cent; see Figure 11.9) changed in a negative way.

The second hypothesis had to be rejected only for the attributed 'efficiency' The change in all other relevant traits confirmed the second hypothesis.

DISCUSSION AND CONCLUSIONS

In this research, the contact hypothesis was tested in 12 Western-European countries. It was hypothesized that intergroup contact between secondary school pupils (based on cooperative, voluntary, informal, and frequently occurring written correspondence) would have a positive effect on their reciprocal stereotypes. In a general sense, the contact hypothesis was confirmed in 12 instances where changes in stereotyping did occur. No confirmation was found in 84 instances. A total of 12 out of 96 possible contact effects (which amounts to a gross net effect of 12.5 per cent) may look moderate. However, it should be noted that these contact effects were found only after a short period of six months. Therefore, it can be presumed that these effects (as opposed to many short-term fluctuations) represent an enduring change in the pattern of stereotyping.

The second hypothesis posited that generalization of changed stereotypes would be limited to the subordinate nation-to-nation level of categorization due to the maintenance of the higher-order level of categorization prototype (Turner, 1987). This was confirmed in 9 out of 12 instances where contact had an effect. The hypothesis was falsified with respect to the generalization of southern respondents' stereotyping of all northern targets as 'religious', the change in northern respondents' stereotyping concerning the 'aggressiveness' of all southern targets, and the change in the stereotyping of big-nation respondents concerning the 'efficiency' of all big nations.

The generalization effect of attributed 'religiousness' might be explained by the fact that Europe is truly religiously divided along lines parallel to the intermediate level of a north-south categorization. During the contact experience, this parallelism may have led to a shift from a national categorization to a religious categorization, resulting in a generalization. With regard to the two remaining generalization effects, no convincing rational explanation could be found.

The conclusion from the research is that individual contact and subsequent exchange of information between members of different national groups reduces negative aspects of nationality stereotypes. Changes in stereotypes are not completely positive since minor negative aspects were also accentuated. Which aspects of stereotypes change, or to what extent, seems to be a contextual effect (that is, the contact situation on a nation-to-nation basis). The level of generalization of the change related mainly to the nation-to-nation contact situation. Individual information from the contact partners was generalized to the national category activated by the contact situation and not the superordinate categorization activated by the intermediate intergroup context. There were some exceptions, however. To better understand the nature of the positive effects of the contact experience and the conditions favoring the effects, further research should concentrate on the various types of context effects, focusing and limiting stereotype change, and should investigate their interaction.

REFERENCES

Allport, G. (1954). *The Nature of Prejudice*. Cambridge/Reading, MA: Addison-Wesley.

Amir, Y. (1976). 'The Role of Intergroup Contact in Change of Prejudice and Ethnic Relations', pp. 245-308 in P. Katz (ed.) *Towards the Elimination of Racism*. Elmford, NY: Pergamon Press.

Biernat, M. (1990). 'Stereotypes on Campus: How Contact and Liking Influence Perception of Group Distinctiveness', pp. 1485-513 in *Journal of Applied Social Psychology*, Vol. 20, No. 18.

Blanchard, F. and S. Cook (1976). 'Effects of Helping a less Competent Member of a Cooperating Interracial Group on the Development of Interpersonal Attraction', pp. 1245-55 in *Journal of Personality and Social Psychology*, Vol. 34, No. 2.

Bornman, E. and J. Mynhardt (1991). 'Social Identity and Intergroup Contact in South Africa with Specific Reference to the Work Situation', pp. 437-62 in *Genetic and General Psychology Monographs*, Vol. 117, No. 4.

Brewer, M. and N. Miller (1984). 'Beyond the Contact Hypothesis: Theoretical Perspectives on Desegregation', pp. 281-302 in N. Miller and M. Brewer (eds.) *Groups in Contact: the Psychology of Desegregation*. New York, NY: Academic Press.

Brown, R. (1984). 'The Effects of Intergroup Similarity and Cooperative Versus Competitive Orientation on Intergroup Discrimination', pp. 21-33 in *British Journal of Social Psychology*, Vol. 23.

Brown, R. and D. Abrams (1986). 'The Effect of Intergroup Similarity and Goal Interdependence on Intergroup Attitudes and Task Performance', pp. 78-92 in *Journal of Experimental Psychology*, Vol. 22.

Caspi, A. (1984). 'Contact Hypothesis and Inter-Age Attitudes: a Field Study of Cross-Age Contact', pp. 74-80 in *Social Psychology Quarterly*, Vol.47.

Clement, R., R. Gardner, and P. Smythe (1977). 'Inter-Ethnic Contact: Attitudinal Consequences', pp. 205-15 in *Canadian Journal of Behavioral Science*, Vol. 9, No. 3.

Commins, R. and J. Lockwood (1978). 'The Effects on Intergroup Relations of Mixing Roman Catholics and Protestants: an Experimental Investigation', pp. 383-6 in *European Journal of Social Psychology*, Vol. 8.

Cook, S. (1978). 'Interpersonal and Attitudinal Outcomes in Co-Operating Interracial Groups', pp. 97-113 in *Journal of Research and Development in Education*, Vol. 12.

Desforges, D., C. Lord, S. Ramsey, J. Mason, M. Van Leeuwen, S. West, and M. Lepper (1991). 'Effects of Structured Cooperative Contact on Changing Negative Attitudes Toward Stigmatized Social Groups', pp. 531-44 in *Journal of Personality and Social Psychology*, Vol 60, No. 4.

Deschamps, J. and R. Brown (1983). 'Superordinate Goals and Intergroup Conflict', pp. 189-95 in *British Journal of Social Psychology*, Vol. 22.

Diab, L. (1970). 'A Study of Intragroup and Intergroup Relations among Experimentally Produced Small Groups', pp. 49-82 in *Genetic Psychology Monographs*, Vol. 82.

Gaertner, S., J. Mann, J. Dovidio, A. Murell, and M. Pomare (1990). 'How Does Cooperation Reduce Intergroup Bias?', pp. 692-704 in *Journal of Personality and Social Psychology*, Vol. 59, No. 4.

Hallinan, M. and S. Smith (1985). 'The Effects of Classroom Racial Composition on Students' Interracial Friendliness', pp. 3-16 in *Social Psychology Quarterly*, Vol. 47.

Hewstone, M. and R. Brown (1986). 'Contact Is Not Enough: an Intergroup Perspective on the "Contact Hypothesis".' pp. 1-44 in M. Hewstone and R. Brown (eds.) *Contact and Conflict in Intergroup Encounters*. Oxford, UK: Basil Blackwell.

Linssen, H. and L. Hagendoorn (1994). 'Social and Geographical Factors in the Explanation of the Content of European Nationality Stereotypes', pp. 165-82 in *British Journal of Social Psychology*, Vol. 33, No. 2.

Marín, G. (1984). 'Stereotyping Hispanics: the Differential Effect of Research Method, Label and Degree of Contact', pp. 17-27 in *International Journal of Intercultural Relations*, Vol. 8.

Miller, N. and G. Davidson-Podgorny (1987). 'Theoretical Models of Intergroup Relations and the Use of Cooperative Teams as an Intervention for Desegregated Settings', pp. 31-65 in C. Hendrick (ed.) *Group Processes and Intergroup Relations*. Beverly Hills, CA: Sage Publications.

Norvell, N. and S. Worchel (1981). 'A Re-Examination of the Relation Between Equal Status Contact and Intergroups Attraction', pp. 902-8 in *Journal of Personality and Social Psychology*, Vol. 41, No. 5.

Revenson, T. (1989). 'Compassionate Stereotyping of Elderly Patients by Physicians: Revising the Social Contact Hypothesis', pp. 230-4 in *Psychology and Aging*, Vol. 4, No. 2.

Riordan, C. (1987). 'Intergroup Contact in Small Cities', pp. 143-54 in *International Journal of Intercultural Relations*, Vol. 11.

Rosch, E. (1978). 'Principles of Categorization', pp. 27-48 in E. Rosch and B. Loyd (eds.) *Cognition and Categorization*. Hillsdale, NJ: Erlbaum.

Rosenfield, D., W. Stephan, and G. Lucker (1981). 'Attraction to Competent and Incompetent Members of Cooperative and Comparative Groups', pp. 416-33 in *Journal of Applied Social Psychology*, Vol. 11.

Schofield, J. (1979). 'The Impact of Positively Structured Contact on Intergroup Behavior: Does it Last under Adverse Conditions?', pp. 280-4 in *Social Psychology Quarterly*, Vol. 42, No. 3.

Spangenberg, J. and E. Nel (1985). 'The Effect of Equal-Status on Ethnic Attitudes', pp. 173-80 in *The Journal of Social Psychology*, Vol. 121.

Stephan, W. (1987). 'The Contact Hypothesis in Intergroup Relations', pp. 13-40 in C. Hendrick (ed.) *Group Processes and Intergroup Relations*. Beverly Hills, CA: Sage Publications.

Stevens, J. (1992). *Applied Multivariate Statistics for the Social Sciences*. Hillsdale, NJ: Erlbaum.

Tajfel, H. (ed.) (1978). *Differentiation Between Social Groups*. London, UK: Academic Press.

Turner, J. (1987). 'A Self-Categorization Theory', pp. 42-67 in J. Turner (ed.) *Rediscovering the Social Group: a Self-Categorization Theory*. London, UK: Basil Blackwell.

Wagner, U., M. Hewstone, and U. Machleit (1989). 'Contact and Prejudice Between Germans and Turks: a Correlational Study', pp. 561-74 in *Human Relations*, Vol. 42, No. 7.

Wilder, D. and P. Shapiro (1989). 'Role of Competition-Induced Anxiety in Limiting the Beneficial Impact of Positive Behavior by an Outgroup Member', pp. 60-9 in *Journal of Personality and Social Psychology*, Vol. 56.

Wilder, D. and J. Thompson (1980). 'Intergroup Contact with Independent Manipulations of Ingroup and Outgroup Interaction', pp. 589-603 in *Journal of Personality and Social Psychology*, Vol. 38, No. 4.

Williams, R. (1964). *Strangers Next Door: Ethnic Relations in American Communities*. Englewood Cliffs, NJ: Prentice-Hall.

12　　The Socialization Process for Hungary's New Political Elites

László Kéri

ABSTRACT

The last few years in the postcommunist transition period provide us with useful and newer insights. For example, in Hungary, the new political elite which has crystallized since 1989 consists of groups that are essentially different from one another. This chapter outlines six basic types among the Hungarian political elites in the 1990s. On the basis of their political cultures, behaviors, and attitudes, we can distinguish the following types: survivors, intellectuals in the humanities tradition, demagogic leaders, professionals, the 'newly-born', and new capitalist entrepreneurs.

It is very instructive to analyze in some detail the socialization experience for each elite type. In the process of political learning, different agent structures were operating in each case. By carrying out comparative analyses of these structures, we can demonstrate that the duality of the previously believed formal-informal socialization model should be fundamentally revised. We should discard some of the criteria we worked out in the 1980s. In connection with changes which political transition has generated, there are now the previous informal political socialization processes, the latent mechanisms which led to the formation of rival political elites, and the fact that this rivalry has become a permanent feature of Hungarian politics. This also means that the hidden mechanisms of political socialization fulfilled not only the function of the traditional transmission of political culture and patterns (to counter the influence of official political indoctrination), but they also fulfilled various other important functions. A detailed description of the Hungarian case will provide new insights into the analysis of the problems of socialization in this recent postcommunist transition period.

INTRODUCTION

After 1989, a climate of unusual rapid change characterized the disintegration of the most important product of socialization in the socialist political establishment that had lasted for more than four decades: the types of ruling politicians. Some 100 000 people belonged to the stratum of professional politicians; from the outside looking in, this stratum seemed to be very homogeneous (that is, a markedly unified group). The formal political socialization process and the major political education institutions had achieved a virtual mass production of these 'model-type' people, constituting only a tiny fraction of the population (some 1-2 per cent). Nevertheless, this group was portrayed for decades as 'role models' for the overwhelming majority to emulate. Their activities were presented as examples to be followed both in the narrow circles of political life and in the public sphere. This group symbolized practically the only political attitude which was universally tolerated as the new orthodoxy.

As for the other ten million people, the authorities considered it sufficient if they displayed the most important external signs of loyalty at special, festive occasions. Even a decade earlier, researchers had already indicated that a great variation in values and political attitudes existed behind the uniform facade of these formal observances. However, this variety could not manifest itself in the official public sphere.

This former model type has disappeared at an incredible rate of speed from the Hungarian public life. In its place stands a group of new competing political elites. Within this new political elite, there is a permanent struggle. Even now, it is difficult to predict which one or more of them will gain long-term ascendancy.

The social background of these various elite groups is quite unstable. We are not far from the truth if we say that, despite the passage of five years, the process in which the major social interest groups ally themselves with the various elite groups has not yet been finished.

The new political elite groups illustrate markedly different socialization patterns. In the course of their struggles for ascendancy, they produced all possible combinations of the features which characterize the political and cultural heritage from recent Hungarian history. Each type represents its own realities which, in turn, have a different social significance. Some of them are rather historical in character, while others represent current interests. However, there is a common feature which all six enumerated types exhibit: none of them can be considered a true product of political socialization processes of the previous regime. One could go further and say that all these types emerged despite the internal logic of the socialist system. Their emergence resulted from the hidden influences which lurked within (or behind) official programs of political socialization. (On these points, see Kéri, 1990, 1991, 1993, and 1994.)

Of course, enumerating the different elite prototypes does not actually mean that we have a basis for identifying their political party loyalties because the various types can be found in practically all the major parties. On the other hand, by studying the characteristics of the six major Hungarian parties, one may predict which of the six enumerated elite groups would actually play a dominant role in their leadership.

Hungarian public opinion regards the leadership of the six parliamentary parties as the dominant agents of the new Hungarian political elite. Therefore, we also attached special importance to the socialization patterns of the new leaders and to their political and cultural heritage when we prepared the following conceptual framework to typify them.

In the course of preparing these types, we relied primarily on personal autobiographies, interviews with the leaders of the new political elite, and results of personal interviews/discussions with almost 100 members of the Hungarian parliament.

THE OLD GUARD OR SURVIVORS

During the last months of the disintegration of the previous political regime, when a period of creative negotiations began, a new group of politicians emerged almost from nothing. Later, at the beginning of the 1990s, this group came to exert decisive influence over Hungary's political life. Their appearance, political style, system of arguments, and behaviors differed radically from what we had previously witnessed. Most of the new political elites were around 60 years old (similar to the age of their major opponents), representing a generation born from 1930-5. But even if they appeared before the public as the politicians of the Communist Party's reform wing, they had much more in common with Hungarian leaders from previous decades.

However, this newly emerging group of politicians (which also came from the older generation) was incredibly far from anything witnessed for decades in the official political life of the country. They were overtly and honestly anticommunist. They despised the failing regime and held values reminiscent of 1948 and, to an even greater degree, of pre-war Hungary. Generally speaking, they were suspicious of the Left and of leftist ideas because they considered them alien to Hungary's political culture. In their eyes, all leftist influence was nothing more than the unavoidable consequences of decades-long Soviet oppression.

In their opinion, Hungary has always been an integral part of Christian Europe and could be separated from it only temporarily. These politicians have fairly good relations with various groups of Hungarian emigres who moved to the West. They also made no secret of their desire to reunite the Hungarians of the diaspora, if only on a symbolic level, but primarily in its cultural aspect. Their avowed ideal is the conservative liberalism of 19th-century Hungary. In connection with this, we can only refer to the fact that these politician types had their golden age at the end of the last and the first half of this century. 'We are all admirers of the 19th century', they often say; this is often emphasized when prominent members of the government speak about themselves.

In the political socialization of the old guard/survivors, we can discern some remarkable similarities. Their autobiographies tend to reveal that famous church schools exerted a crucial influence on their lives. These grammar schools (which were allowed to exist without restraint until 1949) and colleges often have 200- or even 300-year-old traditions. The level of educational requirements are similar to that of the German, northern Italian, and Dutch institutions (gymnasia). After 1949, these church schools were reined in and anybody who had studied at such a school was treated with suspicion when communist 'personnel politicians' did their clearance reports.

The other important channel for their political socialization was the family. More often than not, their families played significant roles in the public, economic, or cultural spheres of pre-1948 Hungary, either on the local or national levels. After 1949, the closed and internal world of these families remained the only social sphere where it was possible to display and represent values, interpretations, and gestures that were diametrically opposed to the regime's officially propagated values. Thus, it is not surprising that in each of these politicians' autobiographies, they emphasized hardships, persecutions, and political punishments their families endured. During the years of Soviet-type rule, these families adopted the strategy of trying to survive the regime with the least possible sacrifice. It was only in the personal micro-sphere of their lives that they considered themselves as the regime's uncompromising enemies. However, they saw no possibility for publicly presenting their own values.

These two features spurred development of isolated, cautious, patient (but intransigent) social-political characters and identities. This personality type holds traditions in high esteem, tries to avoid direct conflicts, but, if necessary, can wait interminably.

THE RESEARCH INSTITUTE INTELLECTUALS

In 1989, the ruling party had to face the challenge the emerging professional-intellectual groups (who had previously dared to express their views and values only in their own very narrow professional circles) of politicians represented. Accustomed to this kind of critical intellectual behavior, they suddenly had to cope with the difficulties which professional politicians face. This proved to be a painful process.

Even after becoming party leaders and members of parliament (or at least public figures), these intellectuals endeavored to preserve their special critical world views. In this framework, they were much more interested in discussing some fundamental, ideological interconnections than in taking part in daily political struggles. They wanted to keep their distance from the direct political activities. Based on their widespread international connections, they know how various national models of modernization have succeeded; they prefer preparing long-range plans rather than the exhausting tasks involved in realizing and implementing them. They clearly see the economic difficulties and all the negative consequences of public alternatives. In general, if we compare them with typical politicians, we find that they perceive much more subtly potential social consequences for probable public decisions. This type of behavior has never been able to become a dominant political force in Hungary. In the light of this observation, it is surprising that the party which best represents this attitude managed to become the second largest parliamentary party in the 1990 election.

The socialization background of this type of political actor (an intellectual) involves training in the humanities and sharing special workplaces. The social-scientific research institutes, university departments, lawyers' offices, and other intellectual workplaces brought together dozens of persons, often of the same age. Later on, they joined with other 'dissidents', who were dependent on the invisible effects and strenuous work of decades in Hungary. These workplaces enjoyed relative independence and freedom because the communist authorities did not assign them any special political importance. One cannot forget that foreign professional literature and the products of the Western press were available at these workplaces. Therefore, it is hardly surprising that this group espoused fundamentally different views from those officially propagated. These places also served as the scenes of continued debates and exchanges of opinion. It is true that those in power dominated the mass media, but the intellectual workshops enjoyed a significant degree of freedom in shaping their own sovereign public sphere. This duality manifested itself in the whole period of the 1970s and 1980s, when the distance between official and nonofficial politics increased.

We can conclude that the previously described field of political socialization benefited the proliferation of behavioral attitudes which encouraged members of this stratum to be constantly ready to criticize, debate, and argue logically. However, this could be converted into collective political action and an intention to participate in public affairs only with serious difficulty since these attempts always collided with the limits from the political system. Features which characterize and define this type of political socialization include a limited political visibility with a background of penetrating intellectual analysis and a subculture that was severely constrained in its scope of action.

LEADERS OF THE PEOPLE

One of the rediscovered traditions of the 1990s has been street politics (that is, street rallies and unrestrained political movements). In this situation, the 'leader of the people' feels secure. He/she loves the audience, which returns the sentiment. The leader of the people is especially fond of the fact that, during a public rally, even the most difficult problems can be explained very simply. Practically everything can be simplified into plus-and-minus or black-and-white questions and answers. The appropriate formulations never fail to elicit immediate applause from those present. The leader of the people is not very fond of the last-mentioned type (the intellectual, trained in the humanities) who keeps on chattering and tattling and who always racks his/her brain over theoretical problems. Disliking the press, he/she is confident that the modern mass media serve the purpose of sheer manipulation. Overall, he/she is extremely critical of the complex and sophisticated institutions of a democracy, based on a division of powers. These democratic institutions represent a way to play for time, to avoid crucial decisions. Consequently, his/her ideal is direct (as compared with indirect) democracy (that is, people participate directly in the management of public affairs). This myth of direct participation is connected with the adoration of national-unity; anybody who threatens to disrupt this unity is a potential traitor. In light of this, it is hardly surprising that the leader of the people does not trust the West and attaches primary importance to centuries of national-historical heritage. The leader of the people believes all our problems can be solved if we rely primarily on the wisdom of our national heritage.

It is almost impossible to explain the socialization background of this politician type without referring to general conditions of Hungarian society in modern history. Hungarian literary life often had to compensate for deficiencies in political life. Therefore, it used to be a widespread custom for writers and poets to represent those political alternatives that were missing from pub-lic/official discussions or that could not be presented openly.

For this reason, literary workshops, creative communities, and voluntary societies served as oral political forums for decades. Such literary and artistic gatherings acted as political groups, but in closed circles. Quite often, the aesthetic aspects of the works of art seemed to be insignificant in comparison with their political importance. Literary and cultural debates concealed real and sharp political differences. Thus, cultural substitutions in overt political discourse resulted in upgrading figurative speech, using symbols, and preferring emotional identification over conceptual learning. The sociological authenticity of opinions, the accuracy of the knowledge conveyed, or the facts were much less important factors than the expressive capacity of the chosen form of discourse and the degree of efficiency in measuring the political weight of the given opinion.

With respect to the field of political socialization, we can sum this up by saying that the political education of this ideal type was based on the community structure of the cultural life. Those symbols and identification forms evolved in the creative communities and artistic groups, which were indispensable for learning political roles. The crucial attribute was assuming responsibility for the people, for the whole of the nation. This kind of behavior could (and can) hardly be interpreted in concrete terms. This attitude/character wishes to grasp the whole. As a matter of fact, this can be understood as the standpoint of the artist. However, in practical politics, this same character will inevitably feel only the extremes. He/she will tend to see everything in either black or white, preferring to understand and emphasize the essence of the things instead of coping with the difficult tasks of making decisions. This prototype is not a Hungarian speciality at all, but is well-known all over Central and Eastern Europe.

THE PROFESSIONALS

The taciturn, well-dressed, polite, professional politicians have a perfect knowledge of how to run various organizations and what is necessary for making a decision. In his/her heart of hearts, this type of politician is convinced that democracy is, after all, a superfluous and clumsy institution which only decreases the speed, efficiency, and implementation of decisions. But he/she also knows that without democracy one is not accepted in 'respectable' circles. Therefore, he/she has no doubt that efficiency is a thousand times more important than democracy.

Based on mutual interest, he/she also thinks it is possible to find a *modus vivendi* with anybody in order to transform any conflicts into mutually advantageous decisions. He/she constantly tries to convince opponents that political life resembles a large, modern factory. There, one can find those neutral managerial and organizational systems of know-how which are absolutely independent of any political or ideological positions. First of all, he/she prefers provision for the technical conditions of modern management, using the well-paid specialist. Although well aware of the probable social consequences of economic and political decisions, these consequences are not the product of a heightened social responsiveness, but derive from his/her ability to see the state of affairs in a broader perspective.

The direct predecessor of this political elite group is not solely the socialist system. Even the world of the former Austro-Hungarian Empire had been familiar with that kind of organizational behavior (in the revitalization of which, the Communist Party came to play such a dominant role after 1949).

The crucial institutions in the political socialization of this type were the previous regime's generation-based political organizations. Among them, the most important was the KISZ (League of Young Communists), the party's youth movement. If one spent some years in the apparatus of the youth organization, then he/she was in a position to choose among top positions either in the public administration or in the party organizations. (Notice that the difference between the two alternatives is not insignificant. Experience gained by working for years in public administration tended to strengthen the ability to manage the affairs of an organization pragmatically, while the party careers promoted the development of ideological-political features.)

There is no doubt that this type of politician most markedly reflects the imprint of the previous regime. Even if he/she does not wish to demonstrate it publicly, his/her gestures undeniably reveal the heritage of the Kádár-era and public activities seem to emphasize the message of the overthrown regime. This situation prevails despite his/her efforts to convince the population that he/she has honestly changed in order to be accepted by the Hungarian society. Nevertheless, his/her previous organizational socialization cannot be wiped out.

If we had to describe the final outcome of this type of political socialization with a single phrase, it would be 'lack of fantasy'. Fully accepting the organization, hiding the persons behind the organization, and depersonalizing public activities as much as possible characterized this type of political socialization. Nevertheless, this is also a reality just as the postwar period cannot be wiped out of Hungary's history (no matter how much some new political elite groups try to do so, even to the extent of eliminating decades from their own history).

THE YOUNG DEMOCRATIC POLITICIANS, 'CLEAN' AND WITH NO PAST AT ALL

Perhaps the most surprising political phenomenon of the post-1989 period was the appearance of a generation whose members were in their twenties and, therefore, had nothing to do with the old communist regime. They only witnessed the socialist system in its final, dying form, though they turned against it with an amazing firmness. Already products of the 1980s, their characters and thought patterns were formed when the higher education system conveyed the regime's ideology only to a very limited extent. This new type can easily manage modern technical equipment, speak and read foreign languages, and stay in tune with reality more readily than previous generations. They are rarely perplexed, are tough negotiators, accept only professionally justified arguments, do not treat ideological debates seriously, and, if compelled to obey a certain ideology, do so pragmatically. They know the mass media better than other politicians and have good relations with domestic and international journalists. They are very well-informed regarding economic questions, support entrepreneurs, but dislike spending time on social problems. They believe the older generation's outlook has been constricted in their ideological and cultural struggles to such an extent that the young democrats do not wish to join a party or participate in these fruitless debates. They are interested in the future instead of the past, though they are able to choose from their heritage and Hungarian political culture those who provide intellectual support for their policy. This behavior simultaneously combines two features: 1) the recent historical tradition which has always seen a certain connection between youth and radical revolutions and 2) the effect of the 'yuppie' tradition (imported from the West) of the 1970s. The political leaders of this new generation are more or less in tune with postmaterialist values, which are pro-democratic, antinuclear, pro-environmental, and community oriented.

It is no coincidence that the overwhelming majority of young democrats came from Budapest's two major universities: the University of Economics and the Faculty of Law of the Eötvös Loránd University. Both universities traditionally attract students whose mental attitudes and behaviors were essentially different from those of the regime. The sense of living a common life, the desire to do something, the criticism of the official educational system, the demand for a larger degree of autonomy, and the constant defense of independence were characteristic features of students in the 1980s. They formed extremely strong links (even stronger than ties among relatives) with one another. In the middle of the 1980s, the intensive cooperation among universities and colleges and the initiation of common activities and workshops allowed these students to participate in the political sphere and openly assume a political role.

No other type of political elites has exhibited such strong generation effects. Therefore, it is no coincidence that present-day Hungarian society (including those generations which accept the FIDESZ, though they are of a different age) consider the political prominence of this political type primarily as a generation-based phenomenon.

ENTREPRENEURS OR POLITICAL DILETTANTES

The last political type has become identifiable only recently. However, it is true that their predecessors and their current leading figures had already appeared in public life by the mid-1980s. Their sphere of action could be extended only after Hungary had officially embraced the idea of market capitalism instead of the previously discredited 'planned economy' (that is, only after Spring 1990).

First of all, this new entrepreneur is a personality whose name is more important than that of the political party. The party does not manage him/her; he/she manages the party. More often than not, he/she has no party affiliations, preferring to maintain good relations with all major political groups to promote entrepreneurial interests. He/she attends all important events (exhibitions, charity balls, diplomatic receptions, and festivals) and is so social that one often asks: When does he/she work or who works instead of him/her? Often, he/she is the principal sponsor of the events. The origin of his/her wealth is usually shrouded in mystery, with various magazines and newspapers typically presenting markedly different explanations concerning this distasteful but tantalizing topic. However, all these stories feature his/her audacity, inventiveness, and ability. One feature these entrepreneurs share is that they could (and dared to) think of something which nobody else had considered.

He/she appears in public life with a moderate, but markedly rich, retinue of friends and associates. The entrepreneur has secretaries, rare automobiles, and legendary hobbies, just as there are legends about the value of his/her successful transactions or failures. Willing to participate in discussions/decisions about political economy and 'economic policy', he/she may meddle in parliamentary, party, and government debates if it seems necessary.

Usually, the entrepreneur has significant stakes in the mass media, but is not interested at all in ideological debates. Personifying the modern ideal of a gentleman/woman, the entrepreneur does not need anybody's support, but by contrast, extends help to those who do. What he/she needs most is fresh and quick information, which can now be purchased along with its source or the means to produce it.

The entrepreneur's socialization background has considerable roots in the post-1978 period, when the 'grey' and 'black' economies gained ground and the failure of the centrally planned economy became more and more apparent. At the start, only a few hundred people were willing to learn the art and take on the risk of running private enterprises, but over the years, their number increased significantly. When the socialist regime was in power, this meant primarily finding loopholes, evading rules, or defeating the inner logic of the system. This flexible attitude served as a guiding pattern for the leading entrepreneurs of those days. Their primary school was the chaotic world of the disintegrating socialist planned economy, where they had to learn the art of survival. They proved to be inventive both in the field of hiding and, at the same time, making long-range plans.

Their primary political socialization came into being during the economic crisis when they developed experience in solving economic problems and dealing with sudden enrichment. We have in mind those kinds of riches which need not be concealed from other people. Their attitudes combined the cruelty of a person who amasses wealth, a desire for stability (as in the case of the bourgeois who is already rich), and the political aspirations of a self-conscious class. It remains to be seen how (and with what kinds of problems) this historic process can be managed or even accelerated when combining the various roles.

ELITES' POLITICAL SOCIALIZATION: SOME CONCLUSIONS

Eastern European researchers often called attention to the fact that during the 1980s, behind the formal-official political socialization process in the socialist system, there were equally important nonofficial socialization trends (with hidden messages) (see Csepeli et al., 1994). Nevertheless, practically all of us were surprised when the most conspicuous product of the official political socialization of the last half century so rapidly disappeared following the fall of the socialist regime. This product was the official political elite, which had its own patterns that predominated for decades.

Even more amazing is the fact that this rapid demise did not result in a vacuum, but involved (as a running parallel to the disappearance of the previously dominant socialist political elite) the emergence of new political elites whose socialization backgrounds were fundamentally different. The rapidity of substitution must make us think about the total failure of previous official socialization mechanisms, even retrospectively. Obviously, this phenomenon could be observed in this form exclusively in the Soviet-type societies and in the postcommunist countries. One may correctly assume that much more importance should be attributed to those hidden and hardly perceptible processes which went on behind officially promoted political socialization mechanisms.

It is the whole of political culture that constitutes the contents of the socialization messages. This statement is true even if the official policy or indoctrination process always chooses selectively from among the political-cultural messages. It tries to establish a hierarchy within the diversity of privileged cultural traditions, supporting certain segments of culture with its own institutions. However, it is possible that (as a boomerang-effect of this official support) an agent can transfer unofficial political-cultural traditions much more effectively than we can measure them with our traditional research methodologies.

In this case, we have to reach a similar conclusion. The socialization backgrounds of the new Hungarian political elite of the early 1990s demonstrate the fact that the differences among the various types can be explained primarily or alternatively by the effects of the different agents. Although it may seem surprising, all the enumerated types show that behind the facade of the seemingly unitary mechanism of political socialization, the various socialization agents produced basically different results during the same decades.

We have tried to demonstrate that the differences among the types of the new political elites can hypothetically be explained by differences in the primary agents of socialization. However, in some cases, it was the family; in others, the age group; while in yet another, the special milieu of the work-place proved to be the decisive factor in political socialization. The most conspicuous fact is that an agent is capable of transferring the whole of political culture continuously, even if the other agents tend to exert influence (simultaneously) on the realization of a fundamentally different system of values. In other words, if (in the process of political socialization) the separate agents possess a continuously relative autonomy, then one can easily imagine that fundamentally different values and patterns (apart from those which the official-formal socialization process/agents promote) can be transferred successfully.

In all probability, these are not findings unique to Hungary; they are probably characteristic features of the whole region. However, one cannot know whether these experiences can be generalized to yet another degree. It is possible that the socialist system, itself, could produce for decades processes of socialization at a very low level and that their (relative) inefficiency was only revealed by the first major international crisis. Certainly, it is remarkable that after decades of intense institutional interventions, the deeper traditions of political culture manifested themselves in such a diversity following the spectacular failure of the official socialization process. We have to add to all this, despite its indisputable failure, that the socialist type of political socialization (which lasted almost half a century) became an integral part of the ensuing diverse world of political culture. Today, we cannot present clear empirically verifiable knowledge to predict the long-term socialization effect of this historical period (which proved to be a major failure once all relevant factors are considered). For example, some of the questions we have yet to consider and answer include: What about the leaders of the social democratic parties (the former communists) in 1994? Are they similar or different compared to the 'old' Communist Party leaders? Is their electoral success related to the effect of successful communist socialization in the past? The interpretation and elaboration of these topics may become a fundamental focus for our further research.

REFERENCES

Csepeli, G., D. German, L. Kéri, and I. Stumpf (eds.) (1994). *From Subject to Citizen*. Budapest, Hungary: Hungarian Center for Political Education and Friedrich Naumann Stiftung.

Kéri, L. (1990). 'About the Possibilities of Interpretation of Problems of Political Socialization', pp. 173-87 in B. Claussen and H. Müller (eds.) *Political Socialization of the Young in East and West*. Frankfurt am Main, FRG: Verlag Peter Lang.

Kéri, L. (1991). 'Facing New Challenges', pp. 29-43 in I. Stumpf and Z. Békés (eds.) *How to be a Democrat in a Post-Communist Society*. Budapest, Hungary: Institute for Political Science and Hungarian Center for Political Education, Hungarian Academy of Sciences.

Kéri, L. (1993). 'Approaching the Year 2000: Prospects for Political Socialization in Hungary and Central Europe', pp. 193-204 in R. Farnen (ed.) *Reconceptualizing Politics, Socialization, and Education*. Oldenburg, FRG: Bibliotheks- und Informationssystem der Universität Oldenburg (BIS).

Kéri, L. (1994). 'An Avalanche of Minorities: Some Unexpected Consequences of Regime Changes in Hungarian Political Culture', pp. 345-55 in R. Farnen (ed.) *Nationalism, Identity, and Ethnicity: Cross-National and Comparative Perspectives*. New Brunswick, NJ and London, UK: Transaction Publications.

13   Identification with Social Groups and Intolerance among Dutch Adolescents
An Empirical Study

Wilma A. M. Vollebergh

ABSTRACT

By definition, 'true' democracy is based on an assumption of equality among group members. On the other hand, social relations between human beings are based on an intuitive sense of inequality. People's social identity (that part of their identity that binds them to a larger community) depends on social relations and perceptions about social groups in society. This leads to an inherent incompatibility between 'true democracy' and social institutions, at least to some extent.

This chapter looks at the social identity of some Dutch adolescents with respect to these issues. We will analyze their affiliation with particular social groups. In addition, we will observe those differences between authoritarian and nonauthoritarian adolescents that throw some light on one's identification with particular groups on the one hand and intolerance toward other groups (as a corollary effect) on the other.

INTRODUCTION

'True' democracy is, by definition, based on an assumption of equality: equal rights, freedom, and opportunities to gain respect, status, or material resources. Alternatively, social relations between human beings are based on an intuitive sense of inequality. That is, the value of friendship, love, or mutual trust seems to lie in the fact that these are not universally shared, but are given only to those whom we choose to love, befriend, or trust.

So far, the picture seems simple and clear. In the private domain and in private matters, 'in-group favoritism' is wanted and needed to guarantee social relations. In the public domain, 'in-group favoritism' is distrusted and forbidden to guarantee social equality.

This dilemma is particularly noticeable in describing or explaining the relations between social groups in society. Identifying with particular social groups is valued as the construction of a positive social identity. Yet simultaneously, it is distrusted in its corollary effect, namely, the construction of 'out-groups'. How are we to value these two aspects? Two major theories exist, but each addresses only one of these aspects. These are authoritarian personality

304

theory (which stresses and studies the construction of out-groups) and social identity theory (that focuses on its positive counterpart).

THE AUTHORITARIAN PERSONALITY

Adorno et al. (1950) regarded authoritarianism as a particular personality type. The suggested characteristics are most apparent in the original description of the authoritarian syndrome itself. Then, it was thought of as comprising nine different aspects: authoritarian submission, conventionalism, superstition, power and toughness, authoritarian aggression, anti-introspection, preoccupation with sex, cynicism and destructive needs, and projection. Together, these aspects were thought to form a quite permanent structure in the person, rendering him/her receptive to antidemocratic thought (Adorno et al., 1950, pp. 228-9). But the way in which these different aspects constituted a personality construct is implied, rather than explained, in the original study.

Throughout the original study, numerous comments suggested that the main organizing forces responsible for the coherence between the different aspects of the F-syndrome are social categorization and in-group/out-group construction. Table 13.1 illustrates that it is possible to assign every aspect of authoritarianism to social categories and in-group/out-group construction. This complies perfectly with the way the different factors were investigated in the original study, namely by converting each into items which addressed particular social groups in a positive or negative way. The in-group thus stands for the social groups that engender submission and identification, while the out-group generates aggression and exclusion. Strictly speaking, only two parts of authoritarianism cannot be applied to this process, namely cynicism and projection. They both pertain to a psychodynamic mechanism characteristic of authoritarians. That is, they tend to be unconscious of their less endearing traits (especially aggression) and externalize these while projecting them onto others. In doing so, they tend to be cynical about human nature.

We will address both social categorization and in-group/out-group construction from the perspective of the authoritarian personality construct.

Table 13.1. The authoritarianism syndrome and in-group/out-group social categorizations

Major Aspects of Authoritarianism	Social Categorization into:	
	In-group	Out-group
1. Conventionalism	disciplinarians	unconventional people
2. Authoritarian submission	social authority powerful groups	
3. Authoritarian aggression		minority groups 'troublemakers'
4. Anti-introspection		intellectuals 'soft' professionals
5. Superstition	God supernatural powers	
6. Power and toughness	'masculinity' army, police	
7. Preoccupation with sex		prostitutes promiscuous people
Psychodynamic characteristics:		
8. Cynicism, destructiveness		
9. Projection		

Social Categorization

There is a tendency to perceive human beings in terms of social categories. This categorization was not seen as a rational or standard way of perceiving social groups in society, but primarily as an irrational need to simplify the social world into stereotypes. Psychologically, this categorization was thought to originate from the deep-lying need to minimize the social world, to render it more predictable, and, at the same time, to create a joint 'enemy', which can serve as a target for the projection of the ego-threatening impulses of the authoritarian personality.

In-group/Out-group Construction

There is a tendency to create a contrast between the two, evaluating the in-group positively and the out-group negatively. The distinction between in-groups and out-groups is the central structure in the categorization process referred to before. This distinction differentiates between 'us' and 'them', good and bad, the morally superior groups in society and the morally inferior, and the acceptable versus the socially unacceptable ones. In this way, the in-group constitutes the moral authority that functions as the main object for identification, while the out-group serves mainly as the target of projection. The psychological function of this in-group/out-group distinction was seen as ego protection; ascribing moral superiority to the in-group rationalizes and legitimizes aggression directed toward the out-groups. Threatening 'id impulses' (which are hard to deal with, especially for authoritarians, since they are generally thought to have weak ego's) within the personality are externalized. That is, they are removed as inner urges and projected onto the out-group, thus appearing to be characteristic only of 'others'. In psychoanalytical terms, this tendency was seen as the result of a failure in the formation of the super-ego. This means that external, social control has not been successfully internalized and, therefore, social adjustment remains dependent on submission to external social authority. Since aggression, which submission to authority provokes, cannot be directed toward the authority figure itself (because this causes anxiety), it is directed toward less dangerous targets by means of projection. These include the weak and the disobedient groups in society. Conventionalism and resistance to social change were thus explained as having a function in authoritarians' continuous struggle to maintain a proper psychological balance between their authoritarian submission and the threatening anger it arouses in them.

Nonauthoritarian personalities are thought to lack this urgent need for an out-group. Their systematic rejection of the items in the different scales was interpreted as the manifestation of an identification with 'everybody'. Nonauthoritarians have no need for out-groups and likewise, presumably, none for in-groups. They are strongly individualized and capable of dealing with ambiguities. Having developed an inner authority (that is, the conscience) they, therefore, do not need to lean on an in-group as a personally external authority. They identify with humanity as a whole and lack the aggressive urges typical of authoritarians.

IN-GROUP FAVORITISM AND SOCIAL IDENTITY

Although the original authoritarian personality theory has been repeatedly and extensively criticized, this idea of in-group favoritism as a central feature of authoritarian thought is still widely accepted in present-day research. It is envisaged as a powerful explanation for ethnocentrist and nationalistic thought (Eisinga and Scheepers, 1989). The idea behind it suggests that only those who favor the culture of their homeland (nationalism, ethnocentrism) show signs of in-group favoritism, while those who reject these particular 'in-groups' (nonauthoritarians) are supposed to abstain from favoring any in-group at all.

The empirical evidence against such statements is almost overwhelming if we interpret in-group/out-group construction in terms of a 'social identity'. According to Tajfel, we can define social identity as that part of the individual's personal identity, which is connected to his/her identification with particular social groups. In other words, in the construction of a social identity, the perception of the social world links with the social dimensions of the individual's self-concept (Turner, 1982). The 'self' thereby functions as a primary schema, which plays a central role in assimilating the relevant social information and protecting, cultivating, or restoring one's self-image (Markus et al., 1985).

Social psychological research points out that this is an almost universal characteristic of the social dimension of human identity (Tajfel, 1981, 1982, 1984; Turner et al., 1987). In social psychological experiments, a simple classification of subjects as members of, for example, a blue or green group only for 'administrative reasons' proved to be enough to produce in-group favoritism, which is strengthened under conditions of perceived interdependence (for example, sharing a 'common fate') (Rabbie and Horwitz, 1969). Both striving for a positive social identity and more economic, instrumental calculations of reciprocity within the in-group seem to be important determinants of this in-group/out-group bias (Rabbie et al., 1989). But even the psychoanalytic theory, itself, can only lead one to assume that for the development of a positive (social) identity, distinctions with other people are not only necessary, but can be even unavoidable, be it on an individual level (where the 'I' is contrasted with other selves) or on a social level (where 'we' are contrasted with other 'we's'). In his 'Psycho-pathology of Everyday Life', Freud suggested that the projection of threatening impulses will always be a corollary of the act of distinguishing oneself from others. The need for projection of undesirable and guilt-inducing feelings is, therefore (even in psychoanalysis), a generalized feature of the human personality.

We could suggest that every positive image of a social or cultural group and the beliefs, customs, values, and cultural lifestyle it represents, tend to be contrasted with counter-images or their negation. Thus, we necessarily tend to find defensive and intolerant reactions present in these situations. These images are not to be seen as only reflecting an inner psychological logic, but as social representations. This means a way of everyday thinking within a particular community that its members share and that reinforces their identity as a group. If so, the characteristic distinguishing authoritarians from nonauthoritarians is to be found in their respective choices for particular in-groups and out-groups. And if so, the F-scale measures the adoption of argumentations legitimizing intolerance toward those out-groups (for example, cultural minorities, unconventional people, and left-wing political activists) that are seen as the counterpart of the authoritarian image of 'us' or 'we', rather than intolerance in general.

RESEARCH METHOD
Research Question

Following social identity theory, it is assumed that when people perceive social groups in society, they will tend to construct an 'in-group/out-group' dimension. The main hypothesis here is that this dimension will be found in both authoritarians and nonauthoritarians perceptions. Both will tend to identify with certain groups and demarcate themselves from groups they regard as their opposites. Thus, both will construct an out-group and use it as a foil against which their own group emerges in a positive light. Constructing an out-group can be seen as the corollary of building a social identity.

The second question is whether authoritarians and nonauthoritarians will use the same dimensions in this construction. Can the out-group for the authoritarians be seen as the in-group of the nonauthoritarians or are other dimensions involved here?

Composition and Selection of the Research Group

The research question was approached in a small, qualitative, in-depth investigation that was part of a larger longitudinal study on political attitudes among youngsters in the Netherlands. Over 2700 youth from different educational levels participated in this study.

For participation in this study, we decided to select students from among lower and higher general secondary education pupils (the Dutch MAVO and HAVO school types), to choose a roughly equal number of high and low scorers from both levels, and to try to ensure a proportional representation of boys and girls. The score on the long authoritarianism scale at the second measurement was adopted as the criterion for our selection.

We telephoned the adolescents who were eligible to participate in the follow-up and asked if they were prepared to come to the University of Utrecht for an interview. However, the following problem occurred during this selection process. As could be expected, the number of eligible boys was relatively large among the high scorers, while the number of eligible girls was relatively large among the low scorers. Therefore, we stopped the selection of high scorers when the pool of male high scorers was emptied (to prevent the girls from forming too small a minority in this category) and vice versa for the low scorers. This limited the front number of potential participants. Finally, 35 adolescents took part in this research project. As can be seen, the HAVO pupils were in the majority both among the high scorers and among the low scorers. High and low scorers, boys and girls, are proportionally represented.

OPERATIONALIZATION
Social Categorization

The concept of 'social categorization' refers to the combination of social groups in larger, more comprehensive categories. The operationalization of social categorization was based on the diagram of the different groups to which the specifics of the original authoritarianism syndrome refer (see Table 13.1). The name of each of these social groups was written on 25 separate cards.

The adolescents were asked to arrange these cards in groups. The instructions stressed that subjects had to make sure the cards within one pile resembled each other more than they resembled one of the cards from another pile. They could make as many piles as they liked. After having done so, we asked them to state their reasons for their categorizations and to give each pile a name. Then, we put each pile of cards into an envelope. The names the students gave to the piles were written on the envelopes.

Table 13.2 Sample characteristics of interviewees by type, gender, school, and (non)participation

Authoritarians*	School Type	Approached	Participated
boys		21	9
	MAVO	12	3
	HAVO	9	6
girls		38	9
	MAVO	24	3
	HAVO	14	6
Nonauthoritarians**			
boys		24	8
	MAVO	9	3
	HAVO	15	5
girls		29	9
	MAVO	14	1
	HAVO	15	8
Total		113	35

Note: * Authoritarians: score on long authoritarianism scale > 3.5
** Non authoritarians: score on long authoritarianism scale < 2.5

Perceived Distance Between Social Groups and the Self

This categorization procedure was also intended to investigate the perceived distance between the adolescents, themselves, and the various social groups. To study this, three cards were added with:

1.   The name of the adolescent him/herself (two cards).

2. The text 'what I would like to be like.' This card represented the so-called 'ideal self' of the person under investigation.

After subjects had finished the categorization procedure described previously, we asked them to put the cards that contained their own names into one of the groups they had made. This procedure resulted in a number of larger categories per adolescent. These could be arranged into a simple matrix of data on similarity, consisting of ones (in cells of two groups, which were grouped together) and zeros (in cells of two groups, which were not grouped together). These matrices were combined to form a matrix for the experimental group as a whole and to develop matrices for the various subgroups of authoritarian and nonauthoritarian adolescents. (This was done by counting the ones in the cells of the matrix of the adolescents from the corresponding [sub]group by cell in the matrix. The totals resulted in the figures which were to be found in the cells of the matrix for the corresponding [sub]group.) The obtained matrices were then used for hierarchical cluster analysis and multidimensional scale analysis (ALSCAL).

Social Identity

The categorization of social groups, itself, need not determine the significance that is attributed to these categories. The most distinguishing characteristic of a social identity is the classification of social categories into so-called 'in-groups' and 'out-groups'.

Questionnaires with several questions per social group (per card) were used. Three different aspects that might be related to the construction of a social identity were distinguished: 1) the perceived similarity between social groups and the self; 2) the construction of in-group/out-group dimensions; and 3) the attribution of masculine or feminine characteristics.

1. The perceived similarity between social groups and the self. In the construction of a social identity, the perception of the social world is linked to the social dimension of the conception of the self. It is assumed that, thereby, a favorable image of self and of one's own group will be constructed. This does not strictly require that one's own group does, in fact, belong to the groups which are presented as a metaphor for 'what is good and worth striving for'. It is also possible for a sort of 'substitute identification' to occur through the construction of similarities between one's own group and the relevant social group. That is, the more one's own group resembles the admired group, the easier it is to identify the two.

The matrices of data on similarity were subjected to cluster analysis and a multidimensional scale technique (ALSCAL) to reveal these resemblances. Thus, it is possible to visualize the underlying structure of the categorizations.

2. The construction of in-group/out-group dimensions. The central dimension in the construction of an 'in-group' refers to the extent to which this group is perceived as a moral authority. In addition to this, it is also important to determine whether this group is experienced as familiar or strange. According to the original theory, authoritarians are, furthermore, inclined to perceive the authorities in power as morally superior. These three aspects (morality, familiarity, power) were operationalized in the questionnaire in a list of semantic differentials. The interviewee had to indicate for each group how he/she would situate this group within the following opposites:

> powerful .... powerless
> strong .... weak
> bad .... good
> fair .... unfair
> deviant .... normal
> strange .... familiar

3. The attribution of masculine and feminine characteristics. The preoccupation of authoritarians with power, toughness, and strength indicates a strong preference for masculinity. As a result of this, authoritarians may perceive 'masculinity' not only as more powerful, but also as worth striving for and as morally superior. Characteristics associated with masculinity or femininity were added to the questionnaire. These adjectives are taken from an investigation of adjectives in the description of females and males by Komter (1977). For this semantic differential, we selected those characteristics which were referred to by more than two-thirds of Komter's respondents as being typically masculine (1) or typically feminine (5). They were operationalized as follows:

> rational .... emotional
> considered .... intuitive
> logical .... mysterious
> tough .... affectionate
> aggressive .... tender

RESEARCH RESULTS
Number of Categories

The categorization of groups was based on perceived similarities between these groups. Therefore, the smaller the number of categories used, the greater the perceived similarity and, thus, the stronger the categorization. The first question was whether authoritarians really do categorize more strongly (that is, use a smaller number of categories than nonauthoritarians). The results indicate that this is not the case. Both authoritarian and nonauthoritarian adolescents use a similar number of categories to classify the relevant groups in a meaningful way.

Table 13.3   Number of social categories by authoritarian and nonauthoritarian interviewees (ANOVA)

	Number of Categories
Authoritarians	6.56
girls	6.89
boys	6.22
Nonauthoritarians	6.82
girls	7.00
boys	6.62
Analysis of Variance	
Authoritarianism	$F(1,34) = .16$, n.s.
Gender	$F(1,34) = .96$, n.s.
2-Way Interaction	$F(2,33) = .05$, n.s.

The Social Representation of Groups in Society: The Clusters

The second question concerns the content of the categories that were created. It is possible that authoritarians create categories different from those created by nonauthoritarians since their classification is based on different dimensions of similarity. Using hierarchical cluster analysis, we investigated which groups were created and whether there were differences in this respect between authoritarian and nonauthoritarian adolescents.

The hierarchical cluster analysis displays a clear pattern. Authoritarian and nonauthoritarian adolescents create similar clusters. The correlation between the content of the cells in the matrices of authoritarian and nonauthoritarian subjects, which was .93, (p<.001), confirmed this finding. In calculating this correlation, the content of the cells in the matrix of authoritarians were taken as one row of scores, which was correlated with the rows representing the content of cells in the matrix of the nonauthoritarians.

Table 13.4 The clusters and composition of social groups

Clusters	Social Group Composition
Private world	Parents, friends
Intellectuals	Scientists, artists, therapists
Upholders of norms	Politicians, magistrates
Upholders of order	Generals, police, soldiers
Supernatural	God, supernatural powers
Minorities	Homosexuals, Turks/Moroccans, Jews, handicapped people
Activists	Political activists, squatters, feminists
Criminals	Criminals, rapists, racists

The Structure in the Perception of Social Groups: Distance from the Self

The distances between the various groups were analyzed using ALSCAL, which was applied to the matrix of data on similarity. The results of this analysis are presented here for their illustrative value, with the proviso that they should be treated with a degree of caution. The three-dimensional solution appears superior on technical grounds (lower stress), but it is more difficult to interpret. Therefore, we present the two-dimensional solution here (see Table 13.5).

It is more difficult to interpret the third dimension than the two-dimensional solution. This was also the case in the pilots. Moreover, the third dimension that we found in the pilots differed from the third dimension that we found in the main research, while the two dimensions found in the pilots and in the main research are comparable. Hence, we present the two-dimensional solution here.

Table 13.5 The RSQ and the stress on the one-dimensional, two-dimensional and three-dimensional solutions of the ALSCAL analysis

Dimension	RSQ	Stress
One	.51	.42
Two	.76	.21
Three	.87	.13
Four	.90	.07

The first dimension discriminates between powerful social groups (such as the upholders of norms and order on the one hand and the sociocultural minorities and, in a certain sense, the activists and supernatural forces on the other). The second dimension differentiates primarily between the private sphere and the criminals. This analysis also confirms the results of the cluster analysis: the groups forming clusters are closely together in this two-dimensional field as well (see Figure 13.1).

Figure 13.1 Two-dimensional ALSCAL configuration

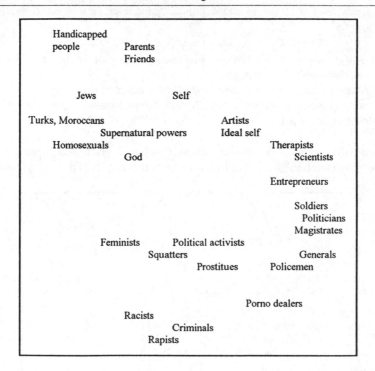

To simplify these data, the next step was a more comprehensive ALSCAL analysis of clusters formed by authoritarian and nonauthoritarian adolescents. The three controversial categories (entrepreneurs, prostitutes, porno-dealers) are excluded here. This analysis also yields a two-dimensional solution displaying a close resemblance with the rough construction in Figure 13.1.

To construct the matrix of data on similarity used for the ALSCAL analysis of the clusters, we calculated the distance between two clusters by taking the average of the distances in the cells which indicate the distances between the original groups from the respective clusters. For example, the distance between the cluster of norm upholders (1. politicians, 2. magistrates) and the cluster of order upholders (3. police, 4. soldiers, 5 .generals) was calculated by adding up the distance in the cells 1-3, 1-4, 1-5, 2-3, 2-4, and 2-5, and then dividing the total by 6. This procedure was followed for each combination of clusters, resulting in a similarity matrix of distances between the clusters which could then be used as input for the ALSCAL procedure.

The advantage of this simplified ALSCAL diagram is not only that it visualizes in a glance the structure of the social groups in society, but also that it is most in accordance with the research procedure. From this point on, the interview was confined to those groups the adolescents, themselves, had constructed.

There are a number of striking features in Figure 13.2:

♦   Activists are regarded as potential criminals in the sense that they are situated closest to criminals.

♦   Minorities are situated close to the private sphere of the adolescents. They are apparently perceived as much more familiar than those who discriminate against them (racists).

Figure 13.2   Differences between authoritarian and nonauthoritarian adolescent categorizations

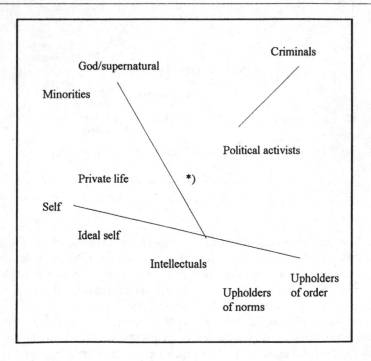

Note: *) = Significant differences between authoritarians and nonauthoritarians.

Differences Between Authoritarians and Nonauthoritarians

Although authoritarian and nonauthoritarian adolescents produced the same clusters, they did not perceive the distances between the clusters or their own position within the clusters in the same way. The distances between the clusters in the similarity matrices of authoritarians and nonauthoritarians displayed significant differences. These are indicated by the lines in Figure 13.2 (the difference in distance was checked with the t-test, p<.05). Nonauthoritarian adolescents created a greater distance between themselves and the upholders of norms and order, while they also perceived a much greater distance between activists and the criminal group than did the authoritarian adolescents. Authoritarian adolescents perceived a smaller distance between the supernatural and the intellectuals. Therefore, separate ALSCAL-analyzes for authoritarians and nonauthoritarians were carried out.

The results of these separate ALSCAL analyzes for authoritarian and non-authoritarian adolescents were as follows:

♦ Both authoritarian and nonauthoritarian adolescents opposed criminals to their 'ideal', thereby revealing that they operated with the same major opposites. Therefore, the difference between authoritarians and non-authoritarians appeared to be gradual, rather than polar (in the sense that the nonauthoritarians were the polar opposite of the authoritarians). It refers to two variations within one and the same dominant culture.

♦ The controversial groups also seem to be given: the activists, whom the authoritarians tended to view as criminals and the nonauthoritarians thought of as intellectuals; God and the supernatural, a category which the non-authoritarians saw as somewhat criminal while the authoritarians 'domesticated' it; and the two categories of upholders of norms and upholders of order, from whom the nonauthoritarians prefer to distance themselves more.

THE CONSTRUCTION OF IN-GROUP/OUT-GROUP DIMENSIONS

The responses to the semantic differentials were analyzed. We calculated an average score per semantic differential for the groups belonging to a cluster. Comparison of the scores per cluster of authoritarian and nonauthoritarian adolescents indicated that the differences between the two groups were only significant for the groups which had already been signalled as controversial in the preceding sections. These differences did not appear in the attribution of power or strength (although authoritarians perceived themselves as more powerful than nonauthoritarians), but rather in the attribution of 'morality' and 'normality'. They matched our expectations: authoritarians had a more positive attitude toward the supernatural and the upholders of order and a more negative one toward activists, while they viewed minorities as more deviant than did the nonauthoritarians. It is striking that the nonauthoritarians attributed themselves greater moral superiority than the authoritarians.

These findings were then combined with the results of the ALSCAL procedure through linear multiple regression analysis (in such a way that the multiple correlation provided an estimate of the extent to which a certain attribute was connected with the dimensions in two-dimensional space (see Kruskal and Wish, 1978; Rosenberg et al.,1968). Once again, this procedure was followed twice: for authoritarians and nonauthoritarians. The results of this analysis can be seen in Figures 13.3 and 13.4. Only the significant correlations are indicated (see Table 13.6).

Figure 13.3 Moral superiority of authoritarians (n = 18)

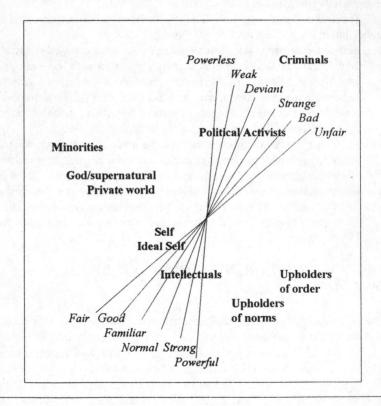

These results confirmed the hypothetical major opposition between criminals and the 'ideal self' of the adolescents under investigation: both authoritarians and nonauthoritarians saw criminals as a metaphor for what was bad and deviant, in contrast to what was good and normal in the form of the person that the adolescents would like to be (their 'ideal self'), and in contrast to the adolescents themselves, their private sphere, and intellectuals. If we distinguish between what was perceived on average as good, on the one hand, and what was perceived on average as not good or as bad, on the other, then the construction of a moral authority as well as the position of the 'out-group' emerges in a recognizable form in the perception of the social field.

Figure 13.4 Moral superiority of nonauthoritarians (n = 17)

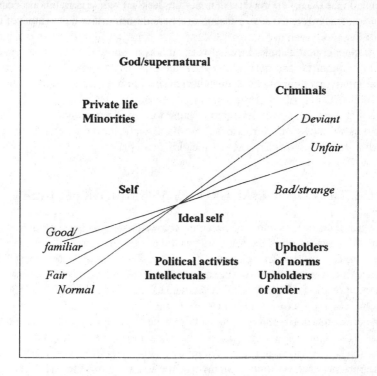

Table 13.6 Multiple correlations between moral superiority and ALSCAL dimensions for authoritarians and nonauthoritarians

	Authoritarians	Nonauthoritarians
Attributes	R^2	R^2
Powerful - powerless	.67**	.26
Strong - weak	.78**	.46
Bad - good	.89***	.75**
Fair - unfair	.81**	.71**
Deviant - normal	.77**	.69*
Strange - familiar	.68*	.68*

Levels of significance: * = p<.05, ** = p<.01, *** = p<.001.

Predictably, there were also some differences between authoritarians and nonauthoritarians in their choice of certain groups: they both shared an aversion to criminals (including racists), but they differed in the construction of resemblances between this universal out-group and other social categories.

Authoritarians classified the supernatural and the upholders of norms and order as being on the side of the good (with minorities less so), while nonauthoritarians appeared to classify activists in particular (as well as minorities) as being on the side of the good.

Another important difference between authoritarians and nonauthoritarians was that authoritarians perceived moral authority as 'powerful', while non-authoritarians saw it differently. Nonauthoritarians did not invert the authoritarians' construction of an in-group/out-group opposition (for example, by evaluating lack of power as morally superior). For nonauthoritarians, the opposites of 'power-powerlessness', as such, were not connected with the construction of the two-dimensional social field at all.

PERCEPTION OF SOCIAL GROUPS AS MALE OR FEMALE

The attribution of masculine or feminine characteristics to the various social groups was dealt with in the same way as the attribution of moral superiority. Here, too, the multiple correlation with the two dimensions in the ALSCAL analysis proved high enough to utilize the attribution of masculinity or femininity as an interpretation of the two-dimensional space. (See Figures 13.5 and 13.6.)

Once again, there were both close resemblances and a number of differences between authoritarians and nonauthoritarians. Masculinity and femininity appeared as minimally two-dimensional concepts, thus contradicting the simple opposition between masculinity and femininity. The two concepts of masculinity and femininity each occupied roughly half the social field (in the adolescents' perceptions). But within that area, there were at least two opposites: the opposition between masculinity and femininity and the opposition between good and bad, which were articulated in a specific way. In general, there was both a good and a bad version of masculinity and femininity: affectionate, tender femininity (good) versus tough, aggressive masculinity (bad); and mysterious or intuitive femininity as a metaphor for the unpredictable and deviant (bad) versus logical, considered masculinity (good). The opposition between 'emotional' and 'rational' covered the more neutral variant of the gender difference (see Table 13.7).

Table 13.7 Multiple correlations between masculinity-femininity for authoritarians and nonauthoritarians

	Authoritarians R^2	Nonauthoritarians R^2
Emotional - rational	.70 **	.77 **
Intuitive - considered	.78 **	.44
Mysterious - logical	.45	.56 *
Affectionate - tough	.87 ***	.75 **
Tender - aggressive	.92 ***	.67 *

Levels of significance: * = $p<.05$, ** = $p<.01$, *** = $p<.001$

Figure 13.5 Masculinity-femininity by authoritarians (n = 18)

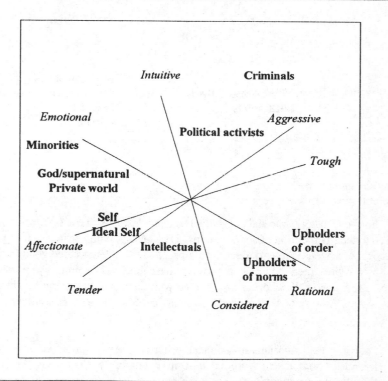

Figure 13.6 Masculinity-femininity by nonauthoritarians (n = 17)

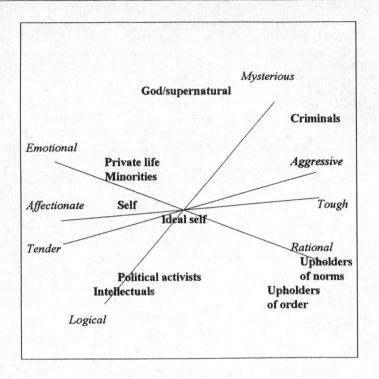

For both authoritarian and nonauthoritarian adolescents, these opposites are linked to their perception of social groups. The corresponding structure in both groups' perceptions is remarkable: the major axis which demarcated good from bad also represented the division between masculine and feminine. However, authoritarians and nonauthoritarians differed with respect to the extent to which these opposites were considered to be applicable to the characteristics of social groups.

1. For both authoritarians and nonauthoritarians, private life (parents and friends of both sexes) symbolized positive femininity. Minorities did too, though more explicitly so far as the nonauthoritarians were concerned. Intellectuals stood for positive masculinity for both groups. Criminals were the symbol of the worst aspects of both masculinity and femininity: aggressive, tough, mysterious, and intuitive.

2. On average, nonauthoritarians held a more positive view of the feminine variant in the opposition between emotionality and rationality, while authoritarians rated the masculine variant (rationality) more highly. The

evaluation of rational masculinity which the upholders of norms and order symbolized was more negative on the part of nonauthoritarians than on the part of authoritarians, while nonauthoritarians considered the feminine pole more applicable to themselves and to their private sphere. On the whole, it seems that the nonauthoritarians saw themselves as more feminine (in its positive facets) - and wanted to be more feminine (see the 'ideal self' scores) than did authoritarians.

3.   God is feminine, or at least endowed with feminine characteristics. This was true of both authoritarians' and nonauthoritarians' perceptions. The only difference was that the nonauthoritarians saw God as a variant of negative femininity, while authoritarians saw God in terms of positive femininity.

These findings seem to indicate that the opposition between good and bad which is at stake in the construction of in-groups and out-groups was associated at both poles with femininity and masculinity in the eyes of both authoritarians and nonauthoritarians. Moral authority (the positive pole) had both a masculine and a feminine representative. Nonauthoritarians seem to place more emphasis on the feminine variant and to reject groups that are associated with masculinity to a greater extent than did authoritarians. Nonauthoritarians were more 'feminine' than authoritarians. This might explain the systematic gender differences found in authoritarianism research on youngsters in the Netherlands. The nonauthoritarian social representation of sociocultural groups appears to be rooted in a more positive attitude toward femininity, as such, and that is probably why it appeals more to girls and women.

THE CHOSEN

As a last test of the validation of our results, we entered the realm of imagination. At the end of the interview, we asked the interviewees to envisage an imaginary island, where existing social problems would have been solved according to their favorite solutions. We then asked which groups they would take with them to this island to organize a better way of living and which groups they would definitely leave behind.

Creating the imaginary island should reveal how the interviewees represented an adequate way of coping with social problems for themselves. However, it could also have provided insight into a number of more psychodynamic aspects of the image which the interviewees had of themselves. The island acted not only as a metaphor of the ideal society, but it could also have been read as a metaphor for the social aspects of their image of themselves. The interviewees identified with the island and its population; the island was a portrait of the person they would have liked to be. This also proved to be the case for both authoritarians and nonauthoritarians. This can be seen in the selection of the island population, the construction of the out-group, and the characteristics of the island as a utopian authority (see Table 13.8).

Table 13.8 Authoritarianism and size of the imaginary island out-group/in-group

	In-group size*	Out-group size**
Authoritarians	15.17	5.78
Nonauthoritarians	16.29	7.76
	$F(1,33) = .47$, n.s.	$F(1,33) = 2.90$, p<.1

Notes: * In-group = number of social groups taken to the island.
** Out-group = number of social groups definitely left behind

The Selection of the Island Population

The island population was composed of the morally superior and familiar groups. This emerged clearly from our processing the 'inclusion score' in the two-dimensional picture of social groups presented earlier. The 'inclusion score' was determined by the response to these questions in the interview:

♦ Which groups would you definitely include on the island? (score: 1)
♦ Which groups would you definitely exclude? (score: 3)
♦ Which groups are more neutral? (score: 2)

Each group was thus given a rating. These scores were averaged for the groups belonging to one of the clusters incorporated in the portrait. Each cluster was thus assigned an average 'inclusion score'. This score was processed with the results of the ALSCAL procedure in the manner described previously (that is, multiple regression). The multiple correlations between the dimension 'taken to the island - left behind' and the two ALSCAL dimensions for authoritarians and nonauthoritarians was .95 for the authoritarians (p<.001) and .80 for the nonauthoritarians (p<.01).

The inclusion or exclusion of groups introduced a distinction between the different clusters in the same way as did the perception of these groups as morally superior. This was illustrated most clearly from the examples of the island populations for the stable authoritarian and stable nonauthoritarian groups (see Figures 13.7 and 13.8). Because our group of interviewees also took part in the longitudinal study, we were able to differentiate between stable and nonstable authoritarians. Stable authoritarians had two high scores on the authoritarianism scale (with two years between the two times of measurement) while nonstable authoritarians had a high score on the second measurement (the selection-criterion), but not on the first. The private sphere (minorities and intellectuals) are above suspicion; they were included by virtually all the adolescents. The stable nonauthoritarians added the activists to this category, while the stable authoritarians added three groups to their island population in place of the activists: the upholders of norms, the upholders of order, and God/the supernatural.

Figure 13.7 The island population of stable authoritarians

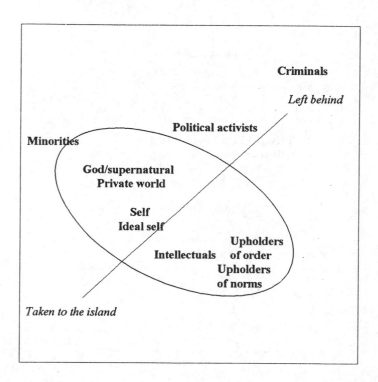

Moral Superiority of the Island Population

The moral superiority of the island population was confirmed using the arguments regarding the inclusion of groups. The included groups were considered necessary for the development of the island society; the interviewees regarded them as reliable enough to have assumed that they would have reflected the ideals to which the interviewees were attached. The groups that were excluded are described as troublesome, redundant, or bad. In Figures 13.7 and 13.8, the ALSCAL configuration and the position of the axis 'taken to the island - left behind' were based on data for all authoritarians (n=18) and all non-authoritarians (n=17). In these figures, the island populations of stable authoritarians and stable nonauthoritarians were encircled for illustrative purposes. The criterion for inclusion in the island population was an 'inclusion score' (see previous description of this measure) of ≤ 1.25.

Figure 13.8 The island population of stable nonauthoritarians

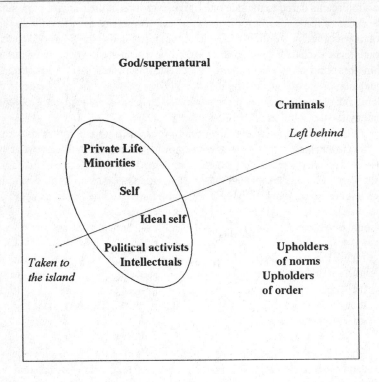

In this respect, the authoritarians and nonauthoritarians were in agreement. Both authoritarians and nonauthoritarians excluded certain groups from their ideal society. Differences were confined to the controversial groups (upholders of order, activists, and God/the supernatural). The size of the out-group (operationalized using the number of groups which interviewees excluded) appeared to be even larger among nonauthoritarians than among authoritarians. Nonauthoritarians excluded a larger number of groups from their utopia than did authoritarians.

The Construction of the Out-Group

All the adolescents excluded criminals. They were the symbol of the 'universal out-group' and were, by definition, viewed with suspicion. Not a single one of the adolescents dared to include one of these groups in their island population. The cause of the kinds of problems (rape, crime, racism) associated with these groups was, hereby, implicitly located in the individuals who belonged to these groups since excluding these groups looked like a strategy to keep the island free from this kind of social problem. It can be interpreted as a mild variant of liquidation of the out-group: the location of responsibility for the occurrence of social problems in certain groups, whose absence was seen as a potential strategy for the solution of these problems.

At the end of the interviews, a mild variant of this liquidation was also found in the erasure of the out-group by making it adapt completely to what was familiar. The interviewees were directly confronted with the excluded categories in the form of a boat story: what would the island residents do if those who had been left behind were to board a boat and come to live on the island as well? The accounts they gave of this confrontation can be read as a metaphor of the struggle between 'self' and 'other', between in-group and out-group:

> I think that it would turn into a fight. Of course, that's not what is supposed to happen, but if they . . . The island people don't want the others to join them. It's a different situation. They aren't island people. They're different; they don't observe the rules of the island (response from a nonauthoritarian girl).

The basis of all the accounts was the assumption of the moral superiority of the island population. There was no difference between authoritarians and non-authoritarians in this respect. None of the interviewees simply allowed the excluded groups onto the island. They argued that the presence of these groups would have created serious problems. Both authoritarians and nonauthoritarians agreed on the conditions under which the boat group might eventually be admitted to the island: they could have come if they adapted to the rules of the island, agreed to the principles of island life, and lived a life based on the same ideals as the island population. Some interviewees suggested a trial period, wherein the boat group had to prove their ability to abide by these conditions. In short, they would allow admission only if every difference between the in-group and out-group disappeared in favor of the in-group.

Utopia and Totalitarianism

This psychological identification of the interviewee with 'my island people' (the island as the operationalization of a social identity) appeared to be a general phenomenon. So did the construction of an out-group in the practically classical sense of the word: the group which is excluded because it is perceived as morally inferior. Of course, this was partly due to the fact that the method we used more or less required the adolescents to have excluded certain groups. However, during the preliminary sessions, the adolescents sometimes refused to do so. Their argument was that it was not right to exclude groups since all groups had the right to share in their island society. It is thus possible to reject this procedure, even though the method tends to favor the exclusion of groups rather than otherwise. The inventor of the island, the author of the island story, had given in to the temptation to assume a position of omnipotence.

CONCLUSIONS AND DISCUSSION

This chapter showed that (contrary to the major assumptions in *The Authoritarian Personality*) categorizing social groups and constructing an in-group/out-group dimension were not the exclusive characteristics of authoritarians. Authoritarian and nonauthoritarian adolescents classified social groups in more comprehensive categories in more or less the same way. Both authoritarians and nonauthoritarians arranged the clusters that they constructed in a two-dimensional space. In this space, the good-bad axis represented the dominant opposites. Authoritarians associated this axis with the attribution of power and strength, while nonauthoritarians did not. The major difference between authoritarians and nonauthoritarians was related to the position of specific controversial groups that were regarded in a more positive light by the authoritarians (upholders of norms and order, God/the supernatural) than by the nonauthoritarians, while for others (activists), the reverse was true.

Thus, both authoritarians and nonauthoritarians differentiated between 'in-groups' (which were perceived as familiar and morally superior) on the one hand and contrasting, morally inferior 'out-groups' on the other, although in doing so, their choice of groups was not exactly the same. They both differentiated between a masculine and a feminine variant of moral superiority. Authoritarians evidenced a slightly more positive attitude to the masculine variant, while nonauthoritarians displayed a greater identification with the feminine variant.

Our results are in line with the original theory of the authoritarian personality, insofar as the in-group of the authoritarians displayed the characteristics that fitted presumed authoritarian preferences: they identified with the powerful and with the more conventional groups, while they displayed a preoccupation with power and toughness in their masculinity. But our conclusions diverged in showing that nonauthoritarians construct in-groups and out-groups as well. As a result of this, the underlying psychodynamic mechanisms of identification, exclusion, and projection may just as well be associated with the target of projection of the more feminine and activist 'in-group' of the nonauthoritarians.

Our results furthermore pointed at a gradual, much more than a polar, difference between authoritarians and nonauthoritarians. The opposition between the 'good' and 'bad' groups in society in their social perception was quite comparable. The construction of in-group favoritism in private life, mentioned previously in our introduction, is a very good example of this, just as is the construction of the 'universal' out-group (including racists!). This 'natural' in-group favoritism is extended into the social domain, where it includes elite groups (like the intellectuals) as if they were noncontroversial as well. Thus, although in *The Authoritarian Personality* and in subsequent research, authoritarians were treated as the opposites of nonauthoritarians (both in their opinions and in their psychological make-up), they are better seen as two different variations of the same psychological and cultural patterns of in-group favoritism.

REFERENCES

Adorno, T., E. Frenkel-Brunswik, D. Levinson, and R. Sanford (1950). *The Authoritarian Personality*. New York, NY: Norton & Company, Inc.

Eisinga, R. and P. Scheepers (1989). *Etnocentrisme in Nederland (Ethnocentrism in the Netherlands)*. Nijmegen, the Netherlands: ITS.

Komter, A. (1977). *Geestelijke gezondheid, verschillende maatstaven voor vrouwen en mannen (Mental Health, Different Criteria for Women and Men)*. Amsterdam, the Netherlands: Masters' thesis, Universiteit van Amsterdam.

Kruskal, J. and M. Wish (1978). *Multidimensional Scaling*. Sage University Paper Series on Quantitative Applications in the Social Sciences, 07-001. Beverly Hills, CA and London, UK: Sage Publications. 4th printing.

Markus, H., J. Smith, and R. Moreland (1985). 'Role of the Self-Concept in the Perception of Others', pp. 1494-512 in *Journal of Personality and Social Psychology*, Vol. 46, No. 6.

Rabbie, J. and M. Horwitz (1969). 'The Arousal of In-Group-Out-Group Bias by a Chance Win or Loss', pp. 223-8 in *Journal of Personality and Social Psychology*, Vol. 69.

Rabbie, J., J. Schot, and L. Visser (1989). 'Social Identity Theory: a Conceptual and Empirical Critique from the Perspective of a Behavioral Interaction Model', pp. 171-202 in *European Journal of Social Psychology*, Vol. 19.

Rosenberg, S., C. Nelson, and P. Vivekananthan (1968). 'Multidimensional Approach to the Structure of Personality Impressions', pp. 283-94 in *Journal of Personality and Social Psychology*, Vol. 9, No. 4.

Tajfel, H. (1981). *Human Groups and Social Categories*. Cambridge, UK: Cambridge University Press.

Tajfel, H. (ed.) (1982). *Social Identity and Intergroup Relations.* Cambridge, UK: Cambridge University Press.

Turner, J. (1982). 'Towards a Cognitive Redefinition of the Social Group', pp. 15-40 in H. Tajfel (ed.) *Social Identity and Intergroup Relations.* Cambridge, UK: Cambridge University Press.

Turner, J., M. Hogg, P. Oakes, S. Reicher, and M. Wetherell (1987). *Rediscovering the Social Group: Self-Categorization Theory.* Oxford, UK: Basil Blackwell.

14 Recent Changes in Polish Youth's Social and Political Consciousness

Barbara Fratczak-Rudnicka

ABSTRACT

This chapter reviews recent changes in Polish youth's attitudes and life orientation. Such changes reveal an increase in educational aspirations, an increase in the estimated value of education and work, a feeling of being more in control of one's life, and a less pessimistic and fearful outlook on the future. These are all symptoms of society's 'healing' process and of positive adaptation to the new market economy and current political reality. However, not the whole young generation evidences these positive changes. Most important in this respect seems to be the economic, cultural, and social 'capital' transmitted through one's family background.

INTRODUCTION

Since 1989, Poland and some other countries in Central and Eastern Europe have implemented major political and economic changes. As a result of these changes, a new economic and political system has emerged. With the introduction of a democratic political system and a market economy came new processes and new structures which did not exist under state socialism, authoritarian society, and a communist economy. Following on these structural changes, democracy and the market economy bring new values and social norms, different from those existing previously. This new economic and political system (in order to function according to its assumptions) requires new patterns of human behavior and different competencies among its individual members.

It has been assumed that decades of living under authoritarian rule and the sociopolitical and economic system of real socialism have led not only to an evolution of a certain kind of political culture, but also to the development of a kind of modal 'socialist' personality, described by the term 'Homo Sovieticus'. This well-known notion infers an attitude of patience and deference to authority, a fear of individual initiative, a feeling of being caught up in a movement which one does not control, and a perception of the outside world as being hostile and threatening. Actually, 'Homo Sovieticus' in its complete or 'ideal' form never existed anywhere. However, many years of communist rule have contributed to a wide acceptance of many beliefs, values, and behavioral patterns which are dysfunctional in a democratic and free market system.

After 1989, it was often maintained that mainly the young generation would be able to understand this new reality and to behave in a rational way since the past least affected them. Many politicians and intellectuals say democracy and a free market economy provide great chances and possibilities especially for youth. In the long run, youth is supposed to be both a major actor and beneficiary of these changes. So several critical questions arise: How do the young people, themselves, perceive these changes? What roles do they want to play in this new reality? Do they perceive these changes as a new chance for themselves, as a challenge, and/or as a threat? How are they prepared to function in this new reality? Will they, in their opinion, be winners or losers after these changes? The answers to these questions are not unequivocal.

The Polish youth population, consisting of people aged 15-25, includes more than 6 million people (more than one-sixth of the total Polish population). This group is internally differentiated according to several features and social characteristics, such as access to education, demographics, socioeconomic factors, and cultural variations. For example, among young people aged 15-18, as many as 80 per cent attend regular schools; however, among young people aged 19-24, only about 20 per cent attend regular schools or other institutions of higher education. Differences in access to an education lead not only to differentiation in terms of knowledge and perceptions about (and emotional evaluations of) the socioeconomic and political order, but also to a differentiation and variations in job market success and opportunities to prosper in life.

Around 40 per cent of young people live in towns. A higher percentage of those who discontinue their education after primary school is found among rural youth. Unemployment (today, approximately 15 per cent of the total labor force) is much more likely for those leaving the school system earlier than it is for those completing secondary or higher education. The previously mentioned group of young people is also differentiated according to the political socialization processes it has been/is undergoing. For example, the two 'border' age groups (the 15- and the 25-year-olds) have gone through historically different socialization processes.

Present-day 15-year-olds were about ten when the system's transition started (in 1989) and were just born in the critical years of 1980-81 (that is, when Solidarity emerged and martial law was introduced). The group that is now 25 years old was about 20 in 1989 and about 11-12 in 1980-81. Thus, they were old enough to remember the powerful political events which occurred then. This also means that (in the case of the oldest age groups) an extensive part of their previous political socialization took place under the 'old system'. At this time, it was in its decadent phase, when the processes which led to a final change in the system were operating at full speed. This also means that an important part of the discussed groups' socialization took part during the initial phase of a new system. Although this new system is being built in an experimental and evolutionary way, much confusion (along with severe political, social, and economic problems) is present during its formative period.

BAD NEWS FIRST APPEARED IN MID-1990

Since mid-1990, public opinion polls in Poland began to register a clear and steady change in the public's mood. Previously overwhelmingly positive feelings toward the recent reforms and optimism about the future were transformed into a dominant conviction that the situation in the country was heading 'in the wrong direction'. Polls documented common complaints about falling living standards, deteriorating social services, and increasing unemployment. All public institutions (including those connected with Solidarity and even the Catholic Church) started to lose their popularity and authority. A massive withdrawal from politics occurred when fewer people participated in elections and other political activities.

In 1992-93, the public mood was so depressed that it gave rise to truly alarmist comments and prognoses. Popular distrust, political apathy, and social insecurity were explained as results of unfulfilled and unrealistic expectations and hopes which the old system's breakdown had stimulated. It was also mentioned that most people lacked the political 'skills' necessary to cope with this new reality. This meant decreasing real income (which dropped 25 per cent in 1990-91), increasing unemployment (totally unknown under the 'old' system), and continuing political turmoil. Similar phenomena were sooner or later observed in all postcommunist countries in Central and Eastern Europe.

The attitudes of Polish young people were subject to changes similar to the rest of the society. At the beginning of the transformation, they were the most supportive group; after three or four years, in some respects, they showed far less support and were the most pessimistic about their country's future. Reports from representative studies of Polish youth conducted in 1991 and 1992 gave a very dramatic picture of young people's state of mind. The two most extensive reports which summed up a vast body of data gathered in studies on youth's 'social and political consciousness' were a 'Report on Polish Youth' (Interpress, 1992) and 'Being Young' (COBOS, 1993). Both are good examples of a larger body of Polish youth research (see Fratczak-Rudnicka, 1994, pp. 117-25). One of the conclusions from the 1992 report was that 'young people are often discouraged and convinced that their chances for success and a career are negligible; they are reluctant to participate in political activity and reject public authorities and personalities. Their typical response to a new reality reveals hedonism, materialism, pragmatism, and concentration on one's own problems' (Interpress, 1992).

In a second report (COBOS, 1993), the authors concluded that a growth of youthful defensive, passive, and escapist reactions and attitudes can be seen.

They attribute it to disappointment with their new freedom which carries with it the threat of unemployment, poverty, lack of social security, and few chances for a 'normal' life. This disappointment was thought to be especially strong among youth since they lacked their parents' realism and experience. Sociologists summarized the general situation of Polish society as 'increasingly anomic', with escapist and ritualistic reactions being much more common than any innovative or responsive ones.

FINALLY, SOME GOOD NEWS TODAY

Although among young people, the pessimists far outnumber the optimists (for example, evaluating the current general 'situation' in Poland in COBOS, BS/119/105/94, 1994) and while in 1994 youth still were much less optimistic concerning their future than in 1990 (COBOS, 3/BS/110/96/94, 1994), some positive changes can definitely be seen today. Compared with their responses in 1992, there is a modest increase in optimism in evaluating their life opportunities (compared to life chances for their parents). Also, a decreasing number of young people declare they would like to emigrate from Poland ('forever'). That is, there was a drop in this response from 19 per cent in 1991 to 10 per cent in 1994 (COBOS, BS/105/92/94, 1994).

Since 1990, there has been a steady increase in youth's educational aspirations. For example, in 1990, 25 per cent of the youth surveyed aspired to a higher education; in 1992, it was 32 per cent; and in 1994, it rose to 36 per cent of similar groups surveyed. Simultaneously, the number of those who said they would be content with only two years of occupational training dropped from 30 per cent in 1990 to 16 per cent in 1994. These views demonstrated the new conviction that education in contemporary Poland 'pays off' and that it is thus worth the effort to pursue further study (COBOS, BS/110/96/94, 1994).

Another big change in young people's attitudes can be reported. This concerns those motives perceived as being crucial when deciding to enroll in a university. Today, university education is perceived more often as a means to secure an interesting job and/or a higher income. Much less often today than was true in 1992, 'escapist' motives are mentioned (such as 'the desire to prolong one's youth' and/or 'a choice for those who don't know what to do with themselves') (COBOS, BS/110/96/94, 1994). Therefore, we see that not only is an increasing number of young people aspiring for better schooling, but education is now clearly perceived as a means for upward social and economic mobility (COBOS, BS/110/96/94, 1994). Also, compared with 1992, young people's career expectations are increasingly connected with the growing private economic sector. There is also a proportionate increase in the number of young people who expect to start a business of their own.

Fear of unemployment among young people who finish school is smaller today than it was two years ago (in 1992, 51 per cent feared unemployment; in 1994, only 31 per cent did so). These results occurred although the overall unemployment rate had risen to almost 15 per cent in 1994 for the total population (COBOS, BS/105/92/94, 1994). Simultaneously, there is less 'fatalism' (compared to the situation in 1992) in identifying factors which facilitate getting a good job (or any job at all) in 1994 compared to 1992. For example, there was an increase of factors connected with qualifications, talents, and intelligence, along with a decrease in factors such as 'luck' or 'chance' (COBOS, BS/105/92/94, 1994). There was also a change in the hierarchy of life's most important goals and aspirations. That is, in 1992, 'a satisfactory family life' held first place, while in 1994, number one was 'a good, interesting job' (COBOS, BS/105/92/94, 1994). Consequently, in just two years, these two values reversed themselves.

Today, the economic (material) expectations of young people for their future are much more pessimistic than two years ago; yet, it can also be said that they are simultaneously more realistic (if the measure we use is the number of people expecting that they will own a house, car, and so on within 10-15 years). At the same time, these 'material values' (compared to the social) are to some extent less important than they were two years ago (COBOS, BS/119/105/94, 1994). Also, a clear majority (more than 66 per cent) believes that success in life depends on oneself (that is, they have a feeling of being in control of their lives) (COBOS, BS/119/105/94, 1994). Today, compared with adults, Polish youth (15-29 years old) are relatively more positive in evaluating the influence of events taking place since 1989 in both the general economic and their own personal situations (in both cases, around 50 per cent) ('Przeglad', DEMOS-KOP, no. 5 [21], 1994). However, as far as politics is concerned, young people are even more uninterested than they were a few years ago. They are also not very well informed politically ('Przeglad', DEMOSKOP, no. 2 [18], 1994). At the same time, they often report that they do not see any political party which can represent their interests (only some 20 per cent see their interests so represented) ('Przeglad', DEMOSKOP, no. 5 [21], 1994). Also, only 6 per cent of youth have a positive opinion about current Polish politicians in general ('Polityka', no. 34, 1994, quoting COBOS).

From a sociological point of view, most of the previously mentioned trends can be interpreted as symptoms of recovery or a positive adaptation to the new market economy and political reality. Material expectations for young people are more realistic. Although many of them are still quite uncertain about their futures, they are also becoming more independent, feel more in control of their own lives, are less fearful about the outside world and the future, and are more willing to accept responsibility for their own life course.

In a 1992 study I conducted among 14-year-old Polish youth, there were already signs of positive changes by the end of that year. In comparison to 14-

year-olds surveyed in 1981 and 1986, those in the 1992 study believed they were more in control of their own futures and evaluated nonconformism more positively. Also, in comparison to the 1981 and 1986 youth, the 14-year-olds in 1992 had a less hostile perception of the 'outer world' (other people and institutions). This implies that changes first began in the younger age group, which is relatively more receptive to new trends and least affected by the 'former system's' political education practices (Fratczak-Rudnicka, 1994).

NOT ALL IS 'BRIGHT' AND OPTIMISTIC: MORE BAD NEWS RESURFACES

Socioeconomic class is still important in Poland. For example, public opinion data show that educational aspirations are highest among children of well-educated, wealthy parents. Many young people who espouse capitalism have parents who already have a private business or plan to start their own enterprises. Children of wealthy, well-educated, or highly qualified parents are most responsive to these ideas of a market economy and liberal democracy. Those coming from this same kind of family feel most often that their family gives them emotional support and a sense of security. But the least independent, most helpless, most threatened, most likely to be unemployed, most fearful for their own future and that of 'their generation', and least likely to receive 'emotional support from their families' are children of parents with low education, low incomes, the unemployed, and those living in small towns or rural areas.

So, despite the 'good news' reported previously, the 'bad news' is that, unfortunately, not every Pole is as yet as well-educated, wealthy, young, and beautiful as we (and they) would like them(selves) to be.

FINAL AND SUMMARY COMMENTS

An important influence on Polish youth's behavior in their new reality seems to be the 'capital' carried over from one's family background. We can speak about three kinds of such capital: socioeconomic, political, and cultural.

The data show that the social situations and attitudes of various groups of young people depend strongly on the social and economic situation (SES) of their parents. This particularly means how well they are doing in the new reality, how 'equipped' they were when they entered it, as well as how this 'equipment' was adequate to meet a new reality. This situation strongly influences all young people's reactions to democracy and a free market economy, in addition to their attitudes about the future (personal and societal).

Sociological studies show that all of the major Polish social groups have become more heterogeneous internally (in comparison to what they used to be under the 'old system'). Also, youth studies from the 1970s and 1980s gave a fairly homogeneous picture of the then 'young generation'. Another common result from those times was that any differences seen were only weakly connected with young people's parents' SES.

Today, connections between young people's opinions and attitudes and their parents' education and material wealth (SES) are becoming much clearer. A sharp division now runs through the total group of all Polish youth (as well as probably through the whole society). This is a division between those who are well 'equipped' to cope with their new reality (that is, children of well-educated parents who are being educated themselves and offspring of those few who gained in the past financially, while others lost), those with more cultural and social competence, and those 'deprived' in these respects (that is, children of less wealthy, poorly educated, occupationally unqualified parents, who are unfamiliar with a new reality which threatens them).

It seems that we cannot make any generalization about today's young generation as a whole. One aspect of this has to do with their feeling of being a 'generation of losers' as well as a degree of their fear for the future of the next generation. However, still another and quite important part of this situation has to do with how the 'winners' fare since they may well be the key representatives of a new society now being built and yet to appear.

REFERENCES

COBOS (1993). 'Being Young.' Warsaw, Poland: Center for Public Opinion Studies (COBOS).

COBOS (1994). 'Youth '94.' Warsaw, Poland: Center for Public Opinion Studies (COBOS).

COBOS bulletins (various dates). Warsaw, Poland: Center for Public Opinion Studies (COBOS). These bulletins (which usually contain data tables and short comments) are designated by code numbers (for example, BS/119/105/94).

Fratczak-Rudnicka, B. (1994). 'Changes in the Political Attitudes of Warsaw's Adolescents 1981-1986-1992', pp. 117-25 in R. Holly (ed.) *Political Consciousness and Civic Education during the Transformation of the System*. Warsaw, Poland: Institute of Political Studies, Polish Academy of Sciences.

Interpress (1992). 'Report on Polish Youth.' Warsaw, Poland: Interpress.

'Przeglad' (DEMOSKOP), No. 2 (18) and No. 5 (21) (1994). Warsaw, Poland: Market and Social Research.

Part IV

Democratization Trends and European Integration

15 How Can the European Union be Democratized?

Rüdiger Meyenberg

ABSTRACT

Above all, democracy means that the authority of the state comes from the people and that it is executed on their behalf. State organs, in turn, have to answer to the people for their actions. Parliamentary representatives only serve as intermediaries and give assistance. They mediate between the population's various opinions and interests to provide the necessary unity in state actions. Simultaneously, they ensure that political decision-making processes remain transparent (without which, public opinion and interest articulation would have no *raison d'être*). But parliaments cannot manage this task on their own; they depend on the mediatory services of public institutions (such as political parties, interest groups, citizen's initiatives, and the mass media). These institutions are lacking in the EU context so that the popular democratic will in EU countries has no way to be represented and may actually be distorted by other political officials, technocrats, and bureaucrats.

WHY DO GERMANS FEAR THE EUROPEAN UNION?

Within Germany, the European integration process has been discredited more now than at any time since its beginning, just after World War II. The idea of a Europe designed by politicians and technocrats gives many German citizens nightmares. Today, the European Union (EU) seems to be producing more problems than solutions. Citizens fear for their bank savings, security, and very ways of life. Naturally, anyone forced to leave safe ground wants to know where their journey will likely end. Yet, political information on this subject is still only vague, indefinite, and risky.

Clear EU objectives are lacking. There is little public discussion about the development of European integration. Although Germans support a 'basic idea of Europe', hardly anyone can define this basic idea accurately. Both Germans and Italians (who strived for national unity in the 19th century), used France and England as models for state building. But where can we find a model for a unified Europe? Nobody I have spoken with has satisfactorily answered this question. The example of the United States of America will not do because a historically based system of European countries cannot be compared to a 'melting pot' of former colonies on a distant shore. Neither the phrases 'Europe

341

of mother-countries' nor 'United Nations of Europe' have been precisely defined to date. There is not even a basic agreement on the planned borders of a unified Europe. Is it (a Europe of 19 or 24 nations) to be organized according to the model of the European Community, with a population of 500 million citizens to be governed from Brussels? Such questions cannot be answered by political scholars, but only by our politicians, themselves. We lack an informed and serious public discussion on this topic. For example, any 'Europe of its citizens' may degenerate into a 'Europe of bureaucrats'.

It seems to have been a simple post-1989 illusion that national states were outmoded, just as it was illusory to pursue a supranational policy (on limited grounds, but with worldwide effects) while forgetting that most people still need to live and deal with their local identities, loyalties, and past. Meanwhile, bureaucrats in Brussels may work on abstruse regulations about the degree of curvature of cucumbers from different parts of the European Community and the statistical requirements for all EC apples. Simultaneously, in both Normandy and the Rhineland, as well as among Flemish and Walloon separatists, these people conjointly seek to change their constitutions, thereby virtually developing their own federal states. For the foreseeable future, we will probably see other evidence of this return to old and divided loyalties and the renaissance of various independence and separation movements. However, regrettably, we will be forced to live with these developments.

The previously described situation engendered strain and fear among Germans. It is not only since the failed (and then successful, with reservations) referendum of the Danes and the narrow consent of the French to 'Maastricht' that Germans have looked skeptically at this European integration process. For example, the Allensbacher Institute opinion polls have revealed that Germans' attitudes about 'Europe' were already reserved. According to Noelle-Neumann in December 1991, an extremely 'pro-European' Eurobarometer poll of the Brussels Commission asked, 'Do you await the Common European Market rather with hope than with fear?' More than half (56 per cent of old *Länder* Germans and 62 per cent of new *Länder* citizens) answered with 'hope' (Noelle-Neumann, 1992).

However, the following question taps the Germans' underlying skepticism about the EU, 'Now, the Bundesrat is considering the rejection of the Maastricht treaty. Should these resolutions be rejected or not?' Most Germans prefer rejection; 42 per cent decided for 'rejection', 25 per cent said 'no rejection', and 33 per cent remained undecided (see Table 15.1).

Consequently, there are numerous reasons which explain the Germans' underlying negative attitudes toward 'Maastricht'. Some people worry about the Deutschmark (DM) currency's stability, others fear the loss of their national identity. Still others see that then there may well be a huge 'democracy deficit' within the present European Community as well as in the proposed EU, itself.

Table 15.1 'Now, the Bundesrat is considering the rejection of the Maastricht treaty. Should these resolutions be rejected or not?' (in %)

Rejection	42
Nonrejection	25
Undecided	33

Source: Adapted from Allensbacher Archiv (16 April 1992) from *Frankfurter Allgemeine Zeitung*, No. 143, p. 11, Frankfurt am Main, FRG.

Responses to the following question illustrate these sentiments: 'Do you think it is possible to keep the future European currency as stable as the DM or do you believe not?' Nearly 70 per cent of 700 business management leaders in western and eastern Germany answered, 'I don't believe so.' There were 26 per cent positive answers. The general population responded quite similarly as the figures in Table 15.2 illustrate.

Table 15.2 'Do you think it is possible to keep the future European currency as stable as the DM or do you believe not?' (in %)

	Population	Business Leaders
It will be kept stable	18	26
I do not believe so	62	69
Undecided	20	5

Source: Adapted from Allensbacher Archiv (16 April 1992) from *Frankfurter Allgemeine Zeitung*, No. 143, p. 11, Frankfurt am Main, FRG.

It seems important for many Germans to maintain the position of 'Germany as it is' today in any future unified Europe. Consider this survey question: 'Assuming that the European countries will join together in a closer network, thus creating a unified Europe, do you believe that Germany as it is will lose its current identity?' For example, in 1992, 39 per cent of the respondents replied 'Germany will gradually lose it' (Table 15.3). As can be seen in both eastern and western Germany, an increasing number of people forecast a loss of national identity.

Currently, any strong movement designed to procure more influence for a directly and popularly elected European Parliament (which cannot determine the domestic policies of member states) cannot be expected to materialize. The following poll question relates to this concern: 'How much influence should the European Parliament have? Is it simply to advise the member states or should it determine the policies of the member states in some or even all areas?' One-third of the German respondents answered, 'Only advise.' They expressed their wish to maintain the greater part of sovereignty for their own government. Only one-tenth of the population supports the obviously least popular position to give full authority to the European Parliament (Table 15.4).

Table 15.3 'Assuming that the European countries will join together in a closer network, thus creating a unified Europe, do you believe that Germany as it is will lose its current identity?' (in %)

| | Western Germany | | | Eastern Germany | | |
	February 1990	October 1990	January 1992	February 1990	October 1990	January 1992
It will lose its identity	26	21	39	16	19	34
I do not believe it will lose its identity	60	63	50	70	67	47
Undecided	14	16	11	14	14	19

Source: Allensbacher Archiv (16 April 1992) from *Frankfurter Allgemeine Zeitung*, No. 143, p. 11, Frankfurt am Main, FRG.

Table 15.4 'How much influence should the European Parliament have? Is it simply to advise the member states or should it determine the policies of the member states in some or even all areas?' (in %)

	Germany	Western Germany	Eastern Germany
Only advise	34	34	36
Determine in some areas	42	43	40
Determine in all areas	10	10	9
Undecided	14	13	15

Source: Allensbacher Archiv (16 April 1992) from *Frankfurter Allgemeine Zeitung*, No. 143, p. 11, Frankfurt am Main, FRG.

The foregoing analysis leads us to consider some basic questions, such as: If criticism of the European Community is as severe as indicated, would it not be better to abstain from EC integration in its present form? Is it not too much of a risk to gamble the present security of a state with all its symbols (such as its own currency) for an uncertain EC future?

The growing trend toward international integration has obviously initiated processes in which basic national policies no longer have a direct impact on a broad scale. The present priorities of national policy seem to disappear in the process of discussing and creating European integration. Therefore, what is needed today is a way to allow country-based politics to play a more creative role in this restructuring process. What this nationally-based reconstruction process would look like may remain unclear until it has been given a chance for initiation, debate, and growth.

IS THERE A SHORTAGE OF DEMOCRACY IN THE EU?

With respect to the theory of a classical democratic constitutional order, the functions and powers of the European Parliament of the EC are rather insufficiently developed. Thus, the Community has often been charged with having a 'democratic deficit'. As a matter of fact, the Community's sparse popular legitimation is based almost exclusively on its support from member states. That is, both member parliaments and their governments have previously consented to the respective EC treaties. However, there are still many decisional areas in which these same national parliaments are not authorized to act competently, popularly, or legally.

Just such a situation became obvious in early 1992, when the opposition in the German Bundesrat turned against the so-called 'tax block', which included increasing the value added tax (VAT) to 15 per cent. In public, these legislators maintained that these proceedings were absolutely under their control, but this was not quite true. The German Federal Minister of Finance had consented to the 15 per cent level in the Council of Ministers in Brussels in June 1991. Yet, his consent did not mean that the 15 per cent rate was definitely accepted. This was because EC regulations had not been passed and made law at that time. What this actually meant was that the German government had made a considerable commitment, something which could not be easily reversed. Such considerations might not have been taken into account by the majority legislators then in office.

Some EC member states have long fought to increase EC parliamentary responsibilities to find a way out of such dilemmas. They seek to introduce actual democratization, which would mean parliamentarizing the Community. But do we really want to deprive the national parliaments of their sovereign powers in favor of a European Parliament whose resolutions must necessarily be compromises among the other parliamentary parties of 12 or more European countries (most of whose decisions still remain both anonymous and obscure to average citizens)? Is it not a fact that EC member countries specifically represent rather different national positions in spite of their many common interests? In the whole debate over the EU's democratization, one observation intentionally or unintentionally has been overlooked. That is, we have no common European democratic political culture or tradition which actually means there really are no comprehensive all-European political parties.

For many observers (both scholars and citizens) of this process, the most important and decisive difficulty to overcome is how not to undermine present national parliamentary processes while both maintaining these political processes and introducing it into an all-European context. Political conflicts over these contrary views were expressed both in the Bundesrat and the Federal states during discussions on the ratification of the Maastricht Treaty. Presently, the EC's 'democracy deficit' is under discussion throughout Europe. Many believe that strengthening the European Parliament would overcome this deficit. Others contend this is a misunderstanding of the real problem. This actually means parliamentary powers may be extended within the EC, but it also requires a discussion of how far the cause of European integration can be advanced without risking the underlying basic principles of democracy (that is, popular sovereignty, representative government, majority rule and minority rights, and so forth).

We need not waste more time describing this 'democracy deficit'. Actually, the EC treaty refers to the European Parliament as the primary political organ of the Community. Nevertheless, its powers and influence are actually inferior to those of other EC organs. The Council of Ministers is the most dominant political actor and decision maker within the entire Community. This Council consists of ministers from all member states. The EC Commission in Brussels (the action center) is appointed by member state governments. It controls the extensive EC administrative apparatus. European Community law is interpreted by the EC Court in Luxembourg. This court acts frequently to protect the overall EC integration course, rather than restricting other EC organs which may have overstepped their basic authority.

The EC Parliament in Strasbourg also offers us no viable alternatives. In fact, since 1979, it has been elected directly by the citizens of the member states. But it does not have the important powers of modern national parliaments. EC Parliament representatives are responsible, among others, for legislation and budgetary policies. Community members' national parliaments also cannot compensate for this lack of democracy. They grant their ruling governments (and, consequently, the regime's representatives in the EC Council) their indirect democratic authorization to act on their behalf. They can, however, not control their government's vote in the EC Council. Since Council decisions need not be unanimous and since the EC Commission shares the legislative power, national parliaments are without any real ongoing influence on EC politics. Does it not seem reasonable to overcome this democratic deficiency by upgrading the status of the European Parliament to bring the EC more in line with the prevailing model of functioning democratic constitutional states?

Strengthening the democratic role for the European Parliament seems to be a necessary next step, especially in light of the Community's development from an international monetary and financial union into an independent locus of the national public's (that is, pseudodemocratic) authority. But it would be an illusion to expect to overcome any deficiency of democracy by such a step alone. That is, parliamentarianism is not identical with democracy!

WHAT DOES DEMOCRACY MEAN IN ITS EUROPEAN CONTEXT?

Above all, democracy means that the state's authority is founded on the sovereign people and that it is executed by the state's organs on these people's behalf. These organs, in turn, have to justify their actions for, and to, the people. Parliamentary representatives are just a means to this end. They mediate between the population's various opinions and interests to formulate the necessary political unity for decision making in the state. Simultaneously, these parliamentary representatives ensure that political decision-making processes remain transparent; without this basis, public opinion expression and interest articulation would have no utility. But parliaments cannot manage this task on their own. Again, they are dependent on the mediatory services of public institutions, such as political parties, interest groups, citizen's initiative, and the mass media.

In view of these extraparliamentary conditions (which are necessarily part of a parliamentary democracy), one has to ask whether the EC would be regarded as fully 'democratized' if the European Parliament received those political competencies which are usually granted to parliaments in their respective national constitutions. Probably not. The European Parliament would still lack the sociopolitical basis (that is, political culture) on which any actual democratic efficiency ultimately depends. Sooner or later, the conversion of the European Parliament from a consulting into a decision-making authority would require the 'Europeanization' of a new party system. Even today, the European Parliament is programmatically divided into parliamentary groups, but they are not nationally-oriented. Furthermore, there are no corresponding all-European political parties. Parties are only organized at a national level and have only joined at a vague level of cooperation at an all-European level. Some new all-European alliances (for example, of greens, Christians, socialists, liberals, or conservatives) would be required to formulate all-European interest articulation and representation in future. However, a parliament with no real decision-making powers has no need for a Europe-wide party system.

Another factor is communication (especially political communication), which is bound to language and to one's experience and interpretation of the world. All of this is mediated by language. Currently, nine languages are used within the EC. If two or three of them should prevail at the political or administrative levels, this does not alter the fact that large sections of the European population are only able to inform themselves and to participate in the opinion-forming process using their native language. It is exceedingly difficult to build a common political culture with more than one or two official languages.

Two basic requirements of democratic systems (information and participation) are always conditioned by language. Thus, there will neither be a common European linguistic public nor a broad public long-term discourse at the all-European level. A 'European people' (to whom a sovereign jurisdiction could be assigned) cannot be expected to develop very soon. But the European Parliament cannot turn into a representative body of the people without a European people and a common European political discourse. This is the basic difference between European integration in the 20th century and the foundation of the German Reich in the 19th century. In Germany, there was a basis for a common language and culture. The perception of a nation developed among the people who insisted on a national state for more than half a century before its actual foundation in 1871. And it differs fundamentally from the foundation of the United States of America in the 18th century. There, the individual constituent parts had never been national states with different languages, varying nationalist traditions, and different ways of political thinking.

In Europe, however, the Maastricht Treaty is setting the course of a European common home and federal state, although there is (neither at present nor to be expected in the near future) no corresponding European people. A 'population of voters' might come into being. Yet, apart from the voting act, they would hardly have anything European in common. The populace would have to disintegrate into national subgroups to form their opinions and articulate their interests, while still being without a national locus to express their political demands. Therefore, the European deficiency of democracy is structurally conditioned. It cannot simply be overcome by superimposing any artificial institutional solutions. For the moment, the achievements of the democratic constitutional state are limited for their expression solely to the national level. If this is true, appropriate steps for a future European restructuring have to follow. If it is not possible to change the EC into a constitutional democratic state in the long run, its development should not be directed toward a federal structure. Instead, it may best remain a functional union, although certain of its authorities might be broadened. What really matters is the sectional integration of existing national states which are related with respect to their shared national convictions and interests, rather than their development into a suprastate. If the United Nations could not develop into a more democratic institution over its 50-year history, how can the EC develop a democratic EU in such a short period of time?

HOW CAN A PROPER BALANCE OF POWER BE ACHIEVED?

If we consider the necessary parliamentarization of the EC, this has to be accompanied by a more detailed separation of competencies among the Community and its member states. Presently, this is missing. Unlike a federal state, the responsibilities of the EC are not objectively (and finitely) limited. The essential goal of the EC is to allow the free movement of persons, goods, services, and capital among member states. Therefore, the EC is in the best position to basically harmonize all national regulations which hinder the achievement of this aim.

Even the principle of subsidiarity (which reduces the locus of public control to the lowest possible functional governmental level) included in the Maastricht Treaty (at Germany's request) cannot stop the imminent danger of EC standardization. This trend has to be stopped in concrete ways. Considering the possibilities for broad governmental expansion allowed in the EC treaty, this can probably only be done in a negative or prohibitive manner. In the broader sense, certain cultural areas (including broadcasting, television, and education) will especially be affected. Assuming that the principles of democracy can most broadly be expressed at the national level, then national parliaments must be better supplied with sufficient political information and power. Moreover, national parliaments need to have a stronger influence on the positions which their national governments take when determining all-European policies (for example, in the Council of Ministers). Actually, the German Federal Constitutional Court has handed down a similar decision in the recent past.

Besides Germany, other European parliaments have a different attitude about EC decisions. The United Kingdom's House of Commons protects its legal rights more stridently when scrutinizing legal decisions from Brussels and when passing on them in Parliament. In London, all legislative bills from Brussels are presented to the respective committees of the House of Commons within 48 hours. Within ten days, the government has to submit a written statement to Commons. In about 10 per cent of these cases, the respective minister has been summoned for questioning and, later, instructed how to vote in Brussels. In Denmark, such things are handled similarly. Germany especially should consider that states with a firm democratic tradition (such as the UK, Denmark, and France) express reservations about a further reduction in their parliamentary rights.

For decades, there has been a strong coalition in Germany in favor of the 'European Question'. But European democracy cannot grow in a vacuum. The more complicated the welfare state and its legislation become, the greater the need to reestablish and maintain closeness between the decision-making bodies and the voters. The European Parliament, which has important controlling functions (over the Commission and, to a limited degree, over the European Council as well), cannot create such public solidarity while substituting their judgement for the separate national democratic development of an informed public opinion. Consequently, the question whether we will be able to 'Europeanize' our national parliaments (which will possibly result in a higher democratization of all European politics) or whether we will 'denationalize' the European Parliament will be crucial for Europe to answer in the late 1990s. It is not easy to say how it will be possible to integrate national parliaments more strongly into the legislative work of the Community. When this problem was discussed in Maastricht, a committee of the regions was established. This advisory committee consists of representatives from regional and local corporate bodies. Nevertheless, one of the questions still remaining is: Was it proper to transfer certain national rights to the European Parliament as was done at Maastricht?

Pursuing German foreign policy (and a German-European policy as well) has become more difficult in the post-Maastricht world. Germany is forced to proceed more selectively and to limit initiatives to feasible goals. Proposing a democratic constitutional initiative could be a valuable German contribution to Europe. Although Germany's partners want the integration of Germany in the Union, we are not relieved of our joint responsibility to pursue an independent, convincing, and reliable all-European policy. Germany needs Europe and Europe needs Germany. But it has to be a Europe which is accepted by everybody, which is close to its citizens, and which is not overly centralist if it wants to endure and preserve our shared and fundamental democratic convictions.

REFERENCES

Bertelsmann Foundation (1990). *The Shaping of a European Constitution*. Gütersloh, FRG: Bertelsmann-Verlag.

Basic Law of the Federal Republic of Germany (1987). Bonn, FRG: Press and Information Office.

Europa wird Eins (Europe Becomes One) (1991): Braunschweig, FRG: Presse und Informationsamt der Bundesregierung, Westermann Druck.

Noelle-Neumann, E. (16 April 1992). 'Die Deutschen beginnen sich zu fürchten: Eine demokopische Bilanz nach Maastricht (The Germans Begin to Fear: Surveying the Balance after Maastricht)', p. 11 in the *Frankfurter Allgemeine Zeitung*, No. 143. Frankfurt am Main, FRG: Frankfurter Verlag.

Vertragstexte von Maastricht (Text of the Maastricht Treaty) (1992). Bonn, FRG: Europa Union Verlag.

16 Elite-Mass Linkages and the European Community
Testing Consensus Explanatory Models

Henk Dekker
Rolf Willemse

ABSTRACT

In this chapter, two questions are posed and answered: Is there a gap or a widespread consensus about the European Union in the Netherlands between the elites and the masses? How are we to explain any existing gap or areas of consensus between these two groups?

To answer the first question, we conducted a survey among Dutch members of Parliament and performed a secondary analysis with data from Eurobarometer polls of 'the mass' public. We observed a consensus between the two sets of findings on most issues and a gap in just two. To explain this resultant consensus and gap, several different models used in the political science literature were tested. Two new models were added to improve our analysis.

INTRODUCTION: ELITE-MASS LINKAGES

The existence of representative or indirect democracies implies the existence of a certain gap between citizens and their representatives. The legitimacy of these representatives (and, in the long term, of the political system, itself) is put in question if the gap between elites and mass becomes too wide. In some publications (popular and scientific) on politics in Western Europe and the US, a widening gap between citizens and politicians is reported; but in other publications, these same perceptions are contradicted. Which perception is true?

If references are to empirical data, several different indicators are used. These relate to the terms 'political', 'gap', and 'widening' differences between elites and masses. Different publications use 'political' to refer to the political system, political parties and politicians, policies, or a combination of one or more of the foregoing terms. 'Gap' indicators related only to citizens or to a comparison of citizens and politicians. Those indicators linked only to citizens are, among others: political misunderstanding; political distrust; political disinterest; political cynicism; lack or low level of political efficacy; lack or low level of party identification or attachment and membership; support for antisystem parties; political dissatisfaction; lack of political confidence; negative opinions on politicians' characteristics or qualities; or low turn-out at elections and other forms of political participation. Citizens could also be directly asked whether they perceive or experience a gap between themselves and 'politicians'. Comparisons between citizens and politicians are made with respect to different levels of political knowledge, opinions or preferences, attitudes, values, or value hierarchies. The concept of 'widening' refers to decreasing levels of political understanding among citizens and to increasing differences between citizens and politicians. Empirical conclusions on 'widening' assume the availability of longitudinal comparable data; but this is rarely the case.

In the Netherlands, the widening gap hypothesis relating to citizens' political orientations has been tested in Andeweg's research (1993), using Euro-barometer data. No clear downward trend was observed in political system satisfaction, subjective political competence, political interest (reading political news and discussing politics with others), and voter turn-out. A growth in support for extreme right-wing parties was found, but it is questionable whether this support indicates a widening gap (that is, not all extreme right-wing parties are antisystem parties, while support for these parties is based on a variety of different motivations). However, a decline in party identification or attachment was clearly observed.

We decided to test the gap hypothesis by using data about opinions and attitudes of both citizens and elites (politicians). Our survey population was restricted to center-left citizens and Members of Parliament (MPs). Moreover, we decided to test the gap hypothesis not with respect to general orientations (such as political interest in general), but only regarding a particular issue. This topic was the outcome of the Danish referendum (2 June 1992) and the French referendum (20 September 1992) on the European Union (Treaty of Maastricht). These referenda indicated that public support for European integration was not as firm as political elites had assumed. In France, a gap was revealed between social-democratic (socialist) politicians (who favored the Treaty) and their traditional supporters (who often opposed it). In the Netherlands, the issue of European integration (in general) and the Treaty on the European Union (in particular) has never been high on the public and political agenda. The Dutch parliament's ratification of the Treaty almost completely escaped public and media attention. As a result, we asked ourselves two questions: Is there a gap or widespread consensus about the European Union in the Netherlands between the mass and the elites? How could any existent gap or consensus between these two groups be explained?

RESEARCH DESIGN
Research Questions

Two questions guided this research: Do the social-democratic Members of Parliament (MPs) and voters in the Netherlands (in contrast to the situation in

France) share the same opinions and attitudes about European integration? How can any existent gap or consensus between these two groups be explained?

A consensus may be operationalized as a situation in which the majority of both groups share the same opinion (pro or con) or attitude (positive or negative) and where the difference between the two percentages is less than 20 per cent (for example 80 per cent of the MPs and 65 per cent of the voters favor a particular policy aim). If the majorities of both the MPs and the voters have the same opinion or attitude, but these majorities differ by more than 20 per cent, we classify the situation as dissention or a political difference. A gap exists if a majority of one of the two groups is in favor of a particular policy aim or has a positive attitude, while a majority of the other group is not in favor or has a negative attitude. Consensus may be explained with the help of several different models of elite-mass political linkages.

Research Methodology and Data Collection/Analysis

Our two research questions will be answered through an analysis of two data sets. These are a Eurobarometer data set ('mass') and our own parliamentary data set ('elites'). Eurobarometer data were used for an analysis of voters' opinions and attitudes. The Eurobarometer is a large-scale, cross-sectional, and cross-national survey which is conducted twice a year, under European Commission auspices. Samples from each EC member state are interviewed about many issues. Here, the Eurobarometer from spring 1992 (No. 37) was used. There were approximately 1000 Dutch respondents 15 years of age and older. From this data set, we selected the respondents who had expressed a preference for the Dutch social-democratic party (the PvdA). However, this number proved to be very small. For statistical reasons, we decided to enlarge the subsample to center-left voters. They were selected by using left-right scaling scores, running from 1 (left) to 10 (right). Those respondents who placed themselves on positions 2, 3 and 4 were characterized as 'center-left'. As a result, not only the 'real' PvdA voters were included in the analysis but, for example, also voters supporting Democrats 66 (D66) and the Green Left who placed themselves within the selected positions. It should be mentioned, however, that at the time of the data collection, Dutch polls predicted a great electoral loss for the PvdA and a great electoral victory for D66. Thus, by selecting positions 2, 3 and 4 from the left-right scale, both the 'lost' and 'potential' PvdA voters were included in our sample. The total number of center-left respondents in our sample was 291. The data on this group were included in our secondary analysis.

Data from the social-democratic Members of the Second Chamber of Parliament were collected using a written questionnaire. It took place between the beginning of July 1993 and the end of August 1993. Our questionnaire contained the same questions which the center-left respondents had answered. Additional questions were asked about MPs' opinions about their responsibilities and functions and their perceptions of the center-left voters' opinions on several EC issues, of party members' EC opinions, and of the importance of their own opinions on EC matters in their party's nomination process (designed to test explanatory models of elite-mass-linkages). Our total response rate was 45 per cent (N = 22). A comparison of the background (gender, level of education, religion, and policy specialization) of this sample with one of the same population (N = 48) from another study (Thomassen et al., 1992) resulted in the conclusion that this sample was both representative and acceptable, only slightly overrepresenting MPs with more higher education.

CONSENSUS, DISSENTION, OR A GAP VIS-À-VIS THE EC?

Does there exist a gap, dissention, or consensus between the Dutch Labor MPs and the center-left voters as far as EC issues are concerned? We answer this question when we compare the 'European' opinions and attitudes of both groups. Answers to many questions (relating to opinions and attitudes of both voters and MPs) were compared. On most EC issues, there is a consensus between the center-left voters and MPs. The specific issues on which there was a consensus varies from efforts to unify Western Europe, Dutch EC membership, and the European Parliament's power to choose between national or EC decision-making options with respect to the rights of workers' representatives on company boards. In almost all cases of consensus, the opinions and attitudes were pro-EC/EU. However, MPs were more outspokenly pro-EC/EU. By comparison, voters' opinions and attitudes may be characterized as 'more permissive, accepting, and benevolent, and less demanding, challenging, pressing, or pushing' (as the Eurobarometer summary concluded about this whole population) (on these points, see Commission, 1987, p. 42). Table 16.1 shows the overall consensus on some of these issues.

Although a consensus prevailed, some dissention and even a gap existed with respect to a few other issues. Dissention existed on minor issues (such as the question whether the EC/EU or the national governments should make decisions regarding protection of computer-based information and scientific and technological research). A gap existed between the opinions of voters and MPs on the Single Market and between voters' and MPs' feelings of being 'European'. In the case of the Single Market, 46.6 per cent of the center-left voters thought that the Single Market was a 'good' idea, while an overwhelming 95.5 per cent of the PvdA-MPs had that opinion. In the case of feeling 'European', 54.2 per cent of the center-left voters 'never' had this feeling (with 29.2 per cent 'sometimes'), while only 4.5 per cent PvdA-MPs reported never having such a feeling (with 77.3 per cent 'sometimes').

Table 16.1 Political issues on which there exists a clear consensus among Dutch voters and MPs (in %)

	Center-left voters	PvdA-MPs
Efforts to unify Western Europe		
For, very much	25.7	40.9
For, to some extent	60.1	59.1
Against, to some extent	11.6	0.0
Against, very much	2.5	0.0
The European Parliament's right to put forward legislation together with the Council of Ministers		
For	81.2	90.0
Against	18.8	10.0
Competency of the national government or the EC/EU in the areas of:		
Security and defense		
National government	21.0	5.0
EC	79.0	95.0
Cooperation with developing countries		
National government	18.8	20.0
EC	81.2	80.0
Value added tax		
National government	21.5	19.0
EC	78.5	81.0
Foreign policy toward countries outside the EC/EU		
National government	21.8	10.0
EC	78.2	90.0
N min. =	266	20
N max. =	286	22

EXPLANATORY MODELS
Models

How can this observed widespread consensus between center-left voters and MPs be explained? And why is there such a wide gap regarding opinions on the Single Market? In the relevant political science literature, we found several different theoretical models of elite-mass linkages. These models are the voters' sanction, the party members' sanction, the pressure group members' sanction, the consensus, and the role models. We added two others, the propaganda and the socialization models, to improve our analysis. With the help of these seven models, we tried to explain the consensus between Labor MPs and center-left voters.

Voters' Sanction Model

The voters' sanction consensus explanatory model assumes that voters usually vote in a rational way. Those politicians are elected whose ideas most correspond to those of the voters. Because of the threat of electoral sanctions, the politicians will adjust their opinions to those of the voters in order to be re-elected. When there was a gap, this adjustment did not take place because the politicians discounted the electoral importance of the issue concerned. Luttberg (1968 and 1981) described this model, also calling it the 'rational-activist model' (see also Berelson, 1981, and compare Downs, 1954). The model can only explain the consensus if, among others, the following conditions are met: the MPs have perceptions of the electors' opinions on the EU, their perceptions are correct, and they acknowledge the electoral importance of EU matters.

The first condition is met here. All MP respondents had perceptions of the center-left voters' opinions on the more general issues, such as the efforts to unify Western Europe, the speed for European integration, the Single Market, and the profit potential from Dutch EU membership. Nearly all MP respondents also had perceptions of the center-left voters' opinions on transfer to the EU of powers in different policy areas (91 per cent had perceptions about public opinion on 12 of 15 such topics). A large majority (68.4 per cent) had perceptions of the center-left voters' opinions on the European Parliament's decision-making powers. The second condition is not met. In general, the PvdA-MPs had incorrect perceptions of relevant center-left voters' opinions. In the case of 13 (out of the 22) relevant opinions, more than 40 per cent of the Labor MPs had incorrect perceptions. The third condition also is not met. More than four out of ten PvdA-MPs (40.9 per cent) said that the center-left voters care 'not at all' about their own opinions on EC matters at the elections, 54.5 per cent said 'very little', and 4.5 per cent said 'little'. None of the MP respondents acknowledged the electoral importance of the voters' opinions on EC issues. To conclude this discussion, two necessary and crucial conditions were not met; therefore, this voters' sanction model cannot be applied in this case.

Party Members' Sanction Model

The inapplicability of the voters' sanction model is not very surprising because it assumes a direct linkage between the electorate and the elected. In the Netherlands, this direct linkage does not exist. The voters have only an indirect influence on the (re-)election of a particular MP due to the system of proportional representation with only one constituency. The total number of votes for a party determines the proportionate number of party seats in the Dutch Second Chamber. A candidate who is too low on the party list will not be elected to Parliament.

People vote in the first place for a party, not for a person. As a consequence, the elected are more dependent on the nomination process in their parties for their re-election than on the direct support of the voters. If the elected are more dependent on the nomination process in their party than on the voters directly, how can the EU consensus be explained? It is imaginable that, to ensure their party's nomination, the MPs adjust their opinions to their perceptions about the opinions of party members because of the threat of sanctions from these party-members. This may explain a consensus between the PvdA-MPs and only a part of their electorate, namely, the party members. This model can only be applied if, among others, the condition is met that the MPs acknowledge the importance of their opinions on EU matters in the party nomination process.

This condition is, however, also not met. None of the MP respondents said that their opinions on EC matters had any weight in the nomination process. One out of three (36.4 per cent) said their EU opinions weighed 'a little', the same percentage answered 'very little', and 27.3 per cent answered 'not at all'. So, just as with perceived electoral importance, a perceived nomination importance of EU matters is not present. This means that this sanction model also cannot explain the consensus between the Labor MPs and (a part of) the center-left voters.

Pressure Group Members' Sanction Model

This model, originally called the pressure group model (Luttberg, 1968), is quite similar to the party members' sanction model. The core of the model is the possibility of positive or negative sanctions from a pressure group against the electoral candidate. Examples of such sanctions are no financial aid for his campaign, negative voting advice to other voters, public criticism, and so forth. In this model, pressure groups become intermediary political actors. Citizens become members of pressure groups to fulfill certain wishes and demands. The pressure group negotiates with the candidate while using the threat of imposing sanctions in the next election. In order to cope with this threat, the candidates adjust their views to the opinions of the pressure group.

The conditions which have to be met for an explanation of the consensus are similar to the conditions in the immediately preceding model. The model works only if the elected take these threats of sanctions seriously. Here, we focused on labor unions as the most relevant pressure group for Labor MPs. Our survey showed that 81.8 per cent think unions' opinions are 'important'. Only 13.6 per cent think these opinions are 'unimportant' and 4.5 per cent think they are 'very unimportant'. There is indication that the Labor MPs do take the possible threat of unions' sanctions very seriously indeed.

But do the Labor MPs adjust their opinions to their perceptions of unions' opinions because they attach great value to these views? To answer this question, we selected the seven most relevant opinions, which receive the most union attention: 1) the Single Market, 2) whether the EC/EU or the national government should decide on the currency, 3) social welfare, 4) participation of the workers' representatives on the company's boards, 5) industrial policy, 6) workers' health and safety, and 7) unemployment policy. We can measure an adjustment in relevant opinions if we compare the PvdA-MPs' opinions with the perceptions they have of the unions' opinions. When a PvdA-MP perceives agreement in such opinions, this could be an indication that he/she adjusted his/her own opinion. Only taking in account the PvdA-MPs who attach high value to the opinions of the unions, it seemed that in the case of four out of the seven mentioned opinions, more than 60 per cent of the PvdA-MPs perceived agreement between themselves and the unions. The MPs who did not attach value to unions' opinions, do not more often perceive a discrepancy between their own and the unions' opinions (this last group consists of only four respondents). In the case of these last respondents, the percentage which percieved agreement in such opinions was, in the case of four of the seven opinions, higher than the percentages of the respondents who attached value to unions' opinions. This last observation indicates that it is doubtful whether or not any adjustment in opinion has taken place. This is even more doubtful when we consider that in the case of workers' representatives participating on the company's board, no consensus was percieved and that in the case of unemployment policy, the MPs perceived a consensus. Why should we believe that an adjustment of opinions took place in the first case and not in the second? It is important to stress that we do not have accurate data about how union members think about the EC. For a proper explanation of the EC consensus between the Labor MP and (this part of) the center-left voters, it would be necessary for us to have such data. It may also be that our assumption about the opinions of union leaders being representative of members' opinions is faulty (Putnam, 1976; Luttberg and Zeigler, 1968; Ippolito et al., 1976).

To conclude, the possible explanation of the EC consensus between PvdA-MPs and the center-left voters who are union members through an adjustment of opinions to the opinions of the unions cannot be excluded, but it could not be tested completely with the available data.

Consensus Model

The consensus model is the empirical translation of reflection theory. This normative theory states that the characteristics of the MPs should mirror the characteristics of the voters. Only then can a real, direct representation be achieved. In this view, representation is based 'on the representative's characteristics, on what he is or is like, on being something rather than doing something' (Pitkin, 1967, p. 61). This is not to say that a representative's actions do not matter. There is an assumed relation between the composition of Parliament and what it does. Such a composition has influence on legislative activities (Thomassen, 1981). The consensus model requires an investigation of what characteristics the representatives and the represented have in common. However, the (empirical) consensus model is still rather unsatisfactory because it is largely descriptive and cannot explain why a consensus exists.

In the literature, we found another model which is also called the consensus model. In his treatment of this model, Luttberg focused strongly on the role of socialization processes. As he said:

> So long as leaders are not treated from their early childhood as a class apart, they will share life experiences and be exposed to a culture similar to that of other men. To the degree that experiences are common and values and beliefs are taught to all, leaders will share with their follow men the goals, values and beliefs of the society (Luttberg, 1968, p. 245).

Because the consensus model, as Luttberg described it, is quite different from Thomassen's (1976 and 1981) empirical consensus model, we prefer to call Luttberg's consensus model the 'socialization' model. Later, we pay more detailed attention to this subject.

Role Model

The role model states that the MP's behavior and his/her role interpretation are related in a determinative way. Three roles can be distinguished. First, there are the so-called delegates, who act according to the opinions, demands, and wishes of the voters. Second, the trustees, who first act according to their own opinions and perceptions of what will be good for the voters. Between these two role interpretations, the politicos can be distinguished. Depending on the situation and the issue which is at stake, the politicos act as either a delegate or as a trustee (Eulau and Wahlke et al., 1962).

This distinction between styles of representation cannot alone explain the EC consensus. The role model only relates MPs' behavior and role interpretations, but it can not explain why candidates and voters share the same opinions. Therefore, this model should be extended. Here, we shall assume that delegates not only act according to voters' wishes, but that they also adjust their own opinions to agree with those of the voters. Since MPs define their role primarily as delegates, this may explain any consensus. However, this is not the case. We asked the PvdA-MPs which role they prefered. None defined him/herself as a delegate, while 63.6 per cent prefered to be a politico, and 36.4 per cent a trustee.

Propaganda Model

The foregoing consensus explanatory models imply an (anticipated) influence of the electors on the elected (candidates). The reverse is also possible: influence from the candidates on the voters, resulting in a consensus. The EU consensus may be the result of effective influence by those to be elected on the electors. In the case of the gap in opinion about the Single Market, then, this influence may not have taken place or it may not have been done effectively. Most of the PvdA-MPs said that they had, indeed, tried to mold the center-left voters' opinions on the EC. Reportedly, 23.8 per cent did this 'often', 52.4 per cent 'sometimes', 19.0 per cent 'rarely', and 4.8 per cent 'never'. Almost all of them said that informing, convincing, and influencing the electors is their task/job (93.8 per cent, 93.8 per cent, and 92.8 per cent, respectively). Whether this influence was responsible for the consensus (and gap) cannot, however, be answered completely with the empirical data that we have. We could have asked on which particular issues the MPs tried to influence the electors and should have applied a longitudinal research design (pre-, and postmeasures, including a control group).

Socialization Model

The propaganda model may be integrated into another new model, which we call the socialization model. In this model, consensus may be explained if we find common political socialization patterns and/or a successful propaganda campaign. A gap is explained by the political elites' additional role socialization and/or less successful propaganda techniques. Consensus is assumed to be a result of the fact that, in general, both the elected (except the specialists) and the electors experience the same socializers' influence. For example, they (have to) rely on the same sources of EC/EU information. Additional political role socialization for the elected, therefore, explains dissention or a gap. This additional political socialization brings the elected into contact with other sources of information, requires the elected to vote for or against a particular proposal (which implies their having definite opinions), and asks the elected to take into account other considerations than those which influence the electorate.

An important difference between MPs and the electorate is that MPs must publicly and regularly vote, while electors lack this responsibility. The Single Market, which is part of the Single Act, is one example when the MPs had to make a definite choice. The fact that they had to vote on the Single Act required them to find other sources of information and forced them to have a clear understanding about the Single Market. Moreover, merely having once expressed a pro or con position may later reinforce and strengthen the previously expressed opinion. That almost all MP respondents thought the Single Market to be a 'good' idea can probably be explained in this way. Among voters, not more than 40 per cent thought that the Single Market was a 'good' idea, but they were not obliged to vote on the matter and were, thus, 'allowed' to have an unchallenged opinion.

The MPs may, due to their job-specific roles, also apply different criteria in the process of opinion formation. They may be more concerned with country/state interests as a whole than with specific and/or private interests. Nearly all PvdA-MPs had the opinion that the Single Market is a good idea, although most of them did not expect any positive effects on their personal lives (65.0 per cent). Voters may be expected to be less concerned about the welfare of the country/state. Instead, they may be more interested in their personal welfare, in the welfare of the region where they live, or in the sector where they work. There are indications that this explanation is valid. A bare majority (51.7 per cent) of the center-left voters did not expect the Single Market to have any effect on their personal lives. It seems that the center-left voters who expected no effect on their personal lives significantly more often thought the Single Market to be neither a good nor a bad idea than did the center-left voters who expected some positive effects from it. The same pattern was found in the case of effects on the region in which the respondent lived and on the sector in which one worked.

Testing this socialization model would require a longitudinal study with an experimental design, using several different political socialization data-acquisition and data-analysis methods. Some of the leading questions in such an analysis would include the following: When, how, and by what means do electors and elected acquire opinions and attitudes with respect to the EC? Does the use of common sources lead to a consensus? How and by what factors are representatives socialized in their political role? When, how and by what means do MPs try to convince the electors of their points of view and how effective are these efforts?

CONCLUSIONS

Many publications claim there is a gap between elites and the mass with respect to European integration as well as expressing concern about it. In this research, a widespread pro-EC consensus between the Labor MPs and the center-left voters in the Netherlands was observed. Dissention exists only with respect to a few issues. An elite-mass gap was observed only with respect to opinions on the Single Market and feelings of being European.

The consensus between elite/mass opinions and attitudes could not be explained using selected models of elite-mass linkages. The so-called consensus model does not provide any plausible explanation. The voters' and party members' sanction model and the role model were contradicted using our own empirical data. Because of a lack in particular data needed (which is not a unique experience in such a secondary analysis), the interest group members' sanction model could not be tested completely. There is, however, not much evidence for (or high expectations about) the explanatory power of this model. The first new model that we introduced, the propaganda model, could also not be tested completely (we did not have an opportunity to employ a longitudinal research design). This model is more promising because almost all the representatives agree their tasks are to inform, convince, and influence the electorate and because many of them have actually done this in practice. The second explanatory model that we introduced here, the socialization model, also seems to be promising. Common political socialization patterns will result in consensus. Political elites' additional role in socialization (for example, in the case of the Single European Act) may result in a gap. Most promising is the combination of the propaganda and socialization models.

Regardless, what fascinates us as an outcome of this study is not so much that there is an elite/mass gap, but rather that there is so much Dutch societal consensus on European integration. How can we explain why it is that so many people of very different ages, genders, levels of education, incomes, places of residence, and so forth, share the same opinions and attitudes on such a complex issue as European integration? Can it be a factor of a generally common political socialization experience characteristic of the Dutch population (which is uncharacteristic of England, France, Denmark, or Germany)? Or is the EC/EU propaganda so successful?

REFERENCES

Andeweg, R. (1993). 'Elite-Mass Linkages in Europe: Legitimacy Crisis or Party Crisis?' Paper prepared for presentation to the Conference on 'Are European Elites Losing Touch with Their Peoples?' at the Institute of European Studies, Oxford University, Oxford, UK . 17-19 September 1993.

Berelson, B. (1981). 'Democratic Practice and Democratic Theory', pp. 15-28 in R. Luttberg (ed.) *Public Opinion and Public Policy. Models of Political Linkage.* Itasca, IL: Peacock Publishers.

Commission of the European Communities (1992). *Eurobarometer No. 37.* Brussels, Belgium: Commission of the European Communities.

Downs, A. (1954). *An Economic Theory of Democracy.* New York, NY: Harper and Row.

Eulau, J., J. Wahlke, W. Buchanan, and L. Ferguson (1962). *The Legislative System. Explorations in Legislative Behavior.* New York, NY: John Wiley and Sons.

Ippolito, D., T. Walker, and K. Kolson (1976). *Public Opinion and Responsible Democracy.* Englewood Cliffs, NJ: Prentice-Hall.

Luttberg, R. (1968). *Public Opinion and Public Policy: Models of Political Linkage.* Itasca, IL: Dorsey.

Luttberg, R. (1981). 'Political Linkage in a Large Society', pp. 1-11 in R. Luttberg (ed.) *Public Opinion and Public Policy. Models of Political Linkage.* Third Edition. Itasca, IL: Peacock.

Luttberg, R. and H. Zeigler (1968). 'Attitude Consensus and Conflict in an Interest Group: an Assessment of Cohesion', pp. 170-83 in R. Luttberg (ed.) *Public Opinion and Public Policy. Models of Political Linkage.* First Edition. Itasca, IL: Dorsey.

Pitkin, H. (1967). *The Concept of Representation.* Berkeley/Los Angeles, CA: University of California Press.

Putnam, R.. (1976). *The Comparative Study of Political Elites.* Englewood Cliffs, NJ: Prentice-Hall.

Thomassen, J. (1976). *Kiezers en Gekozenen in een representatieve democratie* (Electors and Elected in a Representative Democracy). Alphen a/d Rijn, the Netherlands: Samsom.

Thomassen, J. (1981). 'Politieke representatie' (Political Representation) in J. Thomassen (red.) *Democratie. Theorie en praktijk* (Democracy: Theory and Practice). Alphen a/d Rijn, the Netherlands: Samsom.

Thomassen, J. and M. Zielonka-Goeij (1992). 'Het Parlement als volks-vertegenwoordiging' (The Parliament as Representative of the People), pp. 195-224 in J. Thomassen, M. van Schendelen, and M. Zielonka-Goeij (red.) *De Geachte Afgevaardigde... Hoe Kamerleden denken over het Nederlandse Parlement* (The MP ... How MPs Think About the Dutch Parliament). Muiderberg, the Netherlands: Coutinho.

Part V

Politics and/of Education

17   The Relevance of Political Philosophy to Educational Theory
Hannah Arendt and 'Active Citizenship'

Siebren Miedema

ABSTRACT

The central question this chapter focuses on is whether Hannah Arendt's political theorizing has relevance for educational thought. Her analysis of totalitarianism serves as the background for dealing with the concepts of intersubjectivity, plurality, space, and unique individuality. It is (contrary to Arendt's own conviction) here maintained that there is, indeed, a relation between politics and pedagogy, a kind of 'natural' alliance with respect to keeping the space of 'appearance in being', and practicing differentiation. With respect to this relation, we distinguish between the political potential of the pedagogical relation and the contribution of education in directing human beings toward politics (that is, toward active citizenship).

INTRODUCTION

On 4 March 1951, after publishing *The Origins of Totalitarianism*, Hannah Arendt wrote a letter to her former professor and friend, Karl Jaspers, about this book:

> What radical evil really is I don't know, but it seems to me it somehow has to do with the following phenomenon: making human beings as human beings superfluous (not using them as means to an end, which leaves their essence as humans untouched and impinges only on their human dignity; rather, making them superfluous as human beings). This happens as soon as all unpredictability - which, in human beings, is the equivalent of spontaneity - is eliminated. And all this in turn arises from - or, better, goes along with - the delusion of the omnipotence (not simply with the lust for power) of an individual man. If an individual man qua man were omnipotent, then there is in fact no reason why men in the plural should exist at all . . . (Kohler and Saner, 1992, p. 166).

Hannah Arendt's political theories are surely not easy to understand. Quite different interpretations have been proposed. Much criticism has been advanced about her supposed theoretical and political stances. We cannot deal here *in extenso* with these different interpretations or critiques based on any misunderstandings, but we can more safely follow Canovan's very convincing interpretation of Arendt's complete oeuvre in her recent book, *Hannah Arendt: A Reinterpretation of her Political Thought* (Canovan, 1992). This book is labelled 'a reinterpretation' because Canovan's latest reconstruction of Arendt's 'life and mind' uses her published work as well as the until-recently unpublished Arendt papers in the US Library of Congress. Consequently, Canovan's interpretation, as she says, 'differs in a number of important respects from other accounts' (Canovan, 1992, p. vii). In many ways, this full-scale reinterpretation is also a revision of her own earlier understanding of Arendt's thought.

Instead of taking Arendt's more systematic, more structured, and most philosophical book, *The Human Condition* (1958) as the starting point for an in-depth reconstruction, Canovan begins with the earlier published *Totalitarianism* (1951) book. According to Canovan, we really miss Arendt's central point if (as so often has been done) we take her theory of action, stress on plurality, and emphasis of things political instead of her socioeconomic framework as a theory about the good life. This is an exercise in Hellenic nostalgia for the Greek polis or Athenian-style participatory politics (Canovan, 1992, pp. 2, 14, 63, and 275). On the contrary, Arendt strove to recoup and rearticulate 'a variety of forgotten experiences of the capacity to make a new beginning, and considering the implications of these experiences for politics' (Canovan, 1992, p. 14). It is only in relation to her analysis of the constituents of totalitarian ideology, that we can understand her plea in *The Human Condition* for 'bulwarks against political evil that can be erected, not in the loneliness of the individual heart, but in the political space between plural men and the lasting institutions they can create there' (Canovan, 1992, p. 15). Arendt's 1951 letter to Jaspers shows precisely the interconnections of her analysis of the phenomenon of totalitarianism with her analysis of human action in terms of intersubjectivity and plurality, which she discussed at length in *The Human Condition* (1958), the book published seven years after *Origins of Totalitarianism* (1951). It is only with the perspective of the earlier ideas she formulated about the phenomenon of totalitarianism that we are fully able to grasp the meaning Arendt gave to the concepts of intersubjectivity, plurality, space, and individuality, or identity. Following this line, it is possible to more adequately answer questions about the contemporary relevance of Arendt's political philosophy for educational thought. In this chapter, we first focus on Arendt's analysis of totalitarianism; then, on the concepts of intersubjectivity, plurality, space, and individuality; and finally, on relationships between politics and pedagogy. The major objective of this chapter is to show how relevant Arendt's political thought is to civic education.

THE ANALYSIS OF TOTALITARIANISM

What precisely are the constituent elements of totalitarian ideology? When using the concept of ideology, Arendt means 'the logical consistency with which it purports to explain the past and the future' (Canovan, 1992, p. 26). The underlying belief in a totally closed system (quite impervious to factual refutation) is the key point. There is no place here for new ideas and spontaneous actions. Central to totalitarian ideology is the belief that 'everything is possible'. Totalitarians want to change human nature in the sense that man is robbed of his nature, his individuality and capacity for action, his free thought and choice, and is turned into a human beast. Totalitarian leaders who believe in the possible without believing in human freedom and responsibility, see themselves as servants of those inhuman laws that govern the universe. So, human plurality and spontaneity become superfluous for followers and victims alike, as well as for the leaders, themselves (Canovan, 1992, p. 27). As Arendt said, 'The totalitarian murderers are all the more dangerous because they do not care if they themselves are alive or dead, if they ever lived or ever were born' (Arendt, 1951, p. 433). The principal elements of the totalitarian amalgam are anti-Semitism, transformation of the national state, racism, societal expansion solely for expansion's sake, and alliance between capitalists and the mob. The drive toward unlimited power and expansionism, as a self-perpetuating momentum (without being the means to any human end) and the pursuit of total domination are at the very core of totalitarian goals (Canovan, 1992, p. 29). Examples of such totalitarian practices are concentration and extermination camps in Germany during World War II or today in the former Yugoslavia. As Arendt said, these are instances 'in which the fundamental belief of totalitarianism that everything is possible is being verified' (Arendt, 1951, p. 414).

Although totalitarianism has never been completely developed, 'its potentiality can be fully realized only if it has conquered the earth, only when no human being can any longer live outside its murderous domination' (Arendt, 1951, p. 429). However, its past challenge to the standards and beliefs of Western civilization has revealed its potential dangers.

By contrast, mankind is faced with an open future. We live in a world without apparent meaning. We are given no guidance. Therefore, we are condemned to freedom. In Arendt's opinion, the alternative to the predicament of modern humanity, or to the 'ideal solution' of totalitarianism, or to Heideggerian inauthenticity or Sartrean *mauvaise foi*, 'lies in a deliberate new beginning, acknowledging that mankind is now a reality with a common fate . . ., in a conscious assumption of responsibility for political acts all over the world . . ., the recognition and punishment of "crimes against humanity," and . . . the guarantee to all human beings of the one fundamental right . . . the right to citizenship' (Canovan, 1992, p. 62). This means that human beings have to 'accept the implications of their humanity, which means accepting the plurality, their freedom to act and to think, and their joint responsibility to establish a world between them, to set limits to the forces of nature and to bestow rights upon one another' (Canovan, 1992, p. 62).

PLURALITY, INTERSUBJECTIVITY, AND IDENTITY

In *The Human Condition* (1958), Arendt writes about the creation of this world, collectively and cooperatively created by all participants having an *interest* in a common public and political space. What we have here is communication in the Deweyan sense since this is the public activity of our making something in common (Dewey, 1938, p. 46). To characterize this political process, Arendt uses the Aristotelian notion of 'philia', pointing to friendships between citizens. This friendship, this solidarity, focuses on 'the furthering of a dialogue and a conversation in which the joint world is at the centre . . . [and] on the willingness to share the world with others' (Prins, 1992, p. 77). Through the unhampered exchange of ideas through communication, the collective public space is shaped. We learn to be human through speaking. In this way, the earth is humanized. Human beings construct their world, civilizations, a home for themselves. This is over and above the natural earth. Humans decide to be plural individuals instead of interchangeable members of a species or animals (Canovan, 1992, p. 106). Their world view or culture (consisting of durable institutions as well as their visible manifestations) is shared between human beings. It 'gathers us together and yet prevents our falling over each other' (Arendt, 1958, p. 52). Individuals can take different positions, see their common world from different points of view and, therefore, talk about their common affairs. 'Only where things can be seen by many in a variety of aspects without changing their identity, so that those who are gathered around them know they see sameness in utter diversity, can worldly reality truly and reliably appear' (Arendt, 1958, p. 57). In this public space, reality can grow and appear in its many-sidedness.

In this organized political space which we call the public sphere (while recognizing the other as other and as equal in a political sense), this previously existing plurality can flourish, along with freedom and public opinion, too. According to Arendt, this public space is (by definition) an intersubjective space. This political/public space is, of course, not situated in a vacuum. Topics under discussion and issues for deliberation are contextualized with a certain historical or political genealogy. The outcomes of such deliberations may influence or determine the resultant political cultures.

The participants in any discussion about a topic of general interest show (and realize by so speaking) their identities (that is, their unique personalities and subjectivities). Speech 'corresponds to the fact of distinctness and is the actualization of the human condition of plurality, that is, of living as a distinct and unique being among equals' (Arendt, 1958, p. 178). This realizing of one's identity (and of one's political self or citizenship) is connected with (and based upon) our speaking and acting together. 'Because the actor always moves among and in relation to other acting beings, he is never merely a "doer" but always and at the same time a sufferer. To do and to suffer are like opposite sides of the same coin. . . .' (Arendt, 1958, p. 190). To act and speak in the presence of others is necessary for human beings to affirm their own reality. It is Arendt's contention that precisely this 'will to appear', to manifest oneself - this action as self-disclosure - transforms a man into a political being (Canovan, 1992, p. 134 note 135). The primary function of political power is to keep this public space open to allow a variety of 'appearances in being' to happen.

In *The Human Condition* (1958), Arendt does not offer a fixed political theory. Instead, she is here concerned with the predicament from which politics must start. She investigates those human activities that have the most bearing on politics, that is those aspects of the human condition from which politics arises. Accordingly, the most politically relevant characteristic of human beings is their plurality: 'Men, not Man, live on the earth and inhabit the world' (Arendt, 1958, p. 7). In this book, she points to the present situation where labor values have become a structural parallel along with totalitarian terror. She says, 'The human world erected by work is being destroyed by an "unnatural growth of the natural"' (Canovan, 1992, p. 103). If nuclear physics and the economic revolution allow modern men to take control over their lives following the liberation of the 'life process' (in the totalitarian belief that everything is possible), the result is our enslavement to pseudo-natural processes. Here, the limits of the human condition become visible. The world is (for Arendt) more a world of cultural objects and milieux than technology, engineering, or industry. She is a critic of modernity and pseudo-nature, because 'modernity represents for her a kind of pseudo-nature [or synthetic versions of natural processes] to which the genuine human world has been sacrificed. . . . The true worldly values of durability and fitness to house mankind have been lost' (Canovan, 1992, p. 110).

Arendt is also critical of 'society', which, in her opinion, is a kind of pseudo-public realm. The essence of society, in her view, is herdlike uniformity and destruction of our plurality. Such binding together is essentially private (that is, by means of production, a 'socialized' mankind from an economic perspective, and consumption [cultural uniformity]) in a common economy and a common mass culture. Instead, the public process means gathering around a common world that allows us to be plural individuals. On the economic side of society, the political order serves as the handmaid for economic purposes, administration, or the management of our collective life processes. As for the cultural side of society, Arendt points to the striking similarity between whole populations obsessed with consuming, conforming to fashion, and aping the behavior of 'high society' or the aristocrats of the *ancien régime* (Canovan,

1992, p. 117 ff.). The core idea of this analysis is the useless subordination of human beings to quasi-natural processes.

The possibility of the human condition (but not 'human nature' because of our openness and plurality as human beings) is the human capacity to act (that is, to start new beginnings, to account for those things given - meaning not man-made - which man cannot change at all, for example, man's subordination to inescapable conditions). Instead of being exercises in nostalgia or a recommendation for idealized versions of democracy, Arendt deals with Homer and the Athenians, Romans and revolution, and Christianity and the Civil Rights movement. She attends to discovering basic sources and examples of natality and to detecting different modi of public/political action (such as, for example, nonviolent politics) (Canovan, 1992, p. 142 ff.).

Just as totalitarianism never completely developed, it is Arendt's opinion that political action is also incompletely developed as she said:

> action is a capacity all humans possess, and one that lies at the root of politics . . . in most of the political systems that ever existed this capacity has been repressed in favor of government and obedience, and that the political spaces in which action has flourished have been very rare. . . . Action is an "unpolitical political" capacity, which drives men in the direction of politics but also makes it very difficult for them to get there. The impulse to take initiatives drives them to politics partly because they need co-operation of others in their enterprises, and also because they want to be seen in action, and need a space of appearance in which to act and institutions to house that space (Canovan, 1992, p. 148).

The moral of *The Human Condition* (1958) is that political solutions are the only possible solutions to the twin predicaments of totalitarianism and modernity. It is the condition of human plurality which makes it possible for human beings to build their world in which they also can appear as unique individuals. Because of this plurality, 'we can found lasting institutions to guard us against the processes we ourselves start, and to rescue us from the darkness of each person's lonely heart' (Canovan, 1992, p. 154).

Arendt's great emphasis on politics had also to do with her thinking 'without a bannister'. She expressed her Rortyean antifoundationalism, *avant la lettre*, with her conviction that political action is possible without the official authorization of philosophy, much like Rorty's later priority for democracy over formal philosophy (Rorty, 1991, p. 175 ff.; Canovan, 1992, p. 278). One's striving for the 'state of being free' on the basis of being born with the gift of freedom (including one's ability to initiate with its heuristic political potential) also has strong structural similarities to Habermas' ethical or practical intersubjective regulative of the 'ideal speech' situation.

POLITICS AND PEDAGOGY

Arendt actually paid little specific attention to the relation of politics and education. It was her opinion that 'Education can play no part in politics, because in politics we always have to deal with those who are already educated. . . . The word "education" has an evil sound in politics; there is a pretense of education, when the real purpose is coercion without the use of force' (Arendt, 1978, p. 177). My argument here is that politics and pedagogy are two practices which determine and limit each other and where the possibility of identity-formation, community, and solidarity is at stake. Both deal with the necessary creation and use of a public (that is, political) space, with reality construction, and with the appearance of uniqueness in subjectivity and identity. Democratic pedagogy as action, as well as democratic politics as action, are incompatible with totalitarian and purely instrumental relations between human beings.

It is precisely Arendt's insight in the dark sides of human action, in the so-often-oppressed possibilities for human plurality as a gift for producing states of freedom, which gives rise to the question of what education can contribute in creating public political space and action potential in that philosophical sense as she conceptualized it. Is there really a useful way to lead from pedagogy to politics? Another question is connected with the presence of politics in education. Is it also possible to interpret the school as one of the 'lasting institutions' which can contribute to action (in Arendt's sense) and where human plurality can flourish?

In recent pedagogical contributions dealing with the process of identity-formation in education, stress is laid on the intersubjective and dialogical nature of the pedagogical relationship (Masschelein, 1991; Miedema, 1993; Biesta, 1996). The final result of the pedagogical process is not a fixed outcome, but an achievement, which all the participants who take part in the process bring about. The starting point is the intersubjective relation in all of education. Inter-subjectivity is not the result of the activities of (two) subjects, but, on the contrary, the intersubjective relation is constitutive for subjectivity. This subjectivity constitutes and unveils itself in communicating, in acting and speaking. In communication, a joint world of meanings and norms is presupposed. Within the intersubjective matrix of the pedagogical relationship, subjectivity is realized in (and through) speaking to other subjects and by the fact that others speak to us. The action of the teacher as well as that of the child contribute to subjectivity production or identity formation and the appearance of separate, unique identities (in its present state) for both the teacher and the child. So, the educational process can be characterized as a cooperative and co-constructive interaction process. Both teacher and child live in this inter-subjective context (that is, Habermas' life world or Arendt's public world), within the interdependence of this pedagogical relation, when acting out and speaking about their respective identities and their subjectivity (Miedema, 1993, pp. 88-90). As I have said elsewhere, 'If we want to keep the democratic [that is, political] potentials of education alive, . . . we must educate from the idea that difference [Arendt's plurality] - not only between teacher and student, but also between students themselves - is not an obstacle to learning, but is an incentive to learning and an incentive to the development of one's own identity, agency and personality' (Miedema and Biesta, Summer 1994).

The educational process and pedagogical action can be a celebration of difference and uniqueness, that is, of plurality in a public space. Here, we have the political potential in pedagogical relations (Masschelein, 1992). There is, however, also another way to approach this matter (that is, the possible impact of education on politics as relations among 'the already educated' as Arendt termed it). Education can be used as that institution where action (as an 'unpolitical political' opportunity) can be practiced and evaluated, experiences shared, and citizen identities disclosed. Education can create an adequate starting point for starting citizens in the direction of practicing real politics, 'active citizenship, that is [based] on the value and importance of civic engagement and collective deliberation about all matters affecting the political community' (d'Entrèves, 1992, p. 146).

Contrary to Arendt's reservations about the traditional relation of education to politics, a new relation can be formulated today using her own conceptualizations of human action and politics. In *The Human Condition* (1958), she does not restrict the public space (or the space of appearances) to a set of institutions or to a specific location. For example, she wrote, 'Where people gather together, it is potentially there, but only potentially, not necessarily and not forever' (Arendt, 1958, p. 199). 'It is therefore always a potential space, which finds its actualization in the actions and speeches of individuals who have come together to undertake some common project' (d'Entrèves, 1992, p. 148). These ideas are fully compatible with an understanding of the pedagogical relation as a inter-subjective process, stressing its cooperative and co-constructive nature as argued in this chapter. The relevance of Hannah Arendt's political theory for educational thought becomes more obvious if we take this more liberal interpretation of her discussions of democracy, totalitarianism, and pedagogy.

REFERENCES

Arendt, H. (1951). *The Burden of Our Time*. London: Secker & Warburg. (The British title of the 1st edition is *The Origins of Totalitarianism*)

Arendt, H. (1958). *The Human Condition*. Chicago, IL/London, UK: University of Chicago Press.

Arendt, H. (1978). *Between Past and Future*. Harmondsworth, UK: Penguin Books.

Biesta, G. (Summer 1994). 'Education as Practical Intersubjectivity', pp. 299-317 in *Educational Theory*, Vol. 44.

Canovan, M. (1992). *Hannah Arendt. A Reinterpretation of her Political Thought.* Cambridge, UK: Cambridge University Press.

Dewey, J. (1938). *Logic: The Theory of Inquiry.* New York, NY: Holt.

Kohler, L. and H. Saner (eds.) (1992). *Hannah Arendt to Karl Jaspers: Correspondence 1926-1969.* New York, NY/San Diego, CA/London, UK: Harcourt Brace Jovanovich.

Masschelein, J. (1991). *Kommunikatives Handeln und pädagogisches Handeln* (Communicative Action and Pedagogical Action). Leuven, the Netherlands/Weinheim, FRG: Leuven University Press/Deutscher Studien Verlag.

Masschelein, J. (1992). 'Wandel der Öffentlichkeit und das Problem der Identität' (Changes in the Public Sphere and the Problem of Identity), pp. 59-75 in J. Oelkers (ed.) *Aufklärung, Bildund und Öffentlichkeit. Pädagogische Beiträge zur Moderne* (Enlightenment, Edification and the Public Sphere). Weinheim, FRG/Basel, Switzerland: Beltz Verlag.

Miedema, S. (1993). 'De autonomie van het subject. Een moderne illusie?' (The Autonomous Subject: A Modern Illusion?), pp. 83-94 in B. van Oers and W. Wardekker (eds.) *De leerling als deelnemer aan de cultuur* (The Student as Participant in Culture). Delft, the Netherlands: Eburon.

Miedema, S. and G. Biesta (1996, in press). 'Democracy and Education: Are the Two Compatible?', in: D. Green (ed.) *The Practice of Education.* New York, NY: Castillo Press International.

Passerin d'Entrèves, M. (1992). 'Hannah Arendt and the Idea of Citizenship', pp. 145-68 in C. Mouffe (ed.) *Dimensions of Radical Democracy: Pluralism, Citizenship, Community.* London, UK/New York, NY: Verso.

Prins, W. (1992). 'Menselijkheid en de traditie van de politieke theorie' (Humaneness and the Tradition of Political Theory), pp. 70-82 in J. de Visscher, M. van den Bossche, and M. Weyemberg (eds.) *Hannah Arendt en de moderniteit* (Hannah Arendt and Modernity). Kampen, the Netherlands: Kok.

Rorty, R. (1991). *Objectivity, Relativism, and Truth: Philosophical Papers Volume 1.* Cambridge, UK: Cambridge University Press.

18   *Socialization for Moral Democracy*

Cees A. Klaassen

ABSTRACT

In the present debate on citizenship, little attention has been paid to our knowledge of the theory and practice of citizenship education. The discussion attempts to redefine the nature and quality of political life and stresses the need to develop a sense of sociocultural identity. This chapter attempts to link changing concepts of citizenship with traditions of political socialization and education. It discusses the call for and meaning of citizenship; describes citizenship and identity in a morally confused world; and revisits education for citizenship.

INTRODUCTION

Lately, the theme of 'citizenship' has received much attention in public debates in the East as well as in the West. Although there is a considerable intellectual tradition behind the idea of citizenship, there seems to be a reluctance for us to agree upon or to simply define what citizenship actually means. The same is true when it comes to the question: What does education for citizenship mean? Admittedly, this is not an easy task. The concept of citizenship is used in many different political discourses and belongs in the standard vocabulary of all sorts of politics and politicians. Another problem is the fact that we have not elaborated on the theory of democratic citizenship until recent debates on the citizenship theme suggested some radical changes in the nature of democratic citizenship here at the end of this century. For example, discussing citizenship seems to be a global concern. Citizenship is high on the political agenda not only of the new, but also of the old, democracies. This is the case because of recent problems regarding dismantling the welfare state, controlling immigration, protecting civil rights, and transforming formerly subject peoples into an active citizenry.

Redefining the meaning of citizenship undoubtedly will have important consequences for political socialization theory and research and for the practice of political education. However, it is not at all clear just what these consequences or their effects will be. At the moment, very few authors are writing about these important questions. There seem to be two separate intellectual lines: one leading the public debate on the changing notions of citizenship and civil society and the other concerning political socialization, education, and citizenship.

This chapter takes a few steps on the road to elaborating the political socialization consequences of reconceptualizing citizenship. Obviously, we also need to develop clearer interconnections between these two intellectual approaches. We need a new framework in which changing concepts of citizenship and the tradition of political socialization and education for citizenship are more closely linked. This chapter does not present a complete theory of citizenship, nor does it examine the historical development of the concepts of citizenship and civil society in a very systematic fashion. It only tries to highlight some of the most important aspects of the historical notions and practices of citizenship to illuminate some major contemporary ideas on the subject. Then, it explores the changing meanings of citizenship and their implications for democratic political socialization. It concludes with some theoretical considerations that may be used in developing a new theory of citizenship education that is consistent with the tenets of modern democratic citizenship in action.

INCREASING CALLS FOR CITIZENSHIP DIALOGUES

Why are so many people interested in citizenship nowadays? What causes so many politicians to be interested in the nature of citizenship in the contemporary world? Some of these different causes and relevant circumstances include the following factors:

♦ First of all, there is the worldwide globalization process which spurs a reconceptualization of citizenship because a transformation in the autonomous role of the national state has been proposed. Citizenship has been closely connected to the idea of the sovereign national state. At present, traditional notions and practices of citizenship are being challenged because international interdependence and new forms of international cooperation (such as intensified European integration) are being implemented. New forms of both regionalism and localism also question citizenship in its usual forms.

♦ A second causative factor is undermining the foundations and, consequently, dismantling the welfare state. Modern concepts of citizenship are also closely connected with the creation of the welfare state. For example, in Great Britain, Marshall (1977) has described the historical development of citizenship rights in relation to the growth of the welfare state. His concept of citizenship consists of three dimensions: civic, political, and social rights. In Western democracies, both the ideology and practice of the welfare state are being criticized. The growth of public spending, the accent on collectivism, the development of a dependence culture (where some citizens are dependent on state social services) are all under attack.

♦ The world-wide emphasis on markets and the development of a world economic system also invites a reconsideration of citizenship in light of the previous discussion. Changes in the social roles of the national state must be reconsidered, along with the idea of citizenship guaranteeing protection against the egoistic values of the market and mitigating the consequent problem of unequally distributed resources.

♦ The collapse of the command economies in Eastern Europe and the former Soviet Union is another important factor that has aroused interest in the notion of citizenship as a binding force in shaping new democracies. In many countries, there seems to be a need for a new form of social solidarity to fill the 'vacuum' since the former Communist Party system's collapse. Any new concept of citizenship must include ethnic, religious, and cultural differences and how to ensure civil rights, toleration, and minority safeguards. The goal is to institutionalize citizenship in the new social order, to internalize it, and to instill it in the minds and hearts of the people so that these new democracies will not be at risk. Alternative undemocratic ideologies, nationalistic chauvinism, right-wing extremism, and new forms of inequality, crime, and injustice are all waiting in the wings to fill this 'vacuum'.

♦ Other important factors behind the new citizenship dialogue are providing guarantees for human rights, acknowledging the rights of individual citizens to shape their own futures in multicultural societies, protecting refugees and stateless people, and developing a new nationalism (which has to be harmonized with democracy and with current concepts of citizenship). These factors are very popular with people espousing individualism and the morality of competition. Those worried about diminishing community feeling or social solidarity in societies where self-interest and competition predominate have also begun to take an interest in these discussions to provide an alternative viewpoint.

THE MEANING OF CITIZENSHIP

If citizenship is to become more than just a word, we must look at the historical development of its concepts and practices. The long and rich Western tradition of civil life and citizenship helps us to define citizenship. In ancient Greece, Aristotle already described a lack of consensus about this term, *Politeia*. In the Greek *polis*, citizenship referred to the relation between citizen and state. Aristotle defined a citizen as 'someone who participates in public affairs'. Citizenship was restricted to a small elite group of the (male) population. They shared some privileges and used a large group of noncitizens to undergird the economy. Citizens were freed of the burden of daily labor and had the right to possess material goods. Citizens took part in public service since this was a privilege for inhabitants of the city state. This elite group had to perform public service as politicians, judges, administrators, or soldiers. In Aristotle's view, the citizen had a dual role: he shared in ruling and was, himself, ruled. A citizen could fulfill his public obligation only if he shared in the common life of the political community. Important for our present conceptualization of citizenship is the fact that in ancient Greece, the citizen had rights and social status, combined with certain duties and the obligation to be loyal, not to one's fellow citizens, but to the city state. In sum, citizenship included loyalty, submission to authority, and obedience to the law.

Heater (1990) demonstrates that the Romans also had a combination of rights (privileges) and duties. Important for our present understanding is the fact that the Romans also made a distinction between public and private rights. For instance, public rights included the right to enlist in the army, to vote for the senate, and to be eligible for public service. Examples of private rights were the right to marry and to trade with other citizens. Links between the concept of citizen, certain geographic locations, and a certain exclusivity were also manifest during the Middle Ages. In those days, the term *citoyen* (*cité*) or *Bürger* (*Burcht*) was reserved exclusively for the inhabitants of a city. Of their own free will, they carried out specific duties and enjoyed certain rights. According to Heater (1990), it was not until the late Middle Ages (with the dawn of the nation state), that the term citizen become less exclusive. At that time, the concept of citizenship benefitted from its more egalitarian and cohesive character than is the case nowadays. Crucial for the concept of citizenship was the period of the great revolutions (French, American, and Industrial). During the French Revolution, the new *citoyen* enjoyed at birth the rights of *liberté, égalité et fraternité* along with the associated duties. This concept of citizenship was also very much oriented to group solidarity and national feelings. The common will (*volonté générale*) and love for one's country went hand in hand with the values of freedom and equality.

Important for our present discussion is the idea that one of the vital tasks for the school was citizenship education. This idea (already mentioned in the *Politeia*) was accentuated when revolutionary spirits like Rousseau and Condorcet wrote about it. The educational idea has never left the stage again as writings of Dewey (1916), Durkheim (1925), and Mannheim (1951) prove. Looking back at this history, we can conclude that the meaning of citizenship is just as problematic today as it was for our predecessors. It may be that key political concepts like citizenship need to be reconstructed for each time and generation. This present discussion attempts to redefine the nature and quality of political life using both older and newer reconceptualizations of citizenship (for example, Turner, 1993). Besides recognizing elements of collectivist views which date back to the 19th century (emphasizing solidarity, political participation, and mutual respect), one finds new viewpoints referring to the social process of individualization, the decline of the welfare state, the 'calculating' citizen, the effective consumer's behavior, and the search for market-based solutions to social problems (Steenbergen, 1991).

CITIZENSHIP AND IDENTITY IN A MORALLY CONFUSED WORLD

In 'postmodern' societies, the concern for the individual is increasing, whereas the relative importance of institutions (such as the family, social class, politics, or the local community) is gradually dwindling. The erosion of these traditional frameworks and an increasing pluralism in values and value systems are occurring simultaneously. It has become difficult for individuals to fall back on one fixed value system; people struggling with existential questions are now having to cope with divergent and conflicting traditions with which they are confronted in different social contexts. As individuals construct their own world, they position themselves somewhere in a multiform universe of opinions, values, and behaviors (Beck, 1992). These processes of individualization and differentiation of values do not occur everywhere at the same rate. In some Western countries, they manifest themselves more clearly than in others. Traditional institutions (such as social class, family, neighborhood, and government) are losing relevance as frames of reference for individuals, especially young citizens (Chisholm et al., 1990).

Around us, we see a state of moral anarchy, chaos, and confusion. The accepted verities that underlay the long-cherished beliefs in progress, instrumental rationality, and universal truths are daily questioned (Bauman, 1992). Universal moral and political principles are being criticized and deconstructed. They have been fiercely disputed. Cultural critics have also been trying to 'deconstruct' our common ways of thinking about ourselves and our world. The flattering self-image of the Western world, with continuing progress and modernity, has been undermined progressively.

These 'grand narratives' (Lyotard, 1984) are coming to an end. The Western philosophical systems about human nature, the foundations of knowledge and history, progress, and political ideologies are no longer taken for granted. Much of our supposed moral understanding falls to pieces as they are perceived as time-and-place-bound beliefs. Due to increasing social fragmentation and pluralism, familiar social relations and institutions are also rapidly changing (Hall et al., 1993). Our everyday environment and our interests are more and more determined in an environment which has no place and time restrictions. As a result of new information technologies which enable us to bridge large distances and time zones, local events and what happens elsewhere in the world are co-dependent. Indeed, the world is gradually becoming 'one global village'. As a result of modernization, globalization, and cultural pluralization, people now have a wider choice of ideas, norms, values, and behavioral patterns. If it holds anything in common, a society shares its ambivalence, contingency, and fragmentation.

A 'restoration' of the traditional concept of citizenship in late or postmodern society is not possible. The crisis in our cultural traditions and ways of thinking about ourselves must have important consequences for the aims and content of professionalized socialization in our schools. The 'taken-for-grantedness' of traditional self-responsibility and self-reflexivity have grown into indispensable competencies. The processes of individualization, fragmentation, and pluralization in postmodern societies require an increased individual self-responsibility for reconstructing one's own identity and for organizing one's personal biography.

At the same time, ideas about the individual subject are also susceptible to change (Jansen and Klaassen, 1994). This process does not guarantee a complete and closed unity which independently gives meaning to his/her life. Becoming a subject is a process which (because of one's dependence on other people) derives meaning from conflicting relations when confronted in various social contexts. The subject's construction of his/her own biography and identity may require a process of active involvement and assimilation. But this does not originate from, nor result in, fulfilling the needs of an 'authentic self'. After positioning the self in pluriform symbolic and material practices, one may produce subjectivity.

Self-production of identity does not mean the individual is 'free' to create frames of identification and orientation. He/she remains connected with the social categories and the interpretations of the world which jointly form his/her universe of material and symbolic reality. But the borders which cause the subject to identify with (narratives of) specific persons, groups, and communities and to distinguish himself/herself from others are no longer fixed. They are social constructions which do not provide the self with an unambiguous and definite image, from which the self originates and to which it belongs. Definitions enabling the subject to express similarities and differences with 'the other' and narratives which give direction to his/her existence, have become poly-interpretable, overlapping, and liable to change. This leads to the inevitability of personal stances and choices amidst a turmoil of alternatives.

There is no discrepancy between these developments and the overall tendency of increased nationalistic feelings, identification with historically grown regional and local traditions, or rejection of 'otherness'. This might be considered a reaction to the uncertainty of the present situation. Today, the processes of globalization are eroding the state's role as the ultimate protector. However, to many other people, the idea of an emotional identification with supra-state organizations is still a fiction (Elias, 1991). Globalization, fragmentation and separatism appear together because 'the nation-state has become "too small for the big problems of life"' (Giddens, 1990, p. 65).

Newly established social and political frames of reference are not the only starting points and criteria directing the modern search for identity. Age, race, and ethnicity also function as our frames of reference. However, all these frames of identification are temporary and partial. They continuously have to articulate their case against their competing frames. They also demand a conscious choice from the subject with regard to his/her own sociocultural identity. This identity is not *a priori* 'given', but is 'principally changeable', largely a matter of choice and not an integral, definitive identification. Identity is both a matter of 'being' and of 'becoming', of past and future, continuously subject to the permanent struggle in which history, culture, and power compete. Our identity forms a never-ending story. It is the ever-provisional result of the different and changing positions of one's self in narratives about the world.

Democratic citizenship stresses the need to develop a sociocultural identity which is oriented to the community and political system. This identity, including its sociopolitical orientations, is constantly recreated. Its hero is the self-actualizing individual. It does not originate from completely closed narratives of the self or from closed traditional political world views. Citizenship and identity are dynamic concepts and processes which necessitate continuous 'self-reflexivity' of the subject. This relationship between citizenship and identity can also be expressed through the mechanism of citizenship education.

EDUCATION FOR CITIZENSHIP REVISITED

If the concept of citizenship produces a diversity of meanings, the same is true about citizenship education. In the present debate on citizenship, little attention has been paid to our abundant knowledge of the theory and practice of citizenship education. To repeat, there seem to be two major, but separate, intellectual streams, each with a particular frame of reference and its different concept of citizenship.

The first and dominant aspect of this debate is the need for a person to develop a sense of identity. The meaning which the phrase 'education for citizenship' evokes has to do with one's personal and cultural identity. In a world which has individualizing and both globalizing and differentiating tendencies as major characteristics, individuals confront many different groups, organizations, communities, and relationships. The groups to which any person belongs are (to a greater or lesser extent) at variance with each other. Individuals always have to live with conflicting loyalties and competing demands. Meanwhile, they have to find their own way to discover their own identities. They must learn to live with conflicting expectations and within a climate of existential ambivalence.

The second meaning of 'education for citizenship' is very close in its concerns to the fields of political socialization and education. Political education in a public education system refers to the body of knowledge (curriculum) about processes, structures, and issues of political decision-making and to the knowledge relevant for understanding political life and culture. It also includes the preparation for the key political skills, such as participation. In many publications on political socialization and education as well as in many school curricula, citizenship is defined solely in political terms. In such a narrow conception of the subject, citizens also operate only in the political domain. As we have seen in the discussion of the history of the concept of citizenship, the separation of the political from the civic or social domain receives little support within the present debate regarding citizenship requisites. Instead, the essence of the present debate expands the citizenship concept to include 'additional arenas for democratic citizenship', such as sex-role egalitarianism, workplace democracy, and environmental concerns (Ichilov, 1990). In this broader definition of citizenship (which includes democratic political socialization practices), there is also place for participatory democracy in various other sociopolitical domains which are apart from representational democracy.

Of course, there are different models of democracy which may (more or less) stress the value of all citizens participating directly in public decision making. Common to all forms of democracy is the shared idea of some kind of citizen participation in public decision making and the necessity to consider a broad range of public choices. In this sense, democracy is 'moral'. It prescribes the moral principles to which any society (which claims to be democratic) should conform. It provides a moral basis for evaluating social relationships, political institutions, and cultural practices (Klaassen, 1993). Democracy, in this respect, is not only a political system, but also a state of mind of the citizens. It is also the political expression of the values of community, self-determination, and self-fulfillment, all of which may be expressed in the history of citizenship. In a 'moral' democracy, citizenship also has an ideal character. Citizenship means participating positively in reshaping society in such a way that existing rights and obligations of citizens will not only just be preserved, but also enhanced. New possibilities for their practical realization will be created and new ways will be developed to make them more widely available in different sociopolitical domains and environments.

Citizenship is a dynamic historical concept and process. The history of the concept reveals that it has always involved social struggle and political conflict so that its original Greek meanings have been gradually transformed. Our present conception of citizenship is largely the result of past struggles of social groups who were denied sufficient legal, social, and political equality. It is important for political socialization and education that there are no 'absolute' standards regarding the supposedly appropriate rights and duties of citizenship. Studying the history of citizenship shows us the transformation process whereby the demand for social justice and a more egalitarian social order has been gradually realized. Political education must not only look at the actual responsibilities and rights of citizenship, but also at its underlying dynamic aspects. This means that the concept of democratic citizenship must also reflect a moral ideal which, as such, can/will never be fully achieved.

Of course, education for citizenship and democracy involves learning factual knowledge and those fundamental concepts necessary to make complicated social and political matters intelligible to students. To improve the relationships among political facts, concepts, and structure of the learning process, more attention should be paid to organizing conceptual frameworks and factual knowledge with the help of principles derived from the psychology of learning and cognitive, developmental, and moral education research (Farnen, 1990). But education for citizenship is not only a matter of knowledge and insight, it is also concerned with the systematic encouragement of opinion formation and the development of certain basic attitudes (and training in certain skills). It is often claimed in discussions on this subject, that the more attention is paid to forming useless opinions in the classroom, the less attention will be paid to useful knowledge. However, an important condition for forming basic democratic attitudes is the appropriate emphasis on cognitive aspects in the educational setting. An attitude regarding an object presupposes both knowledge and the formation of an opinion. In other words, this means a judgement about the object as well as a willingness to act with regard to the object. Standards and values play an important role *vis-à-vis* our opinions and judgments. With respect to social and political problems and phenomena, different groups have various interests and opinions, founded on values and principles. Communicating about values presupposes that students must learn to check on information in a critical fashion for its reliability and consistency. It also implies a knowledge of other standards and values which different groups in a society may endorse. Education for citizenship means that students must be stimulated to form opinions of their own, to learn to answer questions, and to pose and discuss dilemmas.

CONCLUSIONS

Citizenship education has never been more demanding than it is today. We see a moral world in disarray around us (Klaassen, 1994). The diminishing personal bonds with traditional social groups and the declining significance of homogeneous (political) value systems and ideological frames of reference today provide individuals with more freedom of choice and decision. We discussed which norms and values may direct the behavior of the individual subject and which educational methods are required to stimulate students to manage political and ethic pluriformity. It was proposed that what is necessary today are methods that both stimulate students' mental processes and enlarge their involvement in values. We need effective value communication methods which treat political problems and conflicts with values and norms as educational topics. Thereby, students can be taught to test their opinions, feelings, and political considerations. Democracy and citizenship can only flourish in a society which contains a knowledgeable and informed citizenry capable of debating cultural politics and coherently expressing their informed political choices.

REFERENCES

Bauman, Z. (1992). *Intimations of Postmodernity*. London, UK and New York, NY: Routledge.

Beck, U. (1992). *Risk Society: Towards a New Modernity*. London, UK: Sage Publications.

Chisholm, L., P. Büchner, H. Krüger, and P. Holm (1990). *Childhood, Youth and Social Change: A Comparative Perspective*. London, UK; New York, NY; and Philadelphia, PA: The Falmer Press.

Dewey, J. (1916). *Democracy and Education*. New York, NY: Macmillan.

Durkheim, E. (1925 and 1961). *Moral Education*. New York, NY and London, UK: The Free Press.

Elias, N. (1991). *The Society of Individuals*. Oxford, UK: Blackwell Publishers.

Farnen, R. (1990). *Integrating Political Science, Education and Public Policy: International Perspectives on Decision-Making, Systems Theory and Socialization Research*. Frankfurt am Main, FRG; Bern, Switzerland; New York, NY; and Paris, France: Verlag Peter Lang.

Giddens, A. (1990). *The Consequences of Modernity*. Cambridge, UK: Polity Press.

Hall, S. et al. (1993). *Modernity and its Futures*. Oxford, UK: Blackwell Publishers.

Heater, D. (1990). *Citizenship: The Civic Ideal in World History, Politics and Education*. London, UK: Routledge.

Ichilov, O. (1990). *Political Socialization, Citizenship Education, and Democracy*. New York, NY and London, UK: Teachers College, Columbia University.

Jansen, T. and C. Klaassen (1994). 'Some Reflections on Individualization, Identity and Socialization', pp. 61-80 in P. Jarvis and F. Pöggeler (eds.) *Developments in the Education of Adults in Europe*. Frankfurt am Main, FRG and New York, NY: Verlag Peter Lang.

Klaassen, C. (1993). 'Education for Citizenship: The Pedagogical Mission of Social Studies Teaching', pp. 59-62 in M. van Riessen and K. Broekhof (eds.) *A Key to the World*. Utrecht and Antwerpen, the Netherlands: GEU-VUNB.

Klaassen, C. (1994). 'Socialization, Values and Citizenship', pp. 15-32 in G. Csepeli, D. German, L. Kéri, I. Stumpf (eds.) *From Subject to Citizen*. Budapest, Hungary: Hungarian Center for Political Education and Friedrich Nauman Stiftung.

Lyotard, J. (1984). *The Postmodern Condition*. Minneapolis, MN: University of Minnesota Press.

Mannheim, K. (1951). *Freedom, Power and Democratic Planning*. London, UK: Routledge and Kegan Paul.

Marshall, T. (1977). *Class, Citizenship and Social Development*. Chicago, IL and London, UK: University of Chicago Press.

Steenbergen, B. van. (ed.) (1991). *The Condition of Citizenship*. London, UK: Sage Publications.

Turner, B. (ed.) (1993). *Citizenship and Social Theory*. London, UK: Sage Publications.

19   *Democratic Citizen Competence*
Political-Psychological and Political Socialization Research Perspectives

Henk Dekker

ABSTRACT

Answering questions about democratic citizenship is an important part of current political discourse and political science research. In Western Europe and the US, the political discourse now includes issues arising from a growing individualization and emancipation at the individual level as well as diversification and pluralization on a national scale. National societies are becoming both more international and more regionalized. The growing scale of public life, the increasing complexity of public policy, the rising level of communications, and the declining political party attachment are all issues for discussion and debate. In Central and Eastern Europe, political discourse includes the question of how elites can build new democracies when the people there have little or no experience with democracy. Two other issues are how democratic citizenship competence can be encouraged and how Western European 'ethnic' and regional diversification tendencies can be managed. The following three questions are particularly absorbing for researchers interested in these topics: What is a democratic citizen? (conceptualizations), How democratic are citizens? (descriptions), and When, how, and as a result of what do citizens acquire democratic citizenship competence? (explanations). This chapter offers the results of a literature analysis as well as a new conceptualization and operationalization of democratic citizenship competence. It presents an explanatory model of how individuals acquire citizenship (answering the first question and taking a step toward answering the second and third questions).

CITIZENSHIP

In most publications, citizenship is a fourfold process: the society/community gives the individual certain rights, the individual has to fulfill certain social duties, the individual enjoys the rights which other individuals respect, and the individual has to fulfill certain duties toward these other individuals.

Rights and duties have several dimensions, which lead to several different types of citizenship. Six dimensions can be distinguished: social, economic, cultural, ecological, civil, and political. Social(-economic) rights and duties are considered part of 'social citizenship' (for example, the rights to housing, food, clothes, education, health care, jobs, membership in trade unions; and the duty to earn a living, be financially independent, respect private property, educate children, and perform one's job at a high level). Civil rights and duties belong to 'civil citizenship' (for example, the freedoms of speech, religion, and movement; equality before the law; and the duty to obey laws, pay taxes, defend the country/enroll for military conscription, serve the community through volunteer work, preserve the environment, and respect public property). Political rights and duties are considered part of 'political citizenship' (for example, the right to/freedom of political thought and conscience; right to form and join political organizations; freedom of assembly and expression; right to take part in the government directly or through freely chosen representatives; eligibility for public office; right to a fair trial; right of leaders to compete for votes; and the duties to vote, participate beyond voting, accept majority decisions, and respect the political rights of others). Here, political citizenship is the focal point of our interest.

Political citizenship is connected with political entities at the local (village, town, city), regional (region, province, or state in a [con]federation), national (country, state, or [con]federation of states), international (cooperation of states, for example, the Council of Europe; cooperation and integration of states, for example, the European Union or EU), and the world (for example, the UN) levels. Multiple citizenship includes citizenship on more than one level. As Heater said:

> The truly good citizen . . . is he who perceives this sense of multiple identity most lucidly and who strives most ardently in his public life to achieve the closest concordance possible between the policies and goals of the several civic levels of which he is a member (Heater, 1990, p. 326).

In this chapter, we shall focus on citizenship at the national level.

'Citizenship' is both a legal and a psychological concept. As a legal concept, it includes the legal status, rights, and duties of an individual, described in national and international constitutions, laws, and/or court decisions. Since citizenship and nationality are not synonymous, an individual can have a particular nationality but have lost his/her legal citizenship (as a result of declaring alternative citizenship, committing treason, and obtaining citizenship illegally). The psychological concept of citizenship refers to the whole of the cognitions, affections, intentions, and behaviors of individuals with respect to their positions as citizens. It includes the individual's knowledge, insights, beliefs, opinions, attitudes, (a hierarchy of) values, emotions, behavioral intentions, and behaviors. The foregoing apply with respect to those political entities of which he/she is a member, the relationship between him/her and those political entities, and one's individual rights and duties in these political entities.

At the core is one's behavior; other components are seen as more or less supporting behavior. We all now focus on the psychological concept of citizenship because of its basic importance.

Citizenship in the political-psychological (contrary to the legal) sense of the word is not an absolute condition. A distinction between people with and people without citizenship cannot easily be made. Rather, it has different (for example, minimal and advanced) levels. There is a scale ranging from 'very bad' to 'very good' citizens. The 'good citizen' is something of an ideal type. His/her characteristics (competence) vary with the values of those defining the construct. These characteristics are often disputed among political philosophers, politicians, and other citizens. The same is true of the 'democratic citizen'. It is an ideal type whose characteristics vary with the definition of democracy.

DEMOCRACY

Two dominant 'ideal types' have, to a large extent, influenced thinking about democracy. On the one hand, there are representative democracy theories; on the other, there are participatory democracy theories. Democracy is only one specific form of political system. The polar opposite of democracy is autocracy.

In representative democracy theories (for example, Schumpeter, 1943; Truman, 1951; Sartori, 1962; Bentley, 1967), politics is connected to the public domain and political authorities (that is, government and/or parliament). The concept is narrowly construed. Democratic theory should be empirical and should offer a realistic definition of democracy. The actual, limited political competence and participation of the different strata in society should be accepted as an empirical basis or starting point for what a democracy can and should be. Democracy is just a political method. In the words of Schumpeter (1943, p. 269), it is: 'That institutional arrangement for arriving at political decisions in which individuals acquire the power to decide by means of a competitive struggle for the people's vote.' Free elections are the key. Voting is the main and only political activity; however, information acquisition and discussion are precedents. It is primarily through elections that the citizens can exercise control over their political leaders. Citizens have the right to control their destiny (popular sovereignty) because of their right to be protected from those decisions which could hurt their private interests. The citizenry should have the ultimate right to replace unacceptable elite members. Political participation is restricted to the choice of decision-makers. Political equality means having an equal access to be involved in choosing political leaders. In arguing for a limited political role for a majority of citizens, it is claimed that every effective organization needs to have a ruling elite. There are serious drawbacks in the governmental process when the whole population is politically active. Furthermore, it is assumed that mass political participation could bring dangerous instability to the political system. The nonparticipating proportion of the population is also where high rates of nondemocratic or authoritarian attitudes prevail. A rise in political activity will bring this lower social-economic group into the political arena. Political participation of the masses should be limited in order to avoid outbursts of populist passions and public violence which would create a deeply divided society. Again, Schumpeter says, 'The electoral mass is incapable of action other than a stampede' (Schumpeter, 1943, p. 283). Sometimes, it is also said that political issues are too complex for most people to understand. Nowadays, in Western Europe, the representative democracy theories seem to be dominant. As Pateman said:

> . . . in the contemporary theory of democracy it is the participation of the minority elite that is crucial and the non-participation of the apathetic, ordinary man lacking in the feeling of political efficacy, that is regarded as the main bulwark against instability (Pateman, 1979, p. 104).

Participatory democracy theories (for example, Rousseau, 1968 edition; Barber, 1984) have the following fundamental elements. Politics includes all social life and thus is not limited to formal government. It is an all-inclusive phenomenon. Politics take place wherever conflicts happen, decisions are made, and power is involved. Citizen participation is directed toward making decisions. It includes political activity beyond voting (such as posting placards, distributing handouts, signing one's name to a petition, taking part in a demonstration, getting involved in a political party or organization, participating in a referendum, and being a member of a protest or interest group). Political equality refers to equality of power and influence in making such decisions. Authority structures must be democratized in all areas of life. Individuals are expected to generalize their experiences in nongovernmental authority structures to the wider, local, regional, national, and international spheres of politics. Maximum popular political participation is desirable because (with practice) people can develop very positive political qualities. Through political participation, the individual can develop his/her democratic 'character' and his/her overall identity. Moreover, better decisions will be made and implemented. Shared decisions will mean shared responsibility and greater acceptability for the entire citizenry. The individual will be more integrated in his/her community through a stronger feeling of belonging. Discredited elected politicians can always be removed or replaced. Explosions of violence resulting from pent-up wrath can be avoided. Since many political decisions are actually moral decisions, there is no reason to believe that political leaders are more capable of sounder public judgements than are ordinary citizens. Participation should take place wherever politics are present, particularly in settings where individuals spend most of their time (that is, in the schools, workplaces, and local communities) (Cole, 1920). As Almond and Verba said, opportunities to 'participate in decisions at one's place of work' are of 'crucial significance' for the development of the sense of political efficacy. And, continuing, 'the structure of authority at the workplace is probably the most significant - and salient - structure of that kind with which the average man finds himself in daily contact' (Almond and Verba 1963, p. 294). Mill had high expectations with respect to local democracy, saying: 'Where local government allows participation, it may foster a sense of competence that then spreads to the national level' (Mill, 1965, p. 145). The more citizens participate politically, the more democratically competent they will become. Stability of the democratic system is thereby guaranteed as an educational consequence of political participation. The citizens' ensuing perception of the political system will be more legitimate and they will believe they have more control over their lives.

The differences between representative and participatory democracy theories regarding basic elements and assumptions are presented through key words in Table 19.1. It includes certain additions to a scheme which Farnen (1993) had proposed in an earlier publication.

In political philosophy, the concept of democracy is continuous. Also, in practice, countries have different degrees of democracy. One country may even have different degrees of democracy at different periods of time. Indicators for measuring the level of democracy in empirical studies relate to political structure, the individuals' political rights/liberties, and one's political culture. Political structural indicators include, for example, the level of separation of powers. Political rights/liberties indicators provide evidence about 'the extent to which the political power of the elites is minimized and that of the nonelites is maximized' (Bollen, 1990, p. 9). Political cultural indicators provide evidence about the level of democracy at the level of civil society (for example, media pluralism) and the individual citizens (for example, their democratic orientations and behaviors).

DEMOCRATIC CITIZENSHIP

Democracy and citizenship are often seen as going hand in hand (Almond and Powell, 1988; and Fukuyama, 1993). Both sets of democracy theories assume a relationship between the development of a democratic political system (establishment, growth, maintenance, and evolution) and a democratic citizenship. Three empirical results stem from this relationship. First, the political system and its elites influence the democratic citizenship orientations and behaviors of the masses. Democratic citizenship reflects or follows the political system's characteristics as well as elites' decisions. Second, citizenship affects the political system as well as its elites and their decisions. And third, the political system and citizenship are interdependent. The survival of a political system and its elites depends on the existence of some degree of demonstrable, popular, and public support. Political elites' decisions also coincide to a certain degree with their constituents' opinions, preferences, and attitudes. In the event of divergent preferences, political elites do their best to influence citizens' orientations and behaviors (that is, to persuade others to adopt their preferences and views). One may say that the first empirical approach mentioned previously is in conflict with the set of representative as well as the set of participatory democracy theory elements. By contrast, the second and third approaches parallel participatory democracy theories or representative democracy theories respectively.

Table 19.1 Representative and participatory democracy theories: comparing basic elements and assumptions

		Representative Democracy Theories	Participatory Democracy Theories
1.	Politics includes	Political authorities Public domain	All social life
2.	Democracy	Method Right to replace un- acceptable elite members Free elections	Decision-making and involvement in outcomes
3.	Key word	Voting	Participation
4.	Focus	Select decision makers	Make decisions
5.	Participation	In elections	Wherever politics is (for example, local communities, schools, and workplaces)
6.	Political equality	Equality of eligibility	Equality of power and in- fluence in decision-making
7.	System stability through	Elite rule	Mass participation; decisions are educa- tional, publicly accept- able, and integrate indi- viduals socially
8.	System instability through	Mass participation	Elite rule
9.	Theory based on	Empirical basis	Values
10.	Democracy and citizen efficacy are	Not completely compatible	Compatible

The two different sets of theories about democracy assume different sets of political rights, duties, and roles for citizens behaving as the ruled or rulers. 'Representative democracy' or 'contractual' citizenship conceptions (Conover et al., 1990) have at their core a strong conception of individualism and individual rights. Citizens are seen as autonomous individuals who make choices, are bound together, share a social and political contract, and are more than just friends and neighbors united in some common activities. The 'calculating citizen' uses his rights and fulfills her duties/responsibilities, not from a moral or ideological obligation, but since it serves his/her own interests. Political participation is mainly instrumental and primarily serves private interests rather than a common good or personal self-development. Preference at elections is expected to be based primarily on the perceived qualities of political leaders. Rights are emphasized and interpreted in terms of protection for the individual (against interference from government or society) to preserve his/her autonomy. Duties are usually relegated to the background because they constitute obligations that restrict one's freedom. One's identity as a citizen involves identification, not with a community of people, but instead with the abstract category of being a 'legal citizen', the bearer of rights. The perception of human nature here is relatively negative.

'Participatory democracy' or 'communal' citizenship conceptions (Conover et al., 1990) have at their core a conception of citizens who are not so much autonomous individuals making private choices, but instead, who are social and political human beings whose lives are intertwined with those of their neighbors and friends, who share common traditions and understandings, and who pursue certain common goals. A 'good' democratic citizen is one who so orders his/her political life that at least a part of it is consciously directed to the benefit of the community in which he/she lives. Citizen engagement in public activities results from common traditions, understandings, and goals, as well as from what people share together. Citizens not only have the right to participate in politics, but also are expected to do so for the sake of themselves as well as the community. Preference at elections (for a particular political party/movement) and other political choices are expected to be based primarily on class or party identification, issue awareness, and conceptions of the public good. Individual rights are regarded as contextually defined and take second place. Duties are obligations which are welcomed rather than scorned; in fact, they are advocated. Citizens' activities have also much to do with their personal identities. Citizens identify themselves with a community of people and, in its most developed form, have a sense of collective consciousness about the meaning of that identity, resulting in an encumbered sense of self. The perception of human nature is relatively positive; human kind is naturally good, exhibits altruism and empathy, and reflects a willingness to accept personal and group responsibilities.

The major differences between representative and participatory democracy citizenship conceptions regarding their basic elements and assumptions are presented (using key words) in Table 19.2. It includes additions to a previously published scheme which Farnen (1994) proposed.

Table 19.2 Major differences between representative and participatory democracy citizenship concepts

		Representative Democracy: Citizenship Concepts	Participatory Democracy: Citizenship Concepts
1.	Core	Individualism	Communitarianism
2.	Human nature is	Autonomous	Social and political
3.	Human nature is valued	Negatively; man is naturally bad	Positively; man is naturally good
4.	Individuals are	Bound together by contract	Intertwined with neighbors, friends; united by common activity
5.	Motivation	One's own interest; protection against interference from state and society	One's own and community's sake; pursuit of common political goals
6.	Individual rights are	Emphasized; placed in foreground	Contextually defined; placed in background
7.	Individual duties are	Restrictions on freedom; negative; placed in background	Part of social responsibility; positive; placed in foreground
8.	Individual identity	As a legal citizens; bearers of rights	With a community of people
9.	Participatory activities is level main purpose	Voting A right Limited Safeguard one's private interest and autonomy	Voting and others A right and duty Maximum/unlimited For one's own and the community's sake; and better decisions; help develop one's democratic competence
10.	Choice of political leaders is based on	Perceived qualities of elite candidates	Class or party identification, issue awareness, the public good
11.	Ideal citizen is	Voter	Decision-maker

DEMOCRATIC CITIZENSHIP COMPETENCE

Each of the two sets of democratic citizenship concepts described previously requires a certain level of competence from the citizenry. Because of differences in the scope and intensity of the desirable level of political participation, the two sets of democratic citizenship conceptions differ in the requirements citizens have to satisfy in terms of democratic citizenship competence. Specific indications of these requirements are (in most cases) relatively general. Therefore, it is not really possible to outline these different requirements for each of the democratic citizenship concepts as was done in Tables 19.1 and 19.2. The specific requirements (and their antitheses) which we found in relevant literature are accordingly listed randomly in Table 19.3.

Following Dahl's (1992) proposal to seek a 'good-enough' citizenship competence level, we selected orientations that may be considered as sufficient or minimum democratic competence requirements (see Table 19.4). The selection was limited to political democracy in a strict sense (democracy in the political system, excluding democracy in other systems, such as the educational and economic institutions/systems). It was based on the points of convergence of the ideal type democracy and democratic citizenship competence theories. In the future, it would be preferable to base such a selection not only on theory but also on empirical findings. Consequently, we have planned to investigate what citizens, themselves, think a 'good' democratic citizen is (for example, what his/her cognitions, affections, intentions, and behaviors are and should be) (Theiss-Morse, 1993).

The first point of convergence is that (ideally) citizens should be informed about politics in order to make (better) decisions. The second point is that (ideally) citizens should be supportive of democracy. The third point is that (ideally) they should have a preference with respect to political actors (parties, personalities) and policy options. The fourth point is that (ideally) citizens should be active in elections (or have this intention) as a voter and/or candidate.

EXPLANATION

How do individuals acquire (or not acquire) democratic citizenship competence? Many studies have revealed that political (in)competence in general is not found in roughly equal proportions in all countries. Differences in political (in)competence were related to differences between the political (and economic and educational) systems of these countries. Democratic citizenship does not exist in a political, economic, and social vacuum. It is closely connected with political, economic, and social circumstances. Unequal political rights, differing resource levels, and social-economic inequalities undermine equality of citizen competence.

Also, within individual countries, differences in political competence exist. Differences may be observed between young and old, boys/men and girls/women, people with different states of health, highly- and less-highly-educated people, those with different social-economic positions, and cultural or 'ethnic' majorities and minorities.

Table 19.3 Major components of democratic citizenship competence and their antitheses

Democratic political competence/positive	Antitheses/negatives
Having knowledge of/insights into conceptions of/about democracy; democratic citizenship; political systems (of one's own state); human rights; actual democratic rights and duties of citizens; major actual political problems and controversies; political parties, pressure, and interest groups; issue positions of political parties/candidates; political leaders; participation opportunities and their limitations in various phases of policy development (preparation, decision, implementation, evaluation).	Political ignorance
Holding beliefs, opinions concerning: democracy; democratic citizenship; political systems (of one's own country); main actual political problems and controversies; political parties, leaders, and candidates; importance of elected institutions.	
Holding the following attitudes: acceptance of human equality in politics; attachment to democracy; supportive of political freedoms and competitive party system; democratic self-identification; acceptance of democratic rules and political protest; attitude toward political leaders; openness to other opinions/information; tolerance of views divergent from one's own; political self-confidence; political interest (including actual major political issues and processes); political efficacy; political satisfaction; political trust; political party identification/attachment; left-right self-identification; ideological self-identification; moderation/non-extremism; feelings of national solidarity and of 'connectedness' with fellow nationals; national pride; positive acceptance of ethnic minorities (toleration and empathy); acceptance of foreign countries and peoples; and internationalism.	Intolerance, political indifference, political fatalism, political distrust, political cynicism
Holding the following values: democracy, freedom, equality, solidarity, tolerance, and nonviolence.	National alienation, nationalism, radicalism; ethnic stereotyping; xenophobia; racism; national stereotyping; anti-other country attitudes
Expressing one's desire/intention for: acquiring political information via mass media; talking about and discussing politics among relatives and friends; questioning information, views, policies; advancing reasons for one's own opinions; changing opinions in case of contrary evidence/argument; selecting political representatives based on who best approximates one's own policy preferences (for the common good); voting; becoming a member of a political party/movement or one-issue group(s); participation beyond voting; becoming a member of a government or parliament; settling differences in nonviolent ways.	

Table 19.3 (continued)

Democratic political competence/positive	Antitheses/negatives
Behaviors, such as: watching political news on television; reading political information; talking about and discussing politics among relatives and friends; voting; membership in a political party/movement or one-issue group(s); participation beyond voting; settling differences in nonviolent ways	Political apathy; violent conflict solution

Table 19.4 Basic democratic citizenship competence

Having the following cognitions:
. Democracy conception
. Democratic citizenship conceptions
. Knowledge of the political system
. Knowledge of political issues

. Positive democratic beliefs
. Positive democratic citizenship beliefs
. Knowledge of political actors (parties and personalities)

Having the following opinions/preferences:
. Support for democracy
. Party/leader/candidate preferences

. Importance of elected institutions

Holding the following attitudes:
. Attachment to democracy
. Supportive of political freedom

. Democratic self-identification

Having the following value:
. Democracy

Having the following intentions/willingness to:
. Vote
. Be a candidate for/member of a representative body

. Be a member of a political party

Political behavior:
. Voting
. Membership in a political party

. Candidate/member for/of a representative body

Age (and each phase of life, for example, childhood, adolescence, young adulthood, mid-life, the young elderly, and the elderly) is an important variable. It is linked to variables such as physiological and psychological (needs) development, cognitive development (ability to conjure with remote and abstract concepts), motivational development (interest in collective realities outside the family, the street, and the neighborhood), moral development, social contacts, social pressures, and social and political experiences. Changes in physiological and psychological needs relate to social expectations and requirements. Identity crises (which are present in all humans from infancy through old age, but in adolescents, par excellence) may facilitate more than otherwise the acquisition of new political orientations or a change in orientations acquired earlier.

Gender is an important variable for political competence. Girls are clearly less interested in politics. Fewer girls than boys say they would like to have the right to vote. Fewer young girls say they would vote if made eligible to do so. The usual explanation is sex role socialization, resulting in a situation in which girls (women) see politics as a male domain because it is a process which unfolds outside the house. They are supposedly more interested in personal (rather than impersonal) issues and are less attracted to the conflict-laden atmosphere and hefty discussions which are typical of politics. The weak political competence of a large number of mothers allegedly strengthens these orientations. Other intervening variables are educational level (in some societies, if not in the US, girls are less likely to complete higher levels of education) and whether or not older girls and women work outside the home.

The social-economic position of the individual is also an important variable. The higher the social-economic position, the greater the political knowledge, the more highly developed the political interest, and the more extensive the level of political participation. In general, individuals with a higher social-economic position have enjoyed more (and a higher level of) education. They have more political information (because of their reading habits, travel experiences, friendship patterns, and leisure activities) and are more familiar with decision-making processes (as a result of their social activities). And this helps them to acquire politically relevant knowledge of political skills and behavioral habits. They acquire more politically relevant attitudes (for example, self-confidence) and, finally, feel that they have more to lose because of their higher social-economic positions.

There is also a strong correlation between the level of education and political competence. The higher the level of education, the more extensive the political competence. An intervening variable is the level of education which a survey respondent's parents achieved. This is an important factor which, in part, determines whether or not an individual completes a higher level of education.

The previously mentioned explanations for the influence of the system's and individual's variables indicate that they are not more than background variables. (This may also be the reason for the low percentages of explained variance of electoral participation in most of the studies reviewed, where these variables serve as explanatory variables).

The main influence must come from something else. Democratic citizens are not born. There are no democratic genes. Thus, the question of how democratic citizens are 'made' arises. Our answer is that democratic citizenship competence comes from one's political socialization. Political socialization indicates the meeting of the individual and politics; it links the political system and general individual variables to political individual orientations and behaviors. Democratic citizenship competence is an effect (intended or unintended) of political socialization. Differences in democratic citizenship competence may be explained if we look to differences in democratic citizenship socialization patterns, practices, and processes.

Political socialization is the whole of those structures and processes through which individuals and groups acquire their political orientations. Direct socialization involves the acquisition of orientations which are specifically political in nature. Indirect socialization involves orientations which are not (in themselves) political, but which exert influence on the subsequent acquisition of specific political orientations (for example, personal self-efficacy -> subjective political efficacy). Explaining differences in (or the absence of) democratic citizenship competence calls for an examination of the political socialization agencies and the contents and designs of their messages (socialization structures). We must also examine the way in which these messages are received and how the individual processes them (socialization processes).

Socialization occurs in the context of a particular political (and economic) system. In all political systems, there is a conscious or unconscious attempt to transfer political knowledge, insights, beliefs, opinions, preferences, attitudes, values, emotions, and behavioral intentions and patterns from one generation to the next. Without some regularity and consistency in the transfer and adoption of these orientations, there would not be any stability in the political culture and political structure.

Several different agencies of socialization are active. The first agency is family. For example, there is a positive correlation between a high score on political efficacy scales and (remembered) opportunities to participate in the family. Opportunities to participate are more frequently provided in middle-class families. Working-class families tend to offer fewer such opportunities or exhibit no consistent pattern. This class difference in childrearing may, in turn, influence the low participatory levels of the fathers. Other agencies include church, schools, mass communications media, peer groups, workplaces, and political and public administrative agencies, structures, and processes. Socialization through the previously listed agencies is, in turn, influenced by the dominant subsystems of the society and political (and economic, cultural, and intellectual) elites. Within the different agencies of socialization are various socializers (that is, persons, groups, institutions, organizations, objects, and events) which contribute to the individual's socialization. The individual agencies (and the socializers within them) possess some relative autonomy. Research has been relatively unsuccessful in determining the relative influence of the various agencies and socializers. The main methodological problem is the difficulty in isolating them in a research design. Agencies function concurrently, are linked to one another, influence one another, and function within different political and social-economic substructures and subcultures. Moreover, in many situations, it is difficult to find a control group. For example, in the Netherlands, the social and political education course is compulsory; as a result, no control group of pupils without such a social and political education can be included in any pre- and post-test.

Related to the various socialization agencies (and, within them, the various socializers) are the several different socialization processes (that is, the individual's political 'learning' processes). There are several different theories about how individuals acquire political cognitions, affections, intentions, and behavioral habits. Basically, there are three types of political socialization processes. Namely, individuals acquire political orientations through their own experiences and observations (how democracy works or does not work in the family, church, schools, youth organizations, workplaces, army, political meetings, and political events, such as demonstrations); through intermediated observations from others (such as parents, deacons/priests/ministers, teachers, and journalists); and through internal psychological processes of the individual him/herself (such as developing a belief through joining the object of the belief with particular characteristics; developing an attitude through joining beliefs with values or through elaborating an earlier developed attitude; or developing an intention through joining an attitude with an impression of social norms and control). The more fundamental and more amorphous the political orientations, the earlier in life they seem to be acquired. Primary agencies of socialization (family, church, primary school, and television) have more influence on affections; the secondary agencies (secondary school, newspaper) have more influence on cognitions. After having received the most rudimentary information, the emotional component of attitudes is developed before the elaboration of the cognitive component (growth in factual knowledge and insights); affective learning has precedence over cognitive learning and is, as a result of that, more resistant to change. Socialization in childhood does not determine the political orientations of adolescents and adults. However, it is plausible to expect a strain toward consistency. This persistence hypothesis is one of the dominant themes within political socialization research. However, recently published critical reviews of political socialization research subject this former consensus to scientific debate. There are periods in the lives of adults when they change their political beliefs and attitudes. Such periods are ones in which significant alterations take place in personal circumstances (for example, marriage, divorce, having children, children leaving home, serious illness, becoming unemployed, retirement, death of immediate family, and so forth), making previously acquired political opinions, attitudes, and behavioral intentions inadequate or of marginal importance for dealing with the new situation. An important change in the social, economic, and political spheres (for example, large-scale unemployment, a stock exchange crash, civil war, revolution, or military occupation of one country by another) can be the immediate cause for alterations in political orientations as well.

In summary, determinants of democratic citizenship competence are outlined in Table 19.5.

Behavioral intentions and the behavior, itself (in general), and the intention to vote (in particular) may be seen as the most relevant elements of democratic citizenship competence. We hypothesize that the best determinants of the intent to vote within a given political system are: political knowledge (knowledge of the body to be elected, the candidates, and the issues); political interest; importance attributed to the body to be elected; party preference/attachment; candidate preference; democratic self-identification; and political efficacy, as well as attitudes about voting (for the body to be elected). Also relevant (for women) is the opinion about emancipation of women. Relevant messages which parents, school, and television pass on are influential. Democratic citizens do not grow out of thin air. Democratic citizenship competence is not inherited. Since it is acquired, democratic behavior is learned.

Political socialization research has not been able to determine completely the relative importance of the various factors and the interactions between/among them for developing various individual democratic citizenship orientations and behaviors in different periods of life (childhood, adolescence, young adulthood, mid-life, young elderly, and elderly). It will be a challenge to contribute to making some real progress in this regard.

FUTURE RESEARCH

The goal of future research into democratic citizenship competence should be to test this explanatory model of democratic citizenship competence acquisition. Questions that should be focussed upon include: At what age do children acquire their first cognitions, affections, and intentions with respect to democracy? What stages do individuals follow in the acquisition of democracy cognitions, affections, and intentions? How do democratic cognitions, affections, and intentions change over time in the different periods of life (childhood, adolescence, young adulthood, mid-life, young elderly, and elderly)? What are the relations among these cognitions, affections, and intentions? What are the best determinants of the intentions or behaviors?

Several previous studies have developed valid and reliable indicators for many of these variables. For example, these studies include the 'Eurobarometer' (Commission of the European Communities, twice a year since 1973), 'Cultural Changes in the Netherlands' (Dekker and Ester, 1993), the 'Dutch Parliamentary Election Studies' (van Holsteyn and Irwin [eds.], 1992), and the 'World Values Survey' (Inglehart, 1992). Explanatory system variables data may be derived from existing data sets (from, among others, the US State Department and Amnesty International) or may be collected using indicators which Bollen (1990) proposed or Gastil's Comparative Survey of Freedom (1990), or

Gasiorowski's Political Regimes Project (1990). Through combining previously used indicators and adding new ones, we developed a new set of indicators for the major components of democratic citizenship competence and for the individual's and socialization's variables named above to be used in our future studies. They are named in the appendix later in this chapter in alphabetical order. Their validities have to be tested in future empirical studies.

Table 19.5 Explanatory variables

System variables:
. Political system: political rights/freedoms; political duties/obligations
. Economic system variables

Individual variables:
. Personal characteristics of the individual, including gender, age, and health self-assessment
. Social characteristics of the individual, including level of education, social-economic status (of parents), (not) living in urbanized area, country of birth, and national-ity/'ethnicity'
. Nonpolitical (but politically relevant) orientations, including religiosity, religious affiliation, self-confidence, self-efficacy, fatalism, attitudes toward those in authority (parents, teachers, clergy), motivation for learning and achieving, fear of failure, social ambition, rejection or acceptance of traditional men and women's roles, worry about the general economic outlook for one's own country
. Other political orientations and behavioral patterns, including political satisfaction, left-right ideological self-identification, materialism/postmaterialism, political interest, political efficacy, political institutions confidence, political self-confidence, political actors trust, political party identification/attachment, worry about the political outlook for one's own country; radicalism, national attitude (national feeling, liking, pride, preference, superiority, and nationalism)

Socialization variables:
. One's own experiences with democracy (democracy experiences);
. Democratic education and political education in general from parents and other relatives, church, school, peers, and mass media; and so forth. Relevant aspects are
  . Reading political information, listening to political programs on radio, watching political items on television, talking/discussing politics with friends
  . Content of information received (in the perception of the individual being socialized)

Obviously, a cross-national, longitudinal panel study is the best method to use when we aim to describe and explain long-term developments in citizens' political orientations. Longitudinal political socialization/citizenship studies are extremely limited in number. Several studies have indicated that direct political socialization starts at a very young age. If we are to understand the development of political orientations and the relative influence of socialization agencies and socializers, we must begin at the earliest possible moment to study citizens, perhaps even by age four. Already, by this time, parents have lost their monopoly over the education of their children and are forced to share it with the school and television. Clearly, any research for young age groups (that is, ages 4, 6, and 8) will pose problems of measurement that must be solved. Considerable pretesting will be necessary to get an idea of what can be asked at what age and how it can be phrased. Children may be interviewed individually using half-open interviews, drawings, photos, and video material as the studies done in the past have suggested (Coles, 1986). When dealing with somewhat older children (that is, ages ten and 12), it may be possible to ask them to write a short essay (about democracy or being a 'good' democratic citizen) in addition to half-open interviews. Such essays can be analyzed in connection with the key variables listed above. Older youngsters (age 14 and older) and adults may be asked to fill out a questionnaire, including the questions listed in the appendix.

The overall question is: When, how, and as a result of whom and/or what, do individuals with which characteristics acquire what democratic citizenship competence and what are the determinants of this competence? Understanding how children, youngsters, and adults develop cognitions, affections, and behavioral intentions with respect to democracy will, perhaps, help us better understand what role citizens can and will play in present and future democratic societies.

ACKNOWLEDGEMENT

Parts of this chapter were published and critiqued earlier in 1992 and 1994. I would like to thank Rudy Andeweg, Galen Irwin, Louk Hagendoorn, Russell Farnen, and Malcolm Cross for their comments on earlier versions of this essay.

REFERENCES

Almond, G. and S. Verba (1963). *The Civic Culture*. Princeton, NJ: Princeton University Press. Also (1965). Boston, MA: Little, Brown & Co.

Almond, G. and G. Powell, Jr. (1988). *Comparative Politics Today: A World View*. Glenview, IL: Scott, Foresman, and Company.

Barber, B. (1984). *Strong Democracy: Participatory Politics for a New Age*. Berkeley, CA: University of California Press.

Bentley, A. (1908, 1967). *The Process of Government*. Cambridge, MA: Harvard University Press.

Bollen, K. (1990). 'Political Democracy: Conceptual and Measurement Traps', pp. 7-24 in *Studies in Comparative International Development*, Vol. 25, No. 1.

Bruszt, L. and J. Simon (1992). *Political Culture and Political and Economic Orientations in Central and Eastern Europe during the Transition to Democracy: The Codebook of the International Survey of Ten Countries*. Budapest, Hungary: Hungarian Academy of Sciences, Institute for Political Science.

Cole, G. (1920). *Social Theory*. London, UK: Methuen. Quoted in Pateman, 1979.

Coles, R. (1986). *The Political Life of Children*. Boston, MA: Houghton Mifflin.

Conover, P., I. Crewe, and D. Searing (1990). *Conceptions of Citizenship Among British and American Publics: An Exploratory Analysis*. Essex papers in politics and government, no. 73. Essex, UK: University of Essex, Department of Government.

Dahl, R. (1992). 'The Problem of Civic Competence', pp. 45-60 in *Journal of Democracy*, Vol. 3, No. 4.

Dekker, P. and P. Ester (1993). *Social and Political Attitudes in Dutch Society: Theoretical Perspectives and Survey Evidence*. The Hague, the Netherlands: VUGA.

Farnen, R. (1994). 'Political Decision Making and Problem Solving Education: American and Cross-National Perspectives', pp. 129-52 in S. Miedema et al. *The Politics of Human Science*. Brussels, Belgium: VUB Press.

Fukuyama, F. (1993). 'Capitalism and Democracy: The Missing Link', pp. 2-7 in *Dialogue*, Vol. 100, No. 2 (reprinted from *Journal of Democracy*, July 1992. Washington, DC: National Endowment for Democracy).

Gasiorowski, M. (1990). 'The Political Regimes Project', pp. 109-25 in *Studies in Comparative International Development*, Vol. 25, No. 1.

Gastil, R. (1990). 'The Comparative Survey of Freedom: Experiences and Suggestions', pp. 25-50 in *Studies in Comparative International Development*, Vol. 25, No. 1.

Heater, D. (1990). *Citizenship: The Civic Ideal in World History, Politics and Education*. London, UK: Longman.

Inglehart, R. (1977). *The Silent Revolution, Changing Values and Political Styles among Western Publics*. Princeton, NJ: Princeton University Press.

Inglehart, R. (1992). 'Changing Values in Industrial Society: The Case of North America, 1981-1990.' pp. 1-30 in *Politics and the Individual*, Vol. 2, No. 2.

Mill, J. (1965). *Collected Works*. J. Robson (ed.). Toronto, Canada: University of Toronto Press.

Pateman, C. (1979). *Participation and Democratic Theory*. Cambridge, UK: Cambridge University Press.

Rousseau, J. (1968 edition). *The Social Contract*. Harmondsworth, UK: Penguin.

Sartori, G. (1962). *Democratic Theory*. Detroit, MI: Wayne State University Press.

Schumpeter, J. (1943). *Capitalism, Socialism and Democracy*. New York, NY: Harper and Row; London, UK: Allen & Unwin.

Sigel, R. and M. Hoskin (1977). 'Perspectives on Adult Political Socialization, Areas of Research', pp. 259-93 in S. Renshon (ed.) *Handbook of Political Socialization: Theory and Practice*. New York, NY and London, UK: The Free Press.

Theiss-Morse, E. (1993). 'Conceptualizations of Good Citizenship and Political Participation', pp. 355-69 in *Political Behavior*, Vol. 15, No. 4.

Truman, D. (1951). *The Governmental Process*. New York, NY: Knopf.

van Holsteyn, J. and G. Irwin (eds.) (1992). *De Nederlandse Kiezer 1989* (The Netherlands Voters 1989). Amsterdam, the Netherlands: Steinmetzarchief, Swidoc, Skon.

Weissberg, R. (1974). *Political Learning, Political Choice, and Democratic Citizenship*. Englewood Cliffs, NJ: Prentice-Hall.

APPENDIX

The indicators are in alphabetical order and include the following variables as well as how the variable could be measured (in parentheses):

Acceptance of political protest (multi-item scale) - condoning sit-down demonstrations, disapproving of demonstrators being arrested or dismissed, disapproving of police breaking up demonstrations, condoning occupation of schools, and condoning occupation of companies.

Candidate for or member of representative body (single-item question) - (not) being a candidate or member.

Democracy as an important value (multi-item scale) - selecting democracy as one of the five most important things in life out of 12 choices (freedom, equality, peace, nice family, good health, a lot of free time, a happy marriage, enjoyable work, high income, many friends and acquaintances, a strong faith, and democracy); selecting being a democrat as one of the five most important qualities which children should be encouraged to learn at home out of a list of 12 choices (good manners, unselfishness, independence, determination, obedience, imagination, willing to work hard, interest in politics, knowledge about politics in [respondent's country], knowledge of foreign politics, being a democrat).

Democracy attachment (multi-item scale) - being strongly in favor of democracy; thinking that democracy is important for respondent to do something about, even if this might involve giving up other things; thinking that democratization offers hope for the future.

Democracy conception (multi-item question) - 'Can you write down five characteristics of a good democracy?' and 'People associate democracy with several different meanings such as those that I will mention. For each of them, please tell me whether, for you, democracy has a lot, something, not much or nothing to do with: political liberties, greater social equality, decisions on the (local) lowest level, less corruption, safeguarding fundamental human rights, freedom in moral matters, equal justice, equal rights for women, more jobs, less unemployment, access to health care, elimination of privileges, pluralistic public debate, improvement of economy, multiparty system' (Bruszt and Simon, 1992).

Democracy education perception (multi-item question) - indicating (not) having had democracy education by the listed several different socializers ('Where have you learned and do you mainly learn what you know about democracy?') and the intensity of influence of the selected democracy socializers ('Where have you mainly learned and do you mainly learn what you know about democracy and the problems and challenges it has to deal with?').

Democracy experiences (multi-item, open-ended question) - 'Can you write down how good or bad your experiences are or were with democracy at your parents' home, in school, at your workplace, and in your local community?'

Democracy satisfaction (multi-item scale) - being 'very' or 'fairly satisfied' with the way democracy works in [respondent's country]; thinking citizens have sufficient democratic influence in [respondent's country]; agreeing with 'Everyone is free to express his opinions when he does not agree with something', 'One may do almost anything one likes so long as it is lawful', 'Everyone is truly equal before the law', and disagreeing with 'Small groups with different ideas or customs from the majority are largely disapproved of', 'The freedom to do as you like has gone too far, creating disorder, and in the long run, disorder could bring out dictatorship.'

Democracy support (single-item question) - (completely) agreeing with 'Democracy is the best form of government.'

Democratic citizenship conception (multi-item question) - 'Can you write down five characteristics of a good democratic citizen?' and 'People associate a good democratic citizen with several different meanings such as those that I will mention. For each of these, please tell me whether, for you, a good democratic citizen has a lot, something, not so much, or nothing to do with: being informed about political leaders, parties, and issues; having a preference for a political leader or party; being attached to democracy; accepting political protest; being interested in politics and political issues; tolerating views divergent from one's own; respecting solidarity, freedom, equality, and nonviolence as a important values; watching political news on television frequently; reading political information in newspaper frequently; talking about and discussing politics among relatives and friends frequently; voting; being a member of a political party or of one-issue political group(s); participating beyond voting; and settling differences in a nonviolent way.'

Democratic self-identification (single-item self-assessment question) - being a very strong or strong democrat (and not: strong or very strong anti-democrat).

Ethnic stereotyping; stereotyping ethnic minorities in respondent's country (multi-item question) - attributing characteristics: see national stereotyping.

Fatalism (single-item, closed question) - (completely) agreeing with: 'History is not constructed freely and rationally, but rather we make it without controlling it or understanding it entirely since there exist secret forces that intervene.'

Health (single-item, closed self-assessment question) - feeling very healthy, healthy, unhealthy, very unhealthy.

Ideological self-identification (single-item, closed self-assessment question) - would consider him/herself a communist, social democrat, progressive liberal, Christian-democrat, conservative liberal, orthodox Christian-nationalist, neofascist.

Importance of elected institutions (multi-item, closed question) - saying that what is discussed and decided upon in local councils, regional councils, national parliament (in EU member states, the European Parliament) is '(very or rather) important' and not '(very, rather) unimportant'.

Internationalism (multi-item scale) - (strongly) agreeing with 'I expect to feel comfortable also in other countries of the world', 'I like people from other countries in the world as much as I like [respondent's fellow-nationals] in general', and 'Cooperation with other countries is a good thing even if it implies that [respondent's country] has to give up part of its independence.'

Left-right self-identification (single-item, self-assessment question) - placing him/herself very left-wing, left-wing, center, right-wing, or very right-wing (question 'In political matters, people talk of "the left" and "the right." How would you place your views on this scale?').

Listening to political news on the radio (multi-item index) - listening to news or current events programs on the radio never, sometimes, or frequently (daily or almost daily, two or three days a week, from time to time, almost never or never).

Materialism (multi-item scale) - considering most important 'maintaining order in the nation' and 'fighting rising prices' and considering less important 'giving the people more say in important government decisions' and 'protecting freedom of speech', or considering most important 'maintaining a high rate of economic growth' and 'making sure that this country has strong defense forces', and considering less important 'seeing that people have more say in how things are decided at work and in their communities' and 'trying to make our cities and countryside more beautiful' (Inglehart, 1977, 1990).

Member of a political party (single-item question) - being a member.

Member of one-issue political group(s) (multi-item index) - being a member of a nature protection association and/or a movement concerned with ecology, human rights, antiwar, or stopping construction or use of nuclear power plants.

National alienation (multi-item scale) - (strongly) agreeing with 'I don't feel at home in [the respondent's country]' and 'I don't feel comfortable being among [respondent's fellow-nationals].'

National feeling (single-item question) - (strongly) agreeing with 'I feel I am [respondent's nationality].'

National liking (multi-item question) - (strongly) agreeing with 'I like it to be [respondent's nationality]', 'I like the [respondent's fellow-nationals] in general', and 'I like [respondent's country].'

National pride (multi-item scale) - (strongly) agreeing with 'I am proud to be [respondent's nationality]', and '[respondent's country] can be proud of what it performs.'

National preference (multi-item scale) - (strongly) agreeing with 'I prefer to live in [respondent's country]', and 'I prefer [respondent's fellow-nationals] in my contacts with other people in general.'

National superiority (multi-item scale) - (strongly) agreeing with '[respondent's country] is the best country to live in', 'I like [respondent's fellow-nationals] more than people from other countries in general', and '[respondent's country] should preserve its independence in contacts with other countries.'

Nationalism (multi-item scale) - (strongly) agreeing with 'All [respondent's fellow-nationals] should live in [respondent's country]', '[another country's part] where people speak [respondent's language] should become part of [respondent's country]', and 'cooperation with other countries is at the cost of [respondent's country] and should therefore be rejected.'

Nationality (single-item question) - 'What nationality are you?'

National stereotyping (multi-item question) - attributing characteristics to one's own nationality and other nationalities through answering the following question: 'In this section, we are interested in how you describe people from your own and from certain other countries. Please enter in the proper space the percentage of the population of each country that you believe to possess the stated characteristic. Democratic, tolerant, prejudiced, nationalistic, helpful, empathic, likable, friendly, self-confident, ambitious, dominant, aggressive, intelligent, scientific, efficient, emotional, religious, enjoys life, proud, independent, individualistic, egoistical, industrious, rich, honest, passionate, quick-tempered.'

Nonelectoral political behavior (multi-item index) - having (not) regularly attended political meetings; distributed handouts; signed own name to a petition; hung up a placard or poster; joined a demonstration; activated a newspaper; contacted the mayor, alderman, or member of a local council; tried to activate a political party; tried to activate a political group; tried to activate a local or national radio or television station; lodged a complaint; participated in a referendum; joined in a boycott or strike; or taken part in occupying a building or factory.

Party preference (single-item question) - indicating political party vote for . . . if there were an election to the parliament today, whether [respondent] is allowed and willing to vote or not.

Political institutions confidence (multi-item scale) - having 'a great deal' or 'quite a lot' of confidence in the following groups in [respondent's country]: armed forces, police, civil service, parliament, and head of state; and having 'a great deal' or 'quite a lot' of confidence in government's handling of economic affairs.

Political efficacy (multi-item scale) - not agreeing with 'people like me do not have any say about what the government does'; and agreeing with 'Do you think, that if things are not going well in [respondent's country], people like yourself can help to bring about a change for the better or not?'

Political interest (multi-item, self-assessment scale) - saying being '(very) interested' in 'politics', being '(very) interested' in some actual political processes, and being '(very) interested' in some actual major political issues.

Political system knowledge (multi-item index) - knowing the main powers of the head of state, the prime-minister, and the parliament (second chamber in case of bicameral parliament); and knowing three major political problems dealt with recently in parliament.

Political actors knowledge (multi-item index) - knowing the names of the prime minister, the ministers, the political parties 'represented' in the government, the political parties in the opposition, and the fraction leaders in parliament.

Political actors trust (multi-item scale) - not agreeing with 'Political parties are only interested in my vote and not in my opinion'; 'Politicians consciously promise more than they can deliver'; 'Ministers are primarily working for their own interests'; 'One becomes MP because of one's political friends, rather than because of skills and ability'; 'MPs care too much for powerful groups instead of general interest'; and 'MPs do not care about the opinions of people like me.'

Political education (multi-item question) - indicating (not) having had political education by the listed several different socializers ('Where have you learned and do you mainly learn what you know about politics?') and indicating the intensity of influence of the selected political socializers ('Where have you *mainly* learned and do you mainly learn what you know about politics?').

Political issues knowledge (multi-item index) - knowledge questions about four actual political issues high on the political agenda.

Political leader preference (single-item question) - giving the highest mark to one of the listed party leaders (ministers or fraction leaders in parliament or the number ones in the list of candidates in next election).

Political party identification/attachment (single-item question) - feeling very or fairly close to a political party.

Political satisfaction (multi-item scale) - answering 'enough' to the last question of a series of three: main problem in [respondent's country]; whether or not government could do little or nothing or (very) much to solve this problem; and whether government did enough or not enough to solve this problem given its more or less limited possible solutions.

Political self-confidence (multi-item, self-assessment scale) - confirming knowledge about politics, having an opinion on main political problems, and finding him/herself often persuading his/her friends and/or relatives to share his/her views on political topics.

Positive belief about democracy (multi-item question) - evaluating positively the characteristics of democracy that are named by the respondent answering the democracy conceptions question.

Positive belief about democratic citizenship (multi-item question) - evaluating positively the characteristics of democratic citizenship that are named by the respondent answering the democratic citizenship conceptions question.

Radicalism (multi-item question) - agreeing with 'The entire way our society is organized must be radically changed by revolutionary action'; disagreeing with 'Our society must be gradually improved by reforms', 'Our present society is on the whole acceptable and need no big changes', and 'Our present society must be valiantly defended against all subversive forces.'

Reading political information (multi-item index) - frequency of reading about politics in and policy of [respondent's country] in the newspaper; and frequency or reading about politics in other countries.

Rejection of traditional women's roles (multi-item scale) - not agreeing with the view that women are best suited to looking after small children, the view that women in charge of men at work is unnatural, and the view that good education is less important for girls.

Religiosity (single-item, self-assessment question) - is very religious, religious, not religious, or totally not religious.

Religious affiliation (single-item question) - claiming to be Catholic, Protestant/Calvinist, Muslim, or other or nondenominational.

Self-confidence (multi-item, self-assessment scale) - declaring knowledge about important things in life, having an opinion on main problems in life, and finding him/herself often persuading his/her friends and/or relatives to share his/her views on several different topics in life; thinking that 'you can get further ahead in life by virtue of your own efforts.'

Self-efficacy (multi-item scale) - not agreeing with 'people like me do not have any say about what parents (ditto other relatives, teachers, and friends) do'; and agreeing with 'Do you think, that if things are not going well in your direct environment, people like yourself can help to bring about a change for the better or not?'

Social-economic class self-identification (single-item, self-assessment question) - lower class, lower middle class, middle class, higher middle class, or higher class.

Supportive of political freedoms (multi-item scale) - being (very strongly) in favor of freedom of demonstration, freedom of open criticism of the royal family/president, freedom of open criticism of the government, freedom to strike, conscientious objection to military service, freedom of speech, freedom of the press, and of judicial recall.

Talking about or discussing politics (multi-item index) - talking about/discussing political matters never, sometimes, or frequently with father, mother, other relatives, friends, or colleagues.

Voting (multi-item index) - has (not) voted at the latest elections for the local council, regional parliament, national parliament (and in EU member states, the European Parliament).

Watching political television items (multi-item index) - watching news or current events program on television never, sometimes, or frequently.

Willingness to be a candidate for/member of representative body (single-item question) - is (strongly) willing.

Willingness to be a member of a political party (single-item question) - will certainly become or continue being a member.

Willingness to be a member of one-issue political group(s) (multi-item question) - will certainly become or continue being a member of a nature protection association and/or a movement dealing with ecology, human rights, antiwar, or concerned with stopping construction or use of nuclear power plants.

Willingness to vote (multi-item question) - will certainly go and vote at the next elections for the local council, regional parliament, national parliament (and in EU member states, the European Parliament).

Willingness to participate in nonelectoral political activities (multi-item question) - will certainly or probably attend political meeting; distribute handouts; sign own name to a petition; hang up a placard or poster; join a demonstration; activate a newspaper; contact the mayor, alderman, or member of a local council; try to activate political party; try to activate political group; try to activate local or national radio or television; lodge a complaint; participate in a referendum; join in a boycott; join in a strike; and/or take part in occupying a building or factory in the future.

Worry about the economic outlook (multi-item scale) - agreeing with 'economy goes worse'; expecting that, within the coming year, the general economic situation in [respondent's country] will be a little or a lot worse (and not a lot or a little better); expecting that the financial situation of respondent's family or household will get a little or a lot worse within the coming year (and not a lot better or a little better); expecting that, within the coming year, the employment situation will get a little or a lot worse; expecting that respondent's own job situation will get a little or a lot worse; being often or sometimes worried about his/her [respondent's] economic future.

Worry about the political outlook (multi-item scale) - indicating 15 or more (main) problems out of a list of 21 issues, including unemployment and/or labor market, wages, income distribution, prices, taxes, health care, social security, housing, environment, energy, crime, education, traffic circulation, foreign affairs, defence, norms and values, abortion, euthanasia, women's rights, minorities, government, parliament, and democracy; agreeing with 'politics is getting worse'; and expecting that, within the coming years, the political situation in [respondent's country] will get a little or a lot worse.

20   *Authoritarianism, 'Nie Wieder'*
Anti-Semitism in the Low Countries

Jos Meloen

ABSTRACT

This is a study of religious-cultural, economic, and political anti-Semitism among high schoolers in the Netherlands and Belgium (Flanders). It also relates anti-Semitism to students' knowledge about World War II, their socioeconomic status, and other personal indicators (for example, having Jews as acquaintances).

The research findings indicate that anti-Semitism was divisible into three parts, that students largely rejected it, and that authoritarianism was linked to and shared common roots with it. The more knowledge students had about the Holocaust and the more they paid attention to details of World War II, the less anti-Semitism they demonstrated. Therefore, knowledge is both directly related to anti-Semitism and indirectly related to it through students' attitudes toward World War II. The other factors measured (SES and acquaintances) were not so closely associated, but authoritarianism was found to be an intermediary factor.

In Belgium (Flanders), anti-Semitism was related to antiminority prejudices, nationalism, xenophobia, authoritarianism, antifeminism, pro-apartheid, and racist party preference. Type of education or school was also related to anti-Semitism and ethnocentrism so that education played a role here as a mediating factor. The conclusion is that, while anti-Semitism may not always be part of the authoritarianism-ethnocentrism syndrome, it often appears that a rise in such attitudes may increase anti-Semitism and vice versa.

INTRODUCTION

Some years ago, we conducted a research project on 'anti-Semitism and authoritarianism among high school students' (van der Grift, de Vos, and Meloen, 1991) on behalf of the Anne Frank Foundation in Amsterdam, the Netherlands, and the Dutch Foundation for Research in Education (SVO). The Anne Frank Foundation provides information on the Holocaust to the general public (more specifically to schools) in addition to maintaining the Anne Frank Museum in Amsterdam.

Our project was related to a long-lasting scientific tradition. Some 50 years ago, in 1943 a Berkeley professor and a graduate student received a $500 grant for a study in anti-Semitism. This was one of the first attempts to understand this

411

phenomenon empirically. They first developed a research instrument on anti-Semitism. Thereafter, two Jewish scientists (exiled from Nazi Germany and Austria) joined them in conducting one of the first studies in prejudice, using American Jewish Committee funds. This study was later published as *The Authoritarian Personality* (Adorno et al., 1950) and called an 'instant classic' (Christie and Jahoda, 1954), However, it soon received much overdone and Cold-War-related criticism (Meloen, 1991). Their major findings were often substantiated in other research (Meloen, 1983, 1993). These findings indicated that anti-Semitism was related to a larger syndrome of prejudices against the powerless in society (usually ethnic minority groups) and that authoritarian attitudes often coincided with this syndrome. Their explanation was mainly psychological (or mass psychological). This work inspired more than 2000 scientific publications (mainly concerned with authoritarianism and ethnocentrism) in some 24 countries in the following three decades (Meloen, 1983, 1991). There were many fewer studies on anti-Semitism. For instance, there was one large, nationwide survey in West Germany in the early 1980s. Silbermann found that nearly 25 per cent of the young and up to 40 per cent of the oldest generations supported anti-Semitic attitudes (Silbermann, 1982, p. 65). In the Netherlands, there were only a couple of studies which indicated that small minorities of the population supported statements like: 'There is still too much influence of Jews in our country' (supported by 3 per cent in a large-scale study of high school students) (Hagendoorn and Janssen, 1983) or 'If you do business with Jews, you have to be extra careful' (supported nationally by 18 per cent of the population) (Eisinga and Scheepers, 1989).

ANTI-SEMITISM IN THE NETHERLANDS

When we started our project, we recognized that there were several aspects to anti-Semitism. Therefore, three types of anti-Semitism were included in this investigation: 1) religious-cultural, 2) economic, and 3) political. The first questions we wanted to address were: Are there still anti-Semitic attitudes in the Netherlands? And if so, what kind(s) of anti-Semitism is (are) present? Is there any relationship between anti-Semitism and knowledge or attitudes about World War II and the persecution of the Jews at that time? Also, is there any relationship between authoritarianism and other indicators such as 'having Jews as acquaintances' or the social/economic status or class of the parents?

The investigation was conducted in the Netherlands among 867 high school students, between 14 and 18 years of age. The schools were randomly selected and included the lowest (LBO: lowest occupational, MAVO: lowest general education) as well as the highest (HAVO: higher general education, VWO: pre-university) types of secondary education. Therefore, students from all social strata were included. In this research project, we developed new and carefully balanced instruments to measure various attitudes using the most sophisticated methodology then available.

Our first task was to investigate the three types of anti-Semitism. It appeared, however, that all three types were so closely associated empirically that one may speak of only one type of general anti-Semitism. For a prejudiced person, it apparently makes little difference of what Jews are accused, as long as it is negative. We also found that students who were inclined to agree with anti-Semitic statements or to disagree with pro-Semitic ones were not absent, although they did not answer in great numbers (that is, only 8 per cent for economic anti-Semitism, 4.5 per cent for political anti-Semitism, and 3.5 per cent for religious and cultural anti-Semitism). On the whole, the great majority of students appeared to reject strongly all types of anti-Semitism. The three types of anti-Semitism all appeared to be related to authoritarianism, thus confirming that both phenomena may have common roots. Most students also demonstrated nonauthoritarian attitudes; only 3 per cent favored authoritarianism.

Relationships between anti-Semitism and knowledge of (as well as attitudes toward) the Holocaust and World War II were assessed. The knowledge test had ten multiple-choice questions about the Holocaust. Attitudes about attention to the Holocaust and World War II were tapped using the ten statements listed in Table 20.1. Only 6 per cent of high school students had negative attitudes about paying attention to World War II and the Holocaust.

After analysis, it appeared that all three types of anti-Semitism (especially political anti-Semitism) were negatively, but moderately to strongly related to knowledge of World War II and the Holocaust ($-.37**$ up to $-.57**$; $** =$ significance level/$p = < 0.01$), as well as to attitudes about paying continuing attention to World War II ($-.13**$ up to $-.34**$). In other words, the more accurate knowledge the students had about the Holocaust and the more favorable attitudes they had toward continued public attention to World War II, the less anti-Semitism they demonstrated. This indicates that knowledge may have a crucial influence. Knowledge has often been ignored in this type of research (or results have often been negative in this respect), with the conclusion that it is not worthwhile to teach about such sensitive issues since attitudinal changes have been the main objective. Instead, without such knowledge, no attitude change with respect to anti-Semitism can be expected and any change that does occur may be only superficial.

To plot out the many possible relations among key variables, we computed a model to find if the hypothesized relations were empirically supported (see Figure 20.1). The results show that knowledge has a two-way effect on anti-Semitism: 1) directly, as well as 2) through attitude about paying continued attention to World War II. Authoritarianism is another intermediating factor. Social status, however does not have any substantial effect. Also, the number of a person's Jewish acquaintances does not seem to have much effect on anti-Semitism. Social desirability (that is, having Jews as acquaintances) appeared to be relatively independent. Our conclusion, therefore, was that knowledge about (and continuing public attention to) World War II and Jewish persecution positively influenced anti-Semitic attitudes. Since this is what the Anne Frank Foundation has been working on for decades, it seems to support their efforts, which are not in vain. Nevertheless, it is also possible that anti-Semitic attitudes may still persist in small marginal groups in Dutch society.

Table 20.1 Support for continuing public attention to World War II (Dutch high school students)

1.	(+)	It is important that there is attention given to World War II every year.
2.	(-)	The celebration of Liberation Day can be abolished. (May 5th is a National Holiday [that is, the day of Nazi-capitulation in The Netherlands] in 1945.)
3.	(-)	There has been enough attention given to the Jewish persecutions in World War II.
4.	(+)	It is understandable that World War II still gets so much attention.
5.	(-)	It is an exaggeration that what happened in World War II still keeps people thinking about it.
6.	(+)	It is only logical that the survivors of the Jewish persecution cannot forget their experiences.
7.	(-)	The commemoration (of those who died in WWII) on May 4th can be abolished. (Each year on May 4th, the Dutch victims of World War II are commemorated and two minutes of silence at 20.00 hours [8:00 p.m.] is observed nationwide.)
8.	(-)	It is right that the (last) two imprisoned elderly Nazi war criminals have been released by the government. (This happened several years ago.)
9.	(+)	War criminals should still be tracked down and punished.
10.	(-)	War crimes of World War II should be declared extinguished by time limits.

Notes: Cronbach's alpha: .77
Mean +0.59 (Standard Deviation .33)
Negative attitudes about attending to World War II and the Holocaust were expressed by 6% of these high school students.

ANTI-SEMITISM IN FLANDERS (BELGIUM)

Since political anti-Semitism was the strongest predictor of authoritarian tendencies, we decided to include it in a similar large-scale survey in the Flemish-Dutch speaking part of Belgium, again among high school students (Meloen, van der Linden, and de Witte, 1994). Our aim was to reveal the interrelations among the many other attitudes that were supposed to be related to anti-Semitism. A second reason was that, in Belgium, an anti-immigrant party (that is, Vlaams Blok) had become quite politically successful. One year after completing this research, it gained 11 per cent of the Flemish seats in the Belgian Parliament, precisely the same percentage we found in this survey. This provided an opportunity to test some hypotheses in the field of predicting racist and xenophobic political party support.

Figure 20.1 LISREL Model for anti-Semitism and authoritarianism among Dutch high school students
Notes: Chi-2 = 29.59, df = 27, p = .33
(Also see van de Grift, de Vos, and Meloen, 1991.)

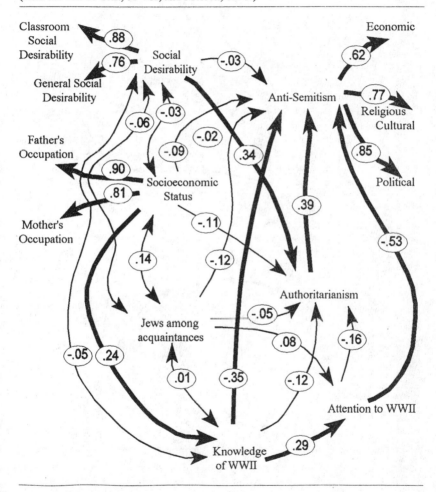

Figure 20.2 LISREL Model: High school students authoritarianism and voting behavior in Flanders, Belgium

Notes: Model 2 final version, Chi-2 = 15.44, df = 16, p = .49; Goodness of Fit Index = .99 (.98); N = 380

(*) .10 > p > .05; * p = < .05; ** p = < .01 *** p = < .001; NS = not significant

Source: Meloen, van der Linden, and de Witte (1994).

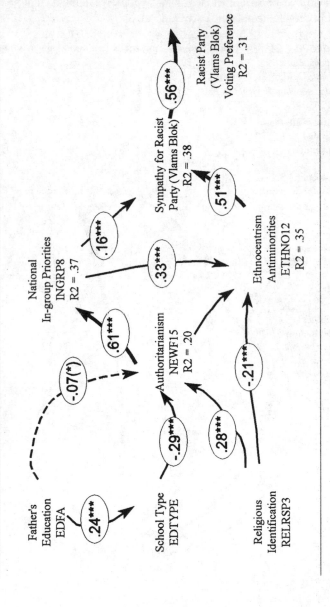

Again, schools of all types of secondary education were randomly chosen. In this case, 901 students from all social classes cooperated. Their parents ranged from unskilled workers up to the managerial elite. Our political anti-Semitism instrument required very little adjustment since Dutch is the official language in Flanders. The eight questions used in the survey are presented in Table 20.2.

Table 20.2 Political Anti-Semitism in Flanders (Belgium) (in %)

Statement		Agree	Neutral	Disagree
1.(+)	Flemish Jews are fine citizens.	58	30	12
2.(-)	Flemish Jews should better go and live in Israel.	17	12	71
3.(+)	The assertion that Jews are very influential in Flemish politics is clearly nonsense.	56	30	14
4.(-)	Every Jew has communist traits.	14	41	45
5.(+)	Its a good thing if Jews feel at ease in Flanders.	66	16	18
6.(-)	Every Jew is a capitalist.	16	33	51
7.(+)	One should respect the Jewish way of life.	69	11	20
8.(-)	Jews are always plotting worldwide.	11	39	50

Notes:
(+) positive direction
(-) negative direction
N = 901 Flemish High School Students
Cronbach's alpha: .84

In our survey of relevant literature and attitude scaling, we found that anti-Semitism is not an isolated phenomenon. In general, a syndrome of related political attitudes (see Table 20.3) was found here, too. Anti-Semitism was related to most other antiminority prejudices, Flemish in-group nationalism, various types of authoritarianism, antifeminism, pro-apartheid attitudes, and voting preference and sympathy for a racist and xenophobic party. However, anti-Semitism was not officially part of this party's propaganda. Party propaganda seen as a direct cause is, therefore, unlikely. In open-ended essays, those students who favored this party only expressed general antiminority views. However, if this anti-Semitism is indirectly a product of antiminority attitudes (in general), of nationalism, and of authoritarianism, then the strong anti-immigrant and racism that this party espouses probably has an indirect effect on increased anti-Semitism. Indeed, this party seems to represent just one idea: a brand of generalized xenophobia including much more than just anti-immigrant statements.

Table 20.3 Intercorrelations between anti-Semitism and other political attitudes (Flanders, Belgium high school students)

Scales	Author(s)	Variable	Political Anti-Semitism PAS8	PAS4+
Pro-Semitism	Van der Grift	PAS4+	-.93***	
Anti-Semitism	Van der Grift	PAS4-	.91***	-.68***
Authoritarianism	Adorno et al.	F15	.40***	
	Middendorp	F7	.33***	
	Eisinga et al.	F8	.35***	
	Altemeyer	RWA10a	.33***	
	Lederer	NGAS10	.42***	
	Meloen	NEWF15	.43***	
	Meloen	NEWF28	.46***	
Democratic Attitudes	Roe	DEMO8	-.20***	
Social Desirability	Reinecke	SD4a	.17**	
Ethnocentrism	Meloen	ETHNO12	.68***	
Apartheid	Meloen	APART8	.48***	
Antifeminism	Vollebergh	AFEM10	.48***	
National In-group Favoritism	Eisinga et al.	INGRP8	.37***	
Sympathy for				
Vlaams Blok	Meloen	VB	.46***	
Greens	Meloen	AGALEV	-.19***	
Nationalists	Meloen	VU	.15**	
Other Parties	Meloen		-.07NS to -.01NS	
Voting Preference				
Vlaams Blok		VBVOTE	.23***	
Not Voting		NOVOTE	-.06NS	
Self Ratings				
Conservative		SELFCONS	.15**	
Right Wing		SELFRGHT	.17**	
Authoritarian		SELFAUT	.13*	
Radical		SELFRAD	.16*	
Education Father		EDFA	-.13*	
Education Mother		EDMO	-.09(*)	
Occupational Status				
Father		STATUSF	-.12*	
Mother		STATUSM	-.23**	
Religious Identification		RELRSP3	-.03NS	
Male/female		SEX	-.18***	
Birth Year		BYR	.05NS	

Notes:
* p = < .05; ** p = < .01; *** p = < .001   NS = not significant
Source: Meloen, van der Linden, and De Witte (1994)
PAS8 (PAS4+ and PAS4-), RWA10a, ETHNO12, APART8 are so called balanced scales; items of all scales randomly distributed in questionnaire; NEWF15 and NEWF28 developed from Adorno et al. (1950), Lederer (1983), and Altemeyer (1988) scales

Anti-Semitism is part of a general antiminority ethnocentrism that plays a part in creating the authoritarianism syndrome which predicts (with other variables) support for this political party. The relations among the main variables were once again computed (see Figure 20.2). What also becomes apparent in Figure 20.2 is that education plays a role here. One's type of education was related to authoritarianism and ethnocentrism, indicating that educational content may be a mediating factor. Indeed, much earlier research also suggests that education is important in the formation of democratic, unprejudiced attitudes (Meloen, 1983) and that the content of education may make a difference (Simpson, 1972).

CONCLUSIONS

From both of these investigations, we may conclude that while anti-Semitism may not always be part of the authoritarianism-ethnocentrism syndrome, it very often will be. An increase in such attitudes may cause a rise in anti-Semitism and vice versa. History is too full of painful examples for us to ignore the Vladamir Zjirinovski's of this world, who complain that there are too many Jews in the Russian government, that Jews should be sent to some far-away island, that Russia should restore its lost empire, and more of this bellicose talk. It may be both impossible and undesirable to silence such political extremists; nevertheless, educating people about the causes/effects of political anti-Semitism and the Holocaust in addition to instilling popular democratic attitudes and behaviors may still be one of the best methods we have to safeguard our answer to 'Authoritarianism? *Nie Wieder!*' (Never again.)

REFERENCES

Adorno, T., E. Frenkel-Brunswik, D. Levinson, and R. Sanford (1950). *The Authoritarian Personality*. New York, NY: Harper and Row. Abridged edition with a new introduction by N. Sanford and D. Levinson (1982). New York, NY: Norton and Co.

Altemeyer, B. (1988). *Enemies of Freedom*. London, UK: Jossey Bass.

Christie, R. and M. Jahoda (1954). *Studies in the Scope and Method of 'The Authoritarian Personality': Continuities in Social Research*. Glencoe, IL: The Free Press.

Eisinga, R. and P. Scheepers (1989). *Etnocentrisme in Nederland* (Ethnocentrism in The Netherlands). Nijmegen, the Netherlands: ITS.

van der Grift, W., W. de Vos, and J. Meloen (1991). *Anti-Semitisme en autoritarisme onder scholieren* (Anti-Semitism and Authoritarianism among secondary school pupils). Utrecht, the Netherlands: Rijksuniversiteit Utrecht and Amsterdam, the Netherlands: Anne Frank Stichting, Academisch Boekencentrum De Lier.

Hagendoorn, A. and J. Janssen (1983). *Rechtsomkeer* (Turn Right!). Baarn, the Netherlands: Ambo.

Lederer, G. (1983). *Jugend und Autorität: Ueber den Einstellungswandel zum Autoritarismus in der Bundesrepublik Deutschland und den USA* (Youth and Authority: Regarding Changes in the Authoritarian Mentality in the FRG and the USA). Opladen, FRG: Westdeutscher Verlag.

Meloen, J. (1983). *De autoritaire reaktie in tijden van welvaart en krisis* (The Authoritarian Response in Times of Prosperity and Crisis). Dissertation. Amsterdam, the Netherlands: University of Amsterdam.

Meloen, J. (1991). 'The Fortieth Anniversary of "The Authoritarian Personality"': Is There New Evidence to Consider the Authoritarian Personality to Be the Backbone of "Left" as Well as "Right Wing" Dictatorships?', pp. 119-27 in *Politics and the Individual*, Vol. 1, No. 1.

Meloen, J. (1993). 'The F Scale as a Predictor of Fascism: An Overview of 40 Years of Authoritarianism Research', pp. 47-69 in W. Stone, G. Lederer, and R. Christie (1993) *Strength and Weakness: The Authoritarian Personality Today*. New York, NY: Springer.

Meloen, J., G. van der Linden, and H. de Witte (1994). 'Authoritarianism and Political Racism in Belgian Flanders: A Test of the Approaches of Adorno et al., Lederer and Altemeyer', pp. 72-108 in R. Holly (ed.) *Political Consciousness and Civic Education during the Transformation of the System*. Warsaw, Poland: Institute of Political Studies, Polish Academy of Sciences.

Meloen, J. and C. Middendorp (1991). 'Authoritarianism in the Netherlands: Ideology, Personality, or Sub-Culture', pp. 49-72 in *Politics and the Individual*, Vol. 1, No. 2.

Middendorp, C. (1978). *Progressiveness and Conservatism: The Fundamental Dimensions of Ideology Controversy and their Relationship to Social Class*. The Hague, the Netherlands: Mouton Publishers.

Raaijmakers, Q., W. Meeus, and W. Vollebergh (1986). 'Extreme Politieke Opvattingen bij LBO en MAVO-scholieren' (Extreme Political Opinions Among High School Students). Paper presented to Dutch Conference on Political Psychology, Nijmegen, the Netherlands.

Reinecke, J. (1989). 'Interviewereffekte und Soziale Erwünschtheit: Theorie, Modell, und Empirische Ergebnisse' (Interview Effect and Social Desirability: Theory, Model, and Empirical Results). Münster, FRG: Institut für Soziologic und Sozialpädagogik, Universität Münster.

Roe, R. (1975). *Links en Rechts in Empirisch Perspectief* (Left and Right-wing in an Empirical Perspective). Dissertation, University of Amsterdam, Amsterdam, the Netherlands.

Silbermann, A. (1982). *Sind wir Antisemiten? Ausmass und Wirkung eines sozialen Vorurteils in der Bundesrepublik Deutschland* (Are We Anti-Semitic? Dimensions and Effects of Social Prejudice in Germany.) Köln, FRG: Verlag Wissenschaft und Politik.

Simpson, M. (1972). 'Authoritarianism and Education: A Comparative Approach', pp. 223-34 in *Sociometry*, Vol. 35, No. 2.

21   *Democratic Socialization in the Schools*

Margaret Conway
Sandra Bowman Damico
Alfonso J. Damico

ABSTRACT

Participation is important for the political education of democratic citizens. But perhaps the strongest factor that explains participatory differences among democratic citizens is the education variable (for example, academic-track/college-bound students are more democratic, participatory, and active). Along with sociodemographic and certain relevant high school variables, our study examines what happens inside schools (for example, extracurricular activities) to measure the effects of this informal education on students' democratic beliefs. We also consider whether or not these beliefs affect patterns of community and political participation among young adults. In the study, we used data from the US National Longitudinal Study of the High School Class of 1972, wherein the National Center for Education Statistics surveyed a representative national sample of all high school seniors. Five follow-up surveys were done. Based on the 1972 base-year survey and the 1974 and 1976 follow ups, our most important finding is that participation in high school activities significantly predicts the holding of democratic beliefs which, in turn, is related to patterns of political and community participation among young adults.

DEMOCRATIC CITIZENSHIP

Democracy is often justified on the basis that citizens can best judge their own interests or, at the very least, that their interests are less likely to be neglected when they do not have to depend on others to look after them. As a political process, democracy is distinctive in that it seeks to guarantee that everyone who is affected by a collective decision will have an equal opportunity to influence the decision taken. This is a protective argument for democracy, one in which men and women need political rights as Mill said, not 'in order that they may govern, but in order that they may not be misgoverned' (Mill, 1951, p. 391). But in addition to empowering people, participation is also thought to improve them when they, thereby, become better citizens. Mill argued not only for trusting people with the power to make their own decisions but also for providing them with the conditions whereby they might come to make better decisions. The advantage of a democratic political system (whatever its flaws) over a hierarchical political system (whatever its merits) is that the means for a political education in self-government exists in the former, but not in the latter. This is called Mill's educative argument for democracy (Thompson, 1976, p. 9). This reason for democracy is still widely championed (Barber, 1984; Mansbridge, 1980). By playing a part in public life, individuals can better understand their own interests, are more likely to accept the public interest as a restraint upon their behavior, and will develop stronger democratic beliefs. This is the democratic promise, one that can be realized through participation in its many forms.

The democratic ideal, then, is one of enlightened democratic citizens cooperating in the collective management of living together. But we all recognize the wide gap between the ideal and the real. No working democracy satisfies such high expectations. There is still a need for equality and room for enlightenment. But this gap between the ideal and the real is hardly surprising; after all, ideals describe a desirable state of affairs as yet unattained. Their function is to bring pressure upon the real, to call attention to the ways in which practice does not match theory. No ordinary citizen is likely to live up to the ideal standards of civic virtue which Rousseau's *citoyen* or Barber's 'strong democrat' (1984) set for us. But there is considerable social science research which supports many of the claims made for political participation. A relationship exists between participation, on the one side, and personal autonomy (Thompson, 1970), democratic values, and political knowledge (Almond and Verba, 1965) on the other.

Participation is important for the political education of democratic citizens. But perhaps the strongest factor that explains differences among democratic citizens is the education variable. Survey research (especially political scientists' findings) points to educational attainment as the single most powerful explanatory variable regarding differences among citizens in voting turnout, political knowledge, democratic commitments, and other political behaviors and values (Berelson et al., 1954; Converse and Campbell, 1972; Rosenstone and Hansen, 1993; and Nie et al., 1994). Our work adds to these findings. Our concern is with what goes on inside schools to measure the effects of informal education on democratic citizenship. We seek to develop a more nuanced conception of how education actually relates to democratic citizenship. So while we discuss formal education and other factors that might be important to democratic citizenship, our major focus is on how student participation within schools later affects adult patterns of participation. It is this other informal or extracurricular education (in the band, on the playing field, in the school newspaper office, in the drama club) that interests us.

PARTICIPATION IN EXTRACURRICULAR ACTIVITIES

The primary way in which schooling, as opposed to formal instruction, contributes to citizenship education is that it provides adolescents with opportunities to participate in a variety of extracurricular activities. Here, students learn about the give and take of social exchanges, leading and following, winning and losing, pleasure and pain, good companions and bad, formal and informal rules, hard work and luck. Given the importance of this citizenship training, it is surprising how little research has actually explored the relationship between such participation in high school and adult community or civic participation (Ehman, Spring 1980). (One previous study of high school seniors suggested that a politicized environment affects political cognition and both low-initiative and high-initiative forms of political participation. On this point, see Sigel and Hoskin, 1981.) Using only articles and conference papers based on empirical data, Holland and Andre (1987) reviewed the literature on the effects of participation in high school extracurricular activities. Their review presents a snapshot of research interests in this area. Half of the reviewed studies were concerned with the relationship between activity participation and educational aspirations and attainment or achievement. Another 15 per cent explored the impact of school size on such participation. Of the 34 studies Holland and Andre reviewed, only three addressed the relationship between activity participation and citizenship behaviors or attitudes: Eyler (1982) explored political attitudes; Hanks (1981) focused on selective forms of political expression; and Lindsay (1984) was concerned with effects on young adults' social participation levels. None of these studies explored whether such participation affected the development of democratic beliefs, nor did they ask whether democratic beliefs were important for understanding which young adults engaged in community or political behavior. Nor did any of them ask which sociodemographic or school variables might account for an adolescent initially deciding to participate in a school activity. These deficiencies define the concerns of our project. That is, our study is designed to examine the effects of high school participation on the holding of democratic beliefs and whether holding such beliefs affects young adults' participation in community and political activities.

METHODS
Data

The data used in this study are from the National Longitudinal Study of the High School Class of 1972. The National Center for Education Statistics surveyed a representative sample of all 1972 high school seniors in the United States. This base-year survey was a two-stage probability sample. Schools were selected with equal probability from over 600 strata, generated by such factors as geographic region, size, income levels, minority enrollments, ethnic make-up, degree of urbanization, and so forth. The subsequent simple random sample of 18 students within two schools from each of the 600 strata produced almost 17 000 completed questionnaires. After this base-year survey, five follow-up studies of the class of 1972 were conducted; the first one in 1973, others in 1974, 1976, 1979, and 1986. Response rates for the follow-ups were high, with 71.1 per cent for the first one and over 90 per cent for the subsequent waves. The base-year survey focused mainly on students' experiences within high school, their personal and family backgrounds, work experiences, plans, goals, and opinions. Each of the follow-up surveys was expanded to take account of likely changes in the circumstances of the sample members. Consequently, over time there is information about postsecondary education experiences, military service, careers, work satisfaction, opinions about gender roles, prejudices, community and political activities, marriage and family.

Since our primary aim is to trace the impact of high school extracurricular activity participation on the acquisition of democratic beliefs and subsequent patterns of young adult community and political participation, we used data from the base-year survey and from the 1974 and 1976 follow-ups. Cases with missing data have been excluded. The resulting sample fluctuates between slightly over 5000 to 5823, depending on the variables included within the analysis. We plan to follow these relationships over time, for instance, looking at the 1986 data when most of the sample members were 32 years old. But we first need a clearer map of the trail that we want to follow. There is, for example, obvious interest in finding out whether the near-term relationship between high school experiences and adult life remains relatively constant or undergoes significant changes. But our first task is to uncover the nature of young adult participation patterns.

Measures

Our study used a series of measures based on questions in the longitudinal surveys of the 1972 senior class. The demographic set for the base-year survey includes standard indicators for socioeconomic status (SES), race, and community size. This initial survey also asked about the number of social studies courses taken and about the sample member's high school program or curriculum track. To measure high school activities, we use questions from the survey that asked, first, whether or not one had participated in a variety of activities and, when the answer was yes, whether the participation was 'active' or as a 'leader or officer'. The experiences sampled ranged from membership and participation in honorary societies and vocational clubs to student government and athletics. The measure of democratic beliefs (a variable that our model posits as an important factor in reenforcing the connection among participation experiences) was constructed out of responses to a question included in the 1974 survey. It asked about the worthwhileness of a number of political practices (such as voting or talking to elected officials) that are usually part of democratic life experiences. Democratic beliefs and high school activities are conceived of as both independent and dependent variables. For example, we want to know, on the one hand, how high school experiences and participation affect having democratic beliefs. But, on the other hand, we also are interested in how holding democratic beliefs might affect young adult community and political participation. In a similar way, we are sometimes interested in factors which explain variations in participation in high school activities. At other times, participation is studied to see if it predicts behavior after graduation.

Both the 1974 and 1976 follow-up surveys asked about community participation. Sample members were asked whether or not they were doing volunteer work, ranging from helping out at a hospital to working in a community center. In addition to volunteer work, the survey measured community participation, such as membership in a church-related activity (beyond attendance at worship services), a service activity (for example, coaching Little League), or a professional activity (for example, belonging to a union, a farmer's organization, or some other type of professional association). Those indicating that they were a member of some community group were asked additional questions about their level of involvement in order to distinguish between those who only belonged to an association and those who were active in it (for example, attended meetings regularly). We refer to the first as a community member and the second more involved actor as a community participant.

The follow-up surveys also asked about political activities. Political discussion is composed out of responses that indicated how frequently one talked about politics and public problems with friends, family members, coworkers, church members, and others. Political participation is similarly based on the frequency with which a person worked in a campaign, contributed money for a political cause, or was in other ways involved in politics. It also sorted registered voters out from nonregistered members of the electorate.

Analysis

To examine whether high school activity participation predicts holding democratic beliefs and, then, whether these beliefs account for patterns of community and political participation, we ran a series of multiple regression analyses. Multiple regression estimates the relative contribution of each of the independent variables, taking into account the correlations between and among all of the other independent variables (Kerlinger, 1979). A set of socio-demographic and high school variables thought to affect participation were included in each of the analyses. We report unstandardized regression coefficients and their standard errors as well as an indicator of the statistical significance of the coefficients. (For a discussion as to why unstandardized as opposed to standardized regression coefficients should be reported, see King, 1986.)

RESULTS
Participation in High School Activities

Before exploring the relationships among participation in high school extracurricular activities, the holding of democratic beliefs, and young adult community and political activity, we looked at how sociodemographic and high school variables might affect participation itself. Table 21.1 indicates that all of the selected sociodemographic and high school variables (except number of social studies courses taken) influence the likelihood of participating in a school's extracurricular activities and (except for race) being a leader in them. Women participate more than men, and although the coefficient is fairly small, women also show up more often than men as leaders in high school activities. Both high school curriculum track and SES are significant predictors of participation and leadership in extracurricular activities. Students enrolled in the academic track and those from higher socioeconomic families are more likely than others to be activity members and leaders. This finding suggests, not surprisingly, a pattern of cumulative inequalities. The coefficient for community size is small, though significant, confirming our more casual impressions of life in small towns. In fact, students who live in smaller communities are more likely than their counterparts from larger ones to be active and leaders in their school's extracurricular activities.

Extracurricular Activity and Democratic Beliefs

We next examined the effects of these sociodemographic and high school variables and patterns of high school participation on the holding of democratic beliefs. This, in turn, brings us closer to our major interest in the relationship between student involvement in high school activities and the valuing of key democratic political activities (for example, voting, writing to legislators, and being an active party member). These coefficients are the most robust of any seen in all the tables. Several of the sociodemographic variables relate to holding democratic beliefs; women and whites are more likely than males or nonwhites to hold democratic beliefs. But community size does not predict democratic beliefs.

Table 21.1 Effects of sociodemographic and high school variables on participation and leadership in high school extracurricular activities

Sociodemographic and School Variables	Participation in High School Extracurricular Activities		Leadership in High School Extracurricular Activities	
Socioeconomic Status	.326***	(.033)	.129***	(.017)
Gender	.469***	(.043)	.063***	(.021)
Race	-.147*	(.080)	-.125	(.040)
Community Size	-.083***	(.010)	-.020***	(.005)
Number of Social Studies Courses Taken	.001	(.013)	.00005	(.006)
High School Curriculum Track	.329***	(.025)	.122***	(.013)
Constant	.551		.110 (ns)	
F =	74.078		32.316	
R^2	.077		.035	
Adj. R^2	.076		.034	
N =	5319		5319	

*Entries are unstandardized regression coefficients. Entries in ( ) are standard errors. One tailed t test: * = $p < .05$; ** = $p < .01$; *** = $p < .005$.

The three high school variables included in Table 21.2 are also meaningfully related to the holding of democratic beliefs: number of social studies courses taken; high school curriculum track; and high school extracurricular activities. The greater the number of social studies courses taken, the more likely the student is to have democratic beliefs. This positive relationship also holds for students enrolled in the curriculum tailored for those who are college bound. Table 21.2 also confirms our hypothesis that high school participation is connected to having democratic beliefs.

From Table 21.2, we know that participation in extracurricular activities is significantly related to the holding of democratic beliefs. But is participation in all types of activities equally predictive of holding these beliefs? To answer this question, extracurricular activities were broken into five categories and, then, included in a multiple regression (see Table 21.3). Participation in three of the five types of high school activities were significantly related to holding democratic beliefs. As might be expected, the coefficients for those who were active in student government or media (for example, a school newspaper) are the largest. Participation in expressive groups (for example, chorus or drama) or athletics/cheerleading was not statistically related to holding democratic beliefs.

Table 21.2 Effects of sociodemographic and high school variables on democratic beliefs

Sociodemographic and High School Variables	Democratic Beliefs	
Socioeconomic Status	.413***	(.079)
Gender	.560***	(.091)
Race	.499*	(.166)
Community Size	.014	(.021)
Number of Social Studies Courses Taken	.101***	(.028)
High School Curriculum Track	.283***	(.053)
High School Extracurricular Activities	.234***	(.028)
Constant	3.230	
F =	38.134	
R²	.044	
Adj. R²	.043	
N =	5823	

*Entries are unstandardized regression coefficients. Entries in ( ) are standard errors. One tailed t test: * = p < .05; ** = p < .01; *** = p < .005.

Duplicating results seen in the previous table, Table 21.3 finds large positive coefficients for gender and race, indicating that females and whites are more supportive of democratic beliefs than others. High SES persons and those following the academic curriculum also are more supportive of democratic beliefs. Number of social studies courses taken in high school is statistically significant, but small in impact.

Membership and Participation in Community Groups

Table 21.4 introduces two new dependent variables: namely, post high school associational membership and community participation in a range of activities from scouting to civic associations to hobby groups. Along with the standard set of sociodemographic and high school factors, we now include for the first time the measure of democratic beliefs as an independent variable. This enables us to address the question of whether the holding of democratic beliefs predicts membership and participation in the community.

In general, the model shown in Table 21.4 is better at predicting membership than participation. This is the first instance in which the community member and the community participant roles of males are significantly greater than that of females. High school curriculum track and participation in extracurricular activities also help to differentiate between members and participants; the number of social studies courses taken does not. Interestingly, we note that holding democratic beliefs is significantly associated with becoming a member of a community association as a young adult and with active participation in adult civic life.

Table 21.3 Effects of participation in different types of extracurricular activities on democratic beliefs

Sociodemographic and High School Variables	Democratic Beliefs	
Socioeconomic Status	.405*	(.072)
Gender	.535*	(.093)
Race	.497***	(.166)
Community Size	.011	(.021)
Number of Social Studies Courses Taken	.095***	(.028)
High School Curriculum Track	.267***	(.054)
Participation by Type of Extracurricular Activity:		
Vocational Education Clubs	.158*	(.089)
Academic Oriented Clubs	.195***	(.067)
Student Government/Media	.404***	(.058)
Expressive Clubs/Groups	.103	(.061)
Athletics/Cheerleading	.030	(.056)
Constant	3.452	
F =	27.086	
R^2	.049	
Adj. R^2	.047	
N =	5823	

*Entries are unstandardized regression coefficients. Entries in ( ) are standard errors. One tailed t test: $*$ = $p < .05$; $**$ = $p < .01$; $***$ = $p < .005$.

During the two to four years after the class of 1972 graduated, they did what many Americans do. They joined a variety of associations organized for many different purposes, some with political goals and others with objectives more civic, recreational, or religious in nature. Table 21.5 reports findings for the effects of participation in specific types of high school extracurricular activities on the associational life of the sample members after they graduated from high school. The findings here are limited to their nonpolitical involvement as a member or as a participant in the community.

Table 21.4 Effects of sociodemographic and high school variables on post high school community membership and participation in community groups in general

Sociodemographic and High School Variables	Community Membership 1974	Community Participation 1974	Community Membership 1976	Community Participation 1976
Socioeconomic Status	-.118***	.111*	.086*	.081**
	(.034)	(.026)	(.038)	(.030)
Gender	-.454***	-.278***	-.425***	-.270***
	(.041)	(.033)	(.048)	(.038)
Race	-.149*	-.080	-.092	-.004
	(.073)	(.060)	(.089)	(.071)
Democratic Beliefs	.075***	.051***	.077***	.048***
	(.006)	(.005)	(.007)	(.005)
Community Size	.011	.008	.009	.018*
	(.009)	(.008)	(.011)	(.009)
Number of Social Studies Courses Taken	.014	.016	.029*	.017
	(.013)	(.010)	(.015)	(.012)
High School Curriculum Track	.138***	.097***	.148***	.099***
	(.024)	(.019)	(.029)	(.022)
High School Extra-curricular Activities	.269***	.193***	.269***	.187***
	(.013)	(.027)	(.015)	(.011)
Constant	.685	.212	.773	.248
F =	119.446	92.214	84.198	64.853
R^2	.148	.118	.117	.093
Adj. R^2	.146	.117	.116	.092
N =	5526	5526	5081	5083

*Entries are unstandardized regression coefficients. Entries in ( ) are standard errors. One tailed t test: * = $p < .05$; ** = $p < .01$; *** = $p < .005$.

Democratic beliefs show up in Table 21.5 as one factor which identifies those who are most likely to have a nonpolitical or community associational life. But it is only one piece of the puzzle; high school participation adds others. Among the five possible categories of high school activities, those participating in athletics/cheerleading are very likely, after graduation, not only to be members but to be participants in their communities. Indeed, all types of school activity participation (except in vocational education clubs) have an impact on subsequent early adult community participation. The academic track and high SES continue to count. Males rather than females are more likely to be members and participants after graduation. Neither the number of social science courses taken nor race are significant for predicting who will be a community member or a community participant.

Table 21.5 Effects of participation in different types of extracurricular activities on post high school membership and participation in nonpolitical community groups

Sociodemographic and High School Variables	Community Membership 1974	Community Participation 1974	Community Membership 1976	Community Participation 1976
Socioeconomic Status	.121***	.093***	.070*	.063*
	(.040)	(.025)	(.038)	(.029)
Gender	-.421***	-.245***	-.386***	-.232***
	(.041)	(.033)	(.049)	(.038)
Race	-.133	-.067	-.077	.008
	(.074)	(.060)	(.089)	(.069)
Community Size	.010	.005	.009	.016
	(.009)	(.008)	(.011)	(.007)
Democratic Beliefs	.074***	.051***	.076***	.048***
	(.005)	(.004)	(.007)	(.011)
Number of Social Studies	.012	.013	.028*	.015
Courses Taken	(.013)	(.010)	(.015)	(.011)
High School Curriculum	.129***	.087**	.134***	.085***
Track	(.024)	(.020)	(.029)	(.022)
Participation by Type of Activity (listed below)				
Vocational Education	.121***	.041	.100*	.014
Clubs	(.039)	(.032)	(.047)	(.036)
Academic-oriented	.203***	.142***	.232***	.162***
Clubs	(.030)	(.024)	(.036)	(.028)
Student Govern-	.200***	.147***	.155***	.095***
ment/Media	(.026)	(.021)	(.031)	(.024)
Expressive Clubs/	.191***	.134***	.224***	.153***
Groups	(.027)	(.022)	(.033)	(.025)
Athletics/	.250***	.210***	.267***	.229***
Cheerleading	(.025)	(.020)	(.030)	(.023)
Constant	.7218	.248	.790	.259
F =	81.049	65.360	58.861	47.616
R^2	.150	.124	.122	.101
Adj. R^2	.148	.123	.120	.099
N =	5526	5526	5085	5085

*Entries are unstandardized regression coefficients. Entries in ( ) are standard errors. One tailed test: * = $p < .05$; ** = $p < .01$; *** = $p < .005$.

Political Discussion and Participation

Becoming a member or a participant in one's community is one component of democratic citizenship (Pateman, 1970). But democratic citizenship is more fully signalled by one's involvement in the public or political life of the community.

Political discussion and political participation are the dependent variables that most interest us. Participation in high school extracurricular activities and democratic beliefs are the independent variables of chief significance here.

In Table 21.6, the independent variables are better able to account for the dependent variables (political discussion and political participation) in 1974 than in 1976. Democratic beliefs show up in all equations as significant, as do SES and curriculum track. The demographic variables point again to gender (males) as an important factor. Interestingly enough, nonwhites report more political behavior than whites. With one exception, enrollment in social studies courses continues to be insignificant.

Table 21.6 Effects of sociodemographic and high school variables on post high school political discussion and participation

Sociodemographic and High School Variables	Political Discussion 1974	Political Participation 1974	Political Discussion 1976	Political Participation 1976
Socioeconomic Status	.088* (.040)	.161*** (.033)	.124*** (.042)	.108*** (.032)
Gender	-.370*** (.052)	-.228*** (.042)	-.412*** (.053)	-.289*** (.041)
Race	-.298*** (.095)	-.155* (.077)	-.329*** (.098)	-.169* (.076)
Democratic Beliefs	.211*** (.008)	.156*** (.006)	.132*** (.008)	.110*** (.006)
Community Size	-.004 (.012)	.042 (.010)	-.001 (.012)	.028*** (.010)
Number of Social Studies Courses Taken	.016 (.016)	.012 (.013)	.034* (.017)	.023 (.013)
High School Curriculum Track	.092*** (.030)	.059* (.024)	.166*** (.031)	.070** (.024)
High School Extracurricular Activities	.180*** (.016)	.152*** (.013)	.177*** (.016)	.109*** (.013)
Constant	3.129	-.248	3.563	.177
F	144.371	133.012	78.720	73.963
R^2	.170	.156	.106	.099
Adj. R^2	.169	.155	.105	.097
N =	5623	5756	5322	5408

Entries are unstandardized regression coefficients. Entries in ( ) are standard errors. One tailed t test: * = $p < .05$; ** = $p < .01$; *** = $p < .005$.

Table 21.7 examines effects of taking part in five types of extracurricular activities on political discussion and participation. The usual patterns are repeated in this table: SES, gender, and race are all significant with higher SES, men, and nonwhites being more active. Support for democratic beliefs and high school curriculum track are significant. Community type is significant in accounting for participation, but not discussion; those in larger communities participate most. Number of social studies courses taken in high school is not significant.

Effects of participating in specific types of high school extracurricular activities are mixed. The consistently more significant coefficients, however, are for those who were active in student government and communications media groups. In both 1974 and 1976, this participation was significantly related to engaging in political discussions and participating in the political process. Coefficients for those who participated in vocational education clubs also were significant for political discussion and participation in both 1974 and 1976. Participation in expressive clubs and groups is significant in accounting for discussion and participation in 1974, but only for discussion in 1976. Membership in academic clubs predicted participating in the political process in 1976, but not discussion in either year. Being an athlete or cheerleader predicted political discussion and participation in 1976 and discussion in 1974.

DISCUSSION
The Reproduction of Democracy

'Democracy' is a noun, but probably should be an adverb. Thought of as a noun, we end up looking for something, a form of government or a set of institutions, that is democracy. But this is misleading insofar as it suggests that democracy is an achievement and, once attained, is completed or finished. In fact, democracy is not something done, but something that exists only in the doing (it is a process). Adverbially, what distinguishes democracy from other political systems is not what is done, but how it is done: making decisions, resolving conflicts, establishing rules, forming judgments, aggregating interests (partisan and common). The list could be expanded, but compiling such an inventory is not the point here. Rather, it is to underscore how much the details of democracy, so to speak, exist in the actual practice of democracy.

As with any practice or business (for example, law or medicine), democracy can be done well or badly. It depends partly on citizens with a willingness and the capacity to participate in the collective management of their life together. We return to our initial premise: democratic citizenship and education are key to maintaining or, as we prefer to say, reproducing democracy. Of course, there are no guarantees; yet, a democratic way of life presupposes citizens equipped with the skills, knowledge, and desire to take part in public life. But none of this can be taken for granted. Thus, both classical and modern theorists of democracy argue that one measure of a political system's worth is the degree to which citizens have the chance to learn the meaning and value of democracy when they experience and practice it. The term 'participatory democracy' describes the process whereby democracy is created and re-created (Gutmann, 1987, p. 39).

Table 21.7 Effects of participation in different types of extracurricular activities on post high school political discussion and participation

Sociodemographic and High School Variables	Political Discussion 1974	Political Participation 1974	Political Discussion 1976	Political Participation 1976
Socioeconomic Status	.088* (.041)	.158*** (.033)	.119** (.042)	.108*** (.033)
Gender	-.357*** (.052)	-.235*** (.043)	-.398*** (.054)	-.301*** (.041)
Race	-.285*** (.094)	-.154* (.076)	-.314*** (.098)	-.164* (.076)
Democratic Beliefs	.208*** (.007)	.153*** (.006)	.129*** (.008)	.107*** (.006)
Number of Social Studies Courses Taken	.010 (.016)	.008 (.013)	.028 (.016)	.021 (.013)
Community Size	-.005 (.011)	.040*** (.010)	-.002 (.012)	.028* (.010)
High School Curriculum Track	.096** (.031)	.051* (.025)	.162*** (.031)	.065** (.025)
Participation by Type of Activity (listed below):				
Vocational Education Clubs	.160*** (.050)	.085* (.041)	.135*** (.052)	.131* (.040)
Academic-oriented Clubs	.024 (.038)	.116 (.031)	.058 (.039)	.087** (.030)
Student Government/Media	.259*** (.033)	.249*** (.027)	.229*** (.033)	.154* (.026)
Expressive Clubs/ Groups	.125*** (.033)	.070* (.028)	.101*** (.035)	.029 (.028)
Athletics/ Cheerleading	.115*** (.031)	.029 (.026)	.155*** (.033)	.065** (.025)
Constant	3.170	-.101	3.608	.234
F =	99.514	92.669	55.285	52.127
R^2 =	.175	.162	.111	.104
Adj. R^2	.174	.160	.109	.102
N =	5623	5756	5322	5408

Entries are unstandardized regression coefficients. Entries in ( ) are standard errors. One tailed t test: * = $p < .05$; ** = $p < .01$; *** = $p < .005$.

Since the earliest period of the American republic, schools have performed the task of civics education. There never has been complete agreement about exactly what it means to be a 'good' citizen; but there has always been widespread agreement that schools have a primary responsibility for preparing students to become one (Mayer, 1964; Welter, 1965). Fostering education for democracy is another way in which people might become democrats. And, as noted earlier, there is no doubt that a person's level of formal education correlates highly with political knowledge, values, interest, and behavior. In all of these cases, the correlation is positive (Converse and Campbell, 1972, p. 234). But, as everyone well knows, there are also informal learning processes that are part of a student's education. Our major focus has been upon this other education for democracy. In this context, our most important findings are, first, that participation in many different forms contributes to valuing democratic practices and, second, that democratic beliefs and high school participation make for 'good' citizens later in life.

Effects of High School Variables

The decision to participate in a high school's extracurricular program is not random. Whites, females, those from higher socioeconomic groups, and students in the academic track are most likely to be members and leaders in these groups. Other research (Damico and Roth, 1993) has confirmed these findings and, then, gone on to describe the ways in which schools (through omission and commission) have failed to broaden the student participant base. Those from lower-SES families in the US frequently rely on the school bus for transportation home. Without alternatives, they are unable to stay after school for meetings. In many schools, there are no explicit policies or procedures for recruiting new club members, leaving undisturbed the tendency of teacher sponsors to invite the academically talented to join their clubs. This is, of course, only one way in which education for democracy, intentionally or unintentionally, becomes a political miseducation. Other instances could be cited. However, what we really need is more discussion and concern for the civics education that is taking place outside of social studies courses. Since participation in high school extracurricular activities importantly contributes to the formation of democratic beliefs and young adult community and civic participation, schools should review their policies on student recruitment and involvement with the explicit goal of finding ways to involve a broader range of adolescents in school activities.

Consistent with other research (Hanks and Eckland, 1976; Holland and Andre, 1987; Lindsay, 1984), we found that the high school curriculum track was significantly associated with participation in high school extracurricular activities. However, using high school curriculum track as an independent variable in all our analyses, we were able to trace the impact of being enrolled in academic, as opposed to general and vocational, courses on young adult beliefs and behaviors. Every table in this study reveals the significant and lasting impact of being assigned to the academic (college/university preparatory) track. Students in this track participated more in extracurricular activities; they also were more likely as young adults to hold democratic beliefs, to participate in their communities, and to be politically active. Our data do not permit us to contrast the experiences of those in the academic track with those in other programs. But, clearly, college-bound adolescents in academic courses are receiving relevant knowledge and/or experiences which predispose them to become active members of a democratic society. Democratic education is faced with a major challenge in that it needs to do more to create similar experiences and opportunities for all (or, at least, more) students.

Research on the effects of civics and social studies courses has tended to focus on consequences of these courses on the development of students' political attitudes and their levels of political knowledge. Far less has been done to trace their impact on adult beliefs and behaviors (see Niemi and Junn, 1993). What research has been conducted in this area has yielded mixed findings. Some studies have demonstrated positive effects of social studies classes (Button, 1974; Liebschutz and Niemi, 1974; Litt, 1963), others have raised questions about the long-term impact of these courses (Jennings, 1968; Merelman, 1971; Patrick, 1972). Niemi and Junn's (1993) recent study, however, argues that civics classes have a small, but resilient, impact on the civic knowledge of seniors. Our analysis of the senior class of 1972 adds weight to this claim; social studies courses do influence the development of democratic beliefs among adolescents. As a less promising result, we found no evidence that the number of social studies courses taken encourages participation in extracurricular activities either during high school or later in the community or political life.

Effects of Sociodemographic Variables

Socioeconomic status, gender, race, and community size were the sociodemographic variables used in all these analyses. There were no surprises here. Our results confirm what others have found out about the impact of these variables on participation in high school activities. Women are more likely than men to participate in all activities except (once again, predictably) for athletics and hobby clubs (Lindsay, 1984; Peng, Fetters, and Kolstad, 1981). In the school political arena, Eyler (1982) found that females were as likely as males to be active in school governance and to be leaders within these groups. By adulthood, though, these gender patterns reverse and we see males significantly more active than females in both the community and civic arena. This finding could also be read as supporting the claim of some feminist political scientists that gender organizes the US adult division of labor in ways that hinder women from participating as fully as men in community and political life (Okin, 1989; Elshtain, 1981).

The effects of SES on participation have also remained fairly constant over time (Holland and Andre, 1987). With the exception of athletics and hobby clubs, students from higher-SES families are most likely to participate in extracurricular activities (Lindsay, 1984). We replicated these results. Again, schools should worry about why so many students (either) shun (or are discouraged from taking part in) such activities.

Community size has little effect on any of our dependent variables. In one instance, attending school in a smaller community was associated with higher participation. In another case, participation in the political process was more likely among those who lived in larger communities. These findings do not allow us to make any definitive statements regarding community size effects. When size has been included in other studies of high school participation, it has generally been confined to size of school. These studies have shown that students in smaller schools participate more than those in larger ones (Barker and Gump, 1964; Lindsay, 1984; Morgan and Alwin, 1980). In smaller schools, there appears to be a good deal of social pressure to be involved in these activities. Barker (1978) found community size to have an effect similar to school size. Kasarda and Janowitz (1974), however, provided contradictory evidence; their study found that community size had little or no effect on social participation in high school.

Race as an independent variable reverses itself in the same way that gender differences did. The early tables indicate that whites are more active in extracurricular activities and more likely to hold democratic beliefs than nonwhites. Race then drops out as a significant factor until we examine the figures in Table 21.6, which portrays political discussion and participation. Here, we find that nonwhites were more likely than whites to engage in political discussions and to be active participants in the democratic process. We have no data to account for these changing patterns, nor were we able to locate other studies using race as an independent variable. Instead, race has been included in research on extracurricular activities as a dependent variable, either as school racial effectiveness (Crain, 1981) or race relationships (Slavin and Madden, 1979). In a democracy that is increasingly being characterized as 'two nations: separate, hostile, unequal' (Hacker, 1992), we recognize the urgent need to look closer at race as a variable in any of our further work examining the class of 1972.

CONCLUSIONS

Perhaps the most important problem of democratic education concerns the relationship between school participation, student beliefs, and their effects on one's adult life. If the learning acquired through participation in school reinforces or augments those democratic values taught at school, there is reason to hope that democratic schooling can strengthen the link between the theory and practice of democracy. When the benefits claimed for being a good citizen in the morning American history class contradict what happens at the afternoon band class or hobby club, then democracy loses positive reinforcement. Where the school provides experiences in associational life, belief in the value of democratic political practices increases. Those experiences and beliefs, in turn, reappear later in young adult civic and political behavior. Clearly, education for democracy is possible; therefore, we should do more of it both in the curriculum and in extracurricular activities.

ACKNOWLEDGEMENT

We would like to acknowledge Angela Halfacre for her work in data preparation and research analysis and Henk Dekker, Wayne Francis, Michael Martinez, and Ken Wald for their comments on an earlier draft of this paper.

REFERENCES

Almond, G. and S. Verba (1965). *The Civic Culture: Political Attitudes and Democracy in Five Nations*. Boston, MA: Little, Brown and Co.

Barber, B. (1984). *Strong Democracy*. Berkeley, CA: University of California Press.

Barker, R. (ed.) (1978). *Habitats, Environments and Human Behavior*. San Francisco, CA: Jossey-Bass.

Barker, R. and P. Gump (1964). *Big School, Small School: High School Size and Student Behavior*. Stanford, CA: Stanford University Press.

Berelson, B., P. Lazarsfeld, and W. McPhee (1954). *Voting*. Chicago, IL: University of Chicago Press.

Button, C. (1974). 'Political Education for Minority Groups', pp. 167-98 in R. Niemi (ed.) *The Politics of Future Citizens*. San Francisco, CA: Jossey-Bass.

Converse, P. and A. Campbell (eds.) (1972). *The Human Meaning of Social Change*. New York, NY: Russell Sage Foundation.

Crain, R. (Summer 1981). 'Making Desegregation Work: Extracurricular Activities', pp. 121-6 in *Urban Review*, Vol. 13, No. 2.

Damico, S. and J. Roth (1993). '"A Different Kind of Responsibility": Social and Academic Engagement of General Track High School Students', pp. 229-45 in R. Donmoyer and R. Kos, *At-Risk Students: Portraits, Policies, Programs, and Practices*. Albany, NY: SUNY Press.

Ehman, L. (Spring 1980). 'The American School in the Political Socialization Process', pp. 99-119 in *Review of Educational Research*, Vol. 50, No. 1.

Elshtain, J. (1981). *Public Man, Private Woman*. Princeton, NJ: Princeton University Press.

Eyler, J. (Spring 1982). 'Test of a Model Relating Political Attitudes to Participation in High School Activities', pp. 43-62 in *Theory and Research in Social Education*. Vol. 10, No. 1.

Gutmann, A. (1987). *Democratic Education*. Princeton, NJ: Princeton University Press.

Hacker, A. (1992). *Two Nations*. New York, NY: Charles Scribner's Sons.

Hanks, M., and B. Eckland (October 1976). 'Athletics and Social Participation in the Educational Attainment Process', pp. 271-94 in *Sociology of Education*, Vol. 49, No. 4.

Hanks, M. (September 1981). 'Youth, Voluntary Associations and Political Socialization', pp. 211-23 in *Social Forces*, Vol. 60, No. 1.

Holland, A. and T. Andre (Winter 1987). 'Participation in Extracurricular Activities in Secondary Schools: What Is Known, What Needs to Be Known?', pp. 437-66 in *Review of Educational Research*, Vol. 57, No. 4.

Jennings, M. (1968). 'Parental Grievances and School Politics', pp. 363-78 in *Public Opinion Quarterly*, Vol. 32.

Kasarda, J. and M. Janowitz (June 1974). 'Community Attachment in Mass Society', pp. 328-39 in *American Sociological Review*, Vol. 39, No. 3.

Kerlinger, F. (1979). *Behavioral Research: A Conceptual Approach*. New York, NY: Holt, Rinehart, & Winston.

King, G. (August 1986). 'How Not to Lie with Statistics: Avoiding Common Mistakes in Quantitative Political Science', pp. 666-87 *American Journal of Political Science* Vol. 30, No. 3.

Liebschutz, S. and R. Niemi (1974). 'Political Attitudes among Black Children', pp. 82-102 in R. Niemi (ed.), *The Politics of Future Citizens*. San Francisco, CA: Jossey-Bass.

Lindsay, P. (Spring 1984). 'High School Size, Participation in Activities, and Young Adult Social Participation: Some Enduring Effects of Schooling', pp. 73-83 in *Educational Evaluation and Policy Analysis*, Vol. 6, No. 1.

Litt, E. (February 1963). 'Civic Education Norms and Political Indoctrination', pp. 69-75 in *American Sociological Review*, Vol. 28, No. 1.

Mansbridge, J. (1980). *Beyond Adversary Democracy*. Chicago, IL: University of Chicago Press.

Mayer, M. (1964). *Social Studies in American Schools*. New York, NY: Harper and Row.

Merelman, R. (1971). *Political Socialization and Educational Climates*. New York, NY: Holt, Rinehart & Winston.

Morgan, D. and D. Alwin (June 1980). 'When Less is More: School Size and Social Participation', pp. 241-52 in *Social Psychology Quarterly*, Vol. 43, No. 2.

Mill, J. (1951). *Utilitarianism, Liberty, and Representative Government*. New York, NY: E. P. Dutton and Company.

Nie, N., J. Junn, and K. Stehlik-Barry (1994). 'Education and Democratic Citizenship.' Paper presented at the annual meeting of the Midwest Political Science Association, Chicago, IL.

Niemi, R. and J. Junn (September 1993). 'Civics Courses and the Political Knowledge of High School Seniors.' Paper presented at the annual meeting of the American Political Science Association, Washington, DC.

Okin, S. (1989). *Justice, Gender, and the Family*. New York, NY: Basic Books

Pateman, C. (1970). *Participation and Democratic Theory*. Cambridge UK: Cambridge University Press.

Patrick, J. (February 1972). 'The Impact of an Experimental Course, "American Political Behavior," on the Knowledge, Skills, and Attitudes of Secondary School Students', pp. 168-79 in *Social Education*, Vol. 36, No. 2.

Peng, S., W. Fetters, and A. Kolstad (1981). *A Capsule Description of High School Students*. Washington, DC: US Department of Education, National Center for Education Statistics.

Rosenstone, S. and J. Hansen (1993). *Mobilization, Participation, and Democracy in America*. New York, NY: Macmillan.

Sigel, R. and M. Hoskin (1981). *The Political Involvement of Adolescents*. New Brunswick, NJ: Rutgers University Press.

Slavin, R. and N. Madden (1979). 'School Practices that Improve Race Relations', pp. 169-80 in *American Educational Research Journal*, Vol. 16, No. 2.

Thompson, D. (1970). *The Democratic Citizen*. Cambridge, UK: Cambridge University Press.

Thompson, D. (1976). *John Stuart Mill and Representative Government*. Princeton, NJ: Princeton University Press.

Welter, R. (1965). *Popular Education and Democratic Thought in America*. New York, NY: Columbia University Press.

Part VI

Conclusions, Synthesis, and Summary Comments

22 *General Conclusions and Overall Findings*

Russell F. Farnen

ABSTRACT

This chapter summarizes and integrates some of the major, specific, and general conclusions drawn from the 20 substantive content chapters in this book. These findings relate to the subjects of authoritarianism, nationalism, political education and socialization, democratization, human rights, stereotyping, elitism, citizenship, anti-Semitism, intolerance, and internationalization or Europeanization. These various contributions make a unique combination of significant findings. This is not possible using a more narrow focus on national or regional (rather than comparative and cross-national) perspectives on these important topics which we discussed and which are of such significant interest today.

INTRODUCTION

The last part of this book discusses specific and general conclusions drawn from the previous parts of the volume. These are divided into concrete conclusions from each of the authors' contributions and more general observations on major topics of analysis (such as ethnonationalism, democratic transitions, human rights, socialization processes, and the like). We shall also discuss the basic trends toward democratization in Central and Eastern Europe based on a Western analysis (for example, Meloen, Watts, Farnen, and German) or from the Central and Eastern European region, itself (for example, Csepeli, Kéri, Stumpf, Golovakha, and Panina). In both these cases, whether from internal or external analyses, the high hopes for a rapid democratization and marketization so prevalent in 1989 and 1990 have proved to be premature. Instead, these processes will probably take a minimum of a decade in the case of politicization and much of a new generation's time and effort in the case of economic reform. We are here speaking of what it will take to accomplish this in Central Europe (for example, Poland, Hungary, Slovakia, and the Czech Republic), but even longer delays may be expected in the Eastern European states (for example, Romania, Albania, Bulgaria, the Ukraine, Russia, and other parts of the Commonwealth of Independent States [CIS]) which formerly comprised the USSR.

SPECIFIC CONCLUSIONS (PARTS I - V)

Some of the most important findings drawn from the studies presented in Parts I through V are:

1. Using measures of authoritarian attitudes over time, it was possible to predict the existence of state authoritarianism (and vice versa) in 70 countries based on key indices of authoritarianism and the results of other studies which assessed democratization levels worldwide.

2. Of all the predictors of individual authoritarianism levels, one's level of education is still the strongest indicator of pro-democratic and anti-authoritarian orientations.

3. Civic/political/democratic education also makes a difference regarding one's knowledge of political topics as well as decreasing anti-Semitism and increasing pro-democratic views. Political education for minorities may not be as effective as it is for majority students, but key factors in explaining these differences are known and may be addressed through schooling, except when they concern unalterable family background factors (such as parental education, SES, or head-of-household questions).

4. Suggested reforms in civic education across the board are directed at an improved school climate more conducive to learning; more study of current events; and a focus on key subject matter, such as civil rights, toleration, authoritarianism, and democracy; greater attention to the middle instructional grades; and other curricular revisions to offset the force of expanding traditional subject matter fields, such as history, economics, and geography.

5. Nationalism is a phenomenon present in postcommunist Central and Eastern Europe. The presentation on Slovakia attempts to measure nationalism in that nation. The evidence is mixed with regard to Hungarians who generally have good feelings toward Slovaks and vice versa. Relationships between these two groups have declined in recent years over the inability of Hungarians to have separate road signs and questions about the use of first names and women's surnames in the original language. Relationships with Gypsies are not good. Some anti-Semitism is present. Due to a lack of longitudinal data, the question of whether or not Slovakia is more nationalistic today than previously could not be answered.

6. The use of elite groups to study democratic transitions in Central and Eastern Europe can produce some useful findings if the groups are large enough, represent different fields of education/professions, and have the

necessary knowledge to respond to survey questions. This is not always true in small-scale studies, which lack the financial means to select national probability samples of the population. The elite study reported in this volume produced relatively reliable findings for some countries (for example, Hungary and Poland) and less credible results in others (for example, in Slovakia), which other survey data and national reports either corroborated (in the former case) or did not (in the latter).

Nevertheless, these results indicate that there is no one, single, or uniform path to democratization in Central and Eastern Europe. Instead, not only do countries take a different route, moving slowly (for example, Albania) or rapidly (for example, Slovenia) along the way, but different societal institutions (politics, economics, communications, and education) also change at different rates both within and across countries in the region. Generally, while there is evidence of increasing political democratization, more democratic communications, and improved civic education (particularly regarding civil rights and minority toleration), the areas of free market reform, environmental safeguards, and the growth of a genuine civil society lag far behind. However, looking at the total picture, there is little change for the overall indices in recent years; minority toleration is at risk (except, perhaps, in Slovenia) everywhere in the region and particularly in Hungary, Poland, the Czech Republic (and most probably the Slovak Republic as well), Serbia, and Croatia.

7. A case study of Germany discarded the class and postmaterialist explanations for the development of political ideology among youth in favor of new left-right divisions based on xenophobia, racism, violence, and ethnic pluralism (with some postmodern individualization influences). The evidence is strong that there is an 'ethnicization' of ideology in both parts of Germany associated with anomie, xenophobia, and rightist views. While out-group conflicts/threats are the sources for these ideological configurations, it is the foreigners' economic competition/threats which are most prominent in the minds of rightist extremists living in the five former GDR states of today's unified Germany.

8. Socialization studies in Hungary indicate the importance of the middle grades when the decentering process (from less-complex/concrete to more-abstract/ideological cognition) occurs. Individual and parental levels of education are also important in this result, just as is maturation, itself. Since modern Hungarian youth are no longer subjected to mandatory (official), voluntary (public, and private), or familial systems of political education, there is less intellectual conflict and more honesty about answering survey questions than was true in the past. These studies in particular found youth

could be placed into five groups based on their state, international, religious, or political views about minorities, loyalties, and national identity.

9. Grouping Hungarian voters using traditional Western categories or models does not seem to work well for analytical purposes. New methods of analysis and different models based on socialization and postmaterial assumptions may be better suited to Hungary's younger or average voters for whom age, religion, and SES variables are more relevant as determinants of party loyalty, support, and identification. In the final analysis, the role of voters under 35 years of age will be critical for determining Hungary's political future.

10. The force of resurgent nationalism in Central and Eastern Europe jeopardizes democratization, especially since self-serving elites there are using ethnic loyalties to forestall threats to their personal power, authority, and influence. With a long history of regional conflict with Russia and among themselves (often involving Western powers), regional states (especially in the Balkans and the Baltic regions) are split between Eastern and Western cultural values (including *Gemeinschaft*, rather than *Gesellschaft*, political orientations which are more compatible with divisive nationalism than with free markets or free societies). The old baggage such former communist-ruled societies carry with them into the future include many of the old *nomenklatura*, abundant police and army security units, and a state-run economy under conditions of a continuing 'foreign-directed' crisis.

11. With the longstanding economic chaos in the Ukraine preventing privatization, marketization, and democratization, their state-of-emergency mentality has produced disenchantment with democracy and desire for the return of the strong authoritarian hand. The public either suffers from anomie or has lost what little faith they had in democratic reform, preferring instead the familiar state paternalism to the perils of starvation, unknown since 1945. Anti-Semitism, xenophobia, ambivalence toward Russia and Russian minority neighbors, and unfamiliarity with the principles and practices of human rights all combine to produce an ideologically inconsistent, naive, sometimes contradictory public which prefers any alternative to their present discontents. This means they are willing to accept almost any option which will put food on the table even if it costs them their recently acquired political freedoms and rights.

12. Since national stereotyping can be diminished with only six months of indirect, written contact, there is hope that casual, frequent, voluntary, and cooperative contacts between students from different nations will have even more beneficial results after a longer period of time. Peer contacts can

influence political socialization in a positive way with respect to nationality stereotypes.

13. Just as it is possible to usefully categorize the politics of Hungarian secondary school students, one can classify Hungarian political elites based on their cultural characteristics as survivors, demagogues, intellectuals, professionals, neophytes, and entrepreneurs. These ideal types of reactionaries, humanists, populists, professionals, democrats, and businessmen grew out of the Hungarian's Marxist/Leninist past just as did the deposed leaders of the pre-1989 period. Consequently, under the seeming homogenization of real socialism's socialization, educational, and propaganda systems, there was more informal and unofficial variety in human behaviors and beliefs than the superficial and surface-thin veneer of communist conformity which appeared instantly to the eye for years on end.

14. Whether it is true of the entire Central and Eastern European region or not, it is clear that in Poland, the traditional Western divisions between the political haves and have-nots is developing among youth. That is, the split between those with cultural capital and those without it has implications for the growth of civil society and the free market. If this dichotomization runs true to form and follows its familiar Western path, there will be class-based social cleavages (which are reflected in political party and cultural divisions) instead of policy or ideological differences on which political choices can be based. Dividing a society on the basis of the economic haves and have-nots is merely a continuation of the old communist system. Then, the political elite became the economic elite. But today, the new economic elite will surely become the new political elite, in part because of the benefits they accrued for themselves and their children under the pre-1989 system. Since Poland, Hungary, Slovakia, the Czech Republic, the Baltics, and the Ukraine are all areas where these old communist elites are cashing in on their new capitalist advantages (education, income, and foreign languages and contacts), the opportunity for a ready-made, class-structured system exists. With all this said, there are no proposals for enlightened political policy, which would incorporate the less fortunate citizenry in their political party and systemic formulations. Therefore, it bears watching to determine the degree of open party competition among mass, broadly representative parties which will develop in the region. For the moment, the prospects for party and systemic democratization seem slim, but they may shift in a more positive way if the rising new elites are pre-equipped with a ready-made social conscience which free enterprise, competition, and self-interest do not combine to corrupt.

15. The strong case we have made for education as an antidote to authoritarianism and the usual connections of authoritarianism to right-wing views, anti-Semitism, ethnocentrism, masculine aggression, deference, and religious convention can be somewhat qualified on the basis of some Dutch research on high school students. While authoritarians may exclude out-group members on the basis of power, order, normality, and religion, yet non-authoritarians also selected 'good' groups to join them based on their assumed moral superiority (though along feminist, nonpower, nonconventional, and less 'tough' lines) to foster in-group favoritism. The specific conclusion stemming from this particular research effort is that, in this regard (ethnocentrism), the differences perceived are more a matter of the rationale therefore or one of degree rather than kind (that is, these are not really opposites or polarized extremes).

16. Two separate views of the European Union are represented in this volume. One depicts the EU as an area where democratic elites and masses substantially agree (in the Netherlands); German doubts are expressed about decreasing democratization, increasing bureaucratization, and continuing Europeanization of member national parliaments while nationalizing the EU to a similar degree. These two studies illustrate that EU member state consensus levels vary considerably by country as the experience with Maastricht ratification indicated in England, France, Denmark, and Germany.

17. The concerns of schooling and politics or the politics and/of education relate to educational and political philosophy (for example, totalitarianism, democratic morality and values, citizenship competence in a democratic society, the important role of political education for developing future citizens, and the contribution which extracurricular involvement in secondary school has on adult political participation levels).

18. Politics and education are inextricably related in any democratic society which stresses active, participatory citizenship within the confines of an open society, which allows minority groups to join with others to become a new political majority, and which agrees not to tyrannize other minorities.

19. Democratic societies have the processes and means at hand to develop workable and functioning moral and ethical principles and standards for a civil society. These values need not be based on religious principles, but they can reflect cultural and civilized tenets (such as the basic worth of the individual; the need for political equality and justice; equal protection of the laws; guarantees for everyone's human rights; and freedom from war, fear,

homelessness, starvation, and other privations which democratic societies can prevent).

20. To ascertain the moral implications for democratic citizenship, we present the following basic list of such requirements. These include valuing democracy, toleration, decision-making skill, party competition, internationalism, and education; enlightened loyalties, reasoned patriotism, and system trust and confidence; political knowledge; gender, racial, and ethnic equality; freedom; service; participation; and other requisites for democratic citizenship.

21. Citizens must also be expected to be able to differentiate between 'strong' and 'weak' democracy, to accept the personal responsibilities of active citizenship, and to recognize the real threat which authoritarianism (from either the left or right) imposes on democrats. It is clear from survey and other large- and small-scale research projects on democracy and authoritarianism that both of these ideologies are very much alive in the US, Europe, and the rest of the world today.

22. Despite some minor limitations or reservations, it is clear that a well-educated and informed citizenry is the best means available today to encourage democracy and to limit authoritarian trends. Basic to this educational project is the need for citizen education in democracy as a principled process which has ideological significance and meaning. By contrast, fascist, rightist, and authoritarian values compete every day with democracy in most societies where deference, convention, and aggression are strongly supported popular alternatives to equality, freedom, and cooperation as public virtues.

23. Anti-Semitism is a perfect example of an antidemocratic value which is one hallmark of fascist beliefs. Whether this exists in societies with only a small group of Jews (for example, in Slovakia or Poland) or in societies with large Jewish minorities (for example, the US) makes little difference; it is still basically a form of stereotyping and prejudice which runs counter to the democratic spirit. Students can study the Holocaust and World War II just as they can learn to participate in secondary school extracurricular activities. Both experiences will benefit the strong democrat in his/her later public life. An informed citizenry will be one best equipped to say 'never again' to the resurgence of any modern fascist trends anywhere in the world.

GENERAL CONCLUSIONS (PARTS I - V)

Some of the general conclusions reached in this edited volume relate to more abstract, higher-level concepts, such as democracy, socialization, nationalism, authoritarianism, CEE democratic transitions, human rights, tolerance, elitism, identity formation, Europeanization, political education, citizenship, and democratic values. Among these are the following:

1. ***Democracy***. The various meanings of democracy across societies and cultures are reflected in the previous pages. For example, in the West (for example, the US and the Netherlands), we are debating participatory versus representative theories of democracy, whereas in the Ukraine, the battle for democracy must overcome anomie and state paternalistic forces. It is also true that in Poland, for example, the conception of democracy is (abstractly) correct both regarding popular sovereignty and majority rule, but faulty (procedurally) with respect to restrictions on minority rights, limits on free speech, a passion for order before liberty (rather than ordered liberty).

The discussions of democratic citizenship and education for democracy indicate that it is possible to hierarchically conceptualize democratic citizenship from the most concrete to the abstract level (which is true for Dutch secondary students who conceive of citizenship in these terms). The moral basis for enlightened democratic citizenship (which espouses both basic substantive goals and procedural due process, for example) does not require any religious or teleological underpinnings other than the society's basic ethical and moral principles, which are applicable to everyday personal and group decision making and problem solving situations. Regarding elite mass linkages, it has also been shown that there is no gap between these two groups regarding the European Community/Union in the Netherlands. However, the same finding may not be true in other EU countries (such as the UK, Denmark, France, or Germany, which have demonstrated widespread social division on the question of the EU). Perhaps Germany may be more nationalistic in its reaction to the EU operations than is true in the Netherlands, with the German goal being to more fully democratize and de-bureaucratize the EU while nationalizing it and simultaneously internationalizing member states.

Continuing with this theme of democratization, it also appears that secondary school extracurricular participation in voluntary activities has its payoff in later life when it comes to adult political involvement and participation. Consequently, participation in the social life of the community is philosophically a key element in practical democratic theory along with antitotalitarianism/antiauthoritarianism, pluralism, individuality, identity, freedom, subjectivity, community, and solidarity. All of the foregoing are

part of democratic schooling in politics and democratic political socialization practices. Different societies are also composed of different types of
democrats, particularly in Central and Eastern Europe, which has no fully
developed tradition of democratic political culture and civil society. From
1989 to 1993, there is a patchwork pattern of development in this region
regarding democratic politics, processes, and institutions, communications,
political education, nationalism, minority rights, and environmental and
market reforms. Some societies (for example, Slovenia) are more environmentally aware, free-market directed, less ethnonationalist oriented, more
tolerant of minorities, further politically developed in civic education, public
communications developed, and have more fully matured democratic
political processes and institutions than do others (for example, Serbia and
Croatia). In certain areas (such as environmental concern), all of the
countries in Central and Eastern Europe are in trouble, whereas in terms of
market development, much the same is true as is also the case for overall
generally low levels of toleration and medium to high levels of ethnonationalism. The levels of democratic communications, political activities,
and political education are also moderate across the board with the overall
pattern for this area from 1991 to 1993 indicating no significant changes in
environment, nationalism, and education and some meaningful changes
occurring in the areas of politics, communications, minority toleration, and
economics.

Similarly, just as political profiles of different Central and Eastern
European countries vary over the years with respect to their democratization
patterns, so do the intrapolitical cultural configurations of elites (as in the
case in Hungary, which exhibits several ideal types running the political
spectrum from naive idealists and intellectuals to the old-guard leaders,
professionals, and entrepreneurs). Of course, many of these same types of
political personalities could be found in other countries as well. Democracy,
if it means anything, allows for the full development of political personalities to suit the needs and requirements of the civil society and political
culture.

2. ***Authoritarianism***. In contrast to the democratic theme, we also have its
    theoretical extreme (although one contribution in this book has shown that
    certain authoritarian/democratic characteristics can be assumed by different
    groups at various times) in the form of authoritarianism and anti- and
    undemocratic alternatives which are very much alive in the world today.
    The key characteristics of aggression, submission, and convention which
    characterize the authoritarian syndrome are readily apparent in Western,
    Central, and Eastern Europe and North America as well as in Asia, Africa,
    and South America. It is also clear that there is a universal preference for
    the abstract principles of democracy (if not for its concrete/procedural

elements) but that undemocratic societies produce authoritarians and that certain characteristics (for example, low education, gender gaps, overpopulation, censorship, minority/ethnic intolerance, and military rule) are associated with this phenomenon worldwide. As a matter of fact, it seems that the education variable is most critical (in the West at least) in forestalling or preventing the widespread emergence of social authoritarianism. However, it is quite clear that, for at least the last half century, the growth of the authoritarian personality syndrome is a crucial part of the dynamics of democratic societies. That is, while democratic civic education and political socialization may promote the growth of the democratic personality in the democratic culture, contrary antidemocratic tendencies in the society promote the growth of right- (or left-) wing radical extremism, which wants to destroy democracy as a process, theory, or system. While democrats may argue about strong or weak democracy and their assets or liabilities, authoritarians prefer to turn out democrats of any stripe so they can serve a strong ruler, dominate over inferiors, and rigidly conform to religious, sexual, or other straitjacket conventions.

One of the other more interesting findings/conclusions we have reached as a result of these cross-national studies is that some other major dimensions of rightist beliefs are also related to authoritarianism. That is nationalism, militarism, anti-internationalism, traditional education, antimulticulturalism, and antiminority toleration/incorporation are all correlates of authoritarianism (that is, those who hold this set of beliefs generally subscribe to authoritarian values). Furthermore, these patterns hold up cross-nationally. Despite the strength of these relationships, civic education in Western countries pretends that authoritarians existed in the past in Nazi Germany or the USSR, but not at home or in other allied states. Consequently, youth are indoctrinated in democratic rituals (such as the need to vote/participate), but they are nearly totally ignorant of those views and persons who would destroy democracy and replace it with neofascism. Forewarned may be forearmed, but many Western citizens are not informed about prominent 'enemies of freedom' who do not live apart from, but rather directly with and among, them.

3. *Democratic political beliefs and attitudes*. Whereas the subject of political behaviors, beliefs, attitudes, and opinions of youth is the subject of much of this volume, society-wide perspectives for youth and young adults in Hungary and the entire adult population in the Ukraine reveal some common political trends in Central and Eastern Europe. In the first place, while the heritage of the communist past of real socialism has had its effects, there were hidden and undocumented political developments in these societies under the seemingly monolithic Marxist-Leninist framework. These trends in political behavioral growth were responsible for both ideal

types discussed previously as well as for several other factors. Among these are the development of a new political generation among those under age 35; the need for a new schematic to conceptualize the political patterns and interests of voters; the continuing heritage/influence of past social, economic, and political dependency; and the quest for the strong authoritarian ruler/oligarchy which typified many former state systems (some since the 19th century or World War I). These trends are not likely to disappear as suddenly as the popular 1989 'silent' revolutions implied. Consequently, we shall have to watch carefully for democratic recidivism to occur as authoritarianism grows in an all too fertile Central and Eastern European political environment. Indeed, although claims to the contrary have been made (for example, in some joint Russian and American research projects; that is, that the Russians are less authoritarian than Americans on the average), our own research indicates quite the opposite. Of course, as the influence and heritage of a 70-year totalitarian regime would certainly predict this result. There is a good chance that the future of many countries in Central and Eastern Europe will conform more with their post-World War II autocratic past rather than with any rosy democratic future which our hopeful Western 'demo-optimism' expectations may have envisioned for them.

In this regard, not only do we need to create new models of voter behavior based on empirical studies in order to properly frame our interpretations and future work, but we also must be prepared for the worst in the Ukraine. Anomie, cynicism, alienation, nostalgia for the Russians and the communist past, and hope for an authoritarian tomorrow are all too real possibilities outlining the parameters for the Ukrainian political future. Poles, Hungarians, Czechs, Slovaks, Slovenes, and Baltic Republics may not share this tendency, but it is one which Albanians, Serbians, Bulgarians, Romanians, Russians and many other Balkan and CIS countries may very well inherit, even making such choices through the ballot box.

4. *National stereotypes, xenophobia, and anti-Semitism.* It appears that preformed national stereotypes can be changed over a relatively short period of time with a minimum amount of effort. If so, this finding has implications for how such prejudices can be addressed in classroom settings which deal with such concerns. With respect to anti-Semitism, it also appears that a modicum of classroom instruction (which helps to increase knowledge and interest in World War II, the Holocaust, and the Jewish diaspora) can reap many rewards. However, when xenophobia is based on economic competition for jobs, influence, and status, it may be an even harder obstacle to overcome. Whatever its cause, it is clear that right-wing radical extremism and xenophobia help to define some western and eastern German youth today. Consequently, this is a reality of the present, rather

than some mass media mirage. However, it may be that all youth (whether democratic or authoritarian) are capable of cultivating in-group/out-group construction and favoritism, developing social distance, framing identities on the basis of similarities and differences, and constructing a morally superior in-group and an inferior out-group. Political educators must also be aware of these possibilities and not merely just know about the authoritarian or democratic character of individual students and educational classes, which is also of importance for proper civic instruction.

5. *National identity and nationalism.* There is no doubt that ethnonationalism has been reborn with a vengeance in Central and Eastern Europe. Whether it was ever totally absent or just in a deep freeze during the communist period is largely irrelevant since it is very much alive and thoroughly defrosted today. This is especially true in countries such as Croatia and Serbia where minority toleration is low (which is also the case in the Czech Republic, Hungary, Poland, but much less so in Slovenia). However, once again, an approved and modern form of multicultural political education may offset these tendencies as they have in some countries in the area (such as Slovenia, but not in Serbia).

Different approaches to the study of conflicting loyalties, national orientations, and identities are equally useful, depending on the country, research orientation, and end in mind (for example, Hungary versus the Netherlands, normative versus empirical, and historical descriptive or follow-up research goals). As in the West, there is no uniform sense of identity/national consciousness, patriotism, or loyalty in Central and Eastern European countries. As yet, there is also less sense of Europeanization in Eastern than in Western Europe. Nevertheless, once again, the growth and dominance of ethnonationalist exclusivity promotes the rise of xenophobia, racism, and authoritarianism, while it limits the growth of human rights, liberal humanism, antielitism, pluralism, and other counters to disorder, barbarism, nativism, provincialism, and war.

Index of Names

Index of Subjects